Praise for *Dismantling Freud*:

"This valuable, timely work lays bare the often dark and pernicious nature of Freudianism, especially insofar as it went beyond the realm of psychoanalysis and morphed into an all-embracing worldview that has greatly abetted the unraveling of the spiritual fabric of today's world."

—SEYYED HOSSEIN NASR, author of *The Need for a Sacred Science* and *Knowledge and the Sacred*, etc.

"In this remarkable work, Samuel Bendeck Sotillos takes us well beyond the familiar image of Sigmund Freud. Calling in part upon primary documents rarely seen, he offers a glimpse of the man: of what or who(!) is driving him. Given the indelible imprint Freud left upon our contemporary, post-modern civilization, this treatise can hardly fail to be of profound interest to everyone still capable of serious, critical thought."

—WOLFGANG SMITH, founder of the Philos-Sophia Initiative Foundation, author of *Rediscovering the Integral Cosmos*, *The Quantum Enigma: Finding the Hidden Key*, etc.

"This book situates Freud's doctrines in their proper context, perhaps for the first time. With great lucidity, depth—even urgency—its author makes clear that our human destiny can be realized only through freedom in and of the Spirit; whereas, in stark contrast to this, Freud (under the guise of liberating us) trapped us in an unconscious determinism, that is, in the most inferior impulses of our soul. This is a work aimed at no less than restoring our human community to health."

—JEAN BORELLA, author of *The Crisis of Religious Symbolism*, *The Sense of the Supernatural*, *Christ the Original Mystery: Esoterism and the Mystical Way*, etc.

"Samuel Bendeck Sotillos, informed by a deep understanding of traditional modes of thought and drawing on prodigious research, develops a searching critique of the very foundations of modern psychoanalysis and exposes the ways in which this totalitarian pseudo-science is symptomatic of the profane worldview which is at the root of our contemporary spiritual crisis. This is a penetrating study of wide-ranging significance and the most urgent relevance."

—HARRY OLDMEADOW, former Coordinator of Philosophy and Religious Studies at La Trobe University, author of *The Betrayal of Tradition: Essays on the Spiritual Crisis of Modernity*, etc.

"Sotillos has garnered a great variety of sources to formulate his critique of Freudianism. His discussion of the scope, the foundation, and the effects of the psychoanalytical movement is very impressive. He illuminates with great insight the deeper meaning and implications of the truths found in different religions of the world. This book will be relevant for those in the fields of Humanities, for therapists, for those who wish to deepen their understanding about the cultural climate of the modern and postmodern worlds."

—*Journal of Transpersonal Psychology*

DISMANTLING FREUD

Dismantling FREUD

FAKE THERAPY
and the
PSYCHOANALYTIC
WORLDVIEW

SAMUEL BENDECK SOTILLOS

Angelico Press

This Angelico Press reprint edition, 2020,
is a reissue of the work originally published as
Psychology Without Spirit: The Freudian Quandary,
by Kazi Publications, Chicago, IL, 2018.
© Samuel Bendeck Sotillos, 2018

For information, address:
Angelico Press, 169 Monitor St.
Brooklyn, NY 11222
angelicopress.com

ISBN 978-1-62138-520-2 (pbk)
ISBN 978-1-62138-541-7 (cloth)

Cover Design: Michael Schrauzer
Cover Image: "Viselec" (Hanging Man), 1997 by David Černý

Contents

Introduction:

Sigmund Freud and the Emergence of the Modern World

"Woe unto those who see in the Law nothing but simple narratives and ordinary words!...Every word of the Law contains an elevated sense and a sublime mystery."[1]—The Zohar

"Seek not things that are too hard for thee and search not things that are hidden from thee. The things that have been permitted thee, think thereupon; thou hast no business with the things that are secret."[2]— The Talmud

"Well, if my powers are not great enough, I shall not hesitate—that's sure—to ask help wherever Help may be found. If the gods above are no use to me, then I'll move all hell."[3]—Virgil

"I regard myself as one of the most dangerous enemies of religion, but they don't seem to have any suspicion of that."[4]—Sigmund Freud

On August 29, 1909, upon arriving on the steamer *George Washington* in the New York Harbor, on Freud's first and only visit to the so-called New World to deliver five introductory lectures[5] on psychoanalysis at the invitation of G. Stanley Hall (1846–1924) for the twentieth anniversary celebration of Clark University in Worcester, Massachusetts, Freud is reported to have commented to his onetime disciples Sándor Ferenczi (1873–1933) and C. G. Jung (1875–1961) in reference to his doctrine of psychoanalysis: "They don't realize we're bringing them the plague."[6] The paradigmatic implications of the Freudian colonization of the human psyche are made palpable in his triumphant pronouncement: "it was no small thing to have the whole human race as one's patient."[7] Freud recognized the full scope of the corrosive impact of the Freudian doctrine on society and civilization: "psychoanalysis is regarded as 'inimical to culture' and has been put under a ban as a 'social danger.'"[8] Freud in no uncertain terms was conscious of the nefarious and destructive implications of his theory that was cloaked in the dress of modern science, which would come to challenge the very foundations of Western civilization.

1

This perplexing declaration articulated above took place one year after Freudian psychology reached a turning point in 1908, becoming a totalizing worldview or *Weltanschauung*. "Psycho-analysis has a special right to speak for the scientific *Weltanschauung*...Its contribution to science lies precisely in having extended research to the mental field."[9] While Freud in the very beginning saw psychoanalysis as "no more than a new medical procedure for influencing certain nervous diseases"[10] or "psycho-analysis originating as a method of treatment"[11] and wished to keep his theories within the realm of science, emphasizing that, "We are doctors and wish to remain doctors,"[12] he was later, however, persuaded otherwise.

Otto Gross's (1877–1920)[13] statements made in 1908 at the first International Congress of Psychoanalysis held in Salzburg, Austria, laid the underpinnings for the all-encompassing application of psychoanalysis beyond the domain of psychology by affirming the "cultural perspectives of science"[14] that Freud was more than ready to incorporate into his messianic mission. On July 5, 1910, Freud wrote to Jung, "I am more and more persuaded of the cultural value of psychoanalysis."[15] Freud wrote to August Stärcke (1880–1954) on February 25, 1912 stressing the utility of psychoanalysis beyond its therapeutic application: "The therapeutic point of view, however, is certainly not the only one for which psychoanalysis claims interest, nor is it the most important. So there is a great deal to be said on the subject even without putting therapy in the forefront."[16] Freud, as British neurologist and psychoanalyst Ernest Jones (1879–1958) reveals, saw the history of humanity in all its diverse fields of inquiry as being in essence distinct "colonies"[17] of psychoanalytic theory. The open-ended application of psychoanalysis beyond the couch was stressed by Freud himself: "nothing that men make or do is understandable without...psycho-analysis"[18] or "we have so often been obliged to venture beyond the frontiers of the science of psychology."[19] Additionally, Freud asserts: "There was...a scientific duty, to apply the...methods of psychoanalysis, in regions far remote from its native soil."[20]

It needs to be very clear from the outset that the psychoanalytic movement was not only seeking to expose how the human psyche was governed by the unconscious and its inner conflicts, but how Freudian therapy extends across all disciplines, human endeavors, and behavior. Professor David Bakan (1921–2004) elaborates on the invasive nature of psychoanalytic theory:

> The psychoanalytic movement seemingly originated as an effort on the part of a physician to cure certain ailments that were resis-

tant to other forms of treatment; and it was in this guise that it first presented itself to the world. Yet, shortly after this introduction, it reached out to touch, infiltrate, and encompass practically every other form of intellectual endeavor. The far-reaching consequences of Freud's thought are paradoxically confirmed by the degree to which his contributions are taken for granted.[21]

Freud explains in his own words how psychoanalytic theory initially began with the study of the mind and how it expanded its inquiry, making connections across wide-ranging fields:

> Its original significance was purely therapeutic: it aimed at creating a new and efficient method for treating neurotic illnesses. But connections which could not be foreseen in the beginning caused psychoanalysis to reach out far beyond its original aim. It ended by claiming to have set our whole view of mental life upon a new basis and therefore to be of importance for every field of knowledge that is founded on psychology.[22]

The psychoanalytic doctrine saw no limits to its scope of knowledge and seized the whole of culture in its therapeutic enterprise, as noted here by German-American historian, Peter Gay (1923–2015): "Freud took all of culture as his providence."[23] Freud emphasizes the importance of the psychoanalytic doctrine beyond its import for modern psychology:

> We do not want to see psychoanalysis swallowed up by medicine...As "psychology of the depths," the theory of the unconscious mind, it may become indispensable to all the branches of knowledge having to do with the origins and history of human culture and its great institutions; such as art, religion, and the social order. It has already contributed to the solution of problems in these fields, but the contribution made is small in comparison with what it will be when historians of civilization, psychologists of religion, etymologists, etc., become willing to use the new weapon for research themselves. Therapy of neuroses [psychopathology] is only one of the uses of analysis; perhaps the future will show that it is not the most important.[24]

Jung also affirms the wide-ranging cultural implications that encompass much more than what is commonly addressed on the psychoanalytic couch:

[P]sychoanalysis in the strictly Freudian sense is not only a therapeutic method but a psychological theory, which does not confine itself in the least to the neurosis and to psychopathology in general but attempts also to bring within its province the normal phenomenon of the dream and, besides this, wide areas of the humane sciences, of literature and the creative arts, as well as biography, mythology, folklore, comparative religion, and philosophy.[25]

Edward Bernays (1891–1995), a nephew of Sigmund Freud who is often referred to as "the father of public relations," was influenced by psychoanalytic theory and interested in how it could be utilized to engineer public consent on a mass scale.[26] In 1928 Bernays published his notorious work *Propaganda* in which he asks the following rhetorical question in the chapter entitled "The Psychology of Public Relations," clueing one into the dangerous reality of the manipulation of the collective mind and behavior: "If we understand the mechanism and motives of the group mind, is it not possible to control and regiment the masses according to our will without their knowing about it?"[27] The innumerable ways in which the human collectivity could be manipulated is alluded to by Bernays himself: "Human nature is readily subject to modification."[28] Freud also recognized this possibility when writing, "A group is extraordinarily credulous and open to influence, it has no critical faculty."[29] Bernays indicates how the human psyche can be manipulated, taking Freudian therapy beyond the psychoanalytic couch:

The conscious and intelligent manipulation of the organized habits and opinions of the masses is an important element in democratic society. Those who manipulate this unseen mechanism of society constitute an invisible government which is the true ruling power of our country. We are governed, our minds molded, our tastes formed, our ideas suggested, largely by men we have never heard of...in almost every act of our daily lives, whether in the sphere of politics or business, in our social conduct or our ethical thinking, we are dominated by the relatively small number of persons...who understand the mental processes and social patterns of the masses. It is they who pull the wires which control the public mind, who harness old social forces and contrive new ways to bind and guide the world.[30]

Regarding the engineering of public consent and suggestibility of the masses, we turn to the discerning words of the French metaphysician René Guénon (1886–1951), who early on the recognized the dangers underlying modernism and its corrosive impact on the human collectivity: "The modern mentality...is no more than the product of a vast collective suggestion"[31] and in fact "the darkest enigmas of the modern world, enigmas which that world itself denies because though it carries them in itself it is incapable of perceiving them, and because this denial is an indispensable condition for the maintenance of the special mentality whereby it exists."[32] Freud himself exposes the manipulative function of his Faustian science, "the intellectual manipulation of carefully verified observations."[33] E. Michael Jones describes the process of desacralizing the sapiential traditions to undermine the centrality of religion in order to manipulate humanity:

> Religious belief meant ipso facto the opposite of opinion, and therefore ideas not subject to the manipulation of the people who controlled the communications media. What needed to be done then was move large areas of thought from the realm of religion to the realm of opinion if any significant breakthroughs in political control through manipulation of the media were to take place. Sexual morality was the most important area of religious thinking that needed to be moved into the realm of "opinion," where it would then be under the control of psychological warriors.[34]

Guénon continues by differentiating the suggestibility of the human collectivity that occurred in the past from the nefarious qualities that it has taken in the modern world:

> It is true that the masses have always been led in one manner or another, and it could be said that their part in history consists primarily in allowing themselves to be led, since they represent a merely passive element, a "matter" in the Aristotelian sense of the word. But, in order to lead them today, it is sufficient to dispose of purely material means, this time in the ordinary sense of the word, and this shows clearly to what depths our age has sunk. At the same time, the masses are made to believe that they are not being led, but that they are acting spontaneously and governing themselves, and the fact that they believe this is a sign from which the extent of their stupidity may be inferred.[35]

French Catholic Philosopher Jacques Maritain (1882–1973) points out the hazardous influences of psychoanalysis propagating on a mass level the suggestion of an imaginary illness that it allegedly cures: "It is likewise true that the diffusion of Freudian interpretations among the general public has had the effect of creating in people the very thing to be discovered in them, and poisoning their imagination."[36]

There were also those who warned against psychoanalysis becoming a totalizing worldview or *Weltanschauung*. Swiss psychiatrist Eugen Bleuler (1857–1939) cautioned his collaborators within the psychoanalytic movement not to employ the "talking cure" beyond the limits of science: "'Who is not with us is against us,' the principle 'all or nothing' is necessary for religious sects and for political parties. I can understand such a policy, but for science I consider it harmful...I do not believe that the [International Psychoanalytical] Association is served by such intransigency. This is not a 'Weltanschauung'..."[37]

It is a common feature of psychoanalytic theory to contradict itself, and so despite the abundant evidence articulated in his own statements, Freud defended himself against claims of universal explanatory power: "It [psychoanalysis] has never dreamt of trying to explain 'everything.'"[38]

The precise date when Freudian psychoanalysis was first inaugurated is uncertain, but it appears to have occurred roughly in the 1890's. We are informed by American psychoanalyst Charles Brenner (1913–2008) that "Its [psychoanalysis's] beginning cannot be dated precisely, since it extended over a period of several years."[39] A former leading disciple, Otto Rank (1884–1939) maintains, "Psychoanalysis was born in the year 1881."[40] What we do know is that the first occurrence of the term *psychoanalysis*[41] appeared on March 30, 1896 in a paper published in French entitled "Heredity and the Aetiology of the Neuroses."[42] A corresponding term frequently used synonymously with *psychoanalysis* to refer to the psychology of the unconscious is *depth psychology* (*Tiefenpsychologie*), whose coinage is often credited to Bleuler.[43] Viktor Frankl (1905–97) in 1938 coined the term *height psychology*[44] to complement rather than to supersede *depth psychology*, as a term that would be more inclusive, embracing the unconscious and also a higher dimension that expands beyond the empirical ego. Jung weighs in and informs us: "What is designated today by the catchword 'psychoanalysis' is not in reality a uniform thing, but comprises in itself many different aspects of the great psychological problem of our age."[45] Sometimes the terms *psychoanalytic* and *psychodynamic* are used interchangeably; however, the term *psychodynamic theory* is generally used in a broad fashion to refer to both Freud's theories and those of the neo- and post-Freudians.

6

In this desacralized and secular epoch that continues to exalt the motto by Nietzsche proclaiming that "God is dead,"[46] the same fate might be proclaimed about the originator of psychoanalytic movement that *Freud is dead*, but such is not the case—far from it—as his cultural influence has proliferated on a mass level.[47] It is all too often assumed that psychoanalysis is an outdated paradigm, and that we now live in "the neurotic aftermath of the Age of Freud,"[48] and while this assumption holds some truth, Freud nonetheless continues to live on. Influential sociologist and cultural critic Philip Rieff (1922–2006) maintains that unorthodox psychoanalysis as found in its neo- and post-Freudian forms is the culprit responsible for Freud's demise: "Vulgar Freudianism has buried Freud."[49] Yet such explanations miss the point and divert the issue at hand, as the core issue is not neo- and post-Freudianism versus orthodox Freudianism, but entails the phenomenon of psychodynamic psychology as a whole. It has been put forward that *Freud is not dead* because as Professor Adolf Grünbaum asserts, "I categorically don't believe Freud is dead. The question is, Are they trustworthy explanations? Have the hypotheses been validated by cogent, solid evidence? My answer to that is no."[50] At the same time, he also held the view that "while psychoanalysis may thus be said to be scientifically alive, it is currently hardly well."[51]

Freudians assert that the more Freud and psychoanalytic psychology are debated, the more their significance is confirmed, as exemplified by the following statement: "the never-ending backlash against Freud confirms...the potency of his theories."[52] Others suggest that an obituary is too preemptive as there is no new psychological paradigm available that supersedes Freudian therapy: "A century's worth of research in psychology, neuroscience, pharmacology and other mind-related fields has not yielded a medical paradigm powerful enough to obviate Freud once and for all."[53] For those individuals who assumed that the psychoanalytic movement would die or fade away with Freud's passing, Freud responded, "how foolish it is to believe that psychoanalysis rests upon my personal existence and will pass with me."[54]

The so-called therapeutic function of psychoanalysis becomes transparent and intelligible, yet alarming to say the least, as what is revealed is not actually therapeutic or hopeful for optimal psychological health and wellbeing, but consists of "transforming your hysterical misery into common unhappiness."[55] Or, "'Happiness,' said Freud, 'is no cultural value.'"[56] Freud pathologized all inquiry into the existential and higher realities: "The moment a man questions the meaning and value of life, he is sick, since objectively neither has any

7

existence."[57] The epistemological and ontological quicksand of psychoanalysis is made apparent here: "Since the criterion of truth...is absent, it is entirely a matter of indifference what opinions we adopt. All of them are equally true and equally false."[58] Freud emphasizes that his burden was to excavate the deepest layers of the human psyche, saying: "I set myself the task of bringing to light what human beings keep hidden within them...the task of making conscious the most hidden recesses of the mind is one which it is quite possible to accomplish."[59]

With this said, Freud did admit to a certain degree of ambivalence regarding the credibility of his psychoanalytic theories. He writes: "I do not know how far I believe in them...It is surely possible to throw oneself into a line of thought and to follow it wherever it leads out of simple scientific curiosity, or, if the reader prefers, as an *advocatus diaboli*, who is not on that account himself sold to the devil."[60] Another reason for his doubt has to do with his confession that "Psychoanalytic material, [is] incomplete as it is and not susceptible to clear interpretation."[61] Here we can glean his outlook from the foundations of his alleged scientific psychology: "Fundamentally, we find only what we need and see only what we want to see."[62] Another telling remark is that "psychoanalysis as a therapy may be worthless."[63]

As for the individuals that Freud treated, he had very little regard for them; in fact he appeared to have a predatory attitude as exemplified by his statements that "Patients are a rabble"[64] and that they are "only any good for making money out of, and for studying."[65] As far as his position on those who critiqued the psychoanalytic "talking cure,"[66] Freud without reservation responded: "They can all go to hell."[67] Why? Because, Freud answered: "We possess the truth."[68] Can anything more be expected of someone whose mission was to "agitate the sleep of mankind"[69] or to "disturb the peace of this world,"[70] which launched the "psychical epidemic"[71] known as the psychoanalytic revolution?

The Freudian antinomianism not only challenged but reversed all human norms, as it was profoundly subversive, as Freud himself attests: "psycho-analysis...itself stands in opposition to everything that is conventionally restricted, well-established and generally accepted."[72] Freud in fact thrived in the face of opposition and in no way hesitated to confront it head on: "Many enemies, much honor."[73] Freud himself unequivocally stated: "we shall in the end conquer every resistance by emphasizing the unshakeable nature of our convictions."[74] These condensed exposés offer an uncanny synopsis of the inner recesses of the psychoanalytic doctrine, underscoring what has been termed a "cul-de-sac of pessimism"[75] by its founder, Sigmund Freud (1856–1939), a central figure of the twentieth century, who has irrevocably shaped the modern world beyond the scope of psychology and psychiatry.

Rather than being just one school of psychology among other schools, whether psychodynamic or depth psychology or another therapeutic approach, psychoanalysis is regarded as the "second force" in contemporary psychology, even though it predates the emergence of behavioristic psychology, known as the "first force."[76] This is because psychoanalysis did not become a mass phenomenon in America until after the Second World War.[77] Prior to World War II, psychoanalysis was for the most part only practiced in Europe and was discredited in America for being unscientific and written off as a "Jewish national affair"[78] or a "Jewish science," as proclaimed by Pierre Janet (1859–1957).[79] Freud recalls his overwhelmingly positive reception during his visit to America, writing:

> In Europe I felt as though I were despised; but over there [in America] I found myself received by the foremost men as an equal. As I stepped onto the platform at [Clark University in] Worcester [Massachusetts] to deliver my *Five Lectures upon Psychoanalysis* it seemed like the realization of some incredible day-dream: psychoanalysis was no longer a product of delusion, it had become a valuable part of reality.[80]

Freud, as is verified by his own impressions above, was overjoyed that psychoanalysis was received with open arms in the New World. Yet, while his popularity rose to prominence in post–World War II America, he was less optimistic about the general fate of America itself, as he remarked late in his life: "America is the most grandiose experiment the world has seen, but, I am afraid, it is not going to be a success."[81] Even with his success in America he was unable to reconcile the fact that the country he detested the most was the one that embraced his ideas most enthusiastically. This presented an inherent tension, if not a contradiction within him. Freud outlines the problems that he had with America in relation to the doctrine of psychoanalysis:

> I often hear that psycho-analysis is very popular in the United States and that it does not come up against the same stubborn resistance there as it does in Europe. My satisfaction over this is, however, clouded by several circumstances. It seems to me that the popularity of the name of psycho-analysis in America signifies neither a friendly attitude to the thing itself nor any specially

wide or deep knowledge of it. As evidence of the former fact I may point out that, although financial support is to be had easily and in plenty for every kind of scientific and pseudo-scientific enterprise, we have never succeeded in obtaining a backing for our psycho-analytic institutions. Nor is it hard to find evidence for my second assertion. Although America possesses several excellent analysts and, in Dr. A. A. Brill, at least one authority, the contributions to our science from that vast country are exiguous and provide little that is new. Psychiatrists and neurologists make frequent use of psycho-analysis as a therapeutic method, but as a rule they show little interest in its scientific problems and its cultural significance. Quite particularly often we find in American physicians and writers a very insufficient familiarity with psycho-analysis, so that they know only its terms and a few catchwords—through this does not shake them in the certainty of their judgment. And these same men lump psycho-analysis with other systems of thought, which may have developed out of it but are incompatible with it to-day. Or they make a hotch-potch out of psycho-analysis and other elements and quote this procedure as evidence of their *broad-mindedness*, whereas it only proves their *lack of judgement*.

Freud's anti-Americanism was barefaced, as exemplified by his comment made to Jones: "Yes, America is gigantic, but a gigantic mistake."[82]

A criticism launched at psychoanalysis by the behaviorists is that "Freud did not discover the mental apparatus but rather invented it."[83] As behaviorism regards the mind and consciousness itself as an epiphenomenon and discards the human psyche and Spirit, the above appraisal is more nuanced than it initially appears. Psychoanalysis, on the other hand, affirms the role of consciousness, as Freud notes: "if anyone speaks of consciousness we know immediately and from our most personal experience what is meant by it."[84] Freud near the age of seventy interestingly professed: "My life has been aimed at one goal only: to infer or to guess how the mental apparatus is constructed and what forces interplay and counteract in it."[85]

Without a doubt the influences of John B. Watson (1878–1958), the founder of behaviorism, like that of Freud, the founder of psychoanalysis, continue to linger in the shadows of contemporary psychology not merely in a peripheral manner, but are principal to it, for they have constructed the foundation of psychology and the mass therapies as a whole.[86] The gospel of secular psychology in many ways, whether it is apparent or not, continues to preach: "Seek ye first the kingdom of Freud and Skinner [including Watson], and all these things will be added unto you,"[87] continuing its allegiance to its erroneous and dehumanizing outlook and becoming a parody of the true psychological wholeness found in the spiritual domain as expressed in the adage: "Seek ye first the kingdom of God, and his righteousness; and all these things shall be added unto you" (Matthew 6:33).

Contemporary psychology continues to be constructed upon this seminal foundation of both systems, and their theories have been infused into the general culture in an indiscernible manner. The impact of these two paradigms is documented here: "Psychoanalysis and behaviorism thus laid the foundations of clinical and experimental psychology, which they dominated for most of the first half of the twentieth century, becoming known as the first and second forces of [contemporary] Western psychology."[88] An important reminder that tends to be overlooked by the more inclusive systems of psychotherapy is that "Psychoanalytic theory doesn't refute the behaviorists so much as put them in their place as custodians of a partial explanation of human behavior."[89]

The contemporary West has been profoundly influenced by Freud and psychoanalytic theory, much more so than many might suspect, for his ideas have been assimilated into the collective mindset in an enduring and virtually unnoticeable manner. This is evident in the recent proliferation of scholarship that has arisen with scores of publications on Freud and the history of psychoanalysis, signifying its colossal impact. While Freud may be one of the twentieth century's most influential figures, likewise, Freud is one of its most controversial figures. With this said, there are those who explicitly uphold that he is: "[T]he greatest con man in the history of medicine."[90] Abundant research is now pushing back against the edifice of the Freudian legend or myth, challenging its monolithic claims by exposing its misdeeds. Frederick Crews emphasizes, "Step by step, we are learning that Freud has been the most overrated figure in the entire history of science and medicine—one who wrought immense harm through the propagation of false etiologies, mistaken diagnoses, and fruitless lines of inquiry."[91] Social psychologist and psychoanalyst Erich Fromm (1900–80) also highlights Freud's deceptive role: "Under the disguise of a therapist and a scientist he was one of the great world reformers of the beginning twentieth century."[92]

So dominant was Freud's influence as one of the chief "architects of the modern age"[93] that it is worth recalling some of the declarations that have been made about Freud and the psychoanalytic doctrine:

"The Twentieth Century is now being called 'The Freudian Century' and 'The Age of the Freudian Revolution.' For a single man to dominate a century his work must affect all manner of thought and human activity."[94] Likewise, "Twentieth-century man is greatly indebted to Freud."[95] Freud's influence is profound because he laid the groundwork for the field of contemporary psychology to be established: "No one in our age can have an image of man which has not been in some decisive way influenced by Freud."[96] "[A]ll nineteenth-century psychiatry really converges on Freud."[97] "It is frequently asserted that in our thinking we all nowadays lie in the shadow of Freud: so powerful, indeed, has his influence been that it is all but impossible for us to imagine ourselves out from under it and to reconstruct the mental habits or attitudes of a pre-Freudian age."[98] "Thus Freud, in his historical existence, stands before us as the paradigmatic man of this century."[99] Again, in one way or another: "Conventional therapy, [is] based either strictly or loosely upon the psychoanalytic beliefs and teachings of Sigmund Freud."[100]

Developmental psychologist Erik H. Erikson (1902–94), writes: "Sigmund Freud's monumental work is the rock on which such exploration and advancement must be based."[101] Bleuler avows: "I consider your teaching [Freudian psychoanalysis] the greatest advancement in the science of psychology."[102] Some may be surprised that Abraham Maslow (1908–70), a pioneer within humanistic ("third force") and transpersonal ("fourth force") psychology, had the highest regard for the founder of psychoanalysis: "Freud was easily the greatest psychologist who ever lived."[103] Likewise, Frankl, an innovator within humanistic psychology and precursor to transpersonal psychology, also held him in great esteem: "the greatest spirit in psychotherapy [is] Sigmund Freud."[104]

The influence of Freudian psychoanalysis is recognized throughout all four "forces" of contemporary psychology, including transpersonal psychology: "However ambivalent most contemporary practitioners of transpersonal psychology may be about Freud, it is safe to say that there would be no transpersonal psychology as we know it without Freud's influence. Freud might be considered the grandfather of the entire movement."[105] For this reason, a key representative of humanistic psychology, James F. T. Bugental (1915–2008), emphasized: "Every psychotherapist is his own Freud today."[106] Influential Scottish psychiatrist R. D. Laing (1927–89), who was an important figure in the anti-psychiatry movement, wrote this on Freud: "I was influenced by Freud more than by any other psychiatrist or anyone else in psychiatry."[107]

Regardless of how far the field has advanced beyond the Freudian "talking cure," its hegemonic influence nonetheless continues within the mainstream outlook: "although the science and theory of psychoanalysis has advanced far beyond Freud, his influence is still strong and pervasive."[108] We are told by a biographer that "we all speak Freud today whether we recognize it or not."[109] A pressing and no doubt thought-provoking question regarding psychoanalysis and its mass propagation thus remains unanswered: "Against what backdrop of the history of ideas shall we place these momentous contributions of Freud?"[110] This being said, the additional follow-up question is paramount: "we can say with confidence that psychoanalysis did not make its way in the world either by curing sick patients or by demonstrating its scientific cogency.

But how did it succeed, then?"[111] Paul M. Churchland elaborates on this perplexing and ambiguous phenomenon that is psychoanalysis:

> The familiar caricature of the bearded and monocled Freudian analyst probing his reclining patient for memories of toilet training gone awry and parentally directing lust is now an anachronism, as is the professional practice of that mostly empty and confabulatory art. How such an elaborate theory could have become so widely accepted—on the basis of no systematic evidence or critical experiments, and in the face of chronic failures of therapeutic intervention in all of the major classes of mental illness (schizophrenia, mania, and depression)—is something that sociologists of science and popular culture have yet to fully explain.[112]

Malcolm Macmillan, an Australian psychologist, provides exhaustive research culminating in some two decades and outlines five reasons as to why psychoanalysis continues to appeal to the contemporary mind:

> Criticism of psychoanalysis is not new, and we should ask why Freud's theory continues to appeal. I believe it does for five main reasons. First, most lay people, as well as large number of nonanalyst professionals, think of psychoanalysis as beyond substantial criticism and as not much changed from the ideas advanced by Freud. Second, the understanding that psychoanalysis gives of the determinants of behavior and personality seems to be especially extensive. Third is the attraction of the irrational, which appeals in and of itself. The psychoanalytic irrational also appeals

13

because many aspects of it are like processes familiar from everyday life and not at all difficult to understand or apply. Fourth, psychoanalysis concentrates on precisely those things in which people have the greatest interest and about which no other discipline says much of anything. Fifth, most people take it for granted that the effectiveness of psychoanalysis as a therapy for a wide range of disorders and problems is well established and certainly not a matter of dispute.[113]

It is a daunting and laborious task to review the current body of psychoanalytical literature, the never-ending stream of anti-Freudian critiques, and no doubt the orthodox Freudian cannon itself to put first things first in order to make sense of it all. Canadian psychiatrist and historiographer of psychiatry Henri F. Ellenberger (1905–93) explains that the challenging nature of this task is due to the mythologizing of the man himself: "The difficulty in writing about Freud stems from the profusion of the literature about him, and from the fact that a legend had grown around him."[114] For this reason Peter J. Swales has suggested that Freud "is surely the most misunderstood figure in all human history."[115]

A major stumbling block for anyone examining the psychoanalytic "talking cure" is the numerous changes that Freud made to his theories and their blatant self-contradictions: "[Freud] constantly rechecked his ideas and concepts, constantly remodeled them. This makes it so difficult when we read in texts quotations from Freud because you always have to look carefully at what time Freud has written this. It's a very easy and endless game to play, to read quotations from different periods of his work and with different meanings."[116] Fromm makes note of another problematic and dubious facet of Freudianism: "the more time passed, the more hypothetical constructs turned into theories upon which new constructions and theories were built. Freud the theorist was very well aware of the doubtful validity of many of his constructs."[117]

Regardless of the obvious inconsistences in his so-called scientific psychology, there are those who are steadfast and still assert the validity of his theories: "While almost every theoretical concept formulated by Freud has been altered or restated, his basic contributions have been reaffirmed and validated."[118] In addition, the understanding that "Freud's career was established on a play on words"[119] presents itself as a conundrum of semantics, rendering the reading and comprehension of psychoanalysis problematic. This is evidenced here by Freud himself: "the one view, which only takes the wording into account, regards it as nonsense; the other view, following the hints that are given, passes through the hearer's unconscious and finds an excellent sense in it."[120]

Freudian psychodynamic theory, again, did not halt at the doors of psychology alone, but aimed at establishing both the foundations of modern psychology and a cultural superstructure that would have no limits, extending its tentacles into the lives of the multitudes. Maritain writes: "The matter is further complicated by the fact that interest in Freud's discoveries and theories has not been restricted to psychological and psychiatric circles."[121] Another difficulty is the lack of consensus from within Freudian orthodoxy itself: "anything that may be said about Freud's ideas can be contradicted by citations from Freud; and no one has yet been able to interpret Freud in a way that is acceptable to all Freudians."[122]

With all of these various factors taken into consideration, there appears to be if not a unanimity, a good amount of consensus, regardless of the unperceived hegemony of psychoanalysis, that there are clear signs indicating a fundamental disintegration of the psychodynamic paradigm. According to Professor Alan A. Stone, a former president of the American Psychiatric Association, "The collapse of conceptual solidarity is now felt at the very center of psychoanalysis—among the self-declared Freudians."[123] The crisis of psychoanalysis is in fact nothing less than the exposing of an illusion that masqueraded as a "science of the soul." It is not a crisis of a true psychology in troubled waters, but of a hoax being exposed for what it is: a fallen psychology or rather an inverted psychology predicated on an upside-down *Weltanschauung*.[124] As American psychologist Frank J. Sulloway emphasizes: "Few theories in science have spawned a following that can compare with the psychoanalytic movement in its cultlike manifestations, in its militancy, and in the aura of a religion that has permeated it."[125]

Chapter 1

The Psychoanalytic Revolution:
The Succession to the Copernican and
Darwinian Revolutions

"The psychology of the unconscious is the philosophy of revolution...because it ferments insurrection within the psyche, and liberates individuality from the bonds of its own unconscious."[1]—*Robert Graham*

Jungian analyst Coline Covington illustrates the subversive intentions of the "talking cure": "Analysis is essentially a tool for revolution."[2] She adds that its subversive uses were well known within the inner circle of the psychoanalytic movement: "Freud and his followers knew this very well."[3] Freud's strategic and no less deliberate positioning of himself on an equal par with canonical figures such as Copernicus and Darwin has considerably aided in the construction of the Freudian myth or legend. Freud in fact was regarded by some of his disciples as the "Darwin of the Mind."[4] Bleuler states, "One compares it [Freud's work] with that of Darwin [and] Copernicus...I believe too that for psychology your [Freud's] discoveries are equally fundamental as the theories of those men are for other branches of science, no matter whether or not one evaluates advancements in psychology as highly as those in other sciences."[5] To understand the broader historical impact of the psychoanalytic revolution it is necessary to situate it in succession to the revolutions of Copernicus and Darwin as Freud himself attests. To this end, Jones writes:

> How one man [Freud] alone could have broken all this new ground, and overcome all difficulties unaided, must ever remain a cause for wonder. It was the nearest to a miracle that human means can compass, one that surely surpasses even the loftiest intellectual achievements in mathematics and pure science. Copernicus and Darwin dared much in facing the unwelcome truths of outer reality, but to face those of inner reality costs something that only the rarest of mortals would unaided be able to give.[6]

Efforts to comprehend it as an independent or isolated phenomenon outside of this historical context will lead to incomplete interpretations of what psychoanalysis signifies in the deepest sense. According to Rabbi Joshua L. Liebman (1907–48), "religion, which already has made its peace with Copernicus and with Darwin, will have to make peace with Freud."[7] Psychoanalysis not only continues but also expands upon the outlook of the revolutions of Copernicus and Darwin; likewise, psychoanalysis continues and expands the theoretical underpinnings of the Renaissance, the Scientific Revolution, and the European Enlightenment, all of which contributed to the advent of the modern and by extension postmodern world of today. It needs to be remembered that "The historical and cultural importance of the Enlightenment cannot be overestimated: it contains the backbone of modern Western civilization."[8] We recall the following quote from a representative of the Enlightenment that planted the seeds of, if not anticipated, the Freudian revolution: "This happy age, which has seen a revolution produced in the human mind."[9]

The psychoanalytic "talking cure" therefore needs to be recognized as a continuation and expansion of one and the same secularism that was born with the Renaissance, the Scientific Revolution, and the so-called Enlightenment. Ellenberger puts forward this association, "The birth of dynamic psychiatry [or psychoanalysis] can also be understood as a manifestation of the victory of the cultural movement of the Enlightenment."[10] Freud's faithfulness to the Enlightenment is captured by one of his key biographers, Peter Gay: "Freud was a loyal son of the Enlightenment."[11] Fromm suggests, "Freud was one of the last representatives of Enlightenment philosophy."[12] When we step back and analyze the broader historical landscape, the same secularizing outlook of the Enlightenment becomes instrumentally connected with the psychoanalytic revolution. An example of this is made evident in Freud's correspondence with Swiss Lutheran minister Oskar Pfister (1873–1956), who writes: "Your substitute for religion is basically the idea of the eighteenth-century Enlightenment in proud modern guise."[13]

The full-scale assault of the psychoanalytic revolt is evident and discernable in Freud's parable of the "three blows," when he attacks what he has diagnosed as "human narcissism" or the traditional belief that the human being is "made in the image of God" (Genesis 1:27) or is theomorphic in essence.[14] The human being was traditionally recognized as a microcosm of the macrocosm, being inseparable from and closely connected to the Spirit: "And God said, Let us make man in our image, after our likeness" (Genesis 1:26).

The first is the "cosmological" blow, more commonly known as the "Copernican revolution" attributed to Nicolaus Copernicus (1473–1543), which severed man from the traditional understanding of the cosmos with man as its miniature, often regarded as the human microcosm. "Man is a little cosmos, and the cosmos is like a big man."[15] According to influential historian of science Alexandre Koyré (1892–1964), "the immediate effect of the Copernican revolution was to spread skepticism and bewilderment."[16] Nasr depicts how it strategically undermined the sense of the sacred: "The Copernican revolution brought about all the spiritual and religious upheavals that its opponents forecasted would happen precisely because it came at a time when philosophical doubt reigned everywhere, and a humanism, already over a century old, had taken away from man his position as the 'divine image' on earth."[17] In the end, this initial cosmological blow was destructive to Western civilization: "the so-called Copernican Revolution...[that] has been depicted...as a victory of science over superstition, is in reality the fateful step that has closed the door to any higher understanding of man and his destiny."[18]

The second is the "biological" blow, or what has been termed the "Darwinian revolution" attributed to Charles Darwin (1809–82) that disconnected man from the traditional understanding of his origin in the Divine, equating what is human with animality. Martin Lings (1909–2005) points out: "There can be little doubt that in the modern world more cases of loss of religious faith are to be traced to the theory of evolution as their immediate cause than to anything else."[19] Fromm discusses the process of dethroning God and the emergence of what he terms "the idolatry of evolution":

> The deep need of man not to feel lost and lonely in the world had, of course, been previously satisfied by the concept of a God who had created this world and was concerned with each and every creature. When the theory of evolution destroyed the picture of God as the supreme Creator, confidence in God as the all-powerful Father of man fell with it...[F]or many of those for whom God was dethroned, the need for a godlike figure did not disappear. Some proclaimed a new god, Evolution, and worshiped Darwin as his prophet...Darwin had revealed the ultimate truth regarding the origin of man; all human phenomena which might be approached and explained by economic, religious, ethical, or political consideration were to be understood from the point of view of evolution.[20]

The third is the "psychological" blow or what can be termed the "psychoanalytic revolution" attributed to Sigmund Freud, who attacked the traditional understanding of the faculties of reason (*ratio*) and the Intellect (*Intellectus*), proclaiming human beings to be controlled by unconscious or instinctual forces that exist beyond the normal reaches of awareness. Freud writes: "man's intellect is powerless in comparison with his instinctual life."[21] This overturns the traditional understanding of the Intellect as being a transcendent faculty immanent within the human being that allows him or her to directly apprehend the Absolute. Freud categorically launches his psychological blow in the following maxim that triumphantly inverts the role of the Intellect and reason, placing the unconscious above the conscious, or the superconscious for that matter: "the Ego is not master in its own house."[22] This subverts the metaphysical and transcendent symbolism of the human being in relation to the cosmos, as is affirmed here: "the terrestrial position of the human being serving as the fixed point to which will be related all the movements of the stars—here symbolises the central role of man in the cosmic whole, of which man is like the goal and the centre of gravity."[23] The human being is both geomorphic and theomorphic: "Man, the transient [in his form], the eternal [in his essence]."[24]

While Freud intentionally dealt a blow traumatizing the so-called "human narcissism" in order to sublimate it to the secular outlook of the modern world, it was in fact a decisive assault on religion and the human collectivity's reliance on the spiritual domain to provide an integral epistemology and ontology. It is the spiritual domain, which is transpersonal in nature and simultaneously immanent within the human being, that alone can provide psychological health and well-being and, more important, the realization of the Absolute. These blows signified to traditional humanity nothing less than a cataclysmic event, as the human being was made in and is centered in the transpersonal. The Freudian revolution was an attempted overthrow of medieval epistemology that defined knowledge as "*adaequatio rei et intellectus*—the understanding of the knower must be *adequate* to the thing to be known."[25] This is to say that in the traditional or premodern world there were levels of reality and corresponding levels of knowledge by which to know these distinct levels. There was a distinction made between relative knowledge and knowledge that is Absolute. The transcendent or noetic faculty immanent within the human being enables him or her to know the fullness of what can be known.

These events were a catalyst that gave rise to the psychological man of the modern world. The psychoanalytic revolution and its historical implications are made abundantly clear in Freud's own description of the "three blows":

> [I]n thus emphasizing the unconscious in mental life we have conjured up the most evil spirits of criticism against psycho-analysis. Do not be surprised at this, and do not suppose that the resistance to us rests only on the understandable difficulty of the unconscious or the relative inaccessibility of the experiences which provide evidence of it. Its source, I think, lies deeper. In the course of centuries the *naïve* self-love of men has had to submit to two major blows at the hands of science. The first was when they learnt that our earth was not the centre of the universe but only a tiny fragment of a cosmic system of scarcely imaginable vastness. This is associated in our minds with the name of Copernicus, though something similar had already been asserted by Alexandrian science. The second blow fell when biological research destroyed man's supposedly privileged place in creation and proved his descent from the animal kingdom and his ineradicable animal nature. This revaluation has been accomplished in our own days by Darwin, Wallace and their predecessors, though not without the most violent contemporary opposition. But human megalomania will have suffered its third and most wounding blow from the psychological research of the present time which seeks to prove to the ego that it is not even master in its own house, but must be content itself with scanty information of what is going on unconsciously in its mind. We psycho-analysts were not the first and not the only ones to utter this call to introspection; but it seems to be our fate to give it its most forcible expression and to support it with empirical material which affects every individual. Hence arises the general revolt against our science, the disregard of all considerations of academic civility and the releasing of the opposition from every restraint of impartial logic.[26]

The destruction caused by Freud's paradigmatic attack still reverberates into the present-day, and paradoxically his psychoanalytic revolt itself does not substantiate its own claims of scientific legitimacy. This does not of course keep Freud from attempting not only to assert legitimacy, but also to claim a monopoly on truth itself regardless of the absence of data confirming his theories. Writer and journalist Janet Malcolm stresses the disastrous consequences of these attempts:

[T]he psychoanalytic revolution with the revolution of Copernicus and then the revolution of Darwin, saying that the first
showed that the earth was not the center of the universe, the second that man was not a unique creation, and the third [the psychoanalytic revolution] that man was not even master of his own
house. It was as if a lonely terrorist working in his cellar on a
modest explosive device to blow up the local brewery had unac-
countably found his way to the hydrogen bomb and blown up half
the world. The fallout from this bomb has yet to settle. It isn't
even clear whether the original target—the neurotic patient—
wasn't overshot; "proof" of the efficacy of psychoanalytic cure
has yet to be established, and no analyst claims it.[27]

Even though he waged his assault in no uncertain terms, Freud's
comprehension of cosmology appears to be limited to say the least,
especially as it applies to that of medieval cosmology. Freud's assessment of traditional cosmology is deeply flawed and erroneous, as is
made clear with further analysis. British historian R. G. Collingwood
(1889–1943) observes:

The crisis of modern cosmology dates to the middle of the six-
teenth century. It was in 1543 that Copernicus's work on the solar
system (*De revolutionibus orbium coelestium*) was posthu-
mously published. The new astronomy expounded in this book
displaced the earth from the center of the world and explained the
planetary movements on a heliocentric hypothesis. The philosophical significance of this new astronomy was profound, but it
has often been misunderstood. It is commonly said that its effect
was to diminish the importance of the earth in the scheme of
things and to teach man that he is only a microscopic parasite on
a small speck of cool matter revolving round one of the minor
stars. This is an idea both philosophically foolish and historically
false...[H]istorically false, because the littleness of man in the
world has always been a familiar theme of reflection.[28]

The fact is that Freud's notion of "human narcissism" was not
unknown as he assumed, but it was not framed within this outlook and
terminology. It is essential to situate the Freudian revolution within
the broader historical context to see how it aided modern science in
undermining the traditional cosmology of the Great Chain of Being
that was a universal norm across the cultures. Historian of ideas Arthur Lovejoy (1873–1962) states:

[T]he conception of the universe as a "Great Chain of Being"...ranging in hierarchical order from the meagerest kind of existents...through "every possible" grade up to the *ens perfectissimum*...has, in one form or another, been the dominant official philosophy of the larger part of...mankind through most of its history.[29]

The littleness of man in the cosmos was not unknown in the Middle Ages, as evidenced by Boethius's (480–524) description contained within the *De Consolatione Philosophiae* (*The Consolation of Philosophy*), considered to be one of the most influential works of this time:

Thou hast learnt from astronomical proofs that the whole earth compared with the universe is no greater than a point, that is, compared with the sphere of the heavens, it may be thought of as having no size at all. Then, of this tiny corner, it is only one-quarter that, according to Ptolemy, is habitable to living things. Take away from this quarter the seas, marshes, and other desert places, and the space left for man hardly even deserves the name of infinitesimal.[30]

Freud's assault on medieval cosmology must not be minimized and does not in any way legitimize the emergence of psychoanalysis. British-born scientist John Wren-Lewis (1923–2006) asserts:

[I]n truth, medieval theology did *not* give man delusions of grandeur about his place in the universe by its placing the earth at the centre of things. On the contrary, this centre was thought of as a very lowly place, to which mankind was supposed to be consigned because of a fall from grace: the only lower place in the medieval view was hell, which was held to be at the centre of the earth itself. The really important regions of the universe were the spheres beyond the sphere of the moon—the spheres of the planets, the sphere of the fixed stars, the *primum mobile* and, most remote of all, the heavenly realm where the Deity was supposed to dwell, the supremely important Being at the greatest distance of all from the centre. The destruction of medieval cosmology by Copernicus and Galileo was therefore in no sense a demotion of man from an exalted position in his own estimation of himself.[31]

Freud misconstrued medieval cosmology's erudite understanding of the human being's place within the Great Chain of Being that encompassed all life forms:

> [I]t is quite untrue to say that medieval theology gave man an exalted view of his place in the scale of living creatures. It actually sets him very near the bottom of the scale, for it envisaged great ranges of living things above man—angels, archangels, thrones, dominations, principalities, powers, cherubim and seraphim—far outnumbering the orders of animal creation inferior to him.[32]

It was the ascendency of a desacralized worldview, which arose through modern science, that undermined traditional cosmology. Foremost philosopher and scholar of Islamic and comparative religion Seyyed Hossein Nasr writes: "The 'great chain of being' of the Western tradition...survived in the West until it became horizontalized."[33] The undermining of the Great Chain of Being through the emergence of modern science is emphasized again by doyen of the world's religions Huston Smith (1919–2016): "Since the Great Chain of Being collapsed with the rise of modern science, something in scientific aims and methods must be inimical to it."[34]

The traditional cosmology—or rather *cosmologia perennis*—while differing on the formal level is unanimous on the supra-formal level, situating the human being and the whole of reality in its rightful place.[35] This is made evident in Philip Sherrard's (1922–95) description:

> The Platonic hierarchy of forms is really a structure of participations stretching from the highest supersensual realities down to those of the visible world. It is this structure of participations which constitutes the great golden chain of being, that unbroken connection between the highest and lowest levels of life. In this structure, there is nothing that is not animate, nothing that is mere dead matter. All is endowed with being...even the least particle...belongs to a living, transmuting whole, each thing is a revelation of the indwelling creative spirit. It was not until the end of the eighteenth century, with Lavoisier and his peers and followers, that the scientific intelligence in Europe became so blunted and whittled down that it lost its sense of the mysterious numinosity of all things, reduced everything either to phenomenon (fact) or to mathematical hypothesis (or, in less polite language,

fiction), and conceived the physical world to be no more than so much inanimate dead matter whose chemical changes were mechanical processes based upon the so-called law of the conservation of mass.[36]

Freud's antagonism toward medieval cosmology is due to its connection with religion. It became necessary for Freud to replace medieval cosmology with a secular theory such as the doctrine of evolution to establish that psychoanalysis was scientific, which no less than paved the way for the secular foundation for the whole of modern psychology.[37] Sulloway submits: "perhaps nowhere was the impact of Darwin, direct and indirect, more exemplary or fruitful outside of biology proper than within Freudian psychoanalysis."[38] The paradigmatic shift that led to a desacralized outlook is made apparent here: "The Darwinian revolution came as a blow to traditional religion not because it degraded man's place in the scale of life...but because it destroyed the notion of the Great System in nature, by exposing the apparent 'order of creation' as merely a by-product of chance."[39]

The narrative of the "three blows" to what is termed "human narcissism" illuminates how Freud's discovery of the "talking cure" takes on its own supernatural character that is viewed as an unparalleled historical event within his inner circle, which gave birth to the Freudian myth or legend as recalled by an official biographer and disciple, Ernest Jones, who writes:

> In the summer of 1897 the spell began to break, and Freud undertook his most heroic feat—a psychoanalysis of his own unconscious. It is hard for us nowadays to imagine how momentous this achievement was, that difficult being the fate of most pioneering exploits. Yet the uniqueness of the feat remains. Once done it is done forever. For no one again can be the first to explore those depths.[40]

Jones not only places the "talking cure" at the acme of human realization, but situates Freud above the saints and sages of all times and places, as it is implicitly he alluded to when he describes Freud as "following a path hitherto untrodden by any human being, by the heroic task of exploring his own unconscious mind."[41]

When we frame the Freudian revolution as the heir of the revolutions of Copernicus and Darwin, Freud's messianic mission to attack and ultimately surmount the domain of religion to deify himself becomes blatantly clear: "Confronting religion, psychoanalysis shows itself for what it is: the last great formulation of nineteenth-century secularism, complete with substitute doctrine and cult."[42] The de-sacralization of the "science of the soul," or psychology that severed the human psyche, from Spirit was certainly a revolution, as it turned the perennial psychology found across the cultures on its head. "The redefinition of psychology was a revolution in the truest sense of the word. What was up went down, and what was down went up. Before that revolution, reason sat on instinct like a rider on a horse."[43]

The doctrine of psychoanalysis has fundamentally eclipsed the way that the human individual was viewed and understood not only in the contemporary West, but across all traditional societies and civilizations. This reverberates with the fact that "Sigmund Freud has changed the image of man."[44] The epistemological limits of psychodynamic theory and its science need to be clearly emphasized: "[M]odern science has produced no cosmology, and is in fact incapable—by virtue of its very methodology—of doing so...[I]t has imposed a kind of pseudo-cosmology, masquerading as science".[45] Freud thus not only sanctified himself into the highest ranks of the demigods of science, but consecrated himself as its final messenger in this temporal cycle as indicated here: "He [Freud] is the Seal of the Prophets of naturalism, heralding the definitive unification of all nature and the final inclusion of humankind, in all their aspects, within it."[46] Rieff confirms, "Freud represents the climax of the nineteenth-century tradition of scientific prophecy as a functional substitute for religious prophecy."[47]

Chapter 2

Psychoanalysis, the Loss of Faith, and the Signs of the Times

"Blessed are they that have not seen, and yet have believed."—John 20:29

"Psychoanalysis is a characteristic expression of [modern] Western man's spiritual crisis, and an attempt to find a solution."[1]—Erich Fromm

The rejection of tradition and the blind adherence to secularization has become a universal dogma of the modern and postmodern world. Jung has identified Freud as the destroyer of tradition: "He is a great destroyer who breaks the fetters of the past."[2]

The contemporary mind has in essence closed itself off to the sacred and the necessity of tradition. Nasr underscores the fundamental distinction between tradition and the ideology of modernism, "that which is cut off from the transcendent, from the immutable principles which in reality govern all things and which are made known to man through revelation in its most universal sense."[3] This intellectual myopia of the modern world has led to a fundamentally distorted meaning of tradition, as Rama P. Coomaraswamy (1929–2006) points out:

> Modern man is...totally unfamiliar with traditional concepts [of religion]...For him the supernatural is vaguely identified with the superstitious, faith with credulity, firmness with fanaticism, the uncompromising with the intolerant, and consistency with narrowness of outlook. The very idea that a given religion should have the "fullness of the truth" appears to him both incongruous and offensive.[4]

It was the conventional wisdom of the premodern or traditional world that "Man cannot live without faith."[5] The implications of the loss of the sense of the sacred for the human collectivity are fatal, as Swiss philosopher Frithjof Schuon (1907–98) points out: "the loss of religion is a disaster for a human society; it is to deprive man of a vital substance and to dehumanize him."[6] Schuon points out that: "Faith [is] the intuition of the transcendent"[7] and "Faith...is the adherence of the intelligence to Revelation."[8] One might ask if there is an inverse correlation between the emergence of Freudian doctrine and the abandoning of one's faith. Freud responds to this query in a vague and rhetorical, if not tongue-and-cheek, manner by writing: "It remains to be considered whether analysis *in itself* must really lead to the giving up of religion."[9] Gay interestingly suggests that "Freud became a psychoanalyst in large part *because* he was an atheist."[10]

Without the contextualization of the emergence of psychoanalysis within the spiritual crisis of the contemporary West, the mass propagation of the doctrine of the "talking cure" remains a curious phenomenon in the history of ideas, appearing as a fluke, as if it originated independent of any temporal or social factors. Yet such is not the case, as Freud's psychoanalytic "talking cure" is firmly rooted in the consciousness of nineteenth-century fin-de-siècle Vienna, even though he himself fought against this notion to perpetuate his own pseudo-myth that it was an ahistorical or atemporal phenomenon. Valer Barbu (1892–1986), corrects this erroneous portrayal by debunking the Freudian legend:

> We must try to see Freud in the perspective of his time. The late nineteenth century was predominantly materialistic and cynical in its thinking. This was partly due to the astounding advances made in the sciences: the progress of physics and chemistry, the discovery of germs as causes of diseases, the progress of pathology and, finally, Darwin's theory of the evolution of man from the animal. The animal nature of man was stressed. Something had to be found in his animal nature to account for his difficulties as a human being. Parts were made to account for the whole. Sexuality appeared to Freud as the foundation of personality and character. Specialization was glorified; larger horizons were lost sight of. Freud's theories fit very well into this so-called scientific period.[11]

The phenomenon that is psychoanalysis becomes intelligible when situated within the gradual decline of religion and spirituality in which it arose that is inseparable from the development of the modern world. "Freudian doctrine aspires quite exactly to take the place left empty by religion."[12] Freudianism is a result of modernism and needs to be understood in this light. Former Professor Emeritus of Psychology and Religious Studies Peter Homans (1930–2009) states: "Freud's therapy was closely related to the predicament of modernity; that predicament was defined as the loss of traditional religious meaning; religion had to be reinterpreted in light of the character of modernity."[13]

Since the birth of the Renaissance, the Scientific Revolution, and the so-called Enlightenment, the West has become increasingly secular in its outlook, which has steadily weakened and marginalized the centrality of religion and spirituality. It is critical to recognize that the Renaissance was not a rebirth in knowledge as is often assumed, but rather a degeneration of the highest order. Lings observes, "the Renaissance...was one of the greatest milestones of decline in Western Europe."[14] Again, "One of the commonplaces of modern historiography is the polemical exaltation of the civilization of the Renaissance over and against medieval civilization."[15]

In the undermining of the centrality of religion and spirituality in the lives of the collectivity, a devastating vacuum has been left in its wake.[16] Hence it is evident and cannot be denied that "Psychoanalysis...has contributed to this crisis."[17] The Freudian revolution has caused significant harm to the Christian tradition, as Professor Wolfgang Smith states: "It has undermined the remaining vestiges of Christian culture and succeeded brilliantly in its program of deconversion."[18] Frank Maraun comments: "First it was psychoanalysis, with its claim to be a new doctrine of salvation for sick minds, that attacked Christianity, declared religion to be out of date, and chose itself as its appointed successor, as the contemporary fulfillment of the religious mission to mankind."[19]

Psychoanalysis was not an innocent bystander observing the unfolding spiritual crisis, but clearly contributed to this crisis and benefited from it in order to usurp its role. Eminent American perennialist author Whitall N. Perry (1920–2005),elaborates on this issue:

> Of the forces at work radically modifying the nature of Western and Christian civilization, there are those which are open and violent and easily discernible, and there are those which are covert and subtle and easily ambiguous. The domain of psychoanalysis with its many ramifications answers particularly well to this second category: in the arts, in the social sciences, indeed in practically every contemporary intellectual movement, and on all levels of society, Freudian concepts and practices have infiltrated to the point where they are so taken for granted that the source is all but ignored.[20]

Psychoanalysis is in many ways an attempt to fill the spiritual void—the loss of the sense of the sacred—both in the outer world of society and in the inner world of the human being. Perry emphasizes that "The loss of religion as Center in the world has left a hole which psychology is trying to fill."[21] This connection is made further here: "Psychoanalysis arose as the result of a long historical mourning process begun centuries ago, with roots in the origins of physical science in the seventeenth century...Secularization has been an ever-so-gradual kind of mourning for the lost symbols and the communal wholeness they organize in the West."[22] From this point of view secularism is then a sign of both individual and social disintegration, as Theodore Roszak (1933–2011) emphasizes: "Secularization is an idolatry of cultural fragments—the part mistaken for the whole, the lesser reality substituted for the greater."[23]

Because of the events of the Renaissance, the Scientific Revolution, and the Enlightenment, the West lost its traditional identity in Christendom or what was known as the Christian world, which many in the present day erroneously assume is still Christian. As C. S. Lewis (1898–1963) emphasizes, we live today in a post-Christian epoch.[24] Professor Louis Dupré further adds that, "the eighteenth century was the first non-Christian century...For the first time, the secular became dominant."[25] Moreover, "The modern West is said to be Christian, but this is untrue: the modern outlook is anti-Christian, because it is essentially anti-religious."[26] For this reason, it has been astutely designated by Smith that: "the post-Christian West may possibly be the first society in human history bereft of a liturgical foundation...And this, to be sure, is the reason why in our secularized Western civilization, culture in the true sense has declined to the point of disappearance."[27] As a result, he further adds, *"Scientism proves in the end to be the idolatry of a post-Christian civilization."*[28]

It is noteworthy to recall that the destructive events of the Second Vatican Council (1962–1965) occurred during the counter-cultural 1960's with events such as the psychedelic revolution[29] and the sexual revolution converged, at a time when many of Freud's theories were available for mass consumption.[30] It is important to draw a connection between the undermining of the Christian tradition by the psychoanalytic revolution and how these events left innumerable individuals lost and without a sacred center maintained by tradition itself: "By exiling the Church a vacuum is created."[31] The secularization of the contemporary West has had a detrimental impact, which is now felt throughout the four directions of the earth, especially so with continual forces of globalization: "nothing is more tragic to a civilization than the loss of its tradition."[32]

Richard M. Weaver (1910–1963) emphasizes the consequences of the vacuum created by the modern world and the importance of realizing its impact to rectify what has transpired, "to establish the fact of decadence is the most pressing duty of our time,"[33] and likewise confirms, "cultural decline is a historical fact."[34] The collective decadence is catastrophic because the inertia builds until it becomes so widespread of a phenomenon that the decadence becomes unnoticeable and untraceable, or in other words normalized into the culture at large. Weaver elaborates on its repercussions for the human collectivity:

> [O]ur most serious obstacle is that people traveling this downward path develop an insensibility which increases with their degradation. Loss is perceived most clearly at the beginning; after habit becomes implanted, one beholds the anomalous situation of apathy mounting as the moral crisis deepens. It is when the first faint warnings come that one has the best chance to save himself; and this...explains why medieval thinkers were extremely agitated over questions which seem to us today without point or relevance. If one goes on, the monitory voices fade out, and it is not impossible for him to reach a state in which his entire moral orientation is lost. Thus in the face of the enormous brutality of our age we seem unable to make appropriate response to perversions of truth and acts of bestiality...We approach a condition in which we shall be amoral without the capacity to perceive it and degraded without means to measure our descent.[35]

There are disastrous consequences when a divine Revelation that is bestowed on a particular human collectivity is destabilized or undermined; seldom explored are its harmful impacts on the psychological health and well-being of that society. When the Christian tradition was still strong in the West, until the late Middle Ages or prior to the Renaissance, it unified and integrated the human psyche into its homogenous spiritual identity; however, this was further hindered with the introduction of Freud's psychoanalysis: "The complexes, anxieties, and fears of the modern soul did not exist to such an extent in previous generations because they were shaken off and integrated in the great social-spiritual organism of Christian Civilization."[36]

Freud and his disciples were fully aware of the weakening of the Christian tradition in the West and the spiritual crisis in their midst as Freud noted: "religion no longer has the same influence on people that it used to."[37] The marginalization of faith in the modern world gave rise to the notion of "homo psychologicus" or psychological man, as Jung explains:

> The modern man has lost all the metaphysical certainties of his mediæval brother...Science has destroyed even the refuge of the inner life...This "psychological" interest of the present time shows that man expects something from psychic life which he has not received from the outer world: something which our religions, doubtless, ought to contain, but no longer do contain—at least for the modern man. The various forms of religion no longer appear to the modern man to come from within—to be expressions of his own psychic life; for him they are to be classed with the things of the outer world. He is vouchsafed no revelation of a spirit that is not of this world; but he tries on a number of religions and convictions as if they were Sunday attire, only to lay them aside again like worn-out clothes.[38]

What in earlier times was recognized as a religious and spiritual phenomenon is now interpreted through the secular lens of modern psychology as mental illness: "in the darkest Middle Ages...they spoke of the devil, today we call it a neurosis."[39] Although modern science challenges the notion of sin, nonetheless, an important correlation between aberrant human behavior and mental illness appears to exist. American psychologist O. Hobart Mowrer (1907–82) elaborates on this point:

> Sin used to be—and, in some quarters, still is—defined as whatever one does that puts him in danger of going to Hell. Here was an assumed cause-and-effect relationship that was completely metaphysical and empirically unverifiable; and it is small wonder that it has fallen into disrepute as the scientific outlook and method have steadily gained in acceptance and manifest power. But there is a very tangible and very present Hell-on-this-earth which science has not yet helped us understand very well; and so I invite your attention to the neglected but very real possibility that it is *this* Hell—the Hell of neurosis and psychosis—to which sin and unexpiated guilt lead us and that it is *this* Hell that gives us *one* of the most, perhaps *the* most realistic and basic criteria for defining sin and guilt. If it proves empirically true that certain forms of conduct characteristically lead human beings into emotional instability, what better or firmer basis would one wish for

labeling such conduct as destructive, self-defeating, evil, sin-ful?[40]

If we return to the original meaning of the term "sin," it denotes the state of missing the mark, of error. Jung's description of neurosis in the form of nervous disorders appears as a psychological reworking of the doctrine of sin, and "consist[s] primarily in an alienation from one's instincts, a splitting off of consciousness from certain basic facts of the psyche."[41] The deviation that is the modern world exists be-cause of the desacralized outlook that dominates our epoch; in this way the following statement made by Jung can be understood: "mod-ern man lives in sin."[42]

In sketching the secular trajectory that began with the Renais-sance and the Scientific Revolution that led to the Enlightenment, we may discern how the steady decline of religion and spirituality brought about a psychological outlook devoid of Spirit: "The reli-gious appeal of Freud's theory was a particular reason for its ac-ceptance in America in the early years of this [the twentieth] century. A revolt was occurring not only against Victorian morality but against traditional Christianity as well."[43] Jung too saw this dilemma and weighs in on the decline of morality due to the loss of the sense of the sacred: "Man...feels in his heart the instability of present-day moral-ity, no longer supported by living religious conviction. Here is the source of most of our ethical conflicts. The urge to freedom beats upon the weakening barriers of morality."[44]

Jung explicitly spells out that "Psychoanalysis stands outside tra-ditional morality."[45] At the same time, it is necessary to point out that Jung argued that tradition was another means of controlling or engi-neering consent of the masses and denied its connection to transcend-ent principles: "The hypnotic power of tradition still holds us in thrall, and out of cowardice and thoughtlessness the herd goes trudging along the same old path."[46] It hardly needs to be illustrated that the opposite is true. This speaks more to Jung's misunderstanding as to what tradition signifies in its truest sense, as sacred tradition is linked to the transcendent and the spiritual domain itself and is not a man-made phenomenon.

Jung erects a dogma of relativism by making an absolute out of the relative, which undermines the metaphysical and transcendent re-ality at the heart of all religions. Sherrard observes:

Indeed, it is precisely this, that he did wish to undermine the tra-ditional basis of religious dogma, as well as of all theological

33

thought of the traditional kind...So long as the great structure of Christian doctrine and dogma, regarded as sacred and inviolate, stood in the way, his own ideas could make little progress. But if he could show that this structure shared in all the necessary limitations of human thought as he conceived them and was in fact essentially subjective and relative and psychic, its authority would be shaken.[47]

Freud as noted previously attempted to fill the spiritual vacuum with his doctrine of the "talking cure," giving rise to the notion of psychological man. Maurice Friedman (1921–2012) credits Freud for this phenomenon: "To Freud, more than to any other single person, goes the credit and the blame for ushering in the age of the Psychological Man."[48] It was not unknown that Freud was one of the most militant enemies of religion and tirelessly pathologized it at every opportunity. A consummate example of Freud's attack on religion was its relegation to the sphere of mental illness: "religion as a universal obsessional neurosis."[49]

An interesting phenomenon about the Freudian "talking cure" is that it lays bare the intrapsychic predicament occurring within the contemporary mind, as it attempts to treat or rather fill the void with the loss of the sense of the sacred and what could alternatively be regarded as the trauma of secularism. Romanian historian of religion Mircea Eliade (1907–86) illustrates the psychological and spiritual predicament of abandoning one's religion:

> Using the very tools and method of modern psychoanalysis, we can lay open some tragic secrets of the modern Western intellectual: for example, his profound dissatisfaction with the worn-out forms of historical Christianity and his desire to violently rid himself of his forefathers' faith, accompanied by a strange sense of guilt, as if he himself had killed a God in whom he could not believe but whose absence he could not bear.[50]

Psychoanalytic theory even in its broader leanings recognizes the vacuum that is left by the marginalization of religion and spirituality in the modern world and the dilemma of a faithless world. Erikson observes,

> The psychopathologist cannot avoid observing that there are millions of people who cannot really afford to be without religion, and whose pride in not having it is that much whistling in the dark. On the other hand, there are millions who seem to derive

faith from other than religious dogmas, that is, from fellowship, productive work, social action, scientific pursuit, and artistic creation. And again, there are millions who profess faith, yet in practice mistrust both life and man. With all of these in mind, it seems worthwhile to speculate on the fact that religion through the centuries has served to restore a sense of trust at regular intervals in the form of faith while giving tangible form to a sense of evil which it promises to ban. All religions have in common the periodical childlike surrender to a Provider or providers who dispense earthly fortune as well as spiritual health; the demonstration of one's smallness and dependence through the medium of reduced posture and humble gesture; the admission in prayer and song of misdeeds, of misthoughts, and of evil intentions; the admission of inner division and the consequent appeal for inner unification by divine guidance; the need for clearer self-delineation and self-restriction; and finally, the insight that individual trust must become a common faith, individual mistrust a commonly formulated evil, while the individual's need for restoration must become part of the ritual practice of many, and must become a sign of trustworthiness in the community. Whosoever says he has religion must derive a faith from it which is transmitted to infants in the form of basic trust; whosoever claims that he does not need religion must derive such basic faith from elsewhere.[51]

With the emergence of the spiritual crisis in the contemporary West came many social problems, which continue to increase in quantity and complexity. In this context, the following assessment by literary scholar Werner Kraft (1896–1991) is apropos: "psychoanalysis is one of those mass movements which are both a cause and consequence of spiritual decay."[52] Although forgotten in the present-day, faith is essential in all human endeavors: "without faith, it is impossible to please God" (Hebrews 11:6) and "If ye love me, keep my commandments" (John 14:15).

Chapter 3

The Secret Inner Circle of the
Psychoanalytic Movement

In 1912, a clandestine group had been formed within the psychoanalytic movement in order "to maintain the faith and to search out deviance,"[1] or essentially for "the cultivation of Freudian Ψa [psychoanalysis]."[2] The secret committee originally consisted of five of Freud's closest collaborators: Ernest Jones, Sándor Ferenczi, Otto Rank, Hanns Sachs (1881–1947), and Karl Abraham (1877–1925). An additional member, Max Eitingon (1881–1943), was added to the committee in 1919. Of all the many peculiar facets of the early formation of modern psychology, perhaps none parallels the origins of psychoanalysis and its code of strict secrecy and silence. Little is it known that "The history of the psychoanalytic movement is littered with suicides, and this pressure-cooker atmosphere of implicit blackmail may have played a role in some of them."[3]

The authoritarianism and abuses of power within the inner circle is striking: "Freud was often deceptive, manipulative, and Machiavellian. He schemed with his favorites to get rid of others for whom he expressed contempt, riding roughshod over them when they got in the way of his grand design."[4] The intention behind the formation of the inner circle becomes apparent, as American psychologist Louis Breger indicates: "The purpose of the Committee was to stifle debate and impose censorship."[5] An essential point about Freud and the psychoanalytic revolution is made available when Freud admonishes his disciple Eva Rosenfeld (1892–1977) by emphasizing the sole purpose of forming the inner circle: "We have only one aim and only one loyalty, to psychoanalysis."[6] In a letter to Jones written on August 1, 1912, Freud expresses:

> What took hold of my imagination immediately is your idea of a secret council composed of the best and most trustworthy among our men to take care of the further development of psycho-analysis and defend the cause against personalities and accidents when I am no more...I know there is a boyish and perhaps romantic element too in this conception, but perhaps it could be adapted to meet the necessities of reality.[7]

Freud emphasizes the necessity of utmost secrecy for the doctrine of psychoanalysis: "First of all: This committee would have to be *strictly secret* in its existence and in its actions."[8] We learn that Freud provided initiatic rings to each member of the secret committee and explains their significance: "Once upon a time these rings were a privilege and a mark distinguishing a group of men who were united in their devotion to psychoanalysis, who had promised to watch its development as a 'secret committee,' and to practice among themselves a kind of analytical brotherhood."[9] Jones informs readers that upon the inner circle's first gathering the following summer: "On May 25, 1913, Freud celebrated the event by presenting us each with an antique Greek intaglio from his collection which we then got mounted in a gold ring."[10] From its very inception it needs to be kept in mind that "Psychoanalysis always was, from the moment Freud found disciples, a semisecret society. This secrecy has never disappeared."[11]

Ferenczi discusses the hierarchical order in a letter to Freud dated February 5, 1910: "the psychoanalytical outlook does not lead to democratic equalizing: there should be an *élite* rather on the lines of Plato's rule of philosophers."[12] Three days later Freud reportedly replied to Ferenczi stating that he had already had the same idea.[13] Jones, who instigated the formation of a secret committee, highlights the requirement of secrecy to protect both the doctrine of psychoanalysis and its master: "The idea of a united small body, designed, like the Paladins of Charlemagne, to guard the kingdom and policy of their master."[14] We are informed that there were disciples of higher and lesser levels whose rank was based on their understanding of the psychoanalytic doctrine: "Freud has come to divide his followers into three grades: those in the lowest have understood no more than *The Psychopathology of Everyday Life* [1901]; those in the second the theories on dreams and neuroses; and those in the third follow him into the theory of sexuality and accept his extension of the libido concept."[15]

Sulloway notes that within the orthodox Freudian atmosphere, "No member of the committee was to depart publicly from any of the fundamental tenets of psychoanalysis without first discussing his views with the others."[16] Attempts to obtain a glimpse or knowledge of the inner workings of psychoanalysis by the uninitiated have been stonewalled, as is made evident in the following example from a fervent disciple: "You are not going to get our secrets!"[17]

It is necessary to understand that Freud was venerated in the highest degree by his inner circle because according to his followers Freud held a deified status, for he did "as much for [humanity] as any other human being who has lived."[18] The hero worship of Freud was palpable within his inner circle, as conveyed by this description of him: "Freud, who possessed what Socrates has called his 'gift from the gods.'"[19] One disciple proclaimed in explicit religious terms, exemplifying the spiritual void the "talking cure" attempted to fill: "I was the apostle of Freud who was my Christ!"[20] It was this faith and zeal that captured the hearts and minds of the Freudian disciples in a way akin to a messianic cult. "Freud's pupils—all inspired and convinced—were his apostles."[21] Jung advised individuals to "Approach him as a great master and rabbi, then all will be well."[22] A. A. Brill (1874–1948), an Austrian-born psychiatrist who was an early evangelizer of the Freudian gospel of psychoanalysis in America, informs those outside of the inner circle that Freud and Jung were referred to as "Allah and his Prophet."[23]

American psychiatrist and neurologist Isador Coriat (1875–1943) proclaimed his faith in the secular religion of psychoanalysis and its prophet Sigmund Freud in a way that mimicked the dual *shahādah* or the essential declaration of faith Islam. This is to bear witness that "There is no god but God" (*Lā ilāha illallāh*) and that "Muhammad is the messenger of God" (*Muḥammadun rasūl Allāh*). Coriat in turn imitates this testimony of faith and proclaims: "there is no psychotherapy but psychoanalysis and Sigmund Freud was its prophet."[24] Regarding Jung and Freud and the tendency to view them as prophets of the modern world, we recall the warning of the appearance of false prophets: "Beware of false prophets, which come to you in sheep's clothing, but inwardly they are ravening wolves" (Matthew 7:15).

Sachs, who treated psychoanalysis as a "revealed religion,"[25] found upon encountering Freud's book *The Interpretation of Dreams* [*Die Traumdeutung*] (1899) that which gave ultimate meaning to his earthly existence. Sachs writes in his portrait of Freud: "My first opening of the *Traumdeutung* (*Interpretation of Dreams*) was the moment of destiny for me...When I finished the book, I had found the one thing worth while for me to live for; many years later I discovered that it was the only thing I could live by."[26] Fritz Perls (1893–1970), who developed Gestalt therapy, observes: "Freud's pupils, fascinated by his greatness, swallowed everything he said as a religion—much as I myself did in former years."[27]

The weekly "Wednesday Psychological Society" or "Psychological Wednesday Society" (*Psychologischen Mittwoch-Gesellschaft*) consisted of meetings of Freud's inner circle or the secret committee that took on the appearance of a religious gathering with the master at the center, as recalled by music critic Max Graf (1873–1958):

The gatherings followed a definite ritual. First, one of the members would present a paper. Then, black coffee and cakes were served; cigar and cigarettes were on the table and were consumed in great quantities. After a social quarter of an hour, the discussion would begin. The last and decisive word was always spoken by Freud himself. There was an atmosphere of the foundation of a religion in that room. Freud himself was its new prophet who made the theretofore prevailing methods of psychological investigation appear superficial.[28]

Sachs, wrote about his indoctrination period as a novice in a manner that confirms the view that psychoanalysis is more of a secular pseudo-religion, and the psychoanalytic movement is more of a church than a science or a professional organization surrounding a scientific psychology. Sachs writes: "Religions have always demanded a trial period, a novitiate, of those among their devotees who desired to give their entire life into the service of the supermundane and the supernatural, those, in other words, who were to become monks or priests...It can be seen that analysis needs something corresponding to the novitiate of the Church."[29]

American anthropologist and psychoanalyst Abram Kardiner (1891–1981) similarly frames it as a quasi-religious or cult-like organization: "For those who are not analysts, this description [of psychoanalysis] can only be compared to a religious dogma. And a source that blocks its own growth tends to resemble a cult."[30] Adolf Meyer (1866–1950), former Professor of Psychiatry at the Johns Hopkins Medical School, confirms the notion of a cult: "My attitude towards Freudianism is that of seeing in it a cult."[31] When Karl Abraham first attended one of the Wednesday Psychological Society meetings in December 1907, he described in a report to his friend Max Eitingon: "*He* [Freud] is all too far ahead of the others. [Isidor] Sadger [1867–1942] is like a Talmud-disciple, he interprets and observes every rule of the Master with orthodox Jewish severity."[32]

The inner circle or "the flock of disciples"[33] did not make a distinction between Freud the man and the psychoanalytic movement; they were one and the same. That the messenger and the message, or in this case, Freud and psychoanalysis, were viewed by Freud's disciples as one and the same is conveyed here by Abraham: "[our work] is identical with your [Freud's] person."[34] And elsewhere it has been written by Fromm that "the origin of psychoanalysis is to be sought in Freud's personality."[35] An apostle of the "talking cure," James Strachey (1887–1967), who was the chief translator of Freud's *oeuvre* into

English, writes: "It *is* curious what a disruptive effect Psycho-Analysis seems to have. Or is it really Freud's private character?"[36] While Strachey answers in the negative, he nonetheless identifies Freud's individuality and idiosyncrasies as directly influencing psychoanalytic theory. Even though Freud himself at times may have minimized his personal influence on the construction of psychoanalysis, his followers, on the other hand did not. Freud writes: "the public has no concern with my personality, and can learn nothing from an account of it."[37]

Because Freud interprets all his theories and discoveries through his own subjectivity, psychoanalysis becomes inseparable from the man himself. A direct consequence of this is the quasi-religious or cult-like atmosphere that surrounded the master: "if Freud had not been impelled by an inner necessity to treat the secular growth of his discovery as an adjunct of his own personality, the external history of the psychoanalytic movement would never have taken the schismatic, cultist course it did."[38] It goes without saying that his statements denying the role of his personality in the creation of the doctrine of the "talking cure" are likely made to dissuade outsiders from giving in to the belief that psychoanalysis was unscientific or was exclusively a "Jewish science" due to the prevailing anti-Semitism in fin-de-siècle Vienna.

Similarly to a cult or a pseudo-religious movement, only those within the inner circle, or as Freud referred to it, "the circle that is closest to me,"[39] had access to its most secret doctrines, as illustrated here: "First of all he is a member of a somewhat esoteric cult; he is one of the 'initiated' who has gone through the ritual of analysis, now knows all the secrets worth knowing, and thus is part of a cult."[40] Much of the details of psychoanalytic history will likely remain unknown and shrouded in secrecy, as Freud made sure to destroy all of his notes, correspondence, and unpublished materials on two different occasions. The question remains, why would such measures need to be taken if psychoanalysis was based on a firm scientific foundation? This will be examined later; however, a wall of secrecy and silence was without question erected regarding the inner circle that formed around Freud and the psychoanalytic movement. Even though its existence is well documented, it is still not common knowledge what lengths were taken to uphold the secrecy that shrouds the origins of psychoanalysis. The following admission is a glimpse into the inner circle of psychoanalysis by its founder:

You can believe me when I [Freud] tell you that we do not enjoy giving an impression of being members of a secret society and of practicing a mystical science. Yet we have been obliged to recognize and express as our conviction that no one has a right to join in a discussion of psycho-analysis who has not had particular experiences which can only be obtained by being analyzed oneself.[41]

Watson criticizes Freud's cult-like workings and quasi-religious theories, which added to the success of behaviorism in America prior to the popularization of psychoanalysis. Watson states: "Freudianism thus became a kind of cult, and the only devotees allowed openly to worship at the shrine were those who had a personal training under Freud."[42] Jung recalls Freud's words that are reminiscent of a cult leader, when Freud would respond, "If they don't understand they must be stamped into Hell."[43]

On May 28, 1910, German psychiatrist Alfred Hoche (1865–1943) made a memorable speech on "A Psychic Epidemic Among Physicians" accusing Freud and the psychoanalytic movement of functioning more like a cult or quasi-religious organization than like a band of scientists:

In a surprising manner, a great number of disciples, some clearly fanatical, have presented themselves to Freud and follow where he leads them. To speak of this as a Freudian school is in reality completely misplaced, as it is a question not of facts which are scientifically provable or demonstrable, but of articles of faith; in truth, if I leave aside a few more considered heads, it is a community of believers, a sort of sect, with all the characteristics which go along with this...To become a member of the sect isn't at all easy. This demands a long novitiate which is ideally terminated by the master himself. At the same time, not anyone can become a disciple, but only those who have faith. He who does not believe has no success, and with few exceptions, cannot speak. What is common with all the members of the sect is the high degree of veneration for the Master, which only perhaps finds its analogue in the personality cult of the circle of Bayreuth [i.e., around Richard Wagner (1813-1883)]...The Freudian movement is in fact a return, under a modern form, of a *medicina magica*, a secret doctrine which can only be practiced by qualified interpreters of signs.[44]

Many might assume that the workings of a secret society would only pertain to Freud and his followers, but Jung also had an inner circle, as the historical record demonstrates.[45] Jung informs us that "the Psychological Club in Zurich...was founded in 1916,"[46] and according to Paul J. Stern this marked the beginning of the Jungian cult: "The founding of the Jungian club meant the social embodiment of Jungian psychology, the genesis of a sect."[47] In 1916, Fanny Bowditch Katz (1874–1967) recorded in her diary: "[Jungian] Analysis is a therapy, and a religion...a going back of Christianity."[48] A close collaborator, Liliane Frey-Rohn (1901–93), who began analysis with Jung in 1934, expressed: "It [Jung's analytic psychology] was like a cult."[49] Not unlike Freud, Jung, according to Jolande Jacobi (1890–1973), a member of the Jungian inner circle, was convinced that "He [Jung] himself behaved as if his psychology was another religion."[50] Christiana Morgan (1897–1967), lay analyst and research associate at Harvard Psychological Clinic, expressed her convictions about Jung in this way: "There is no question about the fact that he is the prophet."[51] Jung's views, to Freud, represented "a new religio-ethical system."[52] It goes without saying that Freud flat-out objected to Jung's grandiosity or messianic tendencies: "a new message of salvation which is to begin a new epoch in psychoanalysis, in fact, reveal a new aspect of the universe for everything else."[53]

Henri F. Ellenberger depicted the Jung Institute in Zurich in the following manner:

> I do not know any place where one breathes the atmosphere of a "theosophical sect" more stifling than at the Jung Institute in Zurich—no other chapel where the master is more divinised or is becoming so. Many of the disciples of Jung openly devote themselves to astrology, to occultism and to divination with the aid of the Chinese oracle, the I Ching. It is often maintained that Jung has, apart from his official doctrine, an esoteric doctrine, following the example of the ancient philosophies, which he always denies.[54]

Viktor von Weizsäcker (1886–1957), a pioneer in psychosomatic medicine, recalls the following in regards to Jung and the dissolution of religion in the modern world:

> C. G. Jung was the first to understand that psychoanalysis belonged in the sphere of religion, more accurately, to the dissolution of religion in our time. To him neurosis was a symptom of the man who loses his support in religion. Publicly he spoke

about that only later, but once he said to me in conversation, *"All* neurotics seek the religious." At first, he may have been under the sway of scientific psychology and the curiosity of the researcher in the history of religion. Later he was prevented from speaking more openly about it by old resentment against Christianity (he was the son of a parson) and probably also by tactical consideration—he was afraid of being identified with a superficial pastoral attitude.[55]

Jung wrote to Freud on August 11, 1910, conveying the need for secrecy within the psychoanalytic movement:

And finally, ΨA thrives only in a very tight enclave of like minds. Seclusion is like a warm rain. Once should therefore barricade this territory against the ambitions of the public for a long time to come...Moreover ΨA is too great a truth to be publicly acknowledged as yet. Generously adulterated extracts and thin dilutions of it should first be handed around. Also the necessary proof has not yet been furnished that it wasn't you who discovered ΨA but Plato, Thomas Aquinas and Kant, with Kuno Fischer and Wundt thrown in. Then Hoche will be called to chair of ΨA in Berlin and Aschaffenburg to one in Munich. Thereupon the Golden Age will dawn.[56]

After all, as Jung declared, only few could fully realize the new psychological religion: "Only a few are capable of individuating."[57] Jones did not hesitate to criticize Jung and the zealotry he perceived in him to the master himself: "Jung is going to save the world, another Christ (with certainly Anti-semitism combined)."[58] Freud responds to Jones's letter and emphasizes his own criticisms of his disciple: "I thank you for your very just remarks about Jung...in fact he behaves like a perfect fool, he seems to be Christ himself, and in the particular things he says there is always something of the *'Lausbub'* [rascal]."[59] In a letter to Ferenczi, Freud again condemns his disciple: "You are right. Our dear Swiss [Jung] [has] gone crazy."[60]

That Freud did not stomach dissent in any shape or form was well known within the inner circle, and this is another reason why psychoanalysis has been compared to a pseudo-religious sect even though it was secular in nature: "No feature of Freud's career has been so widely deplored as his suppression of dissent. Visitors to the Vienna Psychoanalytical Society [formerly the Wednesday Psychological Society] complained that orthodoxy was enforced in an atmosphere of almost religious exaltation."[61] Fromm discusses how all dissenting voices within the inner circle were squelched or banished:

> Those of his [Freud] students who dared to criticize fundamental aspects of his theories left him or were squeezed out in one way or another. Those who built the movement were mostly pedestrian men, from the standpoint of their theoretical capacity, and it would have been difficult for them to follow Freud through basic theoretical changes. They needed a dogma in which they believed and around which they could organize the movement. Thus Freud the scientist became to some extent the prisoner of Freud the leader of the movement; or to put it differently, Freud the teacher became the prisoner of his faithful, but uncreative disciples.[62]

If a Freudian disciple proposed an alternative interpretation that was incompatible with the master and his psychoanalytic orthodoxy, this would likely be received with fierce retaliation. Freud writes: "My inclination is to treat those colleagues who offer resistance exactly as we treat patients in the same situation."[63] It is worth recalling the following rule within psychoanalysis that "whatever interrupts the progress of analytic work is a resistance."[64]

A double standard became apparent to the Freudian disciples; however, they dared not challenge the master and face the consequences. Sándor Ferenczi conveys this double standard of the master: "But what is valid for *you* [Freud] is not valid for the rest of us."[65] According to Vienna psychiatrist Erwin Stransky (1877–1962), "the systematic refusal of opening themselves to the criticisms is one of the distinctive traits of psychoanalytic obedience...The most fatal error [of Freudian theory] resides in the interpretive mania without restraint and in the confusion between interpretation and proof."[66] Hungarian-American psychiatrist Thomas Szasz (1920–2012) illustrates the authoritarian structure of Freudianism:

> Overt tyranny can be appraised for what it is, and there are many ways of resisting it. Freud's leadership, however, was deceitful. He created a pseudo-democratic, pseudo-scientific atmosphere, but was careful to retain for himself the power to decide all important issues...Freud's essential concept of leadership seemed to be to bestow tokens of power on his competitors, only to discredit them if they dared to use it.[67]

Swales exposes the myriad abuses caused by exercising "undue influence" that have occurred throughout the history of the psychoanalytic movement:

> [T]he phenomenon of "undue influence"—be it in matters of donations, legacies, interminable analyses, sexual relations, or the consensual counterfeiting of early memories—is virtually endemic to a profession which, after all, owes its very existence and propagation to a plethora of credulous individuals ready and able to pay out good money for the luxury of abdicating their mental sovereignty to another, all too often in a desperate bid to unburden themselves of moral responsibility for the wreckage of their lives. They are individuals who gladly if unwittingly collude with a highly organized group of mercenary professionals, smug in their institutional accreditations and arrogant in the blind conviction that, with years of costly training behind them, their own "repressions" have been lifted and they possess special insight into the inner workings of mind of a sort denied the ordinary layperson...the profoundly sinister role of "undue influence" in modern psychoanalytic history—a topic rarely discussed in the professional literature...[68]

The cultic and quasi-religious ambiance that surrounded the inner circle of Freud "permitted no deviations from his orthodox teaching."[69] Phyllis Grosskurth tells us: "Jones had grasped the fact that to be a friend of Freud's meant being a sycophant. It meant opening oneself completely to him, to be willing to pour out all one's confidences to him."[70] Freudian whistleblower Jeffrey Moussaieff Masson suggests:"Jones believed that to disagree with Freud (the father) was tantamount to patricide (father murder)."[71] When Ferenczi believed that children had been sexually abused, which Freud denied, because of this disagreement Jones branded Ferenczi a "homicidal maniac."[72]

The Freudian "talking cure" has been described in the following manner: "psychoanalysis is the name of a militant sect, not of a medical science, of a cult, not a cure—is irrefutable."[73] Some might challenge the assertion that Freud wanted to be deified, suggesting rather that Freud did not want to be idolized and that this was the working of his disciples and not the master. Freud defends this position when writing "a transference on a religious basis would strike me as most disastrous; it could end only in apostasy...I [shall do my best to show you that I am unfit to be an object of worship.[74] The master paradoxically states: "I am certainly not fitted for the role of leader."[75]

It appears that Freud wanted to be venerated in an explicit manner and at the same time remain behind the scenes to exhort influence in an invisible manner or in the shadows of the psychoanalytic movement. To whatever degree that this may have been the case, there is significant proof that there was much more occurring within the secret committee than a scientific work group would generally suggest. In this connection, E. Michael Jones adds: "Psychoanalysis...can only function as a form of manipulation from behind the scenes. Because of this, it is quintessentially conspiratorial."[76] The "happy band of brothers"[77] known as the secret committee existed until 1927, when it was incorporated into the board of the International Psychoanalytical Association.

Freud explains that his motive for organizing the International Psychoanalytical Association was to defend authentic psychoanalysis from its counterfeits: "It appeared to me necessary to create an organization with a central office which would conduct its external policies and give authentic information about what should be permitted to be called psychoanalysis."[78] Freud additionally defends his rationale for founding the International Psychoanalytical Association, which he constructed because of the criticism that he and the psychoanalytic movement were facing:

> I can only repeat that these motives were of practical nature and have nothing to do with stifling divergent opinions within our group. The Society does not serve this purpose. The reasons for organizing a Society were: First, the need to present to the public genuine psychoanalysis and protect it for imitations (counterfeits) which soon would arise, and second what Ferenczi emphasized in his speech which he prepared together with me, that we must be ready now to answer our opponents and that it is not proper to leave these answers up to the whim of individuals. It is in the interest of our cause to bring a personal sacrifice and relegate polemics to a central office.[79]

On researching and analyzing mass movements, Eric Hoffer (1902–1983), makes pertinent observations that aid in framing the phenomenon of psychoanalysis more on the level of a mass movement than of a scientific theory:

> This enemy—the indispensable devil of every mass movement—is omnipresent. He plots both outside and inside the ranks of the faithful. It is his voice that speaks through the mouth of the dissenter, and the deviationists are his stooges. If anything goes

wrong within the movement, it is his doing. It is the sacred duty of the true believer to be suspicious. He must be constantly on the lookout for saboteurs, spies and traitors.[80]

Mass movements not only require leaders, but also followers: "Freud's own messianic impulses could not have transformed psychoanalysis into the [Psychoanalytic] Movement had it not been for the needs of his followers and eventually those of the wide public which became enthusiastically attracted to psychoanalysis."[81]

Chapter 4

The Censoring and Mythologizing of Psychoanalytic History

"[P]sychoanalytic treatment is founded on truthfulness"[1] is a statement made by Freud, but this could not be further from the truth. Russell Jacoby observes an essential point regarding contemporary psychology: "the history of [modern] psychology is the history of forgetting."[2] Although true, this assessment applies differently in the case of Freudian psychology, as there has been a deliberate and concerted effort to obstruct and conceal psychoanalytic history by those within the inner circle, not only to hide what they want to keep from those uninitiated, but also to attempt to engineer what has been termed "psycho-history: this is to say *the creation of a pseudo-myth*—a fictitious rewriting of events and realities that never transpired, but thatwere interpreted through the psychoanalytic prism in order to fit the interests and validate its own theory.

"Psychohistory, in a word, is ahistorical. That is its ultimate failing."[3] This is because "Psychoanalytic theories, in sum, are not competing versions of timeless, immutable truth. They are time-bound."[4] The attempts made by Freud and the psychoanalytic movement to deny that the doctrine of the "talking cure" was influenced and shaped by the social milieu of nineteenth-century fin-de-siècle Vienna, alternatively rewriting the historical facts, stating that it stands outside any temporal context, is blatantly untrue. It would also be erroneous, as Jones points, out to treat the historical record of the master in the same way: "Freud's personality cannot, any more than that of anyone else, be studied *in vacuo*."[5] Fromm also confirms that "Freud could not but conceive his new findings in the concepts and terminology of his own time."[6] German-born English psychologist Hans J. Eysenck (1916–97) sketches the problematic issues of the phenomenon of psychohistory: "psycho-history inverts the usual procedure of science; it interprets facts in terms of a theory prior to demonstrating the applicability or indeed the truth-value of that theory, even disregarding the mounting evidence that such truth-value is almost completely lacking."[7]

While *historicism* is one of many reductionist trends, psycho-history is another brand of reductionism. After conducting extensive research on Sigmund Freud and the psychoanalytic movement, Sulloway contends irrefutably:

> [T]he expedient denial and refashioning of history has been an indispensable part of the psychoanalytic revolution. Perhaps more remarkable still is the degree to which this whole process of historical censorship, distortion, embellishment, and propaganda has been effected with the cooperation of psychoanalysis who would instantly proclaim such phenomena as "neurotic" if they spotted them in anyone else.[8]

The psychoanalytic movement attempts to interpret all human history through the psychoanalytic lens, and not as it actually transpired. Partial truths, half-truths, pseudo-myths, and fiction itself are all blurred together as reality. Although it is damaging and no less discrediting to psychoanalysis, Freud himself refers to his theory curiously as: "our mythology."[9] Freud attempted to codify his own brand or privatized version of science and epistemology, regarding them as "our science"[10] and "our knowledge,"[11] all of which are key facets of his totalizing worldview or *Weltanschauung*.

Szasz points out that "To Freud, psychoanalysis was like an invention, which the inventor could patent, thus restricting the rights of others in its use. Thus, Freud insisted that psychoanalysis was to be dispensed only in accordance with his specifications. But he went even further: he declared that only he, and no one else, could change or modify the original formula."[12] With this noted, Freud is at other moments less grandiose, as exemplified by his letter to Berlin nose-and-throat specialist Wilhelm Fliess (1858–1928), on July 27, 1904, emphasizing that science cannot be privatized, "nor can ideas be patented...Once they have been let loose, they go their own way."[13]

Freud apparently did not distinguish between his construction of pseudo-myth or pseudo-science, which is to say that he either could not discern between reality and fiction or intentionally chose to ignore this fundamental distinction. Freud asserts that "truth cannot be tolerant,"[14] but what he does not inform us is that he is interpreting truth according to a very narrow understanding of his own subjective speculations, which do not consider ways of knowing that discern between the relative and the Absolute. Freud acknowledges that his science is essentially a subjective construction or reconstruction of the facts, which he himself regards as a unique psychoanalytic myth, asking "does not every science come in the end to a kind of mythology[?]"[15] He adds: "The theory of the instincts is so to say our mythology. Instincts are mythical entities, magnificent in their indefiniteness."[16] Theodor W. Adorno (1903–69) was the leading figure of the Frankfurt School or the Institute for Social Research (Institute für Sozialforschung) who adamantly expressed the inherent limitations of all claims made about the psychoanalytic "talking cure" and advised people not to believe them: "In psycho-analysis nothing is true except the exaggerations."[17]

A curious and unfortunate facet of Freud's legacy is that he destroyed his personal papers at least twice, the first time in 1885 and the second time in 1907. For this reason and others, it has been stated: "He is a master of covering his intellectual trail."[18] According to his official biographer, Jones, "It was Freud's custom to destroy both his manuscript and the notes on which it was based, of any paper he published."[19] We learn that much of what was recorded by Jones in the official biography of Freud was incorrect or embellished. As Ellenberger learned through his extensive research, "I found 80 percent of Jones' facts to be either completely false or greatly exaggerated."[20] Rieff writes: "Jones has imposed his own interpretation not merely upon those curious about a great man's life but upon all future honest biographers of Freud."[21] Jones's task when understood more fully appears similar to the creation of psycho-history rather than to the documenting of actual historical events that transpired: "Jones's 'rewriting' of history."[22] This is why it has been said that "Jones's version of Freud's intellectual biography itself belongs to the realm of legend rather than fact."[23] As Swales adds, there are many problems with Jones's official biography, as it contradicts the available facts: "The fact that so much testimony about Freud by those who knew him—family, friends, colleagues, and patients—has long been restricted from public inspection is a major hindrance to any assessment of the fidelity of Jones's portrait. However, it is certainly the case that the biographer tended to overlook much about Freud that did not accord with his own pietistic conception of the man."[24]

For this reason, Freud's life and the early formation of psychoanalysis to a certain degree remain hidden and unknown. Jones adds: "Freud preferred to give an unfavorable impression of himself rather than disclose something of his private life. What he revealed of his life was far more carefully selected and censored than is generally supposed."[25] Freud alludes to the secrecy of his doctrine of the "talking cure" that he had to maintain given the antagonism he faced: "I should not even claim that every case of hysteria can be cured by it [the psychoanalytic method], let alone all the states that go by that name...It is not possible to explain anything to a hostile public; accordingly I have kept certain things that might be said concerning the limits of the therapy and its mechanism to myself."[26]

Freud made a concerted effort to seal the inner details of psychoanalytic history in secrecy and silence forever. Additionally, whatever was not destroyed, such as notes, personal correspondence, and unpublished work, was closely guarded by the Sigmund Freud Archives and was only available to the inner circle of the psychoanalytic movement. Some, but not all, of the previously restricted material of the Sigmund Freud Archives has now been declassified and is available to researchers. The archives themselves were erected to safeguard and preserve Freud's documents and those of the inner circle and were not intended for free and open access.

The goal of the Freud Archives had never been to make the documents of Freudianism available to the public, as Luther Evans, the Librarian of Congress, undoubtedly believed when Eissler approached him. In reality, the Library of Congress and the American people had been duped. What Anna Freud and the Freudian Family sought, quite simply, was a safety deposit box where they could lock up the archives, *their* archives, and protect them from the curiosity of outsiders.[27]

To this end, all outsiders were stonewalled from gaining access to the vaults of psychoanalytic history:

> Freud's successors did all they could to impede the work of historians, through censuring [sic] documents, blocking access to the archives of the psychoanalytic movement and launching campaigns of denunciation against scholars. It was essential to protect Freud's narrative monopoly against the alternative accounts proposed by some of his patients, his rivals and historians. Without this, psychoanalysis would have soon returned to being one therapeutic narrative amongst others in the competing and burgeoning private-sector marketplace for psychological well-being. Psychoanalysis would have dissolved into a plethora of divergent contested accounts rather than laying claim to being the sole science of the mind and the pre-eminent form of psychotherapy.[28]

An important letter written by Freud to his fiancée Martha Bernays (1861–1951) has survived that explains Freud's reservations regarding biographers and the rationale behind the obstruction of psychoanalytic or modern psychology's origins. The first systematic destruction took place on April 28, 1885:

> One intention...I [Freud] have almost finished carrying out, an intention which a number of as yet unborn and unfortunate people will one day resent. Since you won't guess what kind of people I am referring to, I will tell you at once: they are my biographers...I couldn't have matured or died without worrying about who would get hold of those old papers...As for the biographers, let them worry, we have no desire to make it too easy for them. Each one of them will be right in his opinion of "The Development of the Hero," and I am already looking forward to seeing them go astray.[29]

Freud further elaborates on his reasons for opposing biography:

> A biography is justified under two conditions. First, if the subject has had a share in important, generally interesting events; second, as a psychological study. Outwardly my life has passed calmly and uneventfully and can be covered by a few dates. A psychologically complete and honest confession of life, on the other hand, would require so much indiscretion (on my part as well as on that of others) about family, friends, and enemies, most of them still alive, that it is simply out of the question.[30]

Like Freud, the founder of behaviorism, Watson also attempted to conceal the history of behavioristic psychology. The parallels between these two figures are striking. Watson emphasizes:

> Everyone has entirely too much to conceal to write an honest [autobiography]—too much he has never learned to put into words even if he would conceal nothing. Thinking of chronicling your adolescent acts day by day—your four years of college—your selfishness—the way you treat other people—your pettiness—your day dreams of sex! Autobiographies are written either to sell the good points about oneself or to vanquish one's critics. If an autobiographer honestly turned himself inside out day by day for six months, he would either commit suicide at the end of the time or else go into a blissful oblivescent depression.[31]

Watson also burned all his unpublished work, notes, and correspondence, reportedly stating: "When you're dead, you're all dead."[32]

Freud makes another interesting disclosure regarding the role of biographers by way of exposing his own motives underlying the invention of his own psycho-history:

> [B]iographers are fixated on their heroes in a very peculiar manner. They frequently select the hero as the object of study because, for personal reasons of their own emotional life, they had a special affection for him from the very outset. They then devote themselves to a work of idealization, which strives to enroll the great man among their infantile models, and to revive through him, as it were, their infantile conception of the father. For the sake of this wish they wipe out the individual features in his physiognomy, they rub out the traces of his life's struggle with inner and outer resistances, and do not tolerate in him anything savoring of human weakness or imperfection; they then give us a cold, strange, ideal form instead of a man to whom we could feel distantly related. It is to be regretted that they do this, for they thereby sacrifice the truth to an illusion, and for the sake of their infantile phantasies they let slip the opportunity to penetrate into the most attractive secrets of human nature.[33]

Not only Freud's resistance, but his sheer antagonism to having the details of the formation of the "talking cure" and the psychoanalytic movement made available for general access is made explicitly clear: "Anyone turning biographer commits himself to lies, to concealment, to hypocrisy, to flattery, and even to hiding his own lack of understanding, for bibliographical truth is not to be had...Truth is unobtainable; humanity does not deserve it."[34] The lengths to which Freud went to conceal and maintain utter secrecy about his life is itself a form of disclosure about the individual himself: "What was intended as an act of concealment may well have succeeded in hiding some episodes in Freud's external biography. But the act reveals a great deal about Freud's inner biography."[35] Eysenck observes:

> It is interesting to see psycho-history turned against its own creator, and the methods of psychoanalysis used to dissect the work of Freud himself. The fact that this has been done by Freud's own followers illustrates the point that Freud's work and his developmental history and personality are in many ways inseparable. The alleged scientific analysis of man which Freud believed himself to have undertaken is little more than a gigantic autobiographical

essay; the miracle is that so many people have taken it seriously as a contribution to science![36]

We might add here that like Freud, Jung also wanted his inner life to be kept secret and did not want its details to be made available to the public until after his death. Rieff suggests that this secrecy was upheld because Jung did not want his messianic mission to be known while he was alive, "Yet, he waited until he was beyond the reach of skeptical reviewers before he published the secret of his life: this burden of prophecy with which he had been charged from the time of his earliest remembered dream."[37]

We recall the admonition found within the Abrahamic monotheisms of Judaism in the Old Testament, "Do not conceal" (Deuteronomy 13:10), from Christianity in the New Testament, "For there is nothing covered, that shall not be revealed; neither hid, that shall not be known (Luke 12:2), and from Islam in the Koran, "Do not dress truth in falsehood and hide the truth, though you know" (2:42). Yet everything pertaining to the psychoanalytic movement is about concealing the truth. This phenomenon concealing and falsification of truth is a much larger issue, which extends beyond psychoanalysis and has to do with the very tenets of modernism itself. Guénon writes: "The falsification of everything has been shown to be one of the characteristic features of our period."[38] In a final synopsis: "psychohistory is readily shown to be both a historical and a psychological sham."[39]

Chapter 5

The Deification of Freud and the Birth of the Freudian Myth of the Hero

"I shall suffer the just punishment that none of the undiscovered provinces of mental life which I was the first mortal to enter will bear my name or follow the laws I have formulated."[1] These messianic-like utterances written by Freud himself read more like a hagiography of a saint than like a description of a scientist solidifying forever what in his mind and that of his disciples was an unparalleled sojourn into the psychic underworld of humanity, liberating it once and for all from bondage and tyranny. Bakan underscores the messianic mission of the master: "One of the critical features of Messianism is its goal of leading people out of slavery and oppression. Thus, Freud's whole effort at the creation of psychoanalysis may be viewed as Messianic in this respect."[2] As a devoted disciple recounts, "for many years, like Moses, he [Freud] stood before the forbidden promised-land with only a guess of what it might look like."[3]

In his pamphlet published in 1914 titled "The History of the Psychoanalytic Movement," Freud speaks with a sense of destiny of almost supernatural proportions regarding his historical role in disseminating the doctrine of the "talking cure" to the world:

> Since, however, my conviction of the general accuracy of my observations and conclusions grew and grew, and as my confidence in my own judgment was by no means slight, any more than my moral courage, there could be no doubt about the outcome of the situation. I made up my mind that it had been my fortune to discover particularly important connections, and was prepared to accept the fate that sometimes accompanies such discoveries.[4]

The messianic impulse underscoring Freud's life and work is to be found in his identification with the biblical figure of Moses has been widely noted throughout the psychoanalytic corpus. In his deified and heroic identity as the new Lawgiver, he becomes infallible within the psychoanalytic church: Helen Walker Puner speaks of "his Messianic conviction that his and his alone was the Word and the Law."[5] Freudian propagandists, by embellishing the facts, also contributed to "his deification as a veritable Moses-figure within modern culture."[6] Jones surmises that "One cannot avoid the pretty obvious conclusion that...Freud had identified himself with Moses,"[7] Rieff likewise confirms: "There is no doubt that Freud, as a great teacher, identified himself with Moses."[8] Professor Reuben Fine adds: "There can be little doubt that Freud had a strong personal identification with Moses."[9] Fromm also stresses Freud's identification with Moses: "under the guise of a scientific school [the psychoanalytic movement], he realized his old dream, to be the Moses who showed the human race the promised land."[10]

It is this deification of Freud as the hero by his inner circle that has catalyzed some of the most fervent criticisms: "Much of the so-called Freud-bashing so prevalent in our time can be understood as a justified backlash to a half-century of idolatrous Freud-laundering."[11] Freud writes: "One can easily understand the hostility to psychoanalysis which destroys cherished illusions and prejudices."[12] Paradoxically, it appears as if the same deification empowered Freud to celebrate the condemnation that he and his ideas have encountered, enhancing the Freudian myth. Peter Gay informs us that he was in fact "proud of his enemies...He likened himself to Hannibal, to Ahasuerus, to Joseph, to Moses, all men with historic missions, potent adversaries, and difficult fates."[13] What becomes apparent and essential in understanding the psychoanalytic revolution is that "Freud's achievement cannot be understood if we treat him simply as a scientist, a psychologist or even as the creator of a biological pseudo-science; it can be understood, finally, only if we regard him in the way in which, deep within his own heart, he saw himself—as a messiah and as the founder of a new religion."[14] The enduring identification of Freud's mission beyond that of pioneering a new scientific psychology appears no less than messianic in nature:

> Certainly the spirit which was to move Freud in his guidance and development of the infant science for the rest of the years of his life would bear out this appearance of ritual and religion. He came to act as if he walked intuitively but no less certainly in the path of his ancestors and in the belief of one of the oldest Jewish traditions—the tradition that all Jews were present on Mount Sinai and there took upon themselves "the yoke of the Law." This yoke rested particularly heavy on Freud. It became a mission, Messianic in character. His psychoanalytic discoveries were to become in his mind and that of some of his devout followers a body of Law as world-shaking and divinely inspired as any ever

promulgated by Moses or Jesus. The dissemination of the psychoanalytic doctrine Freud was to handle in the manner of a high priest and prophet dedicated to the missionary task of spreading the gospel.[15]

Regardless of the facts contained in the mass of historical and biographical material on the psychoanalytic movement and its founder that contradict the notion of the Freudian myth of the hero, the myth nonetheless continues. Richard Webster attributes its perpetuation to the cultic or quasi-religious beliefs that displaced true religion: "The Freud-myth has been sustained in the very midst of the facts which ought to undermine it, not by embargoes or restrictions, but by something much more potent—by the power of faith and legend and by the deep need of countless twentieth-century intellectuals for a system of over-arching certainties and doctrines which could replace the religious beliefs of the common culture they had lost."[16]

The mythologizing of Freud to the status of hero-worship is quite astounding when put into context, but it did not stop his disciples from erecting the Freudian myth or legend. Kurt R. Eissler asserts:

The heroism—one is inclined to describe it so—that was necessary to carry out such an undertaking has not yet been sufficiently appreciated. But anyone who has ever undergone a personal analysis will know how strong the impulse is to take flight from insight into the unconscious and the repressed...Freud's self-analysis will one day take a place of eminence in the history of ideas, just as the fact that it took place at all will remain, possibly for ever, a problem that is baffling to the psychologist.[17]

Sachs presents another example of Freud as the hero: "Freud's intuitive understanding of the unconscious reached as far as psychological insight can delve. He was able to trace its most intricate mazes which, but for him, might have long remained unknown and unexplored. This guidance by his intuition was needed for the begging of the great adventure, as well as for every step that led further into dark and dangerous regions."[18]

Strachey speaks to Freud's role in the grand schema and presents the rationale for the continued mythologizing of Freud as the hero:

[T]hough it may flatter our vanity to declare that Freud was a human being of a kind like our own, that satisfaction can easily be carried too far. There must in fact have been something very extraordinary in the man who was the first able to recognize a whole field of mental facts which had hitherto been excluded from normal consciousness, the man who first interpreted dreams, who first accepted the facts of infantile sexuality, who first made the distinction between the primary and secondary process of thinking—the man who first made the unconscious mind real to us.[19]

Those outside the inner circle and uninitiated into the psychoanalytic doctrine also perpetuate the Freudian myth or legend. The following is an account provided by a French journalist, Raymond Recouly (1876–1950) who describes Freud as an old rabbi appearing with a mystical aura:

We see an extremely accentuated Jewish type, the air of an old rabbi just arrived from Palestine, the thin and emaciated face of a man who has passed days and nights discussing with his initiated followers on the subtleties of the Law, in whom one feels a very intense brain life and the power of playing with ideas as an Oriental plays with the amber beads of his chaplet. When he speaks of his doctrine, of his disciples, he does so with a mixture of pride and detachment. However, it is pride that dominates.[20]

Freud, however, did have his less messianic moments, downplaying his role, as is made evident here: "I [Freud] have a high opinion of what I have discovered, but not of myself. Great discoverers are not necessarily great men. Who changed the world more than Columbus? What was he? An adventurer. He had character, it is true, but he was not a great man. So you see that one may find great things without its meaning that one is really great."[21]

Freud's own appraisal of his signature "talking cure" varied and was not always consistent. At times psychoanalysis produced positive results and was considered the only effective treatment and at other times he was ambivalent or even pessimistic about its curative abilities. Statements by Freud such as the following are not uncommon: "I...do not...think anything of my therapy."[22] When challenged by Karl Abraham for comparing himself with Copernicus and Darwin, Freud responded: "You are right in saying that the enumeration in my last paper may give the impression of claiming a place beside Copernicus and Darwin. But I didn't want to give up the interesting train of thought on that account."[23]

The Freudian myth avows that Freud was the first psychoanalyst—"the revolution effected by one man"[24]—and that there was no one prior to himself to initiate him into the occult art of his "talking cure," yet the question remains: from what source did psychoanalysis originate? A central predicament that Freud's psychoanalysis faces when it is analyzed through the metaphysics and sacred science of the perennial psychology is that it does not originate *in divinis* as the psychologies found within each of the world's religions. Although an iconoclast and fervently against tradition, Freud no doubt recognized the importance of tradition, as all things originated from a source prior to their own manifestation. Although Freud was hostile to tradition, he himself confirmed that everything proceeds from it: "Everything new must have its roots in what was before."[25] Therefore it was essential to subvert it for his and the psychoanalytic movement's own beliefs and propagation.

If Freud could destabilize the spiritual roots of tradition, he could in turn substitute the sacred with the profane and forge his own Promethean science. Burckhardt explains how this profane science differs from sacred science that is rooted in metaphysical principles:

[M]odern science displays a certain number of fissures that are due to the fact that the world of phenomena is indefinite and that therefore no science can ever hope to exhaust it; these fissures derive above all from modern science's systematic exclusion of all the non-corporeal dimensions of reality. They manifest themselves right down to the foundations of modern science, and in domains as seemingly "exact" as that of physics; they become gaping cracks when one turns to the disciplines connected with the study of life, not to mention psychology, where an empiricism that is relatively valid in the physical order encroaches in bizarre fashion on a foreign field. These fissures, which do not merely affect the theoretical domain, are far from harmless; on the contrary, in their technical consequences, they constitute so many seeds of catastrophe.[26]

Psychoanalysis, like the emergence of modern psychology, originated with the severing of itself from the sacred. The predicament then remains, as Guénon emphasizes here: "the requirement [is] imposed on anyone who wants to practice psychoanalysis as a profession of being first 'psychoanalyzed' himself...so from what source did the first psychoanalyst obtain the 'powers' that they communicate to their disciples, and by whom were they themselves 'psychoanalyzed' in the first place?"[27] This is to ask in a slightly different manner, "If every analyst derived their authority from their training analysis, from where did Freud derive his?"[28]

While it is true that Freud requires that "everyone who wishes to carry out analysis on other people shall first himself undergo an analysis by someone with expert knowledge,"[29] he does not, however, provide the details of the origins of his "talking cure." It needs to be made clear that Freud himself was never analyzed. Rieff confirms this: "Nobody psychoanalyzed the first psychoanalyst."[30] What we find is that all of Freud's theories are then not only filtered or colored through his own unconscious mind but in fact began and end there.

For Jung, contemporary psychology filled the epistemological and ontological void created with the eclipse of religion in the modern world, Jung and saw his analytical psychology as a valid initiation analogous to the world's religions: "The transformation of the unconscious that occurs under analysis makes it the natural analogue of the religious initiation ceremonies, which do, however, differ in principle from the natural process in that they forestall the natural course of development and substitute for the spontaneous production of symbols a deliberately selected set of symbols prescribed by tradition."[31]

Lacan suggests that "Psychoanalysis is an anti-initiation."[32] Yet, Rieff informs us: "Analysis is not an initiation but a counter-initiation, to end the need for initiations."[33]

Upon closer examination, the so-called truths that Freud's "talking cure" is alleged to have discovered were in reality already known by the perennial psychology, not to mention that the "talking cure" has appropriated the function of the religions and spiritual traditions: "Psychoanalysis doubly deserves to be classed as an imposture, firstly because it pretends to have discovered facts which have always been known and could never have been otherwise than known, and secondly and chiefly because it arrogates to itself functions that in reality are spiritual, and thus poses practically as a religion."[34]

Another issue that tarnishes the Freudian myth is its claim to be the sole originator of the psychoanalytic "talking cure," as though Freud stood outside of time and of any temporal considerations. Freud writes:

We have all heard of the interesting attempt to explain psychoanalysis as a product of the peculiar character of Vienna as a city...This inspiration runs as follows: psychoanalysis, so far as it consists of the assertion that the neuroses are traceable to disturbances in the sexual life, could only have come to birth in a town like Vienna...and it simply contains a reflection, a projection into theory, as it were, of these peculiar Viennese conditions. Now honestly I am no local patriot; but this theory about psychoanalysis always seems to me quite exceptionally stupid.[35]

What we learn is that while Freud was delivering his lectures in America he curiously gave full credit to the formation of psychoanalysis to Josef Breuer (1842–1925), which he later retracted:

> In 1909, in the lecture hall of an American university, I [Freud] had my first opportunity of speaking in public about psychoanalysis; the occasion was a momentous one for my work, and moved by this thought I then declared that it was not I who had brought psychoanalysis into existence. The credit for this was due to another, to Josef Breuer, whose work had been done at a time when I was still a student occupied with my examinations (1880–82).[36]

Regardless of such statements, let there be no confusion: Freud without question takes full ownership of and credit for his psychoanalytic "talking cure": "psychoanalysis is my creation; I was for ten years the only person who concerned himself with it."[37] Freud further clarifies that it is not Breuer but himself who is the true and sole originator of the "talking cure":

> [P]sychoanalysis is always without question my work alone. I have never heard that Breuer's great share in psychoanalysis has earned him a corresponding measure of criticism and abuse; and as it is long ago now since I recognized that to stir up contradiction and arouse bitterness is the inevitable fate of psychoanalysis, I conclude that I must be the real originator of all that is particularly characteristic in it.[38]

In what Jones calls "The Breuer Period" spanning from 1882 to 1894, he clarifies that the psychoanalytic doctrine without question belongs solely to Freud:

> It has not been found easy to estimate Breuer's significance for Freud and his work. Freud certainly overestimated it in the latter connection, though probably not in the former. When at times he would style Breuer the Founder of Psychoanalysis, he was for some reason modestly transferring that title to him from himself, since the essentials of psychoanalysis—both the method and the discoveries—belong entirely to Freud and were made at a time when the two men had already separated for good.[39]

For historical posterity Jung points out that "Freud, [is] the true discoverer [of psychoanalysis] and founder of the [psychoanalytic] movement."[40] Freud does say this about Breuer's role in the formation of psychoanalysis: "Breuer's 'cathartic procedure' [is] a forerunner of psychoanalysis,"[41] yet Freud unequivocally reminds readers that, "no one can know better than I what psychoanalysis is."[42] Despite his later ambivalence about the therapeutic effectiveness of his psychological theory, Freud informs us that "when I alone represented psycho-analysis...I assured my patients that I knew how to relieve them permanently of their sufferings."[43]

Freud discusses how he himself became a victim of the critics outside of the psychoanalytic movement, which further supports the pseudo-myth of Freudianism: "opponents regarded psychoanalysis as a product of my speculative imagination and were unwilling to believe in the long, patient and unbiased work which had gone to its making."[44] When analyzed outside the Freudian circles, a more realistic portrayal of the man Freud and psychoanalysis comes into clarity. According to Sulloway,

> Such myths about Freud the psychoanalytic hero are far from being just a casual by-product of his highly charismatic personality or eventual life. Nor are these myths merely random distortions of the biographical facts. Rather, Freud's life history has lent itself to an archetypal pattern shared by almost all hero myths, and his biography has often been remolded to fit this archetypal pattern whenever suggestive biographical details have first pointed the way.[45]

Ellenberger exposes the legends and myths that the Freudian disciples constructed around the master in a way that deconstructs the hagiographical portrayal provided by his inner circle:

> A rapid glance at the Freudian legend reveals two main features. The first is the theme of the solitary hero struggling against a host of enemies, suffering "the slings and arrows of outrageous fortune" but triumphing in the end. The legend considerably exaggerates the extent and role of anti-Semitism, of the hostility of the academic world, and of alleged Victorian prejudices. The second feature of the Freudian legend is the blotting out of the greatest part of the scientific and cultural context in which psychoanalysis developed, hence the theme of the absolute originality of the achievements, in which the hero is credited with the achieve-

ments of his predecessors, associates, disciples, rivals, and the contemporaries.

The legend discarded, we are permitted to see the facts in a different light. Freud is shown as having an average career of the contemporary academic man in central Europe, a career whose beginnings were only slightly hampered by anti-Semitism, and with no more setbacks than many others. He lived in a time when scientific polemics had a more vehement tone than today, and he never suffered the degree of hostility as did men such as Pasteur and Ehrlich. The current legend, on the other hand, attributes to Freud much of what belongs, notably, to Herbart, Fechner, Nietzsche, Meynert, Benedikt, and Janet, and overlooks the work of previous explorers of the unconscious, dreams, and sexual pathology. Much of what is credited to Freud was diffuse current lore, and his role was to crystallize these ideas and give them an original shape.[46]

It is also worthwhile to point out that Jungians, like Freudians, participated in the erecting of a mythic hero. The distinction between them regarding the mythologizing of these heroes is, as Richard Noll points out, that "Freudians are interested in securing Freud's place in history as a major cultural figure, a scientific genius as cult-hero, whereas Jungians seem to place more value on preserving an image of Jung as a divinely inspired human vessel for dispensing the eternal truths of the spirit."[47]

Freud's messianic vision was as he himself informs us to achieve the "integration of Jews and anti-Semites on the soil of ΨA."[48] Jones tirelessly attempts to immortalize the master by conveying that "If our race is lucky enough to survive for another thousand years the name of Sigmund Freud will be remembered."[49]

Chapter 6

The Making of Psychological Man:
From *Imago Dei* to *Homo Naturalis*

"[T]he emergence of psychological man, whose passion in life has been for lowering what is high and raising what is low."[1]—*Philip Rieff*

"Freudianism has become...more than a theory of the causes of mental disorders and a therapy claimed to resolve them. It has become, as Freud so obviously hoped that it would, a doctrine of the nature of man that its adherents believe applicable to all mankind."[2]—*Richard LaPiere*

To change the image of the human being is no minor undertaking, as it requires changing one's entire view and understanding of Reality itself. This is made evident here: "the critical battles between approaches to psychology and psychoanalysis in our culture in the next decades, as always, will be on the battleground of the image of man. That is to say, the conception of man which underlies the empirical research."[3] What does the Freudian metapsychology inform us about the nature of man? Fromm notes, "As for his concept of man, it is important to point out first that Freud [is] rooted in the philosophy of humanism and enlightenment."[4] It is here that we can find the roots of the destructive Freudian epistemology and ontology that dehumanizes the human being by reducing it to what is less than human.

The view taken within psychotherapy, whatever school or form it may be, defines how human nature is understood and no less treated. The image of the human being and how this is understood within a given civilization or society also distinguishes what is considered healthy and normal from what is perceived as unhealthy and abnormal. The notion that modern psychology can be neutral or value-free in its outlook is untrue. "Psychoanalysis is not value-neutral."[5] Fromm holds that "The concept of mental health depends on our concept of the nature of man."[6] Psychopathology requires a concept of health and without knowing what health signifies, a true or integral diagnosis is not only improbable, but cannot be made. As Gai Eaton

(1921–2010) points out: "To diagnose the ills of the time one must possess standards of health."[7]

The desacralized image of the human being as framed by the truncated epistemology and ontology of psychoanalytic theory severs the fundamental relationship between the human and the Divine, making it not only ineffective but even harmful. Logically, psychoanalytic theory focuses on a very limited facet of the human condition: "Classical psychoanalytic theory is based quite explicitly on a specific, highly materialistic view of man's nature."[8] As a consequence, "Freudianism institutionalized the underestimation of human possibility."[9] Psychological man no longer seeks the Absolute or sees himself as a microcosm of the macrocosm, but searches solely for the relief of psychological symptoms. As prominent American historian and social critic Christopher Lasch (1932–94) observes:

> Plagued by anxiety, depression, vague discontents, a sense of inner emptiness, the "psychological man" of the twentieth century seeks neither individual self-aggrandizement nor spiritual transcendence but peace of mind, under conditions that increasingly militate against it. Therapists, not priests...become his principle allies in the struggle for composure; he turns to them in the hope of achieving the modern equivalent of salvation, "mental health"...Therapy constitutes an antireligion.[10]

It is the "psychological blow" dealt by Freud, which positions himself directly on the shoulders of Darwin, that equates the human being with the animal, and while similarities certainly exist between the human and the animal, they are not the same. Meister Eckhart (1260–1328) observes that the human being is inseparably linked to the animal: "it is still always true that man is an animal."[11] Yet, this should not confuse the human being's integral identity in the Divine, as Meister Eckhart also points out: "Where the creature stops, there God begins to be."[12] For a human being to be disconnected from the transpersonal dimension is to be less than human: "In the unconscious we are still animals."[13]

Just as the doctrine of the "talking cure" attempted to fill the void left by the marginalization of the sacred, the evolutionary theory of Darwin attempted to do the same, as Victor Tausk emphasizes: "Darwinism...was a scientific religion just as psychoanalysis is."[14] Charles Darwin pronounced in 1859 the idea of this new psychology rooted in the doctrine of evolution: "[modern] psychology will be based on a new foundation, that of the necessary acquirement of each mental power and capacity by gradation."[15] We might also add that according to Freud, "Lamarck's theory of evolution coincides with the final outcome of psychoanalytical thinking."[16] Jung too adhered to this outlook: "I interested myself primarily in evolutionary theory."[17] In a similar fashion, behaviorism, like psychoanalysis, relies on Darwin's evolutionary theory that reduces the human to the animal.

Even though human nature does share in animal nature, it is not defined by it, and this is what makes what makes the human unique in the created order. Schuon distinguishes human nature from animal nature: "When we speak of man, what we have in mind first of all is human nature as such, that is, inasmuch as it is distinguished from animal nature. Specifically human nature is made of centrality and totality, and hence of objectivity; objectivity being the capacity to step outside oneself, while centrality and totality are the capacity to conceive the Absolute."[18] Freudian psychoanalysis disfigures the human being and presents him in a way that is so fragmented that the human ceases to be human in its archetype *in divinis* and becomes inhuman or infrahuman.

Although the human collectivity has without question benefited from the advancements of modern science and technology, these have also had very negative consequences, as human beings have become alienated from themselves and others, and moreover from the transcendent reality that gives ultimate meaning and purpose for existence itself. By borrowing the evolutionary schema laid out by Darwin, Freud depicts man's ability to become a god himself, but according an inverted and Promethean prototype:

> These things that, by his [modern] science and technology, man has brought about on this earth, on which he first appeared as a feeble animal organism and on which each individual of his species must once more make its entry...as a helpless suckling...are an actual fulfillment of every—or of almost every—fairy-tale wish. All these assets he may lay claim to as his cultural acquisition. Long ago he formed an ideal conception of omnipotence and omniscience which he embodied in his gods. To these gods he attributed everything that seemed unattainable to his wishes, or that was forbidden to him. One may say, therefore, that these gods were cultural ideals. To-day he has come very close to the attainment of this ideal, he has almost become a god himself. Only, it is true, in the fashion in which ideals are usually attained according to the general judgment of humanity. Not completely; in some respects not at all, in others only half way. Man has, as

it were, become a kind of prosthetic God. When he puts on all his auxiliary organs he is truly magnificent; but those organs have not grown on to him and they still give him much trouble at times...Future ages will bring with them new and probably unimaginably great advances in this field of civilization and will increase man's likeness to God still more.[19]

Some have attempted to frame the world's religions and their mystical dimensions within an evolutionary context as if the sages and saints all held an evolutionary outlook. Yet such is not the case, as evolutionism (the notion that the greater can derive from the lesser) is a reversal of traditional principles.[20] Śrī Ramana Maharshi (1879–1950), consummate exponent of Advaita Vedānta, in no uncertain terms proclaimed: "There is no evolution for that which is Eternal."[21] Likewise, Ananda K. Coomaraswamy (1877–1947) writes: "An 'evolution' in metaphysics is impossible."[22] German statistician and economist E. F. Schumacher (1911–1977) dissects the problems with the evolutionist *Weltanschauung*: "Evolutionism is not a science; it is a science fiction, even a kind of hoax...that has...imprisoned modern man in what looks like an irreconcilable conflict between 'science' and 'religion.' It has destroyed all faiths that pull mankind up and has substituted a faith that pulls mankind down...[I]t is the most extreme product of the materialistic utilitarianism of the nineteenth century."[23]

The perennial psychology asserts the fundamental relationship between the human and the Divine. The human being is *Homo spiritualis* or *Homo religiosus*, which is to say that the task of this integral psychology as it participates directly within a religious form is to reintegrate into our primordial nature (*fitrah*) the "image of God" (*imago Dei*), Buddha-nature (*Buddha-dhātu*), or the Self (*Ātmā*), our true identity *in divinis*. Schuon writes: "To see man, is to see not only the image of God, but also a door open towards *Bodhi*, liberating Illumination [Enlightenment]; or let us say towards a blessed fixing [centering] in the divine Proximity."[24]

An example of transcendence becoming immanence is found in the biblical verses: "In the beginning was the Word...and the Word was made flesh" (John 1:1, 14). This is to recognize the principle that "The kingdom of God is within you" (Luke 17:21) or "I am seated in the hearts of all" (Bhagavad-Gītā 15:15). Psychoanalysis, in contradistinction, pathologizes transcendence in a way that cannot but lead to imbalance in the human psyche: "In the beginning was psychopathology...and psychopathology was made manifest." Other versions of this parody have been suggested, such as "In the beginning was the

Word, and that Word may well have been 'Anxiety.'"[25] Or "In the beginning was the Word, and that Word may well have been 'Sex.'"[26] Lacan follows in the footsteps of the master alluding to religion as the genesis of mental illness when he writes: "It is when the Word is incarnated that things really start going badly."[27] In contradistinction, Larchet clarifies that originally there was balance and unity between the human being and the Divine, but it was the human being's desire for other than the Divine that ruptured this balance:

> In the first condition of Adam, man's desire was perfectly unified, having God as its sole object and never ceasing to yearn entirely for Him. Man desired nothing but God, and had but one desire—for God. When desire was turned away from God, it lost its unity, and by being turned towards the sensible world considered independently of God, desire is scattered amongst a myriad of things in which the fallen intellect henceforth beholds it. Desire becomes multiform and is divided up amid a multitude of heterogeneous—and at times even contradictory—particular desires.[28]

The perennial philosophy could be summarized in the following metaphysical description: "God became man so that man could become God"[29] or alternatively "The Logos became man, so that man might become Logos."[30] Similarly, the perennial psychology could be described as the sacred science of "The Self became *ego* in order that the *ego* might become Self";[31] this is to say, "In man the Spirit becomes the ego in order that the ego may become pure Spirit."[32] The same principle could be also illustrated as, "*Ātmā* became *Māyā* so that *Māyā* might realize *Ātmā*."[33] According to Shankara (788–820), "Only the Self [*Ātmā*] knows the Self [*Ātmā*]."[34]

Freud not only affirmed animality as the nature of the human being, but denied the theomorphic identity of the human condition: "We human beings are rooted in our animal nature and could never become godlike."[35] Without holding what is fully human in the forefront of consciousness, namely what is transpersonal, the psychotherapist or mental health professional is not only limited in his or her subjective clinical opinion, but also, although likely well intended, capable of causing harm to the individual undergoing treatment. We recall the often-quoted words: "If the blind lead the blind, both fall into the pit" (Matthew 15:14).

The traditional image of the human being held within Jewish mysticism recognizes the integral human relationship with the Divine, as the human is fashioned in its image. Leo Schaya (1916–1986) writes:

> Man is the most perfect image of universal reality in the whole of creation; he is the "incarnated" recapitulation of all the cosmic degrees and of their divine archetypes...he represents the most evident symbol of the ten *Sefiroth*, and his integral personality embraces all the worlds: his pure and uncreated being is identified with the Sefirothic "world of emanation" (*olam ha'atsiluth*); his spirit, with the prototypical "world of creation" (*olam haberiyah*); his soul with the subtle "world of formation" (*olam hayetsirah*); and his body, with the sensory "world of fact" (*olam ha'asiyah*).[36]

Freud's metapsychology defines man as *Homo naturalis* or psychological man, which in essence is *homo irreligiosus*, disavowing the existence of transcendence and what is Divine: "the deepest essence of man is instinctual impulse, whose elemental nature is the same in all men and which directs him to the satisfaction of certain primal needs."[37] According to the perennial psychology the opposite is true. Gregory of Nyssa (332–395) insists: "Man, governed by instinct, likens himself to an animal."[38] Human identity is defined in Freudian anthropology in the following way: "a chaos, a cauldron full of seething excitations...it has no organization, produces no collective [unified] will."[39] An unintegrated human being is fragmented and cannot be true to himself or others, as Freud confirms: "betrayal oozes out of him at every pore."[40]

This precarious disposition leaves the human being to be consumed by his or her own vices. Freud tells us: "Among these instinctual wishes [of humanity] are those of incest, cannibalism and lust for killing."[41] Joseph Jastrow explains: "Freud proceeded to reconstruct psychology in the image of psychoanalysis. The Freudian *homo* is composed of *Id, Ego*, and *Super-ego*."[42] Freud elaborates on what is signified by psychological man is as he envisions it, a strikingly stark portrayal:

> Not merely is this stranger in general unworthy of my love; I must honestly confess that he has more claim to my hostility and even my hatred. He seems not to have the least trace of love for me and shows me not the slightest consideration. If it will do him any good he has no hesitation in injuring me, nor does he ask

himself whether the amount of advantage he gains bears any proportion to the extent of the harm he does to me. Indeed, he need not even obtain an advantage; if he can satisfy any sort of desire by it, he thinks nothing of jeering at me, insulting me, slandering me and showing his superior power; and the more secure he feels and the more helpless I am, the more certainly I can expect him to behave like this to me...

The element of truth behind all this, which people are so ready to disavow, is that men are not gentle creatures who want to be loved, and who at the most can defend themselves if they are attacked; they are, on the contrary, creatures among whose instinctual endowments is to be reckoned a powerful share of aggressiveness. As a result, their neighbor is for them not only a potential helper or sexual object, but also someone who tempts them to satisfy their aggressiveness on him, to exploit his capacity for work without compensation, to use him sexually without his consent, to seize his possessions, to humiliate him, to cause him pain, to torture and to kill him. *Homo homini lupus* ["Man is a wolf to man"].[43]

Freud wrote to Pfister, stating: "I have found little that is 'good' about human beings on the whole. In my experience most of them are trash."[44] Freud's nihilism as it applies to the human condition shines through in this statement: "That man can't be helped, he must become a pessimist!"[45] Likewise: "One feels inclined to say that the intention that man should be 'happy' is not included in the plan of 'Creation.'"[46] Jung, once the foremost disciple of Freud, affirmed a point of view similar to that of his master with regard to psychological man: "*Homo homini lupus* is a sad yet eternal truism."[47] Jung also had a pessimistic view of humanity: "It is only with great difficulty that I can muster a belief in man's natural goodness."[48]

Freud's distrust of human qualities such as virtue goes to the opposite extreme, in an inverted or antinomian manner, where he views such qualities as comprising the worst in humanity. Freudian psychology declares: "the more virtuous a man is, the more severe and distrustful is its behaviour, so that ultimately it is precisely those people who have carried saintliness furthest who reproach themselves with the worst sinfulness."[49] Yet, in striking contrast St. Isaac the Syrian affirms the opposite: "Virtue is naturally the soul's health."[50] Titus Burckhardt (1908–84) illustrates the erroneous nature of this thinking: "The man who desires to realize Divine Knowledge while despising virtue is like a robber wanting to become righteous without restoring the product of his robbery."[51] Metaphysics, which is universal across the religions, requires virtue: "Metaphysical Truth as such is impersonal and motionless; virtue translates it into a 'personal' mode."[52] This is to say, "The spiritual virtues are...supports in man for the Divine Truth (*al-Ḥaqīqah*); they are also reflections of that Truth."[53]

Freud postulated the "death drive" or "death instinct" (*Todestrieb*), suggesting that all human beings have an innate propensity for destruction. This bleak prognosis for humanity is articulated as "the aim of all life is death."[54] He further outlines this notion and introduces what he has unfortunately termed "the Nirvana-principle":

> Whatever it is, we must perceive that the Nirvana-principle, which belongs to the death-instincts, underwent a modification in the living organism through which it became the pleasure-principle, and henceforth we shall avoid regarding the two principles as one. It is not difficult to infer what force it was that effected this modification, that is, if one has any interest at all in following this argument. It can only be the life-instinct, the libido, which has thus wrested a place for itself alongside the death-instinct in regulating the processes of life. In this way we obtain a series, a small but an interesting one: the *Nirvana*-principle expresses the tendency of the death-instincts, the *pleasure*-principle represents the claims of the libido and that modification of it, the *reality*-principle, the influence of the outer world.[55]

Fromm writes: "The use of 'Nirvana principle' is unfortunate inasmuch as it misinterprets the Buddhist Nirvana."[56] He elaborates further in the following passage:

> The use of "Nirvana" principle is unfortunate inasmuch as it misinterprets the Buddhist Nirvana. Nirvana is precisely not a state of lifelessness brought about by nature (which, according to Buddhism has the opposite tendency), but by the spiritual effort of man who finds salvation and the completion of life if he has succeeded in overcoming all greed and egoism and is filled with compassion for all sentient beings. In the state of Nirvana the Buddha experienced supreme joy.[57]

It is apparent that Freud's notion of the Nirvana-principle is limited to the horizontal domain of the empirical ego and does not transcend or reintegrate the human ego back to its source in the Divine, as Freud confirms by referring to "the extinction...of the tensions of the instinctual needs."[58] The so-called Nirvana-principle is a fundamental misinterpretation of universal spiritual teaching found within all of the sapiential traditions. Arthur Osborne (1906–70) writes:

> This Freudian postulate is a misrepresentation of a truth inherent in all sacred traditions. The truth is that man has an intuition of the unreality of his unsatisfactory state as a separate individual being and therefore an urge to break its bounds and emerge into universal being, which is at the same time pure consciousness and undiluted happiness. Doing so would, of course, involve the death of the ego (using the word not in its Freudian sense but to mean the illusory individual being).[59]

While the spiritual teachings unanimously confirm the Prophet Muhammad's dictum "Die before you die," this is a testament to the death of the empirical ego or to profane existence in the Spirit, and not a call for a premature death or a pessimistic outlook. Rūmī (1207-1273) affirms:

> Go die, O man of honor, before you die,
> So that you will not suffer the pangs of death,
> Die in such a way as to enter the abode of light,
> Not the death that places you in the grave.[60]

This is far from being a nihilistic doctrine, as Meister Eckhart writes: "it behooves us to emulate the dead in dispassion towards good and ill and pain of every kind."[61] While Buddha was reticent about speculating on the nature of Reality and preferred to avoid speaking about such intangible themes, there is a well-known Buddhist passage within the Pali Cannon (Udana 7:1–3) that clearly affirms what is metaphysical or transcendent:

> There is, O monks, an unborn, an unbecome, an unmade, an uncompounded; if, O monks, there were not here this unborn, unbecome, unmade, uncompounded, there would not here be an escape from the born, the become, the made, the compounded. But because there is an unborn, an unbecome, an unmade, an uncompounded, therefore there is an escape from the born, the become, the made, the compounded.[62]

Freud, according to Bruno Goetz, may have had some working ideas about what emptiness signifies within the Buddhist tradition, but it did not appear, however, to dissuade him from constructing erroneous theories such as the Nirvana principle, as can be seen here: "Do you know what it means to be confronted by nothingness? Do you know what that means? And yet this very nothingness is simply a European misconception: the Hindu Nirvana is not nothingness, it is that which transcends all contradictions."[63]

Freudian metapsychology put forward the claim that human sexuality was originally "bisexual," which could be interpreted to coincide with the traditional doctrine of primordial human nature of androgyny. Freud speaks of "the poetic fable which tells how the original human beings were cut up into two halves—man and woman—and how these are always striving to unite again in love."[64] He writes of "Bisexuality in Man"[65] and continues: "The conception which we gather from this long known anatomical fact is that there is an original predisposition to bisexuality, that in the course of development this changes to monosexuality, leaving only slight remnants of the stunted sex."[66] Freud elsewhere observes, "*bisexuality*...an individual is not a man or a woman but always both"[67] and speaks of "the bisexuality of all human beings."[68]

As is often the case with Freudian theory, it appears to be taking a purely sexual perspective on a traditional doctrine, as is made evident when he writes: "The theory of bisexuality...[suggests that] each individual seeks to satisfy both male and female wishes in his sexual life...[as] those [two sets of] demands are not fulfilled by the same object."[69] What becomes apparent is that modern man, and postmodern man for that matter, is fundamentally lost, and it is through the remaining remnants of the sacred that man unknowingly attempts to find himself through sex. Sherrard points out that "[Man's] sexual life is a sad search for his lost androgynous state."[70]

Freud confuses or ignores the differentiation of human beings from the original identity in the primordial androgyne, which is consequently a result of humanity's fallen or *saṃsāric* consciousness. The androgyne cannot be restored by giving in to one's lower nature or by doing away with traditional morality. Kathleen Raine (1908–2003) speaks of "[T]he realization of the first-created humanity, the *anthropos*, as imagined by the Creator before the Fall; which Fall is the result of Adam's "sleep," a loss of consciousness, a "descent," as the Greeks would say, from a spiritual to a natural mode of consciousness, with a consequent self-identification not with the spiritual but with the natural body."[71]

For this reason, it has been said that "the primordial androgyne, survives in each of us"[72] and that "each of us carries within ourselves, however observed, the image of the *anthropos*."[73] We need to be skeptical and vigilant of any claims suggesting that "the next step in personal evolution is a transcendence of both masculinity and femininity to general humanness."[74] This would be a fundamental subversion of the two poles of manifestation known in Hindu metaphysics as *Purusha* and *Prakriti*, the creative polarizations of masculine and feminine. While each human being is comprised of varying degrees of both male and female—"each sex, being equally human, shares in the nature of the other"[75]—this does not therefore mean that they can be arbitrarily merged or unified in the absence of a transcendent principle. Where Freud radically departs from the perspective of the perennial psychology is with regard to the notion of psychological man or *homo naturalis*, who is not a liberated human being, but once again a caricature of fallen or *saṃsāric* humanity that has lost its connection with the Divine and has no center.

In contradistinction to Freudian psychoanalysis, the traditional understanding of the androgyne confirms that originally the human being was neither male nor female, but was comprised of both, that an "archetypal reality is the androgyne reflected in both the male and female."[76] This is asserted here: "there is neither male nor female" (Galatians 3:28) and similarly "neither is the man without the woman, neither the woman without the man, in the Lord" (1 Corinthians 11:11). The book of Genesis states: "So God created man in His own image; in the image of God He created him; male and female He created them" (Genesis 1:27). The Midrash clarifies this point: "When the Holy One, Blessed be He, created the first man, He created him androgynous" (Genesis Rabbah 8:1). The Zohar also speaks to this original human state of the androgyne: "'He blessed him and called his name Adam.' A human being is only called Adam when male and female are as one."[77] The Divine pairing of male and female is found in the Koran: "Glory to God, Who created in pairs all things" (36:36), and also: "We have created you in pairs" (78:8). The human being originated in Spirit and was the original *anthrōpos* or androgyne, both male and female, before the sexes were divided, prefixed in the Divine Archetype prior to being born into the world of duality.

Freud goes beyond diagnosing the individual to commenting on the abnormal state of the human collectivity, which paradoxically appears to be a caricature of psychological man itself: "the mob gives vent to its appetites, and we deprive ourselves. We deprive ourselves in order to maintain our integrity, we economize in our health, our capacity for enjoyment, our emotions; we save ourselves for something, not knowing for what."[78] Freud's construction of the image of man has fundamentally disfigured the traditional viewpoint that connected the human with the transpersonal. Nasr discusses the corrosive ramifications of Freudianism: "[Freud] in fact originated a view of human nature which is among the most anti-religious known in the modern world."[79] These Freudian descriptions are in fact a reflection of fallen or *saṃsāric* humanity and not an authentic reflection of what is truly human. The attempt to create a "science of the soul" through this distorted image of the human being is a parody and is in reality none other than a fallen psychology. It depicts the predicament of living in the *Kali-Yuga* or "Dark Age," where the human collectivity has in many ways dissociated itself from the sacred and exists without a center. To extract the transpersonal nature of the human individual and to replace it with unconscious or instinctual drives is to undermine and furthermore destroy what is human.

French Orthodox researcher Jean-Claude Larchet articulates the human being's original health *in divinis* and the loss of the sense of the sacred that has led to the turning away from the Divine, causing a fundamental forgetting of what the human condition is:

> By original sin, Adam turned from the path on which God had set him at his creation. Man missed the goal intended for him by his very nature. When Adam stopped directing his whole being towards God and opening all his faculties to God's uncreated grace, the mirror of his soul was darkened and ceased to reflect its Creator. Since Adam stopped participating in the Source of his perfection, the virtues within him became weak and he lost the likeness of God which he had begun to realize from the moment of his creation. God's image remains in man, and cannot be lost. But since it is no longer brightened by man's active union with God and no longer finds its fulfillment in the likeness's realization, which constitutes its true aim, the image is altered and veiled. Whereas man's advancement towards perfection in the Light of the Spirit made the image radiant, sin suddenly darkened it. Since then, man has forgotten what his authentic nature is. He is ignorant of his true destiny, no longer knowing what his real life is, and has lost almost every idea of what his original health was.[80]

The destructive forces of the human psyche become more evident in the later phases of the temporal cycle, which the psychoanalytic "talking-cure" exemplifies: "It really seems as though it is necessary for us to destroy some other thing or person in order not to destroy ourselves, in order to guard against the impulsion to self-destruction.

A sad disclosure indeed for the moralist!"[81] Due to the fallen or *saṃsāric* consciousness, the human collectivity has lost sight of the sacred, and each human being has turned against each other: "Get you all down, each of you an enemy of each" (Koran 2:36). This is also a view held by Plato, where Clinias condemns the ability of the human collectivity to realize that "Humanity is in a condition of public war of every man against every man, and private war of each man with himself."[82] The behaviorist outlook keeps company with that of psychoanalytic theory in that the human being is viewed inherently against man and that the forces of civilization or society systematically oppress these fundamental urges: "Each of us is engaged in a pitched battle with the rest of mankind...Each of us has interests which conflict with the interests of everybody else. That's our original sin, and it can't be helped."[83]

What has been forgotten is that the human psyche has at all times and places been situated within the spiritual domain and presents a completely different understanding of the "science of the soul" or psychology:

> The image of man presented to us by modern psychology is not only fragmentary, it is pitiable. In reality, man is as if suspended between animality and divinity; now modern thought—be it philosophical or scientific—admits only animality, practically speaking.

> We wish, on the contrary, to correct and perfect the image of man by insisting on his divinity; not that we wish to make a god of him, *quod absit*; we intend simply to take account of his true nature, which transcends the earthly, and lacking which he would have no reason for being.

> It is this that we believe we can call—in a symbolist language— the "transfiguration of man."[84]

While the human being is both theomorphic and geomorphic of the Spirit and the earth, Freudianism reduces the human being to what is less than human or pure nothingness: "God made man out of dust. The analyst reduces him to it."[85] As psychological man no longer has a center, he searches within the sensory or physical world for release, unable to discern what is in reality a spiritual crisis: "Religious man was born to be saved; psychological man is born to be pleased."[86] After examining the notion of psychological man put forth by the psychoanalytic doctrine, it becomes apparent that it is not only an anomaly, but a creation of one man, that being Freud, with his own unbalanced mind: "the Freudian doctrine of man is at best a delusion of Freud's."[87] If it is true, as the perennial psychology teaches, that "Man becomes what he believes himself to be,"[88] it is essential that a transpersonal identity of the human being be cultivated within a traditional spiritual framework rather than according to his fallen or *saṃsāric* identity: "Psychological man is, of course, a myth."[89] For the perennial psychology, it is essential to recognize that the human being was made for the Divine and finds peace and resolution alone in the Divine: "Thou madest us for Thyself, [O Lord] and our heart is restless, until it repose in Thee."[90]

Chapter 7

Psychologism: The Reduction of Reality to Psychological Criteria

Psychodynamic approaches to psychotherapy are quintessentially rooted in the phenomenon of *psychologism*, as has been decisively brought to our attention by its own adherents, who speak of the "psychologism with which Freud and his followers began."[1] Freud himself was tirelessly attempting to plumb the wisdom traditions of the world in search for "the psychical origin of the religious ideas"[2] with no avail, as these principles do not pertain to the psychological order. Psychologism is defined as the reduction of the spiritual to the psychological—the objective to the subjective—which is to say the psychologization of the spiritual domain. In this light psychoanalysis can be equated with the phenomenon of psychologism: "psychologism attempts to explain the greater in terms of the lesser and excludes all that goes beyond its own limits."[3] This process can be further illustrated as follows: the confusion of the Absolute with the relative, the Spirit with the psyche, the Intellect or *Intellectus* with reason or *ratio*, the Self with ego, and the Personality with individuality.[4]

In the same way that behavioristic psychology epitomizes *scientism*, psychoanalytic psychology is the consummate example of *psychologism*. Nonetheless both behaviorism and psychoanalysis are, to be sure, entrenched in scientism. Both scientism and psychologism seek to reduce reality and the psyche to their own measure rather than see them according to what binds them to the Divine. Nasr identifies this psychological reductionism within psychoanalysis and modern psychology: "The modern psychological and psychoanalytical point of view tries to reduce all the higher elements of man's being to the level of the psyche, and moreover to reduce the psyche itself to nothing more than that which can be studied through modern psychological and psychoanalytical methods."[5] Jung reminds us that Freudianism is rooted in the reductionistic outlook of scientific materialism: "Freud's psychology moves within the narrow confines of nineteenth-century scientific materialism."[6] Mark Perry speaks to the destructiveness of psychologism, as reductionism in all of its manifestations undermines any integral society or civilization:

Psychologism, all told, is an outlook born finally from the disease or relativity undermining modern civilization, a perspective that places people onto the unstable ground of ever-shifting reference points which allows man to modify or even to improvise, namely to rewrite rules to fit his behavior *post facto*; thus rules and principles are now molded to man, not man to rules and principles as is the case in traditional religious morality.[7]

Behaviorism denied the existence of the human soul and is regarded as a "psychology without a soul." Psychoanalysis has been charged with the same, as it characterizes a movement that converges and continues with prior revolutions to achieve its destructive mission: "a long and systematic destruction of our religious soul."[8] Former disciple Rank writes: "Psychoanalysis cannot be a...psychology without a soul. Yet as science it denies the soul."[9] While Freud did recognize the inner dimension of the human being, it was to the exclusion of the spiritual domain. According to Jones, "[Freud] never had any belief in the immortality of the soul—or indeed in its existence."[10] He fabricated a psychology or a "science of the soul" but paradoxically "Freud shut out the soul."[11] The harm caused by the doctrine of the "talking cure" can be regarded as destructive as behavioristic psychology: "Freudian psychoanalysis...has set itself the task of laying siege to the religious soul in its depths and very inferiority."[12]

To recognize what is unconscious in the human being and make it conscious is not the same as recognizing the soul or what is transcendent in nature. This predicament is made sense of here: "Recognizing the unconscious, Freud acknowledged the soul; but by explaining the soul materialistically, he denied it."[13] The central challenge within psychoanalysis regarding the human psyche is not limited to the Freudian "talking cure," but reverberates for the most part throughout all forms of contemporary psychology:

To know psychology one has to know its object, the soul. But given its peculiar nature, psychology finds itself in a unique position: it must provide the object of its study—a scientific concept of soul. In fact, psychology does not know its own object, and flatly denies the object that tradition hands down. The soul...does not exist for scientific psychology, yet research goes on as if it did. Ironically, psychology purports to determine the validity of the soul-concept, but its research only confirms that there is no soul...[14]

Contrary to the conventional wisdom of the present day, modern science is not neutral or value-free in its own dogma, or rather authoritarianism, which becomes *scientism* when it no longer remains within the realm of its own inquiry, as indicated in the following: "Every science...must have its dogmatists; otherwise, all questions would be forever first questions—and forever remain unanswerable."[15] Schuon masterfully discerns the reductionistic phenomenon of psychologism:

What we term "psychological impostor" [or psychologism] is the tendency to reduce everything to psychological factors and to call into question not only what is intellectual or spiritual—the first being related to truth and the second to life in and by truth—but also the human spirit as such, and therewith its capacity of adequation and, still more evidently, its inward illumination and transcendence. The same belittling and truly subversive tendency rages in all the domains that "scientism" claims to embrace, but its most acute expression is beyond all doubt to be found in psychoanalysis. Psychoanalysis is at once an endpoint and a cause, as is always the case with profane ideologies, like materialism and evolutionism, of which it is really a logical and fatal ramification and a natural ally.[16]

Psychoanalysis attempts to treat the human psyche through the human psyche, yet it requires a principle higher than the horizontal or psychic realm. Burckhardt asserts that "the psychic cannot be treated by the psychic";[17] this is to say: "The soul, like every other domain of reality, can only be truly known by what transcends it."[18] Freudianism abolishes the role of Spirit by pathologizing the sacred and relegates everything to the psychological order or the empirical ego. Jung writes: "Psychoanalysis is a method which makes possible the analytical reduction of psychic contents to their simplest expression, and for discovering the line of least resistance in the development of a harmonious personality."[19]

Freud emphasizes the unique phenomenon that emerges within psychoanalytic psychology between the individual being analyzed (or the analysand) and the analyst, known as "transference" and "countertransference." Freud writes:

The patient is not satisfied with regarding the analyst in the light of reality as a helper and adviser who, moreover, is remunerated for the trouble he takes...On the contrary, the patient sees in him the return, the reincarnation, of some important figure out of his childhood or past, and consequently transfers on to him feelings and reactions which undoubtedly applied to this prototype.[20]

Freud explains how the psychoanalyst deliberately influences the therapeutic encounter: "The mechanism of our curative method is indeed quite easy to understand; we give the patient the conscious idea of what he may expect to find (*bewusste Erwartungsvorstellung*), and the similarity of this with the repressed unconscious one leads him to come upon the latter himself."[21] In contrast, Freud asserts that so-called positive transference "alters the whole analytic situation; it pushes to one side the patient's rational aim of becoming healthy and free from his ailments. Instead of it there emerges the aim of pleasing the analyst and of winning his applause and love."[22] The mechanism of transference intersects with that of suggestion, as Freud confirms: "our influence rests essentially on transference—that is, on suggestion."[23] Freud observes:

> The treatment is made up of two parts—what the physician infers and tells the patient, and the patient's working-over of what he has heard. The mechanism of our assistance is easy to understand: we give the patient the conscious anticipatory idea [the idea of what he may expect to find] and he then finds the repressed unconscious idea in himself on the basis of its similarity to the anticipatory one. This is the intellectual help which makes it easier for him to overcome the resistance between conscious and unconscious.[24]

The mechanism of transference and suggestion not only challenges the objectivity of the findings of psychoanalytic theory, but also puts the individual in harm's way by placing him or her under the questionable influence of the psychoanalyst. Smith writes "even a perfectly normal person who subjects himself to psychoanalysis is bound to contract a *bona fide* neurosis as a direct consequence of the psychoanalytic process. And it is needless to say that the more confused and wretched the patient becomes, the more susceptible he will be to the promptings of his analyst."[25] The precarious transferential and suggestive process is immanent in the therapeutic relationship, as exposed by Andrew Salter: "With the harpoon of the transference in the patient, the analyst can give him any interpretation, however preposterous, and the patient will usually go along with it."[26] Gail Kennedy discusses the distorting effects of transference and countertransference:

When the analyst makes interpretations, the patient's unconscious may all too willingly comply by furnishing associations in
the form of fantasies, dreams, and selected memories which serve
either submissively to corroborate the interpretation (though it
may be wrong) or defiantly to corroborate the interpretation *because* it is wrong. And under the influence of the countertransference the analyst himself may be seduced into accepting the
patient's own subtly and indirectly proffered interpretations, or
he may project his own unconscious conflicts on to the patient
and end up by treating the wrong person. How is it possible to
get out of this quagmire?[27]

It becomes apparent that the phenomenon of "transference" and
"countertransference" are in fact unavoidable as these are challenges
implicit to the horizontal realm of the human psyche and cannot be
transcended or integrated without a vertical dimension. This dilemma
is a product of dualism and can only be understood within a metaphysical framework. Schuon points out that "The ego as such cannot
logically seek the experience of what lies beyond egoity."[28]

Pope Pius XII (1876–1958) challenges the reductionistic outlook
within modern psychology by outlining the necessity of a transcendent criterion for any true discussion on the subject: "Psychotherapy
and clinical psychology must always consider man (1) as a psychic
unit and totality, (2) as a structured unit in itself, (3) as a social unit,
and (4) as a transcendent unit, that is to say, in man's tending towards
God."[29]

The restricted terrain of modern psychology as it applies to the
Freudian doctrine is further elaborated here:

The competence of psychoanalysis remains restricted to the field
of psychological reality. Psychoanalysis, therefore, may not reduce all reality to the psychological sphere, if it is to avoid the
danger of a "reductionist hermeneutic." Psychoanalysis can remove neurotic guilt feelings, but it cannot liberate a person from
real sin. It can eliminate psychosomatic illnesses, but it cannot
answer ultimate questions about meaning and meaninglessness,
life and death. Its aim is to bring things into consciousness, not
to forgive; it is healing, not salvation.[30]

There are discernable boundaries that exist between the psychic
and spiritual domains, which are not interchangeable or synonymous.
While the Freudian "talking cure" is the quintessence of psychologism, the situation does not necessarily fare better for the rest of mod-

ern psychology, as the phenomenon of psychologism is in many ways embedded in its theoretical tenets. Freud writes:

> Every science is based on observations and experiences arrived at through the medium of our psychical apparatus. But since *our* science has as its subject that [psychical] apparatus itself, the analogy ends here. We make our observations through the medium of the same perceptual apparatus, precisely with the help of the breaks in the sequence of "psychical" events: we fill in what is omitted by making plausible inferences and translating it into conscious material.[31]

Jung was correct in stating that "the human psyche, be it sick or healthy, cannot be explained *solely* by reduction."[32] Yet this should not therefore be interpreted to suggest that Jung was not also reductionistic in his outlook and did not assert his own variation of psychologism. Fromm writes: "Jung reduces religion to a psychological phenomenon and at the same time elevates the unconscious to a religious phenomenon."[33] Jung suggests that "The psyche is a self-regulating system,"[34] and yet he encapsulates the predicament surrounding modern psychology as the limitations of comprehending and treating the human psyche by its own means. What is required is a vertical or spiritual dimension to resolve the inherent impasse that is modern psychology:

> All conceivable statements are made by the psyche...The psyche cannot leap beyond itself. It cannot set up any absolute truths, for its own polarity determines the relativity of its statements...In saying this we are not expressing a value judgment, but only pointing out that the limit is very frequently overstepped...In my effort to depict the limitations of the psyche I do not mean to imply that *only* the psyche exists. It is merely that, so far as perception and cognition are concerned, we cannot see beyond the psyche...All comprehension and all that is comprehended is in itself psychic, and to that extent we are hopelessly cooped up in an exclusively psychic world.[35]

Jung erroneously equates the psychic phenomenon with metaphysical reality, as he confirms here: "It is the soul [psyche] which, by the divine creative power inherent in it, makes the metaphysical assertion; it posits the distinctions between metaphysical entities. Not only is it the condition of all metaphysical reality, it *is* that reality."[36] Ultimately, as Jung points out, all contemporary psychological systems that do not originate *in divinis* are relative and subjective in nature: "philosophical criticism has helped me to see that every psychology—my own included—has the character of a subjective confession...Even when I deal with empirical data, I am necessarily speaking about myself."[37]

That psychoanalysis is limited to the empirical ego and cannot go beyond it is outlined in detail here:

> Psychoanalysis works on the intensive exposure of emotions. They are brought out into the daylight with the object of cleaning out the subconscious, and thus are lived over again, which means that each of them is amplified. Instead of belonging only to the damaged part of the being, they invade the whole field of *prakriti* as the tares spread over a wheat-field. The very structure of emotion must be denied as such, for it arises only from one's subjective view of external elements...The traditional [spiritual] techniques pay no attention to emotion...Several levels have to be passed through before one can know how to minimize emotion at its very source, to know it, to isolate and master it, and finally to be able to get rid of it. The lower stage is to realize once and for all that emotions are a debt to be paid; this realization is the beginning of a process that uproots them. This is the process of eradication...to conceive of emotion as a surrender, an always recurring pattern. It is part of the automatism which becomes evident and really does not exist...Renunciation (*vairāgya*) is the voluntary giving up of all emotions whatsoever...To be capable of mastering an emotion, one has first to evaluate it and dispose of it for what it really is—the distortion of an uncontrolled and misplaced sensation...This [spiritual] method is exact opposite of psychoanalysis, which digs about the ego...Emotion does not enter into any spiritual discipline, because in itself emotion had not consistency. It is only a movement of *prakriti*. When the mind is perfectly calm it is like the still water of a mountain lake. The slightest ripple on the surface is an emotion.[38]

Treating the human psyche outside of an authentic religious or spiritual framework can be very dangerous to the individual being treated, a danger that goes unnoticed when viewed purely through a secular lens; nonetheless, the danger still prevails on a spiritual level, as Schuon notes:

> Analogically speaking: if a man is distressed by a flood and seeks a way to escape from it, psychoanalysis would remove the dis-

tress and let the patient drown...This is not to say that it never happens that a psychoanalyst discovers and dissolves a dangerous complex without at the same time ruining the patient; but we are here concerned with the principle, in which the perils and errors involved infinitely outweigh the contingent advantages and fragmentary truths.[39]

Smith also suggests that the harmful impacts extend not only to the individual being analyzed, but to the psychoanalyst as well: "[T]he psychoanalytic patient opens himself up to forces which even the analyst himself does not understand. It also means that somewhere along the line the analyst, too, may have become victimized by occult influences which are not under his conscious control. And this seems all more likely if one recalls that, according to the Freudian tradition, the psychoanalyst is first of all to be analyzed himself."[40]

Psychologism reaches its apex with attempts to integrate the psychic with the spiritual without a vertical dimension, as exemplified here: "in broad terms, we want to integrate Freud and Buddha, we want to integrate lower 'depth psychology' with 'height psychology'...If you don't befriend Freud, it will be harder to get to Buddha."[41] Schuon underscores the fallacies underlying the myriad psychodynamic therapies:

One of the most insidious and destructive illusions is the belief that depth psychology [or psychoanalysis]...has the slightest connection with spiritual life, which these teachings persistently falsify by confusing inferior elements [psychic] with superior [spiritual]. We cannot be too wary of all the attempts to reduce the values vehicled by tradition to the level of phenomena supposed to be scientifically controllable. The spirit escapes the hold of profane science in an absolute fashion.[42]

Central to psychoanalytic theory is the principle of psychic determinism, or the notion that mental processes are not spontaneous and that nothing happens by chance, as they are determined by the unconscious. As Brenner notes: "in the mind, as in physical nature...nothing happens by chance, or in a random way. Each psychic event is determined by the ones which preceded it."[43] Freud discusses his doctrine of psychic determinism:

Many people, as is well known, contest the assumption of complete psychical determinism by appealing to a special feeling of conviction that there is a free will. This feeling of conviction exists; and it does not give way before a belief in determinism. Like every normal feeling it must have something to warrant it. But so far as I can observe, it does not manifest itself in the great and important decisions of the will: on these occasions the feeling that we have is rather one of psychical compulsion, and we are glad to invoke it on our behalf. ("Here I stand: I can do no other.") [as Luther said before the Diet.] On the other hand, it is precisely with regard to the unimportant, indifferent decisions that we would like to claim that we could just as well have acted otherwise: that we have acted of our free—and unmotivated—will. According to our analyses it is not necessary to dispute the right to the feeling of conviction of having a free will. If the distinction between conscious and unconscious motivation is taken into account, our feeling of conviction informs us that conscious motivation does not extend to all our motor decisions. *De minimis non curat lex*. But what is thus left free by the one side receives its motivation from the other side, from the unconscious; and in this way determination in the psychical sphere is still carried out without any gap.[44]

The following reflection underscores this general idea as it extends to the broader field of mental health: "what is never said about Freudianism, or about the whole of modern psychology, is that the help it offers is directed solely to the automatic part of the human psyche."[45]

A central challenge that Freud recognized in his study of the "psychic apparatus" was its unreliability due to its entrenched relativism, depicting endless shades of gray that are indistinguishable from each other. Freud observes: "in the unconscious...one cannot distinguish between truth and fiction that has been cathected with affect."[46] This embedded relativism also applies to clinical work, as is highlighted by Karl Popper (1902–94): "'Clinical observations,' like all other observations, are *interpretations in the light of theories*; and for this reason alone they are apt to seem to support those theories in the light of which they were interpreted."[47] The "psychic apparatus" is so unreliable that one cannot verify and know with certainty what is true and what is fiction, which is the crux of Freud's dilemma when he writes: "the unconscious never overcomes the resistance of the conscious, the expectation that in treatment the opposite is bound to happen, to the point where the unconscious is completely tamed by the conscious, also diminishes."[48] Perhaps the only thing certain regarding the empirical ego is its illusive nature that cannot be relied upon with any certainty: "the ego will seek to turn even illness to its advantage."[49] As Freud remarked: "we have noticed that no psycho-analyst goes further than his own complexes and internal resistances permit."[50] Jung also echoes something similar in the following: "In the end no one can completely outgrow his personal limitations; everyone is more or less imprisoned by them—especially when he practices psychology."[51]

The method of treatment relies heavily if not exclusively on the resistance of the empirical ego devoid of a vertical or spiritual domain: "The whole theory of psychoanalysis...in fact [is] built up on the perception of the resistance offered to us by the patient when we attempt to make his unconscious conscious."[52] Jung, we might add, makes a similar proposition about the nature of psychopathology: "the neurotic is ill because he is unconscious of his problems,"[53] and therefore: "The...goal of the analysis...is to reach a state where the unconscious contents no longer remain unconscious."[54] Pope Pius XII takes issue with the notion that making unconscious contents conscious is a panacea: "The trite principle that sexual trouble of the unconscious, as all other inhibitions of identical origin, can be suppressed only by their being brought to the level of consciousness, is not valid if it is generalized without distinction."[55] Due to the horizontal and relativistic outlook of psychoanalysis, which for the most part extends throughout contemporary psychology, a Prometheanism becomes apparent as the psychic realm is elevated and given the highest validity.

Chapter 8

Freudianism: The Counter-Religion to Replace
Sacred Tradition

"It is on the subject of religion that the judicious clinician grows ve-hement and disputatious. Against no other strong-point of the repres-sive culture are the reductive weapons of psychoanalysis deployed in such open hostility."[1]—Philip Rieff

The emergence of psychoanalysis is inseparable from the vacuum cre-ated by the marginalization of the sacred, and yet psychoanalysis was also complicit in systematically undermining religion and was itself an attempt to fill this void. Jones confirms this: "Moreover, in the nineteenth century the belief in scientific knowledge as the prime sol-vent of the world's ills—a belief that Freud retained to the end—was beginning to displace the hopes that had previously been built on re-ligion, political action, and philosophy in turn."[2] Homans confirms this process of subversion: "Psychology has arisen in direct propor-tion to the decline of the power of religion. Thus a substitutive relation obtains between the two: psychology is modern man's 'invisible reli-gion.'"[3]

The integral psychology of the perennial philosophy radically de-parts from this perspective since it recognizes the sacred as infused into all domains of reality. From this point of view, sacred tradition signifies the following as Perry indicates:

Tradition is the continuity of Revelation: an uninterrupted trans-mission, through innumerable generations, of the spiritual and cosmological principles, sciences, and laws resulting from a re-vealed religion: nothing is neglected, from the establishment of social orders and codes of conduct to the canons regulating the arts and architecture, ornamentation and dress; it includes the mathematical, physical, medical, and psychological sciences, en-compassing moreover those deriving from celestial movements. What contrasts it totally with our modern learning, which is a closed system materially, is its reference of all things back to superior planes of being, and eventually to ultimate Principles; considerations entirely unknown to modern man.[4]

It is also necessary to clarify what myth signifies within the sapiential traditions. The traditional idea of myth is additionally captured here: "*Myth* [is] *the penultimate truth, of which all experience is the temporal reflection. The mythical narrative is of timeless and placeless validity, true nowhere and everywhere...*Myth embodies the nearest approach to absolute truth that can be stated in words."[5] Similarly: "The content of folklore is metaphysical."[6]

With the marginalization of religion in the contemporary world mental health professionals have encroached upon domains that were traditionally reserved for religion. Rollo May elaborates on this dilemma:

> Therapists belong to a strange profession. It is partly religion. Since the time of the Paracelsus in the Renaissance the physician—and afterward the psychiatrist and psychological therapist—has taken on the mantle of the priest. We cannot deny that we who are therapists deal with people's moral and spiritual questions and that we fill the role of father-confessor as part of our armamentarium, as shown in Freud's position *behind* and unseen by the person confessing.[7]

It is unsurprising that Freud who proclaimed, "I have no religion"[8] has been regarded in the following manner: "That Freud is one of the great atheists of contemporary culture is beyond doubt."[9] Freud's antipathy for religion is reminiscent no doubt of another central architect of the modern world, Karl Marx (1818–83),[10] who made well known the often cited statement about religion: "Religion is...the opium of the people."[11] A similar statement that reduces religion to a man-made phenomenon is: "man makes religion; religion does not make man."[12]

There is also the phenomenon of what has been termed the New Atheism, which appears to be more of a contemporary prolongation of one and the same atheism that has already existed.[13] This form of atheism is advanced by individuals such as Richard Dawkins (b. 1941),[14] Christopher Hitchens (1949–2011),[15] Sam Harris (b. 1967)[16] and Daniel C. Dennett (b. 1942).[17] With further analysis, atheism itself appears to take on the form of a secular pseudo-religion: "The atheist is a religious person. He believes in atheism as though it were a new religion."[18] Smith highlights this conundrum when applied to the concept of psychological man: "'psychological man'—the person who instinctively rejects all absolutes except the absolute of unbelief itself."[19]

Freud discloses what he views as the foremost challenge to the scientific worldview: "religion alone is to be taken seriously as an enemy."[20] The battleground for psychoanalysis is described as "The struggle of the scientific spirit against the religious *Weltanschauung.*"[21] Freud qualifies this attack on religion as "an attack on religion only in so far as any scientific investigation of religious belief presupposes disbelief."[22] As one of Freud's principal biographers confirmed, the Freudian agenda was without question "To demolish religion with psychoanalytic weapons."[23] Gay additionally writes: "Freud was a consistent, aggressive, dogmatic atheist, a child of the Enlightenment who saw a world at war to the death between science and religion."[24]

Whether recognized or not, present-day therapists, psychologists, and psychiatrists are engaged in the "secular priesthood of soul doctors,"[25] or as Freud termed it, "a secular spiritual guide."[26] For "Psychologists and psychoanalysts...have become the priests of a godless age."[27] Nietzsche asks the provocative question suggesting that a novel or updated form of treatment of the human psyche is now needed: *"Where are the new physicians of the soul?"*[28] Little did he know that Sigmund Freud was just the one who would respond to this call. Freud himself confirmed this when writing: "the words, 'secular pastoral worker,' might well serve as a general formula for describing the function [of] the analyst."[29] Elsewhere, he adds, "Indeed, these words, 'a secular spiritual guide,' might well serve as a general formula for describing the function which the analyst, whether he is a doctor or a layman, has to perform in his relation to the public."[30]

While the overwhelming outlook of contemporary therapies is secular in nature and does not recognize the centrality of the Spirit as necessary for psychological health and well-being, paradoxically we are informed by Freudian apologists or revisionists the very opposite, that "the aim of the psychoanalytic cure of the soul is to help the patient attain the attitude...described as religious."[31] While some may still cling to the pretense that the Freudian "talking cure" is or ever was a *bona fide* science and is in some way neutral to religion or spirituality, this perception is far from the case, as the psychoanalytic movement took on characteristics that were more like a secular pseudo-religion. Freud at times makes rare exceptions, and downplays his militant hostility toward religion, presenting it at times with a certain neutrality; this not only contradicts many of his core beliefs, but is deceptive and erroneous in nature:

In itself psycho-analysis is neither religious nor nonreligious, but an impartial tool which both priest and layman can use in the service of the sufferer. I am very much struck by the fact that it never occurred to me how extraordinarily helpful the psycho-analytic method might be in pastoral work, but that is surely accounted for by the remoteness from me, as a wicked pagan, of the whole system of ideas.[32]

Szasz points out that "Despite its deceptive terminology, psychoanalysis is not a science but a religion—the faith of a generation incapable of any other."[33] Be not deceived by appearances, for the substitute religion is, as Hoffer writes, none other than a secular pseudo-religion which has its equally fervent followers: "For though ours is a godless age, it is the very opposite of irreligious."[34]

Freud's assault on religion is well-known and documented; however, the way in which psychoanalytic psychology attempted to substitute itself for the role of religion to become a secular pseudo-religion in its place is less known and requires more attention. Freudianism functions as a counterfeit religion to usurp the role of religion, which is to say it became a parody of religion for the modern world. Prominent historian Egon Friedell (1878–1938) emphasizes:

> Psycho-analysis is in truth a sect, with all the signs and symbols of one—rites and ceremonies, oracles and mantic, settled symbolism and dogmatism, secret doctrine and popular edition, proselytes and renegades, priests who are subjected to tests, and daughter sects which damn each other in turn. Just as the whale, though a mammal, poses as a fish, so psycho-analysis, actually a religion, poses as a science. This religion is pagan in character: it embraces nature-worship, demonology, chthonian belief in the depths, Dionysian sex-idolization. This connection of religion with therapy, hygiene, and the interpretation of dreams existed in the ancient world also, as for example the healing sleep for the sick in the temples of Asklepios. And we have here a seer and singer working for the powers of darkness in most enticing tones, an Orpheus from the Underworld: it is a new world-wide revolt against the Gospel.[35]

Knight Dunlap (1875–1949), psychologist and a past president of the American Psychological Association, deems that the Freudian "talking cure" is another brand not of religion but of pseudo-mysticism itself: "One of the most important if not the most important mystical movement of the nineteenth century is currently known as psychoanalysis."[36] Without exaggerating the role of Freudian therapy, "the practice of psychoanalysis...has come to replace religion in the lives of many people."[37] For this reason, "psychoanalysis succeeded in becoming for many a surrogate religion."[38] This is exemplified by Perls's own therapeutic disclosure: "I had tried to make psychoanalysis my spiritual home, my religion."[39]

An important facet in making sense of this has to do with Freud's enduring interest in if not sheer obsession with religion that lasted throughout his lifetime, up until his death, while he was at the same time one of its most ruthless antagonists. Freud's focus on religion nonetheless persisted until the final year of his life as is visible in the list of publications that are dedicated to this theme: *Totem and Taboo* (1913), *The Future of an Illusion* (1927), *Civilization and Its Discontents* (1930), and *Moses and Monotheism* (1939), as well as other lesser known writings on religion, myth and ritual.[40]

Among some of Freud's private notes obtained from 1905, he concisely and provocatively presents his theories on this theme: "Religion as ob[sessive] neurosis—Private religion."[41] Two years later, Freud's idea germinated into his initial exploratory article "Obsessive Actions and Religious Practices" (1907), comparing religious practices with obsessive behaviors:

> I am certainly not the first person to have been struck by the resemblance between what are called obsessive actions in sufferers from nervous affections and the observances by means of which believers give expression to their piety...It is easy to see where the resemblances lie between neurotic ceremonials and the sacred acts of religious ritual: in the qualms of conscience brought on by their neglect, in their complete isolation from all other actions (shown in the prohibition against interruption) and in the conscientiousness with which they are carried out...[42]

Early on Freud viewed the "ultimate basis" of religion as "the infantile helplessness of mankind."[43] He elaborates further: "The last contribution to the criticism of the religious *Weltanschauung* was effected by psycho-analysis, by showing how religion originated from the helplessness of children and by tracing its contents to the survival into maturity of the wishes and needs of childhood."[44] Freud's monograph *Leonardo Da Vinci: A Study in Psychosexuality* published in 1910 conveys the psychologizing of religion, reducing in principle transcendence or the Absolute with what is termed the "father complex":

> Psychoanalysis, which has taught us the intimate connection between the father complex and belief in God, has shown us that the personal God is psychologically nothing but an exalted father, and daily demonstrates to us how youthful persons lose their religious belief as soon as the authority of the father breaks down. In the parental complex we thus recognize the roots of religious need; the almighty, just God and kindly nature appear to us as grand sublimations of father and mother, or rather as revivals and restorations of the infantile conceptions of both parents. Religiousness is biologically traced to the long period of helplessness and need of help of the little child.[45]

The centrality of the Oedipus complex within Freud's metapsychology, especially its cultural-historical implications, was captured in *Totem and Taboo*, where he reduces the whole of religion to psychological criteria:

> There can be no doubt that in the Christian myth the original sin was one against God the Father. If, however, Christ redeemed mankind from the burden of original sin by the sacrifice of his own life, we are driven to conclude that the sin was a murder. The law of talion, which is so deeply rooted in human feelings, lays it down that a murder can only be expiated by the sacrifice of another life: self-sacrifice points back to blood-guilt. And if this sacrifice of a life brought about atonement with God the Father, the crime to be expiated can only have been the murder of the father. In the Christian doctrine, therefore, men were acknowledging in the most undisguised manner the guilty primeval deed, since they found the fullest atonement for it in the sacrifice of this one son. Atonement with the father was all the more complete since the sacrifice was accompanied by a total renunciation of the women on whose account the rebellion against the father was started. But at that point the inexorable psychological law of ambivalence stepped in. The very deed in which the son offered the greatest possible atonement to the father brought him at the same time to the attainment of his wishes *against* the father. He himself became God, beside, or, more correctly, in place of, the father. A son-religion displaced the father-religion. As a sign of this substitution the ancient totem meal was revived in the form

of communion, in which the company of brothers consumed the flesh and blood of the son—no longer the father—obtained sanctity thereby and identified themselves with him.[46]

Among many of Freud's misunderstandings about religion is that in the Christian tradition, the Son does not in any way replace the Father, which Jesus confirms when proclaiming his Divinity: "I and my Father are one" (John 10:30) and "He that hath seen Me hath seen the Father" (John 14:9). Nonetheless, the Son also asserted that "my Father is greater than I" (John 14:28).

Freud in fact gives the highest praise for his discovery of the Oedipus complex, demonstrating its importance for his theory: "if psychoanalysis could boast of no other achievement than the discovery of the repressed Oedipus complex, that alone would give it a claim to be included among the precious new acquisitions of mankind."[47] Fromm also holds this view: "In seeing the Oedipus complex as the central phenomenon of psychology Freud has made one of the most important discoveries in psychology."[48]

By 1919 Freud had further developed his psychoanalytic metapsychology to usurp the role of religion and spirituality within the doctrine of the Oedipus complex:

God the father once walked upon earth in bodily form and exercised his sovereignty as chieftain of the primal human horde until his sons united to slay him. It emerges further that this crime of liberation and the reactions to it had as their result the appearance of the first social ties, the basic moral restrictions and the oldest form of religion, totemism. But the later religions too have the same content, and on the one hand they are concerned with obliterating the traces of that crime or with expiating it by bringing forward other solutions of the struggle between the father and sons, while on the other hand they cannot avoid repeating once more the elimination of the father.[49]

Freud emphasizes that "man's sense of guilt springs from the Oedipus complex and was acquired at the killing of the father by the brothers banded together."[50] According to Fromm, "This theory [the Oedipus complex] is the secularized version of the concept of 'original sin.'"[51] It is here worth noting that it was Jung who proposed the female equivalent of the Oedipus complex, coining the term "Electra complex" in 1913.[52]

We recall an often-quoted and powerfully expressed passage from *The Future of an Illusion* that underscores Freud's extreme contempt for religion and that interprets it as mental illness itself: "Religion would thus be the universal obsessional neurosis of humanity."[53] Elsewhere he interprets religion as a childhood neurosis: "Religion arises out of the need and anxiety of children and of early mankind, there is no doubt about it."[54]

Freud predicts the demise of religion by making a connection with evolutionary theory and humanity's inevitable embrace of a desacralized worldview:

[L]ike the obsessional neurosis of children, it arose out of the Oedipus complex, out of the relation to the father. If this view is right, it is to be supposed that a turning-away from religion is bound to occur with the fatal inevitability of a process of growth, and that we find ourselves at this very juncture in the middle of that phase of development...If, on the one hand, religion brings with it obsessional restrictions, exactly as an individual obsessional neurosis does, on the other hand it comprises a system of wishful illusions together with a disavowal of reality, such as we find in an isolated form nowhere else but in amentia, in a state of blissful hallucinatory confusion.[55]

Paradoxically Freud attacked religion not on the grounds of the scientific findings and theories of psychoanalysis, but, we have to assume, on the basis of his own personal predilections, as he explicitly states: "Let us be quite clear on the point that the views expressed in my book [*The Future of an Illusion*] form no part of analytic theory."[56] It is interesting how certain psychoanalytic theories are deemed speculative and others are delineated as strictly scientific. Unless one combed through the entire Freudian corpus, how would one know what is considered speculative psychoanalytic literature and what consists of allegedly scientific findings in the official Freudian cannon? Are there then two differing ways to interpret the doctrine of the "talking cure"?

Freud has expressed: "[religious ideas] are illusions, fulfillments of the oldest, strongest and most urgent wishes of mankind."[57] Freud argues that all manifestations of religion, beginning with the religion of the First Peoples and shamanic traditions, emerged from the doctrine of the Oedipus complex:

The father of the primal horde, since he was an unlimited despot, had seized all the women for himself; his sons, being dangerous to him as rivals, had been killed or driven away. One day, however, the sons came together and united to overwhelm, kill, and devour their father, who had been their enemy but also their ideal. After the deed they were unable to take over their heritage since they stood in one another's way. Under the influence of failure and remorse they learned to come to an agreement among themselves; they banded themselves into a clan of brothers by the help of the ordinances of totemism, which aimed at preventing a repetition of such a deed, and they jointly undertook to forgo the possession of the women on whose account they had killed their father. They were then driven to finding strange women, and this was the origin of the exogamy which is so closely bound up with totemism. The totem meal was the festival commemorating the fearful deed from which sprang man's sense of guilt (or 'original sin') and which was the beginning at once of social organization, of religion and of ethical restrictions.[58]

Freud suggests that the "totem meal" of the religion of the First Peoples continues to exist into the present day within Christianity as the rite of communion. Freud writes: "This view of religion throws a particularly clear light upon the psychological basis of Christianity, in which, as we know, the ceremony of the totem meal still survives with but little distortion, in the form of Communion."[59]

Freudian theory had a profound impact on the discipline of anthropology, as Lasch points out: "it was the work of Freud...that most deeply influenced American anthropology in its formative years."[60] As Jung informs us, the psychoanalytic literature views the First Peoples in a very degraded light: "the Freudian school...looks on primitive man as little better than a wild beast."[61] Linguist and anthropologist Edward Sapir (1884–1939) writes of "the violence with which Freud and his followers have torn many of the facts of primitive behavior out of their natural cultural setting."[62] Psychologist Harry K. Wells (1911–76) provides six essential concepts that outline the Freudian anthropology and its understanding of human nature:

(1) *The primal horde myth* on which Freud based his theories of the id and of the super-ego and hence of society. (2) *The doctrine of phylogenetic memories* which maintains that remote primitive experiences such as the original patricide, incest, fear of castration, remorse, guilt, and taboos against incest and patricide become biologically hereditary memories existing in each and every modern child and adult. (3) *The concept of biologically innate infantile sexual phases* through which every child must pass

between birth and the age of five or six. These phases are said to center around erotogenic zones and to be expressed in innate drives—the mouth and its oral cannibalistic drives; the anus and its anal-sadistic-aggressive drives, and the primary sexual organs and their genital drives. It is maintained that the manner in which the child passes from one to another of these phases, or remains fixed in or regresses to them, determines in large part the future character, personality, criminality, normalcy, and relative health or illness of the adult. (4) *The biologically predetermined Oedipus complex* in which the child of two to four or five years finds a sexual object for his infantile sexual drives in the parent of the opposite sex. The manner in which the child resolves the Oedipus complex determines much of his future life. Phylogenetic memories of fear of castration, elicited by current threats from the father, and penis envy are said to play decisive roles in the masculine and feminine solution of the complex. (5) *A primordial language composed of archaic symbols in the form of imagery* is held to be a biologically hereditary feature of human nature, a legacy from primal horde and tribal man. It is that symbolic racial language which allows the analyst or the anthropologist or student of folk lore to translate and interpret dreams and other alleged phenomena of the unconscious. (6) *A biologically inherited racial unconscious* is posited which is the repository of all the phylogenetic memories, infantile sexual phases, and Oedipus drives and taboos against them, as well as of the primordial symbolic language. This unconscious is said to be passed down from generation to generation and thus to belong to the race rather than the individual. The latter is merely the transmitter to future generations. It is this racial unconscious with its irresistible drives and impulses and memories and taboos which dominates the mind and nature of man.[63]

French anthropologist and ethnologist Claude Lévi-Strauss (1908–2009) makes a connection between the religion of the First Peoples and the shamanic traditions and the psychoanalytic doctrine, but he also points out that shamanism is diametrically different from the psychoanalytic method:

Both cures aim at inducing an experience, and both succeed by recreating a myth which the patient has to live or relive. But in one case, the patient constructs an individual myth with elements drawn from his past; in the other case, the patient receives from the outside a social myth which does not correspond to a former personal state...When a transference is established, the patient puts words into the mouth of the psychoanalyst by attributing to him alleged feelings and intentions; in the incantation, on the contrary, the shaman speaks for the patient. He questions her and puts into her mouth answers that correspond to the interpretation of her condition, with which she must become imbued...[64]

Early anthropologists and research into the lives of the First Peoples has been heavily shaped by psychoanalytic theory, causing some to conclude that Freud's ideas were applicable to understanding the traditional peoples of the world. Hungarian psychoanalyst and anthropologist Géza Róheim (1891–1953) claims that "We then proceed to analyze the cultures of various human groups...we find an essentially Oedipal culture."[65] Another example of this is given here by Lévi-Strauss: "The cure would consist, therefore, in making explicit a situation originally existing on the emotional level and in rendering acceptable to the mind pains which the body refuses to tolerate...The shaman provides the sick woman with a *language*, by means of which unexpressed, and otherwise inexpressible, psychic states can be immediately expressed."[66]

German-American anthropologist Franz Boas (1858–1942), however, had the following to say about Freudian speculations:

While, therefore, we may welcome the application of every advance in the method of psychological investigation, we cannot accept as an advance in ethnological method the crude transfer of a novel, one-sided method of psychological investigation of the individual to social phenomena the origin of which can be shown to be historically determined and to be subject to influences that are not at all comparable to those that control the psychology of the individual.[67]

Freud goes on to present his evolutionary perspective on humanity's need to grow out of the neurosis that is religion:

Religion is an attempt to master the sensory world in which we are situated by means of the wishful world which we have developed within us as a result of biological and psychological necessities. But religion cannot achieve this. Its doctrines bear the imprint of the times in which they arose, the ignorant times of the childhood of humanity. Its consolations deserve no trust...If we attempt to assign the place of religion in the evolution of mankind, it appears not as a permanent acquisition but as a counter-part to the neurosis which individual civilized men have to go through in their passage from childhood to maturity.[68]

In contradistinction, it is crucial to recall the work of Wilhelm Schmidt (1868–1954), linguist, ethnologist, and historian of religions, who rigorously challenged the evolutionist presuppositions found among the nineteenth- and twentieth-century anthropologists, ethnologists, and sociologists. Furthermore, through his extensive research Schmidt found that since time immemorial there was the principle of monotheism among the First Peoples' religion. This contradicts the evolutionist presupposition that most contemporaries hold, viewing monotheism or the belief in one God or Supreme Deity as a product of evolution.[69]

The timeless wisdom of the diverse cultures of the world speaks in a unified voice on the nature of the Absolute or Spirit, and this unified vision is known as the perennial philosophy. Joseph Epes Brown (1920–2000), renowned scholar of the Native American Traditions and World Religions, writes:

> It has long been necessary to situate correctly the so-called primitive religions in the context of the world's historical religions, and in so doing to recognize that in spite of many elements unfamiliar to the outsider, Native American traditions, at least where there has not been excessive compromise to the modern world, are in no sense inferior, but indeed are legitimate expressions of the *philosophia perennis*.[70]

Freud clarifies that because of the collective pathology due to the adherence to religion, the faithful are protected from acquiring an individual pathology: "devout believers are safeguarded in a high degree against the risk of certain neurotic illnesses; their acceptance of the universal neurosis spares them the task of constructing a personal one."[71] Freud's attacks on religion relegating it to mental illness or considering it delusional in nature were again in no way discreet or roundabout:

> [W]e call a belief an illusion when a wish-fulfillment is a prominent factor in its motivation, and in doing so we disregard its relations to reality, just as the illusion itself sets no store by verification.

Having thus taken our bearings, let us return once more to the question of religious doctrines. We can now repeat that all of them are illusions...Some of them are so improvable, so incompatible with everything we have laboriously discovered about the reality of the [modern] world, that we may compare them...to delusions.[72]

According to psychoanalytic theory, "religion is an illusion and it derives its strength from its readiness to fit in with our instinctual wishful impulses."[73] Freud states elsewhere: "The whole thing is so patently infantile, so foreign to reality, that to anyone with a friendly attitude to humanity it is painful to think that the great majority of mortals will never be able to rise above this view of life."[74] Rieff emphasizes that the Freudian paradigm pathologizes the role of religion because it seeks a remedy for what does not exist: "To be religious is to be sick, by definition: it is the effort to find a cure where none can possibly exist. For Freud, religion can be only a symptom of what it seeks to cure."[75] Rieff then goes on to situate the role of the psychoanalytic doctrine, illustrating that it too cannot remedy what the human being seeks: "Psychoanalysis does not cure; it merely reconciles."[76]

Albert Ellis (1913–2007), who is recognized as one of the most influential figures in contemporary psychology,[77] was a precursor of the cognitive revolution and is considered by many as the grandfather of cognitive-behavioral therapy. While influenced early on by Freud and his theories, Ellis later became critical of Freudian therapy. Ellis nonetheless holds an analogous position on the role of religion and spirituality and is one of the most outspoken figures against religion. Ellis depicts the continued attack on religion that began with Freud:

In the final analysis...religion is neurosis...religion goes hand in hand with the basic irrational beliefs of human beings. These keep them dependent, anxious, and hostile, and thereby create and maintain their neuroses and psychoses. What then is the role of psychotherapy in dealing with the religious views of disturbed patients? Obviously, the sane and effective psychotherapist should not—as many contemporary psychoanalytic Jungian, client-centered, and existentialist therapists have contended he should—go along with the patients' religious orientation and try to help these patients live successfully with their religions, for this is equivalent to trying to help them live successfully with their emotional illness.[78]

Perls also holds what appears to be a verbatim outlook of the Freudian doctrine, when he states: "Religion tends to prevent the growing up of mankind, tends to keep believers in an infantile state."[79]

Freud minced no words when suggesting the complete overthrow of religion by modern science by his psychoanalytic "talking cure" in February 6, 1899, when he stated: "the religion of science...is supposed to have replaced the old religion."[80] For this reason Jean Borella emphasizes: "Psychoanalysis in fact pursues the declared project of substituting itself for religion, of taking its place, of occupying the terrain where the transcendent and sacred held sway until then. And it has actually become the religion of western humanity."[81] Like Freud, Jung asserted that only religion could replace the human need for the sacred, which he conveys in a most revealing letter to Freud on February 11, 1910: "Religion can be replaced only by religion."[82] The disciples of Freud were in some cases more eager than the master to usurp the place of religion for modern psychology, as Jung confirms:

I imagine a far finer and more comprehensive task for ΨA than alliance with an ethical fraternity. I think we must give it time to infiltrate into people from many centres to revivify among intellectuals a feeling for symbol and myth, ever so gently to transform Christ back into the soothsaying god of the vine, which he was, and in this way absorb those ecstatic instinctual forces of Christianity for the *one* purpose of making the cult and the sacred myth what they once were—a drunken feast of joy where man regained the ethos and holiness of an animal. That was the beauty and purpose of classical religion.[83]

If true religion can be replaced with psychology, then psychology in turn can be utilized to inform what the function of religion once was. Jung suggests: "The religious point of view always expresses and formulates the essential psychological attitude and its specific prejudices."[84] Jung further elaborates on his version of a psychological religion that specifically addresses those that have defected from their faith traditions:

I am not...addressing myself to the happy possessors of faith, but to those many people for whom the light has gone out, the mystery has faded, and God is dead. For most of them there is no going back, and one does not know either whether going back is always the better way. To gain an understanding of religious matters, probably all that is left us today is the psychological approach. That is why I take these thought-forms that have become historically fixed, try to melt them down again and pour them into moulds of immediate experience.[85]

Freud appears to have been put off by Jung's zealotry and the use of Christian and Dionysian imagery and replied two days later to Jung's letter by admonishing Jung: "But you mustn't regard me as the founder of a religion. My intentions are not so far-reaching...I am not thinking of a substitute for religion; this need must be sublimated."[86] In a letter to Eugen Bleuler, dated September 28, 1910, Freud also attempts to disarm the notion that he was attempting to create a secular pseudo-religion out the psychoanalytic movement: "I am represented as the founder of a religion, as one who is worshipped and whose word is infallible."[87]

With this said, there are numerous examples of Freud's attempt to usurp the role of religion and replace it with the psychoanalytic church, as is found here: "[T]he theory of dreams has remained what is most characteristic and peculiar about the young science [of psychoanalysis], something to which there is no counterpart in the rest of our knowledge, a stretch of new country, which has been reclaimed from popular beliefs and mysticism."[88]

Ferenczi reported to the Swiss physician Alphonse Maeder (1882-1971) that in America Jung had declared: "ΨA is not a science but a religion."[89] While Jung is often presumed to be a friend of the world's religions and spiritual traditions, unlike Freud, Jung no less than Freud wanted to create a secular pseudo-religion of modern psychology: "His [Jung's] psychology is virtually a new religion."[90] To Jung's credit, given the errors that he made, he no less recognized the human being's need for the sacred: "Freud has unfortunately overlooked the fact that man has never yet been able single-handed to hold his own against the powers of darkness—that is, of the unconscious. Man has always stood in need of the spiritual help which each individual's own religion held out to him...Man is never helped in his suffering by what he thinks for himself, but only by revelations of a wisdom greater than his own."[91]

Freud's role in replacing religion with the doctrine of the "talking cure" and its psychoanalytic church in the modern world is outlined in the following by Fromm: "Under the disguise of a therapist and a scientist he was one of the great world reformers of the beginning twentieth century...Freud's aim was to found a...new secular and scientific religion for an elite which was to guide mankind."[92]

Just what kind of religion did the psychoanalytic "talking cure" purport to be? As early as 1916, Robert S. Woodworth (1869–1962), an American academic psychologist, highlighted psychoanalysis as an "uncanny religion."[93] Behaviorists such as Watson criticized Freud and charged psychoanalytic psychology as being "Voodooism."[94] He assessed the Freudian metapsychology of the unconscious in the following manner: "The scientific level of Freud's concept of the unconscious is exactly on a par with the miracles of Jesus."[95] Similarly, Webster affirms that Freudianism is a quasi-religious movement: "psychoanalysis...is quintessentially a religion and should be treated as such."[96]

Freud does not attempt to disarm his detractors by reassuring them that they have no cause for concern regarding the emergence of the "talking cure"; on the contrary he confirms that their concerns are real and valid:

> Psychoanalytic research is...the subject of suspicious attention from Catholicism. I do not maintain that this suspicion is unmerited. If our research leads us to a result that reduces religion to the status of a neurosis of mankind and explains its grandiose powers in the same way as we should a neurotic obsession in our individual patients, then we may be sure we shall incur...the greatest resentment of the powers that be.[97]

Within the Freudian corpus one can find positive references made to religion, although they are few and far between, such as in his correspondence with Pfister: "you are in the fortunate position of being able to lead them to God and bringing about what in this one respect was the happy state of earlier times when religious faith stifled the neuroses."[98] While Freudian therapy wages its assault on religion and spirituality, it paradoxically recognizes the curative power of faith among the traditions. Freud admonished psychoanalysts to "model themselves during psycho-analytic treatment on...a surgeon of earlier times [who] took as his motto the words: 'Je le pansai, Dieu le guérit.' [I dressed his wounds, God cured him]."[99] If the analyst fails to adopt this attitude, Freud warns, the analyst "will not only put him[self] into a state of mind which is unfavourable for his work, but will make him[self] helpless against certain resistances of the patient, whose recovery, as we know, primarily depends on the interplay of forces in him."[100]

In rare moments, Freud even goes so far as to defend religion: "Religion has clearly performed great services for human civilization."[101] Freud defends it elsewhere in a backhanded manner: "the beauty of religion certainly does not belong to psycho-analysis";[102] or "I do not think our [cures] can compete with those of Lourdes. There are so many more people who believe in the miracles of the Blessed Virgin than in the existence of the unconscious."[103] This last statement was made a few years prior to his death and may on the other hand not be about religion *per se*, but rather a reflection of his own pessimistic outlook on the therapeutic validity of psychoanalytic psychology. Freud interestingly also writes:

> In point of fact psycho-analysis is a method of research, an impartial instrument, like the infinitesimal calculus, as it were...If the application of the psycho-analytic method makes it possible to find a new argument against the truths of religion, *tant pis* for religion; but defenders of religion will by the same right make use of psycho-analysis in order to give full value to the affective significance of religious doctrines.[104]

Jones in his biography attempts to tackle this problem head on to dissuade outsiders from giving credence to the notion that the psychoanalytic movement attempted to manufacture a new secular pseudo-religion, yet his very characterization gives credibility to the idea that he is trying to dispel:

> It was this element that gave rise to the general criticism of our would-be scientific activities that they partook rather of the nature of a religious movement, and amusing parallels were drawn. Freud was of course the Pope of the new sect, if not a still higher Personage, to whom all owed obedience; his writings were the sacred text, credence in which was obligatory on the supposed infallibilists who had undergone the necessary conversion, and there were not lacking the heretics who were expelled from the church.[105]

Without a doubt, psychoanalytic metapsychology dared to replace the sapiential traditions with its own secular pseudo-scientific discoveries. Freud writes" "analysis leads to no new philosophy of life, but it has no need to, for it rests on the general scientific outlook, with which the religious outlook is incompatible."[106] Freud illustrates this here:

> Our knowledge of the historical worth of certain religious doctrines increases our respect for them, but does not invalidate our

proposal that they should cease to be put forward as the reasons for the precepts of civilization. On the contrary! Those historical residues have helped us to view religious teachings, as it were, as neurotic relics, and we may now argue that the time has probably come, as it does in an analytic treatment, for replacing the effects of repression by the results of the rational operation of the intellect.[107]

Jung wrote as a faithful disciple of Freud on November 11, 1908, confirming his unshakable faith in the psychoanalytic gospel: "*Magna est vis veritatis tuae et praevalebit!*" (Great is the power of your truth and it shall prevail.)[108] Bernard Hart (1879–1966), English psychiatrist and proponent of psychoanalysis, confirms that it cannot be proven empirically, but submits that this secular pseudo-religion needs to be accepted on the grounds of personal faith: "Freudianism is strictly speaking a religion; you can't *prove* it, but you have to accept it because it works."[109]

In a paradoxical manner, the findings of the Freudian doctrine validate fallen or *saṃsāric* humanity, as psychoanalyst and historian of psychiatry Gregory Zilboorg (1891–1959) writes: "the concept of original sin or of the original fall of man finds its empirical counterpart in the findings of psychoanalysis."[110] Freud stresses: "Psychoanalysis has never set itself up as a panacea and has never claimed to perform miracles."[111] Regardless of the similarities that may exist, it is essential to make an important and fundamental distinction between psychoanalysis and religion: "In spite of the many parallels between Freudianism and religion, the Freudian doctrine is in function if not in form the antithesis of a religion."[112] The doctrine of Freudianism and its psychoanalytic church is unequivocally the "[secular pseudo-]religiosity that will at the same time debunk all revelations."[113] In this sense, "Freud has systematized our unbelief; his is the most inspiring anti-creed yet offered a post-religious culture."[114]

Chapter 9

From Metaphysics to Metapsychology

"There are those who...accentuate the opposition between the metaphysical and the psychological. A completely wrong approach! The psychic itself belongs to the domain of the ontological and metaphysical."[1] These discerning words by Pope Pius XII underscore the predicament that is a contemporary psychology that attempts to operate outside a metaphysical framework. What this points to is the predicament of fallen consciousness that no longer sees the necessity of what is beyond the sensorial and psychological realm to understand the fullness of the human condition. Coomaraswamy writes, "Modern man has become completely indifferent to metaphysical principles."[2] Freud discards metaphysics, or the science of the Real, and fabricates what he has termed *metapsychology*, which is the "psychology of the unconscious,"[3] or the processes underlying mythical and religious experiences. Jones confirms the appropriation and inversion of traditional metaphysics: "what was metaphysics becomes metapsychology."[4] Gay upholds the claim that Freudian metapsychology was an attack on traditional or integral metaphysics, as he writes: "metapsychology was [a] rival...[to] that grandiose and futile philosophical daydream, metaphysics."[5] Freud does appears not to have known or to have overlooked the fact that the very principles of modern science emerged from inspiration from or a basis in metaphysics.[6]

Rieff points out that Freud's "metapsychology...can...imply, to its devoted adherents, a cosmology."[7] Freud submits that the mythical and religious experiences are "nothing but psychology projected into the external world."[8] Freudian metapsychology, as the science of the unconscious, returns the projection "back...into the *psychology of the unconscious*,"[9] so that mythical and religious experiences can be understood from a psychodynamic perspective. Psychological metaphysics, according to Freud, concludes that "One could venture to explain in this way the myths of paradise and the fall of man, of God, of good and evil, of immortality, and so on, and to transform *metaphysics* into *metapsychology*."[10] By undermining and reinterpreting the traditional exegesis of the world's religions at their innermost level, Freud was then able to appropriate metaphysics and in its place, establishes his metapsychology. Freud's metapsychology provides him with free rein to speculate on all and everything in an attempt to frame it within his own brand of science. The contrast between sacred science that is rooted in metaphysical principles and profane science rooted in a materialistic worldview could not be starker. Guénon situates these distinct scientific paradigms:

> In assuming its modern form, science has lost not only in depth, but also, one might say, in stability, for its attachment to principles enabled it to share in their immutability to the extent that its subject-matter allowed, whereas being now completely confined to the world of change, it can find nothing in it that is stable, and no fixed point on which to base itself...[A]s far as modern science is concerned, the conclusions in question can only belong to the realm of hypotheses, whereas the teachings of the traditional sciences had a very different character, coming as the indubitable consequences of truths known intuitively, and therefore infallibly, in the metaphysical order.[11]

Sherrard delineates the limits of modern science, in contrast with traditional metaphysics:

> [T]he modern sciences are always dependent to some extent upon some form of experimentation; but metaphysical knowledge is essentially that of which no experimental or external investigation of this kind is possible: being "beyond physics" it is also beyond experiment, beyond every kind of statistical or mathematical verification or demonstration. Consequently, the scope of every separate science can be extended indefinitely without it ever reaching a point of contact with metaphysical knowledge. This is something of which certain modern scientists, who claim that quantum physics, for example, is approaching the state of Eastern metaphysics, appear to be unaware. They do not appear to realize that by definition physics can never be metaphysical—or, at least, can only become metaphysical by ceasing to be physics. Metaphysical knowledge is a supra-rational, intuitive, and immediate knowledge; the domain of metaphysical knowledge is the domain of eternal and immutable principles revealed directly by God and apprehended by human beings only when they have attained the state of contemplation or intellectual vision.[12]

That science is unable to flourish outside an integral metaphysical framework is explained by Burckhardt in the following passage:

The connection with the metaphysical order provides spiritual psychology with qualitative criteria such as are wholly lacking in profane psychology, which studies only the dynamic character of phenomena of the psyche and their proximate causes. When modern psychology makes pretensions to a sort of science of the hidden contents of the soul it is still for all that restricted to an individual perspective because it has no real means for distinguishing psychic forms which translate universal realities from forms which appear symbolical but are only vehicles for individual impulsions. Its "collective subconscious" [collective unconscious] has most assuredly nothing to do with the true source of symbols; at most it is a chaotic depository of psychic residues somewhat like the mud of the ocean bed which retains traces of past epochs.[13]

Metaphysics is as Schuon explains "the science of the Absolute and of the true nature of things."[14] Correspondingly, it could be added, "The true problems of men are metaphysical."[15] The attempt to become who one is or to become whole in the absence of the Divine itself has the potential for causing mental illness and prevents the possibility of obtaining psychological health and well-being: "The anxiety underlying all modern anxieties arises from someone's trying to be himself without God or from his trying to get beyond himself without God."[16] And this is because "Metaphysics is the study of the first and final reality that underlies all phenomena."[17] It is not therefore surprising that Freud belittled the spiritual domain and its integral metaphysics: "I not only have no talent for it [metaphysics] but no respect for it, either. In secret—one cannot say such things aloud—I believe that one day metaphysics will be condemned as a nuisance, as an abuse of thinking, as a survival from the period of the religious *Weltanschauung*."[18]

The well-known dictum by Socrates asserts that "The unexamined life is not worth living."[19] Yet according to Freud, to inquire into the ultimate questions of human existence is itself equivalent to psychopathology. Freud insists: "The moment a man questions the meaning and value of life, he is sick, since objectively neither has any existence."[20] A key biographer tells us: "Freud's passion to get at the truth with the maximum of certainty was, I again suggest, the deepest and strongest motive of his nature."[21]

Even though Freud was searching for the "truth" by plumbing the depths of the unconscious to corroborate his psychoanalytic metapsychology, with a closer look we find that this is not truth as it is normally implied in its ultimate sense, but a relative and alternative truth, if not a distorted truth constructed by his own unbalanced mind. It goes without saying that psychoanalytic epistemology does not approximate the one and the same truth of the ancients, and what is implied by Self-Knowledge for making the unconscious conscious does not equate with the gnosis of the Self. Yet this point is often overlooked or misunderstood within the field of modern psychology: "One does not become enlightened by imagining figures of light, but by making the darkness conscious."[22]

The inscription of the temple at Delphi "Know thyself" (*Gnóthi seautón*) is a testament to this gnosis, as is the following from the Gospels: "The kingdom of God is within you" (Luke 17:21). Similarly, the Koran declares: "We are nearer to him than his jugular vein" (50:16). The famous *hadīth* within the Islamic tradition conveys: "He who knows himself knows his Lord." Clement of Alexandria (150–215) states: "if one knows himself, he will know God."[23] Ibn 'Arabī (1165–1240) writes about the interdependence of Self-Knowledge and the transcendent knowledge of the Divine: "I think—and God knows best—that He commanded us to know Him and turned us over to ourselves in gaining this knowledge only because He knew that we do not perceive and do not know the reality of ourselves and that we are incapable of knowing ourselves. Hence we come to know that we are even more incapable of knowing Him. This is knowledge of Him/not knowledge."[24] He further observes: "The Man is not he who realizes his Lord. The Man is he who realizes his own entity."[25]

Within the Buddhist tradition this process is known as "seeing into your true nature."[26] William C. Chittick qualifies the necessity of Self-Knowledge as the basis for all knowledge: "Self-knowledge is an absolutely necessary precondition for any real knowledge, that is, any knowledge of the Real."[27] True knowledge requires going beyond all dualism, as Guénon affirms: "the only genuine knowledge is that which implies an identification of the subject with the object"[28] or "all true knowledge essentially consists in identification with its object."[29] Ramana Maharshi teaches: "To know the Self is to be the Self—as there are not two separate selves."[30] Shankara teaches: "Nothing exists except the Self."[31] The "science of the soul" through its metaphysics sees the Self as the intrinsic identity in all human beings, as Meister Eckhart has said: "Loving thy Self, thou lovest all men as thy Self."[32]

True knowledge according to Freud is not to be found in consciousness itself, but in what is beneath it, in the psychic underworld, what is unconscious: "Turn your eyes inward, look into your own depths, learn first to know yourself! Then you will understand why you were bound to fall ill; and perhaps, you will avoid falling ill in the future."[33] Within the Freudian orthodoxy, Freud is mythologized as the sole human being in history to have realized the deepest significance of what it means to be human: "Future generations of psychologists will assuredly wish to know what manner of man it was who, after two thousand years of vain endeavour had gone by, succeeded in fulfilling the Delphic injunction: know thyself...Few, if any, have been able to go as far as he did on the path of self-knowledge and self-mastery..."[34]

The harm caused to others and the disastrous impact of an individual's inability to follow the maxim "know thyself" are lamentable, yet in contradistinction, human understanding and behavior when integrated into the spiritual domain can be transformed. Maimonides (1135–1204) writes:

> These great evils that come about between the human individuals who inflict them upon one another...derive from ignorance...Just as a blind man, because of the absence of sight, does not cease stumbling, being wounded, and also wounding others, because he has nobody to guide him on his way [so does] every individual according to his ignorance [do] to himself and to others great evils...If there were knowledge...they would refrain from doing any harm to themselves and to others. For through cognition of the truth, enmity and hatred are removed and the inflicting of harm by people on one another is abolished.[35]

We are informed by Siegfried Bernfeld (1892–1953) that Freud was reported to have been "greatly impressed by his theory of anamnesis and that he had, at one time, given it a great deal of thought."[36] Freud utilizes the Greek term *anamnesis* (recollection or remembrance), but not in the way that the doctrine of anamnesis is utilized by Plato as a function of knowledge recalling the truths latent within the human soul. The Freudian or psychoanalytic use of anamnesis has nothing in common with the original doctrine. Within the Freudian context, it is a reconstruction of truth based on partial memories or inferred memories to construct a reality that suits the theories of the psychoanalytic paradigm. Freud states that successful treatment of psychoanalysis is as follows: "The task of the cure is to remove the amnesias."[37] Although Freud does not make an explicit reference to the Platonic doctrine of anamnesis, it appears to be a very similar reconstruction of this teaching:

The task which the psychoanalytic method seeks to perform may be formulated in different ways, which are, however, in their essence equivalent. It may, for instance, be stated thus: the task of the treatment is to remove the amnesias...Or the formula may be expressed in this fashion: all repressions must be undone. The mental condition is then the same as one in which all amnesias have been removed. Another formulation reaches further: the task consists in making the unconscious accessible to consciousness, which is done by overcoming the resistances.[38]

Jung emphasizes that a common prejudice regarding the Freudian "talking cure" is that "psychoanalysis is nothing but a rather deep and complicated form of *anamnesis*."[39] Jung disagrees with this and in the defense of pschoanlaysis stresses that "psychoanalysis is not an *anamnesis*...It is essentially a way of investigating unconscious associations which cannot be got at by exploring the conscious mind."[40] Even though Jung fights against this conclusion, Freud himself makes statements confirming this conclusion: "the task of a psycho-analytic treatment can be expressed in this formula: its task is to make conscious everything that is pathogenically unconscious."[41] Freud writes: "If a pathological idea...can be traced back to the elements in the patient's mental life from which it originated, it simultaneously crumbles away and the patient is freed from it."[42] Likewise: "To abolish the symptoms it becomes necessary to go back to their origin, to renew the conflict out of which they emerged."[43] Freudian metapsychology asserts that it traces phenomena or symptoms back to their sources"[44]— this cannot be confused with sacred science and quintessential metaphysics, which aim at "tracing a thing back to its source, to its archetype."[45] Freud admits that the task of the "talking cure" is to construct or reconstruct the analysand's memories: "its task is to fill up all the gaps in the patient's memory, to remove his amnesias."[46]

For Freud, everything important to know about the human being is what occurred in the past, and the power of the present moment and what is occurring in the now is disregarded:

So long as we trace the development from its final stage backwards, the connection appears continuous, and we feel we have gained an insight which is completely satisfactory or even exhaustive. But if we proceed the reverse way, if we start from the premises inferred from the analysis and try to follow these up to the final result, then we no longer get the impression of an inev-

itable sequence of events which could not be otherwise determined.[47]

The Sage of Arunachala, Ramana Maharshi, provides a metaphysical analysis of the mind that exposes its mechanisms and the
limits of exploring thought and its relationship with the past in order
to liberate the human being:

> Seek for the Self through meditation in this manner, trace every
> thought back to its origin which is only the mind. Never allow
> thought to run on. If you do, it will be unending. Take it back to
> its starting place—the mind—again and again, and it and the
> mind will both die of inaction. The mind exists only by reason of
> thought. Stop thought and there is no mind. As each doubt and
> depression arises, ask yourself, "Who is it that doubts? What is it
> that is depressed?" Go back constantly until there is nothing but
> the source of all left. And then, live always in the present and
> only in it. There is no past or future, save in the mind.[48]

Freud appears to have first used the term "metapsychology" (*met-
apsychologie*) in February 13, 1896, when corresponding with Fliess:
"I am continually occupied with psychology—really *meta*psychology...I hope something will come of it."[49] He described to Fliess in
his letter dated December 17, 1896 the challenges with constructing
such a theory, speaking of "my ideal and woebegone child—metapsychology."[50] Freud writes Fliess again in March 10, 1898, asking him
what he thinks of the use of this term: "I am going to ask you seriously
whether I should use the term 'metapsychology' for my psychology
which leads behind consciousness."[51] An alternate version of this letter provided by Jones defines metapsychology not as that which
"leads behind consciousness," but as that which "takes one beyond
consciousness."[52] These definitions are very different, the first alluding to the unconscious and the second to the supraconscious. Freud,
however, confirms the first rather than the second: "The unconscious
is *metaphysical*."[53] This is a complete inversion of metaphysics and
exposes psychoanalysis as an inverted psychology.

In a similar reductionistic trend, Jung introduces the term "unconscious metaphysics," which he defines as "expressions of undifferen-
tiated psychic activity which may often contain the germs of conscious thought."[54] Jung, like his former master, reduced metaphysics
to psychological criterion, as is evidenced here: "Metaphysical assertions...are *statements of the psyche*, and are therefore psychological."[55] According to Jung, metaphysics is psychological in nature, and

he emphasizes the impossibility of attaining metaphysical truth: "Psychology accordingly treats all metaphysical claims and assertions as mental phenomena, and regards them as statements about the mind and its structure that derive ultimately from certain unconscious dispositions. It does not consider them to be absolutely valid or even capable of establishing a metaphysical truth."[56]

Freud returns to the theme of his psychological metaphysics in "The Unconscious" written in 1915. He discusses what is implied by his metapsychology and gives it the highest priority within psychoanalytical research: "It will be only right to give a special name to the way of regarding things which is the final result of psychoanalytic research. I propose that, when we succeeded in describing a mental process in all its aspects, dynamic, topographic and economic, we shall call this a *metapsychological* presentation."[57]

It is evident that Freud's metapsychological speculations were distinct from the findings obtained by pure observation, which was precisely why he needed to establish metapsychology in the first place. In *An Autobiographical Study* written in 1924, Freud outlines the broader grasp of his metapsychology, calling it "a method of approach according to which every mental process is considered in relation to three co-ordinates, which I described as *dynamic, topographical*, and *economic* respectively; and this seemed to me to represent the furthest goal that psychology could attain."[58]

The Promethean attempt to subvert integral metaphysics and supplant it with Freudian metapsychology is outlined here by the master himself:

> We can only say: "*So muss denn doch die Hexe dran!*" ["We must call the Witch to our help after all!" Goethe, *Faust*]—the Witch Metapsychology. Without metapsychological speculation and theorizing—I had almost said "phantasying"—we shall not get another step forward. Unfortunately, here and elsewhere, what our Witch reveals is neither very clear nor very detailed.[59]

While metaphysics is beyond all definitions and categorizations, the following by Guénon provides the depth of what integral or traditional metaphysics signifies in its truest sense:

> It may now be stated that metaphysics...is essentially the knowledge of the Universal, or, if preferred, the knowledge of the principles belonging to the universal order, which moreover alone can validly lay claim to the name of principles; but in mak-

ing this statement we are not really trying to propose a definition of metaphysics, for such a thing is a sheer impossibility by reason of that very universality which we look upon as the foremost of its characteristics, the one from which all the others are derived. In reality, only something that is limited is capable of definition, whereas metaphysics is on the contrary by its very nature absolutely unlimited, and this plainly does not allow our enclosing it in a more or less narrow formula; and a definition in this case would be all the more inaccurate the more exact one tried to make it.[60]

As the domain of metaphysics is transcendent and not relativistic it is paramount to recall that "metaphysics can only be studied metaphysically."[61] In the final analysis, the human search for transcendent knowledge according to Freud is a futile endeavor, as has been astutely pointed out: "No man can, in the Freudian view, know himself."[62] It cannot be stressed enough that there can be no psychology without metaphysics, as Schuon writes: "There is no science of the soul without a metaphysical basis to it and without spiritual remedies at its disposal."[63]

Chapter 10

The Freudian Colonization of the Human Psyche: Id, Ego, and Super-Ego

"The unconscious is the true psychical reality."[1]—*Sigmund Freud*

Freud was under the delusion that he alone, unlike any other human being who had ever preceded him, had excavated the human psyche at its deepest core, revealing to humanity what Angelus Silesius (1624–77) has described with "all is hidden in all, and is therein concealed."[2] Freudian metapsychology constructs the "psychical apparatus,"[3] "the hierarchy of agencies, which seems to govern the structure of the apparatus"[4] as consisting of the id, ego, and super-ego. This tripartite structure of the human microcosm radically departs from that of the perennial philosophy and the perennial psychology, which consists of Spirit/Intellect, soul, and body, as the Freudian structure levels the vertical dimension of the human psyche by jettisoning the Spirit within psychology.[5]

We recall that Freud asserted that "There is no appeal to a court above that of reason"[6] and recognized the "omnipotence of thought."[7] This again indicates that Freud and the psychoanalytic movement denied modes of knowing that transcend reason or empirical ego. Freud argues: "the higher nature of man [is] a substitute for a longing for the father...acquired phylogenetically...through the process of mastering the Oedipus complex."[8] Because of this truncated outlook that is anti-metaphysical and undermines the spiritual domain, the human being feels as though he or she is incarcerated within his or her own skin:

> People now find that they are locked up within themselves, their own prisoners. Jailed by [the psychic apparatus of the id, ego, and super-ego], they now attempt to compensate for the loss of the three-dimensional universe of faith by finding three new dimensions within their own mind. Above their *ego*, their conscious level, they discover, in place of heaven, an inexorable tyrant whom they call the *superego*. Below their consciousness, in place of hell, they substitute a hidden world of instincts and urges, primitive longings and biological needs, which they call the *id*.[9]

One author makes a case for the usurpation of the Christian doctrine of the Holy Trinity within Freudian metapsychology and the psychic apparatus:

> [T]he marked similarity between the Christian concept of the Holy Trinity and the Freudian theory of the trinitarian nature of the human psyche...is not only that both systems divide the whole into three parts—that might be a simple coincidence—but that the parts have somewhat similar functions in both systems of thought. Thus the Freudian id is father of the self; and, like God, the id is never known directly. The Freudian ego is largely known to consciousness; and the Holy Trinity the one part known directly by man is the Son, who came, and suffered, and so on. In both systems the functions of the third part, the Holy Ghost and the superego, are the same. They strengthen, they comfort, they protect.[10]

The isthmus that divides the outlook of psychoanalysis from that of the integral psychology of the perennial philosophy becomes increasingly distinguishable as Smith observes: "The essential difference, however, between the traditional [or perennial psychology] and the Freudian psychology, lies in the fact that the former envisions a hierarchic order which entails not only a 'below'—made up of subconscious psychic layers—but also an 'above' consisting of what might be termed the spiritual degrees."[11] Smith continues,

> Hence, symbolically speaking, it is possible in principle both to ascend or to descend from the plane of the ego. To ascend, moreover, is to draw closer to the actual core of our being: it is to attain a higher degree of self-knowledge. And so, to, it is by way of a "descent"—a deviation from the archetypal nature and a certain lapse into oblivion—that we have arrived at a familiar level of psychic existence—the ego, which we normally take to be our self.[12]

The unconscious, many would argue, was Freud's greatest contribution to modern psychology, except that he did not invent it; he rather placed this concept at the center of his theoretical model. Fromm confirms this point: "To be sure, Freud was not the first to discover the phenomenon that we harbor thoughts and strivings which we are not aware of—that is to say, which are unconscious—and live a hidden life in our psyche. But Freud was the first to have made this discovery the center of his psychological system."[13]

"It is generally held," writes Jones, "that Freud's greatest contribution to science...was his conception of an *unconscious mind*."[14] Yet, Freud himself disclosed during his seventieth birthday celebration that it was not he, but "The poets and philosophers before me [who] discovered the unconscious."[15] Eysenck comments: "the notion of 'the unconscious' is one which has been held by philosophers and psychologists for many centuries, and to credit Freud with the discovery of the unconscious is absurd."[16] Gay also confirms this point: "Freud did not discover the unconscious."[17] What is important here is to recognize that the notion of the unconscious was known prior to the birth of psychoanalysis. What did Freud discover then? Freud clarifies for the historical record: "What I discovered was the scientific method by which the unconscious can be studied."[18]

Psychoanalytic theory is thus an inversion of the traditional understanding of the "science of the soul" known across the diverse societies and civilizations, as is made abundantly clear here:

> Freud's main contribution, therefore, lies in the fact that he has elevated this particular element of our psychic make-up to the status of a first principle: he has made it "the core of our being." What appears on the traditional maps as the lowest fringe of psychic existence—a mere shadow of that supra-physical light which resides within us as an image of God—has become in Freud's eyes our very *soul*. On closer inspection the Freudian doctrine turns out to be an inversion of the Christian truth.[19]

We are told that conflicts arise between the demands of the id and the ego, as psychoanalytic theory illustrates: "The ego's relation to the id might be compared with that of a rider to his horse. The horse supplies the locomotive energy, while the rider has the privilege of deciding on the goal and of guiding the powerful animal's movement. But only too often there arises between the ego and the id the not precisely ideal situation of the rider being obliged to guide the horse along the path by which it itself wants to go."[20]

The ego, we are told, needs to mediate between the id and the super-ego. According to Freud, the mechanisms of defense within psychoanalytic theory work in the following way,

> For the ego has to try from the very outset to fulfil its task of mediating between its id and the external world in the service of the pleasure principle, and to protect the id from the dangers of the external world. If, in the course of these efforts, the ego learns to adopt a defensive attitude towards its own id as well and to

treat the latter's instinctual demands as external dangers, this happens, at any rate in part, because it understands that a satisfaction of instinct would lead to conflicts with the external world. Thereafter, under the influence of education, the ego grows accustomed to removing the scene of the fight from outside to within and to mastering the *internal* danger before it has become an *external* one; and probably it is most often right in doing so. During this fight on two fronts—later there will be a third front as well—the ego makes use of various procedures for fulfilling its task, which, to put it in general terms, is to avoid danger, anxiety and unpleasure. We call these procedures "*mechanisms of defence.*"[21]

Fromm adds here: "Freud sees pathology essentially in the failure to find a proper balance between the Id and Ego, between instinctual demands and the demands of reality."[22] Freud elucidates on this point: "ego as a poor creature owing service to three masters and consequently menaced by three dangers: from the external world, from the libido of the id, and from the severity of the super-ego...As a frontier-creature, the ego tries to mediate between the world and the id, to make the id pliable to the world and, by means of its muscular activity, to make the world fall in with the wishes of the id."[23]

However, upon further investigation, Freud points out:

We are warned by a proverb against serving two masters at the same time. The poor ego has things even worse: it serves three severe masters and does what it can to bring their claims and demands into harmony with one another. These claims are always divergent and often seem incompatible...Its three tyrannical masters are the external world, the super-ego and the id.[24]

Psychoanalytical theory overlooks the biblical significance of "No man can serve two masters,"[25] confirming the plight of Freud's psychic apparatus, as no inner peace or integration can prevail when the human being solely focuses on his or her lower nature.

The centrality of Freudian therapy consists in bringing what is unconscious into the light of consciousness. Freud lays this process out: "The task which the psycho-analytic method tries to perform may...be stated thus:...the problem consists in making the unconscious accessible to consciousness, which is done by overcoming the resistances...the aim of the treatment will never be anything else but the practical recovery of the patient."[26]

The empirical ego itself is the problem. as Freud illustrates: "the ego is the real locus of anxiety."[27] Elsewhere Freud writes: "The ego is the actual seat of anxiety."[28] He additionally suggests two functions of the ego: "the ego alone can produce and feel anxiety."[29] The Freudian maxim can be summarized as follows: "Where id was, there ego shall be."[30] This is why he notes that the analyst's effort is "constantly swinging backwards and forward like a pendulum between a piece of id-analysis and a piece of ego-analysis."[31] While unconscious or instinctual drives certainly exist and were known by the ancients, to exclusively focus on them and to define human beings in this way is to dehumanize what it means to be human.

The psychological limitations of Freudianism are made obvious with the following disclosure of the aims of psychoanalysis: "to strengthen the ego...to widen its field of perception and enlarge its organization, so that it can appropriate fresh portions of the id. Where id was, there ego shall be."[32] The psychoanalytic assumption of making the "unconscious conscious" in and of itself is insufficient for psychological integration, as Muriel Ivimey (1888–1953) illustrates:

> "Is it sufficient for a person to become aware of his neurotic trends and conflicts?" is a question that is frequently brought up in discussions. No, it is not enough. In addition to becoming aware of his neurotic trends, a person needs to become aware of their purposes and aims, the forces involved, and the interrelations, interactions, and repercussions of neurotic elements and forces. He also needs to discover the constructive forces within himself which make it possible for him to bring about necessary changes. Awareness of the existence of neurotic trends is only the first step toward extricating oneself from neurotic patterns of living.[33]

A vertical or spiritual dimension is needed to be fully human; for this reason the perennial psychology, contrary to Freudian psychology, teaches that "wherever God is, there also is the soul; and wherever the soul is, there is God."[34] This point of view exemplifies how the psychoanalytic ways of knowing fundamentally differ from the sapiential traditions of the world.

Psychodynamic theory radically subverts the role of the transcendent organ of the Intellect/Spirit and how this faculty not only supersedes the psycho-physical domain but also situates the world of the senses. The Intellect has been formulated as being "naturally supernatural" and "supernaturally natural."[35] Maimonides recognizes the noetic faculty of the Intellect when he declares: "God is the *intellectus*."[36] Correspondingly, Rūmī affirms: "the Universal Intellect is the founder of every thing."[37] According to a *ḥadīth* of the Prophet, "The first thing that God created was the Intellect" and "The first thing God created was the Spirit." Both of these sayings point to one and the same reality. By the same token, the limits of reason when it is disconnected from the Divine are also to be recognized, as Maimonides confirms: "A boundary is undoubtedly set to the human mind which it cannot pass."[38] Similarly, there is a Koranic passage that affirms this same truth: "He knows all that is beyond the reach of a created being's perception as well as all that can be witnessed by a creature's senses or mind—the Great One, the One far above anything that is or could ever be!" (13:9). It is this transcendent organ of the Intellect or the "Eye of the Heart" that Meister Eckhart refers to here: "The eye in which I see God is the same eye in which God sees me. My eye and God's eye are one eye."[39]

This is to say that transcendence is to be found at the center of the human psyche: "There is something in the soul which is uncreated and uncreatable; if the whole soul were such, it would be uncreated and uncreatable; and this is the Intellect."[40] The Gospel refers to this "heart-intellect" here: "Blessed are the pure in heart: for they shall see God" (Matthew 5:8). This spiritual organ is further illuminated by the remarkable sage of the Lakota Sioux, Hehaka Sapa or Black Elk (1863–1950), who writes:

> I am blind and do not see the things of this world; but when the Light comes from Above, it enlightens my heart and I can see, for the Eye of my heart (*Chante Ista*) sees everything. The heart is a sanctuary at the center of which there is a little space, wherein the Great Spirit dwells, and this is the Eye (*Ista*). This is the Eye of the Great Spirit by which He sees all things and through which we see Him. If the heart is not pure, the Great Spirit cannot be seen, and if you should die in this ignorance, your soul cannot return immediately to the Great Spirit, but it must be purified by wandering about in the world. In order to know the center of the heart where the Great Spirit dwells you must be pure and good, and live in the manner that the Great Spirit has taught us. The man who is thus pure contains the Universe in the pocket of his heart (*Chante Ognaka*).[41]

The myopic outlook upon which the psychoanalytic doctrine defines the human being is really an illustration of what is beneath the human condition and not representative of what it means to be truly human. Freud writes: "The core of our being...is formed by the obscure *id*,"[42] and similarly "Originally...everything was id; the ego was developed out of the id."[43] Freud additionally states that "the oldest of these psychical provinces or agencies we give the name of *id*. It contains everything that is inherited, that is present at birth, that is laid down in the constitution—above all, therefore, the instincts, which originate from the somatic organization and which find the first psychical expression here [in the id] in forms unknown to us."[44]

Freudian metapsychology teaches that the ego arises from the id: "It is easy to see that the ego is that part of the id which has been modified by the direct influence of the external world"[45] and "the ego is formed to a great extent out of identifications which take the place of abandoned cathexes by the id."[46] This contradicts the transpersonal identity of the human being that originates in the Spirit and not within the subterranean instinctual drives. Freud also adds "The ego represents what may be called reason and common sense, in contrast to the id, which contains the passions."[47] If this were the case, the greater would then derive from the lesser, but it is the other way around: the lesser derives from the greater.

Huston Smith articulates the fundamental inversion or reductionism within psychoanalysis: "in psychology (with Freud) the rational ego comes after and out of the irrational id. Even when the higher has appeared, the thrust is to understand and interpret its working in terms of the lower. The name for this mode of explanation is, of course, reductionism, and the growth of the [modern] scientific world view can be correlated with its advance."[48] The following is an important reminder: "to claim to derive the 'greater' from the 'lesser'...[is] one of the most typical of modern aberrations."[49]

Key representatives within modern psychology have exposed the inherent limitations and flawed nature of the doctrine of the id. Erikson asserts:

> To return to the id: while it was a step of inestimable import when Freud applied concepts of physical energy to psychology, the exclusive emphasis on the theoretical model by which *instinctual energy* is transferred, displaced, and transformed in analogy to the preservation of energy in a closed system no longer suffices to help us manage the date which we observe when looking at man in his historical and cultural setting.[50]

Freudian metapsychology exposes itself for what it is, an inverted psychology attempting to claim the source of divine Revelation for the id (alternatively known as the "it"). A pioneer of psychosomatic medicine, Georg Groddeck (1866–1934), claims: "Religions are creations of the It."[51] He also states: "About the It itself we know nothing whatever."[52] This of course is a Promethean attempt to undermine the true source of religion and to stake out more ground for the psychoanalytic doctrine to further marginalize the centrality of the sacred. Let there be no question about it: "The Freudian id does in fact represent an infernal realm."[53] About the super-ego Freud writes: "the ego ideal [super-ego] answers to everything that is expected of the higher nature of man. As a substitute for a longing for the father, it contains the germ from which all religions have evolved."[54]

Jung discloses that Freud was unable to access the psychic underworld of the collective unconscious,[55] but emphasizes that this in no way repudiates the master's fame and legacy that is rightfully his: "Freud has not penetrated into that deeper layer [of the collective unconscious] which is common to all men. He could not have done so without being untrue to his historical task. And this task he has fulfilled—a task enough for a whole life's work, and fully deserving the fame it has won."[56] Jung adds: "What I designate as the collective unconscious is completely overlooked by Freud, that is, he interprets it as wholly personal, as merely repressed contents."[57] Freud, however, argues that psychoanalysis does include the doctrine of the collective unconscious; he writes: "the content of the unconscious is collective anyhow."[58]

Freud radically misconstrued what is transcendent in nature and turned it upside-down. The psychoanalytical "talking cure" is confined to the horizontal realm of the empirical ego without access to the vertical domain. According to former clinical professor of psychiatry Arthur J. Deikman (1929–2013):

> In fact, most of modern psychology, of which traditional [Freudian] psychotherapy is a part, denies the possibility of intuition in the strict sense: knowing by means other than the sensory pathways. Intuition in academic psychology means unconscious inference, not direct knowing. Yet the entire spiritual enterprise is based on the possibility of intuitive access to the transcendent.[59]

With so many mistaken ideas about what religion and spirituality authentically are, it is not difficult to see how Freud concluded that "God is nothing but the projection of an individual's father image."[60]

Yet according to Freud, making the "unconscious conscious" does not require the spiritual domain. But this is untrue; the horizontal cannot know the vertical. Through Freud's construction of metapsychology, he tried to assert that it can. Integral or traditional metaphysics teaches that it is only the vertical that can know the horizontal or psychological. Schuon clarifies this matter:

> [I]ts error consists in reducing the spiritual to the psychological and in believing there is nothing beyond the realm of psychology—in other words, that this very limited science can attain to all inner realities, which is absurd. This view would imply that psychology, or even psychoanalysis, could comprehend *Satori* or *Nirvāna*. Modern science, like modern civilization as a whole, is thoroughly profane, having lost all sense of the sacred, reducing everything to merely individual and trivial dimensions.[61]

The point of view that Freudian psychoanalysis, like that of contemporary psychology for the most part, is that human identity is synonymous with the empirical ego. According to the perennial psychology of the world's religions, the empirical ego is ultimately illusory or limited at best, as it cannot constitute a true identity devoid of the Spirit. Jean Klein (1912–98) elaborates on the distinctions between the empirical ego as affirmed by psychoanalysis and that of the transpersonal:

> All [modern] psychological therapies, psychoanalysis among them, are based on a point of view which, for *Vedanta*, is the very cause of what one might call a fundamental neurosis, a metaphysical neurosis, which is the arising of an ego believing itself to be separate.

> The aim of psychoanalysis is to restore health and balance to this separate ego which it considers as a justified reality. The psychoanalyzer wishes to restore a balanced and harmonious ego, an ego in harmony with its surroundings and with other creatures. This ideal appears on second thoughts to be entirely naïve. When we wish to be a balanced self we, in fact, wish to prolong an imbalance under the best possible conditions by appealing to energies which may reinforce, fix and establish an egotistic state which is really the basic imbalance, the source of all others. This is just as absurd as fighting the symptoms of an illness without applying oneself to the illness itself. The psychoanalytical cure is therefore not really a cure. It does not rid the sick man of his sickness, it

helps him to live it, with the ego. His sickness is an imaginary one.[62]

From another point of view, the Freudian metapsychology of the psychic apparatus is not the great novelty that it appears to be, as Allen Esterson illustrates: "[Freud] observes that the ego's 'three tyrannical masters are the external world, the super-ego and the id', but since this is saying little more than that man's consciousness is governed by his environment, his conscience, and his innate instincts, it is hardly a great revelation."[63] From this point of view it can be surmised that "the 'unconscious mind'...does not exist,"[64] at least not in the way that Freudianism interprets it.

Chapter 11

The "Oceanic Feeling":
Mysticism versus Regression

"Freud...and his followers have persistently confused all ideas of transcending the ego with mere loss of 'ego strength.'"[1]—Alan W. Watts

A fundamental dilemma facing Freud's doctrine of the "talking cure" is that it does not recognize the decisive boundary that distinguishes the psychic realm from the spiritual, and it trespasses beyond its own scope of knowledge and what it is allegedly capable of treating. Perry states: "The mischief starts where psychology invades that portion of the soul which belongs to divinity and works consciously or unconsciously to discountenance the sacred and render it to all appearance nugatory, sterile, or void."[2] Some have attempted to trace the rudiments of a spiritual psychology to what Freud referred to as the "oceanic feeling"[3] in his book *Civilization and Its Discontents* (1930). Yet this is again futile, as the Freudian system is anti-metaphysical and anti-spiritual in essence. With this said, the case is made on the basis of the following passage by Freud: "[O]riginally the ego includes everything, later it separates off an external world from itself. Our present ego-feeling is, therefore, only a shrunken residue of a much more inclusive—indeed, an all-embracing—feeling which corresponded to a more intimate bond between the ego and the world about it."[4]

Freud goes on to add,

> Normally, there is nothing of which we are more certain than the feeling of our self, of our own ego. This ego appears to us as something autonomous and unitary, marked off distinctly from everything else. That such an appearance is deceptive, and that on the contrary the ego is continued inwards, without any sharp delimitation, into an unconscious mental entity which we designate as the id and for which it serves as a kind of facade—this was a discovery first made by psycho-analytic research, which should still have much more to tell us about the relation of the ego to the id. But towards the outside, at any rate, the ego seems

to maintain clear and sharp lines of demarcation. There is only one state—admittedly an unusual state, but not one that can be stigmatized as pathological—in which it does not do this. At the height of being in love the boundary between ego and object threatens to melt away. Against all the evidence of his senses, a man who is in love declares that "I" and "you" are one, and is prepared to behave as if it were a fact.[5]

From this notion, it has been hypothesized that Freud had planted the seeds for a spiritual psychology, even though there is nothing to sustain the idea that this was the case; in fact, the above statement likely refers to the primary narcissistic state of union or fusion between the infant and mother and not a unitive state with the Absolute.

The concept of the "oceanic feeling" did not originate with Freud, but with a French writer, Romain Rolland (1866–1944). Freud and Rolland exchanged letters from 1923 to 1936. In a letter dated December 5, 1927, Rolland writes Freud describing the "oceanic feeling":

> Your analysis of religions [presented in *The Future of an Illusion*] is a just one. But I would have liked to see you doing an analysis of *spontaneous religious sentiment* or, more exactly, of religious *feeling*, which is wholly different from *religions* in the strict sense of the word, and much more durable.

> What I mean is: totally independent of all dogma, all credo, all Church organization, all Sacred Books, all hope in a personal survival, etc., the simple and direct fact of *the feeling of the "eternal"* (which can very well not be eternal, but simply without perceptible limits, and like oceanic, as it were).[6]

The notion of the "oceanic feeling" or *la sensation océanique*, as Romain Rolland regarded it, was about the mystical oneness or unity of existence found unanimously across the spiritual traditions, and not a regressive or narcissistic state. Rolland wrote a biography on Śrī Rāmakrishna (1836–86) titled *Vie de Ramakrishna* (*The Life of Ramakrishna*) in 1929 and sent a copy of the book to Freud. Freud read the book; however, he did not change his point of view, as he continued to hold his reductionistic interpretation of religion and its mystical dimension. Freud interestingly responds to Rolland's correspondence on July 14, 1929, stressing that Rolland's mystical perspective troubles him:

Your letter of December 5, 1927, containing your remarks about
a feeling you describe as "oceanic" has left me no peace...in a
new work [*Civilization and Its Discontents*]...I mention this "oceanic" feeling and am trying to interpret it from the point of view
of our [psychoanalytic] psychology...I don't mention your name
but nevertheless drop a hint that points toward you.[7]

Freud wirtes later: "he [Romain Rolland] was sorry I had not properly
appreciated the true source of religious sentiments."[8] Freud confesses:
"To me mysticism is just as closed a book as music."[9] Freud confesses
in a letter to Rolland dated January 19, 1930 that "it isn't easy to pass
beyond the limits of one's nature."[10] Freud further adds:

We seem to diverge rather far in the role we assign to intuition.
Your mystics rely on it to teach them how to solve the riddle of
the universe; we believe that it cannot reveal to us anything but
primitive, instinctual impulses and attitudes—highly valuable for
an embryology of the soul when correctly interpreted, but worthless for orientation in the alien, external world."[11]

Freud clarifies the limited scope of psychoanalysis, suggesting that if
focuses exclusively on the empirical ego and does not touch upon the
transpersonal dimension, as some have claimed: "psychoanalysis [has
as] its sole aim...the enhanced harmony of the ego, which is expected
successfully to mediate between the claims of the instinctual life (the
'id') and those of the external world; thus between inner and outer
reality."[12] While Freud refutes the possibility of an "oceanic feeling"
that is not regressive in nature, he curiously confesses the limited
scope of his knowledge: "Of one thing I am absolutely positive: there
are things we cannot know now."[13] Earlier in Freud's correspondence
with Rolland he reminded him of the role he saw himself playing: "A
great part of my life's work...has been spent [trying to] destroy illusions...of mankind."[14] Yet Freud does lament that he is impervious to
this mystical intuition, as he writes: "I cannot discover this 'oceanic'
feeling in myself."[15]

Reductionist attempts to psychologize the saints and sages of the
world's religions, such as Rāmakrishna,[16] cannot by their very nature
grant insights into their inner lives because of their profane point of
view. Because of the rise in secularism, some have considered the
saints and sages to be suffering from mental illness or psychopathology and have pathologized them, as is evidenced below:

Psychiatric literature contains numerous articles and books that discuss what would be the most appropriate clinical diagnoses for many of the great figures of spiritual history. St. John of the Cross has been called "hereditary degenerate," St. Teresa of Avila dismissed as a severe hysterical psychotic, and [Prophet] Mohammed's mystical experiences have been attributed to epilepsy. Many other religious and spiritual personages, such as the Buddha, Jesus, Ramakrishna, and Shri Ramana Maharshi have been seen as suffering from psychoses, because of their visionary experiences and "delusions."[17]

Spiritual or mystical experiences are often regarded within psychodynamic theory as a form of "regression in the service of the ego,"[18] to use the well-known term attributed to psychoanalyst and art historian Ernst Kris (1900–1957). Maslow, a pioneer within both humanistic and transpersonal currents of modern psychology, also held a similar view on regression: "the path to health is via turning into the fantasies, the primary processes, that is, via the recovery of the intrapsychic in general."[19] This understanding is limited to the horizontal and does not speak to the vertical or transpersonal dimension of what it means to be human. The domain of the human psyche or psychology is always subordinate to the spiritual domain and not the other way around; likewise reductionism, in whatever its form, can never transcend beyond its own limits, just as the human psyche cannot leap beyond itself. Rieff writes, "To achieve psychological freedom through some form of repression is a contradiction in terms."[20]

Here we have a quintessential mystical experience as recorded by Saint Teresa of Ávila (1515–82) that would be interpreted by Freudian metapsychology as a regression rather than a unitive state with the Divine:

> The way in which this that we call union comes, and the nature of it, I do not know how to explain...[T]he soul becomes conscious that it is fainting almost completely away, in a kind of swoon, with an exceeding great and sweet delight. It gradually ceases to breathe and all its bodily strength beings to fail it: it cannot even move its hands without great pain; its eyes involuntarily close, or, if they remain open, they can hardly see...It is futile for him to attempt to speak: his mind cannot manage to form a single word...For in this condition all outward strength vanishes, while the strength of the soul increases so that it may the better have fruition of its bliss...But this state in which they

[the faculties] are completely lost, and have no power of imagining anything—for the imagination, I believe, is also completely lost—is, as I say, of brief duration, although the faculties do not recover to such an extent as not to be for some hours, as it were, in disorder, God, from time to time, gathering them once more to Himself...I was wondering what it is the soul does during that time, when the Lord said these words to me: "It dies to itself wholly, daughter, in order that it may fix itself more and more upon Me; it is no longer itself that lives, but I. As it cannot comprehend what it understands, it is an understanding which understands not."[21]

Similarly, to be childlike is to be innocent and pure and is not in any way to be confused with a regressive fusion. We recall the providential words: "Verily I say unto you, except ye be converted, and become as little children, ye shall not enter into the Kingdom of Heaven" (Matthew 18:3).

Although Freud was militantly opposed to religion and spirituality, he was interested in the psychic phenomenon of the occult or paranormal. Freud is reported to have written the following to the well known psychic investigator Hereward Carrington (1880–1958) regarding his interest in the occult or paranormal: "If I had to live my life over again, I should devote myself to psychical research, rather than psychoanalysis."[22] Freud wrote a letter to Carrington clarifying his position on the occult or paranormal: "I am not one of those who dismiss *a priori* the study of so-called occult psychic phenomena as unscientific, discreditable or even as dangerous."[23] Freud became a corresponding member of the Society for Psychical Research on January 2, 1911 and makes an interesting disclosure: "Alliance and cooperation between analysts and occultists might thus appear both plausible and promising."[24] He also suggests that psychoanalytic theory has itself advanced research in the occult or paranormal: "It would seem to me that psycho-analysis, by inserting the unconscious between what is physical and what was previously called 'psychical,' has paved the way for the assumption of such processes as telepathy."[25] Freud confided to Jones his belief in "clairvoyant visions of episodes at a distance" and "visitations from departed spirits."[26] If fact, Freud was willing to discard psychoanalysis altogether if the "occult procedures" proved to be successful:

If spiritual beings who are the intimate friends of human enquirers can supply ultimate explanations of everything, no interest can be left over for the laborious approaches to unknown mental forces made by analytic research. So, too, the methods of analytic technique will be abandoned if there is a hope of getting into direct touch with the operative spirits by means of occult procedures, just as habits of patient humdrum work are abandoned if there is a hope of growing rich at a single blow by means of a successful speculation.[27]

It is well known that his former disciple Jung was very much interested in the research on the occult, as is indicated by the title of his doctoral dissertation for his medical degree, *On the Psychology and Pathology of So-called Occult Phenomena* (1902).[28]

The dangers of occultism need to be emphasized: "modern occultism is by and large no more than the study of extrasensory phenomena, one of the most hazardous of pursuits by reason of its wholly empirical character and its lack of any doctrinal basis."[29] The essential transgression is that psychodynamic theory does not remain within the domain of its inquiry and encroaches upon what is transpersonal in nature. Schuon writes:

> The spiritual and social crime of psychoanalysis is therefore its usurpation of the place of religion or of the wisdom that is the wisdom of God, and the elimination from its procedures of all consideration of our ultimate destiny...Like every solution that avoids the supernatural, psychoanalysis replaces in its own way what it abolishes: the void it produces by its intentional or unintentional destructions expands it, and condemns it to postulate a false infinite or to function as a pseudo-religion.[30]

That psychoanalysis conflates the empirical ego with the unconscious and the superconscious or transpersonal domain is apparent in the following description made by Freud: "Mysticism is the obscure self-perception of the realm outside the ego, of the id."[31] Freud additionally writes, "We must avoid...the distinction between 'supraconscious' and 'subconscious'...for such a distinction seems precisely calculated to stress the equivalence of what is psychical to what is conscious."[32] Yet the opposite is the case: "the 'subconscious,' thanks to its contacts with psychic influences of the lowest order, effectively 'apes' the 'supraconscience'...[resulting in] an 'inverse spirituality.'"[33] It is essential for any true or integral psychology to include both a horizontal and a vertical dimension. Osborne emphasizes:

Just as physical science can attain only to Prakriti without Purusha, so psychology can only to the subconscious without the superconscious. Some psychologists are indeed coming to suspect and some even to admit openly that there is a superconscious, but that is not enough. What is needed is to have access to it, to have traversed it in oneself and to be able to guide the aspirant in doing so. Treating patients on the psychological level without access to the spiritual may produce a superficial amelioration or an aggravation but can lead to no permanent cure.[34]

It is this confusion, the confusion of the psychic with the spiritual, that epitomizes the relationship of the unconscious and the transpersonal. Guénon elaborates on this essential conflation:

[I]t is impossible to be too mistrustful of every appeal to the "subconscious" [or unconscious]...in a sort of "cosmic consciousness"[35] that shuts out all "transcendence" and so also shuts out all effective spirituality...but what is to be said of someone who flings himself into the ocean and has no aspiration but to drown himself in it? This is very precisely the significance of a so-called "fusion" with a "cosmic consciousness" that is really nothing but the confused and indistinct assemblage of all the psychic influences...these influences have absolutely nothing in common with spiritual influences...

Those who make this fatal mistake either forget about or are unaware of the distinction between the "upper waters" and the "lower waters"; instead of raising themselves toward the "ocean above," they plunge into the abyss of the "ocean below"; instead of concentrating all their powers so as to direct them toward the formless world, which alone can be called "spiritual," they disperse them in the endlessly changeable and fugitive diversity of the forms of subtle manifestation...with no suspicion that they are mistaking for a fullness of "life" something that is in truth the realm of death and of a dissolution without hope of return.

Guénon further explains that the confusion between the psychic and the spiritual occurs in two ways: "confusion...appears in two contrary forms: in the first, the spiritual is brought down to the level of the psychic...in the second, the psychic is mistaken for the spiritual."[36]

The fundamental distinction between the psychic and the spiritual appears to be completely overlooked by Jung when he writes the following about the unconscious: "The unconscious is not just evil by nature, it is also the source of the highest good: not only dark but also light, not only bestial, semi-human, and demonic but superhuman, spiritual, and, in the classical sense of the word, 'divine.'"[37]

Guénon illustrates that it is "the appeal to the 'subconscious' [or unconscious] that marks the complete reversal of the normal hierarchy, and brings us down, in fact to the infra-human."[38] He further adds that contemporary psychology and its limitations are again due to the absence of a vertical dimension: "present-day psychology considers nothing but the 'subconscious' [or unconscious], and never the 'superconscious,' which ought logically to be its correlative."[39] The following further clarifies these points:

> Freud's psychoanalysis is the last thing one should associate with *Yoga*; it takes a certain part, the most obscure, the most dangerous, and the most unhealthy part of nature—the lower vital subconscious—then isolates a few of its most morbid phenomena and attributes to them an action out of all proportion with their true role in nature...I find it difficult to take these psychoanalysts seriously when they try to examine spiritual experience under the flickering light of their torches; however, perhaps it is necessary to do so, for half-knowledge can be a great obstacle to the manifestation of truth. This new psychology reminds me of children learning a basic and incomplete alphabet, confusing with an air of triumph their "a b c" of the subconscious with the mysterious superconscious, and imagining that their first book of obscure rudiments is the very heart of real knowledge. They look from below above and explain the higher lights by the lower darkness; but the foundation of things is above and not below, in the superconscious and not the subconscious...One must know the whole before one can know the part, and the higher before one can understand the lower. The promise of a great psychology awaits its hour, before which all this meager experimentation will disappear and be reduced to nothing.[40]

Given the profound unreliability of the human psyche, which Freud himself recognizes, he curiously, nonetheless, still affirms his utter reliance on this epistemological and ontological quicksand: "The interpretation of dreams is the royal road to a knowledge of the unconscious activities of the mind."[41] The utilization of dreams is found across the cultures of the world, yet dreams were not limited to the psychological level as Freud assumed: "Dreams are completely egotistical."[42] According to the Talmud: "A dream that is not interpreted is like a letter that is not read" (Berakhot 55a). Black Elk affirmed that "Sometimes dreams are wiser than waking."[43] In the Old Testament it is written: "If there be a prophet among you, I the Lord will make myself known unto him in a vision, and will speak unto him in a dream" (Numbers 12:6).

Freud criticized the ancient and traditional belief in prophetic dreams, by reducing them to contents of the unconscious. In response to the question: "[what of] the value of dreams for giving us knowledge of the future?"[44] Freud writes:

> There is of course no question of that. It would be truer to say instead that they give us knowledge of the past. For dreams are derived from the past in every sense. Nevertheless the ancient belief that dreams foretell the future is not wholly devoid of truth. By picturing our wishes as fulfilled, dreams are after all leading us into the future. But this future, which the dreamer pictures as the present, has been moulded by his indestructible wish into a perfect likeness of the past.[45]

Freud continues, "I confess that I feel no necessity for making any mystical assumptions in order to fill the gaps in our present knowledge, and accordingly I have never been able to find anything to confirm the prophetic nature of dreams."[46] Freud goes further and equates dreams with psychopathology itself: "A dream, then, is a psychosis, with all the absurdities, delusions and illusions of a psychosis."[47] We find the following description in the Old Testament that is fitting for Freud: "Behold, I am against them that prophesy false dreams, saith the Lord, and do tell them, and cause my people to err by their lies, and by their lightness; yet I sent them not, nor commanded them: therefore they shall not profit this people at all, saith the Lord" (Jeremiah 23:32).

The "unconscious" of psychoanalysis was known in the premodern world, yet it is often wrongly assumed to be a contemporary invention. An example can be provided from the Hindu tradition that dates to time immemorial and that made note of the unconscious: "Long before psychoanalysis, yoga had shown the importance of the part played by the subconscious [or unconscious]."[48] Rūmī recognized, "man is unconscious of himself and does not know himself."[49] The diverse religious traditions and their corresponding psychologies knew not only about the existence of what was beneath consciousness, but they also knew what was beyond it as well. Schuon argues:

What [in Christianity] is called [the] "examination of conscience" or, by the Moslems, "the science of humors" (*'ilm al-
khawāṭir*), or "investigation" (*vichara*) by the Hindus...is nothing
other than an objective analysis of the near and distant causes of
ways of acting and reacting that we repeat automatically without
being aware of their real motives...To be healed, he must detect
these complexes...become conscious of subconscious errors and
neutralize them by means of contrary affirmations. Lao Tzu said:
"To feel [be conscious of] an illness is to have it no longer."[50]

While the perennial psychology restores the empirical ego to its
rightful place in what transcends it, psychoanalysis begins and ends
within the *cul-de-sac* of the psychic underworld of the empirical ego.
The "talking cure" rules out the possibility of transcendence or a vertical dimension: "Psychoanalysis denies the possibility of ego transcendence."[51] Psychoanalysis is in fact unable to go beyond the horizontal identity: "Freud never got to the self—always getting stuck
with the ego."[52] Put differently, "Psychotherapy's goal is to resolve
the conflicts only on the psychological level."[53]

Nevertheless, Freud's position on religion and spirituality was
made explicitly clear, even with vague references to the transpersonal
dimension such as the "oceanic feeling," as his reductionism is limited to the "psychic apparatus," and such references should not be interpreted to suggest that he is alluding in some way to a sacred or
spiritual psychology. The Freudian depth-psychology did not plant
the seeds for a height-psychology or a transpersonal psychology. In
fact, Freud himself debunks all attempts to reinterpret the doctrine of
the "talking cure" in a spiritual context:

I have never ventured beyond the ground floor and basement of
the building.—You maintain that if one changes one's point of
view one can also see a higher floor, in which there live such
distinguished guests as religion, art, etc. You are not alone in this;
most cultivated specimens of *homo natura* think likewise. You
are the conservative in this respect, and I the revolutionary. If I
still had a lifetime of work ahead of me, I should dare to assign a
home in my lowly little house to those highborn personages. I
have already done so for religion since coming across the category "neurosis of mankind."[54]

We again emphasize Freud's own statements in order for it to become explicitly clear that he was not pioneering a "science of the

soul," but was establishing a psychology based on a materialistic science: "I [Freud] have always confined myself to the ground floor and basement of the edifice."[55] It is through the traditional spiritual practice that an authentic integration of the psychic faculty in the Spirit can occur, as Professor Harry Oldmeadow clarifies: "In a traditional discipline the psychic can be reintegrated with the spiritual but without the necessary metaphysical framework and religious supports psychism becomes wholly infra-intellectual and anti-spiritual."[56]

Chapter 12

The Eclipse of the Sacred and the Rise
of Psychopathology

*"[F]or psychoanalysis to extrapolate its understanding of neuroses
to the field of religion is a transgression of the epistemological limits."[1]—Mark Perry*

Freud's attack on religion and transcendence relegating it to psychopathology is by all estimations unmatched: "The religions of mankind
must be classed among the mass-delusions."[2] Freud's dethroning of
religion in the modern world led him to the corresponding discovery
of the rise of mental illness: "The extraordinary increase in the neuroses since the power of religion has waned."[3] In the current temporal
cycle of the *Kali-Yuga* or "Dark Age," the human psyche is in crisis:
"In our time the psyche has become something of a problem for everyone."[4] The loss of the sense of the sacred has left an epistemological
and ontological void with severe consequences for the human collectivity that contemporary psychology cannot fill: "the ego is sick for
the very reason that it is cut off from the whole, and has lost its connection not only with mankind but with the spirit."[5] We live in an era
that is akin to what Saint John Chrysostom identifies as an inversion
of all things: "everything is turned upside down."[6] The mind of the
contemporary human being has been astutely assessed in light of the
ascendency of this desacralized outlook: "The almost universally unnoticed fact is that we, denizens of the modern age, have been unwittingly plunged into a state of collective schizophrenia, a condition
scarcely compatible with authentic sanity."[7]

The destructive impacts of scientism or materialistic science
themselves also need to be noted here, as Jung affirms: "As scientific
understanding has grown, so our world has become dehumanized."[8]
Freud observed that the sanctuaries of prayer and contemplation
within the Christian tradition have been replaced with psychological
imbalance: "To-day neurosis takes the place of the monasteries which
used to be the refuge of all whom life had disappointed or who felt
too weak to face it."[9] With each passing day, the disorder within the
human psyche appears to increase to such a heightened degree that it

now encompasses the human collectivity where abnormality reigns and has become gradually normalized, not only within the dominant culture of the contemporary West, but extending throughout all parts of the world. "[T]he disorder of [the contemporary human being's] own mind...has become his main preoccupation."[10] The historical trajectory of the epidemic of mental illness is remarkable as it applies to the present day: "At the end of the seventeenth century, insanity was of little significance and was little discussed. At the end of the eighteenth century, it was perceived as probably increasing and was of some concern. At the end of the nineteenth century, it was perceived as an epidemic and was a major concern. And at the end of the twentieth century, insanity was simply accepted as part of the fabric of life."[11]

According to Borella, the rise of psychopathology is directly correlated with the desacrilization of the cosmos and is the human being's response to this predicament:

> [T]he seventeenth century witnessed an increase in the number of the insane, itself resulting from the progressive disappearance of the medieval mythocosm and religion's cultural universe. The frantic and permanent exclusion of insanity, and the never-satisfied desire for a totally pure reason, are themselves only a kind of desperate wish to conjure away the threat of a "sacred madness" ever reborn at the very heart of the human spirit.[12]

Psychopathology on a collective level is therefore unavoidable and is in essence an inevitable consequence of the loss of the sense of the sacred or what Freud terms "psychical epidemics, of historical mass convulsions."[13] From the perspective of traditional cosmology as it is known across the diverse cultures, time is recognized to be cyclical rather than linear, and the current crisis in the human psyche is a spiritual crisis of being cut off from the sacred. Modern or postmodern human beings mirror the gravity of the *Kali-Yuga*. Larchet writes: "the sickly state of fallen man in all its forms is essentially due to the fact that man has turned away from God, thus perverting all his faculties which by nature were oriented towards Him and mutilating his being, which was made to find fullness in and through God."[14] According to Fromm, "Neurosis itself is, in the last analysis, a symptom of moral failure (although 'adjustment' is by no means a symptom of moral achievement)."[15] The normalization of mass psychopathology in our era is in fact: "The normalization of crisis."[16] Perry links the loss of the sense of the sacred with the undermining of what is considered "normal":

> [T]his loss of the sense of the sacred norm explains the immense change in things and customs that the average person today typically considers to be "normal," but that are normal merely for being subscribed to passively by the majority. The desensitization of the soul of modern man, assaulted by the abnormal on a daily and relentless basis, has skewed the perception of what Reality is, to the point that no one really knows anymore what the term "normal" should connote, when in fact it is a term that, far from mirroring ever-shifting customs dictated by inertia and popularity, derives from a world founded on the notion of the True, the Beautiful, and the Good. Indeed, the terms "knowledge," "norm," and "nobility" are cognate terms that have become dissociated over time. Thus a noble person is really a person who knows, just as to know—truly to know—is to be noble, and therefore to be normal.[17]

Freud on the other hand reduces the present-day crisis to an intrapsychic phenomenon holding no external or verifiable reality in the outer world: "The end of the world is the projection of this internal catastrophe."[18]

Perennialist author Tage Lindbom (1909–2001) describes the inevitable psychological disintegration alongside the marginalization or destruction of religion within the human collectivity:

> Religion is not a stifling neurosis and the elimination of the last religious opinions is not the equivalent of liberating humanity from its last neurotic vestiges. On the contrary, it is the secular world surrounding us which is stamped with a growing psychic insecurity; and if it is incapable of giving to men psychic security, it is an effect of growing rationalism. Instead of disappearing from the world illuminated by luciferian light, neuroses increase.[19]

Lindbom additionally illustrates Freud's role in the rise of psychopathology: "we encounter neurosis as mass phenomena. Never before has there been so much talk of 'healing,' never before so many practitioners of the healing arts. How could it be otherwise? No one affirms more explicitly the downward direction attention and consciousness in the modern world than the father of psychoanalysis, Sigmund Freud."[20]

Freudianism did not give any value to the aesthetic dimension and did not recognize its connection to a higher order, to the spiritual domain. The role of beauty serves a tremendous purpose for individual and collective psychological health and well-being and can be found across the diverse cultures of the world. As Plato affirmed, "Beauty is the splendor of Truth." Freud belittles the role of beauty, yet curiously states that civilization cannot do without it: "Beauty has no obvious use; nor is there any clear cultural necessity for it. Yet civilization could not do without it."[21] Freud writes: "Psychoanalysis...has scarcely anything to say about beauty either."[22]

Freud reveals that the human being is mentally ill if he or she is identified with his faith tradition, and likewise individuals attach themselves to a religion because of their mental illness. As Paul Ricoeur (1913–2005) frames it, "man is neurotic insofar as he is *homo religiosus* and religious insofar as he is neurotic."[23] We are informed by Rieff that "Religion may have been the original cure; Freud reminds us that it was also the original disease."[24]

Contrary to Freudian psychology, Professor Emeritus of Psychology at New York University Paul C. Vitz asserts that disbelief itself is the source of psychopathology: "atheism [is] a more probable symptom of neurosis than theism"[25] and "atheism certainly may often be an expression of a psychological pathology."[26] To ignore or minimize the human being's inseparable link to the sacred is to lose sight of what is integrally human, which has disastrous implications on the human collectivity. Sherrard explains:

> Man can be truly human only when he is mindful of his theomorphic nature. When he ignores the divine in himself and in other existences he becomes sub-human. And when this happens not merely in the case of a single individual but in the case of society as a whole, then that society disintegrates through the sheer rootlessness of its own structure or through the proliferation of psychic maladies which it is powerless to heal because it has deprived itself of the one medicine capable of healing them.[27]

The following statement by Jung, reminiscent of his onetime master, makes more sense when situated in a traditional cosmological context: "The attitude of modern civilized man sometimes reminds me of a psychotic patient."[28] Jung also recognized the decline of the sacred gave rise to mental illness: "[S]ide by side with the decline of religious life, the neuroses grow noticeably more frequent...We are living undeniably in a period of the greatest restlessness, nervous tension, confusion and disorientation of outlook...[M]odern man has an ineradicable aversion for traditional opinions and inherited truths...religious truths have somehow or other grown empty."[29]

Therefore the human psychopathology that Freud perseverated on is a consequence of fallen or *saṃsāric* consciousness, as Laing points out: "The relevance of Freud to our time is largely his insight and to a very considerable extent his *demonstration* that the *ordinary* person is a shriveled, desiccated fragment of what a person can be."[30] According to Rank, the emergence of Freudian psychology is a sign of a civilizational crisis: "psychoanalysis as the psychology of the neurotic type—but not the cure for it—is in itself a sign of a decadent civilization."[31] American psychologist Arthur Janov (1924–2017) argues that: "Freud bequeathed us two most unfortunate notions which we have taken as gospel truth. One is that there is no beginning to neurosis—that, in other words, to be born a member of the human race is to be born neurotic. The other is that the person with the strongest defense system is necessarily the one who can best function in society."[32]

Disillusioned, Freud reduces all human beings to that of psychopathology or at best dismisses the possibility of mental health and contextualizes all states of mind within a spectrum of the abnormal. Freud suggests: "a normal ego...is, like normality in general, an ideal fiction. The abnormal ego...is unfortunately no fiction. Every normal person, in fact, is only normal on the average. His ego approximates to that of the psychotic in some part or other and to a greater of lesser extent."[33] Freud again continually dissolves the distinction between the normal and the abnormal, mental health and psychopathology: "psycho-analytic research finds no fundamental, but only quantitative, distinctions between normal and neurotic life."[34] Likewise, "our patients tell us about themselves nothing that we could not also hear from healthy people."[35] He adds: "Thus a healthy person, too, is virtually a neurotic."[36]

From the time the human being is born into the world, he or she, according to Freud, suffers from mental illness: "the act of birth is the first experience of anxiety, and thus the source and prototype of the affect of anxiety."[37] For this reason the originator of the "talking cure" has also been identified in no uncertain terms: "The greatest psychopathologist has been Freud."[38] Jung speaks to Freud's preoccupation with psychopathology: "he [Freud] is somehow fascinated by the almost pathological manifestations of the unconscious mind."[39] While the role of psychopathology is abundant within the psychoanalytic *Weltanschauung* of the "talking cure," the notion of psychological health and well-being is virtually nonexistent in Freudian psychoanalysis. An example of this is made abundantly clear in the following: "[in] the Index to the *Standard Edition of the Complete Psychological Works of Sigmund Freud*, the word 'neurosis' has over 400 references. In contrast, 'health' is not even listed."[40] Psychoanalytic theory suggests that by knowing what mental illness is, it is then possible to know what is "normal" or not psychopathology. Freud observes: "pathology, by making things larger and coarser, can draw our attention to normal conditions which would otherwise have escaped us."[41] This is a false argument, as the reverse is true: to know what integral human health and well-being is, is to know what is not aberrant in nature.

It was his tunnel vision focused on human sickness that led Freud to what he assumes as the most logical conclusion, that everyone is suffering from psychopathology. As Friedell writes: "the false conclusion which is sustained all through psycho-analysis: the neurotic—and the exceptionally difficult neurotic case at that—is hypostasized as the archetype of humanity."[42] Freud did not appear to differentiate between mental health and mental illness; everyone was suffering from psychopathology: "It only shows us how neurotic our whole cultural life is, when people apparently normal behave no differently from neurotics."[43]

A chilling aspect of psychoanalysis is that even if an individual seeking treatment did not suffer from mental illness prior to undergoing analysis, the "talking cure" itself would give him or her a neurosis: "I [Freud] think there is little doubt that here the correct technique can only be to wait until the treatment itself has become a compulsion, and then with this counter-compulsion forcibly to suppress the compulsion of the disease."[44] Freud reflects on the connection between individual psychopathology and collective psychopathology in the following:

> If the development of civilization has such a far-reaching similarity to the development of the individual and if it employs the same methods, may we not be justified in reaching the diagnosis that, under the influence of cultural urges, some civilizations, or some epochs of civilization—possibly the whole of mankind—have become "neurotic"?...In an individual neurosis we take as our starting-point the contrast that distinguishes the patient from his environment, which is assumed to be "normal." For a group all of whose members are affected by one and the same disorder no such background could exist; it would have to be found else-

where...we may expect that one day someone will venture to embark upon a pathology of cultural communities.[45]

While Freud opens this door for work to be conducted in the future, it needs to be remembered that psychoanalysis as a theory is not limited to an individual, but sets out to analyze human existence *in toto*. Freud's one-time disciple Jung has no reservations about explicitly emphasizing the relationship between the individual and collective psychopathology:

We always find in the patient a conflict which at a certain point is connected with the great problems of society. Hence, when the analysis is pushed to this point, the apparently individual conflict of the patient is revealed as a universal conflict of his environment and epoch. Neurosis is thus nothing less than an individual attempt, however unsuccessful, to solve a universal problem...[46]

Freudian metapsychology cannot help but reduce the whole of reality to mental illness and what is psychological, as he himself confesses: "No matter where I start, I always am right back with the neurosis and with the Ψ [psychic] apparatus."[47] The spectrum of abnormality from abnormal to normal is virtually nonexistent within Freudian psychology: "Pathology has always done us the service of making discernible by isolation and exaggeration conditions which would remain concealed in a normal state."[48] In a similar fashion with regard to dreams, Freud emphasizes: "Dreams of neurotics differ in no essential point from the dreams of normal persons; you might even say they cannot be distinguished."[49]

It may perplex readers to know that while the Freudian "talking cure" focused on psychopathology and not human health and well-being, Freud nonetheless states that it would do the most good for those that are not suffering from mental illness. Freud himself puts this assertion forward: "psychoanalysis meets the optimum of favorable conditions where its practice is not needed—i.e., among the healthy."[50] Yet, in another place, he contradicts this position and affirms: "There are people who cannot be analyzed—often perfectly normal people."[51] The final product of an individual analyzed is someone fundamentally dissociated and enclosed within him or herself: "Psychoanalyzed man is inwardly alienated."[52] We recall the wise and timeless words of the Old Testament that aim to remedy the state of alienation: "For to him that is joined to all the living there is hope" (Ecclesiastes 9:4). While on one hand Jung states, "A therapist with a neurosis is a contradiction in terms,"[53] he on the other hand ironically remarks that psychological imbalance does not have to be something negative; it can in fact be advantageous: "A neurosis is by no means merely a negative thing, it is also something positive."[54]

Chapter 13

The Couch and the Confessional

"The secret of Confession may never be revealed."[1]—*Pope Pius XII*

The Sacrament of Penance and Reconciliation, more commonly known as confession, is one of the seven sacraments of the Catholic Church. We recall the instruction of Apostle James: "Confess your sins to one another, and pray for one another, that you may be healed" (James 5:16). That Freud appropriated this sacrament and profaned it by incorporating it into his secular and pseudo-religious "talking cure" is noted in several areas of his work. An example of this can be found in a candid interview conducted with Freud when he disclosed the religious roots of his "talking cure" in clear terms: "[Of] what consists my method of curing hysteria [the cathartic method or abreaction] save in making the patient tell everything to free him from the obsession?...Confession is liberation and that is cure. The Catholics knew it for centuries...I boldly substituted myself for the confessor."[2]

It becomes therefore apparent that Freudian psychoanalysis has decisively usurped this sacrament of the Christian tradition, attempting to create a secular counterfeit of it within modern psychology. Karl Kautsky (1854–1938) recognized the doctrine of the "talking cure" as the usurpation of the traditional rite of confession: "Freudian psychoanalysis in medical practice seems to me fundamentally nothing other than the transfer of some techniques of the Catholic confessional into the physician's consulting room."[3] The act of psychoanalysis trespasses upon the sacred and appropriates its function in the life of the human being and the collectivity, without recognizing this fact: "In the same way a priest receiving confessions must make confession himself; and a psychoanalyst must himself have been analysed. This shows that his discipline, however much he may deny it, is not purely technical but belongs to a spiritual order."[4]

Freud discusses the doctrine of the "talking cure," which as can be observed has its parallels with the sacrament of confession, as it is applied within the psychoanalytic church:

> [Freud or the psychoanalyst] treats his patients as follows. Without exerting any other kind of influence, he invites them to lie

down in a comfortable attitude on a sofa, while he himself sits on a chair behind them outside their field of vision. He does not even ask them to close their eyes, and avoids touching them in any way, as well as any other procedure which might be reminiscent of hypnosis. The session thus proceeds like a conversation between two people equally awake, but one of whom is spared every muscular exertion and every distracting sensory impression which might divert his attention from his own mental activity.[5]

In other instances, Freud suggests that while similarities between the doctrine of the "talking cure" and confession can be found, they also differ in certain respects:

This looks as though we were only aiming at the post of a secular father confessor. But there is a great difference, for what we want to hear from our patient is not only what he knows and conceals from other people; he is to tell us too what he does *not* know...We pledge him to obey the *fundamental rule* of analysis, which is henceforward to govern his behavior towards us. He is to tell us not only what he can say intentionally and willingly, what will give him relief like a confession, but everything else as well that his self-observation yields him, everything that comes into his head, even if it is *disagreeable* for him to say it, even if it seems to him *unimportant* or actually *nonsensical*.[6]

Webster discusses the intrapsychic dynamics occurring within Freud's own mind and the rationale for appropriating the rite of confession:

In placing what was, in effect, a confessional ritual at the very heart of the psychoanalytic movement, it seems clear that Freud was not, as he himself believed, engaging in a form of scientific innovation. Rather he was unconsciously institutionalizing his own profound religious traditionalism at the same time that he was creating for himself a ritual stage on which he could play out his own "God complex" in relation to patients he regarded as inferior and in need of redemption. Just as, through his history of infantile sexuality, he had revised in disguised technical form the doctrine of Original Sin, so he also brought back to life, under a clinical disguise, the most important ecclesiastical ritual which had traditionally helped to sustain that doctrine, and to create a

150

psychological dependency among those who unburdened themselves in the secrecy of the confessional.[7]

Anna O. (Bertha Pappenheim), who through her own albeit failed treatment aided in the development of the "talking cure," herself compared the Freudian doctrine with Catholic confession: "Psychoanalysis in the hands of the physician is what confession is in the hands of the Catholic priest. It depends on its user and its use, whether it becomes a beneficial tool or a two-edged sword."[8] As Ellenberger concludes in his findings on the Anna O. case study, "the famed 'prototype of a cathartic cure' was neither a cure nor a catharsis."[9]

Burckhardt exposes the Freudian psychoanalytic parody of confession for what it is:

[T]he psychiatrist replaces the priest, and the bursting of complexes that had previously been repressed takes the place of absolution. In ritual confession the priest is but the impersonal representative—necessarily discreet—of the Truth that judges and pardons; the penitent, by admitting his sins, in a sense "objectivizes" the psychic tendencies that these sins manifest. By repenting, he detaches himself from them, and by receiving sacramental absolution, his soul is virtually reintegrated in its primitive equilibrium and centered on its diving essence. In the case of Freudian psychoanalysis, on the other hand, man lays bare his psychic entrails, not before God, but to his fellow. He does not distance himself from the chaotic and obscure depths of his soul, which the analyst unveils or stirs up, but on the contrary, he accepts them as his own, for he must say to himself: "This is what I am like in reality." And if he does not overcome, with the help of some salutary instinct, this kind of disillusionment from below, he will retain from it something like an intimate sullying; in most cases it will be his self-abandonment to collective mediocrity that for him will play the part of absolution, for it is easier to endure one's own degradation when it is shared with others. Whatever may be the occasional or partial usefulness of such an analysis in certain cases, the state described above is its more usual result, its premises being what they are.[10]

In 1926, Freud retracted statements that he made elsewhere regarding the "talking cure" being synonymous with the confession of the Christian tradition, as he notes here: "Confession enters into analysis, as its introduction, as it were. But it is far from being the same thing as analysis, and it cannot serve to explain its effect. In confession the sinner tells what he knows, in analysis the neurotic must tell more. Besides, we have no knowledge that the system of confession has developed the power to get rid of direct symptoms of illness."[11]

Psychoanalyst Alexander Reid Martin (1896–1983) also pushes back on this assertion, emphasizing the distinction between psychoanalysis and confession:

> There is a common belief that psychoanalysis is analogous to confession, to the bringing out of certain experiences and behavior of which the patient is fully conscious, but which he has felt to be socially so unacceptable and blameworthy that he has never been able to reveal them to anyone. Many who feel this way will not see the need for psychoanalysis and will be inclined to say: "Why be psychoanalyzed? Just let go and confide in someone. Confession is good for the soul!" Analysis, while interested in all the motives for and the value of confession, is in no sense a confessional procedure.[12]

Former disciple Rank comments on the parallels between the rite of confession and that of psychoanalysis:

> [M]an confesses in one or another way that he is himself sinful, guilty, bad. Exactly the same process of justification and self-accusation we see unroll itself in psychoanalysis only here it appears in the therapeutic and psychological terminology of our natural science age, although it seems unavoidable to bring in the contentually richer ideas and symbols of earlier systems. In its technique, psychoanalysis is exactly as much a matter of consolation and justification as therapy must be according to its nature. That is, it quiets man concerning his badness, since it says to him that all others are thus also and that it lies grounded in human nature.[13]

While the doctrine of the "talking cure" appropriates the traditional sacrament of confession, it is limited to the horizontal and psychological domain. It becomes apparent that psychoanalysis, as Swiss physician Paul Tournier (1898–1986) indicates, "does not eliminate [guilt] but shifts it."[14] What is commonly misunderstood in the contemporary era is that rather than being a hindrance, "guilt is the driving force towards healing."[15]

Jung suggests that "every psychological theory [is] in the first instance...subjective confession."[16] He also draws on the parallels between psychoanalysis and confession:

The first beginnings of all analytical treatment are to be found in its prototype, the confessional. Since, however, the two practices have no direct causal connection, but rather grow from a common psychic root, it is difficult for an outsider to see at once the relation between the groundwork of psychoanalysis and the religious institution of the confessional.17

Jung continues:

The confession of her sinful thoughts may have given considerable relief to the patient. But it seems unlikely that the cure can be ascribed entirely to their verbal expression or to the "abreaction." Pathological ideas can be definitely submerged only by a strong effort. People with obsessions and compulsions are weak; they are unable to keep their ideas in check. Treatment to increase their energy is therefore best for them. The best energy-cure, however, is to force the patients, with a certain ruthlessness, to unearth and expose to the light the images that consciousness finds intolerable. Not only is this severe challenge for the patient's energy but also his consciousness begins to accept the existence of ideas hitherto repressed.[18]

Lindbom underscores the dangers of utilizing confession within a secular context, such as that of psychoanalysis:

Psychoanalysis has signaled the break-through of psychic surgery. The human soul must be "opened" to the new "scientific vision." One is assured that mental health consists in directing the luciferian light to the depths of the "hidden recesses" of the soul and in the drawing out of materials which will then be treated rationally. What hides in these dark depths especially is the constraining neurosis which constitutes religion; especially where religious opinions are encountered under the form of neurotic survivals. They must be destroyed, Freud said. Surely man possesses an immortal soul which can neither be analyzed nor verbalized in terms of psychological science, but this objection is thrust aside by saying that it is a question precisely, of one of the most important veils to be rent: religion, not only as illusion, but as foyer of neurosis.[19]

The rite of confession again occurs between the penitent and the priest who is the mediator between the human being and God; however, in psychoanalysis this process becomes horizontal or psychological, if not potentially infernal in nature, as it is devoid of any transcendent criterion. According to Perry:

> Modern face-to-face confessions, in which the priest listens to a penitent in the capacity of a friendly advisor, are trivial and worthless, if not frankly Luciferian in cases where the priest starts playing the role of a kind of psychoanalyst, because then the ego of the believer is likely to be mollified instead of mortified. It should not be difficult for anyone to understand that a face-to-face confession ruins—utterly and irrevocably—the idea of the penitent placing himself before Christ.[20]

Psychoanalysis sets out to analyze the hidden forces that drive behavior, but even with these unconscious impulses identified, it is not enough for them to be analyzed. By the faculty of reason alone psychoanalysis attempts to discover what these latent forces are; yet it is beyond the faculty of reason or talking about something that will reintegrate the human psyche. "It is not enough to analyze the sin in order to break down the consciousness of sin or to cure it."[21] A higher faculty of the Spirit/Intellect is needed to restore psychological health and well-being:

> To uncover the motives of sin, by studying the patient's past, is no cure. Sin is not in the understanding alone, nor in the instincts; sin is in the will. Hence it cannot be broken up as another complex may be broken up by dragging it into the consciousness. Psychic diseases may arise from repressed complexes; but sin must be regarded as an act of the will that implicates the whole personality. Mere [rational] comprehension will not destroy its effects or restore the patient's health.[22]

Ultimately without what is above or transcendent, no true therapy is possible. The distinction between the doctrine of the "talking cure" that is horizontal and that which goes beyond the psychological is found here: "Psychoanalysis is the probing of the mind by mind; confession is the communion of conscience and God."[23] It has been suggested that all mental illness has a metaphysical origin, and therefore an integral psychology actively linked with the Spirit is necessary for true efficacy of treatment: "The root of every psychological tension is basically metaphysical."[24] Perry writes: "all human problems stem, in the last analysis, from our separation from God...man cannot be helped lastingly until he is restored virtually if not effectively to his prototype *in divinis*."[25] This is likely why it has been stated: "Healing may be called a religious problem."[26]

Jones describes the disposition of an orthodox psychoanalyst when providing treatment:

> He makes himself as *inaccessible* as possible, and surrounds his personality with a *cloud of mystery*...the broad tendency of aloofness displays itself by the desires, on the physical side of being inaccessible, on the mental side of being mysterious. The person aims at wrapping himself in an impenetrable cloud of mystery and privacy. Even the most trivial pieces of information about himself, those which an ordinary man sees no object in keeping to himself, are invested with a sense of high importance, and are parted with only under some pressure. Such a man is very loth to let his age be known...let alone to talk about his private affairs...The veil of mystery and obscurity that he casts over himself is naturally extended so as to cover all those pertaining to him. Thus he never spontaneously refers to his family, speaking of them reluctantly when any inquiries are made about them, and the same applies to any affairs in which he may have become concerned.[27]

The German philologist Jacob Bernays (1824–81) in 1857 wrote an influential article that changed the way that catharsis (from the Greek *katharsis*, "purification" or "purgation") was understood until that time as employed by Aristotle in his *Poetics*. Bernays reinterprets Aristotelian catharsis within a psychological outlook, definitively altering the classical interpretation. Jacob Bernays was the uncle of Freud's wife, Martha Bernays, and both Josef Breuer and Sigmund Freud were influenced by Jacob Bernays's reinterpretation of Aristotelian catharsis.

This reinterpretation was essential for the early formation of the "talking cure." The cathartic method or the mechanism of abreaction was a precursor of the psychoanalytic "talking cure" as Freud again illustrates: "Breuer's 'cathartic procedure' [is] a forerunner of psychoanalysis."[28] Just how does psychoanalytic psychology bring about a curative effect? Breuer and Freud inform us that its effectiveness is due to the cathartic method or abreaction:

> It brings to an end the operative force of the idea which was not abreacted in the first instance, by allowing its strangulated affect to find a way out through speech; and it subjects it to associative correction by introducing it into normal consciousness (under

light hypnosis) or by removing it through the physician's suggestion, as is done in somnambulism accompanied by amnesia.

In our opinion the therapeutic advantages of this procedure are
considerable...[I]t seems to us far superior in its efficacy to re-
moval through direct suggestion, as it is practiced to-day by psychotherapists.[29]

Freud appears to have first mentioned the "abreaction theory" in
a letter to Fliess on June 28, 1892.[30] As Freud explained in 1898:
"Basing myself on the 'cathartic' method introduced by Josef Breuer,
I have in recent years almost completely worked out a therapeutic
procedure which I propose to describe as 'psycho-analytic.'"[31] In
1903, Freud emphasized that "The particular psychotherapeutic procedure which Freud practices and describes as 'psycho-analysis' is an
outgrowth of what was known as the 'cathartic' method and was discussed by him in collaboration with Josef Breuer in their *Studies on
Hysteria* (1895)."[32] In 1904, Freud identifies the term that distinguishes his work from Breuer's: "the method which Breuer called *cathartic*, but which I myself prefer to call 'analytic.'"[33] Almost twenty
years later, in 1923, Freud still affirmed that "The cathartic method
was the immediate precursor of psychoanalysis; and, in spite of every
extension of experience and of every modification of theory, is still
contained within it as its nucleus."[34]

Jung suggests a common origin of catharsis known in the mystery
religions and the emergence of the psychoanalytic "talking cure":

[A] saying from the Greek mysteries: "Give up what thou hast,
and then thou wilt receive."

We may well take this saying as a motto for the first age in psychotherapeutic treatment. It is a fact that the beginnings of psychoanalysis were fundamentally nothing else than the scientific
rediscovery of an ancient truth; even the name catharsis (or
cleansing), which was given to the earliest method of treatment,
comes from the Greek initiation rites.[35]

In examining the essential functions of the cathartic method or
abreaction it is easy to see its parallels with the sacred rite of confession and how it was implemented to have the same effect within a
desacralized context. "Psychoanalytic probing, like religious confession, is a psychic cathartic—a way of getting disturbing products out
of one's system."[36] While not wishing to digress, we see that even

though Freud gave up the cathartic method or abreaction, it nonetheless influenced many of the twentieth-century therapies beyond that of Freudian psychoanalysis, such as the human potential movement and humanistic psychology, including group psychotherapies, encounter groups, sensitivity groups, Reichian therapy, bioenergetics, gestalt therapy, primal therapy and so on.

In analyzing the perennial psychology found within each of the revealed religions, it becomes apparent that contemporary psychology not only proves to be nothing new, but is a pale reflection of the perennial psychology found within each of the world's religions: "To study souls is nothing new; in the whole gamut of modern psychology there is nothing written on frustration, fears, and anxieties that can even faintly compare in depth or breadth with Saint Thomas's treatise on the Passions, Saint Augustine's *Confessions*, or Bossuet's treatise on Concupiscence."[37] The sapiential traditions also warned individuals about putting their psychic and spiritual lives in the hands of those who are ignorant or charlatans. Saint Symeon the New Theologian (949–1022) writes: "Do not put yourself in the hands of an inexperienced master...for he will sooner initiate you into the diabolic life."[38] Similarly, Abba Poemen (340–450) adjures: "Do not confide your conscience in someone whom your heart does not fully trust."[39] A central challenge in demarcating where the psychological and spiritual domains begin and end regarding the rite of confession is that they are intimately aligned and are almost inseparable from one another: "every psychological confession has religious significance, and every religious confession, whether ritual and sacramental or free, its psychological effects."[40]

Chapter 14

The Satanic Pact and the Psychologizing of Evil

"When reason fails, the devil helps!"[1] These are memorable words from Fyodor Dostoyevsky's (1821–81) novel *Crime and Punishment* (1866). "Woe unto them that call evil good, and good evil; that put darkness for light, and light for darkness; that put bitter for sweet, and sweet for bitter!" (Isaiah 5:20). It is apparent that "psychoanalysis was itself based on Faustian principles."[2] The Devil served a principal function within Freudian psychology, as the theme captivated Freud on a profound level, as did religion. Because of the existing secular outlook of the times where belief in the Devil was discarded, Freud could reduce the Devil and evil itself to a psychological phenomenon. Freudian orthodoxy upholds that "we are ruled by external reality rather than by our inner demons."[3]

The desensitization of the masses to evil and its indulgence is due to the relativizing of truth itself. An important question has been put forth by psychologist Bernie Zilbergeld (1939–2002), which he addresses by the same token as exposing the contemporary mindset: "*Whatever Became of Sin?* The answer is simple: it was psychologized away."[4] He goes on to say: "Evil has suffered a fate similar to sin's."[5] This is to say that evil has been psychologized. Jung also confirms this: "Sin has for them become something quite relative: what is evil for the one, is good for the other."[6]

While the existence of evil, like the existence of the Devil or the notion of sin for that matter, is questioned and often denied in the present-day secular milieu that is antagonistic to Spirit, what is needed is an ever-present vigilance in order not to be deceived by the disintegrating forces of the times that cause doubt and confusion in the minds of the faithful. Guénon points out that "Satanism...is always characterized by a reversal of the normal order"[7] and reminds us that "the supreme craft of the devil, however he may be conceived, is to make us deny his existence."[8] As Schuon maintains: "The evil one wants us to doubt the Most High."[9]

It is the very materialistic way in which reality is understood today that prevents transcendence and the existence of evil from being understood as it was in previous eras: "That in this day and age...men no longer take either God or Satan seriously, arises from the fact that they have come to think of both alike only objectively, only as persons external to themselves and for whose existence no adequate proof can be found."[10] Because of the loss of this essential discernment, the presence of evil can, as Seraphim Rose (1934–82) states, freely infiltrate the heart and minds of the human collectivity: "Satan...is now entering naked into human history."[11] From this perspective the notion of "malefic influences"[12] and the phenomenon of "unconscious satanism"[13] can be better understood, as they reflect the hidden forces that remain in large part undetected and misunderstood. With this said, this deceptive presence is not limited to a single entity as is often assumed, but can take on a host of myriad forms, as Ananda K. Coomaraswamy (1877–1947) writes: "Satan is not a real and single Person, but a severally postulated personality, a 'Legion.'"[14] Freud wrote to Fliess on January 24, 1897 with a description of what he hopes psychoanalysis may become, at least for its inner circle or secret committee: "I dream, therefore, of a primeval devil religion with rites that are carried on secretly, and understand the harsh therapy of the witches' judges."[15]

The first place where we find attempts to psychologize the origin of the Devil is in the classic study by Breuer and Freud, *Studies on Hysteria* (1893–95): "The split-off mind is the devil with which the unsophisticated observation of early superstitious times believed that these patients were possessed. It is true that a spirit alien to the patient's waking consciousness holds sway in him; but the spirit is not in fact an alien one, but a part of his own."[16]

Freud attributes the birth of evil to a psychological cause in a paper entitled "A Neurosis of Demonical Possession in the Seventeenth Century" published in 1922. Freud writes:

> What in those days were thought to be evil spirits to us are base and evil wishes, the derivatives of impulses which have been rejected and repressed. In one respect only do we not subscribe to the explanation of these phenomena current in mediaeval times; we have abandoned the projection of them into the outer world, attributing their origin instead to the inner life of the patient in whom they manifest themselves.[17]

It was Russian-born psychoanalyst Immanuel Velikovsky (1895–1979) who first referred to the Freudian "Faust-pact" in 1941. It was the idea that Freud had a secret wish to enter the Roman Catholic Church in order to achieve his worldly ambitions. Velikovsky writes:

"the most important determination of almost all dreams mentioned by Freud is his inner struggle for unhampered advancement: In order to get ahead he would have to conclude a Faust-pact; he would have to sell his soul to the [Catholic] Church."[18] Freud analyzes a painter named Christoph Haitzmann (1652–1700) who made a Satanic Pact with the Devil. Freud proposes three factors needed to enter a Satanic Pact: (1) that the individual suffer from depression; (2) that the depression be associated with the death the individual's father; and (3) that the individual be preoccupied about how to earn a livelihood. What is important to note here is that Freud met these criteria, as is evident in the Freudian corpus.

(1) *Freud struggled with depression.* Freud refers to his condition as a "deep inner crisis" of "depression."[19] Elsewhere he writes: "I do not enjoy anything, for weeks I haven't borne a cheerful expression, and in short I am so unhappy."[20] At other times he has expressed: "I am now having a fit of gloom."[21] Jones confirms in his authorized biography that Freud was challenged by depression when he writes: "For many years he suffered from periodic depressions and fatigue or apathy, neurotic symptoms which later took the form of anxiety attacks."[22] Bakan suggested: "Freud suffered from acute depressions. His self-analysis, and his development of psychoanalysis, were the cure for his depression."[23]

(2) *The death of Freud's father was severe for him.* Freud regarded the death of his father as "the most poignant loss."[24]

(3)*Freud was preoccupied with money.*[25] Freud disclosed his financial dilemma with his then-fiancée Martha Bernays: "I have no money"[26] and elsewhere: "it is too painful for me to admit my lack of money."[27] He also writes of "the worry about holding one's own, finding something new to make the world sit up and bring not only recognition from the few but also attract the many, the well-paying public."[28] At other times, he speaks about his fear of poverty due to his family's financial troubles during his upbringing: "My state of mind also depends very much on my earnings...I once knew helpless poverty and have constant fear of it."[29] He also describes "poverty, long struggle for success, little favor among men, oversensitiveness, nervousness, and worries."[30] In a letter to Jung he refers to his preoccupation with his finances as a "money complex"[31] and expresses the following about both Jung and himself: "You see, we both of us had nothing."[32] Freud appeared to be consciously obsessed with generating more money, as he writes: "Money is laughing gas for me."[33]

The question remains, as Freud asks, "Why does one sell oneself to the Devil"[34] or make a pact with the Devil? Bakan suggests: "precisely because Freud did not accept the supernatural reality of the Devil, he could permit himself the full exploitation of the metaphor."[35] Christoph Haitzmann, according to Freud, "sold himself to the Devil, therefore, in order to be freed from a state of depression. Truly an excellent motive, in the judgment of those who can understand the torment of these states and who appreciate, moreover, how little the art of medicine can do to alleviate the malady."[36] Vitz suggests that Freud's cocaine use was linked to his Satanic Pact: "it is clear that cocaine for Freud was thoroughly linked to the Devil, and, indeed, was connected from the beginning to some kind of pact."[37] At the very least for those that may deny Freud's Satanic Pact with the Devil, it could be supported that "malefic influences"[38] consumed his interior life: "Freud's psyche was to some extent fractured into separate centers, and...at least one significant part of him was identified with the Devil."[39] We are reminded of the well-known dictum: "For what shall it profit a man, if he shall gain the whole world, and lose his own soul?" (Mark 8:36).

Leonard Shengold, Clinical Professor of Psychiatry at the New York University School of Medicine, analyzes Freud's struggle with Jung as documented in their correspondence and confirms Freud's involvement with the diabolical: "Freud discovered that he was Mephistopheles as well as Faust; the devils were not without but within."[40] Freud could be seen as having made a Satanic Pact with the Devil in order to individuate, as Jungian psychology instructs: "the devil is a preliminary stage of individuation."[41] With this noted, Jung clearly demonstrates how the Devil and evil itself can be reduced to a psychological phenomenon: "The devil is a variant of the 'shadow' archetype, i.e., of the dangerous aspect of the unrecognized dark half of the personality."[42] As a Freudian apologist or revisionist stated: "In terms of the devil's pact, the abandoning of self corresponds to the selling of one's soul. In psychiatric terms we call it the 'alienation from self.'"[43]

Freud elaborates further on the healing powers of the Devil by way of defending the doctrine of the "talking cure":

> Why should we hold aloof from this obvious and natural explanation? The state of affairs would then simply be that someone in a helpless state, tortured with melancholic depression, sells himself to the Devil, in whose healing powers he reposes the greatest confidence. That the depression was caused by the father's demise would then be quite irrelevant: it could quite conceivably have been due to some other cause. This seems a force-

ful and reasonable objection. We hear once more the familiar criticism of psychoanalysis that it regards the simplest affairs in an unduly subtle and complicated way, discovers secrets and problems where none exist, and that it achieves this by magnifying the most insignificant trifles to support far-reaching and bizarre conclusions.[44]

Freud ignores the essential reminder about not being seduced by the world of forms and the quest for power which leads to the forfeiting one's connection with the Divine: "For what shall it profit a man, if he shall gain the whole world, and lose his own soul?" (Mark 8:36).

In the same paper, Freud emphasizes that today "neuroses appear in a hypochondriacal guise, masked as organic diseases...the neurosis of olden times masquerad[ed] in demonological shape."[45] Freud further adds: "Despite the somatic ideology of the era of 'exact' science, the demonological theory of these dark ages has in the long run justified itself."[46]

The subheading for the third part of this paper is "The Devil as a Father-Substitute,"[47] as it is here that Freud further outlines his psychodynamic theory of "the Devil as a substitute for the loved parent."[48] Freud expands upon this theory:

> God is a father-substitute, or more correctly, an exalted father, or yet again, a reproduction of the father as seen and met with in childhood—as the individual sees him in his own childhood and as mankind saw him in prehistoric times in the father of the primal horde...It requires no great analytic insight to divine that God and the Devil were originally one and the same, a single figure which was later split into two bearing opposed characteristics...The father is thus the individual prototype of both God and the Devil. The fact that the figure of the primal father was that of a being with unlimited potentialities of evil, bearing much more resemblance to the Devil than to God, must have left an indelible stamp on all religions.[49]

Psychoanalysis exploits the conscious utilization of the super-ego in the transference process. Bakan explains: "In the course of psychoanalysis the patient learns that the expected punishment will not materialize. The transference is essential; for unless the patient identifies the figure of the psychoanalyst with the superego, then the permissiveness is essentially ineffectual. The psychoanalyst listens to the patient's discussion of his deepest 'sins' and does not blame."[50]

Bakan continues by providing a further glimpse into the inner workings of psychoanalysis and how the Devil aids in absolving the individual of his or her guilt:

> More prosaically this can be stated as follows: The disease of the neurotic is his guilt. This guilt is, in itself, an evil and its removal is good. However, within the neurosis the guilt is a punishment for evil. Within the neurosis a counterforce to the punishing imago is required. Hence there is an alliance with such a counter-imago as will allow all to become open, accessible to consciousness. If God is the guilt-producing imago, then the Devil is the counterforce. But the Devil's very permissiveness is the cause of his own destruction. Having permitted all to become open, the infantile character of both imagos is revealed and "distance" with respect to each is won.[51]

Perry explains how the Devil acts as counterforce to the integral function with which God facilitates the human psyche: "God allegorically speaking holds the suppressed material, which is at the origin of a person's neurosis, subjectively in the 'unconscious.' A counter-force, the Devil allegorically speaking, is needed to render the material conscious. Through an alliance of the ego with this metaphorical Devil, objectivity is achieved and the neurosis liquidated."[52]

"Now what is the Devil, psychologically? The answer is eminently simple, on one level. *The Devil is the suspended superego*...The Devil is that part of the person which permits him to violate the precepts of the superego."[53] Bakan notes that "If Moses was the super-ego, then the Devil was Freud's necessary ally in his fight against him."[54]

Here is where it is visible that Freudian therapy trespasses upon the domain of religion and the precious function that it plays in this secular context that pathologizes and denies the existence of the Divine. The diabolical nature of this outlook, is further suggested: "The manifestations of compulsion to repeat...exhibit to a high degree an instinctual character and, when they act in opposition to the pleasure principle, give the appearance of some 'daemonic' force at work."[55]

Freud's official biographer makes an interesting observation, providing a clue into the architect behind the psychoanalytic revolution: "What a daemonic intuition must have been at work!"[56] Jones continues: "Perhaps we are nearing a clue to the mysterious problem of how it was that just this man was destined to discover psychoanalysis and reveal the unconscious mind of man."[57] Freud, while hailed as a genius by his inner circle, clearly suffered from a "diabolical cleverness."[58]

Freud was keenly interested in a book published in 1914 by French poet and novelist Anatole France (1844–1924), entitled *The Revolt of the Angels*. He encouraged his disciples to deepen their knowledge of its contents. Freud is reported to have commented upon this book, making the following statement: "War will produce war and victory defeat. God defeated will become Satan, Satan victorious will become God."[59] This reveals Freud's reversal of the spiritual order, which appears to be a doctrine at the heart of the psychoanalytic "talking cure." We could also provide another example of this when the master writes in a letter to Jung: "When the day of 'recognition' comes, it will be to the present what the gruesome magic of the Inferno is to the holy boredom of the Paradiso. (That is, of course, the other way around.)"[60]

Critiques leveled at Freudian psychology have made comparisons between the "talking cure" and possession: "psychoanalysis is already demonology."[61] Likewise Freud makes an interesting comparison between psychoanalysis and possession: "Do you remember that I always said that the medieval theory of possession held by the ecclesiastical courts was identical with our theory of a foreign body and the splitting of consciousness?"[62] To the surprise of those who assume that Jung was more balanced in his outlook, he interestingly attributes the origins of modern psychology to the Devil, as he illustrates in the following: "It is a technique [psychoanalysis or analytic psychology] we have learnt from the devil...The menacing and dangerous thing about analysis is that the individual is apparently understood: the devil eats his soul away."[63] The Promethean agenda underlying psychoanalysis takes on the appearance of being a secular and pseudo-religious exorcism in modern guise: "No one who, like me [Freud], conjures up the most evil of those half-tamed demons that inhabit the human breast, and seeks to wrestle with them, can expect to come through the struggle unscathed."[64]

In closing, we might add that Freud interestingly commented to one of his associates: "Do you not know that I am the Devil? All my life I have had to play the Devil, in order that others would be able to build the most beautiful cathedral with the materials that I produced."[65] In a similar fashion, Sherrard observes: "Jung regarded it as his task to redeem the devil."[66] Perhaps this is what Jung meant when he referred to "our Promethean conquest."[67]

[T]he one thing certain in any case is that there is something here that fits in perfectly with the exigencies of a "control" exerted over inferior psychic influences, themselves already essentially "malefic," in order that they may be used more directly with certain defined ends in view, in conformity with the pre-established "plan" of the work of subversion, for which purpose they are now being "unchained" in our world.[68]

An individual who is captive to the empirical ego, who has not cultivated a sufficient level of self-domination, not only is unable to navigate on his or her own through the psycho-spiritual labyrinth, but can unknowingly deliver himself up to what is essentially diabolical. Within Islamic spirituality there is the following Sufi adage: "He who does not have a shaykh [guide] has Satan for his shaykh [guide]."[69]

We refer to the biblical passage regarding the presence of evil that has become widely disseminated in the present day and that provides a sense of hope: "For there shall be no hereafter for evil, illumination of the wicked shall be extinguished" (Proverbs 24:20). The relativization of truth has absolutized evil, and the consequences have been detrimental to the whole of civilization and society. As Burckhardt writes, "Man, by virtue of his own central position in the cosmos, is able to transcend his specific norm; he can also betray it, and sink lower; *corruptio optimi pessima* [corruption of the best is the worst]."[70]

Chapter 15

The Ethical Void and the Crisis of
the Super-Ego

"Psychoanalysis is out, under a therapeutic disguise, to do away entirely with the moral faculty in man."[1]—D. H. Lawrence

Freud himself writes, "But even ordinary normal morality has a harshly restraining, cruelly prohibiting quality."[2] The doctrine of the "talking cure" intentionally and decisively uproots the human being's connection with his or her community, sacred tradition, and the Divine, essentially alienating the individual from the cosmos. He emphasizes: "There is no golden rule which applies to everyone: every man must find out for himself in what particular fashion he can be saved."[3] Lasch underscores that the predicament of the present day is a moral dilemma: "the crisis of contemporary culture, in effect, [is] a crisis of the superego."[4] This is to say in Freudian terms the triumph of the id is equivalent to the decay of the super-ego. Within psychoanalytic structural theory of the human psyche, morality derives from the super-ego and pertains to feelings of guilt and conscience. As Freud confirms, "the *super-ego...*functions as our *conscience.*"[5] He adds that the demise of the Oedipus complex gave birth to the super-ego: "The super-ego is in fact the heir to the Oedipus complex and is only established after that complex has been disposed of."[6]

"Freud conceived of a 'revolutionary' psychology, according to which the passions would at first subvert and finally overwhelm rational control."[7] The destructive repercussions of undergoing the psychoanalytic initiation are underscored by Rieff: "'man below man' of...psychoanalytic instinctualists...set loose by Freud."[8] According to Freud, "the price we pay for our advance in civilization is a loss of happiness through the heightening of the sense of guilt."[9] Herbert Marcuse (1898–1979),[10] a prominent figure within the Frankfurt School or The Institute for Social Research (Institute für Sozialforschung), writes: "According to Freud, the history of man is the history of his repression."[11]

Freud explains how the super-ego develops during an individual's earliest years from the social environment until it transfers and becomes part of the makeup of an individual's outlook: "When we were little children we knew these higher natures, we admired them and feared them; and later we took them into ourselves."[12] Yet, as cultural critic Neil Postman (1931–2003) asserts, Freud's theory is destructive and antagonistic to childhood itself: *"without a well-developed idea of shame, childhood cannot exist."*[13] Freud's antinomianism not only attacked the foundations of traditional morality as found within religion, but also was an instrumental attack and subversion of Western civilization. "Therapy no longer seeks merely to bring unconscious wishes to light, so as to analyze the consequences of their repression; instead, it seeks to dissolve the very machinery of repression. It assumes that psychic health and personal liberation are synonymous with an absence of inner restraints, inhibitions, and 'hangups.'"[14]

Freud asserts: "The great ethical element in ΨA work is truth and again truth and this should suffice for most people. Courage and truth are of what they are mostly deficient."[15] He adds: "We can present society with a blunt calculation that what is described as its morality calls for a bigger sacrifice than it is worth and that its proceedings are not based on honesty and do not display wisdom."[16] This is what Rieff regarded as the Freudian "ethic of honesty."[17] Freud was again adept at playing with words, and more important what he considers to be "truth" cannot be taken as truth as it is commonly understood or as that which is affirmed by the sapiential traditions.

"Freud's discarding of moral values...has contributed toward making the analyst just as blind as the patient."[18] Due to the ethical vacuum that has been created by the undermining and subverting of traditional morality, as known across the faith traditions of the world, the notions of good and evil, right and wrong have been made into relative concepts. Likewise, the norms rooted in the sacred have also been uprooted, so that the binary terms of normal and abnormal no longer have meaning for most individuals. The ethical vacuum is a systemic dilemma within the mental health field, as psychiatrist Nathaniel S. Lehrman indicates:

> The tendency to avoid moral issues is widespread and deep throughout the world of mental health, in a great measure because its primary orientation is individualistic. This in turn is largely the result of at least two fundamental scientific errors made by Freud and subsequently carried over into the entire field. These errors are the confusion of harsh enforcement of the moral codes with the existence of the codes themselves, and the belief that

individual needs stand in permanent, irreconcilable conflict with social laws.[19]

The psychoanalytic doctrine does not aim at the transformation of the human being but at his adjustment to a culture or civilization that is psychologically unbalanced. Marcuse states: "while psychoanalytic theory recognizes that the sickness of the individual is ultimately caused and sustained by the sickness of his civilization, psychoanalytic therapy aims at curing the individual so that he can continue to function as part of a sick civilization without surrendering to it altogether."[20] Freud's daughter Anna Freud (1895–1982) also confirms that the doctrine of the "talking cure" is about adaptation to the individual's environment: "In working with an adult we have to confine ourselves entirely to helping him to adapt himself to his environment."[21]

What we are left with is relativism on a mass scale, leading to what has been termed as the "tyranny of psychology,"[22] as Rieff explains: "Normality is not a statistical conception, for the majority is no longer normal. Normality is an ethical ideal, pitted against the actual abnormal...Being essentially negative, normality is an ever-retreating ideal...Nor can the psychological man forget himself in pursuit of the normal, for his normality consists of a certain kind of self-awareness...psychoanalysis is an expression of a popular tyranny."[23]

Jung discloses that following the morality of the faith traditions of the world is no longer necessary and that salvation is impossible for those who do not participate in his secular pseudo-religion of Jungian psychology: "If we are conscious, morality no longer exists. If we are not conscious, we are still slaves, and we are accursed if we obey not the law. He [Jung] said that if we belong to the secret church, then we belong, and we need not worry about it, but can go our own way. If we do not belong, no amount of teaching or organization can bring us there."[24]

To be human is to be aware of one's conduct and to act accordingly: "Assuredly man is conscious of himself [or of his own soul] even if he offers excuses" (Koran 75:14–15). Unless the human being cultivates self-domination, he or she is under the control of the lower tendencies: "a man's foes shall be they of his own household" (Matthew 10:36). Freud has inverted traditional morality as it was known across the diverse societies and civilizations of the world. In a letter written on November 17, 1911 to Sándor Ferenczi, Freud states: "A man should not strive to eliminate his complexes but to get into accord with them: they are legitimately what directs his conduct in the world."[25] It is also worth citing Jung, who expresses a similar point of view: "The patient has not to learn how to get rid of his neurosis, but how to bear it."[26] Freud does not make a distinction between what is a natural human limitation and a vice or a complex. He in fact emphasizes the impossibility of being able to live in accordance with traditional morality, as is indicated here: "The commandment, "Love thy neighbor as thyself,"[27] is the strongest defense against human aggressiveness and an excellent example of the unpsychological [expectations] of the cultural super-ego. The commandment is impossible to fulfil...anyone who follows such a precept in present-day civilization only puts himself at a disadvantage *vis-à-vis* the person who disregards it."[28]

Aḥādīth such as the following confirm the need for good actions in accordance with the Divine: "Among the best of you is the most beautiful in character traits." And similarly, "I was sent to complete the beautiful character traits." Only the Divine is absolutely good: "None is good but God alone" (Luke 18:19). Both religion and its mystical or inner dimension confirm the necessity for noble character, which corresponds to the Divine and defines what it means to be human: "Assuming the character traits of God—that is Sufism."[29] After all, which virtue is the most important? According to Saint Makarios of Egypt, "the virtues are linked one to the other, and follow as it were a sacred sequence, one depending on the other."[30]

A way of overcoming the individual's lower impulses has been known since the earliest times throughout the world's plenary traditions as "spiritual warfare." For example, the Guatama Buddha himself confirms the following in the *Dhammapada*: "One may conquer in battle a thousand times a thousand men, yet he is the best of conquerors who conquers himself."[31] Within Christianity, spiritual warfare may be exemplified with: "For we wrestle not against flesh and blood, but against principalities, against powers, against the rulers of darkness of this world, against spiritual wickedness in high places" (Ephesians 6:12).[32] The concept of spiritual warfare has also been used within the Shamanic or primordial religion of the First Peoples:

> [T]he sun dancer and the Sun Dance itself will bless all of the tribe and all creation through the inner, spiritual warfare...The warrior fights an enemy who is on the outside; the sun dancer wages a war on an enemy within himself. Each of us must fight a continuing battle to keep to the spiritual values that represent our traditional heritage. If we fail to be continually alert in our prayers and our attitudes and to use good sense in all that we do,

then we will fail in our interior war. In olden days, this interior warfare had the support of the whole tribe, and our life itself helped to guide us in our personal struggle. Nowadays, we must follow the Sun Dance way all the more carefully, because it contains the key to our sacred warfare.[33]

The conflict between the human being and the world that Freudian psychology depicts is in reality a spiritual battle between the higher and lower nature of the human being; animality seeks the world of form by gravitating to the sensory, while the theomorphic identity seeks transcendence and gravitates to the Divine. Rūmī observes,

> Outside this world of which we are speaking there is another world for us to seek. This world and its delights cater to the animality of man; these all feed his animality, whilst the root principle, man, goes into a decline. After all, they say, "Man is a rational animal." So man consists of two things. That which feeds his animality in this material world is these lusts and desires. But as for that which is his true essence, its food is knowledge and wisdom and the sight of God. The animality in man flees away from God, whilst his humanity flees away from this world. ["One of you is an unbeliever, and one of you a believer" (Koran 64:2).] Two persons are warring within this one entity.[34]

Ramana Maharshi verifies the universal practice of subduing the passions by stilling or quieting the mind as it applies across the religions, pointing to the interconnectedness of mental health and spirituality as expressed by the perennial psychology: "All scriptures without any exception proclaim that for attaining Salvation the mind should be subdued."[35] And it could likewise be said that without reliance on the Spirit/Intellect the human being is unable to manage baser impulses: "Without the aid of trained emotions the intellect is powerless against the animal organism."[36]

"Surely the soul commands to evil, save whom my Lord may show mercy" (Koran 12:53). The doctrines and methods of the perennial philosophy and its perennial psychology do not advocate *suppression*, but rather self-domination, as informed by the sapiential traditions. Within Islamic spirituality, known as Sufism, there are four degrees of the human psyche ascending from the animal soul (*al-nafs al-ḥaywāniyah*), the passional soul (*al-nafs al-ammārah* or the "soul which incites" to evil), the discerning or intelligent soul (*al-nafs al-lawwāmah* or "the soul which blames"), and the intellective soul (*al-*

nafs al-mutma'innah or "the soul at peace," the human psyche reintegrated in Spirit or *Rūḥ*).[37]

"One way to train the *nafs* is to resist its desires. However, if we wish to resist, we know that we must not resist by opposing or suppressing it, for when we do, it will rear up somewhere else, seeking gratification of its desires. Thus, it has been said that to resist the *nafs* through the *nafs* is an error."[38] Similarly, "Resistance to the *nafs* is the basis of all spiritual practice and the perfection of all spiritual endeavor. Only through this can the devotee find the way to God, for conformity with the *nafs* is destruction for the devotee, while resistance to it is salvation."[39] From the earliest times diverse human communities were instructed to conduct themselves in the following way: "So vie with one another in good deeds" (Koran 2:148).

Without the inclusion of what transcends and integrates the human psyche into Spirit, no psychotherapy can be effective. Schuon points out: "The fallen soul is like an untamed animal."[40] Richard Krafft-Ebing, a contemporary of Freud, held a similar view on the battling forces within the human being: "Life is a never-ceasing duel between the animal instinct and morality."[41] Freud himself lamented the fundamental limitations of his psychoanalytic "talking cure": "As a rule the repression is only temporarily removed and is promptly reinstated."[42] Ironically, Freud claims that "The doctrine of repression is the foundation-stone on which the whole structure of psychoanalysis rests."[43]

What is needed is to go to the transpersonal root of human identity and not focus solely on the empirical ego. That simplistic notions of repression do not work was known by the sapiential traditions as indicated here: "When we repress our desires, they do not disappear but stay beneath the surface and continue to exert their influence. Prohibition arouses desire and suggests stratagems for satisfying it."[44] Osborne indicates the essential role of spiritual practice for not only rising above the lower tendencies, but integrating them into the higher nature: "the process of *sadhana* [spiritual practice] squeezes out the lower tendencies in a person and brings them to the surface in the process of casting them out, just as psycho-analysis is supposed to [in theory but is incapable of doing so]."[45]

The void that is felt in the outer world is one and the same void that is felt within the human being. It is the human search to remedy this vacuum that can either lead individuals on the quest of reintegrating into the Divine or of pursuing the gratification of endless and confusing desires. Larchet writes,

Man believes he can remedy this frustration by the very means which in truth is its cause: instead of recognizing that the void he senses is the absence of God in him, and that consequently only God can fill it, he wants to see therein the call to possess and delight in new sensible objects that he believes could satisfy this void. So as to avoid the pain following every pleasure, and to put an end to the deep frustration of his desire for infinite delight, fallen man perseveres in his search for new pleasures, not resting in his unbridled running after desires. He gathers and multiplies his pleasures in an attempt to reconstitute the totality, continuity, and absoluteness for which he is nostalgic, believing in his delusion to find the infinite in the indefinite.[46]

Paradoxically within Freudian psychology exists the notion of sublimation, which appears to be a defense of morality and the super-ego. Jung avows: "Freud has invented the idea of sublimation to save us from the imaginary claws of the unconscious."[47] Sublimation is defined as "the power to exchange its [the sexual instinct's] nearest aim for others of higher value which are not sexual."[48] Freud wrote to James J. Putnam explaining that "Sublimation, that is striving toward higher goals, is of course one of the best means of overcoming the urgency of our drives. But one can consider doing this only after ΨA work has lifted the repressions."[49] Elsewhere, while not utilizing the term *sublimation*, Freud implies this concept when he explains: "Psycho-analysis is an instrument to enable the ego to achieve a progressive conquest of the id."[50]

Freud illustrates how society, civilization, and social order itself, while contributing to progress, undermine the individual desires of human sexuality: "historians of civilization seem to be unanimous in opinion that such deflection of sexual motive powers from sexual aims to new aims, a process which merits the name of *sublimation*, has furnished powerful components for all cultural accomplishments. We will, therefore, add that the same process acts in the development of every individual, and that it begins to act in the sexual latency period."[51]

Again, psychoanalytic theory upholds:

We believe that civilization was forged by the driving force of vital necessity, at the cost of instinct-satisfaction, and that the process is to a large extent constantly repeated anew, since each individual who newly enters the human community repeats the sacrifices of his instinct-satisfaction for the sake of the common good. Among the instinctive forces thus utilized, the sexual impulses play a significant role. They are thereby sublimated, i.e., they are diverted from their sexual goals and directed to ends socially higher and no longer sexual.[52]

Freud stresses that there is a clash between human sexuality and social order that cannot be remedied, as they are antithetical to each other: "Society can conceive of no more serious menace to its civilization than would arise through the satisfying of the sexual instincts by their redirection toward their original goals."[53]

Likewise, Freud warns that human beings can become ill if they attempt to sublimate beyond their individual capacity: "It must further be borne in mind that many people fall ill precisely from an attempt to sublimate their instincts beyond the degree permitted by their organization and that in those who have a capacity for sublimation the process usually takes place of itself as soon as their inhibitions have been overcome by analysis."[54]

Again, Freud upholds that "Holding back aggressiveness is in general unhealthy and leads to illness."[55] Fromm suggests that the Freudian theory of sublimation is problematic: "The concept of 'sublimation' is questionable even when Freud applied it to sexual, and especially to pregenital instincts."[56] Freud again overlooks the fact that "God tasks no soul beyond its capacity" (Koran 2:286).

Through the spiritual practices offered by the sapiential traditions, authentic self-domination becomes possible through an operative spiritual method.

The denial of the existence of evil as an objective entity—to say nothing of the existence of God—is to assume that religion has no supernatural basis. Moreover, what is lost sight of in this assumption that repression leads to neurosis is, firstly, that every human being has to overcome himself otherwise he will become a devil, and, secondly, that archetypally the process of repression is related to the principle of conversion as fermentation. Indeed, one of the most cogent images for the principle of "self-domination" or for the *noble* "repression" of baser instincts is the alchemist's athanor, or oven (symbol of the prayer cell), in which the precious elixir (our vital but still unconverted substance) is hermetically sealed, upon which it is then heated (the fire of concentrated prayer directed by the vow of commitment to God) so as to convert it from mortal bitterness to immortal sweetness.[57]

Modern psychology, with very few exceptions, is limited to the horizontal domain and cannot be a complete psychology without a vertical or spiritual dimension. Perry explains why the vertical or spiritual domain in the "science of the soul" is not only needed, but a prerequisite for any complete psychology:

> To explain man through [modern] psychology when what is really needed is a pneumatology or a "science of the Spirit," without which psychology—or the study of the soul—can only amount to the blind leading the blind because no matter how erudite or subtle our analysis will be we cannot escape the conundrum of the mortal attempting to define the Immortal; we cannot escape by our own means the narrow labyrinth of human observations and speculations unless we can appeal to a higher principle.[58]

Pope Pius XII emphasizes that "The moral struggle to remain on the right path does not prove that it is impossible to follow that path, nor does it authorize any drawing back."[59] The destructive nature of psychoanalysis on the individual and the human collectivity is made abundantly clear in the following: "That desire, if not fulfilled, will lead to pathology makes of self-indulgence man's highest goal. It is a kind of treason to the self, and possibly to others, to deny one-self anything."[60] We are reminded by the Islamic tradition that "Virtue is to worship God as if you see Him, and if you see Him not, surely He sees you!" (*Ḥadīth* of Gabriel). Likewise, within the Christian tradition, "Ye shall know the Truth and the Truth shall make you free" (John 8:32).

Chapter 16

Freud and the Question of Jewish Identity

"[P]sycho-analysis clothed in the ancient language which has been awakened to a new life by the will of the Jewish people."[1]—Sigmund Freud

Freud quotes a verse from Goethe alluding to the role of the Jewish tradition in his life and its usurpation for his own messianic mission: "What thou hast inherited from thy fathers, / Acquire it to make it thine."[2] The loss of faith within the Jewish tradition has in turn led to the secular pseudo-religion of psychoanalysis. Scholar of Jewish History Yosef Hayim Yerushalmi (1932–2009) writes: "Jews who had lost faith in the God of their fathers sought and found a spectrum of novel secular Jewish surrogates."[3] Those that defected from the Jewish tradition found their home in the secular faith of psychoanalysis: "Jews alienated from the synagogue began to congregate in the temple of Freud."[4] Much has been written about Freud and his relationship to Judaism, which has underscored the complexity of this relationship, and yet we are told that "it is impossible to understand psychoanalysis...without taking into account the role of Judaism."[5]

What is known is that Freud's Jewish identity prevailed until his death, as has been documented by Freud himself: "My parents were Jews, and I have remained a Jew myself."[6] And elsewhere: "I have never disowned my Jewishness."[7] Freud also admits that the problem of Jewish character "has pursued me throughout the whole of my life."[8] According to Jones, Freud "felt himself to be Jewish to the core, and it evidently meant a great deal to him. He had the common Jewish sensitiveness to the slightest hint of anti-Semitism and he made very few friends who were not Jews."[9]

Freud recognized the supremacy of his own ethnic makeup, as he speaks of the "superior Jewish race."[10] American psychologist Kevin MacDonald adds, "An attitude of Jewish superiority to gentiles not only characterized Freud but pervaded the entire movement."[11] Professor Dennis B. Klein additionally supports this notion and its negative impact on the development of psychoanalysis: "The feeling of

Jewish superiority alienated many non-Jews within the [psychoanalytic] movement and encouraged many outside the movement to dismiss as hypocritical the humanitarian claims of the psychoanalysts."[12]

While Freud's Jewish identity is well documented, it has been contrasted with his militant disbelief in all religion, including Judaism: "He discovered that although he was not a believing Jew, he remained a psychological one."[13] Yet, the matter is not as straightforward as might be imagined. What is unclear is whether Freud had a secret devotional life, practicing Judaism privately, and how this influence has informed the creation of psychoanalysis, as he often portrayed himself as a staunch atheist in his public life and denied such an influence. Because of the ambiguity of Freud's religious affiliation, it could be assumed that what is presented by the inner circle of the Freudian orthodoxy or the official biographical accounts contains the exclusive and verbatim information of his life without researching further. Portraying this narrative, Gay indicates: "Freud had grown up with no religious instruction at home, came to Vienna University as an atheist, and left it as an atheist—with persuasive scientific arguments."[14] The official biography similarly documents his atheism: "[Freud] went through his life from beginning to end as a natural atheist: that is to say, one who saw no reason for believing in the existence of any supernatural Being and who felt no emotional need for such a belief."[15] Jones adds: "He grew up devoid of any belief in a God or immortality, and does not appear ever to have felt the need of it."[16]

In 1925, Freud wrote a letter to the Jewish Press Centre in Zürich indicating:

> I can say that I stand as far apart from the Jewish religion as from all other religions: that is to say, they are of great significance to me as a subject of scientific interest, but I have no part in them emotionally. On the other hand I have always had a strong feeling of solidarity with my fellow-people, and have always encouraged it in my children as well. We have all remained in the Jewish denomination.[17]

In 1926, due to the prevailing political situation, Freud avowed his Jewish identity in an interview with George Sylvester Viereck (1884–1962): "My language is German. My culture, my attainments are German. I considered myself a German intellectually, until I noticed the growth of anti-Semitic prejudice in Germany and in German Austria. Since that time, I consider myself no longer a German. I prefer to call myself a Jew."[18]

Elsewhere, Jones contradicts the official narrative and confirms the opposite regarding Freud and religion: "Freud himself was certainly conversant with all Jewish customs and festivals."[19] Freud himself informs us that "My deep engrossment in the Bible story (almost as soon as I had learnt the art of reading) had, as I recognized much later, an enduring effect upon the direction of my interest."[20] On Freud's thirty-fifth birthday his father, who had grown up as an Orthodox Jew, gave him a Bible with a Hebrew inscription:

My dear Son,

It was in the seventh year of your age that the spirit of God began to move you to learning. I would say the spirit of God speaketh to you: "Read in My book; there will be open to thee sources of knowledge and of the intellect." It is the Book of Books; it is the well that wise men have digged and from which lawgivers have drawn the waters of their knowledge.

Thou hast seen in this Book the vision of the Almighty, thou hast heard willingly, thou hast done and hast tried to fly high upon the wings of the Holy Spirit. Since then I have preserved the same Bible. Now, on your thirty-fifth birthday I have brought it out from its retirement and I send it to you as a token of love from your old father.[21]

While Freud does not definitively confirm the Jewish origins of psychoanalysis, at the same time he does not completely deny these claims: "I am not sure that your opinion, which looks upon psychoanalysis as a direct product of the Jewish mind, is correct, but if it is I wouldn't be ashamed. Although I have been alienated from the religion of my forebears for a long time, I have never lost the feeling of solidarity with my people."[22] Freud adds: "the Jews altogether, have celebrated me like a national hero, although my service to the Jewish cause is confined to the single point that I [Freud] have never denied my Jewishness."[23]

It also remains ambiguous to what extent the mystical roots of Judaism, Hasidism, and the Kabbalah have played in the formation of psychoanalysis; this was something that Jung alludes to when writing: "one would have to take a deep plunge into the history of the Jewish mind. This would carry us beyond Jewish orthodoxy into the subterranean workings of Hasidism...and then into the intricacies of the Kabbalah, which still remains unexplored psychologically."[24] Freud himself made references to Jewish mysticism, yet they were ambiguous and infrequently made, such as the following example: "You will see in this another confirmation of the specifically Jewish nature of my mysticism."[25] Yet he contradicts this when he writes elsewhere in reference to Jung: "We Jews have an easier time [than Jung], having no mystical element."[26]

A distinction needs to be made between Freud's Jewish identity and his acceptance of the religious doctrines of the Jewish tradition, as Bakan asserts:

> It is important to distinguish between Freud's sense of identity as a Jew and his acceptance of Jewish religious doctrines. The intensity of his feelings on his Jewish identity was matched by his rejection of religious doctrine and practice. His works on religion are *against* the classical Judeo-Christian religious doctrines. Yet his sense of Jewish identity was so strong that we might consider his *genetic* conception of the Jew, most clearly asserted in his *Moses and Monotheism*, as the theoretical counterpart of his deep feeling of Jewish identity.[27]

Freud posed a central and yet ironic question regarding the birth of psychoanalysis to Pfister in 1918 regarding his Jewish identity: "why was it that none of all the pious ever discovered psycho-analysis? Why did it have to wait for a completely godless Jew?"[28] Freud's admission establishes his Jewish identity, and yet he makes an interesting point: why was the founder of psychoanalysis a Jew rather than a member of one of the other Abrahamic monotheisms, a Christian or a Muslim? Given that the presence of Muslims living in Vienna or Europe at that time reflected a rather small makeup of the population, the task of developing psychoanalysis would have been left to either a Jew or a Christian. With this said, Freud does confirm that the origins of psychoanalytic psychology by a Jew were not accidental. Freud himself remarks: "Nor is it perhaps entirely a matter of chance that the first advocate of psychoanalysis was a Jew."[29] Alphonse Maeder asserts a similar position as that of the master: "I am convinced that ΨA had to be discovered by a Semite, that the Semitic spirit is particularly suited for analysis."[30] A. A. Brill notes the exclusive Jewish consciousness behind the creation of the psychoanalytic revolution:

> One of the arguments that has been hurled at psychoanalysis on a few occasions is that its originator was a Jew, implying thereby that the theories expressed by Freud do not apply to the rest of

mankind...Freud's Jewish decent—constitution—as well as the environment to which he was subjected because of it—fate—exerted considerable influence on his personality. One might say that only a Jewish genius, forged in the crucible of centuries of persecution, could have offered himself so willingly on the altar of public opprobrium for the sake of demonstrating the truths of psychoanalysis.[31]

Despite his lack of religious observance growing up, we learn through his correspondence with Fliess and from Jones's biography that Freud was a member of B'nai B'rith (Sons of the Covenant).[32] It was through his membership with B'nai B'rith, which began on September 23, 1897 and not in 1895 as reported by Jones and Strachey, that Freud was provided with a platform and sounding board for his emerging psychoanalytic theories. This period was prior to his having a following or disciples, and occurred when he was in a rather isolated situation in which his first lecture, "On Dream Interpretation," was delivered, on December 7, 1897, to the Vienna Lodge brothers.[33] Freud recalls the significance of what it meant to belong to the B'nai B'rith and its place in the birth of psychoanalysis: "There was no question whatever of my convincing you of my new theories; but at a time when no one in Europe listened to me and I still had no disciples even in Vienna, you have me your kindly attention. You were my first audience."[34] Freud additionally writes: "That you are Jews could only be welcome to me, for I was myself a Jew, and it has always appeared to me not only undignified, but outright foolish to deny it."[35]

However, former protégé and Freudian renegade Wilhelm Reich (1897–1957) fundamentally challenges the belief that Freud was Jewish either in his religious outlook or his personal identity:

Freud had a severe conflict with Judaism. Here, he was bound down, too. On the one hand, out of protest against the persecution he had suffered, he maintained very bravely and very courageously that he was a Jew. But he wasn't. Freud was not Jewish...He didn't want to be a Jew. Never. He wasn't Jewish. I never felt he was Jewish. Neither did I feel Anna Freud as Jewish. They had nothing Jewish in them, either characterologically, religiously, or nationally.[36]

Freud interprets the phenomenon of anti-Semitism through a sexual lens: "The castration complex is the deepest unconscious root of anti-semitism; for even in the nursery little boys hear that a Jew has something cut off his penis—a piece of his penis, they think—and this gives them a right to despise Jews."[37]

In his prefatory notes to his revolutionary thesis made in his final book, *Moses and Monotheism*, he writes without reservation: "With the audacity of one who has little or nothing to lose."[38] However, earlier in his life, Freud was not without concern about how his attack waged on religion would negatively impact the psychoanalytic movement, as he comments: "whether the publication [*The Future of an Illusion*] of this work might not after all do harm. Not to a person, however, but to a cause—the cause of psycho-analysis."[39] This is a striking statement to make regarding the concluding work of the Freudian corpus, as this book intended "To deny a people the man [Moses] whom it praises as the greatest of its sons."[40] It challenges the very foundations of Jewish identity, asserting that the "original" Moses was an Egyptian. What does this say about Jewish identity and how Freud envisions it? Freud, however, was ambivalent about the book's publication, yet he unabashedly admits to his creative utilization of psycho-history in forging a new portrayal of Judaism: "I am quite prepared to hear anew the reproach that I have put forward my reconstruction of the early history of the tribe of Israel with undue and unjustified certitude. I shall not feel this criticism to be too harsh, since it finds an echo in my own judgment."[41]

It has been suggested that *Moses and Monotheism* is not a continuation of his thesis that religion and spirituality are an illusion and to be equated with psychopathology, but rather that the motivation for writing such a book is much more complex and nefarious: "this book [*Moses and Monotheism*] stands as an exorcism. It marks the renouncement on the part of Sigmund Freud the Jew of the value that his narcissism could still rightfully claim, the value of belonging to the race that engendered Moses and imparted ethical monotheism to the world."[42] Freud illustrates how central Moses is to the Jewish tradition:

> I started asking myself how the Jews acquired their particular character, and following my usual custom I went back to the earliest beginnings. I did not get far. I was astounded to find that already the first so to speak embryonic experience of the race, the influence of the man Moses and the exodus from Egypt, conditioned the entire further development up to the present day—like a regular trauma of early childhood in the case history of a neurotic individual. To begin with, there is the temporal conception

of life and the conquest of magic thought, the rejection of mysticism, both of which can be traced back to Moses himself...[43]

Bakan suggests that not only does Freud identify himself with Moses, to become the Lawgiver, but he ultimately destroys Moses, thereby appointing himself as the new Lawgiver: "If Freud conceives of himself as the new Lawgiver, then the new Lawgiver must at one and the same time be like unto Moses, the previous Lawgiver, whose place he must preempt, and must be destructive of Moses. The new Lawgiver must revoke the older Law. The identification with Moses turns into its opposite, the destruction of Moses."[44]

Having turned Moses into a Gentile, Freud then takes up the task of converting the biblical narrative. Freud states the following regarding this feat and its significance: "The distortion of a text is not unlike a murder."[45] Freud, however, sees his task as restoring the scriptural account to fit into psycho-history: "we may count on finding the suppressed and abnegated material hidden away somewhere, though in an altered shape and torn out of its original connection...it is not always easy to recognize it."[46]

R. M. Jurjevich emphasizes Freud's identity with Moses and that of his messianic mission to overthrow the old Lawgiver and to resurrect himself as the new Lawgiver:

> Freud suffered, among other psychological maldevelopments, from a messianic complex. He aspired to be the new Moses who would lead humanity out of the alleged wilderness of repressions, neuroses, sexual misperceptions and all kinds of unwisdom. He deluded himself that he would be the founder of scientifically acceptable morals, whatever they might be. In the process he unwittingly created a cult, a new sect, disguised under the cloak of science. His sect proved to be more destructive than salutary. In retrospect, Freud appears as anti-Moses.[47]

Gay describes Freud's relationship with the Jewish tradition in the following manner: "It was a Judaism without religion."[48] Freud discloses that "it would not be my fault if I remained to the end of my life what I now was—'an infidel Jew.'"[49] That is to say, as Freud put it, "I [Freud] was always an unbeliever."[50] A year before his death Freud confessed his career as an atheist: "Neither in my private life nor in my writings have I ever made a secret of my being an out-and-out unbeliever."[51]

Chapter 17

Anti-Semitism and the Vengeance
on Christianity

"Vengeance is mine, saith the Lord, I will repay."—Romans 12:19

Fromm provides a thought-provoking interpretation that, while not speaking directly about Freud, highlights potential motives underlying Freud's messianic mission that pivoted upon, or were even fueled by, his vengeance on Christianity: "It is as if in his passion for vengeance he elevates himself to the role of God...The act of vengeance may be his greatest hour just because of this self-elevation."[1] In 1937, French psychoanalyst René Laforgue (1894–1962) went to Vienna to advise Freud to leave the county because of the imminent threat of the Nazis, and Freud perplexingly responded with: "The Nazis? I am not afraid of them. Help me rather to combat my true enemy...Religion, the Roman Catholic Church."[2]

Regarding Freud's relationship with the Christian tradition, it has been suggested: "One of Freud's most powerful motives in life was...to inflict vengeance on Christianity."[3] Freud's hostility toward the Catholic Church is palpable when he speaks of "The Catholic Church, which so far has been the implacable enemy of all freedom of thought and has resolutely opposed any idea of this world being governed by advance towards the recognition of truth!"[4] Freud observes, "Christendom is very indecent."[5] Jewish scholars Stanley Rothman and S. Robert Lichter have also arrived at a similar conclusion: "Though it is sometimes forgotten today, Freud's work was profoundly subversive of the cultural underpinnings of European Christian society, a subversiveness of which he was not unaware. There is evidence that some of the impetus for the creation of psychoanalysis lay in his hostility to Christianity."[6]

Psychoanalysis was a quintessential tool to probe the Gentile or non-Jewish psyche to and obtain its subterranean secrets, giving Freud and the psychoanalytic movement a remarkable advantage in their subversive mission to fracture Western civilization. MacDonald concludes that "Freud's real analysand was gentile culture, and that

185

psychoanalysis was fundamentally an act of aggression toward that culture."[7]

In a broader context, it has been emphasized by Andrew R. Heinze that "Jewish thinkers introduced their ideas in tension with Christian society"[8] in order "to purge the evils they associated with Christian civilization."[9] Fritz Wittels believed that all gentiles, especially Christian civilization, would ultimately be conquered, as he writes here: "the spirit of the Jews would conquer the world."[10] The attack on the Christian tradition is made evident in the following statement made at a secret B'nai B'rith meeting held in Paris in 1936: "As long as there remains among the Gentiles any moral conception of the social order, and until all faith, patriotism and dignity are uprooted, our reign over the world shall not come..."[11]

Max Horkheimer (1895–1973) and Theodor W. Adorno, two key representatives of the Frankfurt School, jointly wrote in their 1947 paper entitled "Elements of Anti-Semitism" attacking Christianity at its roots: "Christ, the incarnated spirit, is the deified sorcerer. The human self-reflection in the absolute, the humanization of God through Christ, is the *proton pseudos* [first substitution]. The progress beyond Judaism is paid for with the assertion that the mortal Jesus was God. The harm is done precisely by the reflective moment of Christianity, the spiritualization of magic."[12] Arnold Zweig (1887–1968), a German writer, announced the dethroning of the Christian tradition to the master himself: "Analysis has reversed all values, it has conquered Christianity, disclosed the true Antichrist."[13]

Freud was sensitive to the realities posed by anti-Semitism and was untrusting of Gentiles or non-Jews. Freud makes an impotant parallel between the struggles that the Jewish people have historically faced and his absolute pledge to psychoanalysis: "I [Freud] have often felt as though I had inherited all the defiance and all the passions with which our ancestors defended their Temple and could gladly sacrifice my life for one great moment in history."[14] Freud writes to Pfister in 1910: "Building the temple with one hand and with the other wielding weapons against those who would destroy it—strikes me as a reminiscence from Jewish history."[15] Freud asserts that it is due to his Jewish identity that he can defy the opposing forces: "Because I was a Jew I found myself free of many prejudices which restrict others in the use of the intellect: as a Jew I was prepared to be in the opposition and to renounce agreement with the 'compact majority.'"[16] It is likewise this Jewish identity that empowered Freud in taking a solitary position in the face of adversity: "To profess belief in this new theory [psychoanalysis] called for a certain degree of readiness to accept a position of solitary opposition—a position with which no one is more familiar than a Jew."[17]

Freud clearly points out in *Moses and Monotheism* that "The hatred for Judaism is at bottom hatred for Christianity."[18] Freud writes: "one asks oneself again how the Jew came to be what he is and why he has drawn upon himself this undying hatred. I soon found the formula: Moses created the Jew."[19] Freud vehemently attacks the notion of redemption as found within the Christian tradition when he writes in no uncertain terms of "the lie of the salvation of mankind."[20] Freud makes an interesting admission regarding the Jewish tradition by way of admitting his animosity for Christianity: "The Christian religion did not keep to the lofty heights of spirituality to which the Jewish religion had soared."[21]

And we can see further verification of this hatred in Freud's own recollections of his childhood, which we cite at length to capture the richness of its detail:

I had actually been following in Hannibal's footsteps. Like him, I had been fated not to see Rome; and he too had moved into the Campagna when everyone had expected him in Rome. But Hannibal, whom I had come to resemble in these respects, had been the favorite hero of my later school days. Like so many boys of that age, I had sympathized in the Punic Wars not with the Romans but with the Carthaginians. And when in the higher classes I began to understand for the first time what it meant to belong to an alien race, and anti-Semitic feelings among the other boys warned me that I must take up a definite position, the figure of the Semitic general rose still higher in my esteem. To my youthful mind Hannibal and Rome symbolized conflict between the tenacity of Jewry and the organization of the Catholic church. And the increasing importance of the effects of the anti-Semitic movement upon our emotional life helped to fix the thoughts and feelings of those early days...At that point I was brought up against the event in my youth whose power was still being shown in all these emotions and dreams. I may have been ten or twelve years old, when my father began to take me with him on his walks and reveal to me in his talk his views upon things in the world we live in. Thus it was, on one such occasion, that he told me a story to show me how much better things were now than they had been in his days. When I was a young man, he said, I went for a walk one Saturday in the streets of your birthplace; I was well dressed, and had a new fur cap on my head. A Christian came up to me and with a single blow knocked off my cap into the mud and shouted: "Jew! get off the pavement!" "And what did you do?" I asked. "I went into the roadway and picked up my cap," was his quiet reply. This struck me as unheroic conduct on the part of the big, strong man who was holding the little boy by the hand. I contrasted this situation with another which fitted my feelings better: the scene in which Hannibal's father, Hamilcar Barca, made his boy swear before the household altar to take vengeance on the Romans. Ever since that time Hannibal had had a place in my phantasies.[22]

His biographer Gay declares that this decisive experience led Freud to develop "fantasies of revenge."[23] In a similar fashion, the psychoanalyst Ernst Simmel (1882–1947) writes: "the Jew, as the object of anti-Semitism, represents the bad conscience of Christian civilization."[24] Freud himself emphasizes that "The deeper motives of anti-Semitism...come from the unconscious."[25] In the eyes of Freud, all were held with suspicion and reservation, the essential reason being that "Basically, all are anti-Semites."[26]

Freud recalls facing anti-Semitism when he began his university studies and remarks on how this experience shaped and empowered his psyche to deal with antagonism and the harsh realities of life:

When, in 1873, I first joined the University, I experienced some appreciable disappointments. Above all, I found that I was expected to feel myself inferior and an alien because I was a Jew. I refused absolutely to do the first of these things. I have never been able to see why I should feel ashamed of my descent or, as people were beginning to say, of my race. I put up, without much regret, with my non-acceptance into the community; for it seemed to me that in spite of this exclusion an active fellow-worker could not fail to find some nook or cranny in the framework of humanity. These first impressions at the University, however, had one consequence which was afterwards to prove important; for at an early age I was made familiar with the fate of being in the Opposition and of being put under the ban of the "compact majority." The foundations were thus laid for a certain degree of independence of judgment.[27]

American psychologist David C. McClelland (1917–1998) presents a thought-provoking question on the paradoxical scenario that the psychoanalytic movement could become a new secular pseudo-religion:

> Has the Christian church become so petrified, so insensitive to the needs of our times, that a new religious movement has again arisen out of Judaism, opposed to orthodoxy and spread by secularized Jews? Certainly psychoanalysis has all of these characteristics. It is essentially individualistic, mystical, and opposed to religious orthodoxy...Would it not be the supreme irony of history if God had again chosen His People to produce a new religious revolt against orthodoxy, only this time of Christian making?[28]

In this connection, it is helpful to understand that the influence of secularism within Judaism is not a new phenomenon that began with Freud; but it is worthwhile to reflect on the ill consequences of the desacralization of the Jewish tradition and its corrosive effects on all the world's religions. Guénon writes:

> [W]hy is it that the principal representatives of the new tendencies, like...Freud in psychology, and many others of less importance, are almost all of Jewish origin, unless it be because there is something involved that is closely bound up with the "malefic" and dissolving aspect of nomadism when it is deviated, and because that aspect must inevitably predominate in Jews detached from their tradition?[29]

Saint John Chrysostom (349–407) further situates this discussion in a broader historical context of Christianity:

> Yet what kind of men were they who set their hands to the task [of rebuilding the temple]? They were men who constantly resisted the Holy Spirit, revolutionists bent on stirring up sedition. After the destruction which occurred under Vespasian and Titus, these Jews rebelled during the reign of Hadrian and tried to go back to the old commonwealth and way of life. What they failed to realize was that they were fighting against the decree of God, who had ordered that Jerusalem remain forever in ruins.[30]

Because of the pervasive anti-Semitism that Freud and the psychoanalytic movement faced in Vienna, where it was perceived to be a "Jewish science," Freud attempted to squelch this notion, as confirmed in a letter to Ferenczi on June 8, 1913 that explicitly states that "there should be no distinct Aryan or Jewish science."[31] While Freud appears to have rejected religion, including Judaism, he nonetheless had a powerful Jewish identity. Professor MacDonald notes: "although recent scholarship is unanimous that Freud had an intense Jewish identity, Freud took pains to conceal this identity from others because of a concern that his psychoanalytic movement would be viewed as a specifically Jewish movement and thus be the focus of anti-Semitism."[32] Despite the fact that Freud did not appear to be in favor of a "Jewish science," his daughter Anna Freud made a famous statement at the inaugural lecture for the Sigmund Freud Chair at the Hebrew University in Jerusalem reinforcing and normalizing the notion of a "Jewish science": "[Psychoanalysis has] been criticized for its methods being imprecise, its findings not open to proof by experiment, for being unscientific, even for being a 'Jewish science.' However the other derogatory comments may be evaluated, it is, I believe, the last-mentioned connotation which, under present circumstances, can serve as a title of honour."[33]

Freud tried to circumvent these hostile forces by soliciting a non-Jewish representative within the fold of the psychoanalytic movement, none other than C. G. Jung, to evangelize on behalf of the "talking cure" to broader audiences. Pfister could also be viewed in a similar context, although not as central to the expansion of the psychoanalytic movement. Jones was also one of the few non-Jewish representatives, who ceaselessly tried to win over the adoration of the master but was always viewed as an outsider for the simple fact that he was a Gentile. "In the eyes of all of [the Jewish members of the inner circle], Jones was a Gentile...[T]he others always seized every opportunity to make him aware that he could never belong. His fantasy of penetrating the inner circle by creating the Committee was an illusion, because he would forever be an unattractive little man with his ferret face pressed imploringly against the glass."[34]

Freud considered Jung to be "a bridge to the Gentile world"[35] and identified him as the successor of the psychoanalytic movement. He referred to Jung as the "crown prince."[36] Helen Walker Puner explains: "Freud had persuaded himself that in Jung he had found the ideal temporal head of his new religion. If Jung would run the secular affairs of the church—take over the external organization and the regulation of psychoanalysis—then he, Freud, could concern himself exclusively with that which was nearest to his heart, the formulation of the dogma."[37]

According to Fritz Wittels (1880–1950), a friend of both Jung and Freud: "His [Freud's] face beamed whenever he spoke of Jung [saying]: 'This is my beloved son, in whom I am well pleased!'"[38] In his letter to Ludwig Binswanger, written on March 14, 1911, Freud explicitly conveyed who would be the new leader of the psychoanalytic movement upon his passing: "When the empire [the psychoanalytic movement] I have founded is orphaned, no one else but Jung must inherit the lot."[39]

> Most of you are Jews, and therefore you are incompetent to win friends for the new teaching. Jews must be content with the modest role of preparing the ground. It is absolutely essential that I should form ties in the world of science. I am getting on in years, and am weary of being perpetually attacked. We are all in danger. [Grasping his coat by the lapels, he expressed:] They won't even leave me a coat to my back. The Swiss will save us—will save me, and all of you as well.[40]

Freud understood very well the need to have non-Jewish representation within the inner circle of the psychoanalytic movement: "After all, our Aryan comrades are quite indispensable to us; otherwise psychoanalysis would fall a victim to anti-Semitism."[41] Freud made Jung's decisive role within psychoanalysis even clearer in a letter to Jung dated February 25, 1908: "You really are the only one capable of making an original contribution [to psychoanalysis]."[42] Freud writes: "if I am Moses, then you are Joshua and will take possession of the promised land of psychiatry [and psychology], which I shall only be able to glimpse from afar."[43] In 1910, Freud appointed Jung president of the International Psychoanalytical Association, a position that Jung held until his resignation on April 20, 1914, due to the insurmountable differences between his views and those of Freud. Jung writes: "The latest developments have convinced me that my views are in such sharp contrast to the views of the majority of the members of our Association that I can no longer consider myself a suitable personality to be president."[44]

Jung's break with his master is captured in his written correspondence with Freud. Jung wrote to Freud on March 3, 1912 asserting his genuineness as a disciple, yet not without also asserting his own role beyond that of a mere disciple:"Let Zarathustra speak for me: 'One repays a teacher badly if one remains only a pupil.'"[45] Jung confesses to his master Freud his own deviant outlook, or apostasy for that matter, which is the rationale he offers for his participation in the psychoanalytic movement to begin with: "I would never have sided with you in the first place had not heresy run in my blood."[46]

The accusations that Jung harbored anti-Semitic views likely stem from Freud's own words on Jung: "he seemed ready to enter into a friendly relationship with me and for my sake to give up certain prejudices in regard to race which he had previously permitted himself."[47] It is worth including the damaging statements made to Jungian psychology regarding Jung's views on race; while they in and of themselves may not confirm that Jung was as some have alleged anti-Semitic, they are nonetheless troubling and not favorable in nature: "The 'Aryan' unconscious has a higher potential than the Jewish";[48] likewise, "The Jew...has never yet created a cultural form of his own...since all his instincts and talents require a more or less civilized nation to act as host for their development."[49]

Jung's remarks on Hitler are extremely troubling, as they demonstrate such an egregious lack of discernment:

> There is no question but that Hitler belongs in the category of the truly mystic medicine man. As somebody commented about him at the last Nürnberg party congress, since the time of [the Prophet] Mohammed nothing like it has been seen in this world. This markedly mystic characteristic of Hitler's is what makes him do things which seem to us illogical, inexplicable, curious and unreasonable...So you see...Hitler is a medicine man, a form of spiritual vessel, a demi-deity or, even better a myth...[50]

Jung responds to the charges of anti-Semitism in the following manner:

> The mere fact that I speak of a difference between Jewish and Christian psychology suffices to allow anyone to voice the prejudice that I am an anti-Semite...This hypersensitivity is simply pathological and makes every discussion practically impossible. As you know, Freud previously accused me of anti-Semitism because I could not abide his soulless materialism. The Jew directly solicits anti-Semitism with his readiness to scent out anti-Semitism everywhere.[51]

It is also worth noting Jung's relationship with the Christian tradition, as it will likely surprise readers to know that while he was allegedly a defender of religion, Jung conveyed the following regarding a disciple who converted to Catholicism: "With me nobody has his place who is in the Church. I am for those people who are out of the Church."[52] Jung's attacks on religion, like Freud's and those made by the post-Conciliar Church of Vatican II, helped undermine traditional Catholicism:

> Jung was exerting a powerful and destructive influence upon the Catholic Church which—having been all but abolished in its traditional form by the Second Vatican Council—was groping for some way to relate to its own rich mythopoetic heritage, so much so that Jungian psychology almost replaced the Church Fathers as the golden key to scriptural exegesis for Novus Ordo Catholics.[53]

Jungian analyst Marie-Louise von Franz (1915–98), designates Jung's apostasy as having occurred sometime in 1912: "In 1912 he came to the conclusion that he personally could not return to the medieval or original Christian myth and set his foot on the path of finding his own myth..."[54] To commit apostasy was no small matter for Jung, as he came from a devout Christian family: "it is by no means irrelevant to recall that eight of Jung's uncles were pastors, and that his father, too, was a pastor, who had partially lost his faith and suffered from attacks of insanity which led to his commitment to an asylum."[55] In Jung's autobiography *Memories, Dreams, Reflections*, he affirms the spiritual wasteland of modernism and his own internal dilemma of having lost his own faith in Christianity:

> But in what myth does man live nowadays? In the Christian myth, the answer might be, "Do *you* live in it?" I asked myself. To be honest, the answer was no. "For me, it is not what I live by." "Then do we no longer have myth?" "No, evidently we no longer have any myth." "But then what is your myth—the myth in which you do live?" At this point the dialogue with myself became uncomfortable, and I stopped thinking. I had reached a dead end.[56]

While Jung abandoned his faith in the Christian tradition, he in turn resurrected his own secular pseudo-religion in his psychological framework of analytic psychology that alone could provide redemption and salvation in the modern world. Regarding the rise of mental illness in the contemporary context, Jung does not advocate the recovery of the sacred as found within the revealed sapiential traditions of the world, but advocates salvation through his own Jungian or analytical psychology: "The neurotic is ill not because he has lost his old faith, but because he has not yet found a new form for his finest aspirations."[57] Jung affirms the saving truth of his new psychological religion: "*magna est vis veritatis et praevalebit.*"[58] ("Great is the power of the truth and it will prevail").

Freud also had a relationship with the Christian tradition that renders an alternate presentation on the Freudian myth or legend. To better comprehend this matter, it is helpful to look at the early religious influences on Freud, especially his devout Catholic nanny, Resi Wittek. Freud writes:

> [M]y "primary originator" [of neurosis] was an ugly, elderly but clever woman who told me a great deal about God and hell, and gave me a high opinion of my own capacities...If...I succeeded in resolving my hysteria, I shall have to thank the memory of the old woman who provided me at such an early age with the means for living and surviving. You see how the old liking breaks through again.[59]

Freud recalls: "I asked my mother whether she remembered my nurse. 'Of course,' she said, 'an elderly woman, very shrewd indeed. She was always taking you to church. When you came home you used to preach, and tell us all about how God conducted His affairs.'"[60]

The foundational role that Freud's Catholic nanny had on his understanding of religion cannot be easily dismissed, as some principal biographers have attempted, especially since a good case has been made that his Catholic nanny did have a powerful influence on Freud. Vitz adds: "Whether Freud was covertly baptized must on the basis of present information remain unknown, but that this nanny was consciously trying to influence Sigmund with respect to becoming a Christian is virtually certain."[61] Because of the subversive nature of the psychoanalytic revolution on Christianity, it is of interest to recall the Talmudic saying "the kingdom [namely, the Roman Empire] will be converted to heresy" (B. Sanhedrin 97a).[62] The Latin phrase *extra ecclesiam nulla salus* means "outside the Church there is no salvation." It is a dogma of the Catholic Church.[63] Yet Freud erected in turn his own secular pseudo-religious dogma that asserted there was no salvation outside the psychoanalytic church.

Chapter 18

Psychoanalysis and the Heretical
Jewish Messianic Movements

"Freud, consciously or unconsciously, secularized Jewish mysticism; and psychoanalysis can intelligently be viewed as such a secularization."[1]—David Bakan

An expanding body of research has been devoted to exploring the influence of Jewish mysticism on the development of psychoanalysis; a monumental work in this regard is David Bakan's *Sigmund Freud and the Jewish Mystical Tradition* published in 1957.[2] According to Bakan, who met with Rabbi Chaim Bloch, it was confirmed to him that Freud was made aware of the Lurianic Kabbalah when he was presented with a manuscript on the work of Chaim Vital's (1543–1620), who was none other than the foremost disciple of Isaac Luria (1534–72). Upon reading the manuscript on Jewish mysticism, Freud is reported to have excitedly stated "This is gold."[3] Bakan adds that the reason why there is so little reference to the Jewish mysticism in Freud's work is that "anti-Semitism, in which Jewish literature was a primary object of attack, was so widespread and so intense at the time that to indicate the Jewish sources of his ideas would have dangerously exposed an intrinsically controversial theory to an unnecessary and possible fatal opposition."[4]

An important clue to understanding the formation of psychoanalysis is its connection between heterodox beliefs and practices of Jewish mysticism, such as the Sabbatian and the Frankist sects, and Sigmund Freud. It is important to contextualize how widespread these movements were within the Jewish world. As Professor Gershom Scholem (1897–1982) notes, the Sabbatian movement was "the largest and most momentous messianic movement in Jewish History."[5] Likewise, "Never before had there been a movement that swept the whole House of Israel."[6] Rabbi Samuel H. Dresner (1923–2000) writes: "Sabbatianism [is] the one movement in Jewish history that not only broke the moral yoke of Sinai but provided a theological justification for it: 'in the transgression is the mitzvah.'"[7] Regarding the distinction between Sabbatianism and Frankism, Scholem indicates that "there is no basic difference between the terms Sabbatianism and Frankism."[8]

Scholem also affirms the secretive and hidden nature of this movement that spread throughout the world: "No chapter in the history of the Jewish people during the last several hundred years has been as shrouded in mystery as that of the Sabbatian movement."[9] He explains the reason for the secrecy and hidden nature of this movement and why it is not more readily known and understood today:

> Secularist historians...have been at pains to de-emphasize the role of Sabbatianism for a different reason. Not only did most of the families once associated with the Sabbatian movement in Western and Central Europe continue to remain afterwards within the Jewish fold, but many of their descendants, particularly in Austria, rose to positions of importance during the nineteenth century as prominent intellectuals, great financiers, and men of high political connections.[10]

Sabbatai Zevi (1626–76) was born in Smyrna (Izmir), received a traditional education in religious and Talmudic training, and appears to have been ordained as a *hakham*, the Sephardi honorific title for rabbi, when he was eighteen years of age. He was self-taught in the Kabbalah, as it is reported that he did not have a teacher or a mentor.

A defining moment in the messianic voyage of Sabbatai Zevi occurred in the spring of 1665 when he met the learned Rabbi and skilled exorcist Abraham Nathan b. Elisha Ḥayyim Ashkenazi, more commonly known as Nathan of Gaza (1643-1680), who Sabbatai Zevi sought out for the healing of his anguished soul. Sabbatai Zevi "struggled with himself and with the demons that possessed his soul, and his one desire was to rid himself of those troublesome mental states that were to him, no doubt, an unbearable affliction."[11] It has been explained that: "Sabbatai did not come as a messiah to his prophet, but, rather, as a sick man to the doctor of souls, who knew the hidden roots of every soul and who could prescribe to each its appropriate *tiqqun*...Nathan announced to him that his was a soul of a very high order which needed no *tiqqun*; he was, in fact, the messiah."[12]

Sabbatai Zevi was informed by Nathan of Gaza that he was not possessed, but was in fact the messiah himself. We are informed that when Nathan of Gaza disclosed to Sabbatai Zevi his prophetic vision, it was not only not taken seriously but scoffed at. The following is reported to have transpired: "Nathan addressed him [Sabbatai Zevi] as the messiah, he laughed at him and said, 'I had it [the messianic vocation], but have sent it away.'"[13] It was only through much discussion and persuasion that Nathan of Gaza was able to convince Sabbatai Ẓevi of his messianic mission. After proclaiming Sabbatai Ẓevi as the messiah, Nathan of Gaza would soon be "at once the John the Baptist and the Paul of the new messiah."[14] In May 31, 1665, Sabbatai Ẓevi proclaimed himself to be the long-awaited Jewish messiah. An early follower, Samuel Primo, announced the advent of the messiah:

> The only and first-begotten Son of God, Sabbatai Zevi, Messiah and Redeemer of the people of Israel, to all the sons of Israel, Peace! Since ye have been deemed worthy to behold the great day and the fulfillment of God's word by the prophets, your lament and sorrow must be changed into joy and your fasting into merriment, for ye shall weep no more. Rejoice with song and melody, and change the day, which was formerly spent in sadness and sorrow, into a day of jubilee, because I have appeared.[15]

He would often sign letters in the following manner: "I am the Lord your God Sabbatai Ṣevi."[16] There are earlier records that confirm that Sabbatianism began as early as 1648 when he initially declared himself the messiah.[17]

Sabbatai Ẓevi, as the alleged awaited messiah, came to reveal a new Law for the Jewish people, a Law that would revoke all previous laws. Scholem points out:

> ...that the King Messiah was to give "a new Torah" and that the commandments of the Law (*mitzvot*) were to be abrogated in Messianic times...Even those visionaries who dreamt through the ages of a new Word of God in a redeemed world did not, in fact, particularly connect this idea with the activities of the Messiah himself, and it was not until it was seized upon by the new "Marranic" doctrine that its latent explosive power was revealed.[18]

It has been pointed out that Nathan of Gaza, the prophet of this messianic movement, was very different in character from Sabbatai Ẓevi. Nathan of Gaza immersed himself in Jewish mysticism and began to have experiences; these experiences eventually culminated in what has been considered a prophetic awakening, which he himself describes in a letter written around 1673:

> When I had attained the age of twenty, I began to study the book Zohar and some of the Lurianic writings. [According to the Talmud] he who wants to purify himself receives the aid of Heaven;

and thus He sent me some of His holy angels and blessed spirits who revealed to me many of the mysteries of the Torah. In that same year, my force having been stimulated by the visions of the angels and the blessed souls, I was undergoing a prolonged fast in the week before the feast of Purim. Having locked myself in a separate room in holiness and purity...the spirit came over me, my hair stood on end and my knees shook and I beheld the *merk-abah*, and I saw visions of God all day long and all night...[19]

Nathan of Gaza received a message from the "angel of the Covenant" expressing that he needed to maintain the faith regardless of confirmation through outward signs: "Moreover I was told that Israel ought to believe [in the messiah] without any sign or miracle. And whoever does not believe, it is evident that his soul contains an admixture of evil from the generations that rebelled against the kingdom of Heaven and against the kingdom of David."[20]

Sabbatai Ẓevi was known to enter altered states of consciousness in which he became possessed, and in these states of possession he advocated the breaking of Jewish religious laws. In exalted states Sabbatai Ẓevi often pronounced in public the Divine Name, the Tetragrammaton in Hebrew of the Ineffable Name of YHVH, which is forbidden to utter by rabbinic law. This was a blatant violation of the third commandment that "Thou shalt not take the name of the Lord thy God in vain; for the Lord will not hold him guiltless that taketh His name in vain" (Exodus 20:7).

The Sabbatian dictum can be summarized as "Praise be to Thee, O Lord, who permittest the forbidden"[21] or "Him who allows the forbidden."[22] The new Law made the unholy holy and the profane sacred. From the Talmudic saying, "David's son comes only in an age which is either completely guilty or completely innocent" (Sanhedrin 98a), the Sabbatians drew the following conclusion: "since we cannot all be saints, let us all be sinners."[23]

The inversion of religion and spirituality was made apparent by Sabbatai Ẓevi's character itself: "during his periods of illumination he felt impelled to commit acts which ran counter to religious law, later called *ma'asim zarim* ('strange or paradoxical actions')."[24] We are told of a story at the end of the *Vision of R. Abraham*, an important document for studies on Sabbatianism, of a dream that he had early on which tormented him throughout his life:

When he [Sabbatai Ẓevi] was six years old a flame appeared in a dream and caused a burn on his penis; and dreams would frighten him but he never told anyone. And the sons of whoredom [the demons] accosted him so as to cause him to stumble and they beat him, but he would not hearken unto them. They were the sons of Na'amah, the scourges of the children of man, who would always pursue him so as to lead him astray.[25]

It has been suggested that Sabbatai Ẓevi suffered from mental illness and that this was the underlying cause of his unconventional or deviant behavior. Scholem affirms: "There is no doubt that Sabbatai Ṣevi was a sick man, and it is worthwhile to try and understand the nature of his illness. His contemporaries speak of him as a madman, a lunatic, or a fool, and even his followers admitted that his behavior, at least from puberty onward, provided ample reason for these appellations."[26] Scholem adds: "The [psychiatric] sources suggest with almost absolute certainty that Sabbatai suffered from a manic-depressive psychosis, possibly combined with some paranoid traits."[27]

Between 1642 and 1648 he lived in semi-seclusion. During this period he began to display a character that conforms largely to what handbooks of psychiatry describe as an extreme case of cyclothymia or manic-depressive psychosis. Periods of profound depression and melancholy alternated with spasms of maniacal exaltation and euphoria, separated by intervals of normality. These states, which are richly documented throughout his life, persisted until his death.[28]

Samuel Gandor, an enthusiastic adherent, prepared the following testimony in the summer of 1665 discussing the psychopathology that Sabbatai Ẓevi suffered from:

It is said of Sabbatai Zevi that for fifteen years he has been bowed down by the following affliction: he is pursued by a sense of depression which leaves him no quiet moment and does not even permit him to read, without his being able to say what is the nature of this sadness which has come upon him. Thus he endures it until the depression departs from the spirit, when he returns with great joy to his studies. And for many years already he has suffered from this illness, and no doctor has found a remedy for it, but it is one of the sufferings which are inflicted by Heaven.[29]

An interesting phenomenon is that rather than deterring followers, these aberrant behaviors confirmed to the faithful the validity of his messianic vocation, for none who was not the messiah would dare to commit such vile and heinous acts:

His strange behavior, far from belying his messianic dignity, actually confirmed it. No ordinary soul, let alone that of a pious ascetic, would ever seek expression in such "strange actions." Clearly these were "hidden acts of *tiqqun.*" The messiah still continued his warfare against the *qelippah,* and he alone who had struggled free from the depth of the abyss knew by what paradoxical ways this realm of darkness, impervious to the power of Torah, could be subdued.[30]

On September 15, 1666, Sabbatai Ẓevi was brought before the Sultan in Adrianople (Edirne) and was given the choice of being put to death or converting to Islam. To the horror of Jews around the world he chose the latter, to convert, and was given the Islamic name of Aziz Mehmed Effendi. In effect, "the Sabbatian movement depended on the paradoxical assumption that the messiah's apostasy was a mystery and—appearances notwithstanding—an essentially positive event. In order to survive, the movement had to develop an ideology that would enable its followers to live amid the tensions between inner and outer realities."[31]

Various rationales were given for the apostasy, and many followers, known as the Dönmeh, a crypto-Jewish sect, followed him in his footsteps into apostasy and embraced Islam.[32] They outwardly lived and appear as devout Muslims, yet they inwardly or secretly lived as Jews. Scholem explains: "The Sabbatians were outwardly Muslims, but inwardly were seeking an esoteric and, in a way, concrete Judaism, the precise nature of which was not yet clear to them."[33] Similarly it was reported that Sabbatai Ẓevi lived a double life, sometimes seen performing rituals of the Jewish tradition, and at other times seen observing rites of the Islamic tradition.

In contrast to the cases of a false messiah committing apostasy or other followers converting to other faiths to infiltrate them, masquerading as believers, the Sabbatian-Frankist movement, as Scholem emphasizes, is a strictly Jewish phenomenon: "Sabbatianism must be regarded...as a single continuous development which retained its identity in the eyes of its adherents regardless of whether they themselves remained Jews or not, but also, paradoxical though it may seem, as a specifically Jewish phenomenon to the end."[34]

Sabbatai Ẓevi is recorded as having expressed the following regarding a commentary on Psalm 143:10, "Teach me to do Thy will; for Thou art my God; Thy spirit is good":

Since I do not as yet know anything of the laws of this religion [Islam], therefore I must be taught...for thou art my God, thou and none other. Thy spirit is good, for the way of this nation [the Ishmaelites] is in madness, for they behave madly in the root of the madman [Muhammad], and when they behave madly they bring upon themselves an evil spirit. *But though I am among them I am not of them*; for Thou, O God, Thy spirit is good, but their spirit is evil.[35]

Jacob Frank (1726–91) expanded upon and continued the messianic movement that began with Sabbatai Ẓevi, "comprising the last stage in the development of the Shabbatean movement."[36] In Frankism one finds what can be termed "radical Sabbatianism" and its fundamental prolongation: "The world of Sabbatianism itself, on the one hand, remains intact, or rather has reached that ultimate stage of its development where it verges on self-annihilation."[37] According to Scholem, Jacob Frank is "one of the most frightening phenomena in the whole of Jewish history: a religious leader who...was in all his actions a truly corrupt and degenerate individual."[38] In another place, he writes that Frank was "the most hideous and uncanny figure in the whole history of Jewish Messianism."[39] Scholem further adds that Frank is "a figure of tremendous...satanic power."[40]

Jacob Frank viewed religion in an extremely antinomian manner and sought to infiltrate and subvert all faiths from within: "the true believer...should go through all religions, rites, and established orders without accepting any and indeed annihilating all from within and thereby establishing true freedom. Organized religion is only a cloak to be put on and be thrown away on the way to the 'sacred knowledge'...where all traditional values are destroyed."[41] Jacob Frank depicts his messianic mission *vis-à-vis* his inverted spirituality: "Christ...said that he had come to redeem the world from the hands of the devil, but I have come to redeem it from all the laws and customs that have ever existed. It is my task to annihilate all this so that the Good God can reveal Himself."[42]

Frankism requires complete submission to their nefarious doctrine that permits all acts of evil without impunity to amass power: "The descent into the abyss requires not only the rejection of all religions and conventions, but also the commission of "strange acts," and this in turn demands the voluntary abasement of one's own sense of self, so that libertinism and the achievement of that state of utter shamelessness which leads to a *tikkun* of the soul are one and the same thing."[43] The followers of the Frankist doctrine are told to do so until the Spirit is utterly and fully eclipsed in order to submit wholeheartedly to the nihilistic void, as described here: "Nevertheless, the way to Life is not easy, for it is the way of nihilism and it means to free oneself of all laws, conventions, and religions, to adopt every conceivable attitude and to reject it, and to follow one's leader step for step into the abyss."[44]

Frank subverted the meaning of the esoteric or mystical dimension of religion, making it utterly destructive and diabolical in principle:

> This "Life," however, is not the harmonious life of all things in bond with God, a world ordered by divine law and submissive to His authority, but something very different. Utterly free, fettered by no law or authority, this "Life" never ceases to produce forms and to destroy what it has produced. It is the anarchic promiscuity of all living things. Into this bubbling cauldron, this continuum of destruction, the mystic plunges. To him it is the ultimate human experience. For Frank, anarchic destruction represented all the Luciferian radiance, all the positive tones and overtones, of the word "Life." The nihilistic mystic descends into the abyss in which the freedom of living things is born; he passes through all the embodiments and forms that come his way, committing himself to none; and not content with rejecting and abrogating all values and laws, he tramples them underfoot and desecrates them, in order to attain the elixir of Life. In this radical interpretation of a symbol, the life-giving element of mystical experience was combined with its potential destructiveness. It goes without saying that from the standpoint of the community and its institutions, such mysticism should have been regarded as demonic possession. And it is indicative of one of the enormous tensions that run through the history of Judaism that this most destructive of all visions should have been formulated in its most unrestrained form by one who rebelled against the Jewish law and broke away from Judaism.[45]

Frank taught that salvation could be obtained through sexual perversions, and so these were sanctioned in full. Scholem observes: "From the standpoint of sexual pathology...Frank himself was a diseased individual."[46] We can find parallels between the psychoanalytic doctrine and the Sabbatian and Frankist movements, as in the following observation: "The principle of the Freudian theory is hedonism."[47]

Jacob Frank, like Sabbatai Ẓevi, enacted apostasy, yet he did not convert to Islam as did Sabbatai Ẓevi, but converted to Catholicism. Scholem argues that Frankism was "for generations nothing other than a particularly radical [off]shoot of the Dönmeh, only with a Catholic façade."[48] It needs to be remembered that neither of these men converted to other faiths because they loved these faiths or because Spirit had guided them to these distinct spiritual homes; nor did they necessarily love their ancestral tradition of Judaism, as is demonstrated by their betrayal of its principal tenets. The matter of religious conversion itself can be looked at from several distinct points of view that do not suggest apostasy. The esoteric or mystical understanding of changing religion is not equivalent to conversion in the usual sense of the word. Guénon makes this clear: "Contrary to what takes place in 'conversion,' nothing here implies the attribution of the superiority of one traditional form over another. It is merely a question of what one might call reasons of spiritual expediency, which is altogether different from simple individual 'preference,' and for which exterior considerations are completely insignificant."[49] With this said, while conversion in and of itself does not equate or suggest apostasy, the conversion of Sabbatai Ẓevi and Jacob Frank and that of their followers was indeed apostasy. Sabbatianism and Frankism are fundamentally ways of subverting and destroying religion all together.

The followers of Jacob Frank were able to penetrate high levels of the Austrian government and aristocracy, making it difficult to measure their enduring influence, "but they preserved a few Frankist traditions and customs, so that a stratum was created in which the boundaries between Judaism and Christianity became blurred, irrespective of whether the members had converted or retained their links with Judaism."[50] What we do know is that Frankism continued after Jacob Frank died, and took on the shape of a secret society hidden from the common view:

The [Frankist] sect's exclusive organization continued to survive in this period through agents who went from place to place, through secret gatherings and separate religious rites, and through the dissemination of a specifically Frankist literature. The "believers" endeavored to marry only among themselves, and a wide network of inter-family relationships was created among the Frankists, even among those who had remained within the Jewish fold. Later Frankism was to a large extent the religion of families who had given their children the appropriate education. The Frankists of Germany, Bohemia, and Moravia usually held secret gatherings in Carlsbad in summer round about the Ninth of Av.[51]

While it has been documented that Sabbatai Ẓevi had contact with various Dervish orders, this does not indicate that he was in any way a Sufi himself.[52] Scholem quotes the famous Sufi mystic al-Junayd (835–910) in an attempt to draw a parallel between the traditions in order to make sense of the astonishing declarations proposing that certain rabbinical laws or transgressions were now sanctified by the bizarre behavior of Sabbatai Ẓevi and Jacob Frank: "God brings upon those that love him a kind of sudden and supernatural madness, in which a man may speak and act against the directions of religion, without his being responsible for his actions and without God caring to make them accord with the religion which He has revealed from heaven."[53]

Within Islamic spirituality this approach is recognized as the "way of blame" or "blameworthy," known as the *malāmatiyya* (the term is derived from the Arabic word *malāma* "to blame"). This approach is not an isolated phenomenon, as it has its corresponding manifestations throughout the world's religions. *Malāmatiyya* are known in Christianity as "Fools for Christ," in Hinduism as Avadhūta, and within the First Peoples and their shamanic traditions as Heyoka. These spiritual representatives were far from being heretics; they were considered to be the spiritual elect: "The People of Blame [*malāmatiyya*] are the masters and leaders of the folk of God's path. Among them is the master of the cosmos, that is, Muhammad, the Messenger of God—God bless him and give him peace!"[54]

It is worth citing several key and well-known ejaculations by Bāyazīd Bisṭāmī (d. 234/848 or 261/875): "Glory be to Me! How great is My majesty!" (*Subḥānī! mā a'ẓama sha'nī*) and "I am He" (*Anā Huwa*),[55] or Manṣūr al-Ḥallāj (858–922), who made his famous pronouncement uttering "I am the Truth" (*anā-l-Ḥaqq*). These were considered blasphemous and heretical, as it was suggested that they meant that these Sufis were claiming to be God, violating the principle of Divine Unity (*al-tawḥīd*), as known in the Abrahamic monotheisms. Professor William Chittick explains that "*Tawhid* is expressed more succinctly in the formula, 'There is no god but God.' God is *wujud* [being or existence], so 'There is no *wujud* but God.' Everything other than God is not *wujud* and can properly be called 'nonexistence' (*'adam*)."[56] According to the esoteric or mystical understanding, it would be blasphemy or heretical not to acknowledge and furthermore fully identify with one's inseparability from the Divine, as the Divine is all that truly is.

While many parallels of ecstatic sayings can be found throughout the comparative religious literature of the world, we could also cite the following by Ḥallāj when he affirms: "I became infidel to God's religion, and infidelity is my duty, because it is detestable to Muslims."[57] Or "May God veil you from the exterior of the religious law, and may he reveal to you the reality of infidelity. From the exterior of the religious law is a hidden idolatry, while the reality of infidelity is a manifest gnosis."[58] These pronouncements were in no way antinomian or nihilistic, but have been interpreted by some in this way, turning the true meaning on its head. These ecstatic sayings were uttered when the identification with the empirical ego was annihilated in the timeless and formless realm of the Supreme Identity, where dichotomies such as self and other no longer exist.

For traditional ecstatic sayings as these to be intelligible, it is necessary to make an essential distinction between the exoteric or outer and esoteric or inner dimensions of religion. In the proceeding ecstatic sayings of Junayd, Bāyazīd and Ḥallāj are speaking to Ultimate Reality that transcends conventional knowledge. The outer and inner dimensions of religion are needed to comprehend such statements, yet what tends to be overlooked is that the inner or exoteric dimension is not accessible without the outer or exoteric dimension. Guénon clarifies this point: "where exoterism and esoterism are directly linked to the constitution of a traditional form in such a way as to be as it were the two faces, exterior and interior, of one and the same thing, it is immediately comprehensible to everyone that one must first adhere to the exterior in order subsequently to be able to penetrate to the interior, and that there can be no other way than this."[59]

All Kabbalistic manuals quote Maimonides's warning about studying the mystical or esoteric dimensions prior to being versed in the formalistic or exoteric aspects of the religion: "No one is worthy to enter Paradise [the realm of mysticism or esoterism] who has not first taken his fill of bread and meat."[60] Emphasizing that sacred tradition cannot be indiscriminately abrogated, the poem *Yigdal* that forms part of the daily Jewish service affirms: "The Law God gave, He never will amend,/Nor ever by another Law replace."[61]

By the same token the exoteric or outer dimension of religion is limited without the esoteric or inner dimension, even though it is sufficient for the salvation of one's soul. With this said, there are potential abuses of this spiritual framework, which become more and more common in the current temporal cycle of the *Kali-Yuga* through the medium of inverted spirituality or New Age counterfeit-spirituality.[62]

While the Sabbatian-Frankist movements made use of the mystical dimension that is the heart of every revealed religion, it is necessary to point out that Sabbatai Ẓevi and Jacob Frank have betrayed and inverted not only the outer forms of their respective religions, but also the inner dimension. Guénon notes that "the confusion between exoterism and esoterism is one of the causes that most frequently gives rise to heterodox 'sects.'"[63] Al-Hujwīrī (d. 465/1072) warns those who violate religious law (*sharī'ah*) and corrupt others to acquire followers:

> He who abandons the law and commits an irreligious act, and says that he is following the rule of "blame," is guilty of manifest wrong and wickedness and self-indulgence. There are many in the present age who seek popularity by this means, forgetting that one must already have gained popularity before deliberately acting in such a way as to make the people reject him; otherwise, his making himself unpopular is a mere pretext for winning popularity.[64]

The *malāmatiyya* are of the highest caliber in their proximity to the Divine and should not be confused with pseudo-mystics or those who deviate from the moral codes of conduct. They are unique and truly gifted individuals; however, their outer observances need a metaphysical perspective to be fully understood.[65] It is mistaken to think that the *malāmatiyya* intentionally violate the *sharī'ah* or disregard religious and moral observances out of a deviation in their understanding or out of self-interest. Ibn 'Arabī clarifies this matter in the following way:

> [The *malāmatiyya*] add nothing to the five daily prayers and the supererogatory exercises (*rawātib*). They do not distinguish themselves from the faithful who perform God's obligations by any extra state whereby they might be known. They walk in the markets, they speak to the people, and none of God's creatures sees any of them distinguishing himself from the common people by a single thing; they add nothing to the obligatory works or the Sunna customary among the common folk. They are alone with God, firmly rooted, not wavering from their servanthood for the blink of an eye. They find no favor in leadership, since Lordship has overcome their hearts and they are lowly before it. God has

given them knowledge of the places of things and of appropriate works and states. They are veiled from the creatures and stay concealed from them by the covering of the common people. For they are sincere and purely devoted servants of their Master. They witness Him constantly in their eating and drinking, their waking and sleeping, and their speaking with Him among the people.[66]

The seeker needs to beware that there are masters and fellow travelers that will be led astray. It is necessary to follow the narrow and steep path, for this is why it has been emphasized: "Enter houses by their doors" (Koran 2:189).

The English occultist and foremost Satanist Aleister Crowley (1875–1947), who styled himself as the "Great Beast 666" and was dubbed by the British press as "the wickedest man in the world," had diabolic maxim similar to that of the Sabbatian-Frankist movements: "Do what thou wilt shall be the whole of the Law."[67] Voltaire, a leading mind of the so-called Enlightenment, had a similar motto, "do what thou wilt."[68] This of course was a fundamental subversion of Saint Augustine's (354–430) dictum: "*Dilige* [deum] *et quod vis fac*" or "Love [God], and do what thou wilt,"[69] meaning that the spiritual aspirant is required not to desire anything that God does not will; it does not mean that the individual is sanctioned to do whatever he or she desires. The Supreme Commandment instructs: "Hear, O Israel: the Lord our God is one Lord. And thou shalt love the Lord thy God with all thine heart, and with all thy soul and with all thy might" (Deuteronomy 6:4–5).

When examined as a whole, the Sabbatian-Frankist movements converge in an uncandid fashion with the corrosive and inverted phenomenon of the psychoanalytic revolution. Freud emphasizes: " [psychoanalysis] is calculated to undermine religion, authority and morals."[70] It cannot also be overlooked that "Sigmund Freud would have to be declared a moral bankrupt in virtue of countless ethical abuses."[71] A connection can also be made between the antinomianism not only of the Sabbatian-Frankist movements and Freudianism, but also of the Frankfurt School or The Institute for Social Research (Institute für Sozialforschung). According to Walter Benjamin (1892–1940): "On the breaking of this cycle maintained by mythic forms of law, on the suspension of law with all the forces on which it depends as they depend on it, finally therefore on the abolition of state power, a new historical epoch is founded."[72]

The heretical Jewish "messiah" who claimed to have come to redeem the inhabitants of the world had in fact delivered himself and
his followers to pure evil and what is Luciferian in essence. "The Sabbatian paradox, however, was not that of a saint who suffers and
whose suffering is a mystery hidden with God, but of a saint who sins.
A faith based on this destructive paradox has lost its innocence."[73] A
significant justification for the Sabbatian apostasy was that "Moses,
the first redeemer, foreshadows the messiah. Even as Moses lived as
an Egyptian at the court of Pharaoh, so Sabbatai too had to apostatize
and live as a Turk in order to reform his people."[74] It could thus be
said that "Sabbatai was assuming the role of Moses *redivivus*."[75]

The psychoanalytic doctrine joins the Sabbatian-Frankist apostasy by erecting in turn its own Freudian apostasy: "In *Moses and
Monotheism*, Freud brings the Sabbatian impulse to its dramatic climax. Sabbatai Zevi *became* a Gentile. Jacob Frank *became* a Gentile.
The ultimate fulfillment of the theme of Sabbatianism, is to have Moses, the most profound Messianic figure of Judaism and the image of
all other Messiahs, already *be* a Gentile."[76] Bakan adds:

> If, as we have seen, Freud strongly identified himself with Mo-
> ses, then his preoccupation with the Moses of Michelangelo, *who
> sits petrified in a church in Rome and graces the tomb of a Pope*,
> and his turning Moses into a Gentile, can be understood as
> Freud's own realization of the Sabbatian act of apostasy.
> Through the image of Moses...Freud becomes a Gentile psycho-
> logically as he makes a Gentile of Moses.[77]

There are scriptural warnings in the book of Revelation about the
synagogue of Satan and those who "say they are Jews, and are not,
but do lie" (Revelation 3:9); we are told that "they delight in lies: they
bless with their mouth, but they curse inwardly" (Psalm 62:4). This
alludes to phenomena of the heretical Jewish messianic movements
of Sabbatianism and Frankism. This inverted spirituality attempted to
subvert sacred tradition and erect its own malevolent parody: "Their
coming was to mark a new age when the rule of Torah was to be superseded—'What was forbidden is now permitted'—and transgressions would become mitzvoth."[78]

Maimonides formulates the following in defense of tradition: "the
truth of the matter: the Torah with all its laws and ordinances is ever-
lastingly valid and nothing will be added to it or taken away from it."[79]
He continues: "do not think that in the days of the messiah there will
be any departure from the normal course of things or any change in

the cosmic order."[80] Hoffer illustrates the broader influence of such inverted movements on the human collectivity: "Heresies have often served as vehicles for the transmission of ideas, attitudes, and ways of life."[81] The Sabbatian-Frankist movement is the negation of all that is sacred: "When the divine is totally denied, the ineluctable consequence is that there is nothing else to take its place but the spirit of negation, the satanic."[82]

Chapter 19

Psychoanalysis as Pseudo-Science

"[P]sychoanalysis is the paradigmatic pseudoscience of our epoch"[1] and "[Freud] was the creator of a complex pseudo-science which should be recognized as one of the great follies of Western civilization."[2] When psychiatrist Richard von Krafft-Ebing (1840–1902) made the following remark about Freud's work, it dealt a powerful blow to the doctrine of the "talking cure": "It [psychoanalytic theory] sounds like a scientific fairy tale"[3] (*Es klingt wie ein wissenschaftliches Märchen*). Szasz went so far as to dismiss the psychoanalytic doctrine as "fake therapy"[4] essentially consisting of "fake case histories."[5] Scores of scholarly journal articles and books have brilliantly illustrated the flaws and grave errors of the Freudian "talking cure," and some argue that Freud's findings are not only inconclusive, but contradictory, as he attempted to give them the appearance of a valid science when pscyhoanalysis was anything but a true science. It has been explained that "It is characteristic of a pseudoscience that the hypotheses which comprise it stand in asymmetrical relation to the expectations they generate, being permitted to guide them and be vindicated by their fulfilment but not to be discredited by their disappointment."[6]

The verdict is not favorable for psychoanalysis. Freud was curiously opposed to or uninterested in scientific data pertaining to the validity of psychoanalytic theory. He reports, "statistics...are in general uninstructive"[7]; and elsewhere, "statistics would be worthless if the collected cases were not comparable."[8] Rather than implementing large-scale controlled experiments, as is consistent with the scientific outlook, he rather suggested: "It is wiser to examine one's individual experiences."[9] Ricoeur attests that "facts in psychoanalysis are in no way facts of observable behaviour."[10] The paradox of Freudian analysis is that only those initiated can verify its truth: "only the psychoanalyzed or the psychoanalysts are entitled to judge the truth of his doctrine."[11]

The endemic *scientism*, "the belief that the scientific method and scientific findings are the sole criterion for truth,"[12] is the rejection of anything that cannot be verified by the five senses. Freud declares his allegiance to scientific fundamentalism: "No, our science is no illusion. But an illusion it would be to suppose that what science cannot give us we can get elsewhere."[13] This overwhelmingly narrow interpretation of science is reminiscent of another well-known scientistic declaration by Bertrand Russell (1872–1970): "what science cannot discover, mankind cannot know."[14] Science, according to Freud, represents the only legitimate means of obtaining true knowledge: "there are no sources of knowledge of the universe other than the intellectual working-over of carefully scrutinized observations—in other words, what we call research—and alongside of it no knowledge derived from revelation, intuition or divination."[15]

What is altogether misunderstood regarding the phenomenon of scientism is that its totalitarian claims negate its essential assertions: "the contention that there are no truths save those of [modern] science is not itself a scientific truth; in affirming it scientism contradicts itself."[16] Scientism thus confines the scope of psychology or the "science of the soul" to what is exclusively horizontal: "scientism encourages man to stop his search for inwardness at the level of psychic contents."[17]

Freud staunchly defended his theorems at all cost, along with the psychoanalytic apologists and revisionists, and was indifferent to the essential questions: "*Is a scientific psychology in the strict sense of the word at all possible?* Can psychoanalysis claim to be such a psychology?...Freud himself paid no attention to these methodological questions and quietly continued to publish his clinical observations; he disliked philosophical discussions."[18]

Freud himself expresses the following regarding the empirical claims of psychoanalytic theory:

> [Y]ou should not for a moment suppose that what I put before you as the psycho-analytic view is a speculative system. It is on the contrary empirical—either a direct expression of observations or the outcome of a process of working them over. Whether this working-over has been carried out in an adequate and justifiable manner will appear in the course of the further advance of the science, and indeed I may assert without boasting, after a lapse of nearly twenty-five years, and having reached a fairly advanced age, that these observations are the result of particularly hard, concentrated and deep-going work.[19]

It is true that many have attested to the master's scientific genius, such as American psychotherapist Ira Progoff (1921–98): "Freud stands out as the great pioneer whose genius created a science where none had been before."[20] Velikovsky describes the master's work as "a masterpiece in the history of the understanding of the human mind."[21] Freud, however, saw himself in a different light. He addresses what he perceived as his innovation of psychoanalysis in a manner that might surprise those who assume his description would speak to his identity as a man of science. It does not. Rather, it ascribes his role as a colonizer of the human psyche: "I [Freud] am actually not at all a man of science, not an observer, not an experimenter, not a thinker. I am by temperament nothing but a conquistador."[22]

This disclosure may appear odd at first; however, the more one analyzes the topsy-turvy or rather constructed scientific foundations of psychoanalysis, the more sense it makes. Freud confides to his disciple Fliess: "As a young man my only longing was for philosophical knowledge, and now that I am changing over from medicine to psychology I am in the process of fulfilling this wish. I became a therapist against my will."[23] Almost two decades later Freud writes: "In short, I am evidently an analyst."[24] At the end of his life he felt comfortable enough to disclose:

> After forty-one years of medical activity, my self-knowledge tells me I have never really been a doctor in the proper sense. I became a doctor through being compelled to deviate from my original purpose; and the triumph of my life lies in my having, after a long and roundabout journey, found my way back to my earliest path. I have no knowledge of having had any craving in my early childhood to help suffering humanity.[25]

When charged by critics with being unscientific, Freud wrote them off with responses such as "We have our own science."[26] When Freud was asked what scientific justification he had for the hypothesis that dreams are not somatic but rather psychic phenomena, he responded: "None; but that alone need not deter us from making it."[27] In a similar way he brushes off the scientific justification for his doctrine of the unconscious: "when anyone wants to bring forward the objection that the unconscious can have no reality for science and is a mere makeshift, (*une façon de parler*), we must simply shrug our shoulders and reject his incomprehensible statement resignedly."[28] When Freud and the psychoanalytic movement encountered obstacles on their path to legitimize their scientific psychology, the master did not hesitate to recall the words of Jesus in John 18:36: "Our kingdom is indeed not of this world."[29]

Former president of the American Psychiatric Association Jules H. Masserman (1905–94) concludes that Freud "demonstrated his utter inability to recognize how his own preconceptions affected his clinical data, skewed his observations, reinforced his predilections, and thus greatly handicapped him as a research scientist."[30] For this reason, allegations of being a pseudo-science or scientific fraud have been launched at psychoanalysis without end. An example of such a critique is highlighted here: "The pseudo-science of psycho-analysis is one of the finest specimens of its kind ever devised by the mind of man."[31]

There is no scientific evidence to support the Freudian idea that man is born with biologically provided urges, needs, or interests that set him at odds with the society in which he lives; there is no real reason to suppose that sex is the dominant, if submerged, force in the life of the individual; there is no reason, aside from Freud's assurances, to think that what a man does is not what it seems to be; and there is no evidence, aside from that adduced by Freud and his disciples in accordance with their interpretive system, that the child inevitably—or even ever—develops an Oedipus complex, followed by a castration complex or penis envy, and that he thereafter goes fumbling and stumbling through life with the balance between his id, his ego, and his superego ever precarious and ever subject to jeopardy. There is not even any scientific evidence that the concepts of id, ego, and superego represent actual components of the individual's psyche.[32]

Although Freud and his disciples presented psychoanalytic theory as a credible science, that was quite far from the case, as reflected in the lack of empirical data provided to substantiate its claims. Eysenck highlights the essential ambivalence regarding the scientific efficacy of Freud's "talking cure": "...Freud and his followers feel under the constraint to give a *causal* explanation, but they are also *afraid* of making any definite statement which could be refuted by an appeal to factual inconsistencies. This ambivalence...pervades all of Freud's world, and that of his followers."[33]

Oddly enough, even with significant consensus on the unsound scientific foundations of the psychoanalytic "talking cure," it is nonetheless still widely embraced. American psychologist Lewis M. Terman (1877–1956) elucidates how widely discredited psychoanalytic theory is, while at the same time acknowledging its paramount contribution: "the Freudian concepts, even when their validity has been discounted about 90 per cent, nevertheless, constitute one of the... most important contributions to modern psychology."[34] Freud himself underscores the theories shortcomings, yet he simultaneously affirms its theoretical integrity: "Though the structure of psycho-analysis is unfinished, it nevertheless presents...a unity."[35] Even those initiated into the occult art of psychoanalysis are curiously unable to verify the validity of its theories. Karen Horney (1885–1962) writes: "It seems to me that analytic experience alone does not sufficiently enable us to judge the soundness of some of the fundamental ideas that Freud has made the basis of his theory."[36]

The efficacy of the psychoanalytic method has been extensively probed and debunked, and yet Freud rigorously attempted to empha-size its stature as a *bona fide* scientific psychology: "Even if psycho-analysis showed itself as unsuccessful in every other form of nervous and psychical disease as it does in delusions, it would still remain completely justified as an irreplaceable instrument of scientific re-search."[37] Jung, like Freud, recognized the need to present psychology within a scientific framework in order to gain wider acceptance: "To-day the voice of one crying in the wilderness must necessarily strike a scientific tone if the ear of the multitude is to be reached."[38] Jung declares that Freud's intention was in influencing the human collec-tivity on a mass scale, or should we say it was the erection of a total-izing worldview or *Weltanschauung*, rather than the propagation of a scientific theory that appears as only a means to an end: "Secretly, psychoanalytic theory has no intention of passing as a strict scientific truth; it aims rather at influencing a wider public."[39]

At the Second International Psychoanalytic Congress at Nürn-berg, Germany, in 1910, Freud expressed to his adherents his unwa-vering belief in his new psychology, which transgresses the bounda-ries of science, becoming a totalitarian ideology: "I will let you go, therefore, with the assurance that you do your duty in more than one sense by treating your patients psychoanalytically. You are not merely working in the service of science, by using the only and irreplaceable opportunity for discovering the secrets of the neuroses; you are not only giving your patients the most efficacious remedy for their suffer-ings..."[40]

The hocus-pocus of psychoanalysis is made apparent by the fact that it itself diagnoses, treats, and determines when the analysis is suc-cessful, and in Freud's case, this determination habitually contra-dicted the actual results of the alleged success in treatment. What has become apparent with the ample scholarship available is that the effi-cacy of psychoanalysis begins and ends with Freud's own subjective theorems and interpretation of his observations rather than the empir-ical evidence: "Freud placed the stamp of his personality on every phase of his discipline."[41] For this reason, a central criticism of Freudian psychoanalysis, and modern psychology for that matter, is that each theory is essentially self-validating. Freud underscores this problem: "The teachings of psycho-analysis are based on an incalculable number of observations and experiences, and only someone who has repeated those observations on himself and on others is in a position to arrive at a judgment of his own upon it."[42]

Freud asserts in his preface to *The Interpretation of Dreams*: "I have not, I believe, trespassed beyond the sphere of interest covered by neuropathology."[43] However, time and time again it is made obvious that his subjective speculations did in fact transgress the boundary of the domain of the scientific method. Freud again paradoxically avows his allegiance to the scientific method: "The theory of psychoanalysis [is] a theory based upon observation."[44] One can only assume that this is done to give the appearance of upholding the scientific standard.

Yet the empirical evidence for psychoanalytic theory and its application is spotty or minimal at best and radically incomplete. Another critique that powerfully portrays the dilemma at hand for the doctrine of the "talking cure" is made by Dunlap: "Psychoanalysis...attempts to creep in wearing the uniform of science, and to strangle it from the inside."[45] Emil Kraepelin (1856–1926), regarded as the "father of modern psychiatry," determined that psychoanalysis is unequivocally unscientific:

> [W]e meet everywhere the characteristic fundamental features of the Freudian trend of investigation, the representation of arbitrary assumptions and conjectures as assured facts, which are used without hesitation for the building up of always new castles in the air ever towering higher, and the tendency to generalization beyond measure from single observations...As I am accustomed to walk on the sure foundation of direct experience, my Philistine conscience of natural science stumbles at every step on objections, considerations, and doubts, over which the likely soaring tower of imagination of Freud's disciples carries them without difficulty.[46]

Heinz Kohut (1913–81), who developed the influential school of self psychology that emerged out of the psychodynamic outlook of psychoanalysis, writes:

> [I] recognize the limits of the applicability of some of the basic [Freudian] analytic formulations. And with regard to the classical

psychoanalytic conceptualization of the nature of man, too—however powerful and beautiful it might be—I have become convinced that it does not do justice to a broad band in the spectrum of human psychopathology and to a great number of other psychological phenomena we encounter outside the clinical situation...And I know...that the suggestion that it is inadequate, or even that in certain respects it leads to an erroneous outlook on man, is bound to arouse opposition.[47]

There is very little if any hard evidence that substantiates the findings of Freud's theories: "All the other great 'facts' of psycho-analysis are found on examination to be mere assumptions...No proofs of any of these assumptions are adduced. But they are all treated as facts."[48] Psychoanalyst Otto Fenichel (1897–1946) makes a perceptive point about psychoanalytic theory: "The psychoanalytic literature is very extensive. It is amazing how small a proportion of it is devoted to psychoanalytic technique and how much less to the theory of technique: an explanation of what the analyst does in psychoanalysis."[49]

Freud was not unaware of the shortcomings of psychoanalytic theory and its implications on the Freudian revolution. He admits that "[the] incompleteness of our premises threatens to bring our calculation to a complete miscarriage."[50] Even though there their doctrine has very little scientific credibility, the neo- and post-Freudians continue to be faithful to the doctrine of the "talking-cure." Horney, for example, defends the Freudian therapy: "There is...only one psychological school that offers...an insight with any high degree of scientific exactness—namely, psychoanalysis."[51] Another apologists or revisionist response has emphasized a less favorable point: "He [Freud] made no claim for their validity and sometimes even spoke deprecatingly of their value. But the more time passed, the more hypothetical constructs turned into theories upon which new constructions and theories were built."[52]

The power of suggestion as a determinant of successful treatment within Freudianism cannot be overlooked: "The possibility that psycho-analytic cures are really due to suggestion must seriously be considered."[53] A powerful example of how Freud refused to take these dangers seriously is provided here: "We need not be afraid...of telling the patient what we think his next...thought is going to be. It will do no harm"[54] or "The principle point is that I [Freud] should guess the secret and tell it to the patient straight out."[55] As Freud himself candidly disclosed to Fliess on August 7, 1901: "My clients are sick people, hence especially irrational and suggestible."[56] Elsewhere, Freud also confirms the suggestibility of his clinical methodology: "You asked me why we do not make use of direct suggestion in psycho-analytic therapy, when we admit that our influence depends substan-tially upon transference, i.e., suggestion, for you have come to doubt whether or not we can answer for the objectivity of our psychological discoveries in the face of such a predominance of suggestion."[57]

He later underscores the essential dilemma facing Freudian doc-trine:

> Now you will say, regardless of whether we call the driving force of our analysis transference or suggestion, there is still the danger that through our influence on the patient the objective certainty of our discoveries becomes doubtful...This objection is most of-ten raised against psychoanalysis...[I]f it were justified, psycho-analysis would be nothing more than an extraordinarily well dis-guised and especially workable kind of treatment by sugges-tion.[58]

Freud downplays the dangers of suggestibility in analysis by appeal-ing to the good will of the psychoanalyst, which ignores the potential abuses and harm that can be done in the name of the alleged "talking-cure":

> The danger of our leading a patient astray by suggestion, by per-suading him to accept things which we ourselves believe but which he ought not to, has certainly been enormously exagger-ated. An analyst would have had to behave very incorrectly be-fore such a misfortune could overtake him; above all, he would have to blame himself with not allowing his patients to have their say. I can assert without boasting that such an abuse of "sugges-tion" has never occurred in my practice.[59]

The psychoanalytic "talking cure" is quintessentially a process of fabrication, as the master himself admits when he calls it the "work of construction, or, if it is preferred, of reconstruction."[60] Freud de-scribes (writing in the third person for a textbook) how the psychoan-alytic method of interpretation can be manufactured:

> Freud has developed...an art of interpretation which takes on the task of, as it were, extracting the pure metal of the repressed thoughts from the ore of the unintentional ideas. This work of interpreta-tion is applied not only to the patient's ideas but also to his dreams, which open up the most direct approach to a knowledge

of the unconscious, to his unintentional as well as to his purpose-less actions (symptomatic acts) and to the blunders he makes in everyday life (slips of the tongue, bungled actions, and so on). The details of this technique of interpretation or translation have not yet been published by Freud. According to indications he has given, they comprise a number of rules, reached empirically, of how the unconscious material may be reconstructed from the associations, directions on how to know what it means when the patient's ideas cease to flow, and experiences of the most important typical resistances that arise in the course of such treatments.[61]

The ambiguity in the distinction between what is already existent in an individual's consciousness and what is in a sense planted there by the therapist is a dilemma that each person appears to resolve within him or herself, as Freud notes:

In view of the very great number of associations produced in analysis to each individual element of the content of a dream, some readers may be led to doubt whether, as a matter of principle, we are justified in regarding as part of the dream-thoughts all the associations that occur to us during the subsequent analysis— whether we are justified, that is, in supposing that all these thoughts were already active during the state of sleep and played a part in the formation of the dream. Is it not more probable that new trains of thought have arisen in the course of the analysis which had no share in forming the dream? I can only give limited assent to this argument. It is no doubt true that some trains of thought arise for the first time during the analysis. But one can convince oneself in all such cases that these new connections are only set up between thoughts which were already linked in some other way in the dream-thoughts.[62]

He continues by further highlighting the necessity of the suggestibility of the mind being analyzed for the success of the analysis:

It must be allowed that the great bulk of the thoughts which are revealed in analysis were already active during the process of forming the dream; for, after working through a string of thoughts which seem to have no connection with the formation of a dream, one suddenly comes upon one which is represented in its content and is insensible for its interpretation, but which could not have been reached except by this particular line of approach.[63]

Freud clears the air and admits to the role of suggestion in psychoanalysis: "It's true that the analyst uses suggestion, but only to help the psychoanalytic procedure."[64] Although Freud later admits that it was an erroneous methodology, he states earlier on that "It was my view at that time...that my task was fulfilled when I had informed a patient of the hidden meaning of his symptoms: I considered that I was not responsible for whether he accepted the solution or not—though this was what success depended on."[65] He then irrevocably contradicts this position and emphasizes that suggestion has never worked for him: "I have never yet succeeded in forcing on a patient a scene I was expecting to find."[66]

Maurice Natenberg takes issue with psychoanalysis because of its "unconditional surrender" and the coercive nature of this doctrine that imposes what can be interpreted as a form of mind control: "His [Freud's] couch became an abyss, a strange, fantastic domain where he manipulated his patients like puppets on strings. This complete surrender permitted Freud to secure acceptance of all his dogma."[67] It becomes evident that the doctrine of the "talking cure" places individuals in a precarious position of extreme vulnerability and subjects them to influences that they can neither understand nor control. Andrew Salter (1914–96) affirms: "the entire analytic procedure fosters the most complete and dangerous sort of dependence."[68]

Not only is the process of Freudian therapy suggestive in what it asks the individual to accept, but it indoctrinates the person into a Freudian prototype:

> The process of interpretation presumably runs throughout the entire analysis. It is, ordinarily, made piecemeal and gradually, and it involves inducting the patient into the Freudian way of thinking about psychic matters. In effect, then, the patient is gently schooled in Freudian doctrine; or, as non-Freudians would be inclined to say, converted to the Freudian faith. Even in Freudian theory, it is quite essential to therapeutic success that the patient come to accept as valid the Freudian concept of him as a person. He must learn to think of himself as composed of id, ego, and superego; as a victim of the Oedipus, castration, and other complexes; as one whose behavior has obscure implications; as one whose natural self and socially imposed self are unceasingly engaged in an unresolvable conflict; and as one who is, as a consequence, psychologically frail. For only if he does come to see himself in this way will the analyst's interpretation of the causes of his mental distress be acceptable to him. And it is, presumably,

through his accepting the analyst's interpretation that he is absolved from the mental consequences of those causes.[69]

Regarding Freud's signature theory of the Oedipus complex, it has been emphasized that "his famous Oedipus-complex theory is based on a total misunderstanding of a myth."[70] It has been likewise been debunked as "a hypnotic myth":[71]

Our surrogate of Greek drama is now psychoanalysis. In a secular society it seems to be the only ritual left us. The patient is supposed to be in search of his Oedipus complex; I suggest he is reenacting the Oedipus drama in a more fundamental sense—he is struggling for light against darkness. He wants, or ought to want, the truth about himself; but sometimes the more earnestly and energetically he sets about it, the more obstacles he puts in his own way. He is not yet free for the truth. All this is the well-known matter of "religion," and the psychoanalysts tell us all about it; we have no need here for the philosopher.[72]

According to American psychiatrist Karl Menninger (1893–1990), one must hold the principle of neutrality in all psychoanalytic work: "Neutrality in the analyst is one of the essentials of psychoanalytic treatment...It means...a hovering attention to what the patient says, with a suspension of expressed moral judgment."[73] However, the alleged neutrality of the Freudian analyst is deceptive, as Marmor writes: "It has become increasingly clear that such 'neutrality' is actually a fiction."[74]

The power of suggestion within Freud's signature "talking cure" is further elaborated:

Psycho-analysts defend their theory by pointing to its practical therapeutic success. People are cured by psycho-analysis, they say; therefore psycho-analysis must be correct as a theory. This argument would be more convincing than it is, if it could be shown: first, that people have been cured by psycho-analysis after all other methods had failed; and secondly, that they have really been cured by psycho-analysis and not by suggestion somewhat circuitously applied through psycho-analytic ritual.[75]

Freud at other times denies any form of suggestion in his doctrine of the "talking cure": "it guarantees to a great extent that no factor in the structure of the neurosis will be overlooked and that nothing will be introduced into it by the expectations of the analyst."[76] Jung argues against the reliance of psychoanalysis on suggestion: "The patient is not an empty sack into which we can stuff whatever we like; he brings his own particular contents with him, with which you have always to reckon afresh."[77] While Freud sometimes admits to or minimizes the suggestive influence of psychoanalysis, at other times he is more adamant about its neutrality. Freud states: "The analyst respects the patient's individuality and does not seek to remould him in accordance with his own—that is, according to the physician's—personal ideals; he is glad to avoid giving advice and instead to arouse the patient's power of initiative."[78]

The ambiguity regarding the realm of the human psyche was also not unknown to Freud, yet this dilemma continues to impact the field at large due to the lack of inclusion of integral metaphysics of the perennial philosophy within contemporary psychology. Freud writes: "I have no inclination at all to keep the domain of the psychological floating, as it were, in the air, without any organic foundation. But I have no knowledge, neither theoretically nor therapeutically, beyond that conviction, so I have to conduct myself as if I had only the psychological before me."[79] Jung adds this about psychic determinism within psychoanalysis: "Analysis is the reduction of actual contents of consciousness, ostensibly of a fortuitous nature, to their psychological determinants."[80]

Without being aware of it, Freud confirms psychoanalysis's inability to see what is beyond the human psyche. The problem is that any theory or theoretical orientation can be self-validating, and this is a real issue not only for psychoanalysis to tackle but for the field in its entirety:

> [D]epending upon the point of view of the analyst, the patients of each school seem to bring up precisely the kind of phenomenological data which confirm the theories and interpretations of their analysts! Thus each theory tends to be self-validating. Freudians elicit material about the Oedipus complex and castration anxiety, Adlerians about masculine strivings and feelings of inferiority, Horneyites about idealized images, Sullivanians about disturbed interpersonal relationships, etc. The fact is that in so complex a transaction as the psychoanalytic therapeutic process, the impact of patient and therapist upon each other, and particularly of the latter upon the former, is an unusually profound one. What the analyst shows interest in, the kinds of questions he asks, the kind of data he chooses to react to or to ignore, and the interpretations he makes, all exert a subtle but significant

suggestive impact upon the patient to bring forth certain kinds of data in preference to others.[81]

In a similar fashion, the theoretical approach that is implemented will catalyze the individual to respond according to the psychological model:

> A patient who has a positive transference to the therapist wants to please him and will talk about what she thinks will interest him...A patient lets himself be known, even though he fears exposing himself to humiliation and punishment, because he wants the therapist's affection and approval, not simply because he wants to get well. To know this about a patient is to be alert to the dangers of the transference relationship. The patient in a positive transference will, unconsciously, do his best to conform to the therapist's wishes as he, the patient, understands them. If the therapist wants to talk in terms of the Oedipus complex and incestuous sexuality, the patient will do his utmost to bring out material in such a way that it will fit that set; if another therapist approaches the same patient in a different framework, the latter will oblige that therapist in turn.[82]

Another unfortunate phenomenon regarding psychoanalysis has to do with how individuals were treated when they disagreed with Freud and how they were coerced into believing that the issue or problem had to do with them and not with psychoanalytic theory itself. Eysenck writes:

> Freud had a very clever ploy for dealing with disagreement. If the patient agreed with his interpretation, then Freud claimed that the interpretation was obviously correct. If the patient disagreed, however, Freud claimed that this was because of psychoanalytic "resistance," which makes interpretation unacceptable precisely *because* it is correct; hence disagreement also indicates the correctness of the theory. Clearly there is no way in which the theory could be disproved—a very fortunate state for a scientific theory to be in, one might have thought. In actual fact, of course, the opposite is true: if a theory cannot be disproved by any observable fact, then...it is not a scientific theory at all.[83]

Similarly, depending on what point of view is taken, the same could be said regarding Freud and Jung: "while the pupils of Freud confirm by their clinical observations the findings of their master, the pupils of Jung, working with weapons forged of much the same material and in a closely similar pattern, have no difficulty in finding ample clinical confirmation for the quite disparate tenets of Jung."[84]

The question as to the scientific validity of the "talking cure" is not only of concern to those within psychoanalysis, but pertains to the entire field of modern psychology or mental health on a structural level:

> Should we therefore conclude that psychoanalysis is a science? My evaluation shows that at none of the different stages through which it evolved could Freud's theory generate adequate explanations. From the very beginning, much of what passed as theory was description, and poor description at that...In every one of the later key developmental theses, Freud assumed what had to be explained...None of his followers, including his revisionist critics who are themselves psychoanalysts, have probed any deeper than he did into the assumptions underlying their practice, particularly the assumptions underlying the basic method—free association. None has questioned whether those assumptions hold in the therapeutic situation; none has attempted to break out of the circle.[85]

This being the case for the Freudian "talking cure," it has little or no defense against accusations of being a pseudo-science. Again, "Whatever it is, psychoanalysis is not a science."[86] Polish-born American psychologist Joseph Jastrow (1863–1944) urges that: "the time has come to make clear that the principles of psychoanalysis are not any such order of realities, but are conjectures, schemes, constructions of Freud's fertile imagination...The *"discoveries" are hypotheses*— and they are nothing more."[87]

A striking and memorable point is made by French psychoanalyst and psychiatrist Jacques Lacan (1901–81) regarding the therapeutic import of the "talking cure": "The basic thing about analysis is that people finally realize that they've been talking nonsense at full volume for years."[88] Szasz, famed critic of pseudo-science, makes this point: "psychotherapy is [merely] talking."[89] For this reason, when the question is asked, how will an individual differ after Freudian analysis? The response is in no way inspiring, as we are told that "the patient will remain essentially the same person after the best analysis."[90]

Hence, the following question answers itself: "If psychanalysis is not a science, in the modern sense of that word, is it—or was it—a [secular pseudo-]religion?"[91] Grünbaum makes an important assessment of the Freudian doctrine: "psychoanalysis must then be deemed a *placebo* therapy."[92]

Chapter 20

Psychoanalysis and Its Discontents:
Corrosive Ideology and Debunked
Case Histories

"[T]he worst enemies of psychoanalysis are the psychoanalysts them-selves."[1]—Jacques Maritain

To say as Karl Menninger does that "Psychoanalysis has its therapeutic failures"[2] is not only an understatement, but a fundamental denial of the facts at hand. "[T]he main objection to all psychotherapies, and psychoanalysis in particular, was their lack of scientific theory or validation. Therapists relied on case histories and did not even pretend at scientific proof."[3] More concerning than the lack of proof of scientific efficacy of its theories is the harm it has caused, as Hoche writes: "In very many cases, psychoanalytic therapy is a direct damage to the patient."[4] Louise Bates Ames (1908–96), a pioneer in child development research, confirms the grave societal harm caused by the psychoanalytic doctrine: "In child care I would say that Freudianism has been the psychological crime of the century."[5] The nihilistic and malignant implications of the Freudian doctrine are highlighted here: "Never has a doctrine of man that is so morbid, so discouraging, so without hope or confidence, and so lacking in inspiration been so widely acclaimed."[6] Jung stresses:

> Freud himself, the founder of psychoanalysis, has thrown a glaring light upon the dirt, darkness and evil of the psychic hinterland, and has presented these things as so much refuse and slag; he has thus taken the utmost pains to discourage people from seeking anything behind them. He did not succeed, and his warning has even brought about the very thing he wished to prevent: it has awakened in many people an admiration for all this filth.[7]

The scope and depth of the misdeeds caused by Freud and the psychoanalytic movement are striking, to say the least. Freud attempts to comfort the weary and skeptical by normalizing the potential harmful uses of the "talking cure": "Misuse of psychoanalysis is possible in various ways...But no professional method of procedure is protected from misuse; a knife that is not sharp is of no use in effecting a cure."[8] A significant obstacle posed by those who launched critiques of Freud and the doctrine of psychoanalysis, especially while he was alive, is that, as Jung points out, "Anything that might make them think is written off as a complex. This protective function of [psychoanalysis] badly need[s] unmasking."[9]

This is the crux of the matter, which is that critics of Freudianism are dismissed as heretics or apostates and are excommunicated from the psychoanalytic church. They are essentially deemed to be mentally ill or psychologically unbalanced per the subjective discretion of the representatives of the psychoanalytic "talking cure." Jung speaks to the actions taken by the psychoanalytic movement to stop all forms dissent: "I am forced to the painful conclusion that the majority of ΨAsts misuse ΨA for the purpose of devaluing others and their progress by insinuations about complexes (as though that explained anything. A wretched theory!)"[10] The following realization regarding psychoanalysis becomes palpable: "the situation is not hopeless, but it *is* grave. We have been living in a fool's paradise, believing that our clinical theory was soundly established when in fact very little of it has been."[11]

William James (1842–1910), often regarded as the "father of American psychology," makes a notable comment about the doctrine of the Freudian "talking cure," referring to it as "[a] most dangerous method."[12] While James did not doubt that psychoanalysis could make contributions to the field of modern psychology, the impression that Freud made on James when they met is worth recalling: "They [Freud and his disciples] can't fail to throw light on human nature; but I confess that he made on me personally the impression of a man obsessed with fixed ideas."[13] Jung adds: "Freud's dogmatism comes very close to the attitude of religious conviction."[14] We are informed that Alfred Adler (1870–1937) gradually distanced himself from Freud because he "came to believe that the whole process of psychoanalysis was inimical to the welfare of mankind."[15] A ruthless "blow" was hurled at psychoanalysis by Perls, a pioneer within humanistic psychology who at one time looked up to and revered the master: "Psychoanalysis turns out to be a closed, unchanged and unchangeable system, full of explanatariness but missing self-evident understanding. Psychoanalysis is an illness that pretends to be a cure. Unsuccessful treatments, from three to over twenty years, far outweigh the scant success."[16] British physician Havelock Ellis (1859–1939) warned American psychiatrist Joseph Wortis (1906–95) about his zealotry toward the psychoanalytic church and the dangers of this doctrine:

> About being psychoanalysed, my own feeling most decidedly is that it would be better to follow his *example* than his precept. *He* did not begin by being psychoanalysed (never was!) or attaching himself to any sect or school, but went about freely, studying the work of others, and retaining always his own independence. If he had himself followed the advice he gives you, he would have attached himself to Charcot with whom he was working, and become his disciple, like Gilles de la Tourette, an able man and now forgotten. If you are psychoanalysed you either become a Freudian or you don't. If you don't, you remain pretty much where you are now; if you do—you are done for!—unless you break away, like Jung or Adler or Rank (and he has done it too late).[17]

After breaking ties with Josef Breuer, Freud only published six detailed case histories attempting to forge the empirical efficacy of psychoanalysis; however, when these cases are critically examined, it is baffling as to why Freud would have wanted them to see the light of day, for they in no way confirm successful treatment as is purported. In fact, the very opposite is true: "It is both curious and striking that Freud chose to demonstrate the utility of psychoanalysis through descriptions of largely unsuccessful cases."[18] And, elsewhere, this pertinent question has been asked: "If Freud did not cure most of his patients or even believe them generally curable, what was the purpose of publishing case histories? Even more to the point, why did Freud choose to publish analyses of individuals who were usually treated only briefly, usually never cured, and sometimes not even seen by him personally?"[19]

The answer to this pressing question is that Freud and the psychoanalytic movement utilized the technique of construction or reconstruction to fictitiously establish their own scientific and therapeutic legitimacy, alternatively known as psycho-history. The therapeutic outcomes were not as Freud recorded; they were rather based on his own reconstructions of how he would have liked them to conclude per psychoanalytic theory, and not on how they achieved in actuality. They betrayed the individual's trust in the therapeutic process. The individuals' feelings about the treatment were silenced. Not only this, but they were told that treatment was successful, and they themselves were put in a precarious situation where they were forced to succumb to Freud's authority:

Freud's "case histories" (*Krankengeschichten*) are no less mythical than the fabulous "history of the psychoanalytic movement" narrated in his autobiographical writings or the history of humanity described in his phylogenetic and anthropological fictions. No matter where we look, we find the same rewriting of history, the same narrativising of arbitrary interpretations, the same transformation of hypotheses into facts.[20]

Although their accounts are extremely troubling and contrary to any authentic form of therapy, Freudians continue in the master's footsteps, reconstructing the unsuccessful cases into successful ones, as a Viennese psychoanalyst who was one of Freud's most faithful adherents, Kurt R. Eissler (1908–99), upholds when he speaks of "the pillars on which psychoanalysis as an empirical science rests."[21] Despite the lack of clinical trials to demonstrate the efficacy of psychoanalytic theory, Brenner faithfully avows: "The psychoanalytic method is the only method so far available which has made possible the scientific observation of the major motivational forces of man's mental life."[22]

To the surprise of many who assumed that the Freudian myth or legend was what it purported to be, it remains doubtful if Freud had any successful case histories since that of "Dora," a pseudonym given by Freud to a patient whose real name was Ida Bauer (1882–1945). Jones has emphasized that "This first case history of Freud's has for years served as a model for students of psychoanalysis."[23] Erikson states that the Dora case became "the classical analysis of the structure and the genesis of a hysteria."[24]

The real story of Dora is very different from the official narrative constructed by Freudian psycho-history, as it was in reality a therapeutic disaster. Dora prematurely terminated treatment in 1900, and her case does not appear to be a confirmation of successful treatment, as Freud recorded for historical posterity. Patrick J. Mahony provides this stark example of psychoanalytic fraud and betrayal:

> The case of Dora has an array of negative distinctions. It is one of the great psychotherapeutic disasters; one of the most remarkable exhibitions of a clinician's published rejection of his patient; spectacular, through tragic, evidence of sexual abuse of a young girl, and her own analyst's published exoneration of that abuse; an eminent case of forced associations, forced remembering, and perhaps several forced dreams...[T]he case, the published history, and the subsequent reception can be called an example of

continued sexual abuse. Dora had been traumatized, and Freud retraumatized her. And for roughly half a century the psychoanalytic community remained either collusively silent about that abuse or, because of blind adoration, simply ignorant of it.[25]

Freud himself confesses to the suggestive or constructive nature of Dora's case that deceitfully pathologized her: "to convince the patient herself of the existence in her of an intention to be ill."[26]

While Freud vaunted that the treatment of Anna O. (Bertha Pappenheim) was a "great therapeutic successes,"[27] such claims are not only inconsistent with the facts derived from the constructed case histories but fundamentally illusory. Professor Mikkel Borch-Jacobsen writes:

> No one today can remain unaware that the treatment of Anna O. (whose real name was Bertha Pappenheim) was very different from what Breuer and Freud have told us about it—so different, in fact, that we can legitimately wonder what remains of modern psychotherapy's origin-myth, now that the historians of psychoanalysis have so thoroughly debunked it. But that hasn't prevented this myth and its derivatives from perpetuating themselves and proliferating in psychotherapeutic discourse...[28]

Webster explains the need to perpetuate the myth of Anna O.'s therapeutic success: "to entertain any serious doubt about the diagnosis of Anna O. would be to deal a devastating blow to the mythology which has traditionally sustained the psychoanalytic church. For, although Anna O. was not one of Freud's own patients, the mystique of her cure rapidly became one of the most important elements in the Freudian legend."[29] The myth of therapeutic success has to be perpetuated, as so much is at stake. Freud in 1917 recalled how "Breuer actually achieved the recovery of his patient [Anna O.], that is, freed her of her symptoms...Breuer's discovery still remains the foundation of psychoanalytic therapy."[30] Gay also regarded Anna O. as "the founding case of psychoanalysis."[31] However, Jones confirms that "The poor patient [Anna O.] did not fare so well as one might gather from Breuer's published account."[32] Apparently, Breuer disclosed to Freud that a year after he had stopped treating Anna O., her symptoms returned, as Jones reveals in his official biography: "[Anna O.] was quite unhinged and...he wished she would die and so be released from her suffering."[33] We learn from Professor Albrecht Hirschmüller, who specializes in research on the history of psychiatry and psychoanalysis, that "Freud's version is an interpretative reconstruction. With increasing lapse of time after the events, this reconstruction became more and more consolidated and condensed, until the mere suspicion that the analysis had not been advanced far enough became the spectacular picture of Breuer's flight from his patient's hysterical birth."[34]

Freud himself confirms in his correspondence the lack of therapeutic success in completing a single case: "I have no case that is complete and can be viewed as a whole."[35] Readers may ask where exactly Freud went wrong, in view of his lack of therapeutic success with the individuals he treated, yet what is important to understand is that the problem lies with the erroneous worldview that informs the theory and practice of psychoanalysis: "Psychoanalysis was never a 'pure psychology'...Freud erected his psychoanalytic edifice on a kind of intellectual quicksand, a circumstance that consequently doomed many of his most important theoretical conclusions from the outset."[36]

With this said, wherever one turns, not only is the evidence of success fundamentally lacking, but the therapeutic failure is demonstrated: "Neither Freudian interpretations that appear to support the theory nor the success of analysis as a therapeutic technique provide scientifically acceptable evidence for the truth of the theory."[37] Paradoxically, the alleged triumph of Freud's psychoanalysis is predicated on the therapist's concealment of his or her suggestive influence and shifting of the blame for unsuccessful treatment onto the individual, rather than taking responsibility for the shortcomings of the treatment itself. Freud discloses a little dark secret about the "talking cure": "talking people into and out of things...is what my work [psychoanalysis] consists of."[38]

Not only is the empirical evidence lacking, but what is reported as successes in treatment cannot be trusted to be accurate reflections of what occurred in analyses and can only be taken at face value. Jung avows: "There is then a certain untrustworthiness about all these earlier cases [of Freud]. Thus again, the famous first case [Dora] that he had with Breuer, which has been so much spoken about as an example of a brilliant therapeutic success, was in reality nothing of the kind."[39] The case of Dora was a therapeutic hazard: "Freud treated Dora as a deadly adversary. He sparred with her, laid traps for her, pushed her into corners, bombarded her with interpretations, gave no quarter, was as unspeakable, in his way, as any of the people in her sinister family circle, went too far, and finally drove her away."[40]

This again brings to light that "Freudian psychology is not after all founded on the analysis obtained, but upon preconceived notions, or, perhaps it would be better to say, on the attractiveness of the conclusions reached."[41] Friedell comments on the challenges of accusing psychoanalysis of erroneous diagnosis:

> Here, as in all other questions, it is impossible to convict the psycho-analysts of a false diagnosis, as they are such adepts in refuting all criticism by means of the catch-words with which they make play—terms like "ambivalent," "inverted," symbolic," "repressed," "transferred," and "sublimated." The convincingness of the argumentation here rests on the assumption that the pettifogging verbal quibble is the organizing principle of all spiritual life, and that the dream-god is of the Mosaic confession.[42]

As to the the case of Little Hans (Herbert Graf, 1904–73), we learn that Freud himself only met with him on one occasion. Jones explains: "It was the father, not Freud, who conducted the analysis. Freud himself had only one interview with the boy during it, but he had frequent consultations with the father, who consented to the case being published."[43] With this stated, it is perplexing that this case was considered an important demonstration of therapeutic success for the validity of psychoanalytic theory:

> Freud's subsequent analysis was not based on any material he himself discovered; the material was collected by little Hans's father, who kept in touch with Freud by regularly writing reports. The father had several discussions with Freud concerning little Hans's phobia, but during the analysis Freud himself saw the little boy only once! This is a curious way of carrying out treatment, and of laying the foundations for child analysis, yet few analysts seem to have found the procedure peculiar.[44]

South African psychiatrist Joseph Wolpe (1915–97) and Professor Stanley Rachman examined the case of Little Hans and conclude that it contains glaring inadequacies that challenge the scientific foundations of psychoanalytic theory:

> The chief conclusion to be derived from our survey of the case of Little Hans is that it does not provide anything resembling direct proof of psychoanalytic theorems. We have combed Freud's account for evidence that would be acceptable in the court of science, and have found none...Freud fully believed that he had obtained in Little Hans a direct confirmation of his theories, for he speaks towards the end of "the infantile complexes that were revealed behind Hans's phobia." It seems clear that although he

wanted to be scientific Freud was surprisingly naive regarding the requirements of scientific evidence. Infantile complexes were not *revealed* (demonstrated) behind Hans's phobia: they were merely hypothesized.[45]

While attributing successful treatment to the case of Little Hans, Freud also highlights the suggestibility required for psychoanalytic reconstruction: "It is true that during the analysis Hans had to be told many things which he could not say himself, that he had to be presented with thoughts which he had so far shown no signs of possessing, and that his attention had to be turned in the direction from which his father was expecting something to come."[46]

Freud goes on to justify this method, which runs throughout his work and no less his case studies: "This detracts from the evidential value of the analysis; but the procedure is the same in every case. For a psychoanalysis is not an impartial scientific investigation, but a therapeutic measure. Its essence is not to prove anything, but merely to alter something."[47]

The following summarizes the case known as Rat Man, a pseudonym for Ernst Lanzer (1878–1914), which was intended to be an exemplary case for the nascent method of Freudianism: "Freud mixed momentous insights with exaggerated claims," some of which "were made in his zeal to protect and promote a new discipline."[48] One of the most famous case studies of psychoanalytic literature has relatively recently surfaced with the case of the Wolf Man, a pseudonym for Sergei Pankejeff (1886–1979), who was interviewed by Viennese journalist Karin Obholzer prior to his death. Jones describes this case in the following way: "The case history known as that of the 'Wolfman' is assuredly the best of the series. Freud was then at the very height of his powers, a confident master of his method, and the technique."[49] The psychoanalytic pseudonym "Wolf Man" was given to the patient by Freud because of a dream that the patient had at the age four. Fromm discusses the case of the Wolf Man case and its shortcomings:

> Freud constructs a childhood neurosis which this man [Wolf Man] did not even experience—he was not sick at all. When this man brought up a dream he had when he was four, in which he saw [a pair of white] wolves sitting in a tree, Freud constructed that this man observed a primal scene, sexual intercourse between his parents, at the age of [one-and-a-half]. Freud develops

almost a need to construct and really does a lot of violation to his empirical observations.[50]

Freud's former patient the Wolf Man expresses some sixty years later that the treatment was far from successful: "That was the theory, that Freud had cured me 100 percent. You see, my memoirs, the entire book is based on that. And that's why [Muriel] Gardiner recommended that I write memoirs. To show the world how Freud had cured a seriously ill person...It's all false."[51] For this reason the patient known as the Wolf Man attempted to set the record straight. In retrospect, the so-called successful treatment appears as a sham of the highest caliber: "In reality, the whole thing looks like a catastrophe. I am in the same state as when I first came to Freud, and Freud is no more."[52] The patient known as the Wolf Man affirms, contrary to psycho-history and its reconstructions: "Instead of doing me some good, psychoanalysts did me harm."[53] Due to the limited recollection of the Wolf Man when undergoing analyses, Freud takes ownership of his psychoanalytic reconstruction: "The gaps...were filled...in a fashion which must be regarded as unexceptionable, if any value at all is attached to the analytic method of work."[54]

The history of psychoanalysis is strewn with horror stories. Between 1902, when the Vienna Psychoanalytic Society (formerly known as the Wednesday Psychological Society) was established, and 1938, at least 9 of the 149 members are known to have committed suicide.[55] To this fact, Freud would likely respond in his customary detached manner: "Do you know, I think we wear out quite a few men."[56]

Many attempts have been made to draw attention to the harm done by psychoanalysis, yet these attempts have been censored through silence or discredited altogether within the inner circle and its creation of psycho-history:

And then there is everything we do not find in the Biography's three thick volumes. We vainly search for the episode of Emma Eckstein's [1865–1924] catastrophic "nasal therapy" (there is only a mention, in passing, that she was one of the women with whom Freud maintained an intellectual relationship). No mention of the unbelievable erotic-analytic triangle of Ferenczi, Gizella Pálos [1863-1949] and her daughter Elma, to which Freud had played the role of family therapist. Nothing about the analysis of Anna Freud by her own father. Nothing about the suicides of Viktor Tausk [1879–1919] and Herbert Silberer [1882–1923], which the analytic rumour attributed to their relationships with Freud. Nothing about the murder of Hermine von Hug-Hellmuth [1871–1924], the pioneer of child psychoanalysis, by her nephew-patient; and nothing either about the fact that the so-called *A Young Girl's Diary* [1919], which she had edited and Freud had glowingly prefaced, was in reality a complete fabrication.[57]

Gay in his biography has regarded Anna Freud placement on the psychoanalytic couch by her own father as "a most irregular proceeding,"[58] and "a calculated flouting of the rules he had laid down with such force and precision."[59] For this reason, "Many Freudians have clearly experienced grave embarrassment over the revelation that Freud analyzed Anna. It is seldom discussed, and some people wish the information had never seen the light of day."[60] We learn, however, that this unethical practice was not an irregular occurrence within the psychoanalytic movement, as Gay reveals here:

> Jung, in his Freudian phase, had tried to psychoanalyze his wife; Max Graf had analyzed his son, Little Hans, with Freud as consultant in the background; Freud had analyzed his friends Eitingon and Ferenczi, and Ferenczi, in turn, his professional colleague Ernest Jones. More: in the early 1920s, years after Freud, in his technical papers, had described the analyst's attitude toward his patient as akin to the cool professional demeanor of the surgeon, the pioneering child analyst Melanie Klein analyzed her own children. When the eldest son of the Italian psychoanalyst Edoardo Weiss, preparing to enter his father's profession, asked him to be his analyst, Weiss consulted Freud. In his reply, Freud called such an analysis a "delicate business."[61]

The tragic case of Horace Frink is also another demonstration of the psychoanalytic abuses of power. Horace Frink (1883–1936) was a founding member of the New York Psychoanalytic Society who was anointed by the master as his protégé to lead the psychoanalytic movement in the New World. During Fink's analysis with the master, Fink informed Freud about his sexual attraction to one of his patients Angelika Bijur, the wealthy banking heiress. Freud encouraged his disciple's sexual liberation and recommended that Frink divorce his wife, Doris Best, and marry the rich patient. In defense of his conduct, Freud wrote in 1921 in a letter to Abraham Bijur's psychoanalyst: "I thought it the good right of every human being to strive for sexual gratification and tender love...both of which he [Frink] had not found with his wife [Doris Best]."[62] Horace Frink and Angelika Bijur were married in Paris on December 27, 1922.

Bijur's husband, Abraham Bijur, was furious about the situation and was threatening to expose this ethical misconduct on the part of Frink and the psychoanalytic movement to the world in an open letter to Freud. Fortuitously for Frink and no less for Freud, Abraham Bijur died of cancer in May 1922 before the letter was published.[63] Angelika Bijur connected the dots and discovered that Freud had promoted her marriage with Frink in order to acquire more funds for the psychoanalytic movement in America. She was correct in thinking this, as Freud wrote to Fink: "If matters turn out all right let us change this imaginary gift into a real contribution to the Psychoanalytic Funds..."[64] Interesting, Freud stresses for the public record that "Real sexual relations between patients and analysts are out of the question."[65]

Freud's flawed intervention, not to mention ethical misconduct, not only disintegrated Fink's marriage and his family and Angelika Bijur's marriage to her husband Abraham Bijur, but was a key factor that led to Fink's psychotic episode. Frink was admitted to the Henry Phipps Psychiatric Clinic, at Johns Hopkins Hospital, and placed in the care of psychiatrist Adolf Meyer in May 1924. It is frightening that Freud had minimized or overlooked Frink's deteriorating mental health and pronounced his analysis to have been completed. Frink had revered the master and was highly vulnerable to Freud's suggestion and consequent manipulation. When Frink was asked by his daughter, Helen Kraft, if he had the opportunity to convey a message to Freud what would it be? Frink responded, "Tell him he was a great man," adding, "even if he did invent psychoanalysis."[66]

In taking a broader look at the available case histories, it is evident that the clinical data regarding therapeutic efficacy of psychoanalysis is lacking, to say the least. British psychiatrist and psychoanalyst Anthony Storr (1920–2001) states: "the evidence that psychoanalysis cures anybody of anything is so shaky as to be practically non-existent."[67] After extensive research, Abraham Myerson (1881–1948) concludes the following about psychoanalytic theory and practice: "I state definitely that as a therapeutic system, psychoanalysis has failed to prove its worth."[68] German-American psychiatrist Fredric Wertham (1895–1981) unequivocally affirms the therapeutic futility of Freudian psychology: "From many years' experience in clinics I have come reluctantly to the conclusion that eight out of ten orthodox psychoanalyses are not indicated, and that six out of ten are more harmful than helpful."[69] Despite the lack of successful outcomes with psychoanalytic treatment, Freud nonetheless still holds strongly that "The psychic life of the patient is permanently changed by overcoming these resistances, it is lifted upon a higher plane of development and remains protected against new possibilities of disease. The work of overcoming resistance is the fundamental task of the analytic cure."[70]

The viability of psychoanalysis according to Freud paradoxically depends on the accurate screening of the likelihood of successful treatment for an individual: "Many attempts at treatment failed in the early years of analysis because they were made on cases that were not at all suited to the procedure."[71] In this same vein he adds: "Psychoanalytic treatment may be compared to a surgical operation, and has the right to be undertaken under circumstances favorable to its success."[72]

When the question is asked about the duration of psychoanalytic treatment, Freud responds in a roundabout manner, emphasizing that such a question is virtually unanswerable:

> Our answer is like the answer given by the Philosopher to the Wayfarer in Aesop's fable. When the Wayfarer asked how long a journey lay ahead, the Philosopher merely answered "Walk!" and afterwards explained his apparently unhelpful reply on the ground that he must know the length of the Wayfarer's stride before he could tell how long his journey would take. This expedient helps one over the first difficulties; but the comparison is not a good one, for the neurotic can easily alter his pace and may at times make only a very slow progress. In point of fact, the question as to the probable duration of a treatment is almost unanswerable.[73]

Although psychoanalysis no doubt attempts to present a total vision of the human being and the world, Freud admits that the "talking cure" is unable to provide one: "It must not be forgotten...that psychoanalysis...cannot offer a complete picture of the world."[74] More evidence points to therapeutic impasses rather than successes for the doctrine of the Freudian "talking cure," but the question needs to be asked, what about the harm caused to patients in the name of therapy?:

> Two of the cases were incomplete and the therapy ineffective. Freud's first case history dealt with an eighteen-year-old hysterical patient named "Dora." Treatment lasted only three months, when the patient, fed up with Freud's badgering manner [and]

insensitive insinuations, fled therapy. Freud's much later case of a female homosexual also terminated after a short time and involved no therapeutic improvement or even real treatment. A third case was not actually treated by Freud. He saw five-year-old "Little Hans" only once, the "analysis" having been conducted by the boy's father, who was a devout Freudian. Moreover, Little Hans, whose statements were repeatedly reinterpreted by his father and Freud to suit psychoanalytic theory, appears to have understood the straightforward traumatic source of his horse phobia, which followed his witnessing a carriage accident, better than either of his two would-be therapists. Using considerable common sense, Little Hans tried his best to resist Freud's oedipal "reconstructions" and interpretations; but his father and Freud, working in concert, gradually wore him down in an effort to get the case history to come out in a psychoanalytically correct fashion. Freud's other three cases reveal even more severe shortcomings.[75]

Jones comments on another perplexing fact, that "The fourth lengthy study, published in 1911, is remarkable inasmuch as Freud had never seen the patient."[76]

When critically assessed, Freud's case studies appear as a mirage of successful treatment, but when the illusion gives way, it becomes evident that the cases histories are constructions or reconstructions of failed treatment, attempting to further solidify the so-called scientific foundation of psychoanalysis and the Freudian myth. Ironically, even when no diagnosis can be made, the Freudian "talking cure" can still be of use, as indicated by Austrian writer and journalist Karl Kraus (1874–1936): "Psychopathology: if there is nothing wrong with a person, the best way to cure him is by explaining to him what illness he suffers from."[77] Or another ironic statement made about psychoanalysis: "Diagnosis: one of the commonest diseases."[78]

Freud's work, along with his case studies, appears to be closer to that of literature depicting the creative and no less subjective exploits of his own mind, as he himself discloses: "it still strikes me myself as strange that the case histories I write should read like short stories and that, as one might say, they lack the serious stamp of science."[79] An apologist or revisionist perspective is provided by Rieff, who exclaims: "It matters little whether Freud's case histories are called science or art. Freud's interpretative science was itself, in practice, an art, aiming at a transformation of the life thus interpreted."[80] There we have it, according to the adherents of psychoanalysis: it no longer appears to matter what actually transpires during the course of treatment as to how the outcome of therapy is interpreted. Fact and fiction are thus blurred indefinitely. An interesting rationale for the existence of the doctrine of the "talking cure" has been summarized in the following manner: "there is only one justification for the existence of psychoanalysis: it is useful for unmasking psychoanalysis."[81]

Chapter 21

Freud on the Psychoanalytic Couch:
A Case History of
Unfinished Self-Analysis

"The minds of others I know well; / But who I am, I cannot tell"[1] reveals Nietzsche. From its very inception, the psychoanalytic doctrine was not a portrayal of clinical observations on and scientific research of the nature of the human mind and behavior, but was rather a crisis within the psyche of one man alone—its founder—and an attempt to resolve this crisis. Psychoanalyst Heinz Hartmann (1894–1970) upheld: "The story of the creation of psychoanalysis is at the same time the story of the creator's crisis."[2] Freud's own self-analysis was imperative to the formation of psychoanalysis, as Wells emphasizes: "Psychoanalysis proper is essentially the product of Freud's self-analysis."[3] Despite this acknowledgment, the belief in the Freudian myth of the hero prevails within orthodox psychoanalytic circles: "Among Freudians, Freud's self-analysis remains singular. Psychoanalysis begins with the heroic exception to the rule that the self may not know the self, the subject not be its own object."[4] Even though Freud is depicted as the hero, who has accomplished something that no other human before him has accomplished, he demonstrated a great deal of reluctance to take his own medicine of lying on the psychoanalytic couch to undergo analysis of his own. Yet the biblical teaching nonetheless instructs: "Physician, heal thyself" (Luke 4:23).

The master's adversity to being analyzed became apparent to his onetime disciple Jung and created an unsurmountable tension in their relationship, which ultimately led to its demise. Jung writes: "Meanwhile you [Freud] remain on top as the father, sitting pretty. For sheer obsequiousness nobody dares to pluck the prophet by the beard and inquire for once what you would say to a patient with a tendency to analyse the analyst instead of himself. You would certainly ask him: 'Who's got the neurosis?'"[5]

Jung fought against Freud's *ad hominem* attempts to pathologize his disciples: "your technique of treating your pupils like patients is a *blunder*. In that way you produce either slavish sons or impudent puppies."[6] Freud's resistance to being analyzed—or his refusal—became exceptionally clear to Jung when on their seven-week voyage to America, Freud was confronted by the undeniable fact that he would not let himself be analyzed by Jung, and Freud immediately ended any such attempts by emphasizing: "I cannot risk my authority!"[7]

Freud did not want others to have access to his intrapsychic world and felt threatened by such attempts to storm the psyche of the master to acquire its secrets. For this reason he selected a less threatening option, and engaged in what he termed "self-analysis." This situation was untenable for Jung and foreshadowed the end of their relationship, as Jung wrote: "Freud was placing personal authority above truth."[8] Jung attempted to have the master look at himself impartially by urging Freud to analyze his own resistance to being analyzed: "If ever you should rid yourself entirely of your complexes and stop playing the father to your sons [disciples] and instead of aiming continually at their weak spots take a good look at your own for a change, then I will mend my ways and at one stroke uproot the vice of being in two minds about you."[9]

Freud verified truth on his own terms as if he were trademarking his own brand of science, knowledge, myth, or worldview, for that matter, and would not budge on this matter. A significant factor in the history of the psychoanalytic movement is that Freud himself never underwent the psychoanalytic initiation, as did his disciples and other psychoanalysts. Lacan speaks to the irony of this situation that Freud, the master, did not live up to the criteria of psychoanalytic orthodoxy as he was unanalyzed: "The truth is perhaps simply one thing, namely, the desire of Freud himself, the fact that something, in Freud, was never analyzed."[10] The fact that Freud did not undergo his own psychoanalytic initiation is not in any way perceived as a flaw according to orthodox psychoanalysis; on the contrary it only adds to the Freudian myth or legend and reaffirms his messianic vocation. Rieff confirms the quasi-supernatural nature of Freud's achievement: "Freud's self-analysis stands outside the tests of his own science; it is like the mystery of the unmoved mover."[11]

Freud again insisted that each analyst first be analyzed before practicing the Freudian doctrine on others, and did not give the option of self-analysis to other disciples or practitioners of psychoanalysis:

> But if the doctor is to be in a position to use his unconscious in this way as an instrument in the analysis, he must himself fulfill one psychological condition to a high degree. He may not tolerate any resistances in himself which hold back from his consciousness what has been perceived by his unconscious; otherwise he

would introduce into the analysis a new species of selection and distortion which would be far more detrimental than that resulting from concentration of conscious attention. It is not enough for this that he himself should be an approximately normal person. It may be insisted, rather, that he should have undergone a psycho-analytic purification and have become aware of those complexes of his own which would be apt to interfere with his grasp of what the patient tells him.[12]

The impetus for engaging in the sojourn of self-analysis was to overcome the psychic obstacles within the master himself: "I [Freud] have...difficulties to overcome, which lie within myself."[13] Freud held the highest expectations for his self-analysis, as he writes: "My self-analysis is the most important thing I have in hand, and promises to be of the greatest value to me, when it is finished."[14] Even though he initially believed that his self-analysis was not only possible but efficacious, this was short lived, as he then hit an impasse and emphasized that it was an impossible feat: "My self-analysis is still interrupted. I have now seen why. I can only analyse myself with objectively acquired knowledge (as if I were a stranger); self-analysis is really impossible, otherwise there would be no [neurotic] illness. As I have come across some puzzles in my own case, it is bound to hold up the self-analysis."[15]

The way in which Freud's psychoanalysis on his patients and his own personal self-analysis were enmeshed and influenced one another was striking and no less puzzling, given the presumed scientific legitimacy of his "talking cure." Rank observes: "To put it bluntly, in one sentence which shakes the foundation of the whole Freudian system and of psychology in general, for that matter: Freud, without knowing it, interpreted the analytical situation in terms of his worldview and did not, as he thought, analyze the individual's unconscious objectively."[16]

Freud comments: "As I have come across some puzzles in my own case, it is bound to hold up the self-analysis."[17] Elsewhere, he discloses that while progress can be made with self-analysis, it is limited at best. Psychoanalysis provided by a qualified therapist who has been initiated into the "talking cure" is more effective: "One learns psycho-analysis on oneself, by studying one's own personality...Nevertheless, there are definite limits to progress by this method. One advances much further if one is analysed oneself by a practiced analyst."[18]

Freud realized the utilization of dreams and their importance on his own therapeutic process: "I soon saw the necessity of an analysis of myself and this I carried out with the help of a series of my own dreams which led me back through all the events of my childhood; I am still to-day of the opinion that this kind of analysis may suffice for anyone who is a prolific dreamer and not too abnormal."[19] Freud informs us that it was his own psychopathology that impeded his self-analysis: "my own neurosis has been obstructing any progress in the understanding of neurosis."[20]

While Freud had the ambition to conquer the world, we can only imagine the hurt and rage that he may have experienced when over-hearing his father expressing: "The boy will come to nothing."[21] The role of Freud's mother was key for both his inner development and that of psychoanalysis. Freud writes: "A single idea of general value dawned on me. I have found, in my own case too, [the phenomena of] being in love with my mother and jealous of my father, and I now consider it a universal event in early childhood."[22] Freud draws quintessential conclusions about the nature of humanity through his own self-analysis: "[Oedipus's] destiny moves us only because it might have been ours—because the oracle laid the same curse upon us before our birth as upon him. It is the fate of all of us, perhaps, to direct our first sexual impulse towards our mother and our first hatred and our first murderous wish against our father. Our dreams convince us that that is so."[23]

Of King Oedipus Freud remarks: "King Oedipus, who slew his father Laïus and married his mother Jocasta, merely shows us the fulfilment of our own childhood wishes."[24] Jones also confirms this: "One must suppose that in Freud's earliest years there had been extremely strong motives for concealing some important phase of his development—perhaps even from himself. I would venture to surmise it was his deep love for his mother."[25]

Fromm illustrates that the construction of the doctrine of the Oedipus complex was a way for Freud to bypass the emotional intensity he felt for his mother:

> This intense attachment of Freud to his mother, most of which he concealed from others, and probably from himself, is of the greatest importance not only for the understanding of Freud's character, but also for the appreciation of one of his fundamental discoveries, that of the Oedipus complex. Freud explained the attachment to the mother—quite rationalistically—as being based on the sexual attraction of the little boy to the woman with whom

he is most intimate. But, considering the intensity of his attachment to his own mother, and the fact that he tended to repress it, it is understandable that he interpreted one of the most powerful strivings in man, the craving for the care, protection and all-enveloping love and affirmation of Mother, as the more limited wish of the little boy to satisfy his instinctual needs through Mother. He discovered one of the most fundamental strivings in man, the wish to remain attached to Mother, and that is to the womb, to nature, to pre-individualistic, pre-conscious existence—and at the same time he negated this very discovery by restricting it to the small sector of instinctual desires. His own attachment to Mother was the basis of his discovery and his resistance to seeing his attachment was the basis for the limitation and distortion of this very discovery.[26]

Many critics of Freud have suggested that his obsession with sexuality stems from his own sexual dysfunction. According to French writer Maryse Choisy (1903–79), "Is not then Freud's theory a rationalization of his own sexual inhibition?"[27]

As we learn, Freud entered many non-ordinary if not pathological states of mind through his sojourn of self-analysis: "in probing the psychic depths of others he was obliged sometimes to descend into regions of his own mind where contact with the chaotic, the incongruous, the uncanny, and the demented required all the strength of his powers to stay sane."[28] Freud, in the course of his own self-analysis, states: "I have been through some kind of a neurotic experience, with odd states of mind not intelligible to consciousness—cloudy thoughts and veiled doubts, with barely here and there a ray of light..."[29] He continues: "I believe I am in a cocoon, and heaven knows what sort of creature will emerge from it."[30] He also writes: "No one can help me in the least with what oppresses me; it is my cross, I must bear it; and God knows that in adapting to it, my back has become noticeably bent."[31] The topsy-turvy terrain of Freud's psyche proved to be exceptionally challenging for him to traverse and left him unable to communicate what he had undergone:

After a spell of good spirits here I [Freud] am now having a fit of gloom. The chief patient I am busy with is myself. My little hysteria, which was much intensified by work, has yielded one stage further. The rest still sticks. That is the first reason for my mood. This analysis is harder than any other. It is also the thing that paralyses the power of writing down and communicating what so far I have learned. But I believe it has got to be done and is a necessary stage in my work.[32]

Hagiographer Jones refers to these non-ordinary states or psychopathology of his master as the "twilight condition of mind":

There is ample evidence that for ten years or so—roughly comprising the nineties—he suffered from a very considerable psychoneurosis...[H]is sufferings were at times very intense, and for those ten years there could have been only occasional intervals when life seemed much worth living...It consisted essentially in extreme changes of mood, and the only respects in which the anxiety got localized were occasional attacks of dread of dying...and anxiety about traveling by rail...The alternations of mood were between periods of elation, excitement, and self-confidence on the one hand and periods of severe depression, doubt, and inhibition on the other. In the depressed moods he could neither write nor concentrate his thoughts...He would spend leisure hours of extreme boredom, turning from one thing to another, cutting open books, looking at maps of ancient Pompeii, playing patience or chess, but being unable to continue at anything for long—a state of restless paralysis. Sometimes there were spells where consciousness would be greatly narrowed: states, difficult to describe, with a veil that produced almost a twilight condition of mind.[33]

Freud attests to the psychological upheavals that he experienced during the period he wrote *The Interpretation of Dreams*: "It is an intellectual hell, layer upon layer or it, with everything fitfully gleaming and pulsating; and the outline of Lucifer-Amor coming into sight at the darkest centre."[34]

The reflections of James, although not specifically referring to Freud, speak broadly to the therapeutic mindset and its idiosyncrasies: "Like most psychologists...he makes of his personal peculiarities a rule."[35] This is an interesting disclosure that provides insight into the fact that mental health professionals work with people in a way that reflects their own individuality and is not neutral or objective as is often assumed. While this makes sense and is logical, it nonetheless presents challenges for the notion of scientific objectivity. Freud comments: "this technique [psychoanalysis] is the only one suited to my individuality."[36]

In the preface of the second edition of *The Interpretation of Dreams*, Freud reveals the subjective source of his alleged scientific psychology, which was in large part obtained through his own personal analysis: "For this book [*The Interpretation of Dreams*] has a further subjective significance for me personally—a significance which I only grasped after I had completed it. It was, I found, a portion of my own self-analysis, my reaction to my father's death—that is to say, to the most important event, the most poignant loss, of a man's life."[37]

Freud discloses that his childhood relationship with a nephew of his had become "the source of all my friendships and all my hatreds."[38] Freud provides a vital glimpse into the intrapsychic workings of his mind:

> My emotional life has always insisted that I should have an intimate friend and a hated enemy. I have always been able to provide myself afresh with both, and it has not infrequently happened that the ideal situation of childhood has been so completely reproduced that friend and enemy have come together in a single individual—though not, of course, both at once or with constant oscillations, as may have been the case in my early childhood.[39]

There were distinguishable signs of interpersonal difficulties in Freud's relationships since his formative childhood years. As an adult Freud appeared to be able to hold an individual as an intimate friend and at the same time a hated enemy; both dynamics could coexist together in the same individual. Jones observes this double-edged tendency in the master: "We know that with Freud intense love and hate were specially apt to go hand in hand."[40] Freud in fact appeared to thrive in the face of hostility and embraced it with open arms: "It is an honour to have plenty of enemies!"[41]

The relationship between Freud and Jung when examined within a psychodynamic lens takes on a more nuanced meaning: "Freud was in 'narcissistic transference,' that he saw in Jung an idealized version of himself,"[42] and conversely in Jung there was a double mix of "idealization of Freud and grandiosity in the self."[43] When Jung referred to the master's disposition with the phrase "[h]is neurotic tendency,"[44] perhaps he was alluding to Freud's own characterization of himself, which appears to have become a self-fulfilling prophecy: "a man with unbridled ambition is bound at some time to break away and, to the loss of science and his own development, become a crank."[45]

We might reflect on what appears to be for Freud a subconscious compulsion to repeat the patterns of interpersonal conflicts as is evident with his former collaborators due to his need to be on top as the master. Although the following does not speak to this phenomenon directly, it nonetheless frames the dynamic well:

> Thus we have come across people all of whose human relationships have the same outcome: such as the benefactor who is abandoned in anger after a time by each of his protégés, however much they may otherwise differ from one another, and who thus seems doomed to taste all the bitterness of ingratitude; or the man whose friendships all end in betrayal by his friend; or the man who time after time in the course of his life raises someone else into a position of great private or public authority and then, after a certain interval, himself upsets that authority and replaces him by a new one.[46]

Freud realized the dangers of unfinished or unsuccessful treatment, concluding that "in self-analysis the danger of incompleteness is particularly great. One is too soon satisfied with a part explanation, behind which resistance may easily be keeping back something that is more important perhaps."[47] Jung addresses what he views as the core dilemma for those wishing to follow in the footsteps of the master to undergo their own self-analysis: "There are analysts who believe that they can get along with a self-analysis...and they will certainly remain stuck. They forget that one of the most important therapeutically effective factors is subjecting yourself to the objective judgment of another."[48]

Jones himself emphasizes that "No self-analysis, it is true, however ruthlessly pursued, can completely resolve the deepest unconscious conflicts."[49] There are those within contemporary psychology who have also come to the same conclusion regarding the limited efficacy of this method: "Self-analysis...has distinct limitations...Rare, almost to the point of being non-existent, are those who fully perform it."[50]

While everyone else was required to undergo the psychoanalytic initiation of analysis, Freud, being the master, alternatively opted out of this fundamental requirement and decided to undertake his own self-analysis. Freud's self-analysis appeared to be at an impasse because of his own internal resistance and was far from being completed, yet Freud comes to the bizarre conclusion that "I have examined myself thoroughly and come to the conclusion that I don't need to change much."[51] This does not reflect the historical record as it stands today. Breuer provides a less-than-positive reflection on Freud: "Freud is a man given to absolute and exclusive formulations: this is a psychical need which, in my opinion, leads to excessive generalization."[52]

As Freud did not have to undergo his own analysis, the question still remains: "Who could guarantee that Freud's analysis had been complete?"[53] Freud then asks a peculiar question that casts doubt on the efficacy of the entire establishment of the psychoanalytic "talking cure," suggesting that the task itself was an impossible feat: "Who, after all, has been sufficiently analyzed?"[54] Self-analysis provided Freud with a way out, so that he did not need to bare the contents of his psyche to another human being. This peering into the inner recesses of the master's psyche, in Freud's eyes, would have fundamentally compromised his role as the master. What becomes apparent is that Freud was unable to take his own psychoanalytic prescription: "Being entirely honest with oneself is a good exercise."[55] According to Puner, it becomes blatantly clear: "For all his will finally to psychoanalyze himself, the father of psychoanalysis met within his own psyche a resistance greater than that with which any patient had confronted him. He looked at himself but he did not see himself whole."[56]

It remains to be analyzed whether the "human megalomania" that Freud emphasized in his parable of the "three blows" that he vehemently attacked and attempted to sublimate through the vices of his psychoanalytic theory was not a projection of his own megalomania stemming from his own psychological imbalance. Professor John Farrell illustrates the imbalance found within the psyche of the master: "The fact that Freudian suspicion respects no limit, the fact that it is total, betrays...that it is a product of compulsive rhetoric and personal imperative rather than observation...For the psychoanalytic mind, nothing is what it seems. Every human act must be reduced within the code of suspicion."[57]

Freud realized that "objective knowledge" was a prerequisite for his self-analysis and no doubt also for the credibility of psychoanalysis itself, yet his understanding of what objective knowledge signifies in its truest sense departs radically from the sapiential traditions of the world. Time and time again, we find that Freud's psychoanalysis is in reality a description of his own journey into the psychic underworld. Professor José Brunner adds: "Freud overexpanded the psychoanalytic framework in order to demonstrate its all-encompassing inclusiveness and to apply to large-scale social processes and institutions the concepts and categories which he had developed in his writings on the private realm."[58] As has been put forward by several writers, rather than being neutral or objective, the psychoanalytic process aimed at deliberately influencing the individual through suggestion and was in reality a form of mind control, as emphasized by E. Michael Jones: "Freud was not interested in freeing people from the slavery of sin. He was much more interested in giving people permission to sin and then reaping financial benefits by absolving them of guilt (or claiming to do so) in psychoanalysis and thereby gaining control over them."[59]

To achieve psychiatric or therapeutic equity, Freudian psychology would need to undergo its own analysis. Friedell remarks: "What should really be done is to psycho-analyse psycho-analysis."[60] Freud would have benefited greatly if he had taken to the traditional maxim that individuals suffering from a sick soul are unable to heal themselves or be their own healers and must entrust themselves to those who know the healing arts. As Marcus Tullius Cicero (106-43) counsels: "The soul that is sick cannot rightly prescribe for itself, except by following the instruction of wise men."[61]

And yet for whatever intrapsychic reasons, he was unable to do so. What remains noteworthy and at the same time very disconcerting is that "Freud himself...is the only man who has been able to impress his own neurosis on the world, and remold humanity in his own image."[62] Jung provides readers with an ironic truth about the doctrine of the "talking cure," which is in alignment with the master's own outlook: "rule 1 of psychoanalysis: principles of Freudian psychology apply to everyone except the analyser."[63] Freud made many errors that on a human level are understandable; however, when he attempted to project these errors onto humanity in the form of ultimate truth, it became blatantly evil. Seneca's teachings speak loud and clear when applied to Freud: *"Errare humanum est, sed perseverare diabolicum"* (To err is human, but to persist in error is diabolical).

Chapter 22

Freud's Cocaine Episode

Freud began researching the therapeutic potential of cocaine isolated from coca leaves in 1884 and considered it a "miracle drug." The importance of Freud's research on cocaine is informative for both the historical posterity of the man himself and the formation of Freudian psychology. Bernfeld makes this point: "The cocaine episode is therefore not only of interest to the biographical consideration of Freud, but also bears directly on the development of psychoanalysis."[1] Freud's monograph "On Coca" (1884) is erroneously titled, as coca leaves are not equivalent to the drug cocaine and are not habit-forming. Coca leaves have been used by the First Peoples of South America since time immemorial and are highly valued and considered sacred. They are used for their myriad medicinal properties and for traditional religious rites and rituals.[2]

The depth of Freud's involvement with cocaine becomes most visible when we read his clinical notebooks, as his preferred experimental subject was himself:

> I realize that such experiments on oneself possess the dubious feature of demanding in the same matter double credibility in the person undertaking them. But for external reasons I had to do it, since none of the individuals at my disposal showed such a regular reaction to cocaine. However, the results of the investigation were also confirmed through my testing of other persons— mainly colleagues.[3]

It needs to be remembered that at the time Freud was researching cocaine it was not illegal or a controlled substance, nor were the harmful aspects of the drug known to the general scientific community. Freud's enthusiasm for the "miracle drug" cocaine is noted when he writes: "On the basis of my experiences with the effects of cocaine, I have no hesitation in recommending the administration of cocaine."[4]

The following provides a sense of how involved he was in his "research" on, or rather unrestrained consumption of, cocaine:

[The psychic effect of cocaine consists of] exhilaration and last-ing euphoria, which in no way differs from the normal euphoria of the healthy person...You perceive an increase of self-control, possess more vitality and capacity for work...In other words, you are simply normal; and it is soon difficult to believe that one is under the influence of any drug... Long-lasting, intensive mental or physical labor is performed without fatigue...You are able—on demand—to eat well and without disgust, but you have the clear impression that the meal was not required...This effect of hardening you against work...is enjoyed without any of the un-pleasant aftermaths which accompany exhilaration through alco-holic means. [And this amazing drug is not habit forming.] Ab-solutely no craving for further use of cocaine appears after the first, or repeated, taking of the drug; rather you feel a certain un-motivated aversion to it.[5]

Freud informs readers as to why he began using cocaine: "I was making frequent use of cocaine at that time to reduce some trouble-some nasal swellings."[6] This is a curious omission, as nasal swellings are a common response to the use of cocaine, therefore suggesting his regular use, if not abuse, of this drug. Eysenck observes: "What is beyond any doubt is that the odd changes that took place in Freud correspond very precisely to the kind of changes, both physical and psychological, which have been noted many times in patients suffer-ing from cocaine addiction."[7] Elsewhere Freud discloses experiencing auditory hallucinations that could also be attributed to cocaine use: "During the days when I was living alone in a foreign city—I was a young man at the time—I quite often heard my name suddenly called by an unmistakable and beloved voice; I then noted down the exact moment of the hallucination and made anxious enquires of those at home about what had happened at the time. Nothing had happened."[8]

Jones states that Freud took the drug to alleviate mental health symptoms that he was experiencing: "Cocaine calmed the agitation and dispelled the depression."[9] The substance also aided Freud in tem-porarily suspending unsolicited thoughts emerging from the uncon-scious entering into the conscious mind: "Freud observed on his own person that cocaine could paralyze some disturbing element and thus release his full normal vitality."[10] Freud openly admitted that with re-peated treatments of the drug that: "I need a lot of cocaine."[11] Accord-ing to his official biographer, Jones, the master appeared to have abused this substance: "I am afraid that Freud took more cocaine than he should though I am not mentioning that [in the biography]."[12]

Freud also realized the erotic potential of cocaine and wrote to Martha Bernays, his fiancée at the time, encouraging her to participate in the use of this substance:

> Woe to you, my Princess, when I come. I will kiss you quite red and feed you till you are plump. And if you are forward you shall see who is the stronger, a gentle little girl who doesn't eat enough or a big wild man *who has cocaine* in *his body*. In my last severe depression I took coca again and a small dose lifted me to the heights in a wonderful fashion. I am just now busy collecting the literature for a song of praise to this magical substance.[13]

Freud provides interesting reflections on the human condition while under the influence of cocaine that disclose how the drug distorts reality, making things appear other than what they truly are: "The bit of cocaine I have just taken is making me talkative, my little woman. I will go on writing and comment on your criticism of my wretched self. Do you realize how strangely a human being is constructed, that his virtues are often the seed of his downfall and his faults the source of his happiness?"[14]

According to medical historian E. M. Thornton, cocaine was the inspiration for the Freudian doctrine of the unconscious, which is the heart of psychoanalytic psychology:

> Freud's concept of the "unconscious" must be attributed to his cocaine usage; death wishes, infantile incestuous desires, perversion, and excrement are not the preoccupations of a normal mind. Constantly recurring throughout the drug literature are the same words and phrases used by Freud and his followers to describe his concept of the unconscious mind...In both psychoanalysis and this literature the same metaphors of "looking down into an abyss" occur.[15]

Within Freud's book *Cocaine Papers* is an essay by Louis Lewin (1850–1929), the eminent German pharmacologist and author of the classic book *Phantastica* (1924) on mind-altering drugs and plants. Lewin's concluding reflections on the drug are powerful and thought-provoking, and certainly speak not only to the use of cocaine but perhaps to that of all mind-altering substances: "Those who believe they can enter the temple of happiness through this gate of pleasure purchase their momentary delights at the cost of body and soul. They speedily pass through the gate of unhappiness into the night of the abyss."[16]

Chapter 23

Childhood Sexual Abuse and the Betrayal of Truth

"[O]ne has demonstrated to them the solution of a more-than-thou-sand- year-old problem, a caput Nili [source of the Nile]!"[1]—*Sigmund Freud*

Perhaps the best-kept secret within the formation of psychoanalysis and that of modern psychology in its entirety is Sigmund Freud's retraction of the "seduction theory" or the idea that neurosis or psychopathology in adults was caused by childhood sexual trauma. Families had brought their little children to be treated by Freud because of what they considered to be symptoms of mental illness, but what Freud discovered was that they were not suffering from mental illness but in fact had been sexually assaulted. Freud initially set out to expose this abuse and stood up for the rights of the voiceless children, demonstrating courage and honesty, but he then took a fundamentally different turn by abandoning this position and denying the occurrence of the sexual abuse. Some have blamed Freud for sowing the seeds for "false memory syndrome." This consists of memories of events or facts that are untrue or did not occur, but are nonetheless strongly believed by the individual to be true.[2]

The epidemic of childhood sexual abuse continues today and has an enormous impact on society.[3] With this said, the repudiation of the seduction theory was a decisive turn that was an assault on the psychological health and well-being of innumerable children. Mental health professionals who were mandated to report such cases of abuse may have stopped or under-reported them because of the Freudian influence that wrote them off as fantasy. Masson speaks to the difficulties faced by those who came to discuss their sexual trauma with Freud:

> Freud's female patients had the courage to face what had happened to them in childhood—often this included violent scenes of rape by a father—and to communicate their traumas to Freud, no doubt hesitating to believe their own memories and reluctant to remember the deep shame and hurt they had felt. Freud

listened and understood and gave them permission to remember and speak of these terrible events.[4]

On October 15, 1895, Freud wrote a letter to Fliess that provides an important disclosure on the seduction theory: "Have I revealed the great clinical secret...Hysteria is the consequence of a presexual *sexual shock*...Obsessional neurosis is the consequence of a presexual *sexual pleasure*...'Presexual' means actually before puberty, before the release of sexual substances..."[5] Prior to 1896 Freud appeared to be convinced that the sexual abuse of young children was due to the betrayal of their innocence by adults. However, after 1896, he had a mysterious change of mind on this matter, which has had immense repercussions not only for psychoanalysis, but for the entire field of psychology.

What caused Freud to abandon the seduction theory and decide that the sexual abuse of children was fantasy or delusion? Here lies one of the most captivating stories to be told regarding modern psychology and the events that transpired within the inner circle of psychoanalysis. What the psychoanalytic movement could have done to be the fearless voice and defender of innumerable children exposed to the horrors of sexual abuse if it were not for the repudiation of the seduction theory, we will never know.

Freud delivered a lecture entitled "The Aetiology of Hysteria" to the Vienna Society for Psychiatry and Neurology on April 21, 1896, in which he broke the silence on the sexual abuse of children amongst his patients. This is noted in the following: "I therefore put forward the thesis that at the bottom of every case of hysteria there are *one or more occurrences of premature sexual experience*, occurrences which belong to the earliest years of childhood."[6] This statement was received negatively and as a result Freud lost some colleagues over it. To Freud's credit he was initially willing to stand alone in the face of this adversity on behalf of the multitude of voiceless children, who experienced this trauma. Freud asserts:

> As regards the controversial matter itself, I will only remark that the singling out of the sexual factor in the aetiology of hysteria springs at least from no preconceived opinion on my part. The two investigators as whose pupil I began my studies of hysteria, Charcot and Breuer, were far from having any such presupposition; in fact they had a personal disinclination to it which I originally shared."[7]

It is from this theory itself that some suggest the science of psychoanalysis derived and yet, it is the same theory that provides the most severe "blow" to the doctrine of the "talking cure." Freud anticipated that he would encounter objections to the seduction theory and tried to appeal to the scientific mindset by asserting that others should take his word and submit to his authority and not empirical evidence. Freud observes:

> Only the most laborious and detailed investigations have converted me, and that slowly enough, to the view I hold to-day. If you submit my assertion that the aetiology of hysteria lies in sexual life to the strictest examination, you will find that it is supported by the fact that in some eighteen cases of hysteria I have been able to discover this connection in every single symptom, and, where the circumstances allowed, to confirm it by therapeutic success.[8]

At first Freud concluded that most adult neurosis was due to sexual abuse in childhood, yet he later recanted this view and decided that patients were recalling fantasies mistaken for reality: "I cannot help concluding that what I am dealing with is something that never happened at all but has been unjustifiably smuggled in among...childhood memories."[9] This reinforced his sexual theory, which postulated that daughters had a secret wish to be seduced by their father and likewise sons secretly wished to be seduced by their mother; this was the Oedipus complex in males and the Electra complex in females, which also asserted that sons and daughters unconsciously wanted to kill their fathers or mothers.

In doing away with the seduction theory, he undermined the real and terrible traumas that his patients as children had experienced, thus regarding their suffering as childish sexual "fantasies." This has caused considerable controversy, calling into question the very scientific premises underlying psychoanalysis, if not modern psychology as a whole.[10] With this said, it is dumbfounding to find those who nonetheless still uphold the erroneous notion that "The nature of infantile sexuality and its importance for the development of the personality structure were never specifically understood before Freud."[11] Crews points to the censoring of the facts and the ongoing revisions made to his theory to cover his tracks:

> [E]ven when [Freud] felt secure enough to admit his seduction mistake and turn it to rhetorical advantage, he continued to adulterate the facts. In 1896 the alleged seducers of infants were said

to have been governesses, teachers, servants, strangers, and sib-
lings, but in later descriptions Freud retroactively changed most
of them to fathers so that a properly oedipal spin could be placed
on the recycled material. At every stage, earlier acts of fakery and
equivocation were compounded by fresh ones.[12]

Freud reveals this ambiguity in the discernment between truth and
falsehood in "traumatic experiences," which highlights the topsy-
turvy nature of his alleged scientific findings:

> If the infantile experiences brought to light by analysis were in-
> variably real, we should feel that we were standing on firm
> ground; if they were regularly falsified and revealed as inven-
> tions, as phantasies of the patient, we should be obliged to aban-
> don this shaky ground and look for salvation elsewhere. But nei-
> ther of these things is the case: the position can be shown to be
> that the childhood experiences constructed or remembered in
> analysis are sometimes indisputably false and sometimes equally
> certainly correct, and in most cases compounded of truth and
> falsehood.[13]

Jones documented this about the rejection of the seduction theory:
"He [Freud] at first accepted his patients' stories of their parents' sexual overtures towards them when they were children, but came to realize that the stories were simply phantasies derived from his patients'
own childhood."[14] Freud himself disclosed "the great secret" to Fliess
in a letter written on September 21, 1897: "I no longer believe in my
neurotic [theory of neurosis]."[15] Yet this is a rather ambiguous confession, for we know nothing as to what this actually implies or what
prompted it. Another significant clue lies in this letter written to
Fliess, when Freud writes of "The continual disappointment in my
efforts to bring a single analysis to a real conclusion."[16]

The suggested proof of these successful cases is in fact, as we
learn, fictional and not true, as Freud confesses to Flies on March 7,
1897: "I have not yet finished a single case."[17] His lack of success
with these cases provoked an inner conflict within Freud. It also needs
to be noted that Freud wanted his personal correspondence with Fliess
destroyed, and with good reason, as much of it contradicts what is
published in his collected writings or the official biography. While we
can hypothesize about what would have occurred if Freud had not
abandoned the seduction theory, Freud's daughter Anna Freud makes
a paramount statement in a letter dated September 10, 1981 about this

subject: "Keeping up the seduction theory would mean to abandon the Oedipus complex, and with it the whole importance of phantasy life, conscious or unconscious phantasy. In fact, I think there would have been no psychoanalysis afterwards."[18]

Freud's paper "Femininity," published in 1932, is representative of his final revisions on the seduction theory, which are worth citing: "In the period in which the main interest was directed to discovering infantile sexual traumas, almost all my women patients told me that they had been seduced by their father. I was driven to recognize in the end that these reports were untrue and so came to understand that hysterical symptoms are derived from phantasies and not from real occurrences."[19]

The above point is deeply troubling and unfortunate, to say the least, given the fact that Freud had acknowledged the seduction theory nearly four years prior to this statement. Regrettable as it may be, Freud did make similar statements earlier, as exemplified by: "Hysterical symptoms are not attached to actual memories, but to phantasies erected on the basis of memories."[20] One can only imagine how many children would have benefited from his initial recognition and validation of childhood sexual abuse and its traumatic effects that can often endure throughout the lifespan of an individual and even become intergenerational.

Many might suggest that Freud's former disciple, Jung, may have viewed things differently, and while this might be the case in some things, we see that regarding childhood sexual trauma, this is far from the case, as he too appears to have colluded that it was fantasy. In a letter dated April 27, 1912, Jung had expressed to Freud: "Like you, I am absorbed in the incest problem and have come to conclusions which show incest primarily as a fantasy problem."[21] Less than a month later, in a letter dated May 17, 1912, Jung acknowledges that Freud took "the so-called sexual trauma" seriously, mistaking fantasies for realities, and expresses a chilling point of view on the matter: "The trauma is *seemingly important* or real," but "*cum grano salis* it doesn't matter whether a sexual trauma really occurred or not, or was a mere fantasy."[22] In a letter dated May 23, 1912, Freud acknowledges to Jung his original mistake about taking the reports of sexual trauma in his patients seriously: "I value your letter for the warning it contains, and the reminder of my first big error, when I mistook fantasies for realities."[23]

Janet Malcolm summarizes the severity of what Freud's abandonment of the seduction theory signified for the doctrine of the "talking cure": "When Freud abandoned the seduction theory, it was the death of psychoanalysis. The received truth is that it was the *birth* of psychoanalysis, but it wasn't; it was the end, and, deep down, all analysts know it was the end. That is why they all feel like such frauds. They do analysis because it's good business, but in their innermost souls they feel utterly fraudulent."[24]

Freud viewed events of a human being's life as all being recorded and kept in a depository of the individual's unconscious to be accessed if they could be released from repression. With this said, the notion of remembering is not as straightforward as one might assume. Professor Elizabeth F. Loftus, a specialist on human memory, writes:

> [H]uman remembering does not work like a videotape recorder or a movie camera. When a person wants to remember something he or she does not simply pluck a whole memory intact out of a "memory store." The memory is constructed from stored and available bits of information; any gaps in the information are filled in unconsciously by inferences. When these fragments are integrated and make sense, they form what we call a memory.[25]

Perls asserts: "The great error of psychoanalysis is in assuming that the memory is reality." He then goes to the other extreme, to steadfastly deny childhood trauma altogether: "the so-called *traumata*...are an invention of the patient...None of these traumata has ever been proved to exist. I haven't seen a single case of infantile trauma that wasn't a falsification. They are all lies to be hung onto in order to justify one's unwillingness to grow."[26]

While Freud insists on the retrieval of the individual's hidden memories of the past, psychoanalysis, as he himself emphasizes, does not always conform to this method and takes a different approach: "Quite often we do not succeed in bringing the patient to recollect what has been repressed. Instead...we produce in him an assured conviction of the truth of the construction which achieves the same therapeutic result as a recaptured memory."[27] This is another astonishing passage as it confirms that the retrieval of authentic memories is practically unnecessary to treatment, as psychoanalytic theory has the power to produce successful treatment regardless of the retrieved memory if the individual can accept the therapeutic construction provided to him or her by the mental health professional.

It is worth noting that Webster emphasizes that there was no abandonment of the seduction theory in the way that Freud critics suggest, because the initial memories of sexual abuse were constructed, suggested, or forced onto individuals by Freud himself. Webster writes:

"The purpose of Freud's therapeutic sessions was not to listen to recollections which patients freely offered, but to encourage them to discover or construct scenes of which they had *no* recollection."[28] This is made evident in his paper "The Aetiology of Hysteria" when Freud writes:

> Before they come for analysis the patients know nothing about these scenes. They are indignant as a rule if we warn them that such scenes are going to emerge. Only the strongest compulsion of the treatment can induce them to embark on a reproduction of them. While they are recalling these infantile experiences to consciousness, they suffer under the most violent sensations, of which they are ashamed and which they try to conceal; and, even after they have gone through them once more in such a convincing manner, they still attempt to withhold belief from them, by emphasizing the fact that, unlike what happens in the case of other forgotten material, they have no feeling of remembering the scenes.[29]

Even after treatment has terminated, the individual may have no recollection of the traumatic experience, yet we are informed that whether it occurred or not is of no importance, leaving the individual extremely vulnerable to the suggestion of the analyst. Freud writes:

> Even when everything is finished and the patients have been overborne by the force of logic and have been convinced by the therapeutic effect accompanying the emergence of precisely these ideas—when, I say, the patients themselves accept the fact that they thought this or that, they often add: "But I can't *remember* having thought it." It is easy to come to terms with them by telling them that the thoughts were *unconscious*.[30]

Freud informs us : "If the first-discovered scene is unsatisfactory, we tell our patient that this experience explains nothing, but that behind it there must be hidden a more significant, earlier, experience...A continuation of the analysis then leads in every instance to the reproduction of new scenes of the character we expect."[31] Freud probes the psychic underworld of the individual until he finds what he is looking for." Years later Freud momentarily concedes that he might have planted these ideas of sexual abuse in the minds of his patients: "I was at last obliged to recognize that these scenes of seduction had never taken place, and that they were only phantasies which my patients had made up or which I myself had perhaps forced on them..."[32] He further admits: "these scenes from infancy are not reproduced during the treatment as recollections, they are the products of construction."[33] Yet Freud then almost immediately contradicts himself when disqualifying this possibility: "I do not believe even now that I forced the seduction-phantasies on my patients, that I 'suggested' them."[34] These so-called memories were not real memories to begin with, but illusions constructed by Freud out of theoretical necessity. Freud adds, "In psycho-analytic treatments we are invariably faced by the task of filling up these gaps in the memory of childhood."[35] Webster affirms: "In short there *were* no truths for Freud to abandon."[36]

However, Freud never, to our knowledge, recognized that it was a mistake to abandon the seduction theory and not take sexual abuse seriously; yet who knows the impact that this decisive decision had upon his inner life. Sulloway makes an important point about the master being the ultimate law giver and conveyer of what is true, which makes more sense of how he first upheld the seduction theory and later denied it without any apparent conflict: "Freud as psychoanalyst...became Freud the prosecuting attorney within his own clinical count of psychoanalytic law."[37]

Chapter 24

Freud, Eros, and the Sexual Revolution

"Freud introduced a great revolution...He destroyed the taboo of sex."[1]—Osho

The rationale for Freud's pansexualism and antinomianism is declared in his statement "Sexual morality...strikes me as very contemptible."[2] For this reason the title of "the prophet for the Victorian age of sexual suppression"[3] has been conferred upon him, as he himself encouraged free inquiry into human sexuality when it was uncommon to do so. He writes: "from the very first what has to do with sexuality should be treated like anything else that is worth knowing about."[4] Jung ambiguously points out the existence of a modern sexual crisis: "Serious-minded people know that there is something of a sexual problem today."[5] Freud is often referred to as a precursor to the *sexual revolution* of the counter-cultural 1960's, and it is well known that human sexuality held a central place in his psychological model. Yet it was Wilhelm Reich, regarded as Freud's onetime "favorite son"[6] and brilliant contributor to the psychoanalytic movement, who first utilized this term, as Reich himself asserts: "I coined the term 'Sexual Revolution' in the 1930's."[7] Similar to the case with his former master, "To Reich, sex was to be equated with life per se."[8]

Perls upholds the centrality of Freud's role in the sexual revolution: "Great [is] the service...which Freud has rendered to mankind by unchaining the sex instinct."[9] The destructive forces that were unleashed during the sexual revolution, like that of the broader counter-cultural movements, had a tremendously negative impact on society and the family. These counter-cultural currents emerged to challenge societal discontent and iniquity with the prevailing power structures, and while they were assumed by many to be positive, they proved to be otherwise. In hindsight, it can be seen that they were harmful to the integrity of the human collectivity.[10]

The pioneering and controversial American sexologist Alfred C. Kinsey (1894–1956) is often regarded as the "father of the sexual revolution."[11] Upon its publication in 1948, his book *Sexual Behavior in the Human Male* was likened to the dropping of an atomic bomb on the cultural and social mores of the time. His follow-up study was published in 1953 as *Sexual Behavior in the Human Female*; both books make up what is considered the "Kinsey Reports." Kinsey expresses a pansexualism that is akin to not only Freudianism, but also the Sabbatian-Frankist movements, and he was also said to have been influenced by the British occultist Aleister Crowley.[12] It is important again to note Crowley's destructive influence as he explicitly transgressed and inverted the social norms of Victorian morality, making inroads for others to follow in his footsteps:

> Mankind must learn that the sexual instinct is...ennobling. The shocking evils which we all deplore are principally due to the perversions produced by suppressions. The feeling that it is shameful and the sense of sin cause concealment, which is ignoble, and internal conflict which creates distortion, neurosis, and ends in explosion. We deliberately produce an abscess, and wonder why it is full of pus, why it hurts, why it bursts in stench and corruption...*The Book of the Law* solves the sexual problem completely. Each individual has an absolute right to satisfy his sexual instinct as is physiologically proper for him. The one injunction is to treat all such acts as sacraments.[13]

The following statement cloaked in what could be termed a conundrum of semantics illustrates Kinsey's nefarious outlook: "The only unnatural sex act is that which you cannot perform."[14] According to a biographer, Paul Robinson Kinsey's work was instrumentally designed to "undermine the traditional sexual order."[15] This point is made evident by Kinsey himself: "Biologically there is no form of outlet which I will admit as abnormal."[16]

There were early indicators of Kinsey's troubled and deviant attitude toward sexuality in his adolescence, as illustrated by James H. Jones in his biography: "Kinsey's behavior was clearly pathological, satisfying every criterion of sexual perversion."[17] Hugh Hefner (1926–2017), the founder of *Playboy* magazine and proponent for the legalization of pornography, was highly influenced by Kinsey's work and its academic appearance. Incidently, the first issue of *Playboy* magazine coincided with the publication of Kinsey's second book, which was published in December 1953. As biographer Thomas Weyr contended: "Hefner recognized Kinsey as the incontrovertible word of the new God based on the new holy writ—demonstrable evidence. Kinsey would add a dash of scientific truth to the *Playboy* mix."[18]

Hugh Hefner was also a militant critic of religion, emphasizing that "It's perfectly clear to me that religion is a myth."[19]

Another precursor to the sexual revolution was British physician Havelock Ellis. Ellis also prides himself on challenging the morality of that time: "I have never repressed anything. What others have driven out of consciousness...as being improper or obscene, I have maintained and even held in honour."[20]

Yet Freud's role in the sexual revolution should not be minimized due to Kinsey's work; on the contrary, as influential sociologist John H. Gagnon (1931–2016) states: "The Freudian tradition was especially influential in general intellectual matters and was probably the most important in the development of twentieth-century sexual ideologies."[21] Wardell Pomeroy (1913–2001), a disciple of Kinsey, points out that it was Freud's pioneering work that later research on sexuality would be understood in light of: "[it was] Sigmund Freud whose genius introduced the idea of *childhood* sexuality—that children are sexual beings was an idea never considered before—an idea that forever affected our conception of human sexual development and thoughts about sex education."[22]

E. Michael Jones highlights the broader historical trajectory of the sexual revolution, which has a much earlier beginning: "the first tentative ideas of how to exploit sex as a form of social control arose during the Enlightenment."[23] And paradoxically: "Sexual liberation leads to anarchy, chaos, and horror, and chaos invariably leads to forms of social control."[24] Indications of the changes in sexual attitudes were already apparent in the year 1660, as is indicated in the following: "almost all the themes of later pornography are present; within a completely amoral attitude, in which all perversions are welcome if they gratify the senses...these take place within a tightly knit family circle, with the shocking suggestion that all the conventional relationships of society are merely a façade for personal gratification."[25] John Cleland's erotic novel *Memoirs of a Woman of Pleasure* (1749) is often also cited as an early forerunner of contemporary pornography.

As several writers have established connections between Freud and the ideology of the European Enlightenment, it is also important to link these connections with the events of the sexual revolution. Webster writes: "Freud's theory of sexuality, which was to be the doctrinal rock on which his own church was founded, certainly bears all the marks of his messianic and profoundly mystical personality."[26] Freudian therapy is equated with sexual theory itself: "Freudian psychoanalysis is sexual psychoanalysis."[27] Freud himself believed that man "should make genital eroticism the central point of his life."[28] Freud's conception of psychopathology was, as he confirmed, in sexuality, as he viewed it as "the key that unlocks everything."[29] Freud's often quoted dictum is that "No neurosis is possible with a normal *vita sexualis*."[30] Freud takes a reductionist approach and defines the human being according to his or her sexual potency, which is considered a mirror reflection of his or her terrestrial existence: "The behaviour of a human being in sexual matters is often a prototype for [his or her] whole...reaction to life."[31]

He identifies the absence of sexual fulfillment as the cause of mental illness: "Psychoanalytic work has furnished us with the rule that people fall ill of a neurosis as a result of *frustration*."[32] Additionally, Freud adds: "human beings fall ill when...the satisfaction of their erotic needs *in reality* is frustrated."[33] He claimed that, "in every case of neurosis there is a sexual aetiology,"[34] and that "anxiety is always libido which has been deflected from its [normal] employment."[35] Freud went as far as stating: "what we call libido...is the drive behind every neurosis."[36] Or as Jung wrote about psychoanalytic theory: "There is an unspoken expectation that it is a fact that neurosis comes only from repressed sexuality."[37] Freud suggests that "[sexuality] is regarded as a more comprehensive bodily function, having pleasure as its goal and only secondarily coming to serve the ends of reproduction."[38]

The psychoanalytic view of human sexuality is exemplified in the following condensed summary made by Freud:

> [N]ormality developed as the result of repression of certain component-instincts and components of the infantile disposition, and of subordination of the remainder under the primacy of the genital zone in the service of the reproductive function; perversions represented disturbances in this process of coalescence caused by an excessive (obsessive, as it were) development of certain of the component-instincts;...neurosis could be traced back to unduly severe repression of libidinal tendencies.[39]

A clear demarcation exists for Freud concerning the faithful, or those who believe in the doctrine of the Oedipus complex, as opposed to the unfaithful, or those that do not give it credibility. Freud draws an allegorical line in the sand for followers and opponents alike to identify themselves:

It has justly been said that the Oedipus complex is the nuclear complex of the neuroses, and constitutes the essential part of their content. It represents the peak of infantile sexuality, which, through its after-effects, exercises a decisive influence on the sexuality of adults. Every new arrival on this planet is faced by the task of mastering the Oedipus complex; anyone who fails to do so falls victim to neurosis. With the progress of psycho-analytic studies the importance of the Oedipus complex has become more and more clearly evident; its recognition has become the shibboleth that distinguishes the adherents of psycho-analysis from its opponents.[40]

Freud claimed the crucial pathogenic role for the Oedipus complex: "the Oedipus complex is the nucleus of the neuroses."[41] Likewise, Jones affirms, "the kernel of any neurosis is the Oedipus complex."[42]

Freud goes on to propose its necessity for any relationship based on love between men and women: "It sounds not only disagreeable but also paradoxical, yet it must nevertheless be said that anyone who is to be really free and happy in love must have surmounted his respect for women and have come to terms with the idea of incest with his mother or sister."[43] Freud suggests that the consequences for overthrowing the reign of the Oedipus complex are as follows: "Conscience and morality arose through overcoming, desexualizing, the Oedipus complex."[44] Freudian metapsychology tirelessly reduces the human condition to what is sexual in nature: "the beginnings of religion, morality, social life and art meet in the Oedipus complex."[45]

In a letter written on May 31, 1897 to Fliess, Freud confides to him: "I am about to discover the source of morality."[46] He then references a dream: "The dream of course fulfils my wish to pin down a father as the originator of neurosis and put an end to my persistent doubts."[47] What becomes evident is that "The Freudian theory of the origin of religion is the cultural and collective dimension of the discovery of the Œdipus complex."[48] Jung comments: "Above all, Freud's attitude towards the spirit seems to me highly questionable. Wherever, in a person or in a work of art, an expression of spirituality (in the intellectual, not the supernatural sense) came to light, he suspected it, and insinuated that it was repressed sexuality."[49]

Freud frames the doctrine of the Oedipus complex within a developmental context:

When a boy (from the age of two or three) has entered the phallic phase of his libidinal development, is feeling pleasurable sensations in his sexual organ and has learnt to procure these at will by manual stimulation, he becomes his mother's lover. He wishes to possess her physically in such ways as he has divined from his observations and intuitions about sexual life, and he tries to seduce her by showing her the male organ which he is proud to own. In a word, his early awakened masculinity seeks to take his father's place with her...His father now becomes a rival who stands in his way and whom he would like to get rid of.[50]

The seminal importance of Freud's discovery, some have suggested, was not the unconscious but the doctrine of the libido theory. Reich writes:

...Freud discovered the principle of energy functioning of the psychic apparatus. *The energy-functioning principle.* This was what distinguished him from all other psychologists. Not so much the discovery of the unconscious. The unconscious, the theory of the unconscious, was, to my mind, a consequence of a principle he introduced into psychology. That was the principle, the natural scientific principle, of energy—the "libido theory."[51]

Freud defines his libido theory in this way:

We have laid down the concept of the libido as a force of variable quantity by which processes and transformations in the spheres of sexual excitement can be measured. This libido we distinguished from the energy which is at the basis of the psychic processes in general as far as their special origin is concerned, and we thus attribute to it also a qualitative character. In separating libidinal from other psychic energy, we give expression to the assumption that the sexual processes of the organism are differentiated from the nutritional processes through a special chemism.[52]

Freud makes a link between eros and libido when he writes: "The greater part of what we know about Eros—that is to say, about its exponent, the libido—has been gained from a study of the sexual function, which, indeed, on the prevailing view, even if not according to our theory, coincides with Eros."[53] It goes without saying that the Freudian notion of eros and love are radically different from those of Platonism and are not compatible, as is emphasized here: "The truth is that Freudian love is very nearly the obverse of Platonic love. In their metaphysical bases, and in their dynamic directions, they not merely differ, but in effect contradict one another. So far are the two interpretations from being (as Freud thought) coincident, that neither could be true if the other were even meaningful."[54]

Reich affirms his own role in continuing this energetic principle that was first articulated by his former master: "I consider my bio-energetic work with the emotions to be a *direct continuation* of that energy principle in psychology."[55] Many of Freud's disciples differed in this regard by extracting this principle from their version of psychodynamic theory. Reich explains: "What is important, however, is what they did—what analysts like Adler, Stekel and Jung did. They took his theory, broke off the most important thing, pulled it out, threw it away and went after fame...it was always the sexuality that they threw out."[56] Freud writes the following regarding his former disciple, Jung, and his deviation from the libido theory: "All that has been gained thus far from psychoanalytic observation would be lost if, following C. G. Jung, one would subtilize the very concept of libido to the extent of making it synonymous with psychic instinctive energy in general."[57] Incidentally, this is one of the reasons why Jung, a chief disciple, broke away from the master:

> There was no mistaking the fact that Freud was emotionally involved in his sexual theory to an extraordinary degree. When he spoke of it, his tone became urgent, almost anxious, and all signs of his normally critical and skeptical manner vanished. A strange, deeply moved expression came over his face, the cause of which I [Jung] was at a loss to understand...
>
> I can still recall vividly how Freud said to me, "My dear Jung, promise me never to abandon the sexual theory. That is the most essential thing of all. You see, we must make a dogma of it, an unshakable bulwark." He said that to me with great emotion, in the tone of a father saying, "And promise me this one thing, my dear son: that you will go to church every Sunday."[58]

Although Freud was preoccupied with religion throughout his life, he never ceased to reduce religion to a regressive child-like fantasy, delusion, or even: "sexual libido"[59] itself. Jung challenges his former master and urges for a theoretical outlook that goes beyond the sexual: "I therefore suggest that psychoanalytic theory should be freed from the purely sexual standpoint. In place of it I should like to introduce an *energetic viewpoint* [libido] into the psychology of neurosis."[60] Jung continues: "All psychological phenomena can be considered as manifestations of energy...I call it *libido*, using the word in its original sense, which is by no means only sexual."[61]

While he criticizes his onetime master, Jung at the same time comes to his defense: "If I accuse the Freudian sexual theory of one-sidedness, that does not mean that it rests on rootless speculation; it too is a faithful picture of real facts which force themselves upon our practical observation."[62] While Jung's portrayal of libido is more nuanced than Freud's, and although he goes further than his master in situating the doctrine of the "talking cure" beyond human sexuality, he nonetheless ends in a reductionistic *cul-de-sac*, albeit more inclusive; he still appears to reduce the spiritual domain to the libido. Jung writes: "The sun is, as Renen remarked, really the only rational representation of God, whether we take the point of view of the barbarians of other ages or that of the modern physical sciences...the sun is adapted as is nothing else to represent the visible God of this world. That is to say, that driving strength of our own soul, which we call libido."[63]

Horney challenges the Freudian orthodoxy, reminding us of the imbalance within psychoanalysis as it privileges a masculine outlook at the expense of the feminine: "Psychoanalysis is the creation of a male genius, and almost all those who have developed his ideas have been men. It is only right and reasonable that they should evolve more easily a masculine psychology and understand more of the development of men than of women."[64] Freud made explicit assumptions about biological determinism, such as the assertion that "anatomy is destiny,"[65] suggesting that female anatomy is inferior to male anatomy and that this in turn shapes the psychic apparatus. Freud informs us: "we have learned that the small girl feels sensitive over the lack of a sex organ equal to the boy's, and holds herself to be inferior on that account; and that this 'penis-envy' gives rise to a whole series of characteristic feminine reactions."[66] Jung also confirms this limitation as the "feminine principle which could find no place in Freud's patriarchal world."[67]

In this context, Freud suggests that the most upsetting occurrence for little girls is the realization that they are without a penis, while boys have one. Freud writes: "The discovery that she is castrated is a turning-point in a girl's growth."[68] In contrast, the perennial philosophy and its corresponding perennial psychology recognize: "O Mankind! Lo! We have created you male and female. The noblest among you, in the sight of God, is the best in conduct" (Koran 46:13).

Horney continues highlighting the inadequacies of Freud's outlook on female psychology:

In this formulation we have assumed as an axiomatic fact that females feel at a disadvantage because of their genital organs, without this being regarded as constituting a problem in itself— possibly because to masculine narcissism this has seemed too self-evident to need explanation. Nevertheless, the conclusion so far drawn from the investigations—amounting as it does to an assertion that one half of the human race is discontented with the sex assigned to it and can overcome this discontent only in favorable circumstances—is decidedly unsatisfying, not only to feminine narcissism but also to biological science.[69]

Freud considered female sexuality as the "dark continent" of the human psyche that challenged his materialistic science, as is written here: "the sexual life of grown-up women...is still a 'dark continent' for psychology."[70] Freud admits to his inability to comprehend the feminine psyche to Princes Marie Bonaparte (1882–1962): "The great question that has never been answered and which I have not yet been able to answer, despite my thirty years of research into the feminine soul, is 'What does a woman want?'"[71] It may also be interesting to note that Freud compares the doctrine of the "talking cure" to a woman: "Psychoanalysis is like a woman who wants to be seduced but knows she will be underrated unless she offers resistance."[72]

Freud maintains the supremacy of masculine sexual potency that he emphasizes is required for the greater good of society: "it is positively a matter of public interest that men should enter upon sexual relations with full potency."[73] Breuer early on recognized that "the great majority of severe neurosis in women have their origin in the marriage bed,"[74] and regarded "sexuality as one of the major components of hysteria."[75] Freud makes a striking statement on the loveless phenomenon of contemporary marriage when proposing its remedy: "the cure for nervous illness arising from marriage would be marital unfaithfulness."[76]

It has been suggested that Freud himself had an affair with his sister-in-law, Minna Bernays.[77] The official biography attempts to squelch this notion, as Jones emphasizes: "There was no sexual attraction on either side, but he found her a stimulating and amusing companion and would occasionally make short holiday excursions with her when his wife was not free to travel."[78] Yet as Gay points out with regard to the Minna Bernays question, Freud "left behind some tantalizing private mysteries."[79] Jones, being a good disciple of the master, writes: "His [Freud's] wife was assuredly the only woman in Freud's love life...Freud no doubt appreciated her [Minna Bernays's] conversation, but to say that she in any way replaced her sister in his affections is sheer nonsense."[80] Jung, who knew Freud more intimately than Jones did, provides an account of his first visit to Vienna in 1907, where Minna Bernays confided in him that "Freud was in love with her and that their relationship was indeed very intimate."[81] In this context, the following becomes clearer: "Minna Bernays's importance for psychoanalysis has been largely overshadowed by controversy over her putative sexual liaison with Freud—a controversy that members of the profession have until recently put down to Freudicidal malice."[82]

Jung justifies his position sanctioning extramarital relations, which he deemed necessary for a successful marriage such as his own; but his wife was exempt from such arrangements: "The prerequisite for a good marriage, it seems to me, is the license to be unfaithful. I in my turn have learnt a great deal."[83] On the issue of monogamy, Horney writes: "We know that the dissociation between 'spiritual' and sensual love, which has so strong a bearing on the possibility of faithfulness, is dominantly—indeed, almost specifically—a masculine characteristic."[84]

Freud also held perversion to be a common feature of normal sexual development, as reflected here: "a disposition to perversions is an original and universal disposition of the human sexual instinct and...[n]o healthy person...can fail to make some addition that might be called perverse."[85] Freud normalizes sexual aberrations: "sexual perversions are very widely diffused among the whole population."[86] One wonders if Freud would have viewed the mass consumption and rise of sexual addiction, pornography, exhibitionism, voyeurism, sadomasochism, fetishism, to name a few, in contemporary life as a normal feature of human sexual development.

The Freudian notion of "polymorphously perverse" is important to recall in this context, as it is the idea that individuals can obtain sexual gratification outside accepted norms of sexual behavior. Freud elaborates how the theory of polymorphously perverse can occur early on: "It is an instructive fact that under the influence of seduction children can become polymorphously perverse, and can be led into all possible kinds of sexual irregularities. This shows that an aptitude for them is innately present in their disposition."[87] E. Michael Jones points out: "Exposure to pornography does not result in satiation"[88] and in fact creates an unbalanced and fragmented outlook, as is specified here:"exposure to pornography creates in the viewer a fundamentally distorted view of sexuality."[89]

There is an interesting Sabbatian-Frankist antinomian trend within the pornography industry, as is made evident in the following: "there's no getting away from the fact that secular Jews have played (and still continue to play) a disproportionate role throughout the adult film industry in America."[90] This point becomes strikingly apparent when American pornographer Al Goldstein (1936–2013) admits: "The only reason that Jews are in pornography is that we think that Christ sucks. Catholicism sucks."[91]

Contemporary brain research shows that the human brain changes through addiction to pornography, as psychiatrist and psychoanalyst Norman Doidge illustrates:

> Pornography, by offering an endless harem of sexual objects, hyperactivates the appetitive system. Porn viewers develop new maps in their brains, based on the photos and videos they see. Because it is a use-it-or-lose-it brain, when we develop a map area, we long to keep it activated. Just as our muscles become impatient for exercise if we've been sitting all day, so too do our senses hunger to be stimulated. The men at their computers [addicted to] looking at porn were uncannily like the rats in the cages of the NIH, pressing the bar to get a shot of dopamine or its equivalent. Though they [do not] know it, they [have] been seduced into pornographic training sessions that [meet] all the conditions required for plastic change of brain maps.[92]

Regarding homosexuality, we might add that while Jung pathologized homosexuality, calling it the "deviation towards homosexuality,"[93] his former master to a varying degree normalizes it and at other times appears to be ambivalent at best: "Homosexuality is assuredly no advantage, but it is nothing to be ashamed of, no vice, no degradation; it cannot be classified as an illness; we consider it to be a variation of the sexual function, produced by a certain arrest of sexual development."[94] In 1905 Freud referred to homosexuality as an "inversion,"[95] and in 1917 emphasized: "in the case of no single neurotic do we fail to obtain evidence of homosexual tendencies"[96] He suggests that the familial causes of homosexuality are due to a prolonged identification with one's mother: "In all our male homosexuals there was a very intensive erotic attachment to a feminine person, as a rule to the mother...This attachment was produced or favored by too much love from the mother herself, but was also furthered by the retirement or absence of the father during the childhood period."[97]

273

Freud also connects homosexuality with narcissistic identification: "Homosexual object-choice originally lies closer to narcissism than does the heterosexual kind."[98] He adds, "[the homosexual] finds the objects of his love along the path of narcissism, as we say; for Narcissus, according to the Greek legend, was a youth who preferred his own reflection to everything else and who was changed into the lovely flower of that name."[99]

The psychoanalytic construction of homosexuality is as follows:

> In the male homosexual there is, as a rule, an overly strong attachment to the mother up to and including the oedipal phase, which is not resolved by identification with the father but rather by partial identification with the mother. Object choice is narcissistic in type, i.e., the loved person must be like the self, and sexual excitation is experienced in regard to men instead of women. Due to strong castration fears the homosexual man cannot tolerate a sexual partner without the tremendously valued male organ. Another common motive for homosexual object choice is the avoidance of rivalry with fathers and brothers.
>
> In female homosexuality (Lesbianism), the woman retains the strong original pre-oedipal attachment to the mother, which is displaced onto the homosexual partner. As a result of an unsatisfactory outcome of oedipal conflicts, her identification with mother is incomplete and she holds on to mother as an object of love.[100]

Ultimately, Freud emphasizes: "It is not for psycho-analysis to solve the problem of homosexuality. It must rest content with disclosing the psychical mechanisms that resulted in determination of the object-choice, and with tracing the paths leading from them to the instinctive basis of the disposition. There its work ends, and it leaves the rest to biological investigation."[101]

It is helpful to recall that in 1973, the American Psychiatric Association depathologized homosexuality by removing it from the second edition of the *Diagnostic and Statistical Manual of Mental Disorders* (DSM). Thus, homosexuality was no longer considered a form of mental illness; it was rather viewed as normal.[102] With this said, the World Health Organization did not remove homosexuality from its *International Classification of Diseases* until 1992 with the publication of the ICD-10.

The escalation of sexual aberrations is considered by the perennial psychology as a reflection of the crisis within the human psyche due to having lost its connection with the sacred. "Psychoanalysis has emphasized the subpersonal primordialism of sex by applying a degrading inversion."[103] In seeking intimacy, connection, and fulfillment solely within the corporeal realm, devoid of what transcends and contains the physical, is futile. Sexual aberrations, like the myriad addictions of the present day, are a symptom of the pathology of fallen man, the human being within *saṃsāra,* who attempts to find wholeness in what is incapable of providing wholeness. These attempts were foretold and known within the religions to be due to the progressive dissociation of the human psyche from the Spirit, acknowledged as the *Kali-Yuga* or "Dark Age." The sexual revolution has desacralized human sexuality, cutting it off from its metaphysical root: "The reaction of the so-called sexual revolution has only led the masses to a regimen of quick, easy, and cheap sex treated as an item of consumption."[104]

We are told that across the board or "practically all modern schools of psychology and psychotherapy inform us [that human happiness and emotional stability] can only be achieved when the individual achieves sexual maturity."[105] Yet what is "sexual maturity" according to modern psychology? Ellis informs readers:

> Sexual maturity [is]...the *realistic acceptance* of the *facts* of human sexuality...so that a maximum number of human beings may satisfy their biosocial sex urges with a minimum of unnecessary stress and strain. [Society must] arrange its customs and mores so that virtually all its males and females obtain a reasonable degree of sex satisfaction during their adolescence, young adulthood, and mature years.[106]

Yet beyond the wish fulfillment of sexual urges is the primordial need for the sacred, as Roshi Philip Kapleau (1912–2004) explains:

> Freud and other psychologists speak of the great harm done to the psyche when sexual desire cannot find an outlet. But far worse is the frustration of the primordial need to know who and what we are and the meaning of our life and death. These questions are barriers you yourself must penetrate; on the other side of them is the Reality you sense. But it is not separate, this Reality—how can there be more than one Reality? When the silt of your delusory thoughts settles, you will gaze into fresh, clear water that is really the same water purged of dirt and impurities.[107]

With the progressive dissociation from the sacred, human relationships, intimacy, and sexuality become ever more desacralized. Schuon writes: "Loving each other, Adam and Eve loved God; they could neither love nor know outside God. After the fall, they loved each other outside God and for themselves, and they knew each other as separate phenomena and not as theophanies; this new kind of love was concupiscence and this new kind of knowing was profanity."[108]

The perennial psychology, as is found across the religions, does not ignore or downplay the role of human sexuality, nor does it take a prudish stance as is often mistakenly believed, but it views integral sexuality as the communion of the human with the Spirit: "In primordial man sexual ecstasy coincides with spiritual ecstasy, it communicates to man an experience of mystical union, a 'remembrance' of the Divine Love of which human love is a distant reflection."[109] Since the earliest times human beings have known that "Traditional man sought to find the secret and essence of sex in divinity itself."[110] Julius Evola (1898–1974) observes: "With regard also to sex, the rediscovery of its [highest] primary and deepest meaning...depend[s] on the possibility of the reintegration of modern man and on his arising once more and betaking himself beyond the psychic and spiritual lowlands into which he has been led by the mirages of his material civilization, for in this lowlands the meaning of being truly a man or woman is doomed to vanish."[111]

Freud's obsessional reductionism of all things to a sexual common denominator prohibited him from him from seeing what was integrally human and normal. This was a significant factor that caused Jung to break with the master. Jung provides a more varied use of symbolism that is not limited to sexuality, and critiques Freud:

A man may dream of inserting a key in a lock, of wielding a heavy stick, or of breaking down a door with a battering ram. Each of these can be regarded as a sexual allegory. But the fact that his unconscious for its own purposes has chosen one of these specific images—it may be the key, the stick, or the battering ram—is also of major significance. The real task is to understand *why* the key has been preferred to the stick, or the stick to the ram. And sometimes this might even lead one to discover that it is not the sexual act at all that is represented, but some quite different psychological point.[112]

An early criticism of Freudian metapsychology, which exclusively sexualizes all phenomena and deems that the root of all human behavior is its resultant, comes from Dunlap:

There is absolutely nothing in the universe which may not readily be made into a sexual symbol...We may explain, by Freudian principles, why trees have their roots in the ground; why we write with pens; why we put a quart of wine into a bottle instead of hanging it on a hook like a ham, and so on...cures resulting from Freudian treatment have no value as evidence in support of the Freudian dogmas.[113]

This speaks to the perversion of integral or traditional symbolism that is rooted in spiritual principles rather than in subjective speculation. The doctrine of Freudianism misunderstood the integral meaning of symbolism and subverted its sacred significance, which extends throughout the work of Freud and his disciples. Freud relegated symbolism to the unconscious, as is indicated here: "symbolism...is characteristic of unconscious ideation."[114] Guénon perceptively observes:

[W]hen Freud spoke of "symbolism," what he thus misnamed was in reality only a simple product of the human imagination, variable from one individual to another and having nothing in common with authentic traditional symbolism. But that was only a first stage, and it remained for other psychoanalysts to modify the theories of their "master" in the direction of a false spirituality, in order that by a more subtle confusion they might apply them to the interpretation of traditional symbolism itself. This was especially the case with Carl Gustav Jung[115]

Guénon further writes,

[E]very true symbol bears its multiple meanings within itself, and this from its very origin, because it is not constituted as such by any human convention but in virtue of the "law of correspondence" that links all worlds together; if some see these meanings while others do not, or see them only in part, they are no less truly contained in the symbol, for it is the "intellectual horizon" of each person that makes all the difference, symbolism being an exact science and not a reverie in which individual fantasies are given free rein.[116]

The symbolism of sacred nudity embraces the correspondence between earthly and heavenly beauty, earthly beauty being "outward" and heavenly beauty being Divine and "inward." Through an integral framework that utilizes both the esoteric and exoteric dimensions, sacred nudity, as it is found across the sapiential traditions, can be more fully understood. Schuon elaborates:

> Sacred nudity—which plays an important role not only with the Hindus but also with the American Indians—is based on the analogical correspondence between the "outermost" and the "inmost": the body is then seen as the "heart exteriorized," and the heart for its part "absorbs" as it were the bodily projection; "extremes meet." It is said in India that nudity favors the irradiation of spiritual influences, and also that feminine nudity in particular manifests Lakshmi and consequently has a beneficial effect on the surroundings. In an altogether general way, nudity expresses and virtually actualizes a return to the essence, the origin, the archetype, thus to the celestial state. "And it is for this that, naked, I dance," as Lalla Yogishvari, the great Kashmiri saint, said after having found the divine Self in her heart. To be sure, in nudity there is a de facto ambiguity because of the passional nature of humanity; but there is not only the passional nature, there is also the gift of contemplativity, which can neutralize it, as is precisely the case with "sacred nudity." Similarly, there is not only the seduction of appearances, there is also the metaphysical transparency of phenomena which permits one to perceive the archetypal essence through the sensory experience. Saint Nonnos, when he beheld Saint Pelagia entering the baptismal pool naked, praised God for having put into human beauty not only an occasion of fall, but also an occasion of rising toward God.[117]

An example of this is also found within the Islamic tradition, as Lings points out:

> Originally there was, for both sexes, an alternative to clothes, namely a return to the nakedness of primordial man. This remained a fully approved mode of *ihrām* until...the last few years of the Prophet's life...as to the traditional alternative, like certain other already mentioned aspects of the precious legacy of the first of the Patriarchs, sacred nudity presupposes a spiritual development which could not be said to characterize more than a very small minority in any one of those three religions which are, in a sense, Abraham's legatees. There could therefore have been no question of Islam's retaining nakedness as the pilgrimal alternative to clothing.[118]

It is again rudimentary to differentiate false or pseudo-symbolism that is reductionistic, being horizontal and psychological in nature, from that which stems from metaphysical principles. What psychodynamic approaches hold to be integral symbolism are pale reflections of a desacralized and psychic residue of the former. Burckhardt explains:

> In every collectivity that has become unfaithful to its own traditional form, to the sacred framework of its life, there occurs a collapse or a sort of mummification of the symbols it had received, and this process will be reflected in the psychic life of every individual belonging to that collectivity and participating in that infidelity. To every truth there corresponds a formal trace, and every spiritual form projects a psychic shadow; when these shadows are all that remains, they do in fact take on the character of ancestral phantoms that haunt the subconscious. The most pernicious of psychological errors is to reduce the meaning of symbolism to such phantoms.[119]

Jiří Langer (1894–1943), in his book published in 1923, *Die Erotik der Kabbala* (*The Eroticism of the Kabbalah*), attempted to interpret the sacred symbolism of Jewish mysticism through the lens of the doctrine of the "talking cure." Yet this attempt, as Scholem points out, was unsuccessful: "An attempt to interpret the 'Eroticism of the Kabbalah' in psychoanalytical terms has actually been made, but the author has not advanced beyond the common catch-phrases which not a few adherents of the school unfortunately seem to regard as a sufficient answer to problems of this nature."[120] Regarding psychoanalytic interpretations of Jewish mysticism, Scholem adds: "there is little hope...that real light can be shed on the matter in this way [through psychoanalysis]."[121]

While Freud shares a belief in the profound significance of sexuality with Kabbalah, his point of departure desacralizes and pathologizes its transcendent symbolism. According to the Zohar, the sexual union between husband and wife symbolizes the union of the spiritual body of the *sefirot* with the Divine:

> When he is male together with female and is highly sanctified and zealous for sanctification; then and only then he is designated one without mar of any kind. Hence a man and his wife should have a single inclination at the hour of their union, and the man should be glad with his wife, attaching her to himself in affection. So conjoined, they make one soul and one body: a single soul

279

through their affection; a single body, for only when male and female are conjoined do they form a single body; whereas, and this we have learned, if a man is not wedded, he is, we may say, divided in two. But when male and female are joined, God abides upon "one" and endows it with a holy spirit; and, as was said, these are called the children of the Holy One, be blessed.[122]

Scholem articulates the sacred dimension of sexuality as it appears in the Kabbalah:

The mystery of sex, as it appears to the Kabbalist, has a terribly deep significance. This mystery of human existence is for him nothing but a symbol of the love between the divine "I" and the divine "You," the Holy one, blessed be He and His Shekhinah. The ἱερὸς γάμος [*hieros gamos*], the "sacred union" of the King and the Queen, the Celestial Bridegroom and the Celestial Bride, to name a few of the symbols, is the central fact in the whole chain of divine manifestations in the hidden world. In God there is a union of the active and the passive, procreation and conception, from which all mundane life and bliss are derived.[123]

The symbolism depicting this embrace traces back to rabbinic writings, to an important Talmudic passage (*Yoma* 54a-b):

Rab Katina said: When the Israelites entered the Temple in Jerusalem [during the three pilgrimage festivals], the curtain [to the Holy of Holies] was opened and they were shown the cherubim in intimate embraces, and they were told: Behold, the love between yourselves and God is like the love between man and woman...Resh Lakish said: When the Gentiles conquered the Temple, they saw the cherubim in intimate embraces. They hauled them out into the marketplace and said: "Behold! Israel, whose blessing is a blessing and whose curse is a curse, concerns itself with such things?!" Then they reviled them, as is said, "All that honored her despise her, because they have seen her nakedness" [Lam. 1:8].[124]

Freudian therapy and its outlook on human sexuality appear then not only as a parody, but as an aberration of how sexuality was viewed within the Jewish mystical tradition. August Forel (1848–1931), a Swiss psychiatrist, concluded that Freudianism was a secular religion by drawing upon its Jewish symbolism, speaking of the "sanctifying sexual church, its infant sexuality, its Talmudic-exegetic-theological interpretations."[125]

Similar examples of sacred sexuality can be found across the diverse societies and civilizations of the world. The traditional Tibetan symbolism of *yab-yum* (father-mother) is known as the primordial union of wisdom and compassion or the feminine and masculine depicted in sexual embrace, two aspects that are fundamental for enlightenment. Sexuality looks very different in this traditional context from the way it looks in Freudian theory:

> The man [sees] the woman as a goddess,
> The woman [sees] the man as a god.
> By joining the diamond scepter and lotus,
> They should make offerings to each other.
> There is no worship apart from this.[126]

> Without meditating, without renouncing the world,
> Stay at home in the company of your mate.
> Perfect knowledge can only be attained
> While one is enjoying the pleasures of the senses.[127]

Within the *Kāma Sūtra* of the Hindu tradition, human sexuality is regarded as a dimension of spiritual practice, which is made apparent here: "Sexual intercourse is a form of yoga in which two beings blend, two hearts are united. Duality always desires unity."[128] The physical embrace is then about communion with the Divine: "Not only can the physical sexual act be transcended, but it is only when it is transcended that the sexual life can attain its highest levels of expression. The sexual life is linked with the deepest roots of man's being—with his metaphysical roots and with the meeting-place in him of the divine and the human."[129]

Alain Daniélou (1907–94), noted Hindu scholar and translator, writes:

> Happiness both given and received is mutual enjoyment. For this shared happiness and pleasure, a man is willing to give himself entirely. For a man as for a woman, the total gift of self is a source of wonderful happiness and luck. Sexual intercourse is not merely a pleasure of the senses: more important is the sacrifice of oneself, the gift of self. To understand the mystery of sexual intercourse, to know and make use of what is fitting is the essential difference between man and beast.[130]

The intention of such a communion is not a promiscuous search for many partners, but the focus of attention on one partner: "Happy is the possessor of a single lover."[131]

In Tantric Buddhism, women are viewed as embodiments of the great goddess, as Vajrayoginī states: "Wherever in the world a female body is seen, / That should be recognized as my body."[132] Rāmakrishna observes: "He who has realized God...perceives clearly that women are but so many aspects of the Divine Mother. He worships them all as the Mother Herself."[133] Within Islamic spirituality, Ibn ʿArabī describes the contemplation of the Divine in the female form as the highest method of contemplation possible. He writes:

> When man contemplates God in woman, his contemplation rests on that which is passive; if he contemplates Him in himself, seeing that woman comes from man, he contemplates Him in that which is active; and when he contemplates Him alone, without the presence of any form whatsoever issued from him, his contemplation corresponds to a state of passivity with regard to God, without intermediary. Consequently his contemplation of God in woman is the most perfect, for it is then God, in so far as He is at once active and passive, that he contemplates, whereas in the purely interior contemplation, he contemplates Him only in a passive way. So the Prophet—Benediction and Peace be on him—was to love women because of the perfect contemplation of God in them. One would never be able to contemplate God directly in absence of all (sensible or spiritual) support, for God, in his Absolute Essence, is independent of all worlds. But, as the (Divine) Reality is inaccessible in respect (of the Essence), and there is contemplation (*shahādah*) only in a substance, the contemplation of God in women is the most intense and the most perfect; and the union which is the most intense (in the sensible order, which serves as support for this contemplation) is the conjugal act.[134]

Within the Christian tradition, Saint John Climacus (c. 579–649), describes this form of contemplation that bears semblance to a Platonic implication:

> A certain man, seeing a woman of unusual beauty, glorified the Creator for her: the mere sight of her moved him to love God and made him shed a flood of tears. It was indeed astonishing to see how what for another could have been a pitfall to perdition was

for him the supernatural cause of crown of glory. If such a man, on similar occasions, feels and acts in the same way, he is already risen, and is incorruptible, even before the general resurrection.[135]

It is also worth recounting the Lakota Sioux story of Pte San Win—the "White Buffalo Calf Woman"—that revealed the seven sacred rites, such as the sacred pipe and the sacred ritual of the Sun Dance. It is recounted that very many winters ago when the White Buffalo Calf Woman appeared, one of the two men who had bad intentions and sexualized the "wakan woman" or holy woman perished because of his profane vision. Black Elk expresses the following on this desacralized mentality: "Any man who is attached to the senses and to the things of this world, is one who lives in ignorance and is being consumed by the snakes which represent his own passions."[136] We recall the teaching conveyed within the Christian tradition: "But I say unto you, that whosoever looketh on a woman to lust after her hath committed adultery with her already in his heart" (Matthew 5:28)

The desacralized image of the human being rooted in scientism misses no opportunity to portray the human state in terms of what is beneath it. Reinhold Niebuhr (1892–1971) makes an astute point regarding this secular outlook and its dehumanizing consequences: "The modern naturalism which seeks to solve the problems of man's sexual life by treating him as an animal, only slightly more complex than other brutes, represents a therapy which implies a disease in our culture as grievous or more grievous than the sickness it pretends to cure."[137] Larchet points out that "Fallen man destroys himself by means of his desires contrary to nature."[138] We turn to the discerning words of Saint Augustine: "Thus, a good man, though a slave, is free; but a wicked man, though a king, is a slave. For he serves, not one man alone, but, what is worse, as many masters as he has vices."[139]

Chapter 25

The Neo- and Post-Freudian Revolution: Apologists, Heretics, and Revisionists

"Revised psychoanalysis, nonetheless, is Freudianism,"[1] as "Both Freudianism and its reformed version [neo- and post-Freudianism] provide the necessary rationalization for the employment of the stock-in-trade techniques of psychoanalytic practice."[2] The neo-Freudians (such as Alfred Adler and C. G. Jung, Erik Erikson, Erich Fromm, Karen Horney, Clara Thompson, Franz Alexander, and Harry S. Sullivan) and post-Freudians (including Abraham Maslow, Gordon Allport, Rollo May, and Carl Rogers) are individuals who have been strongly influenced by Freud and agree with the essential postulates of psychoanalytic theory, yet who have expanded the doctrine of the "talking cure" beyond "the straightjacket of orthodox psychoanalytic theory"[3] to include their own theories and practices, which often differ from orthodox psychoanalytic interpretations. While they disagree with and at times express strong dissent from Freud and certain psychoanalytic doctrines, they have not discarded the original doctrine of the "talking cure," and in many ways remain loyal to Freudianism.[4]

The neo- and post-Freudians tend to downplay the malaise of Freudianism, which is very deceptive, given its corrosive influence. An example of this can be found when Fromm writes: "Freud's revolution was to make us recognize the unconscious aspect of man's mind and the energy which man uses to repress the awareness of undesirable desires."[5] While apologist and revisionist attempts present the psychodynamic theory as less focused on sex and more driven by empathy and regard for the other, this is not in alignment with how the master presented or constructed his theories, which is deceptive in nature: *"The awareness of human separation, without reunion by love—is the source of shame. It is at the same time the source of guilt and anxiety."*[6] Far from vanishing, the Freudian revolution is perpetuated through the neo- and post-Freudians, who remain devoted to the essential *Weltanschauung* or totalizing worldview of Freudianism.

"Not Freud but Fromm, Maslow and Rollo May are the psychological gurus of the present day. And in certain respects their doctrine is very much opposed to the orthodox Freudian teaching which is not at all concerned with offering consolations. Nonetheless, it is clear that these later authorities are still following in the footsteps of the master, and that if it were not for the breach achieved by Freud, they could not have exerted any comparable influence upon society."[7]

This revisionist *Weltanschauung* goes beyond what is generally accepted to be the scope of modern psychology and in this way holds true to its roots in Freudianism: "This undertaking goes beyond what is called 'psychology.' It should more properly be called a 'science of man,' a discipline which deals with the data of history, sociology, psychology, theology, mythology, physiology, economics, and art, as far as they are relevant to the understanding of man."[8]

The need for revision to orthodox psychoanalysis is qualified here: "Many of Freud's observations have a sound bases and have been epoch making. Many of his theoretical formulations, on the other hand, have been misleading and in the course of time a radical revision became necessary."[9] Some examples of criticisms that the neo- and post-Freudians would embrace are expressed in the following quotations: "Psychoanalysis is bound down by its method"[10]; "the incompleteness or insufficiency of his system [psychoanalytic theory]"[11]; "Freud's therapeutic formula is correct but incomplete."[12] Nevertheless, many of the Freudian apologists, heretics, and revisionists continue to construct upon the erroneous foundations of psychoanalytic theory. Even though these more updated therapeutic modalities, which appear to have a more scientific basis than their predecessor, they are nevertheless hindered by the same problematic and erroneous epistemology. Professor Morris Eagle asserts: "the different variants of so-called contemporary psychoanalytic theory [the neo- and post-Freudians]...are on no firmer epistemological ground than the central formulations and claims of Freudian theory...There is no evidence that contemporary psychoanalytic theories have remedied the epistemological and methodological difficulties that are associated with Freudian theory."[13]

From this perspective, the neo- and post-Freudian revolution can be viewed as a prolongation, although more discrete and much less problematic in theory, of orthodox Freudianism, but the neo- and post-Freudians nonetheless hold tightly to its rudimentary principles. A. H. Almaas makes this point:

Psychoanalysis in particular, starting with the monumental discoveries and formulations of Sigmund Freud, has contributed the primary and most useful understanding of the human mind in this century...Later psychologists such as Jung, Reich and Perls developed other systems, but in general their work was not in contradiction to Freud's basic formulations about the psychic structure, and the basic Western approach to mind was retained.[14]

Freud's doctrine of the "talking cure" splintered into myriad other schools and movements within modern psychology, yet according to Freud no matter what form they may take they are inseparable from the legacy of Freudianism. Freud explicitly speaks to the mistaken attempts to revise or present psychoanalytic theory outside of its orthodoxy: "whatever form this psychotherapy for the people may take, whatever the elements out of which it is compounded, its most effective and most important ingredients will assuredly remain those borrowed from strict and untendentious psycho-analysis."[15]

Brill defends the master, emphasizing the futility of the revisionist efforts for altering the official doctrine of the psychoanalytic church: "Reflecting on the works of the Freudian secessionists, I feel that none of them has contributed anything of real value to mental science since they separated themselves from the master."[16] Brill continues by affirming Freud's role as the master who cannot be superseded: "His disciples, of whom there are many the world over, have made impressive contributions to the mental sciences, but a deep study of these productions will show nothing that is so novel as not to have been anticipated or implied by the master himself."[17]

Yet it was Freud himself who confirmed that psychoanalytic theory was not yet complete and was not a closed system; in fact he affirmed that it was "open to revision."[18] The master adds: "Psychoanalysis is founded securely upon the observation of the facts of mental life; and for that very reason its theoretical superstructure is still incomplete and subject to constant alteration."[19] With statements like these made by the master himself, it was logical that neo- and post-Freudians would construct upon the preexisting psychoanalytic foundations. This is due to the simple reason that the Freudian apologists and revisionists were "building on the foundations that he [Freud] has laid."[20] Nevertheless, as it can be imagined with Freud, nothing is as straightforward as it may initially appear. Freud on the contrary has also confirmed that nothing in psychoanalytic theory is to be revised. Freud writes: "In regard to *fundamental* discoveries I have hitherto found nothing to alter, and I hope this will remain true in the future."[21]

While it is true that Freudian psychoanalysis has in large part been superseded by other therapeutic modalities, one can see how those who were influenced by Freud and came to the field later on are essentially continuators of one and the same theoretical trajectory. Horney elaborates on this:

> If one believes that it [psychoanalysis] is constituted entirely by the sum total of theories propounded by Freud, then what is presented here is not psychoanalysis. If, however, one believes that the essentials of psychoanalysis lie in certain basic trends of thought concerning the role of unconscious processes and the ways in which they find expression, and in a form of therapeutic treatment that brings these processes to awareness, then what I present is psychoanalysis.[22]

The apologist and revisionist position is presented in the following: "The complete refutation of psychoanalysis which...critics often resort to is regrettable because it leads to discarding the valid with the dubitable and thereby prevents a recognition of what psychoanalysis essentially has to offer."[23] Furthermore, Horney writes: "the more I took a critical stand toward a series of psychoanalytical theories, the more I realized the constructive value of Freud's fundamental findings."[24]

Some would argue that the psychoanalytic revolution was never a unified whole and since its inception it has reflected disunity. Tournier observes: "And yet, if there is a discipline which ought to impress upon its adepts the relativity of all human doctrines, is it not psychoanalysis?"[25] It is essential to recall that many onetime disciples of Freud had revolted against the reductionistic outlook of their master and in turn borrowed in varying degrees from the master to construct their own brand of a more progressive psychology to supplement the limitations of the master's outlook. Czech psychiatrist and pioneer within transpersonal psychology Stanislav Grof explains:

> The psychological orientation in psychiatry was inspired by the pioneering research of Sigmund Freud and his followers. Some of them, such as Carl Gustav Jung, Otto Rank, Wilhelm Reich, and Alfred Adler, left the psychoanalytic association or were expelled from it and started their own schools. Others stayed within the organization, but developed their own variations of psychoanalytic theory and technique. In the course of the twentieth century, his collective effort resulted in a large number of schools of "depth psychology," which differ significantly from each other in terms of their understanding of the human psyche and the

nature of emotional disorders, as well as the therapeutic techniques they use.[26]

From this perspective, it becomes evident, as Rank states: "Each grasps different parts, claiming to explain the whole; each discounts and excludes some phenomena; each fails to weigh the explanation, which itself is just an interpretation of phenomena."[27] Again, it was the imperative reductionism of orthodox psychoanalytic theory that urged Freud's key disciples to develop more comprehensive theories and practices:

The chief objections of the revisionists to Freud may be summed up as follows: Freud has grossly underrated the extent to which the individual and his neurosis are determined by conflicts with his environment. Freud's "biological orientation" let him to concentrate on the phylogenetic and ontogenetic *past* of the individual: he considered the character as essentially fixed with the fifth or sixth year (if not earlier), and he interpreted the fate of the individual in terms of primary instincts and their vicissitudes, especially sexuality. In contrast, the revisionists shift the emphasis "from the past to the present," from the biological to the cultural level, from the "constitution" of the individual to his environment. "One can understand the biological development better if one discards the concept of libido altogether" and instead interprets the different stages "in terms of growth and of human relations." Then the subject of psychoanalysis becomes the "total personality" in its "relatedness to the world," and the "constructive aspects of the individual," his "productive and positive potentialities" receive the attention they deserve. Freud did not see that sickness, treatment, and cure are a matter of "interpersonal relationships" in which total personalities are engaged on both sides. Freud's conception is predominantly relativistic: he assumed that psychology can "help us to understand the motivation of value judgments but cannot help in establishing the validity of the value judgments themselves." Consequently, his psychology contains no ethics or only his personal ethics. Moreover, Freud had a "static" concept of society and thought that society developed as a "mechanism for controlling man's instincts," whereas the revisionists know "from the study of comparative cultures" that "man is not biologically endowed with dangerous fixed animal drives and that the only function of society is to control these." They insist that society "is not a static set of laws instituted in the past at the time of the murder of the primal father, but is rather a growing, changing, developing network of interpersonal experiences and behavior."[28]

Lasch highlights the dilemma of Freudian revisionism and its attempts to scrub and sanitize the orthodox canon of the psychoanalytic church:

> Revisionism was full of ironies. Attempting to radicalize Freud, the revisionists eliminated what was radical from his thought, the articulation of contradictions without any attempt to resolve them: the contradiction between the bourgeois myth of the autonomous individual and the evidence of unconscious determinism uncovered by the analysis of dreams and neurosis; the contradiction between "civilized sexual morality" and the rampant, insatiable sexuality underlying it; above all, the conflict between nature of culture.[29]

This revisionism erects a watered-down version of Freudianism, as Lasch writes: "The term 'revisionism' is used...for lack of a better one, but it does not accurately describe the relation between Freud and Fromm, Horney, Sullivan, Thompson, et al. Those writers did not 'revise' Freudian theory; they substituted a new theory of their own, which bore only a superficial resemblance to Freud's."[30] Fromm provides a case in point:

> If we stay within the Freudian system, well-being would have to be defined in terms of the libido theory, as the capacity for full genital functioning, or, from a different angle, as the awareness of the hidden Oedipal situation, definitions which...are only tangential to the real problem of human existence and the achievement of well-being by the total man. Any attempt to give a tentative answer to the problem of well-being must transcend the Freudian frame of reference and lead to a discussion, incomplete as it must be, of the basic concept of human existence, which underlies humanistic psychoanalysis.[31]

With a closer examination of psychoanalysis, it is possible to identify the origins of many schools, therapeutic approaches, and movements within contemporary psychology. Freud perceived early on the mind-body connection and the important role of the body, prior to what has become known as somatic psychology: "Psychoanalysis hopes to discover the common ground on which the coming together of bodily and mental disturbances will become intelligible."[32] Freud predicted the relevance of the "talking cure" in conjunction with the role of psychopharmacology, as is recorded here: "This future is still far distant, but one should study analytically every case of psychosis because this knowledge will one day guide the chemical therapy."[33]

Paradoxically, while Freud held extremely pessimistic and nihilistic views on human nature, it has been suggested that he was a forerunner of humanistic psychology because he had made the following statement about the psychoanalytic method: "the cure is effected by love."[34] Some even went as far as asserting that the germinating impulse for spiritual or transpersonal psychology also had its roots in Freud: "Freudian renegades...have made a significant impact on the development of the New Age, in particular on that aspect known as the Human Potential Movement."[35] Similarly, Rollo May holds that, "Existential psychotherapy is...owed chiefly to the genius of Freud,"[36] and Bugental writes, "Existential theory is deeply indebted to Freud's pioneer discoveries."[37] In the broader context of the emergence of mass therapies, American psychiatrist and schizophrenia researcher E. Fuller Torrey suggests: "The personal growth movement is thus the ultimate Freudianization of America."[38]

Freud's fundamentalism or anti-spiritual approach to the "science of the soul" or psychology that pathologized the sacred thwarted others' attempt to correct the errors in his theoretical outlook. Tournier observes, "Freud thought it possible to derive from his newly discovered science a definitive explanation of religion...which he proposed to reduce to simple psychic functions...his most faithful disciples have been obliged to depart from him on this central point and recognize that the world of true spiritual values eludes psychological analysis."[39]

Jung vehemently expressed the claim that Freud's work was antagonistic to the sacred, writing: "Freud's view is a sinful violation of the sacred. It spreads darkness, not light..."[40] Even though Jung rightly criticized Freud for pathologizing the sacred, when analyzed more closely, Jung is also guilty of many of the same criticisms he launched at Freud, and when it comes to his embrace of the sacred, this is often misunderstood. Respected author on Tibetan Buddhism Marco Pallis (1895–1989) frames the impasse of both Freudian and Jungian depth psychology in the light of the spiritual traditions:

The latest and in many ways deadliest addition to this process of subversion is the psychological interpretation of religion, of which the Freudian and Jungian schools provide two representative forms, the one being avowedly materialistic and hostile, while the other affects a sympathetic attitude on the strength of a deftly nurtured system of equivocations, as between things of a spiritual and of a psychic order.[41]

The following assessment by Jung speaks not only about his master's outlook on the "science of the soul" or psychology, but also his own analytic psychology: "Error is just as important a condition of life's progress as truth."[42] In conclusion, Jung confirms that his analytical psychology should not be viewed as a deviation of psychoanalysis, but a continuation of Freudian therapy: "It has never been my purpose to criticize Freud...I have been far more interested in the continuation of the road he tried to build..."[43]

What must be understood is that Freud's own rebellion that brought about the psychoanalytic revolution cannot avoid continual "divergent schools of thought," as seen throughout the history of modern psychology. The disconnection of the revolutionary impulse in all its forms from the Spirit provokes a truncated outlook, as Schuon confirms: "Relativism engenders the spirit of rebellion and is at the same time its fruit."[44] We are left with a final reflection on the neo- and post-Freudian revolution: "All the [neo- and] post-Freudians...became modes of consolation."[45]

Conclusion:

Founder of the Greatest Revolution in Psychology or "the Greatest Con Man in the History of Medicine"?

Many might assume that the influence of Freud and psychoanalysis have faded into the enigmatic history of the annals of contemporary psychology or have vanished altogether, given the newer developments; however, like behaviorism, or the "first force" of modern psychology, this is far from the case. It would be naïve to assume that someone who has been hailed as "The greatest psychologist of our century"[1] would enigmatically vanish in this way. The theoretical tenets or rather ideology of Freudianism is so widespread in the popular culture that it is akin to the air that we breathe, the way in which we see the world, or the lexicon that is spoken: "Psychoanalysis and its ideas about the unconscious mind have spread to every nook and cranny of the culture."[2] For this reason, Freud and the psychoanalytic "talking cure" continue to live among us. The following contextualizes this point within the broader historical trajectory of contemporary psychology: "Without question Freud was a man of a thousand mistakes, many illusions, and colossal arrogance, and many of his theories are best forgotten...Long after Abraham Maslow, Carl Rogers, and Fritz Perls are relegated to footnotes in the history of [modern] psychology, Freud will remain a permanent resident in the Hall of Exemplars."[3]

The very foundations of contemporary psychology for better or worse begin with Freud and Watson. Freud asserts: "Psycho-analysis is a part of psychology...It is certainly not the whole of psychology, but its substructure and perhaps even its entire foundation."[4] Putting all Freudian condemnation aside, Swedish psychiatrist Poul Bjerre (1876–1964) illustrates that the field of contemporary psychology has been so impregnated with Freud and his findings that no one can discuss or provide treatment without utilizing the legacy that Freud has left:

All criticisms coming from without and all inner scientific differences, do not so much harm what Freud brought forth, as does his infelicitous tendency to drive one-sidedness to absurdity. It is depressing to see such a movement work upon its own annihilation. For it can never be denied that it was first through the ideas which came from this direction, that psychotherapy was able to lift itself up to importance and become a general life-factor. Freud with one stroke has given the study of the soul-life such breadth and such surety, that we have obtained a foundation upon which to build for all time. One may be never so bitter against him for the blunders he has made—yet no one can carry out a single simple treatment without making use of some thing he discovered. It devolves upon those who will take the scientific inheritance after him to see to it that all his daring ingenious ideas are followed out with every conceivable freedom from prejudice.[5]

Whatever critiques may be launched at Freud and psychoanalytic movement they have nonetheless paradigmatically influenced the creation of contemporary psychology and the field of mental health in an indisputable manner. Even with the innumerable, insightful, and persuasive critiques now available, the influence of Freudianism continues, as Jung establishes: "Everybody derided and criticized Freud's psychoanalysis, because they had neither applied nor even understood the method, and yet it ranks among the greatest achievements of modern psychology."[6] Jung also affirms: "You see, Freudian theory goes much deeper, right into the glands, it is the most profound statement that can ever be made about human psychology."[7]

With this noted, it is imperative not to downplay the errors of psychoanalysis, because alongside behaviorism, it has erected the ground floor or structure for the development of modern psychology to be erected. Should the foundations of modern psychology be proved to be theoretically unsound, it would reflect negatively upon the entire efficacy of the field, as all of the constituent parts are constructed with the same essential architecture and building materials. Myriad examples have already been provided; however, the following identifies the dilemma of relying on psychoanalysis, not unlike the quandary of behaviorism in establishing the foundation of contemporary psychology: "considered in its entirety, psychoanalysis won't do. It is an end product, moreover, like a dinosaur or a zeppelin; no better theory can ever be erected on its ruins, which will remain for ever one of the saddest and strangest of all landmarks in the history of twentieth-century thought."[8]

Regarding the predicament facing behavioristic psychology, we are reminded:

There can be no doubt about it, contemporary American scientific psychology is the sterilest of the sterile. Years of arduous labour and the assiduous enterprise of hundreds of professors and thousands of students has yielded precisely nothing...In the fifty-three years that have passed since that "momentous" occasion [John B. Watson, *Psychology as the Behaviorist Views It* (1913)] can *one* positive contribution towards any increased knowledge of man be pointed to? None such can be found; no substantive contribution can be named. The canard that "psychology is a new science" has long outlived its explanatory-away usefulness; the unpleasant and discouraging facts must be faced honestly.[9]

One of the many dangers of Freudian psychoanalysis is that its theories are not contained within the scope of modern psychology or modern science for that matter. Freudianism is a *reductio ad absurdum*, for it makes myriad unwarranted and speculative assumptions that include but are not limited to grammar, art, literary criticism, mathematics, politics, history, jurisprudence, mythology, folklore, religion, anthropology, sociology—attempting to exert its influence into all facets of the human condition. There does not appear to be any set parameters for the doctrine of the "talking cure"; hence it has been emphasized that it is "trying to swallow everything in psychoanalysis."[10] As unsettling as it may be, "Freud's theories are now a basic part of our cultural substance."[11]

With the widespread dissemination of the doctrine of the "talking cure" that has fashioned itself as a mass movement, it is essential not to lose focus on its subversive nature that is inseparable from the emergence of the modern world itself:

> [T]here is, within the modern world itself, a secret that is better kept than any other: it is that of the formidable enterprise of suggestion that has produced and that maintains the existing mentality, that has constituted it and as it were "manufactured" it in such a way that it can only deny the existence and even the possibility of any such enterprise; and this is doubtless and best conceivable means, and a means of truly "diabolical" cleverness, for ensuring that the secret shall never be discovered.[12]

Psychoanalysis is a definitive trademark of modernism, as an epistemological and ontological *cul-de-sac* that seeks to purge religion of its centrality, making it a separate category equal to all others, which ultimately undermines the sacred altogether. The marginalization of religion inevitably leads to its becoming less significant and a perfect target to be attacked and ultimately expunged from the lives of the human collectivity. A vacuum is left in the absence of religion, and religion is replaced by a secular pseudo-religion: this is to say psychoanalysis or "Freudianism as a religion."[13] Szasz indicates that the issue is not limited to Freudian psychoanalysis, but applies to contemporary psychology in its entirety: "Herein lies one of the supreme ironies of modern psychotherapy: it is not merely a religion that pretends to be a science, it is actually a fake religion that seeks to destroy true religion."[14] The same could be said for contemporary psychiatry, as "psychiatry takes on the characteristics of a new religion or antireligion."[15]

Although psychoanalysis is a byproduct of the materialistic outlook in which it incubated and from which it emerged, its all-encompassing assertions are a novel development in the history of ideas. Psychoanalysis does not seek to make comparisons between the different disciplines, let alone build bridges between them, but rather asserts the singularity of its own point of view inaugurating an imperialism of the human mind and behavior by refuting and squelching all dissenting positions. For those who were sitting on the fence or ambivalent about the doctrine of the "talking cure," the verdict on psychoanalysis has been rendered and made explicitly clear by Crews: "there is literally nothing to be said, scientifically or therapeutically, to the advantage of the entire Freudian system."[16]

Fromm argues that only if one recognizes Freud's messianic impulse to bring a new message to the human collectivity can his mass appeal and the insurgency of the psychoanalytic movement be grasped:

> What a strange phenomenon, this psychoanalytic movement! Psychoanalysis is a therapy, that of neurosis, and it is at the same time a psychological theory, a general theory of human nature and specifically of the existence of the unconscious and its manifestations in dreams, symptoms, in character and in all symbolic productions. Is there any other case of a therapy or of a scientific theory transforming itself into a movement, centrally directed by a secret committee, with purges of deviant members, with local organizations in an international superorganization? No therapy in the field of medicine was ever transformed into such a movement.[17]

In recapping the myriad errors and harm caused, the following summarizes the predicament that the "second force" within modern psychology known as psychoanalysis faces:

> Consider some of the damaging charges that have been brought against Freud in recent years: that he lied about his role in promoting the use of cocaine for morphine addiction; that he propagated false and demeaning stories about Breuer's grounds for aborting their collaboration; that he boasted in 1898 of "innumerable" therapeutic successes which were nonexistent; that having concealed for eight years that his imputation of infantile molestations to his patients was a mistake, he then falsely boasted of having discovered how to distinguish the aftermath of genuine molestations from the aftermath of fancied ones; that he gave distorted and self-serving accounts of the procedure which led him to mistakenly impute molestations in the first place and that he did this to obscure the fact that it was the same procedure on which he based his "discovery" of the Oedipus complex and infantile polymorphous perversity; that in order to undercut the objection that apparent clinical corroboration of his theories was due to his patient's compliance he falsely denied that he had formulated these theories before his patients corroborated them; that he claimed to have validated his theses concerning infantile sexuality 'in every detail' by independent investigations of infantile behaviour, which had in fact never been undertaken; that while publicly insisting that his grounds for the privileged etiological role of sexuality were purely empirical and forced on him by his clinical experience, he privately acknowledged that they were *a priori* assumptions that he was unwilling to dispense with; that a careful scrutiny of his texts reveal inconsistencies so gross that they point to a profoundly opportunistic cast of mind.[18]

Fromm warns against the nefarious potentials of mind control within the mental health field that manifests as the inversion of the timeless injunction of "Know thyself": "Today the function of psychiatry, psychology and psychoanalysis threatens to become the tool in the manipulation of man."[19] Yet the malevolent and totalitarian implications of psychoanalysis to be used as mind control that began with Freud continue forth:

> Resistance to self-insight and resistance to social facts are contrived, most essentially, of the same stuff. It is here that psychology may play its most important role. Techniques for overcoming

resistance, developed mainly in the field of individual psychotherapy, can be improved and adapted for use with groups and
even for use on a mass scale...Thus, we need not suppose that
appeal to emotion belongs to those who strive in the direction of
fascism, while democratic propaganda must limit itself to reason
and restraint. If fear and destructiveness are the major emotional
sources of fascism, *eros* belongs mainly to democracy.[20]

In his book *The Impact of Science on Society* (1951) Bertrand
Russell reveals the parallels between behaviorism and psychoanalysis
as the bedrock of contemporary psychology and how they have sown
the seeds for the utilization of mass social engineering and mind control on the collectivity:

> Physiology and psychology afford fields of scientific technique
> which still await development. Two great men, Pavlov [including
> Watson] and Freud, have laid the foundation. I do not accept the
> view that they are in any essential conflict, but what structure will
> be built on their foundations is still in doubt. I think the subject
> which will be of most importance politically is mass psychol-
> ogy...Its importance has been enormously increased by the
> growth of modern methods of propaganda. Of these the most in-
> fluential is what is called "education." Religion plays a part,
> though a diminishing one; the Press, the cinema and the radio
> play an increasing part...It may be hoped that in time anybody
> will be able to persuade anybody of anything if he can catch the
> patient young and is provided by the State with money and equip-
> ment.

> Although this science will be diligently studied, it will be rigidly
> confined to the governing class. The populace will not be allowed
> to know how its convictions were generated. When the technique
> has been perfected, every government that has been in charge of
> education for a generation will be able to control its subjects se-
> curely without the need of armies or policemen.[21]

Lewis makes an interesting and memorable comment about social
engineering: "the power of Man to make himself what he pleases
means, as we have seen, [is] the power of some men to make other
men what *they* please."[22]

Even though Freud was attempting to achieve scientific credibility for his signature "talking cure," he curiously selected the following
Promethean epigram from Virgil's *Aeneid* to preface his famed book

The Interpretation of Dreams (1899), which speaks to the nefarious quality of a science broken away from its sacred source: "If I cannot bend the higher powers, I shall stir up Hell" (*Flectere si nequeo superos, Acheronta movebo*). This statement seems to suggest that if modern psychology cannot gain access to what is above or transcendent, it will unleash the subterranean forces of what is below or infernal to acquire influence and legitimacy. The dark and nefarious science of Freudianism is impregnated with what Freud has termed the "psychical underworld,"[23] and adds that "The psychoanalytic expectation is of the sinister; the signposts all point downward, into the dark."[24]

It needs to be remembered that neither psychologism nor scientism, or any other form of reductionism, can produce an integral therapy of the human psyche in the absence of Spirit, soul and body, when eclipsing Spirit and exclusively focusing on a very narrow dimension of the soul.[25] Psychoanalytic doctrine is essentially founded on an epistemological and ontological quicksand that is destructive to its own existence: "The crowning paradox of psychoanalysis is the near-uselessness of its insights. To 'make the unconscious conscious'—the program of psychoanalytic therapy—is to pour water into a sieve. The moisture that remains on the surface of the mesh is the benefit of analysis."[26] Such a psychology cannot be a true psychology, and yet the shibboleths of behaviorism and psychoanalysis make up the very underpinnings of modern psychology, being an antithesis of the "science of the soul." Yeats's famous phrase comes to mind regarding the quandary that Freudianism finds itself in: "Things fall apart; the centre cannot hold."[27] This point is further elaborated upon: "Psychoanalysis seems to be in particular disarray...while there have always been dissenting voices and even new schools, the organized center seems to be less and less a majority viewpoint. Fragmentation appears to be the order of the day..."[28]

Freud himself conceded that "One has an impression that one ought not to be surprised if it should turn out in the end that the difference between a person who has not been analyzed and the behavior of a person after he has been analyzed is not so thorough-going as we aim at making it and as we expect and maintain it to be."[29] This admission verifies the bitter fruit that was born with the doctrine of the "talking cure." As the often-cited verse of the Apostle Matthew reads: "Ye shall know them by their fruits" (Matthew 7:16–17).

Despite its apparent decline and less perceivable role amidst the present-day arsenal of therapies, the hegemonic dominance of the Freudian paradigm continues its fervent presence within modern psychology. Psychoanalysis needs to be understood for what it truly is—

one of the greatest theoretical deviations of the twentieth century. The hoax that psychoanalysis was somehow an effective scientific theory in treating the human psyche—with myth-making trickeries of successful treatment, metanarratives speculating on the nature of reality and the human condition, the insurgence of a subversive secular pseudo-religion for modern human beings traumatized by the loss of the sense of the sacred—is no longer credible and is none other than a fabrication of an illusion that is psychoanalysis. And if we dare to explore the psychodynamic implications of what this illusion is according to its own theory, we risk being ensnared and trapped once again in an ideological relativism.

Jung asks: "By what criterion do we judge something to be an illusion? Does there exist for the psyche anything which we may call 'illusion'? ...the psyche does not trouble itself about...categories of reality...It is highly probable that what we call illusion is actual for the psyche."[30] An imperative recognition is that "psychoanalytic theory, in any and all of its guises, is an illusion—ironically enough, in the Freudian sense of that word."[31] Jastrow writes:

> The signs of the times converge; they compose the writing on the wall. The decisive verdict cannot but be influenced by the violations of the fundamentals of psychology and the rules of logic, at all stages of construction, from foundation to finish. So considered, the house that Freud built is built upon sand, and with crumbly cement. There is, say those who have lifted psychology from an uncertain discipline to a secure position among the sciences, no place in the psychology of the future for a house of fictions, myths, and dreams...Freudianism may come to be regarded as the most glamorous delusion of a scientific age, a modern mirage...[32]

American author John Kerr (1950–2016) reminds us "psychoanalysis early ceased to be merely a clinical method—it was never a science—and became instead both a movement and a *Weltanschauung*."[33] An essential and critical factor is that psychoanalytic theory did not limit its inquiry to the scientific pursuit of psychology alone but attempted to erect both the foundations of contemporary psychology and a cultural superstructure based on his theory that aimed at destroying Western civilization. Freud supplied modern man with an upside-down *Weltanschauung* that is psychodynamic theory. Eysenck provides a necessary forewarning about the dangers of analysis: "a prototype of Freudian therapy...often makes a patient worse, rather than better!"[34]

Knowing the dark and ominous forces within the human psyche, Freud utilized his subversive therapeutic knowledge to manipulate these hidden forces within the masses, to lead them to abandon their faith, substituting the role of religion with his doctrine of the "talking cure" and the psychoanalytic church. Freud writes: "And, finally, groups have never thirsted after truth. They demand illusions, and cannot do without them. They constantly give what is unreal precedence over what is real; they are almost as strongly influenced by what is untrue as by what is true. They have an evident tendency not to distinguish between the two."[35]

Freud was not interested in the human being lying on the couch of his consulting room or humanity struggling to make sense of the epistemological and ontological void of modernism and its consequent spiritual crisis; rather, he was attempting to psychoanalyze himself. The doctrine of the "talking cure" is thus not a science as such, but a derivative or rather a symptom of Freud's own psychological imbalance and his attempt to cure himself: "Freudian psychoanalysis...is a psychic symptom which has proved to be more powerful than the analytical art of the master himself."[36] Freud not only ventured to analyze himself, he went on to project his psychoanalytic therapy upon the whole of humanity. Cloaking his theories and discoveries in scientific dress, he propagated the notion that these findings were universal in order to erect a cultural superstructure based on his theories and subsequently to destroy Western civilization.

Bakan observes: "Freud's psychoanalysis reached out from the healing of individuals to the healing of society."[37] Ultimately, the mirage and hoax that is psychoanalysis gives way to make it self-evident that the "talking cure" is a symptom rather than a therapeutic modality: "Psychoanalysis is an illness that pretends to be a cure."[38] Freud is exposed as "a false and faithless prophet" whose "theories were baseless and aberrational."[39] Psychoanalysis is essentially the nefarious legacy of an inverted psychology becoming an inverted spirituality for modern man. The memorable words of the Gospel are worth recalling anew: "Offense must needs come, but woe unto him through whom offense cometh" (Matthew 18:7). For this reason, it has been emphasized by Guénon that "while nineteenth century materialism closed the mind of man to what is above him [Spirit]...twentieth century [modern] psychology opened it to what is below him."[40] And yet we must never be led into despair or nihilism, forgetting what is foremost and essential: *Vincit omnia Veritas*—"Truth conquers all" (I Esdras 3:12.)

Sources

Abhedānanda, Swami and Joseph A. Fitzgerald (eds.). *The Original Gospel of Rāmakrishna: Based on M.'s English Text, Abridged.* Bloomington, IN: World Wisdom, 2011.

Abrams, Nathan. "Triple Exthnics," *Jewish Quarterly*, vol. 51, No. 4 (2004), pp. 27–30.

Adler, Mortimer J. *What Man Has Made of Man: A Study of the Consequences of Platonism and Positivism in Psychology.* New York, NY: Frederick Ungar Publishing, 1938.

Adorno, Theodor W. *Minima Moralia: Reflections on a Damaged Life*, trans. E.F.N. Jephcott. London, UK: Verso, 2005.

Adorno, Theodor W., Else Frenkel-Brunswik, Daniel Levinson, and Nevitt Sanford, *The Authoritarian Personality*. New York, NY: Harper & Row, 1950.

Alexander, Franz and Sheldon T. Selesnick, "Freud-Bleuler Correspondence," *Archives of General Psychiatry*, vol. 12 (January 1965), pp. 1–9.

Almaas, A.H. *Essence: The Diamond Approach to Inner Realization.* York Beach, ME: Samuel Weiser, 1986.

———. *The Void: Inner Spaciousness and Ego Structure*. Boston, MA: Shambhala, 2003.

Angell, James Rowland. "The Influence of Darwin on Psychology," *Psychological Review*, vol. 16, No. 3 (May 1909), pp. 152–69.

Anonymous. "Freud Is Not Dead," *Newsweek* (March 27, 2006).

———. "Is Freud Dead?" *Time* (November 29, 1993).

———. "The Jewish Peril and The Catholic Church," *Catholic Gazette* (February 1936), pp. 46–47.

Antelman, Marvin S. *To Eliminate the Opiate, Vol. 1*. Jerusalem, Israel: Zionist Book Club, 1974.

———. *To Eliminate the Opiate, Vol. 2*. Jerusalem, Israel: Zionist Book Club, 2002.

Arberry, A.J. *Discourses of Rumi*. London, UK: RoutledgeCurzon, 2004.

Augustine, Saint. *City of God*. New York, NY: Image Books, 1953.

———. *The Confessions of Saint Augustine*, trans. E.B. Pusey. Oxford, UK: John Henry Parker, 1853.

Azevedo, Mateus Soares de. *Men of a Single Book: Fundamentalism in Islam, Christianity, and Modern Thought*. Bloomington, IN: World Wisdom, 2010.

Azevedo, Mateus Soares de (ed.). *Ye Shall Know the Truth: Christianity and the Perennial Philosophy*. Bloomington, IN: World Wisdom, 2005.

Badcock, Christopher. *PsychoDarwinism: The New Synthesis of Darwin and Freud*. London, UK: Flamingo, 1995.

Baer, Marc David. *The Dönme: Jewish Converts, Muslim Revolutionaries, and Secular Turks*. Stanford, CA: Stanford University Press, 2010.

Bakan, David. *Sigmund Freud and the Jewish Mystical Tradition*. London, UK: Free Association Books, 1990.

Barrett, William. *The Illusion of Technique: A Search for Meaning in a Technological Civilization*. Garden City, NY: Anchor Books, 1979.

Basch, Michael Franz. *Doing Psychotherapy*. New York, NY: Basic Books, 1980.

Bentinck van Schoonheten, Anna. *Karl Abraham: Life and Work, a Biography*, trans. Liz Waters. London, UK: Karnac Books, 2016.

Bendeck Sotillos, Samuel. *Behaviorism: The Quandary of a Psychology without a Soul*. Chicago, IL: Kazi Publications, 2017.

———. "New Age or the Kali-Yuga?" *AHP Perspective* (April/May 2013), pp. 15–21.

———. "Prometheus and Narcissus in the Shadows of the Human Potential Movement," *AHP Perspective* (December 2012/January 2013), pp. 6–12.

———. (ed.). *Psychology and the Perennial Philosophy: Studies in Comparative Religion*. Bloomington, IN: World Wisdom, 2013.

———. "The Self and the Other in the Light of the One: The Metaphysics of Human Diversity," *Sacred Web: A Journal of Tradition and Modernity*, Vol. 41 (Summer 2018), pp. 34–76.

Benjamin, Walter. *Reflections: Essays, Aphorisms, Autobiographical Writing*, ed. Peter Demetz. New York, NY: Schocken Books, 1986.

Benvenuto, Bice. *Concerning the Rites of Psychoanalysis: Or the Villa of the Mysteries*. New York, NY: Routledge, 1994.

Bernays, Edward. *Crystallizing Public Opinion*. New York, NY: Liveright Publishing Corporation, 1961.

Bernays, Edward. "The Engineering of Consent," *Annals of the American Academy of Political and Social Science*, vol. 250, no. 1 (March 1947), pp. 113–20.

———. *Propaganda*. Brooklyn, NY: Ig Publishing, 2005.

Bernfeld, Siegfried. "Freud's Scientific Beginnings," *American Imago*, vol. 6, No. 3 (September 1949), pp. 163–96.

————. "Freud's Studies on Cocaine, 1884–1887," *Journal of the American Psychoanalytic Association*, vol. 1, No. 4 (October 1953), pp. 581–613.

Bettelheim, Bruno. *Freud and Man's Soul*. New York, NY: Vintage Books, 1984.

Billinsky, John M. "Jung and Freud (The End of a Romance)," *Andover Newton Quarterly*, vol. 10, no. 2 (1969), pp. 39–43.

Binswanger, Ludwig. *Being-in-the-World: Selected Papers of Ludwig Binswanger*, trans. Jacob Needleman. New York, NY: Basic Books, 1963.

————. *Sigmund Freud: Reminiscences of a Friendship*, trans. Norbert Guterman. New York, NY: Grune & Stratton, 1957.

Bjerre, Poul. *The History and Practice of Psychoanalysis*, trans. Elizabeth N. Barrow. Boston, MA: Richard G. Badger, 1920.

Boas, Franz. "The Methods of Ethnology," *American Anthropologist*, vol. 22, no. 4 (October/December 1920), pp. 311–21.

Bonaparte, Marie, Anna Freud and Ernst Kris (eds.). *The Origins of Psychoanalysis: Letters to Wilhelm Fliess, Drafts and Notes: 1887–1902*, trans. Eric Mosbacher and James Strachey. New York, NY: Basic Books, 1954.

Borch-Jacobsen, Mikkel. *Making Minds and Madness: From Hysteria to Depression*. New York, NY: Cambridge University Press, 2009.

Borch-Jacobsen, Mikkel and Sonu Shamdasani. *The Freud Files: An Inquiry into the History of Psychoanalysis*. Cambridge, UK: Cambridge University Press, 2012.

Borella, Jean. *The Crisis of Religious Symbolism and Symbolism & Reality*, trans. G. John Champoux. Kettering, OH: Angelico Press/Sophia Perennis, 2016.

Bottome, Phyllis. *Alfred Adler: A Biography*. New York, NY: G.P. Putnam's Sons, 1939.

Breger, Louis. *Freud: Darkness in the Midst of Vision*. New York, NY: John Wiley and Sons, 2000.

Brenner, Charles. *An Elementary Textbook of Psychoanalysis*. New York, NY: Anchor Books, 1974.

Breuer, Josef and Sigmund Freud, *Studies on Hysteria*, trans. and ed. James Strachey. New York, NY: Basic Books, 2000.

Brill, A. A. *Freud's Contribution to Psychiatry*. New York, NY: W. W. Norton & Company, 1944.

Brown, J.A.C. *Freud and the Post-Freudians*. Baltimore, MD: Penguin Books, 1967.

Brown, Joseph Epes. *The Sacred Pipe: Black Elk's Account of the Seven Rites of the Oglala Sioux*. Norman, OK: University of Oklahoma Press, 1989.

————. *The Spiritual Legacy of the American Indian: Commemorative Edition with Letters While Living with Black Elk*, eds. Marina Brown Weatherly, Elenita Brown and Michael Oren Fitzgerald. Bloomington, IN: World Wisdom, 2007.

Brunner, José. *Freud and the Politics of Psychoanalysis*. New Brunswick, NJ: Transaction Publishers, 2001.

Bucke, Richard Maurice. *Cosmic Consciousness*. New York, NY: Arkana Books, 1991.

Buckley, Kerry W. *Mechanical Man: John Broadus Watson and the Beginnings of Behaviorism*. New York, NY: Guilford Press, 1989.

Bugental, James F. T. *The Search for Authenticity: An Existential-Analytic Approach to Psychotherapy*. New York, NY: Holt, Rinehart and Winston, 1965.

Burckhardt, Titus. *Introduction to Sufi Doctrine*, trans. D. M. Matheson. Bloomington, IN: World Wisdom, 2008.

————. *Mirror of the Intellect: Essays on Traditional Science and Sacred Art*, trans. and ed. William Stoddart. Albany, NY: State University of New York Press, 1987.

————. *Mystical Astrology According to Ibn 'Arabi*, trans. Bulent Rauf. Louisville, KY: Fons Vitae, 2001.

Burtt, E. A. *The Metaphysical Foundations of Modern Science*. Mineola, NY: Dover Publications, 2003.

Carotenuto, Aldo. *A Secret Symmetry: Sabina Spielrein between Jung and Freud*, trans. Arno Pomerans, John Shepley and Krishna Winston. New York, NY: Pantheon Books, 1982.

Casey, Deborah. "The Basis of Religion and Metaphysics: An Interview with Frithjof Schuon," *The Quest*, vol. 9, no. 2 (Summer 1996), pp. 74–84.

Chapelle, Daniel. *Nietzsche and Psychoanalysis*. Albany, NY: State University of New York Press, 1993.

Charet, F.X. *Spiritualism and the Foundations of C. G. Jung's Psychology*. Albany, NY: State University of New York Press, 1993.

Chittick, William C. *Ibn 'Arabi: Heir to the Prophets*. Oxford, UK: Oneworld, 2007.

————. *Science of the Cosmos, Science of the Soul: The Pertinence of Islamic Cosmology in the Modern World*. Oxford, UK: Oneworld, 2009.

————. *The Self-Disclosure of God: Principles of Ibn al-'Arabī's Cosmology*. Albany, NY: State University of New York Press, 1998.

————. *The Sufi Path of Knowledge: Ibn al-'Arabī's Metaphysics of Imagination*. Albany, NY: State University of New York Press, 1989.

Choisy, Maryse. *Sigmund Freud: A New Appraisal*. New York, NY: Philosophical Library, 1963.

Churchland, Paul M. *The Engine of Reason, the Seat of the Soul*. Cambridge, MA: Massachusetts Institute of Technology Press, 1996.

Cioffi, Frank. *Freud and the Question of Pseudoscience*. Chicago, IL: Open Court, 1998.

Clement of Alexandria, Saint. *The Writings of Clement of Alexandria*, trans. Rev. William Wilson. Edinburgh: T. & T. Clark, 1884.

Cohen, David. *Psychologists on Psychology*. New York, NY: Taplinger Publishing Company, 1977.

Cohen, Patricia. "Freud Is Widely Taught at Universities, Except in the Psychology Department," *New York Times* (November 25, 2007).

Collingwood, R. G. *The Idea of Nature*. London, UK: Oxford University Press, 1970.

Collis, John Stewart. *An Artist of Life: A Study of the Life and Work of Havelock Ellis*. London, UK: Cassell & Company, 1959.

Coomaraswamy, Ananda K. *Coomaraswamy, Vol. 1: Selected Papers: Metaphysics*, ed. Roger Lipsey. Princeton, NJ: Princeton University Press, 1977.

————. *Coomaraswamy, Vol. 2: Selected Papers, Traditional Art and Symbolism*, ed. Roger Lipsey. Princeton, NJ: Princeton University Press, 1978.

————. *Hinduism and Buddhism*. New York, NY: Philosophical Library, 1943.

Coomaraswamy, Rama P. *The Destruction of the Christian Tradition: Updated and Revised*. Bloomington, IN: World Wisdom, 2006.

Corbin, Henry. "The Question of Comparative Philosophy: Convergences in Iranian and European Thought," *Spring: An Annual of Archetypal Psychology and Jungian Thought* (1980), pp. 1–20.

Corydon, Bent and L. Ron Hubbard, Jr., *L. Ron Hubbard: Messiah or Madman*. Secaucus, NJ: Lyle Stuart, 1987.

Covington, Coline. "The Future of Analysis," *Journal of Analytical Psychology*, vol. 46, no. 2 (April 2001), pp. 325–34.

Cranefield, Paul F. "Josef Breuer's Evaluation of His Contribution to Psycho-Analysis," *International Journal of Psycho-Analysis*, vol. 39 (1958), pp. 319–22.

Crews, Frederick C. *Follies of the Wise: Dissenting Essays.* Emeryville, CA: Shoemaker and Hoard, 2006.

———. *Freud: The Making of an Illusion.* New York, NY: Metropolitan Books, 2017.

———. *The Memory Wars: Freud's Legacy in Dispute.* New York, NY: New York Review of Books, 1995.

———. (ed.). *Unauthorized Freud: Doubters Confront a Legend.* New York, NY: Viking, 1998.

———. "The Verdict on Freud," *Psychological Science*, vol. 7, no. 2 (March 1996), pp. 63–68.

Crowley, Aleister. *The Book of the Law.* Boston, MA: Red Wheel/Weiser Books, 1976.

———. *The Confessions of Aleister Crowley: An Autobiography*, eds. John Symonds and Kenneth Grant. New York, NY: Arkana Books, 1989.

Dalrymple, Theodore. *Admirable Evasions: How Psychology Undermines Morality.* New York, NY: Encounter Books, 2015.

Daniélou, Alain. *The Complete Kāma Sūtra: The First Unabridged Modern Translation of the Classic Indian Text by Vātsyāyana*, trans. Alain Daniélou. Rochester, VT: Park Street Press, 1994.

Darwin, Charles. *The Origin of Species.* London, UK: John Murray, 1866.

Dawkins, Richard. *The God Delusion.* New York, NY: Houghton Mifflin, 2006.

Deikman, Arthur J. "Spirituality Expands a Therapist's Horizons," *Yoga Journal*, Issue 88 (September/October 1989), pp. 49, 115.

Dennett, Daniel C. *Breaking the Spell: Religion as a Natural Phenomenon.* New York, NY: Viking, 2006.

Dikshit, Sudhakar S. (ed.). *I Am That: Talks with Sri Nisargadatta Maharaj*, trans. Maurice Frydman. Durham, NC: Acorn Press, 1999.

Doidge, Norman. *The Brain That Changes Itself: Stories of Personal Triumph from the Frontiers of Brain Science.* New York, NY: Penguin Books, 2007.

Dostoyevsky, Fyodor. *Crime and Punishment.* New York, NY: P.F. Collier & Son, 1917.

Dresner, Samuel H. *Can Families Survive in Pagan America?* Lafayette, LA: Huntington House Publishers, 1995.

Dryden, Windy and Colin Feltham. *Psychotherapy and Its Discontents*. Buckingham, UK: Open University Press, 1992.

Dunlap, Knight. *Mysticism, Freudianism and Scientific Psychology*. St. Louis, MO: C.V. Mosby Company, 1920.

———. "The Pragmatic Advantage of Freudo-Analysis: (A Criticism)," *Psychoanalytic Review*, vol. 1, no. 2 (1913–14), pp. 149–52.

Dupont, Judith (ed.). *The Clinical Diary of Sándor Ferenczi*, trans. Michael Balint and Nicola Zarday Jackson. Cambridge, MA: Harvard University Press, 1988.

Dupré, Louis. "Spiritual Life and the Survival of Christianity," *Cross Currents*, vol. 48, no. 3 (Fall 1998), pp. 381–90.

Earman, John, Allen I. Janis, Gerald J. Massey and Nicholas Rescher. *Philosophical Problems of the Internal and External Worlds: Essays on the Philosophy of Adolf Grünbaum*. Pittsburgh, PA: University of Pittsburgh Press, 1993.

Eaton, Gai. *King of the Castle: Choice and Responsibility in the Modern World*. Cambridge, UK: Islamic Texts Society, 1990.

Eberstadt, Mary. "The Zealous Faith of Secularism," *First Things*, vol. 279 (January 2018), pp. 35–40.

Eckhart, Meister. *Meister Eckhart: Teacher and Preacher*, ed. Bernard McGinn. Mahwah, NJ: Paulist Press, 1986.

———. *Meister Eckhart, Vol. 1*, trans. C. de B. Evans, ed. Franz Pfeiffer. London, UK: John M. Watkins, 1924.

———. *Meister Eckhart: The Essential Sermons, Commentaries, Treatises, and Defense*, trans. Edmund Colledge, O.S.A. and Bernard McGinn. Mahwah, NJ: Paulist Press, 1981.

Editors of Executive Intelligence Review, *The Ugly Truth about the Anti-Defamation League*. Washington, DC: Executive Intelligence Review, 1992.

Edmunds, Lavinia. "His Master's Choice," *John Hopkins Magazine*, vol. 40, no. 2 (April 1988), pp. 41–49.

Eisen, Arnold M. and Gideon Lewis-Kraus (eds.). *The Jew of Culture: Freud, Moses, and Modernity*. Charlottesville, VA: University of Virginia Press, 2008.

Eissler, Kurt R. *Medical Orthodoxy and the Future of Psychoanalysis*. New York, NY: International Universities Press, 1965.

———. *Talent and Genius: The Fictitious Case of Tausk contra Freud*. New York, NY: Quadrangle Books, 1971.

Eliade, Mircea. *Occultism, Witchcraft, and Cultural Fashions: Essays in Comparative Religions*. Chicago, IL: University of Chicago Press, 1976.

————. *Patanjali and Yoga*, trans. Charles Lam Markmann. New York, NY: Schocken Books, 1976.

Ellenberger, Henri F. *The Discovery of the Unconscious: The History and Evolution of Dynamic Psychiatry*. New York, NY: Basic Books, 1970.

Ellis, Albert. *The American Sexual Tragedy*. New York, NY: Lyle Stuart, 1962.

————. *The Case Against Religion: A Psychotherapist's View and The Case Against Religiosity*. Austin, TX: American Atheist Press, 1980.

————. "Is Psychoanalysis Harmful?" *Psychiatric Opinion*, vol. 5, no. 1 (January 1968), pp. 16–25.

Ellis, Albert and Robert A. Harper, *A Guide to Rational Living*. Hollywood, CA: Wilshire Book Company, 1971.

Ellis, Havelock. *Studies in the Psychology of Sex: The Evolution of Modesty, the Phenomena of Sexual Periodicity Auto-Erotism*. Philadelphia, PA: F. A. Davis Company, 1904.

Erikson, Erik H. *Identity and the Life Cycle*. New York, NY: W. W. Norton & Company, 1994.

————. *Identity: Youth and Crisis*. New York, NY: W. W. Norton & Company, 1968.

————. "Reality and Actuality," *Journal of the American Psychoanalytic Association*, vol. 10, no. 3 (July 1962), pp. 451–74.

————. *Young Man Luther: A Study in Psychoanalysis and History*. New York, NY: W. W. Norton & Company, 1993.

Ernst, Carl W. *Words of Ecstasy in Sufism*. Albany, NY: State University of New York Press, 1985.

Esterson, Allen. *Seductive Mirage: An Exploration of the Work of Sigmund Freud*. Chicago, IL: Open Court, 1993.

Evola, Julius. *The Metaphysics of Sex*. New York, NY: Inner Traditions, 1983.

————. *Revolt Against the Modern World*, trans. Guido Stucco. Rochester, VT: Inner Traditions International, 1995.

Eysenck, Hans J. *Decline and Fall of the Freudian Empire*. New York, NY: Penguin Books, 1991.

Falzeder, Ernst (ed.). *The Complete Correspondence of Sigmund Freud and Karl Abraham, 1907–1925*, trans. Caroline Schwarzacher, Christine Trollope, and Klara Majthényi King. London, UK: Karnac, 2002.

Falzeder, Ernst, Eva Brabant, and Patrizia Giampieri-Deutsch (eds.). *The Correspondence of Sigmund Freud and Sándor Ferenczi,*

Vol. 1: 1908–1914, trans. Peter T. Hoffer. Cambridge, MA: Belknap Press of Harvard University Press, 1993.

―――. (eds.). *The Correspondence of Sigmund Freud and Sándor Ferenczi, Vol. 2: 1914–1919*, trans. Peter T. Hoffer. Cambridge, MA: Belknap Press of Harvard University Press, 1996.

Farrell, John. *Freud's Paranoid Quest: Psychoanalysis and Modern Suspicion*. New York, NY: New York University Press, 1996.

Felitti, Vincent J., Robert F. Anda, Dale Nordenberg, David F. Williamson, Alison M. Spitz, Valerie Edwards, Mary P. Koss, and James S. Marks, "Relationship of Childhood Abuse and Household Dysfunction to Many of the Leading Causes of Death in Adults: The Adverse Childhood Experiences (ACE) Study," *American Journal of Preventive Medicine,* vol. 14, no. 4 (May 1998), pp. 245–58.

Fenichel, Otto. *Problems of Psychoanalytic Technique*. New York, NY: *Psychoanalytic Quarterly*, 1941.

Fernando, Ranjit (ed.). *The Unanimous Tradition: Essays on the Essential Unity of All Religions*. Colombo: Sri Lanka Institute of Traditional Studies, 1999.

Fichtner, Gerhard (ed.). *The Sigmund Freud–Ludwig Binswanger Correspondence, 1908–1938*, trans. Arnold J. Pomerans and Thomas Roberts. New York, NY: Other Press, 2003.

Fine, Reuben. *History of Psychoanalysis*. New York, NY: Jason Aronson, 1990.

Fisher, Seymour and Roger P. Greenberg. *The Scientific Credibility of Freud's Theories and Therapy*. New York, NY: Columbia University Press, 1985.

Fitzgerald, Michael Oren. *Frithjof Schuon: Messenger of the Perennial Philosophy*. Bloomington, IN: World Wisdom, 2010.

―――. *Yellowtail, Crow Medicine Man and Sun Dance Chief: An Autobiography*. Norman, OK: University of Oklahoma Press, 1994.

Forleo, Romano and Willy Pasini. *Medical Sexology: The Third International Congress*. Littleton, MA: PSG Publishing, 1980.

Foucault, Michel. *Madness and Civilization: A History of Insanity in the Age of Reason*, trans. Richard Howard. New York, NY: Vintage Books, 1988.

Foxon, David F. Libertine. *Literature in England, 1660–1745*. New Hyde Park, NY: University Books, 1966.

Frankl, Viktor E. *The Unheard Cry for Meaning: Psychotherapy and Humanism*. New York, NY: Touchstone, 1978.

Freud, Anna. "Inaugural Lecture for the Sigmund Freud Chair at the Hebrew University, Jerusalem," *International Journal of Psycho-Analysis*, vol. 59 (1978), pp. 145–48.

———. *The Psychoanalytical Treatment of Children: Lectures and Essays*. New York, NY: Schocken Books, 1964.

Freud, Ernst L. (ed.). *Letters of Sigmund Freud*, trans. Tania Stern and James Stern. New York, NY: Basic Books, 1975.

———. (ed.). *The Letters of Sigmund Freud and Arnold Zweig*, trans. William Robson-Scott and Elaine Robson-Scott. London, UK: Hogarth Press and the Institute of Psycho-Analysis, 1970.

Freud, Sigmund. *An Autobiographical Study*, trans. and ed. James Strachey. New York, NY: W. W. Norton & Company, 1989.

———. *The Basic Writings of Sigmund Freud*, trans. and ed. A. A. Brill. New York, NY: Modern Library, 1938.

———. *Beyond the Pleasure Principle*, trans. and ed. James Strachey. New York, NY: WW. Norton & Company, 1989.

———. *Character and Culture*, ed. Philip Rieff. New York, NY: Collier Books, 1963.

———. *Civilization and Its Discontents*, trans. and ed. James Strachey. New York, NY: W. W. Norton & Company, 1989.

———. *Cocaine Papers*, ed. Robert Byck. New York, NY: Stonehill, 1974.

———. *Collected Papers of Sigmund Freud, Vol. 1*, trans. Joan Riviere. London, UK: Hogarth Press and the Institute of Psycho-Analysis, 1950.

———. *Dora: An Analysis of a Case of Hysteria*, ed. Philip Rieff. New York, NY: Touchstone, 1997.

———. *The Ego and the Id*, trans. Joan Riviere, ed. James Strachey. New York, NY: W. W. Norton & Company, 1989.

———. *Five Lectures on Psycho-Analysis*, trans. and ed. James Strachey. New York, NY: W. W. Norton & Company, 1989.

———. *The Future of an Illusion*, trans. and ed. James Strachey. New York, NY: W. W. Norton & Company, 1989.

———. *A General Introduction to Psychoanalysis*. New York, NY: Horace Liveright, 1920.

———. *General Psychological Theory: Papers on Metapsychology*, ed. Philip Rieff. New York, NY: Touchstone, 2008.

———. *Group Psychology and the Analysis of the Ego*, trans. James Strachey. New York, NY: W. W. Norton & Company, 1989.

———. *The History of the Psychoanalytic Movement*, ed. Philip Rieff. New York, NY: Collier Books, 1963.

———. *The Interpretation of Dreams*, trans. and ed. James Strachey. New York, NY: Science Editions, 1963.

———. *Introductory Lectures on Psychoanalysis*, trans. and ed. James Strachey. New York, NY: W. W. Norton & Company, 1977.

———. *Jokes and Their Relation to the Unconscious*, trans. and ed. James Strachey. New York, NY: W.W . Norton & Company, 1989.

———. *Leonardo Da Vinci: A Study in Psychosexuality*, trans. A. A. Brill. New York, NY: Vintage Books, 1947.

———. *Leonardo da Vinci and a Memory of His Childhood*, trans. Alan Tyson, ed. James Strachey. New York, NY: W. W. Norton & Company, 1989.

———. *Moses and Monotheism*, trans. Katherine Jones. New York, NY: Vintage Books, 1967.

———. *New Introductory Lectures on Psycho-Analysis*, trans. and ed. James Strachey. New York, NY: W. W. Norton & Company, 1989.

———. *On the History of the Psycho-Analytic Movement*, trans. Joan Riviere, ed. James Strachey. New York, NY: W. W. Norton & Company, 1989.

———. *An Outline of Psycho-Analysis*, trans. and ed. James Strachey. New York, NY: WW. Norton & Company, 1969.

———. *The Problem of Anxiety*, trans. H. A. Bunker. New York: W. W. Norton & Company, 1963.

———. "The Psychogenesis of a Case of Female Homosexuality," *International Journal of Psycho-Analysis*, vol. 1, no. 2 (1920), pp. 125–49.

———. *The Psychopathology of Everyday Life*, trans. and ed. James Strachey. New York, NY: W. W. Norton & Company, 1989.

———. *The Question of Lay Analysis*, trans. and ed. James Strachey. New York, NY: W. W. Norton & Company, 1989.

———. *Sexuality and the Psychology of Love*, ed. Philip Rieff. New York, NY: Collier Books, 1978.

———. *The Standard Edition of the Complete Psychological Works of Sigmund Freud, Vol. 3*, trans. and ed. James Strachey. London, UK: Hogarth Press and the Institute of Psycho-Analysis, vols. 3 and 9, 1981; vols. 7, 14, and 22, 1953; vol. 10, 1962; vol. 11, 1956; vol. 12, 1958; vol. 17, 1955; vol. 18, 1975; vol. 20, 1959; vol. 21, 1961; vol. 23, 1964.

———. *The Standard Edition of the Complete Psychological Works of Sigmund Freud, Vol. 19*, trans. and ed. James Strachey. London, UK: Vintage Books, 2001.

———. *Studies in Parapsychology*, ed. Philip Rieff. New York, NY: Collier Books, 1966.

———. *Therapy and Technique*, ed. Philip Rieff. New York, NY: Collier Books, 1963.

———. *Three Essays on the Theory of Sexuality*, trans. and ed. James Strachey. New York, NY: Basic Books, 2000.

———. *Totem and Taboo*, trans. and ed. James Strachey. New York, NY: W. W. Norton & Company, 1989.

Friedell, Egon. *A Cultural History of the Modern Age, Vol. 3: The Crisis of the European Soul*, trans. C.F. Atkinson. New York, NY: Alfred A. Knopf, 1932.

Friedman, Maurice. *Contemporary Psychology: Revealing and Obscuring the Human*. Pittsburgh, PA: Duquesne University Press, 1984.

———. *The Hidden Human Image: A Heartening Answer to the Dehumanizing Threats of our Age*. New York, NY: Delta Book, 1974.

Fromm, Erich. *The Anatomy of Human Destructiveness*. New York, NY: Holt, Rinehart and Winston, 1974.

———. *The Art of Loving*. New York, NY: Bantam Books, 1963.

———. *Beyond the Chains of Illusion: My Encounter with Marx and Freud*. New York, NY: Simon & Schuster, 1962.

———. *Beyond Freud: From Individual to Social Psychoanalysis*, ed. Rainer Funk. Riverdale, NY: American Mental Health Foundation, 2010.

———. *The Crisis of Psychoanalysis*. Greenwich, CT: Fawcett, 1970.

———. *The Dogma of Christ: And Other Essays on Religion, Psychology and Culture*. Greenwich, CT: Fawcett, 1973.

———. *Escape from Freedom*. New York, NY: Henry Holt and Company, 1994.

———. *Greatness and Limitations of Freud's Thought*. New York, NY: Mentor Books, 1981.

———. *Man for Himself: An Inquiry into the Psychology of Ethics*. New York, NY: Rinehart and Company, 1947.

———. *The Pathology of Normalcy*, ed. Rainer Funk. Riverdale, NY: American Mental Health Foundation, 2010.

———. *Psychoanalysis and Religion*. New Haven, CT: Yale University Press, 1974.

————. *The Revolution of Hope: Toward a Humanized Technology*. New York, NY: Bantam Books, 1971.

————. *The Sane Society*. Greenwich, CT: Fawcett, 1955.

————. *Sigmund Freud's Mission: An Analysis of His Personality and Influence*. New York, NY: Grove Press, 1963.

Gagnon, John H. "Sex Research and Social Change," *Archives of Sexual Behavior*, vol. 4, no. 2 (March 1975), pp. 111–41.

Gathorne-Hardy, Jonathan. *Sex the Measure of All Things: A Life of Alfred C. Kinsey*. Bloomington, IN: Indiana University Press, 2000.

Gay, Peter. *Freud: A Life for Our Time*. New York, NY: Anchor Books, 1989.

————. (ed.). *The Freud Reader*. New York, NY: W. W. Norton & Company, 1995.

————. *A Godless Jew: Freud, Atheism, and the Making of Psychoanalysis*. New Haven, CT: Yale University Press, 1987.

————. "Sigmund and Minna? The Biographer as Voyeur," *New York Times Book Review*, January 29, 1989, pp. 1, 43–45.

Gelfand, Toby and John Kerr (eds.). *Freud and the History of Psychoanalysis*. Hillsdale, NJ: Analytic Press, 1992.

Gill, Merton M. *Psychoanalysis in Transition: A Personal View*. Hillsdale, NJ: Analytic Press, 2000.

Glasser, William. *Reality Therapy: A New Approach to Psychiatry*. New York, NY: Harper & Row, 1975.

Glover, Edward. *Freud or Jung?* New York, NY: Meridian, 1956.

Goetz, Bruno. "That Is All I Have to Say about Freud: Bruno Goetz's Reminiscences of Sigmund Freud," *International Review of Psycho-Analysis*, vol. 2 (1975), pp. 139–43.

Graetz, Heinrich. *History of the Jews, Vol. V*, trans. Bella Löwy. London, UK: David Nutt, 1892.

Graf, Max. "Reminiscences of Professor Sigmund Freud," *Psychoanalytic Quarterly*, vol. 11 (1942), pp. 465–76.

Graham, Robert (ed.). *Anarchism: A Documentary History of Libertarian Ideas, Vol. 1: From Anarchy to Anarchism (300 CE to 1939)*. Montreal: Black Rose Books, 2005.

Graves, Robert. "A Motley Hero," *Sewanee Review*, vol. 57, no. 4 (Autumn 1949), pp. 698–99.

Gray, Paul. "The Assault on Freud," *Time*, vol. 142, no. 23 (November 29, 1993), pp. 47–51.

Groddeck, Georg. *The Book of the It*. New York, NY: Vintage Books, 1949.

Grof, Stanislav. *Psychology of the Future: Lessons from Modern Consciousness Research*. Albany, NY: State University of New York Press, 2000.

Gross, Martin L. *The Psychological Society: A Critical Analysis of Psychiatry, Psychotherapy, Psychoanalysis and the Psychological Revolution*. New York, NY: Random House, 1978.

Grosskurth, Phyllis. *Melanie Klein: Her World and Her Work*. London, UK: Hodder and Stoughton, 1986.

———. *The Secret Ring: Freud's Inner Circle and the Politics of Psychoanalysis*. Reading, MA: Addison-Wesley Publishing, 1991.

Grünbaum, Adolf. *The Foundations of Psychoanalysis: A Philosophical Critique*. Los Angeles, CA: University of California Press, 1985.

Guénon, René. *The Crisis of the Modern World*, trans. Arthur Osborne, Marco Pallis and Richard C. Nicholson. Hillsdale, NY: Sophia Perennis, 2004.

———. *The Great Triad*, trans. Henry D. Fohr, ed. Samuel D. Fohr. Hillsdale, NY: Sophia Perennis, 2004.

———. *Initiation and Spiritual Realization*, trans. Henry D. Fohr, ed. Samuel D. Fohr. Ghent, NY: Sophia Perennis, 2001.

———. *Insights into Christian Esoterism*, trans. Henry D. Fohr, ed. Samuel D. Fohr. Ghent, NY: Sophia Perennis, 2001.

———. *Introduction to the Study of the Hindu Doctrines*, trans. Marco Pallis. Ghent, NY: Sophia Perennis, 2001.

———. *Man and His Becoming According to the Vedanta*, trans. Richard C. Nicholson. New York, NY: Noonday Press, 1958.

———. *Miscellanea*, trans. Henry D. Fohr, Cecil Bethell, Patrick Moore and Hubert Schiff. Hillsdale, NY: Sophia Perennis, 2001.

———. *The Multiple States of the Being*, trans. Henry D. Fohr, ed. Samuel D. Fohr. Ghent, NY: Sophia Perennis, 2001.

———. *The Reign of Quantity and the Signs of the Times*, trans. Lord Northbourne. Ghent, NY: Sophia Perennis, 2001.

———. *The Spiritist Fallacy*, trans. Alvin Moore, Jr. and Rama P. Coomaraswamy. Hillsdale, NY: Sophia Perennis, 2004.

———. *Studies in Hinduism*, trans. Henry D. Fohr, ed. Samuel D. Fohr. Ghent, NY: Sophia Perennis, 2001.

———. *Symbols of Sacred Science*, trans. Henry D. Fohr, ed. Samuel D. Fohr. Hillsdale, NY: Sophia Perennis, 2004.

———. *Theosophy: History of a Pseudo-Religion*, trans. Alvin Moore, Jr., Cecil Bethell, Hubert and Rohini Schiff. Hillsdale, NY: Sophia Perennis, 2004.

Haeckel, Ernst. *The History of Creation: Or, The Development of the Earth and Its Inhabitants by the Action of Natural Causes, Vol. 1*, trans. Sir E. Ray Lankester. New York, NY: D. Appleton and Company, 1914.

Hale, Nathan G. Jr. *James Jackson Putnam and Psychoanalysis: Letters between Putnam and Sigmund Freud, Ernest Jones, William James, Sándor Ferenczi, and Morton Prince, 1877–1917*, trans. Judith Bernays Heller. Cambridge, MA: Harvard University Press, 1971.

Hamilton, Edith and Huntington Cairns (eds.). *The Collected Dialogues of Plato: Including the Letters*. Princeton, NJ: Princeton University Press, 1980.

Hanly, Charles and Morris Lazerowitz (eds.). *Psychoanalysis and Philosophy*. New York, NY: International Universities Press, 1970.

Harms, Ernest. "Carl Gustav Jung—Defender of Freud and the Jews: A Chapter of European Psychiatric History under the Nazi Yoke," *Psychiatric Quarterly*, vol. 20, no. 2 (April 1946), pp. 199–230.

Harris, Sam. *The End of Faith: Religion, Terror, and the Future of Reason*. New York, NY: W. W. Norton & Company 2004.

Hart, Bernard. *Psychopathology: Its Development and Its Place in Medicine*. Cambridge, UK: Cambridge University Press, 1950.

Haynal, André and Ernst Falzeder (eds.). *100 Years of Psychoanalysis, Contributions to the History of Psychoanalysis*. Geneva: Cahiers Psychiatriques Genevois, Special Issue, 1994.

Hearnshaw, L.S. *The Shaping of Modern Psychology*. London, UK: Routledge, 1989.

Heelas, Paul. *The New Age Movement*. Oxford, UK: Blackwell Publishers, 2003.

Heinze, Andrew R. *Jews and the American Soul: Human Nature in the Twentieth Century*. Princeton, NJ: Princeton University Press, 2004.

Heuer, Gottried. "The Devil Underneath the Couch: The Secret Story of Jung's Twin Brother," *Harvest*, vol. 49, no. 2 (2003), pp. 130–45.

Higgins, Mary and Chester M. Raphael (eds.). *Reich Speaks of Freud: Wilhelm Reich Discusses His Work and His Relationship with Sigmund Freud*, trans. Therese Pol. New York, NY: Farrar, Straus and Giroux, 1972.

Hitchens, Christopher. *God Is Not Great: How Religion Poisons Everything*. New York: Twelve, Hachette Book Group, 2007.

Hoffer, Eric. *The Ordeal of Change*. New York, NY: Harper & Row, 1963.

———. *The True Believer: Thoughts on the Nature of Mass Movements*. New York, NY: Harper & Row, 1966.

Hoffman, Edward. *The Right To Be Human: A Biography of Abraham Maslow*. Los Angeles, CA: Jeremy P. Tarcher, 1988.

Holt, Robert R. "The Current Status of Psychoanalytic Theory," *Psychoanalytic Psychology*, vol. 2, no. 4 (1985), pp. 289–315.

Homans, Peter. *The Ability to Mourn: Disillusionment and the Social Origins of Psychoanalysis*. Chicago, IL: University of Chicago Press, 1989.

———. *Jung in Context: Modernity and the Making of a Psychology*. Chicago, IL: University of Chicago Press, 1979.

Hook, Sidney (ed.). *Psychoanalysis, Scientific Method, and Philosophy*. New York, NY: New York University Press, 1964.

Horgan, John. "Why Freud isn't Dead," *Scientific American*, vol. 275, no. 6 (December 1996), pp. 106–111.

Horkheimer, Max and Theodor W. Adorno, *Dialectic of Enlightenment: Philosophical Fragments*, trans. Edmund Jephcott, ed. Gunzelin Schmid Noerr. Stanford, CA: Stanford University Press, 2002.

Horney, Karen. *Feminine Psychology*, ed. Harold Kelman. New York, NY: W. W. Norton & Company, 1973.

———. *Neurosis and Human Growth: The Struggle Toward Self-Realization*. New York, NY: W. W. Norton & Company, 1950.

———. *The Neurotic Personality of Our Time*. New York, NY: W. W. Norton & Company, 1964.

———. *New Ways in Psychoanalysis*. New York, NY: W. W. Norton & Company, 1966.

———. *Our Inner Conflicts: A Constructive Theory of Neurosis*. New York, NY: W. W. Norton & Company, 1972.

Horney, Karen (ed.). *Are You Considering Psychoanalysis?* New York, NY: W. W. Norton & Company, 1962.

Hornstein, Gail A. "The Return of the Repressed: Psychology's Problematic Relations with Psychoanalysis, 1909–1960," *American Psychologist*, vol. 47, no. 2 (February 1992), pp. 254–63.

al-Hujwīrī, 'Alī b. 'Uthmān al-Jullābī. *The Kashf al-Mahjub: The Oldest Persian Treatise on Sufism*, trans. R. A. Nicholson. London, UK: Luzac and Company, 1976.

Huxley, Aldous. "Our Contemporary Hocus-Pocus," *Forum*, vol. 73 (March 1925), pp. 313–20.

Ibn al-'Arabī. *The Bezels of Wisdom*, trans. R.W.J. Austin. New York, NY: Paulist Press, 1980.

―――. *The Wisdom of the Prophets (Fusus al-Hikam)*, trans. Titus Burckhardt and Angela Culme-Seymour. Gloucestershire, UK: Beshara, 1975.

Jacoby, Russell. *Social Amnesia: A Critique of Conformist Psychology from Adler to Laing*. Boston, MA: Beacon Press, 1975.

James, Henry (ed.). *The Letters of William James, Vol. II*. Boston, MA: Atlantic Monthly Press, 1920.

James, William. *The Principles of Psychology, Vol. 2*. New York, NY: Dover, 1950.

―――. *The Varieties of Religious Experience*. New York, NY: Penguin Books, 1985.

Janov, Arthur. *The Primal Scream: Primal Therapy, The Cure for Neurosis*. New York, NY: Dell Publishing, 1970.

Janzen, Bernard. *Unmasking the Faces of Antichrist: Interview with Dr. Wolfgang Smith*. Davidson, Saskatchewan, Canada: Triumph Communications, 2017.

Jastrow, Joseph. *Freud: His Dream and Sex Theories*. Cleveland, OH: World Publishing Company, 1948.

Jeffries, Stuart. *Grand Hotel Abyss: The Lives of the Frankfurt School* London, UK: Verso, 2017.

John Chrysostom, Saint. *Discourses Against Judaizing Christians*, trans. Paul W. Harkins. Washington, D.C.: Catholic University of America Press, 1999.

Johnston, William M. *The Austrian Mind: An Intellectual and Social History, 1848–1938*. Berkeley, CA: University of California Press, 2000.

Jones, E. Michael. *The Jewish Revolutionary Spirit and Its Impact on World History*. South Bend, IN: Fidelity Press, 2008.

―――. *Libido Dominandi: Sexual Liberation and Political Control*. South Bend, IN: St. Augustine's Press, 2000.

Jones, Ernest. *Essays in Applied Psycho-Analysis*. London, UK: International Psycho-Analytical Press, 1923.

―――. *Free Associations: Memories of a Psychoanalyst*. New York, NY: Basic Books, 1959.

―――. *The Life and Work of Sigmund Freud, Vol. 1: The Formative Years and the Great Discoveries, 1856–1900*. New York, NY: Basic Books, 1959.

―――. *The Life and Work of Sigmund Freud, Vol. 2: Years of Maturity, 1901–1919*. New York, NY: Basic Books, 1955.

———. *The Life and Work of Sigmund Freud, Vol. 3: The Last Phase, 1919–1939*. New York, NY: Basic Books, 1957.

Jones, James H. *Alfred C. Kinsey: A Life By*. New York, NY: W. W. Norton & Norton, 2004.

Jordan, Nehemiah. *Themes in Speculative Psychology*. New York, NY: Routledge, 2014.

Jung, C. G. *Analytical Psychology: Notes of the Seminar Given in 1925*, ed. William McGuire. London, UK: Routledge, 1992.

———. *C. G. Jung Letters, Vol. 1: 1906–1950*, trans. R.F.C. Hull, eds. Gerhard Adler and Aniela Jaffé. New York, NY: Routledge, 1992.

———. *C. G. Jung Letters, Vol. 2: 1951–1961*, trans. R.F.C. Hull, ed. Gerhard Adler. London, UK: Routledge, 2011.

———. *C. G. Jung Speaking: Interviews and Encounters*, eds. William McGuire and R.F.C. Hull. Princeton, NJ: Princeton University Press, 1993.

———. *Children's Dreams: Notes from the Seminar Given in 1936–1940*, trans. Ernst Falzeder and Tony Woolfson, eds. Lorenz Jung and Maria Meyer-Grass. Princeton, NJ: Princeton University Press, 2008.

———. *The Collected Works of C. G. Jung, Vol. 1: Psychiatric Studies*, trans. R.F.C. Hull, ed. Gerhard Adler. Princeton, NJ: Princeton University Press, 1983.

———. *The Collected Works of C. G. Jung, Vol. 2: Experimental Researches*, trans. Leopold Stein and Diana Riviere. Princeton, NJ: Princeton University Press, 1981.

———. *The Collected Works C. G. Jung, Vol. 7: Two Essays on Analytical Psychology*, trans. R.F.C. Hull, eds. Sir Herbert Read, Michael Fordham and Gerhard Adler. Princeton, NJ: Princeton University Press, 1972.

———. *The Collected Works of C. G. Jung, Vol. 8: Structure and Dynamics of the Psyche*, trans. Gerhard Adler and R.F.C. Hull. Princeton, NJ: Princeton University Press, 1972.

———. *The Collected Works of C. G. Jung, Vol. 10: Civilization in Transition*, trans. R.F.C. Hull. Princeton, NJ: Princeton University Press, 1970.

———. *The Collected Works of C. G. Jung, Vol. 11: Psychology and Religion: West and East*, trans. R.F.C. Hull, ed. Gerhard Adler. Princeton, NJ: Princeton University Press, 1975.

———. *The Collected Works C. G. Jung, Vol. 13: Alchemical Studies*, trans. R.F.C. Hull, ed. Gerhard Adler. Princeton, NJ: Princeton University Press, 1983.

————. *The Collected Works of C. G. Jung, Vol. 15: The Spirit in Man, Art and Literature*, trans. R.F.C. Hull. Princeton, NJ: Princeton University Press, 1971.

————. *The Collected Works of C. G. Jung, Vol. 16: The Practice of Psychotherapy*, trans. R.F.C. Hull. Princeton, NJ: Princeton University Press, 1985.

————. *The Collected Works of C. G. Jung, Vol. 18: The Symbolic Life: Miscellaneous Writings*, trans. R.F.C. Hull. Princeton, NJ: Princeton University Press, 1980.

————. *The Collected Works of C. G. Jung, Supplementary Volume A: The Zofingia Lectures*, trans. Jan van Heurck, eds. Sir Herbert Read, Michael Fordham, and Gerhard Adler. New York, NY: Routledge, 2014.

————. *Critique of Psychoanalysis*, trans. R.F.C. Hull. Princeton, NJ: Princeton University Press, 1975.

————. *Essays on Contemporary Events: The Psychology of Nazism*, trans. R.F.C. Hull. Princeton, NJ: Princeton University Press, 1989.

————. "The Letters of C. G. Jung to Sabina Spielrein," *Journal of Analytical Psychology*, vol. 46, no. 1 (January 2001), pp. 173–99.

————. (ed.). *Man and His Symbols*. New York, NY: Laurel, 1968.

————. *Memories, Dreams, Reflections*, trans. Richard Winston and Clara Winston, ed. Aniela Jaffé. New York, NY: Vintage Books, 1965.

————. *Modern Man in Search of a Soul*, trans. W. S. Dell and Cary F. Baynes. New York, NY: Harcourt, Brace & World, 1933.

————. "Psychological Commentary," in *The Tibetan Book of the Dead*, ed. W. Y. Evans-Wentz. London, UK: Oxford University Press, 1968, pp. xxxv–lii.

————. "Psychological Commentary," in *The Tibetan Book of the Great Liberation*, ed. W. Y. Evans-Wentz. London, UK: Oxford University Press, 2000, pp. xxix–lxiv.

————. *Psychology and Religion*. New Haven, CT: Yale University Press, 1938.

————. *Psychology of the Unconscious*, trans. Beatrice M. Hinkle. New York, NY: Moffat, Yard and Company, 1917.

————. *Selected Letters of C. G. Jung, 1909–1961*, ed. Gerhard Adler. Princeton, NJ: Princeton University Press, 1984.

————. *The Theory of Psychoanalysis*. New York, NY: Journal of Nervous and Mental Disease Publishing Company, 1915.

————. *Two Essays on Analytical Psychology*, trans. R.F.C. Hull. New York, NY: Meridian, 1956.

Jurjevich, R. M. *The Hoax of Freudism: A Study of Brainwashing the American Professionals and Laymen*. Philadelphia, PA: Dorrance and Company, 1974.

Justman, Stewart. "Freud and His Nephew," *Social Research*, vol. 61, no. 2 (Summer 1994), pp. 457–76.

Kanzer, Mark and Jules Glenn (eds.). *Freud and His Self-Analysis*. New York, NY: Jason Aronson, 1983.

Kapleau, Philip. *Zen: Dawn in the West*. Garden City, NY: Anchor Books, 1980.

Kardiner, Abram. *My Analysis with Freud: Reminiscences*. New York, NY: W. W. Norton & Company, 1977.

Kaye, Howard L. "Why Freud Hated America," *Wilson Quarterly*, vol. 17, no. 2 (Spring 1993), pp. 118–25.

Keen, Sam. *Fire in the Belly: On Being a Man*. New York, NY: Bantam Books, 1991.

Kerr, John. *A Most Dangerous Method: The Story of Jung, Freud, and Sabina Spielrein*. New York, NY: Alfred A. Knopf, 1993.

Klein, Dennis B. *Jewish Origins of the Psychoanalytic Movement*. Chicago, IL: University of Chicago Press, 1985.

Klein, Jean. *Be Who You Are*, trans. Mary Mann. Salisbury, UK: Non-Duality Press, 2006.

Knickerbocker, H.R. "Diagnosing the Dictators: An Interview with Dr. Jung," *Hearst's International-Cosmopolitan*, vol. 106 (January 1939), pp. 22–23, 116–20.

Knight, Robert P. "Evaluation of the Results of Psychoanalytic Therapy," *American Journal of Psychiatry*, vol. 98, no. 3 (November 1941), pp. 434–46.

Knoepfmacher, Hugo. "Sigmund Freud and the B'nai B'rith," *Journal of the American Psychoanalytic Association*, vol. 27, no. 2 (April 1979), pp. 441–49.

Kohut, Heinz. *The Restoration of the Self*. Chicago, IL: University of Chicago Press, 2009.

Koyré, Alexandre. *From the Closed World to the Infinite Universe*. Kettering, OH: Angelico Press, 2016.

Kraepelin, Emil. *Dementia Praecox and Paraphrenia*, trans. R. Mary Barclay, ed. George M. Robertson. Edinburgh, UK: E & S Livingstone, 1919.

Krafft-Ebing, Richard. *Psychopathia Sexualis*. New York, NY: Rebman Company, 1906.

Kripal, Jeffrey J. *Kali's Child: The Mystical and the Erotic in the Life and Teachings of Ramakrishna*. Chicago, IL: University of Chicago Press, 1998.

Kris, Ernst. *Psychoanalytic Explorations in Art*. New York, NY: International Universities Press, 1952.

Kuby, Gabriele. *The Global Sexual Revolution: Destruction of Freedom in the Name of Freedom*, trans. James Patrick Kirchner. Kettering, OH: Angelico Press/LifeSite, 2015.

Küng, Hans. *Freud and the Problem of God*, trans. Edward Quinn. New Haven, CT: Yale University Press, 1979.

Lacan, Jacques. *Écrits: The First Complete Edition in English*, trans. Bruce Fink with Héloïse Fink and Russell Grigg. New York, NY: W. W. Norton & Company, 1999.

———. *The Four Fundamental Concepts of Psychoanalysis*, trans. Alan Sheridan, ed. Jacques-Alain Miller. New York, NY: W. W. Norton & Company, 1998.

———. *My Teaching*, trans. David Macey. London, UK: Verso, 2008.

———. *The Triumph of Religion*, trans. Bruce Fink. Malden, MA: Polity, 2013.

Laing, R. D. *The Divided Self: An Existential Study in Sanity and Madness*. New York, NY: Penguin Books, 1976.

———. *The Politics of Experience*. New York, NY: Ballantine Books, 1972.

Landis, Bill. *Anger: An Unauthorized Biography of Kenneth Anger*. New York, NY: HarperCollins, 1995.

LaPiere, Richard. *The Freudian Ethic*. New York, NY: Duell, Sloan and Pearce, 1959.

Larchet, Jean-Claude. *Therapy of Spiritual Illnesses: An Introduction to the Ascetic Tradition of the Orthodox Church*, vols. 1, 2, and 3, trans. Fr. Kilian Sprecher. Montréal: Alexander Press, 2012.

Lasch, Christopher. *The Culture of Narcissism: American Life in an Age of Diminishing Expectations*. New York, NY: W. W. Norton & Company, 1978.

———. *Haven in a Heartless World: The Family Besieged*. New York, NY: WW. Norton & Company, 1995.

———. *The Minimal Self: Psychic Survival in Troubled Times*. New York, NY: W. W. Norton & Company, 1984.

Lawrence, D.H. *Psychoanalysis and the Unconscious*. New York, NY: Thomas Seltzer, 1921.

Lehrer, Ronald. *Nietzsche's Presence in Freud's Life and Thought: On the Origins of a Psychology of Dynamic Unconscious Mental Functioning*. Albany, NY: State University of New York Press, 1995.

Lehrman, Nathaniel S. "Moral Aspects of Mental Health," *The Humanist*, vol. 22, nos. 2–3 (1962), pp. 58–61.

Levenson, Edgar A. *The Fallacy of Understanding: An Inquiry into the Changing Structure of Psychoanalysis*. New York, NY: Basic Books, 1972.

Lévi-Strauss, Claude. *Structural Anthropology*, trans. Claire Jacobson and Brooke Grundfest Schoepf. New York, NY: Basic Books, 1963.

Lewis, C. S. *The Abolition of Man*. New York, NY: Collier Books, 1986.

———. *De Descriptione Temporum: An Inaugural Lecture*. Cambridge, UK: Cambridge University Press, 1955.

Lewisohn, Leonard (ed.). *The Heritage of Sufism, Vol. 1: Classical Persian Sufism from Its Origins to Rumi (700–1300)*. Oxford, UK: Oneworld, 1999.

Liebman, Joshua L. *Peace of Mind: Insights on Human Nature that can Change your Life*. New York, NY: Citadel Press, 1994.

Lindbom, Tage. *The Tares and the Good Grain or the Kingdom of Man at the Hour of Reckoning*, trans. Alvin Moore, Jr. Macon, GA: Mercer University Press, 1983.

Lings, Martin. *Ancient Beliefs and Modern Superstitions*. Cambridge, UK: Archetype, 2001.

———. "Book Review—The Transformist Illusion," *Studies in Comparative Religion*, vol. 4, no. 1 (Winter 1970), p. 59.

———. *The Eleventh Hour: The Spiritual Crisis of the Modern World in the Light of Tradition and Prophecy*. Cambridge, UK: Archetype, 2002.

———. *Mecca: From Before Genesis Until Now*. Cambridge, UK: Archetype, 2004.

Loftus, Elizabeth F. *Memory*. New York, NY: Ardsley House, 1988.

Loftus, Elizabeth F. and Katherine Ketcham, *The Myth of Repressed Memory: False Memories and Allegations of Sexual Abuse*. New York, NY: St. Martin's Press, 1996.

Loftus, Elizabeth F. and Jacqueline E. Pickrell. "The Formation of False Memories," *Psychiatric Annals*, Vol. 25, No. 12 (December 1995), pp. 720–25.

Lovejoy, Arthur. *The Great Chain of Being: A Study of the History of an Idea*. Cambridge, MA: Harvard University Press, 1964.

McCall, W. Vaughn. "Psychiatry and Psychology in the Writings of L. Ron Hubbard," *Journal of Religion and Health*, vol. 46, no. 3 (September 2007), pp. 437–47.

McClelland, David C. "Religious Overtones in Psychoanalysis," *Princeton Seminary Bulletin*, vol. 52, no. 3 (January 1959), pp. 40–64.

McDonald, Barry (ed.). *Every Branch in Me: Essays on the Meaning of Man*. Bloomington, IN: World Wisdom, 2002.

MacDonald, Kevin. *The Culture of Critique*. Bloomington, IN: 1stBooks, 2002.

McGuire, William (ed.). *The Freud/Jung Letters: The Correspondence Between Sigmund Freud and C. G. Jung*, trans. Ralph Manheim and R.F.C. Hull. Princeton, NJ: Princeton University Press, 1994.

Maciejewski, Franz. "Freud, His Wife, and His 'Wife'," *American Imago,* vol. 63, no. 4 (Winter 2006), pp. 497–506.

McLynn, Frank. *Carl Gustav Jung: A Biography*. New York, NY: St. Martin's Press, 1996.

Macmillan, Malcolm. *Freud Evaluated: The Complete Arc*. Cambridge, MA: Massachusetts Institute of Technology Press, 1997.

McNeill, John T. *A History of the Cure of Souls*. New York, NY: Harper & Row, 1977.

Madhavananda, Swami. *Vivekachudamani of Sri Sankaracharya: Text with English Translation, Notes and an Index*. Almora: Advaita Ashrama, 1921.

Mahony, Patrick J. *Freud and the Rat Man*. New Haven, CT: Yale University Press, 1986.

———. *Freud's Dora: A Psychoanalytic, Historical, and Textual Study*. New Haven, CT: Yale University Press, 1996.

Maimonides, Moses. *The Guide for the Perplexed*, trans. Michael Friedländer. New York, NY: Dover, 1956.

———. *The Guide of the Perplexed, Vol. 2*, trans. Shlomo Pines. Chicago, IL: University of Chicago Press, 1963.

Makari, George. *Revolution in Mind: The Creation of Psychoanalysis*. New York, NY: HarperCollins, 2008.

Malcolm, Janet. *In the Freud Archives*. New York, NY: Vintage Books, 1985.

———. *Psychoanalysis: The Impossible Profession*. New York, NY: Alfred A. Knopf, 1981.

Mango, Andrew. *Atatürk: The Biography of the Founder of Modern Turkey*. New York, NY: Overlook Press, 2002.

Mannoni, Octave. *Freud: The Theory of the Unconscious*. London, UK: Verso, 1985.

Marcuse, Herbert. *Eros and Civilization: A Philosophical Inquiry into Freud*. New York, NY: Vintage Books, 1962.

———. "The Social Implications of Freudian 'Revisionism,'" *Dissent: A Quarterly of Socialist Opinion*, vol. 2, no. 3 (Summer 1955), pp. 226–27.

Maritain, Jacques. "Freudianism and Psychoanalysis," *CrossCurrents*, vol. 6, no. 4 (Fall 1956), pp. 307–324.

Marmor, Judd. *Psychiatry in Transition: Selected Papers*. New Brunswick, NJ: Transaction Publishers, 1994.

Marx, Karl. *Critique of Hegel's 'Philosophy of Right,'* trans. Annette Jolin and Joseph O'Malley. Cambridge, UK: Cambridge University Press, 1982.

Maslow, Abraham H. *Toward a Psychology of Being*. Princeton, NJ: Van Nostrand, 1968.

———. "Was Adler a Disciple of Freud? A Note," *Journal of Individual Psychology*, vol. 18, no. 2 (1962), pp. 126–35.

Maslow, Abraham H. and Béla Mittelmann, *Principles of Abnormal Psychology: The Dynamics of Psychic Illness*. New York, NY: Harper & Brothers Publishers, 1941.

Masserman, Jules H. "Sexuality Re-Evaluated," *Canadian Journal of Psychiatry*, vol. 11, no. 5 (October 1966), pp. 379–88.

Masson, Jeffrey Moussaieff. *The Assault on Truth: Freud's Suppression of the Seduction Theory*. New York, NY: Farrar, Straus and Giroux, 1984.

———. *A Dark Science: Women, Sexuality, and Psychiatry in the Nineteenth Century*. New York, NY: Farrar, Straus and Giroux, 1986.

———. (ed.). *The Complete Letters of Sigmund Freud to Wilhelm Fliess,*
1887–1904, trans. Jeffrey Moussaieff Masson. Cambridge, MA: Belknap Press of Harvard University Press, 1985.

———. *Final Analysis: The Making and Unmaking of a Psychoanalyst*. Reading, MA: Addison-Wesley Publishing Company, 1990.

———. *The Oceanic Feeling: The Origins of Religious Sentiment in Ancient India*. Dordrecht, Netherlands: D. Reidel, 1980.

Matt, Daniel Chanan. *Zohar: The Book of Enlightenment*. Mahwah, NJ: Paulist Press, 1983.

May, Rollo. *The Cry for Myth*. New York, NY: Delta Book, 1992.

———. *The Discovery of Being: Writings in Existential Psychology*. New York, NY: W. W. Norton & Company, 1983.

Meerloo, Joost A.M. *The Rape of the Mind: The Psychology of Thought Control, Menticide, and Brainwashing*. New York, NY: Grosset & Dunlap, 1956.

Medawar, Peter B. *The Hope of Progress: A Scientist Looks at Problems in Philosophy, Literature and Science*. London, UK: Methuen, 1972.

———. "Victims of Psychiatry." Review of *The Victim Is Always the Same*, by I. S. Cooper. *The New York Review of Books* (January 23, 1975), p. 17.

Meisel, Perry and Walter Kendrick (eds.). *Bloomsbury/Freud: The Letters of James and Alix Strachey, 1924–1925*. New York, NY: Basic Books, 1985.

Menaker, Esther. "Anna Freud's Analysis by Her Father: The Assault on the Self," *Journal of Religion and Health*, vol. 40, no. 1 (Spring 2001), pp. 89–95.

Menninger, Karl. *Man Against Himself*. New York, NY: Harcourt, Brace and World, 1938.

———. *Theory of Psychoanalytic Technique*. New York, NY: Harper & Row, 1964.

Meitlis, Jacob. "The Last Days of Sigmund Freud," *Jewish Frontier*, vol. 18, no. 9 (September 1951), pp. 20–22.

Meng, Heinrich and Ernst L. Freud (eds.). *Psychoanalysis and Faith: The Letters of Sigmund Freud and Oskar Pfister*, trans. Eric Mosbacher. New York, NY: Basic Books, 1963.

Meyer, Adolf. "Thirty-Five Years of Psychiatry in the United States and Our Present Outlook," *American Journal of Psychiatry*, vol. 8, no. 1 (July 1928), pp. 1–31.

Micale, Mark S. (ed.). *Beyond the Unconscious: Essays of Henri F. Ellenberger in the History of Psychiatry*, trans. Françoise Dubor and Mark S. Micale. Princeton, NJ: Princeton University Press, 1993.

Miller, Russell. *Bare-Faced Messiah: The True Story of L. Ron Hubbard*. New York, NY: Henry Holt and Company, 1987.

Minnicino, Michael. "The Frankfurt School and 'Political Correctness,'" *Fidelio*, vol. 1, no. 1 (Winter 1992), pp. 4–27.

———. "Freud and the Frankfurt School," *Executive Intelligence Review*, vol. 21, no. 16 (1994), pp. 36–38.

Mommsen, Wolfgang J. and Jürgen Osterhammel (eds.), *Max Weber and His Contemporaries*. New York, NY: Routledge, 2006.

Moore, Alvin Jr. and Rama P. Coomaraswamy (eds.). *Selected Letters of Ananda K. Coomaraswamy*. Oxford, UK: Oxford University Press, 1988.

Moore, Burness E. and Bernard D. Fine. *A Glossary of Psychoanalytic Terms and Concepts*. New York, NY: American Psychoanalytic Association, 1968.

Morgan, Douglas N. *Love, Plato, the Bible and Freud*. Englewood Cliffs, NJ: Prentice-Hall, 1964.

Mortimer, William Golden. *Peru: The History of Coca, "The Divine Plant" of the Incas*. New York, NY: J. H. Vail & Company, 1901.

Mousseau, Jacques. "Freud in Perspective: A Conversation with Henri F. Ellenberger," *Psychology Today*, vol. 6, no. 10 (March 1973), pp. 50–60.

Mowrer, O. Hobart. *The Crisis in Psychiatry and Religion*. Princeton, NJ: D. Van Nostrand Company, 1961.

Murchison, Carl (ed.). *A History of Psychology in Autobiography, Vol. 2*. Worcester, MA: Clark University Press, 1932.

Murphy, Gardner. *Psychological Thought from Pythagoras to Freud: An Informal Introduction*. New York, NY: Harcourt, Brace and World, 1968.

Myerson, Abraham. "The Attitude of Neurologists, Psychiatrists and Psychologists Towards Psychoanalysis," *American Journal of Psychiatry*, vol. 96, no. 3 (November 1939), pp. 623–41.

Nasr, Seyyed Hossein. *The Encounter of Man and Nature: The Spiritual Crisis of Modern Man*. London, UK: George Allen and Unwin, 1968.

———. *The Garden of Truth: The Vision and Promise of Sufism, Islam's Mystical Tradition*. New York, NY: HarperCollins, 2008.

———. *Islam and the Plight of Modern Man, Revised and Enlarged Edition*. Chicago, IL: ABC International Group, 2001.

———. (ed.). *Islamic Spirituality: Foundations*. New York, NY: Crossroad, 1997.

———. *Knowledge and the Sacred*. Albany, NY: State University of New York Press, 1989.

———. "The Recovery of the Sacred: Tradition and Perennialism in the Contemporary World," *Sacred Web: A Journal of Tradition and Modernity*, vol. 19 (Summer 2007), pp. 15–37.

———. "Reflections on Islam and Modern Thought," *Studies in Comparative Religion*, vol. 15, nos. 3 & 4 (Summer–Autumn 1983). pp. 164–76.

———. *A Young Muslim's Guide to the Modern World*. Chicago, IL: Kazi Publications, 1994.

Natarajan, A. R. *Timeless in Time: Sri Ramana Maharshi*. Bloomington, IN: World Wisdom, 2006.

Natenberg, Maurice. *Freudian Psycho-Antics: Fact and Fraud in Psychoanalysis*. Chicago, IL: Regent House, 1953.

Needleman, Jacob. *Lost Christianity*. Garden City, NY: Doubleday, 1980.

———. *A Sense of the Cosmos: The Encounter of Modern Science and Ancient Truth*. New York, NY: E. P. Dutton and Company, 1976.

Needleman, Jacob and George Baker (eds.). *Understanding the New Religions*. New York, NY: Seabury Press, 1978.

Needleman, Jacob and Dennis Lewis (eds.). *On the Way to Self Knowledge*. New York, NY: Alfred A. Knopf, 1976.

Neihardt, John G. *Black Elk Speaks: Being the Life Story of a Holy Man of the Oglala Sioux*. Lincoln, NE: University of Nebraska Press, 1988.

Nelson, Benjamin (ed.). *Freud and the 20ᵗʰ Century*. New York, NY: Meridian, 1958.

Nicholson, Reynold A. *Rūmī: Poet and Mystic*. London, UK: George Allen and Unwin, 1978.

Niebuhr, Reinhold. *The Nature and Destiny of Man: A Christian Interpretation, Vol. I: Human Nature*. Louisville, KY: Westminster John Knox Press, 1996.

———. "Sex Standards in America," *Christianity and Crisis*, vol. 8, no. 9 (May 1948), pp. 65–66.

Nietzsche, Friedrich. *Daybreak: Thoughts on the Prejudices of Morality*, trans. R. J. Hollingdale, eds. Maudemarie Clark and Brian Leiter. New York, NY: Cambridge University Press, 2003.

———. *The Gay Science*, trans. Walter Kaufmann. New York, NY: Vintage Books, 1974.

Nikhilananda, Swami. *The Gospel of Ramakrishna: Originally recorded in Bengali by M., a disciple of the Master*. New York, NY: Ramakrishna-Vivekananda Center, 1977.

Noll, Richard. *The Aryan Christ: The Secret Life of Carl Jung*. New York, NY: Random House, 1997.

———. *The Jung Cult: Origins of a Charismatic Movement*. Princeton, NJ: Princeton University Press, 1994.

Nunberg, Herman and Ernst Federn (eds.). *Minutes of the Vienna Psychoanalytic Society, Vol. II: 1908–1910*, trans. Margarethe Nunberg. New York, NY: International Universities Press, 1967.

Nurbakhsh, Javad. *The Psychology of Sufism* [Del wa Nafs]. London, UK: Khaniqahi-Nimatullahi Publications, 1992.

Obholzer, Karin. *The Wolf-Man: Conversations with Freud's Controversial Patient—Sixty Years Later*, trans. Michael Shaw. New York, NY: Continuum, 1982.

Oldmeadow, Harry (ed.). *The Betrayal of Tradition: Essays on the Spiritual Crisis of Modernity*. Bloomington, IN: World Wisdom, 2005.

———. *Journeys East: 20th Century Western Encounters with Eastern Traditions*. Bloomington, IN: World Wisdom, 2004.

Osborne, Arthur. *Be Still, It Is the Wind That Sings*. Tiruvannamalai, India: Sri Ramanasramam, 2003.

———. (ed.). *The Collected Works of Ramana Maharshi*. Boston, MA: Weiser Books, 1997.

———. *For Those with Little Dust: Selected Writings of Arthur Osborne*. Sarasota, FL: Ramana Publications, 1990.

Osho [Bhagwan Shree Rajneesh], *Sex Matters: From Sex to Superconsciousness*. New York, NY: St. Martin's Press, 2002.

Pallis, Marco. *A Buddhist Spectrum: Contributions to Buddhist-Christian Dialogue*. Bloomington, IN: World Wisdom, 2003.

———. *The Way and the Mountain: Tibet, Buddhism, and Tradition*, ed. Joseph A. Fitzgerald. Bloomington, IN: World Wisdom, 2008.

Palmer, G.E.H., Philip Sherrard, and Kallistos Ware. *The Philokalia, Vol. 1: The Complete Text; Compiled by St. Nikodimos of the Holy Mountain and St. Makarios of Corinth*. London, UK: Faber and Faber, 1983.

———. *The Philokalia, Vol. 3: The Complete Text; Compiled by St. Nikodimos of the Holy Mountain and St. Makarios of Corinth*. London, UK: Faber and Faber, 1995.

Parsons, William B. *The Enigma of the Oceanic Feeling: Revisioning the Psychoanalytic Theory of Mysticism*. New York, NY: Oxford University Press, 1999.

Paskauskas, R. Andrew (ed.). *The Complete Correspondence of Sigmund Freud and Ernest Jones, 1908–1939*. Cambridge, MA: Belknap Press of Harvard University Press, 1993.

Perls, Frederick S. *Ego, Hunger and Aggression*. New York, NY: Vintage Books, 1969.

———. *The Gestalt Approach and Eye Witness to Therapy*. Palo Alto, CA: Science and Behavior Books, 1973.

———. *Gestalt Therapy Verbatim*. Lafayette, CA: Real People Press, 1969.

———. *In and Out of the Garbage Pail*. Lafayette, CA: Real People Press, 1969.

———. "A Life Chronology," *Gestalt Journal*, vol. 16, no. 2 (1993), pp. 5–9.

Perry, Mark. *The Mystery of Individuality: Grandeur and Delusion of the Human Condition*. Bloomington, IN: World Wisdom, 2012.

Perry, Whitall N. *Challenges to a Secular Society*. Oakton, VA: Foundation for Traditional Studies, 1996.

—————. (ed.). *A Treasury of Traditional Wisdom*. New York, NY: Simon and Schuster, 1971.

Pfeiffer, Ernst (ed.). *Sigmund Freud and Lou Andreas-Salomé Letters*, trans. William Robson-Scott and Elaine Robson-Scott. New York, NY: W. W. Norton & Company, 1985.

Pius XII, Pope. *On Psychotherapy and Religion: An Address of His Holiness Pope Pius XII to the Fifth International Congress on Psychotherapy and Clinical Psychology, April 13, 1953*. Washington, DC.: National Catholic Welfare Conference, 1953.

Polit, Gustavo. *Breaking the New Atheist Spell in the Light of Perennial Wisdom*. London, UK: Matheson Trust, 2017.

Pomeroy, Wardell B. *Dr. Kinsey and the Institute for Sex Research*. New Haven, CT: Yale University Press, 1982.

Popper, Karl. *Conjectures and Refutations: The Growth of Scientific Knowledge*. New York, NY: Routledge, 2002.

Postman, Neil. *Amusing Ourselves to Death: Public Discourse in the Age of Show Business*. New York, NY: Penguin Books, 1988.

—————. *The Disappearance of Childhood*. New York, NY: Vintage Books, 1994.

Prince, Raymond and Charles Savage. "Mystical States and the Concept of Regression," *Psychedelic Review*, no. 8 (1966), pp. 59–75.

Prinz, Joachim. *The Secret Jews*. New York, NY: Random House, 1973.

Progoff, Ira. *The Death and Rebirth of Psychology: An Integrative Evaluation of Freud, Adler, Jung and Rank and the Impact of Their Insights on Modern Man*. New York, NY: McGraw-Hill, 1969.

Puner, Helen Walker. *Freud: His Life and His Mind*. New York, NY: Howell, Soskin, 1947.

Rabinbach, Anson and Sander L. Gilman (eds.). *The Third Reich Sourcebook*. Los Angeles, CA: University of California Press, 2013.

Rahula, Walpola. *What the Buddha Taught*. New York, NY: Grove Press, 1974.

Raine, Kathleen. *'What is Man?'*. Ipswich, UK: Golgonooza Press, 1980.

Rank, Otto. *Beyond Psychology*. New York, NY: Dover, 1958.

————. *Psychology and the Soul: A study of the Origin, Conceptual Evolution, and Nature of the Soul*, trans. Gregory C. Richter and E. James Lieberman. Baltimore, MD: Johns Hopkins University Press, 1998.

————. *A Psychology of Difference: The American Lectures*, ed. Robert Kramer. Princeton, NJ: Princeton University Press, 1996.

————. *Truth and Reality*, trans. Jessie Taft. New York, NY: W. W. Norton & Company, 1978.

Rao, B. Sanjiva. "Bhagavan Sri Ramana and the Modern Age," in *Golden Jubilee Souvenir*. Tiruvannamalai, India: Sri Ramanasramam, 1995, pp. 82–99.

Recouly, Raymond. "A Visit to Freud," *Outlook* (September 5, 1923), pp. 27–28.

Reich, Ilse Ollendorff. *Wilhelm Reich: A Personal Biography*. New York, NY: Avon Books, 1970.

Reich, Wilhelm. *The Function of the Orgasm*, trans. Theodore P. Wolfe. New York, NY: Noonday Press, 1970.

————. *The Sexual Revolution: Toward a Self-Regulating Character Structure*, trans. Therese Pol. New York, NY: Farrar, Straus and Giroux, 1986.

Reisman, Judith A. "The Homosexual in America," *Time*, vol. 87, no. 3 (January 21, 1966), p. 52.

————. *Kinsey: Crimes and Consequences*. Crestwood, KY: Institute for Media Education, 2003.

————. *Sexual Sabotage: How One Mad Scientist Unleashed a Plague of Corruption and Contagion on America*. Washington, D.C.: WND Books, 2010.

Reisman, Judith A. and Edward W. Eichel, *Kinsey, Sex and Fraud: The Indoctrination of a People*, eds. J. Gordon Muir and John H. Court. Lafayette, LA: Huntington House, 1990.

Reitman, Janet. *Inside Scientology: The Story of America's Most Secretive Religion*. New York, NY: Houghton Mifflin Harcourt, 2011.

Reymond, Lizelle. *To Live Within*, trans. Nancy Pearson and Stanley Spiegelberg. New York, NY: Penguin Books, 1973.

Ricoeur, Paul. *Freud and Philosophy: An Essay on Interpretation*, trans. Denis Savage. New Haven, CT: Yale University Press, 1970.

————. *Hermeneutics and the Human Sciences: Essays on Language, Action and Interpretation*, trans. John B. Thompson. Cambridge, UK: Cambridge University Press, 1998.

—————. *On Psychoanalysis: Writings and Lectures, Vol. 1*, trans. David Pellauer. Cambridge, UK: Polity Press, 2012.

Rieff, Philip. *Freud: The Mind of the Moralist*. Chicago, IL: University of Chicago Press, 1979.

—————. *The Triumph of the Therapeutic: Uses of Faith After Freud*. Chicago, IL: University of Chicago Press, 1987.

Roazen, Paul. *Brother Animal: The Story of Freud and Tausk*. New York, NY: New York University Press, 1986.

—————. *Erik H. Erikson: The Power and Limits of a Vision*. Northvale, NJ: Jason Aronson, 1997.

—————. *Freud and His Followers*. New York, NY: Meridian, 1974.

Robinson, Paul. *The Modernization of Sex: Havelock Ellis, Alfred Kinsey, William Masters and Virginia Johnson*. New York, NY: Harper & Row, 1976.

Rogow, Arnold A. *The Dying of the Light: A Searching Look at America Today*. New York, NY: G.P. Putnam's Sons, 1975.

Róheim, Géza. *Psychoanalysis and Anthropology: Culture, Personality and the Unconscious*. New York, NY: International Universities Press, 1968.

Rose, Seraphim. *Orthodoxy and the Religion of the Future*. Platina, CA: Saint Herman of Alaska Brotherhood, 1990.

Rosen, R. D. *Psychobabble: Fast Talk and Quick Cure in the Era of Feeling*. New York, NY: Atheneum, 1977.

Rosenbaum, Max and Melvin Muroff (eds.). *Anna O.: Fourteen Contemporary Reinterpretations*. New York, NY: Free Press, 1984.

Rothman, Stanley and S. Robert Lichter, *Roots of Radicalism: Jews, Christians, and the Left*. New Brunswick, NJ: Transaction Publishers, 1996.

Ruitenbeek, Hendrik M. (ed.). *Freud as We Knew Him*. Detroit, MI: Wayne State University Press, 1973.

Rush, John A. (ed.). *Entheogens and the Development of Culture: The Anthropology and -Neurobiology of Ecstatic Experience*. Berkeley, CA: North Atlantic Books, 2013.

Russell, Bertrand. *The Impact of Science on Society*. New York, NY: Routledge, 1976.

—————. *Religion and Science*. Oxford, UK: Oxford University Press, 1997.

Rycroft, Charles (ed.). *Psychoanalysis Observed*. Baltimore, MD: Penguin Books, 1968.

Sachs, Hanns. *Freud, Master and Friend*. Cambridge, MA: Harvard University Press, 1945.

―――. "'The Man Moses' and the Man Freud," *Psychoanalytic Review*, vol. 28 (1941), pp. 156–62.

Sadock, Benjamin J., Virginia A. Sadock, and Pedro Ruiz. *Kaplan and Sadock's Synopsis of Psychiatry: Behavioral Sciences/Clinical Psychiatry*. Philadelphia, PA: Wolters Kluwer, 2015.

Safran, Jeremy D. (ed.). *Psychoanalysis and Buddhism: An Unfolding Dialogue*. Somerville, MA: Wisdom Publications, 2003.

Salter, Andrew. *The Case Against Psychoanalysis*. New York, NY: Citadel Press, 1963.

Salzman, Leon and Jules H. Masserman (eds.). *Modern Concepts of Psychoanalysis*. New York, NY: Philosophical Library, 1962.

Sapir, Edward. "The Contribution of Psychiatry to an Understanding of Behavior in Society," *American Journal of Sociology*, vol. 42, no. 6 (May 1937), pp. 862–70.

Sargant, William. *Battle for the Mind: A Physiology of Conversion and Brain-Washing*. Cambridge, MA: Malor Book, 1997.

Schaff, Philip (ed.). *A Select Library of the Nicene and Post-Nicene Fathers of the Christian Church*. New York, NY: Christian Literature Company, 1888.

Schaya, Leo. The Universal Meaning of the Kabbalah, trans. Nancy Pearson. Baltimore, MD: Penguin Books, 1974.

Schimmel, Annemarie. *Deciphering the Signs of God: A Phenomenological Approach to Islam*. Albany, NY: State University of New York Press, 1994.

Schmidt, Wilhelm. *The Origin and Growth of Religion*, trans. H. J. Rose. New York, NY: Cooper Square Publishers, 1971.

Scholem, Gershom. *Kabbalah*. New York, NY: Meridian, 1978.

―――. *Major Trends in Jewish Mysticism*. New York, NY: Schocken Books, 1974.

―――. *The Messianic Idea in Judaism: And Other Essays on Jewish Spirituality*. New York, NY: Schocken Books, 1995.

―――. *On the Kabbalah and Its Symbolism*, trans. Ralph Manheim. New York, NY: Schocken Books, 1969.

―――. *On the Mystical Shape of the Godhead: Basic Concepts in the Kabbalah*. New York, NY: Schocken Books, 1991.

―――. *Sabbatai Ṣevi: The Mystical Messiah, 1626–1676*, trans. R. J. Zwi Werblowsky. Princeton, NJ: Princeton University Press, 2016.

―――. (ed.). *Zohar: The Book of Splendor*. New York, NY: Schocken Books, 1977.

Schumacher, E. F. *A Guide for the Perplexed*. New York, NY: Harper & Row, 1977.

Schuon, Frithjof. *Art from the Sacred to the Profane: East and West*, ed. Catherine Schuon. Bloomington, IN: World Wisdom, 2007.

————. *Esoterism as Principle and as Way*, trans. William Stoddart. Bedfont, Middlesex, UK: Perennial Books, 1981.

————. *The Eye of the Heart*. Bloomington, IN: World Wisdom Books, 1997.

————. *The Feathered Sun: Plains Indians in Art and Philosophy*. Bloomington, IN: World Wisdom Books, 1990.

————. *From the Divine to the Human*, trans. Gustavo Polit and Deborah Lambert. Bloomington, IN: World Wisdom Books, 1982.

————. *Gnosis: Divine Wisdom*, trans. G.E.H. Palmer. Bedfont, Middlesex, UK: Perennial Books, 1990.

————. *Islam and the Perennial Philosophy*, trans. J. Peter Hobson. London, UK: World of Islam Festival Publishing Company, 1976.

————. *Language of the Self*. Bloomington, IN: World Wisdom Books, 1999.

————. *Light on the Ancient Worlds*, trans. Lord Northbourne. Bloomington, IN: World Wisdom Books, 1984.

————. *Light on the Ancient Worlds: A New Translation with Selected Letters*, trans. Deborah Casey, Mark Perry, Jean-Pierre Lafouge, and James S. Cutsinger, ed. Deborah Casey. Bloomington, IN: World Wisdom, 2005.

————. *Logic and Transcendence*, trans. Peter N. Townsend. London, UK: Perennial Books, 1984.

————. *The Play of Masks*. Bloomington, IN: World Wisdom Books, 1992.

————. *Roots of the Human Condition*. Bloomington, IN: World Wisdom Books, 1991.

————. *Stations of Wisdom*. Bloomington, IN: World Wisdom Books, 1995.

————. *Survey of Metaphysics and Esoterism*, trans. Gustavo Polit. Bloomington, IN: World Wisdom Books, 1986.

————. *To Have a Center*. Bloomington, IN: World Wisdom Books, 1990.

————. *The Transcendent Unity of Religions*. Wheaton, IL: Quest Books, 1993.

————. *The Transfiguration of Man*. Bloomington, IN: World Wisdom Books, 1995.

————. *Understanding Islam*. Bloomington, IN: World Wisdom, 1998.

————. *World Wheel, Volumes IV–VII*. Bloomington, IN: World Wisdom, 2006.

Schur, Max. *Freud: Living and Dying*. New York, NY: International Universities Press, 1972.

Scotton, Bruce W., Allan B. Chinen and John R. Battista (eds.). *Textbook of Transpersonal Psychiatry and Psychology*. New York, NY: Basic Books, 1996.

Scruton, Roger. *Fools, Frauds and Firebrands: Thinkers of the New Left*. London, UK: Bloomsbury, 2016.

Scupoli, Lorenzo. *Unseen Warfare: The Spiritual Combat and Path to Paradise of Lorenzo Scupoli*, ed. Nicodemus of the Holy Mountain and revised by Theophan the Recluse, trans. E. Kadloubovsky and G.E.H. Palmer. Crestwood, NY: St. Vladimir's Seminary Press, 2000.

Shah-Kazemi, Reza. *Paths to Transcendence: According to Shankara, Ibn Arabi, and Meister Eckhart*. Bloomington, IN: World Wisdom, 2006.

————. "Tradition as Spiritual Function: A 'Perennialist' Perspective," *Sacred Web: A Journal of Tradition and Modernity*, vol. 7 (Summer 2001), pp. 37–58.

Shakow, David and David Rapaport, *The Influence of Freud on American Psychology*. Cleveland, OH: World Publishing Company, 1968.

Shamdasani, Sonu. *Cult Fictions: C. G. Jung and the Founding of Analytical Psychology*. London, UK: Routledge, 1998.

Shaw, Miranda. *Passionate Enlightenment: Women in Tantric Buddhism*. Princeton, NJ: Princeton University Press, 1994.

Sheen, Fulton J. *Peace of Soul*. Liguori, MO: Liguori/Triumph, 1996.

Sheldrake, Rupert. *The Science Delusion*. London, UK: Coronet, 2013.

Sherrard, Philip. "The Christian Understanding of Man," *Sophia Perennis*, vol. 2, no. 1 (Spring 1976), pp. 38–57.

————. *Christianity and Eros: Essays on the Theme of Sexual Love*. Limni, Evia, Greece: Denise Harvey, 1995.

————. *Christianity: Lineaments of a Sacred Tradition*. Brookline, MA: Holy Cross Orthodox Press, 1998.

————. *The Rape of Man and Nature: An Inquiry into the Origins and Consequences of Modern Science*. Ipswich, UK: Golgonooza Press, 1991.

Silesius, Angelus. *The Cherubinic Wanderer*, trans. Maria Shrady. Mahwah, NJ: Paulist Press, 1986.

Simmel, Ernst (ed.). *Anti-Semitism: A Social Disease*. New York, NY: International Universities Press, 1946.

Sisman, Cengiz. *The Burden of Silence: Sabbatai Sevi and the Evolution of the Ottoman-Turkish Dönmes*. New York, NY: Oxford University Press, 2015.

Skinner, B. F. "Critique of Psychoanalytic Concepts and Theories," *Scientific Monthly*, vol. 79, no. 5 (November 1954), pp. 300–5.

———. *Walden Two*. New York, NY: Macmillan, 1962.

Smith, Darrell. "Trends in Counseling and Psychotherapy," *American Psychologist*, vol. 37, no. 7 (July 1982), pp. 802–9.

Smith, Dinitia. "Freud May Be Dead, But His Critics Still Kick," *New York Times* (December 10, 1995), p. E14.

Smith, Huston. *Beyond the Post-Modern Mind*. New York, NY: Crossroad, 1982.

———. *Forgotten Truth: The Common Vision of the World's Religions*. New York, NY: HarperCollins, 1992.

———. "Introduction," to Frithjof Schuon, *The Transcendent Unity of Religions*. Wheaton, IL: Quest Books, 1993, pp. ix–xxvii.

Smith, Wolfgang. *Cosmos & Transcendence: Breaking Through the Barrier of Scientistic Belief*. Peru, IL: Sherwood Sugden & Company, 1990.

———. (ed.). *In Quest of Catholicity: Malachi Martin Responds to Wolfgang Smith*. Kettering, OH: Angelico Press, 2016.

———. *Science and Myth: What We Are Never Told*. San Rafael, CA: Sophia Perennis, 2010.

———. *Teilhardism and the New Religion: A Thorough Analysis of the Teachings of Pierre Teilhard de Chardin*. Rockford, IL: Tan Books and Publishers, 1988.

———. *Theistic Evolution: The Teilhardian Heresy*. Tacoma, WA: Angelico Press/Sophia Perennis, 2012.

Socarides, Charles W. "Sexual Politics and Scientific Logic: The Issue of Homosexuality," *Journal of Psychohistory*, vol. 19, no. 3 (Winter 1992), pp. 307–29.

Sonnenschein, Allan. "Inside the Church of Scientology: An Exclusive Interview with L. Ron Hubbard, Jr.," *Penthouse* (June 1983), pp. 110–13, 166, 170, 172–75.

Stannard, David E. *Shrinking History: On Freud and the Failure of Psychohistory*. New York, NY: Oxford University Press, 1980.

Stark, Rodney and William Sims Bainbridge. *The Future of Religion: Secularization, Revival and Cult Formation*. Berkeley, CA: University of California Press, 1985.

Stekel, Wilhelm. *The Autobiography of Wilhelm Stekel: The Life Story of a Pioneer Psychoanalyst*, ed. Emil A. Gutheil. New York, NY: Liveright, 1950.

Stern, Paul J. *C. G. Jung: The Haunted Prophet*. New York, NY: Dell, 1977.

Stoddart, William. *Remembering in a World of Forgetting: Thoughts on Tradition and Postmodernism*, eds. Mateus Soares de Azevedo and Alberto Vasconcellos Queiroz. Bloomington, IN: World Wisdom, 2008.

Stone, Alan A. "Where Will Psychoanalysis Survive?" Harvard Magazine, vol. 99, no. 3 (January/February 1997), pp. 35–39.

Storr, Anthony. *Feet of Clay: Saints, Sinners, and Madmen: A Study of Gurus*. New York, NY: Free Press, 1997.

Sullivan, Harry Stack. *Conceptions of Modern Psychiatry*. New York, NY: W. W. Norton & Company, 1953.

Sulloway, Frank J. *Freud, Biologist of the Mind: Beyond the Psychoanalytic Legend*. New York, NY: Basic Books, 1979.

———. "Reassessing Freud's Case Histories: The Social Construction of Psychoanalysis," *Isis*, vol. 82, no. 2 (June 1991), pp. 245–75.

Suzuki, D. T., Erich Fromm, and Richard De Martino (eds.). *Zen Buddhism and Psychoanalysis*. New York, NY: Grove Press, 1963.

Swales, Peter J. "Freud, Filthy Lucre, and Undue Influence," *Review of Existential Psychology and Psychiatry*, vol. 23, nos. 1–3 (1997), pp. 115–41.

———. "Freud, Minna Bernays, and the Conquest of Rome: New Light on the Origins of Psychoanalysis," *New American Review*, vol. 1 (Spring/Summer 1982), pp. 1–23.

Symonds, John. *The Magic of Aleister Crowley*. London, UK: Frederick Muller, 1958.

Szasz, Thomas. "Freud as a Leader," *Antioch Review*, vol. 23, no. 2 (Summer 1963), pp. 133–44.

———. *Karl Kraus and the Soul-Doctors: A Pioneer Critic and His Criticism of Psychiatry and Psychoanalysis*. Baton Rouge, LA: Louisiana State University Press, 1976.

———. *The Myth of Psychotherapy: Mental Healing as Religion, Rhetoric, and Repression*. Garden City, NY: Anchor Press, 1979.

Teresa of Ávila, Saint. *The Complete Works of Saint Teresa of Jesus, Vol. 1: General Introduction, Life, Spiritual Relations*, trans. and ed. E. Allison Peers. New York, NY: Sheed & Ward, 1946.

Thornton, E. M. *The Freudian Fallacy: An Alternative View of Freudian Theory*. Garden City, NY: Dial Press, 1984.

Torrey, E. Fuller. *Freudian Fraud: The Malignant Effects of Freud's Theory on American Thought and Culture*. New York, NY: HarperCollins, 1992.

Torrey, E. Fuller and Judy Miller, *The Invisible Plague: The Rise of Mental Illness from 1750 to the Present*. New Brunswick, NJ: Rutgers University Press, 2007.

Tournier, Paul. *Guilt and Grace: A Psychological Study*, trans. Arthur W. Heathcote, J. J. Henry and P. J. Allcock. New York, NY: Harper & Row, 1962.

———. *The Whole Person in a Broken World*, trans. John and Helen Doberstein. New York, NY: Harper & Row, 1964.

Trilling, Lionel. *The Liberal Imagination: Essays on Literature and Society*. New York, NY: *New York Review of Books*, 2008.

Trosman, Harry and Ernest S. Wolf, "The Bernfeld Collaboration in the Jones Biography of Freud," *International of Journal of Psycho-Analysis*, vol. 54 (1973), pp. 227–33.

Tyagananda, Swami and Pravrajika Vrajaprana. *Interpreting Ramakrishna: Kali's Child Revisited*. India: Motilal Banarsidass Publishers, 2010.

Upton, Charles. *The Science of the Greater Jihad: Essays in Principial Psychology*. San Rafael, CA: Sophia Perennis, 2011.

———. *The System of the Antichrist: Truth and Falsehood in Postmodernism and the New Age*. Ghent, NY: Sophia Perennis, 2001.

———. *Vectors of the Counter-Initiation: The Course and Destiny of Inverted Spirituality*. San Rafael, CA: Sophia Perennis, 2012.

Velikovsky, Immanuel. "The Dreams Freud Dreamed," *Psychoanalytic Review*, vol. 28 (October 1941), pp. 487–511.

Viereck, George Sylvester. *Glimpses of the Great*. New York, NY: Macaulay Company, 1930.

Virgil. *The Aeneid*, trans. C. Day Lewis. Oxford, UK: Oxford University Press, 1986.

Vitz, Paul C. *Sigmund Freud's Christian Unconscious*. New York, NY: Guilford Press, 1988.

Voltaire. *The Works of Voltaire: A Contemporary Version, Vol. XII*, trans. William F. Fleming. New York, NY: St. Hubert Guild, 1901.

———. *The Works of Voltaire: The Dramatic Works of Voltaire, Vol. 5*. New York, NY: E. R. DuMont, 1901.

Waddell, Norman. *The Essential Teachings of Zen Master Hakuin*. Boston, MA: Shambhala Publications, 1994.

Walsh, Michael. *The Devil's Pleasure Palace: The Cult of Critical Theory and the Subversion of the West.* New York, NY: Encounter Books, 2015.

Walsh, Roger and Deane H. Shapiro (eds.). *Beyond Health and Normality: Explorations of Exceptional Psychological Well-Being.* New York, NY: Van Nostrand Reinhold, 1983.

Walsh, Roger N. and Frances Vaughan (eds.). *Paths Beyond Ego: The Transpersonal Vision.* New York, NY: Jeremy P. Tarcher/Putnam, 1993.

Warner, Silas L. "Freud's Antipathy to America," *Journal of the American Academy of Psychoanalysis,* vol. 19, no. 1 (1991), pp. 141–55.

Washburn, Michael. *Transpersonal Psychology in Psychoanalytic Perspective.* Albany, NY: State University of New York Press, 1994.

Watson, John B. "Feed Me on Facts," *Saturday Review of Literature,* vol. 4, no. 47 (June 1928), pp. 966–67.

———. "The Myth of the Unconscious: A Behavioristic Explanation," *Harper's Magazine* (September 1927), pp. 502–8.

———. "The Psychology of Wish Fulfilment," *Scientific Monthly,* vol. 3, no 5 (November 1916), pp. 479–87.

———. *The Ways of Behaviorism.* New York, NY: Harper & Brothers Publishers, 1928.

Watts, Alan W. *Psychotherapy East and West.* New York, NY: Mentor Books, 1963.

Weaver, Richard M. *Ideas Have Consequences.* Chicago, IL: University of Chicago Press, 1984.

Webb, James. *The Occult Establishment.* La Salle, IL: Open Court, 1976.

Webster, Richard. *Why Freud Was Wrong: Sin, Science, and Psychoanalysis.* New York, NY: Basic Books, 1995.

Weisskopf, Walter A. "Existential Crisis and the Unconscious," *Journal of Humanistic Psychology,* vol. 7, no. 1 (Spring 1967), pp. 58–65.

Wells, H. G., Julian S. Huxley, and G.P. Wells, *The Science of Life.* New York, NY: Literary Guild, 1931.

Wells, Harry K. *The Failure of Psychoanalysis: From Freud to Fromm.* New York, NY: International Publishers, 1963.

———. *Pavlov and Freud, Vol. 2: Sigmund Freud: A Pavlovian Critique.* New York, NY: International Publishers, 1960.

Wertham, Fredric. "What to Do Till the Doctor Goes," *The Nation* (September 2, 1950), pp. 205–7.

Weyr, Thomas. *Reaching for Paradise: The Playboy Vision of America*. New York, NY: Times Books, 1978.

Wilber, Ken. *A Brief History of Everything*. Boston, MA: Shambhala, 1996.

Wilson, Colin. *New Pathways in Psychology: Maslow and the Post-Freudian Revolution*. New York, NY: Taplinger Publishing Company, 1972.

Wittels, Fritz. *Sigmund Freud: His Personality, His Teaching, and His School*, trans. Eden Paul and Cedar Paul. New York, NY: Routledge, 2014.

Wollheim, Richard (ed.). *Freud: A Collection of Critical Essays*. Garden City, NY: Anchor Books, 1974.

———. *Sigmund Freud*. New York, NY: Cambridge University Press, 1995.

Wolpe, Joseph and Stanley Rachman, "Psychoanalytic 'Evidence': A Criticism Based on Freud's Case of Little Hans," *Journal of Nervous and Mental Disease*, vol. 131, no. 2 (August 1960), pp. 135–48.

Woodworth, Robert S. "Followers of Freud and Jung," *The Nation*, vol. 103, no. 2678 (October 26, 1916), p. 396.

———. "Some Criticisms of the Freudian Psychology," *Journal of Abnormal Psychology*, vol. 12, no. 3 (August 1917), pp. 174–94.

Wortis, Joseph. *Fragments of an Analysis with Freud*. New York, NY: Simon & Schuster, 1954.

———. "Fragments of a Freudian Analysis," *American Journal of Orthopsychiatry*, vol. 10, no. 4 (October 1940), pp. 843–49.

Yalom, Irving *The Theory and Practice of Group Psychotherapy*. New York, NY: Basic Books, 1975.

Yeats, W. B. *The Collected Poems of W. B. Yeats*. London, UK: Wordsworth Editions, 2000.

Yerushalmi, Yosef Hayim. *Freud's Moses: Judaism Terminable and Interminable*. New Haven, CT: Yale University Press, 1991.

Young-Bruehl, Elisabeth. *Anna Freud: A Biography*. New Haven, CT: Yale University Press, 2008.

———. (ed.). *Freud on Women: A Reader*. New York, NY: W. W. Norton & Company, 1990.

Zehme, Bill. "Playboy Interview: Hugh M. Hefner," *Playboy*, vol. 47, no. 1 (January 2000), pp. 63–64, 67–69, 72, 76, 78, 80, 240–45.

Zilbergeld, Bernie. *The Shrinking of America: Myths of Psychological Change*. Boston, MA: Little, Brown and Company, 1983.

Zilboorg, Gregory. *Mind, Medicine, & Man*. New York, NY: Harcourt, Brace & Company, 1943.

Notes

Introduction: Sigmund Freud and the Emergence of the Modern World

[1] *The Zohar*, vol. 1, trans. Harry Sperling and Maurice Simon (New York, NY: Soncino Press, 1984), pp. xiii–xiv.

[2] The Talmud, *Tractate Chagigah*, quoted in David Bakan, *Sigmund Freud and the Jewish Mystical Tradition* (London, UK: Free Association Books, 1990), pp. 70–71.

[3] Virgil, "Book Seven," in *The Aeneid*, trans. C. Day Lewis (Oxford, UK: Oxford University Press, 1986), p. 199.

[4] Sigmund Freud, "Letter to Marie Bonaparte—April 26, 1926," quoted in Ernest Jones, "Fame and Suffering," in *The Life and Work of Sigmund Freud, Vol. 3: The Last Phase, 1919–1939* (New York, NY: Basic Books, 1957), p. 124.

[5] See Sigmund Freud, *Five Lectures on Psycho-Analysis*, trans. and ed. James Strachey (New York, NY: W. W. Norton & Company, 1989).

[6] Sigmund Freud as remembered by C. G. Jung, quoted in Jacques Lacan, "The Freudian Thing, or the Meaning of the Return to Freud in Psychoanalysis," in *Écrits: The First Complete Edition in English*, trans. Bruce Fink with Héloïse Fink and Russell Grigg (New York, NY: W. W. Norton & Company, 1999), p. 336; Sigmund Freud, quoted in Octave Mannoni, "Afterward: The Future of a Dissolution," in *Freud: The Theory of the Unconscious* (London, UK: Verso, 2015), p. 168.

[7] Sigmund Freud, "The Resistances to Psychoanalysis" (1925), in *Character and Culture*, ed. Philip Rieff (New York, NY: Collier Books, 1963), p. 261.

[8] Ibid., p. 260.

[9] Sigmund Freud, "The Question of a *Weltanschauung*" (1933 [1932]), in *New Introductory Lectures on Psycho-Analysis*, trans. and ed. James Strachey (New York, NY: W. W. Norton & Company, 1989), pp. 196–97. "[P]sychoanalysis is compatible with various *Weltanschauungen*" (Sigmund Freud, "Letter to James J. Putnam—July 8, 1915," in Ernst L. Freud (ed.), *Letters of Sigmund Freud*, trans. Tania and James Stern [New York, NY: Basic Books, 1975], p. 309).

[10] Sigmund Freud, "A Short Account of Psycho-Analysis" (1924 [1923]), in *The Standard Edition of the Complete Psychological Works of Sigmund Freud*, vol. 19, trans. and ed. James Strachey (London, UK: Vintage Books, 2001), p. 194.

[11] Sigmund Freud, "Explanations, Applications and Orientations" (1933 [1932]), in *New Introductory Lectures on Psycho-Analysis*, trans. and ed. James Strachey (New York, NY: W. W. Norton & Company, 1989), p. 187.

[12] Sigmund Freud, quoted in Wolfgang Schwentker, "Passion as a Mode of Life: Max Weber, the Otto Gross Circle and Eroticism," in Wolfgang J. Mommsen and Jürgen Osterhammel (eds.), *Max Weber and His Contemporaries* (New York, NY: Routledge, 2006), p. 488.

[13] "Otto Gross was one of the most dangerous men of his generation—a threat to the bourgeois-Christian universe of German Europe…Gross was the great breaker of bonds, the loosener, the beloved of an army of women he had driven mad—if just for a short time. He coaxed one lover/patient to suicide, and then another patient died under similar circumstances. His contemporaries described him as brilliant, creative, charismatic, and troubled. He was a Nietzschean physician, a Freudian psychoanalyst, and anarchist, the high priest of sexual liberation, a master of orgies, the enemy of patriarchy, and a dissolute cocaine and morphine addict. He was loved and hated with equal passion, an infectious agent to some, a healing touch to others. He was a strawberry-blond Dionysus" (Richard Noll, "Polygamy," in *The Aryan Christ: The Secret Life of Carl Jung* [New York, NY: Random House, 1997], pp. 70–71). See also Gottfried Heuer, "The Devil Underneath the Couch: The Secret Story of Jung's Twin Brother," *Harvest*, vol. 49, no. 2 (2003), pp. 130–45.

[14] Otto Gross, quoted in Wolfgang Schwentker, "Passion as a Mode of Life: Max Weber, the Otto Gross Circle and Eroticism," in Wolfgang J. Mommsen and Jürgen Osterhammel (eds.), *Max Weber and His Contemporaries* (New York, NY: Routledge, 2006), p. 488.

[15] Sigmund Freud, "Letter to C. G. Jung—July 5, 1910," quoted in Ernest Jones, "Appendix," in *The Life and Work of Sigmund Freud, vol. 2: Years of Maturity, 1901–1919* (New York, NY: Basic Books, 1955), p. 448. "I am becoming more and more convinced of the cultural value of ΨA [psychoanalysis]" (Sigmund Freud, "Letter to C. G. Jung—July 5, 1910," in William McGuire (ed.), *The Freud/Jung Letters: The Correspondence Between Sigmund Freud and C. G. Jung*, trans. Ralph Manheim and R.F.C. Hull [Princeton, NJ: Princeton University Press, 1994], p. 340).

[16] Sigmund Freud, "Letter to August Stärcke—February 25, 1912," quoted in Ernest Jones, "Opposition," in *The Life and Work of Sigmund Freud, Vol. 2: Years of Maturity, 1901–1919* (New York, NY: Basic Books, 1955), p. 125.

[17] Ernest Jones, "Dissensions," in *The Life and Work of Sigmund Freud, Vol. 2: Years of Maturity, 1901–1919* (New York, NY: Basic Books, 1955), p. 140.

[18] Sigmund Freud, "Explanations, Applications and Orientations" (1933 [1932]), in *New Introductory Lectures on Psycho-Analysis*, trans. and ed. James Strachey (New York, NY: W. W. Norton & Company, 1989), pp. 179–80.

[19] Sigmund Freud, "The Psychical Apparatus and the External World" (1940 [1938]), in *An Outline of Psycho-Analysis*, trans. and ed. James Strachey (New York, NY: W. W. Norton & Company, 1969), p. 52.

[20] Sigmund Freud, "Psychoanalysis and Religious Origins" (1919), in *Character and Culture*, ed. Philip Rieff (New York, NY: Collier Books, 1963), p. 224.

[21] David Bakan, "The Problem of the Origins of Psychoanalysis," in *Sigmund Freud and the Jewish Mystical Tradition* (London, UK: Free Association Books, 1990), p. 4.

[22] Sigmund Freud, "The Resistances to Psychoanalysis" (1925), in *Character and Culture*, ed. Philip Rieff (New York, NY: Collier Books, 1963), pp. 253–54.

[23] Peter Gay, "Sigmund Freud: A Brief Life," in Sigmund Freud, *An Autobiographical Study*, trans. and ed. James Strachey (New York, NY: W. W. Norton & Company, 1989), p. xvi.

[24] Sigmund Freud, "Chapter Seven," in *The Question of Lay Analysis*, trans. Nancy Procter-Gregg (New York, NY: W. W. Norton & Company, 1950), p. 121.

[25] C. G. Jung, "Introduction to Kranefeldt's 'Secret Ways of the Mind'" (1930), in *Critique of Psychoanalysis*, trans. R.F.C. Hull (Princeton, NJ: Princeton University Press, 1975), p. 216. "The funnelling of the individual conflict into the general moral problem puts psychoanalysis far outside the confines of a merely medical therapy. It gives the patient a working philosophy of life based on empirical insights, which, besides affording him a knowledge of his own nature, also make it possible for him to fit himself into this scheme of things" (C. G. Jung, "New Paths in Psychology" (1912), in *The Collected Works C. G. Jung, Vol. 7: Two Essays on Analytical Psychology*, trans. R.F.C. Hull, eds. Sir Herbert Read, Michael Fordham and Gerhard Adler [Princeton, NJ: Princeton University Press, 1972], p. 267).

[26] See Stewart Justman, "Freud and His Nephew," *Social Research*, vol. 61, no. 2 (Summer 1994), pp. 457–76.

[27] Edward Bernays, "The Psychology of Public Relations," in *Propaganda* (Brooklyn, NY: Ig Publishing, 2005), p. 71. See also Edward Bernays, "The Engineering of Consent," *Annals of the American Academy of Political and Social Science*, vol. 250, no. 1 (March 1947), pp. 113–20.

[28] Edward Bernays, "An Outlining of Methods Practicable in Modifying the Point of View of a Group," in *Crystallizing Public Opinion* (New York, NY: Liveright Publishing Corporation, 1961), p. 150.

[29] Sigmund Freud, "Le Bon's Description of the Group Mind," in *Group Psychology and the Analysis of the Ego*, trans. James Strachey (New York, NY: W. W. Norton & Company, 1989), p. 13.

[30] Edward Bernays, "Organizing Chaos," in *Propaganda* (Brooklyn, NY: Ig Publishing, 2005), pp. 37–38.

[31] René Guénon, "Tradition and Traditionalism," in *The Reign of Quantity and the Signs of the Times*, trans. Lord Northbourne (Ghent, NY: Sophia Perennis, 2001), p. 209.

[32] René Guénon, "Introduction," to *The Reign of Quantity and the Signs of the Times*, trans. Lord Northbourne (Ghent, NY: Sophia Perennis, 2001), p. 5.

[33] Sigmund Freud, quoted in Philip Rieff, "The Emergence of Psychological Man," in *Freud: The Mind of the Moralist* (Chicago, IL: University of Chicago Press, 1979), p. 331.

[34] E. Michael Jones, "Part III, Chapter 9: South Bend, Indiana, 1962," in *Libido Dominandi: Sexual Liberation and Political Control* (South Bend, IN: St. Augustine's Press, 2000), p. 416.

[35] René Guénon, "A Material Civilization," in *The Crisis of the Modern World*, trans. Arthur Osborne, Marco Pallis, and Richard C. Nicholson (Hillsdale, NY: Sophia Perennis, 2004), p. 88.

[36] Jacques Maritain, "Freudianism and Psychoanalysis," *CrossCurrents*, vol. 6, no. 4 (Fall 1956), p. 310.

[37] Eugen Bleuler, "Letter to Sigmund Freud—March 11, 1911," quoted in Franz Alexander and Sheldon T. Selesnick, "Freud-Bleuler Correspondence," *Archives of General Psychiatry*, vol. 12 (January 1965), p. 5.

[38] Sigmund Freud, "Psychoanalysis" (1922), in *Character and Culture*, ed. Philip Rieff (New York, NY: Collier Books, 1963), p. 249. "Our observations hold true for a certain society—if the society changes, then the phenomena will be different." (Sigmund Freud, quoted in Joseph Wortis, "Fragments of a Freudian Analysis," *American Journal of Orthopsychiatry*, vol. 10, no. 4 [October 1940], p. 846).

[39] Charles Brenner, "Two Fundamental Hypotheses," in *An Elementary Textbook of Psychoanalysis* (New York, NY: Anchor Books, 1974), p. 1.

[40] Otto Rank, "Psychoanalysis as General Psychology" (1924), in *A Psychology of Difference: The American Lectures*, ed. Robert Kramer (Princeton, NJ: Princeton University Press, 1996), p. 51.

[41] "One could describe the psychology inaugurated by him [Freud] as 'analytical psychology.' Bleuler suggested the name 'depth psychology,' in order to indicate that the Freudian psychology was concerned with the deeper regions or hinterland of the psyche, also called the unconscious. Freud himself was content just to name his method of investigation: he called it psychoanalysis" (C. G. Jung, "New Paths in Psychology" (1912), in *Two Essays on Analytical Psychology*, trans. R.F.C. Hull [New York, NY: Meridian, 1956], p. 259).

[42] Ernest Jones, "The Breuer Period," in *The Life and Work of Sigmund Freud, Vol. 1: The Formative Years and the Great Discoveries, 1856–1900* (New York, NY: Basic Books, 1959), p. 244.

[43] Henri F. Ellenberger, "Notes," in *The Discovery of the Unconscious: The History and Evolution of Dynamic Psychiatry* (New York, NY: Basic Books, 1970), p. 562.

[44] Viktor E. Frankl, "The Unheard Cry for Meaning," in *The Unheard Cry for Meaning: Psychotherapy and Humanism* (New York, NY: Touchstone, 1978), p. 29.

[45] C. G. Jung, "Introduction to Kranefeldt's 'Secret Ways of the Mind'" (1930), in *Critique of Psychoanalysis*, trans. R.F.C. Hull (Princeton, NJ: Princeton University Press, 1975), p. 218.

[46] Friedrich Nietzsche, "The Madman," in *The Gay Science*, trans. Walter Kaufmann (New York, NY: Vintage Books, 1974), p. 181. While Freud does not confirm Nietzsche's influence on psychoanalysis, he does, however, confirm the common ground that exists between them: "Nietzsche...agree[s] in the most astonishing way with the...findings of psychoanalysis" (Sigmund Freud, "An Autobiographical Study" (1925 [1924]), in *An Autobiographical Study*, trans. and ed. James Strachey [New York, NY: W. W. Norton & Company, 1989], p. 67). Jones reports that Freud several times said: "Nietzsche...had a more penetrating knowledge of himself than any other man who ever lived or was ever likely to live" (Ernest Jones, "Non-Medical Applications of Psychoanalysis," in *The Life and Work of Sigmund Freud, Vol. 2: Years of Maturity, 1901–1919* [New York, NY: Basic Books, 1955], p. 344). At the same time, Jones denies this influence and affirms: "Nietzsche had in no way influenced his ideas" (Ernest Jones, "Non-Medical Applications of Psychoanalysis," in *The Life and Work of Sigmund Freud, Vol. 2: Years of Maturity, 1901–1919* [New York, NY: Basic Books, 1955], p. 344). "Freud himself had told me that he had never read Nietzsche" (C. G. Jung, "Sigmund Freud," in *Memories, Dreams, Reflections*, trans. Richard Winston and Clara Winston, ed. Aniela Jaffé [New York, NY: Vintage Books, 1965], p. 153). Jung on the other hand affirms Nietzsche's influence on his own work: "I approach from the side of psychiatry, well prepared for modern psychology by Nietzsche" (C. G. Jung, "General Remarks on the Therapeutic Approach to the Unconscious," in *Two Essays on Analytical Psychology*, trans. R.F.C. Hull [New York, NY: Meridian, 1956], p. 128). See also Ronald Lehrer, *Nietzsche's Presence in Freud's Life and Thought: On the Origins of a Psychology of Dynamic Unconscious Mental Functioning* (Albany, NY: State University of New York Press, 1995); Daniel Chapelle, *Nietzsche and Psychoanalysis* (Albany, NY: State University of New York Press, 1993).

[47] See "Is Freud Dead?" *Time* (November 29, 1993); "Freud Is Not Dead," *Newsweek* (March 27, 2006).

[48] Neil Postman, "The Medium Is the Metaphor," in *Amusing Ourselves to Death: Public Discourse in the Age of Show Business* (New York, NY: Penguin Books, 1988), p. 6.

[49] Philip Rieff, "Preface to the Third Edition," in *Freud: The Mind of the Moralist* (Chicago, IL: University of Chicago Press, 1979), p. xxiv.

[50] Adolf Grünbaum, quoted in Paul Gray, "The Assault on Freud," *Time*, vol. 142, no. 23 (November 29, 1993), p. 51.

[51] Adolf Grünbaum, "Critique of Freud's Final Defense of the Probative Value of Data from the Couch: The Pseudo-Convergence of Clinical Findings," in *The Foundations of Psychoanalysis: A Philosophical Critique* (Los Angeles, CA: University of California Press, 1985), p. 278.

[52] Dinitia Smith, "Freud May Be Dead, But His Critics Still Kick," *New York Times* (December 10, 1995), p. E14.

[53] John Horgan, "Why Freud isn't Dead," *Scientific American*, vol. 275, no. 6 (December 1996), p. 108.

[54] Sigmund Freud, "Letter to Eugen Bleuler—September 28, 1910," quoted in Franz Alexander and Sheldon T. Selesnick, "Freud-Bleuler Correspondence," *Archives of General Psychiatry*, vol. 12 (January 1965), p. 2.

[55] Sigmund Freud, "The Psychotherapy of Hysteria," in Josef Breuer and Sigmund Freud, *Studies on Hysteria*, trans. and ed. James Strachey (New York, NY: Basic Books, 2000), p. 305.

[56] Sigmund Freud, quoted in Herbert Marcuse, *Eros and Civilization: A Philosophical Inquiry into Freud* (New York, NY: Vintage Books, 1962), p. 3.

[57] Sigmund Freud, "Letter to Marie Bonaparte—August 13, 1937," in Ernst L. Freud (ed.), *Letters of Sigmund Freud*, trans. Tania and James Stern (New York, NY: Basic Books, 1975), p. 436.

[58] Sigmund Freud, "The Question of a *Weltanschauung*" (1933 [1932]), in *New Introductory Lectures on Psycho-Analysis*, trans. and ed. James Strachey (New York, NY: W. W. Norton & Company, 1989), p. 217.

[59] Sigmund Freud, "The Clinical Picture" (1905 [1901]), in *Dora: An Analysis of a Case of Hysteria*, ed. Philip Rieff (New York, NY: Touchstone, 1997), p. 69.

[60] Sigmund Freud, "Beyond the Pleasure Principle" (1920), in *Beyond the Pleasure Principle*, trans. and ed. James Strachey (New York, NY: W. W. Norton & Company, 1989), p. 71.

[61] Sigmund Freud, "Chapter Three," in *Civilization and Its Discontents*, trans. and ed. James Strachey (New York, NY: W. W. Norton & Company, 1989), p. 42.

[62] Sigmund Freud, "The Question of a *Weltanschauung*" (1933 [1932]), in *New Introductory Lectures on Psycho-Analysis*, trans. and ed. James Strachey (New York, NY: W. W. Norton & Company, 1989), p. 217.

[63] Sigmund Freud, quoted in Sándor Ferenczi, "Diary Entry—August 4, 1932," in *The Clinical Diary of Sándor Ferenczi*, trans. Michael Balint and Nicola Zarday Jackson, ed. Judith Dupont (Cambridge, MA: Harvard University Press, 1988), p. 186. "We certainly cannot help them" (Sigmund Freud, quoted in Sándor Ferenczi, ibid., p. 93).

[64] Sigmund Freud, quoted in Sándor Ferenczi, ibid., p. 93.

[65] Sigmund Freud, quoted in Sándor Ferenczi, ibid., p. 118. Freud once remarked the following about a woman who had terminated treatment: "Of course she is right [to do so], because she is beyond any possibility of therapy, but it is still her duty to sacrifice herself to science" (Sigmund Freud,

"Letter to C. G. Jung—December 17, 1911," in William McGuire (ed.), *The Freud/Jung Letters: The Correspondence Between Sigmund Freud and C. G. Jung*, trans. Ralph Manheim and R.F.C. Hull [Princeton, NJ: Princeton University Press, 1994], pp. 473–74).

[66] "She [Anna O., pseudonym for Bertha Pappenheim (1859–1936)] aptly described this procedure [psychoanalysis], speaking seriously, as a 'talking cure,' while she referred to it jokingly as 'chimney-sweeping'" (Josef Breuer, "Fräulein Anna O.," in Josef Breuer and Sigmund Freud, *Studies on Hysteria*, trans. and ed. James Strachey [New York, NY: Basic Books, 2000], p. 30). "If someone speaks, it gets lighter" (Anonymous Child, quoted in Sigmund Freud, "Anxiety" (1916–17 [1915–17]), in *Introductory Lectures on Psychoanalysis*, trans. and ed. James Strachey [New York, NY: W. W. Norton & Company, 1977], p. 407).

[67] Sigmund Freud, "Letter to Wilhelm Fliess—April 26, 1896," in *The Complete Letters of Sigmund Freud to Wilhelm Fliess, 1887–1904*, trans. and ed. Jeffrey Moussaieff Masson (Cambridge, MA: Belknap Press of Harvard University Press, 1985), p. 184.

[68] Sigmund Freud, quoted in Ernest Jones, "Dissensions," in *The Life and Work of Sigmund Freud, Vol. 2: Years of Maturity, 1901–1919* (New York, NY: Basic Books, 1955), p. 148.

[69] Sigmund Freud, quoted in Peter Gay, "Preface," to *Freud: A Life for Our Time* (New York, NY: Anchor Books, 1989), p. xvii. "[D]isturbed the sleep of the world" (Sigmund Freud, "On the History of the Psychoanalytic Movement" (1914), in *The History of the Psychoanalytic Movement*, ed. Philip Rieff [New York, NY: Collier Books, 1963], p. 55). Elsewhere the quote reads as, "disturb the sleep of the World" (Hanns Sachs, "Vienna," in *Freud, Master and Friend* [Cambridge, MA: Harvard University Press, 1945], p. 36).

[70] Sigmund Freud, "Fixation to Traumas—The Unconscious" (1916–17 [1915–17]), in *Introductory Lectures on Psychoanalysis*, trans. and ed. James Strachey (New York, NY: W. W. Norton & Company, 1977), p. 285.

[71] Alfred Hoche, quoted in Sigmund Freud, *The History of the Psychoanalytic Movement*, ed. Philip Rieff (New York, NY: Collier Books, 1963), p. 61.

[72] Sigmund Freud, "Psycho-Analysis and Telepathy" (1941 [1921]), in *The Standard Edition of the Complete Psychological Works of Sigmund Freud, Vol. 18*, trans. and ed. James Strachey (London, UK: Hogarth Press and the Institute of Psycho-Analysis, 1975), p. 178.

[73] Sigmund Freud, quoted in Ernest Jones, "The Beginning of International Recognition," in *The Life and Work of Sigmund Freud, Vol. 2: Years of Maturity, 1901–1919* (New York, NY: Basic Books, 1955), p. 44.

[74] Sigmund Freud, "Sexuality in the Aetiology of the Neuroses" (1898), in *The Standard Edition of the Complete Psychological Works of Sigmund Freud*, vol. 3, trans. and ed. James Strachey (London, UK: Hogarth Press and the Institute of Psycho-Analysis, 1981), p. 269.

[75] Reinhold Niebuhr, "The Problem of Vitality and Form in Human Nature," in *The Nature and Destiny of Man: A Christian Interpretation, Vol. I: Human Nature* (Louisville, KY: Westminster John Knox Press, 1996), p. 53.

[76] See Samuel Bendeck Sotillos, *Behaviorism: The Quandary of a Psychology without a Soul* (Chicago, IL: Kazi Publications, 2017); Samuel Bendeck Sotillos, "The Impasse of Modern Psychology: Behaviorism, Psychoanalysis, Humanistic, and Transpersonal Psychology in the Light of the Perennial Philosophy," in *Psychology and the Perennial Philosophy: Studies in Comparative Religion*, ed. Samuel Bendeck Sotillos (Bloomington, IN: World Wisdom, 2013), pp. 60–86.

[77] See Gail A. Hornstein, "The Return of the Repressed: Psychology's Problematic Relations with Psychoanalysis, 1909–1960," *American Psychologist*, vol. 47, no. 2 (February 1992), pp. 254–63; David Shakow and David Rapaport, *The Influence of Freud on American Psychology* (Cleveland, OH: World Publishing Company, 1968).

[78] Sigmund Freud, "Letter to Karl Abraham—May 3, 1908," in *The Complete Correspondence of Sigmund Freud and Karl Abraham, 1907–1925*, trans. Caroline Schwarzacher, Christine Trollope and Klara Majthényi King, ed. Ernst Falzeder (London, UK: Karnac, 2002), p. 38.

[79] See Peter Gay, "The Question of a Jewish Science: 'A Title of Honor,'" in *A Godless Jew: Freud, Atheism, and the Making of Psychoanalysis* (New Haven, CT: Yale University Press, 1987), pp. 117–54.

[80] Sigmund Freud, "An Autobiographical Study" (1925 [1924]), in *An Autobiographical Study*, trans. and ed. James Strachey (New York, NY: W. W. Norton & Company, 1989), p. 58.

[81] Sigmund Freud, quoted in Hanns Sachs, "'That Due of Many Now Is Thine Alone,'" in *Freud, Master and Friend* (Cambridge, MA: Harvard University Press, 1945), p. 86.

[82] Sigmund Freud, quoted in Peter Gay, *Freud: A Life for Our Time* (New York, NY: Anchor Books, 1989), p. 563. See also Howard L. Kaye, "Why Freud Hated America," *Wilson Quarterly*, vol. 17, no. 2 (Spring 1993), pp. 118–25; Silas L. Warner, "Freud's Antipathy to America," *Journal of the American Academy of Psychoanalysis*, vol. 19, no. 1 (1991), pp. 141–55.

[83] B. F. Skinner, "Critique of Psychoanalytic Concepts and Theories," *Scientific Monthly*, vol. 79, no. 5 (November 1954), p. 301.

[84] Sigmund Freud, "Psychical Qualities" (1940 [1938]), in *An Outline of Psycho-Analysis*, trans. and ed. James Strachey (New York, NY: W. W. Norton & Company, 1989), p. 28.

[85] Sigmund Freud, quoted in Ernest Jones, "The Medical Student," in *The Life and Work of Sigmund Freud, Vol. 1: The Formative Years and the Great Discoveries, 1856–1900* (New York, NY: Basic Books, 1959), p. 45.

[86] See Samuel Bendeck Sotillos, *Behaviorism: The Quandary of a Psychology without a Soul* (Chicago, IL: Kazi Publications, 2017).

[87] Viktor E. Frankl, "The Unheard Cry for Meaning," in *The Unheard Cry for Meaning: Psychotherapy and Humanism* (New York, NY: Touchstone, 1978), p. 20.

[88] Roger N. Walsh and Frances Vaughan, "Introduction," to *Paths Beyond Ego: The Transpersonal Vision*, eds. Roger N. Walsh and Frances Vaughan (New York, NY: Jeremy P. Tarcher/Putnam, 1993), pp. 1–2.

[89] R. D. Rosen, "Psychobabble," in *Psychobabble: Fast Talk and Quick Cure in the Era of Feeling* (New York, NY: Atheneum, 1977), p. 8. "Behavior is never determined only by external forces; there are impulses from within" (Karl Menninger, "The Motives," in *Man Against Himself* [New York, NY: Harcourt, Brace and World, 1938], p. 17).

[90] Quoted in Reymond Greene, "Foreword," to E. M. Thornton, *The Freudian Fallacy: An Alternative View of Freudian Theory* (Garden City, NY: Dial Press, 1984), p. vii.

[91] Frederick Crews, "Afterword: Confessions of a Freud Basher," in *The Memory Wars: Freud's Legacy in Dispute* (New York, NY: New York Review of Books, 1995), p. 298.

[92] Erich Fromm, "Freud, the World Reformer," in *Sigmund Freud's Mission: An Analysis of His Personality and Influence* (New York, NY: Grove Press, 1963), p. 87.

[93] Erich Fromm, "Some Personal Antecedents," in *Beyond the Chains of Illusion: My Encounter with Marx and Freud* (New York, NY: Simon & Schuster, 1962), p. 11.

[94] Benjamin Nelson (ed.), *Freud and the 20th Century* (New York, NY: Meridian, 1958), quote is taken from the front cover of book.

[95] Anthony Storr, "Sigmund Freud," in *Feet of Clay: Saints, Sinners, and Madmen: A Study of Gurus* (New York, NY: Free Press, 1997), p. 125.

[96] Maurice Friedman, "Psychotherapy and the Human Image," in *The Hidden Human Image: A Heartening Answer to the Dehumanizing Threats of our Age* (New York, NY: Delta Book, 1974), p. 81.

[97] Michel Foucault, "The Birth of the Asylum," in *Madness and Civilization: A History of Insanity in the Age of Reason*, trans. Richard Howard (New York, NY: Vintage Books, 1988), p. 277.

[98] Richard Wollheim, "Introduction," to *Freud: A Collection of Critical Essays*, ed. Richard Wollheim (Garden City, NY: Anchor Books, 1974), p. ix.

[99] Ludwig Binswanger, "Freud's Conception of Man in the Light of Anthropology," in *Being-in-the-World: Selected Papers of Ludwig Binswanger*, trans. Jacob Needleman (New York, NY: Basic Books, 1963), p. 178.

[100] William Glasser, "The Difference between Reality Therapy and Conventional Therapy," in *Reality Therapy: A New Approach to Psychiatry* (New York, NY: Harper & Row, 1975), p. 51.

[101] Erik H. Erikson, "Preface," to *Young Man Luther: A Study in Psychoanalysis and History* (New York, NY: W. W. Norton & Company, 1993), p. 8.

[102] Eugen Bleuler, "Letter to Sigmund Freud—February 17, 1925," quoted in Franz Alexander and Sheldon T. Selesnick, "Freud-Bleuler Correspondence," *Archives of General Psychiatry*, vol. 12 (January 1965), p. 8.

[103] Abraham H. Maslow, quoted in Colin Wilson, *New Pathways in Psychology: Maslow and the Post-Freudian Revolution* (New York, NY: Taplinger Publishing Company, 1972), pp. 129–30. See also Abraham H. Maslow and Béla Mittelmann, "Psychoanalytic Therapy," in *Principles of Abnormal Psychology: The Dynamics of Psychic Illness* (New York, NY: Harper & Brothers Publishers, 1941), pp. 314–59.

[104] Viktor E. Frankl, "Preface," to *The Unheard Cry for Meaning: Psychotherapy and Humanism* (New York, NY: Touchstone, 1978), p. 14.

[105] Mark Epstein, "Freud's Influence on Transpersonal Psychology," in *Textbook of Transpersonal Psychiatry and Psychology*, eds. Bruce W. Scotton, Allan B. Chinen and John R. Battista (New York, NY: Basic Books, 1996), p. 29.

[106] James F. T. Bugental, "Psychotherapy and Emergent Man," in *The Search for Authenticity: An Existential-Analytic Approach to Psychotherapy* (New York, NY: Holt, Rinehart and Winston, 1965), p. 377.

[107] R. D. Laing, quoted in David Cohen, "Interview with R. D. Laing," in *Psychologists on Psychology* (New York, NY: Taplinger Publishing Company, 1977), p. 203.

[108] Benjamin J. Sadock, Virginia A. Sadock, and Pedro Ruiz, "Theories of Personality and Psychopathology," in *Kaplan and Sadock's Synopsis of Psychiatry: Behavioral Sciences/Clinical Psychiatry* (Philadelphia, PA: Wolters Kluwer, 2015), p. 151.

[109] Peter Gay, "Preface," to *Freud: A Life for Our Time* (New York, NY: Anchor Books, 1989), p. xvii.

[110] David Bakan, "The Problem of the Origins of Psychoanalysis," in *Sigmund Freud and the Jewish Mystical Tradition* (London, UK: Free Association Books, 1990), p. 4.

[111] Frederick C. Crews, "Overview," in *Unauthorized Freud: Doubters Confront a Legend*, ed. Frederick C. Crews (New York, NY: Viking, 1998), p. 215.

[112] Paul M. Churchland, "The Brain in Trouble: Cognitive Dysfunction and Mental Illness," in *The Engine of Reason, the Seat of the Soul* (Cambridge, MA: Massachusetts Institute of Technology Press, 1996), p. 181.

[113] Malcolm Macmillan, "The Appeal of Psychoanalysis," in *Freud Evaluated: The Complete Arc* (Cambridge, MA: Massachusetts Institute of Technology Press, 1997), p. 617.

[114] Henri F. Ellenberger, "Sigmund Freud and Psychoanalysis," in *The Discovery of the Unconscious: The History and Evolution of Dynamic Psychiatry* (New York, NY: Basic Books, 1970), p. 427.

[115] Peter J. Swales, "Freud, Minna Bernays, and the Conquest of Rome: New Light on the Origins of Psychoanalysis," *New American Review*, vol. 1 (Spring/Summer 1982), p. 1.

[116] Harald Leupold-Löwenthal, quoted in David Cohen, "Interview with Harald Leupold-Löwenthal," in *Psychologists on Psychology* (New York, NY: Taplinger Publishing Company, 1977), p. 229.

[117] Erich Fromm, "Appendix: Freud's Theory of Aggressiveness and Destructiveness," in *The Anatomy of Human Destructiveness* (New York, NY: Holt, Rinehart and Winston, 1974), p. 478.

[118] Leon Salzman, "Modern Concepts of Psychoanalysis," in *Modern Concepts of Psychoanalysis*, eds. Leon Salzman and Jules H. Masserman (New York, NY: Philosophical Library, 1962), p. 5.

[119] Octave Mannoni, "My Life Is of No Interest Except in Its Relation to Psychoanalysis..." in *Freud: The Theory of the Unconscious* (London, UK: Verso, 1985), p. 14.

[120] Sigmund Freud, "Jokes and the Species of the Comic" (1905), in *Jokes and Their Relation to the Unconscious*, trans. and ed. James Strachey (New York, NY: W. W. Norton & Company, 1989), p. 266.

[121] Jacques Maritain, "Freudianism and Psychoanalysis," *CrossCurrents*, vol. 6, no. 4 (Fall 1956), p. 307.

[122] Richard LaPiere, "The Freudian Doctrine of Man," in *The Freudian Ethic* (New York, NY: Duell, Sloan and Pearce, 1959), p. 34.

[123] Alan A. Stone, "Where Will Psychoanalysis Survive?" *Harvard Magazine*, vol. 99, no. 3 (January–February 1997), p. 36.

[124] "In all domains psychoanalysis intends to realize a displacement or, more exactly, a symmetrical inversion, in such a way that what is below is above and what is above is below" (Jean Borella, "The Topological Conditioning of the Freudian Critique," in *The Crisis of Religious Symbolism and Symbolism & Reality*, trans. G. John Champoux [Kettering, OH: Angelico Press/Sophia Perennis, 2016], p. 206).

[125] Frank J. Sulloway, "The Myth of the Hero in the Psychoanalytic Movement," in *Freud, Biologist of the Mind: Beyond the Psychoanalytic Legend* (New York, NY: Basic Books, 1979), p. 480. "Freud and his followers frequently suggested that all religion was a mass delusion, a communal neurosis, or even a shared psychosis. Of course, Freud's circle consisted of well-educated, highly secular persons who prided themselves on their scientific attitudes. But we suggest that the main reason for this hostility to conventional religion was the fact that Psychoanalysis itself was a client cult, struggling to establish itself at the very border of religion. Surely, it offered a package of compensators, some of which were very general, totally outside the prevailing Christian culture. In attacking conventional religions, Psychoanalysis explicitly sought to replace them. For many of Freud's followers, indeed, for an embarrassingly prominent set of his most famous disciples, Psychoanalysis did develop into a religious cult." (Rodney Stark and William Sims Bainbridge, "Who Joins Cult Movements?" *The Future of*

Religion: Secularization, Revival and Cult Formation [Berkeley, CA: University of California Press, 1985], p. 419).

Chapter 1: The Psychoanalytic Revolution: The Succession to the Copernican and Darwinian Revolutions

[1] Robert Graham, "Otto Gross: Overcoming Cultural Crisis (1913)," in *Anarchism: A Documentary History of Libertarian Ideas, Vol. 1: From Anarchy to Anarchism (300 CE to 1939)*, ed. Robert Graham (Montréal: Black Rose Books, 2005), p. 281.

[2] Coline Covington, "The Future of Analysis," *Journal of Analytical Psychology*, vol. 46, no. 2 (April 2001), p. 331.

[3] Ibid.

[4] Ernest Jones, "Biology," in *The Life and Work of Sigmund Freud, Vol. 3: The Last Phase, 1919–1939* (New York, NY: Basic Books, 1957), p. 304. "Sigmund Freud's name is as cardinal in the history of human thought as Charles Darwin's" (H.G. Wells, Julian S. Huxley and G.P. Wells, "Psycho-Analysis," in *The Science of Life* [New York, NY: Literary Guild, 1931], p. 1368).

[5] Eugen Bleuler, "Letter to Sigmund Freud—October 19, 1910," quoted in Franz Alexander and Sheldon T. Selesnick, "Freud-Bleuler Correspondence," *Archives of General Psychiatry*, vol. 12 (January 1965), p. 5.

[6] Ernest Jones, "Character and Personality," in *The Life and Work of Sigmund Freud, Vol. 2: Years of Maturity, 1901–1919* (New York, NY: Basic Books, 1955), p. 423.

[7] Joshua L. Liebman, "Two Strategies, One Goal," in *Peace of Mind: Insights on Human Nature that can Change your Life* (New York, NY: Citadel Press, 1994), p. 20.

[8] Henri F. Ellenberger, "The Background of Dynamic Psychiatry," in *The Discovery of the Unconscious: The History and Evolution of Dynamic Psychiatry* (New York, NY: Basic Books, 1970), p. 197.

[9] Voltaire, "The Age of Louis XIV," in *The Works of Voltaire: A Contemporary Version, Vol. XII*, trans. William F. Fleming (New York, NY: St. Hubert Guild, 1901), p. 277.

[10] Henri F. Ellenberger, "The Background of Dynamic Psychiatry," in *The Discovery of the Unconscious: The History and Evolution of Dynamic Psychiatry* (New York, NY: Basic Books, 1970), p. 245. "[T]he birth of dynamic psychiatry can thus be understood as a manifestation of the Enlightenment in both its rational and irrational aspects" (Henri F. Ellenberger, "The Background of Dynamic Psychiatry," in *The Discovery of the Unconscious: The History and Evolution of Dynamic Psychiatry* [New York, NY: Basic Books, 1970], p. 198).

[11] Peter Gay, "The Last Philosophe: 'Our God Logos'," in *A Godless Jew: Freud, Atheism, and the Making of Psychoanalysis* (New Haven, CT: Yale University Press, 1987), p. 41.

[12] Erich Fromm, "The Instinctivists," in *The Anatomy of Human Destructiveness* (New York, NY: Holt, Rinehart and Winston, 1974), p. 32. "Freud was in many respects a typical representative of the Enlightenment" (Erich Fromm, "The Moral Powers in Man," in *Man for Himself: An Inquiry into the Psychology of Ethics* [New York, NY: Rinehart and Company, 1947], p. 213).

[13] Oskar Pfister, "Letter to Sigmund Freud—November 24, 1927," in *Psychoanalysis and Faith: The Letters of Sigmund Freud and Oskar Pfister*, trans. Eric Mosbacher, eds. Heinrich Meng and Ernst L. Freud (New York, NY: Basic Books, 1963), p. 115.

[14] German biologist Ernst Haeckel (1834–1919), known for propagating the Darwinian doctrine, predates Freud's parable of the "three blows" by critiquing the Copernican and Darwinian revolutions that laid the groundwork for psychoanalytic theory: "[The] two great fundamental errors are asserted in [the Abrahamic monotheisms teaching that the human being was made in the image of the Divine] it, namely, first, the *geocentric* error that the earth is the fixed central point of the whole universe, round which the sun, moon, and stars move; and secondly, the *anthropocentric* error, that man is the premeditated aim of the creation of the earth, for whose service alone all the rest of nature is said to have been created. The former of these errors was demolished by Copernicus' System of the Universe in the beginning of the 16th century, the latter by Lamarck's [and Darwin's] Doctrine of Descent in the beginning of the 19th century" (Ernst Haeckel, "The Mosaic Cosmogeny," in *The History of Creation: Or, The Development of the Earth and Its Inhabitants by the Action of Natural Causes, Vol. 1*, trans. Sir E. Ray Lankester [New York, NY: D. Appleton and Company, 1914], p. 40).

[15] Sufi adage quoted in Ibn 'Arabi, "Of the Divine Wisdom (*al-hikmat al-ilāhiyah*) in the Word of Adam," in *The Wisdom of the Prophets (Fusus al-Hikam)*, trans. Titus Burckhardt and Angela Culme-Seymour (Gloucestershire, UK: Beshara Publications, 1975), p. 11.

[16] Alexandre Koyré, "The New Astronomy and the New Metaphysics," in *From the Closed World to the Infinite Universe* (Kettering, OH: Angelico Press, 2016), p. 29.

[17] Seyyed Hossein Nasr, "The Intellectual and Historical Causes," in *The Encounter of Man and Nature: The Spiritual Crisis of Modern Man* (London, UK: George Allen and Unwin, 1968), p. 66.

[18] Wolfgang Smith, "Cakra and Planet: O. M. Hinze's Discovery," in *Science and Myth: What We Are Never Told* (San Rafael, CA: Sophia Perennis, 2010), p. 143.

[19] Martin Lings, "Book Review—The Transformist Illusion," *Studies in Comparative Religion*, vol. 4, no. 1 (Winter 1970), p. 59. See also Wolfgang Smith, *Theistic Evolution: The Teilhardian Heresy* (Tacoma, WA: Angelico Press/Sophia Perennis, 2012).

[20] Erich Fromm, "The Instinctivists," in *The Anatomy of Human Destructiveness* (New York, NY: Holt, Rinehart and Winston, 1974), pp. 30–31.

[21] Sigmund Freud, "Chapter Ten," in *The Future of an Illusion*, trans. and ed. James Strachey (New York, NY: W. W. Norton & Company, 1989), p. 68. "Nothing influences our conduct less than do intellectual ideas" (C. G. Jung, "Problems of Modern Psychotherapy," in *Modern Man in Search of a Soul*, trans. W. S. Dell and Cary F. Baynes [New York, NY: Harcourt, Brace & World, 1933], p. 42); "[T]he totality of the psyche can never be grasped by intellect alone" (C. G. Jung, "Conclusion," to *Two Essays on Analytical Psychology*, trans. R.F.C. Hull [New York, NY: Meridian, 1956], p. 130); "Man is guided by his intellect to make right choices. But we know also how weak and unreliable this instrument is. It is easily influenced by man's desires and passions and surrenders to their influence" (Erich Fromm, "Malignant Aggression: Premises," in *The Anatomy of Human Destructiveness* [New York, NY: Holt, Rinehart and Winston, 1974], p. 224).

[22] Sigmund Freud, "A Difficulty in the Path of Psycho-Analysis" (1917), in *The Standard Edition of the Complete Psychological Works of Sigmund Freud, Vol. 17*, trans. and ed. James Strachey (London, UK: Hogarth Press and the Institute of Psycho-Analysis, 1955), p. 143. "[W]e soon discover that the man is not master in his own house" (C. G. Jung, "The Autonomy of the Unconscious Mind," in *Psychology and Religion* [New Haven, CT: Yale University Press, 1938], p. 18); "He should learn that he is not master in his own house and that he should carefully study the other side of his psychic world which seems to be the true ruler of his fate." (C. G. Jung, "Letter to Miguel Serrano—September 14, 1960," in *C. G. Jung Letters, Vol. 2: 1951–1961*, trans. R.F.C. Hull, ed. Gerhard Adler [London, UK: Routledge, 2011], pp. 594–95).

[23] Titus Burckhardt, "Chapter One," in *Mystical Astrology According to Ibn 'Arabi*, trans. Bulent Rauf (Louisville, KY: Fons Vitae, 2001), p. 10.

[24] Ibn al-'Arabī, "The Wisdom of Divinity in the Word of Adam," in *The Bezels of Wisdom*, trans. R.W.J. Austin (New York, NY: Paulist Press, 1980), p. 51.

[25] E. F. Schumacher, "'*Adaequatio*': I," in *A Guide for the Perplexed* (New York, NY: Harper & Row, 1977), p. 39.

[26] Sigmund Freud, "Fixation to Traumas—The Unconscious" (1916–17 [1915–17]), in *Introductory Lectures on Psychoanalysis*, trans. and ed. James Strachey (New York, NY: W. W. Norton & Company, 1977), pp. 284–85. See also Sigmund Freud, "A Difficulty in the Path of Psycho-Analysis" (1917), in *The Standard Edition of the Complete Psychological Works of Sigmund Freud, Vol. 17*, trans. and ed. James Strachey (London, UK: Hogarth Press and the Institute of Psycho-Analysis, 1955), pp. 135–44.

[27] Janet Malcolm, "Chapter Four," in *Psychoanalysis: The Impossible Profession* (New York, NY: Alfred A. Knopf, 1981), p. 23.

[28] R. G. Collingwood, "Copernicus," in *The Idea of Nature* (London, UK: Oxford University Press, 1970), pp. 96–97.

[29] Arthur Lovejoy, *The Great Chain of Being: A Study of the History of an Idea* (Cambridge, MA: Harvard University Press, 1964), pp. 59, 26.

[30] Boethius, (Book ii, Prosa vii) quoted in R.G. Collingwood, "Copernicus," in *The Idea of Nature* (London, UK: Oxford University Press, 1970), p. 97.

[31] John Wren-Lewis, "Love's Coming of Age," in *Psychoanalysis Observed*, ed. Charles Rycroft (Baltimore, MD: Penguin Books, 1968), pp. 84–85.

[32] Ibid., p. 85.

[33] Seyyed Hossein Nasr, "The Cosmos as Theophany," in *Knowledge and the Sacred* (Albany, NY: State University of New York Press, 1989), p. 197.

[34] Huston Smith, "Introduction," to Frithjof Schuon, *The Transcendent Unity of Religions* (Wheaton, IL: Quest Books, 1993), p. xviii.

[35] "The traditional vision of things is above all 'static' and 'vertical'. It is static because it refers to constant and universal qualities, and it is vertical in the sense that it attaches the lower to the higher, the ephemeral to the imperishable. The modern vision, on the contrary, is fundamentally 'dynamic' and 'horizontal'; it is not the symbolism of things that interests it, but their material and historical connections" (Titus Burckhardt, "Traditional Cosmology and Modern Science: Cosmologia Perennis," in *Mirror of the Intellect: Essays on Traditional Science and Sacred Art*, trans. and ed. William Stoddart [Albany, NY: State University of New York Press, 1987], p. 25).

[36] Philip Sherrard, "The Christian Understanding of Man," *Sophia Perennis*, vol. 2, no. 1 (Spring 1976), pp. 42–43.

[37] "[T]he scientific basis of psychoanalysis was evolutionary biology" (Otto Rank, "The Irrational Basis of Modern Psychologies," in *Beyond Psychology* [New York, NY: Dover, 1958], p. 28); "[T]he influence of Darwinism on psychoanalysis is manifold...Freud followed Darwin in the shaping of a psychology based on the biological concept of the instincts...Freud's theory of the instincts is obviously derived from Darwin" (Henri F. Ellenberger, "The Background of Dynamic Psychiatry," in *The Discovery of the Unconscious: The History and Evolution of Dynamic Psychiatry* [New York, NY: Basic Books, 1970], p. 236). See also Christopher Badcock, *PsychoDarwinism: The New Synthesis of Darwin and Freud* (London, UK: Flamingo, 1995).

[38] Frank J. Sulloway, "The Darwin Revolution's Legacy to Psychology and Psychoanalysis," in *Freud, Biologist of the Mind: Beyond the Psychoanalytic Legend* (New York, NY: Basic Books, 1979), p. 275.

[39] John Wren-Lewis, "Love's Coming of Age," in *Psychoanalysis Observed*, ed. Charles Rycroft (Baltimore, MD: Penguin Books, 1968), p. 86.

[40] Ernest Jones, "Self-Analysis," in *The Life and Work of Sigmund Freud, Vol. 1: The Formative Years and the Great Discoveries, 1856–1900* (New York, NY: Basic Books, 1959), p. 319.

[41] Ernest Jones, "The Fliess Period," in *The Life and Work of Sigmund Freud, Vol. 1: The Formative Years and the Great Discoveries, 1856–1900* (New York, NY: Basic Books, 1959), p. 287.

[42] Philip Rieff, "The Religion of the Fathers," in *Freud: The Mind of the Moralist* (Chicago, IL: University of Chicago Press, 1979), p. 257.

43 E. Michael Jones, "The Third Session of the Council," in *The Jewish Revolutionary Spirit and Its Impact on World History* (South Bend, IN: Fidelity Press, 2008), p. 921.

44 Nathan M. Pusey, quoted in Gardner Murphy, "Sigmund Freud: Psychoanalysis," in *Psychological Thought from Pythagoras to Freud: An Informal Introduction* (New York, NY: Harcourt, Brace and World, 1968), p. 182.

45 Wolfgang Smith, quoted in Bernard Janzen, "Science, Scientism and Christological Cosmology," in *Unmasking the Faces of Antichrist: Interview with Dr. Wolfgang Smith* (Davidson, Saskatchewan, Canada: Triumph Communications, 2017), pp. 19–20.

46 Ernest Gellner, "Psychoanalysis, Social Role and Testability," in *Psychotherapy and Its Discontents*, eds. Windy Dryden and Colin Feltham (Buckingham, UK: Open University Press, 1992), p. 43.

47 Philip Rieff, "The Triumph of the Therapeutic," in *The Triumph of the Therapeutic: Uses of Faith After Freud* (Chicago, IL: University of Chicago Press, 1987), p. 260.

Chapter 2: Psychoanalysis, the Loss of Faith, and the Signs of the Times

1 Erich Fromm, "Values and Goals in Freud's Psychoanalytic Concepts," in *Zen Buddhism and Psychoanalysis*, eds. D. T. Suzuki, Erich Fromm, and Richard De Martino (New York, NY: Grove Press, 1963), p. 80.

2 C. G. Jung, "Sigmund Freud in His Historical Setting" (1934), in *The Collected Works of C. G. Jung, Vol. 15: The Spirit in Man, Art and Literature*, trans. R.F.C. Hull (Princeton, NJ: Princeton University Press, 1971), p. 36.

3 Seyyed Hossein Nasr, "Reflections on Islam and Modern Thought," *Studies in Comparative Religion*, vol. 15, Nos. 3 & 4 (Summer-Autumn 1983), p. 164.

4 Rama P. Coomaraswamy, "Modernism in the Church: The Road to Hell Is Paved with Good Intentions," in *The Destruction of the Christian Tradition: Updated and Revised* (Bloomington, IN: World Wisdom, 2006), p. 391.

5 Erich Fromm, "Faith as a Character Trait," in *Man for Himself: An Inquiry into the Psychology of Ethics* (New York, NY: Rinehart and Company, 1947), p. 210.

6 Frithjof Schuon, "The Twofold Discernment," in *Roots of the Human Condition* (Bloomington, IN: World Wisdom Books, 1991), p. 97.

7 Frithjof Schuon, "No Initiative without Truth," in *The Play of Masks* (Bloomington, IN: World Wisdom Books, 1992), p. 82.

8 Frithjof Schuon, "The Nature and Arguments of Faith," in *Stations of Wisdom* (Bloomington, IN: World Wisdom Books, 1995), p. 45.

9 Sigmund Freud, "Letter to Max Eitingon—June 20, 1927," quoted in Peter Gay, *A Godless Jew: Freud, Atheism, and the Making of Psychoanalysis* (New Haven, CT: Yale University Press, 1987), p. 12.

356

[10] Peter Gay, "The Last Philosophe: 'Our God Logos,'" in *A Godless Jew: Freud, Atheism, and the Making of Psychoanalysis* (New Haven, CT: Yale University Press, 1987), p. 41.

[11] Valer Barbu, "What Schools of Psychoanalysis Are There?" in *Are You Considering Psychoanalysis?*, ed. Karen Horney (New York, NY: W. W. Norton & Company, 1962), p. 57. "Freud was so imbued with the spirit of his culture that he could not go beyond certain limits which were set by it" (Erich Fromm, "Freedom—A Psychological Problem?" in *Escape from Freedom* [New York, NY: Henry Holt and Company, 1994], p. 7).

[12] Jean Borella, "Freud and the Inversion of the Sacred," in *The Crisis of Religious Symbolism and Symbolism & Reality*, trans. G. John Champoux (Kettering, OH: Angelico Press/Sophia Perennis, 2016), p. 199.

[13] Peter Homans, "The Structure of Jung's Mature Thought: Its Three Themes," in *Jung in Context: Modernity and the Making of a Psychology* (Chicago, IL: University of Chicago Press, 1979), p. 172.

[14] Martin Lings, "The Political Extreme," in *The Eleventh Hour: The Spiritual Crisis of the Modern World in the Light of Tradition and Prophecy* (Cambridge, UK: Archetype, 2002), pp. 43–44.

[15] Julius Evola, "Decline of the Medieval World and the Birth of Nations," in *Revolt Against the Modern World*, trans. Guido Stucco (Rochester, VT: Inner Traditions International, 1995), p. 309.

[16] See Erich Fromm, "The Religious Vacuum," in *The Pathology of Normalcy*, ed. Rainer Funk (Riverdale, NY: American Mental Health Foundation, 2010), pp. 31–36.

[17] Walter A. Weisskopf, "Existential Crisis and the Unconscious," *Journal of Humanistic Psychology*, vol. 7, no. 1 (Spring 1967), p. 64.

[18] Wolfgang Smith, "The Ego and the Beast," in *Cosmos & Transcendence: Breaking Through the Barrier of Scientistic Belief* (Peru, IL: Sherwood Sugden & Company, 1990), p. 103.

[19] Frank Maraun, "Christianity and Psychoanalysis" (1933), in *The Third Reich Sourcebook*, eds. Anson Rabinbach and Sander L. Gilman (Los Angeles, CA: University of California Press, 2013), p. 384.

[20] Whitall N. Perry, "The Revolt Against Moses: A New Look at Psychoanalysis," in *Challenges to a Secular Society* (Oakton, VA: Foundation for Traditional Studies, 1996), p. 17.

[21] Whitall N. Perry, "The Zodiac of the Soul: Observations on the Differences between Traditional and Empirical Psychology," in *Challenges to a Secular Society* (Oakton, VA: Foundation for Traditional Studies, 1996), p. 200.

[22] Peter Homans, "Introduction," to *The Ability to Mourn: Disillusionment and the Social Origins of Psychoanalysis* (Chicago, IL: University of Chicago Press, 1989), p. 4.

[23] Theodore Roszak, "Ethics, Ecstasy, and the Study of New Religions," in *Understanding the New Religions*, eds, Jacob Needleman and George Baker (New York, NY: Seabury Press, 1978), p. 51.

[24] See C.S. Lewis, *De Descriptione Temporum: An Inaugural Lecture* (Cambridge, UK: Cambridge University Press, 1955).

[25] Louis Dupré, "Spiritual Life and the Survival of Christianity," *Cross Currents*, vol. 48, no. 3 (Fall 1998), p. 381.

[26] René Guénon, "A Material Civilization," in *The Crisis of the Modern World*, trans. Arthur Osborne, Marco Pallis and Richard C. Nicholson (Hillsdale, NY: Sophia Perennis, 2004), p. 95.

[27] Wolfgang Smith, "Letter to Father Malachi Martin—May 19, 1999," in *In Quest of Catholicity: Malachi Martin Responds to Wolfgang Smith*, ed. Wolfgang Smith (Kettering, OH: Angelico Press, 2016), p. 117.

[28] Wolfgang Smith, "Modern Science and Guénonian Critique," in *Science and Myth: What We Are Never Told* (San Rafael, CA: Sophia Perennis, 2010), p. 41.

[29] See Samuel Bendeck Sotillos, "Drug-Induced Mysticism Revisited: Interview with Charles Upton," in *Psychology and the Perennial Philosophy: Studies in Comparative Religion*, ed. Samuel Bendeck Sotillos (Bloomington, IN: World Wisdom, 2013), pp. 130–54. Jan Irvin, "R. Gordon Wasson: The Man, the Legend, the Myth: Beginning a New History of Magic Mushrooms, Ethnomycology, and the Psychedelic Revolution," in *Entheogens and the Development of Culture: The Anthropology and Neurobiology of Ecstatic Experience*, ed. John A. Rush (Berkeley, CA: North Atlantic Books, 2013), pp. 565–619.

[30] See Michael Minnicino, "The Frankfurt School and 'Political Correctness'," *Fidelio*, vol. 1, no. 1 (Winter 1992), pp. 4–27; Gabriele Kuby, *The Global Sexual Revolution: Destruction of Freedom in the Name of Freedom*, trans. James Patrick Kirchner (Kettering, OH: Angelico Press/LifeSite, 2015).

[31] Rama P. Coomaraswamy, "Modernism in the Church: The Road to Hell Is Paved with Good Intentions," in *The Destruction of the Christian Tradition: Updated and Revised* (Bloomington, IN: World Wisdom, 2006), p. 392.

[32] Fulton J. Sheen, "Frustration," in *Peace of Soul* (Liguori, MO: Liguori/Triumph, 1996), p. 9.

[33] Richard M. Weaver, "Introduction," to *Ideas Have Consequences* (Chicago, IL: University of Chicago Press, 1984), p. 10.

[34] Ibid.

[35] Ibid.

[36] Fulton J. Sheen, "Frustration," in *Peace of Soul* (Liguori, MO: Liguori/Triumph, 1996), p. 6.

[37] Sigmund Freud, "Chapter Seven," in *The Future of an Illusion*, trans. and ed. James Strachey (New York, NY: W. W. Norton & Company, 1989), p. 48.

[38] C. G. Jung, "The Spiritual Problem of Modern Man," in *Modern Man in Search of a Soul*, trans. W. S. Dell and Cary F. Baynes (New York, NY: Harcourt, Brace & World, 1933), pp. 204–6.

[39] C. G. Jung, "The Meaning of Psychology for Modern Man" (1934), in *The Collected Works of C. G. Jung, Vol. 10: Civilization in Transition*, trans. R.F.C. Hull (Princeton, NJ: Princeton University Press, 1970), p. 146.

[40] O. Hobart Mowrer, "Some Constructive Features of the Concept of Sin," in *The Crisis in Psychiatry and Religion* (Princeton, NJ: D. Van Nostrand Company, 1961), p. 42.

[41] C. G. Jung, "The Soul and Death" (1934), in *The Collected Works of C. G. Jung, Vol. 8: Structure and Dynamics of the Psyche*, trans. Gerhard Adler and R.F.C. Hull (Princeton, NJ: Princeton University Press, 1972), p. 410.

[42] C. G. Jung, "The Spiritual Problem of Modern Man," in *Modern Man in Search of a Soul*, trans. W. S. Dell and Cary F. Baynes (New York, NY: Harcourt, Brace & World, 1933), p. 198.

[43] E. Fuller Torrey, "An Audit of Freud's American Account," in *Freudian Fraud: The Malignant Effects of Freud's Theory on American Thought and Culture* (New York, NY: HarperCollins, 1992), pp. 255–56.

[44] C. G. Jung, "New Paths in Psychology" (1912), in *Two Essays on Analytical Psychology*, trans. R.F.C. Hull (New York, NY: Meridian, 1956), pp. 270–71.

[45] C. G. Jung, "Therapeutic Principles of Psychoanalysis" (1912), in *Critique of Psychoanalysis*, trans. R.F.C. Hull (Princeton, NJ: Princeton University Press, 1975), p. 114.

[46] C. G. Jung, "New Paths in Psychology" (1912), in *The Collected Works C. G. Jung, Vol. 7: Two Essays on Analytical Psychology*, trans. R.F.C. Hull, eds. Sir Herbert Read, Michael Fordham and Gerhard Adler (Princeton, NJ: Princeton University Press, 1972), p. 261.

[47] Philip Sherrard, "Christianity and the Religious Thought of C. G. Jung," in *Christianity: Lineaments of a Sacred Tradition* (Brookline, MA: Holy Cross Orthodox Press, 1998), p. 137.

[48] Maurice Friedman, "Psychological: Sigmund Freud and Carl G. Jung," in *Contemporary Psychology: Revealing and Obscuring the Human* (Pittsburgh, PA: Duquesne University Press, 1984), p. 43.

[49] Sigmund Freud, "Obsessive Actions and Religious Practices" (1907), in *The Standard Edition of the Complete Psychological Works of Sigmund Freud, Vol. 9*, trans. and ed. James Strachey (London, UK: Hogarth Press and the Institute of Psycho-Analysis, 1981), pp. 126–27.

[50] Mircea Eliade, "Cultural Fashions and History of Religions," in *Occultism, Witchcraft, and Cultural Fashions: Essays in Comparative Religions* (Chicago, IL: University of Chicago Press, 1976), p. 5.

[51] Erik H. Erikson, "Growth and Crisis of the Healthy Personality," in *Identity and the Life Cycle* (New York, NY: W. W. Norton & Company, 1994), pp. 66–67.

[52] Werner Kraft, quoted in Thomas Szasz, "Karl Kraus Today," in *Karl Kraus and the Soul-Doctors: A Pioneer Critic and his Criticism of Psychiatry and Psychoanalysis* (Baton Rouge, LA: Louisiana State University Press, 1976), p. 93.

Chapter 3: The Secret Inner Circle of the Psychoanalytic Movement

[1] Phyllis Grosskurth, "Prologue," to *The Secret Ring: Freud's Inner Circle and the Politics of Psychoanalysis* (Reading, MA: Addison-Wesley Publishing, 1991), p. 23.

[2] Sigmund Freud, "Letter to Karl Abraham—November 6, 1913," in *The Complete Correspondence of Sigmund Freud and Karl Abraham, 1907–1925*, trans. Caroline Schwarzacher, Christine Trollope and Klara Majthényi King, ed. Ernst Falzeder (London, UK: Karnac, 2002), p. 206.

[3] Richard Noll, "Religion Can Only Be Replaced by Religion," in *The Aryan Christ: The Secret Life of Carl Jung* (New York, NY: Random House, 1997), pp. 59–60. See also John Kerr, *A Most Dangerous Method: The Story of Jung, Freud, and Sabina Spielrein* (New York, NY: Alfred A. Knopf, 1993); Paul Roazen, *Brother Animal: The Story of Freud and Tausk* (New York, NY: New York University Press, 1986); Peter J. Swales, "Freud, Filthy Lucre, and Undue Influence," *Review of Existential Psychology and Psychiatry*, vol. 23, Nos. 1–3 (1997), pp. 115–41.

[4] Robert R. Holt, "Freud's Parental Identifications as a Source of Some Contradictions Within Psychoanalysis," in *Freud and the History of Psychoanalysis*, eds. Toby Gelfand and John Kerr (Hillsdale, NJ: Analytic Press, 1992), pp. 21–22.

[5] Louis Breger, "The King and His Knights: The Committee," in *Freud: Darkness in the Midst of Vision* (New York, NY: John Wiley and Sons, 2000), p. 209.

[6] Sigmund Freud, quoted in Ernest Jones, "Fame and Suffering," in *The Life and Work of Sigmund Freud, Vol. 3: The Last Phase, 1919–1939* (New York, NY: Basic Books, 1957), p. 153.

[7] Sigmund Freud, "Letter to Ernest Jones—August 1, 1912," quoted in Ernest Jones, "The Committee," in *The Life and Work of Sigmund Freud, Vol. 2: Years of Maturity, 1901–1919* (New York, NY: Basic Books, 1955), p. 153.

[8] Sigmund Freud, "Letter to Ernest Jones—August 1, 1912," quoted in Ernest Jones, "The Committee," in *The Life and Work of Sigmund Freud, Vol. 2: Years of Maturity, 1901–1919* (New York, NY: Basic Books, 1955), p. 153.

[9] Sigmund Freud, "Letter to Ernst Simmel—November 11, 1928," in Ernst L. Freud (ed.), *Letters of Sigmund Freud*, trans. Tania Stern and James Stern (New York, NY: Basic Books, 1975), pp. 382–83.

[10] Ernest Jones, "The Committee," in *The Life and Work of Sigmund Freud, Vol. 2: Years of Maturity, 1901–1919* (New York, NY: Basic Books, 1955), p. 154.

[11] Jeffrey Moussaieff Masson, "Epilogue," to *Final Analysis: The Making and Unmaking of a Psychoanalyst* (Reading, MA: Addison-Wesley Publishing Company, 1990), p. 209.

[12] Sándor Ferenczi, "Letter to Sigmund Freud—February 5, 1910," quoted in Ernest Jones, "The International Psycho-Analytical Association," in *The*

Life and Work of Sigmund Freud, Vol. 2: Years of Maturity, 1901–1919 (New York, NY: Basic Books, 1955), p. 69.

[13] See Ernest Jones, "The International Psycho-Analytical Association," in *The Life and Work of Sigmund Freud, Vol. 2: Years of Maturity, 1901–1919* (New York, NY: Basic Books, 1955), p. 69.

[14] Ernest Jones, "Letter to Sigmund Freud—August 7, 1912," in *The Complete Correspondence of Sigmund Freud and Ernest Jones, 1908–1939*, ed. R. Andrew Paskauskas (Cambridge, MA: Belknap Press of Harvard University Press, 1993), p. 149.

[15] Karl Abraham, "Letter to Max Eitingon—January 1, 1908," quoted in Anna Bentinck van Schoonheten, *Karl Abraham: Life and Work, a Biography*, trans. Liz Waters (London, UK: Karnac Books, 2016), p. 50.

[16] Frank J. Sulloway, "Reassessing Freud's Case Histories: The Social Construction of Psychoanalysis," *Isis*, vol. 82, no. 2 (June 1991), p. 269.

[17] Herman Nunberg, quoted in Paul Roazen, "Introduction: Meeting Freud's Patients and Pupils," in *Freud and His Followers* (New York, NY: Meridian, 1974), p. xxxiii.

[18] Richard Wollheim, "The Last Phase," in *Sigmund Freud* (New York, NY: Cambridge University Press, 1995), p. 252.

[19] Hanns Sachs, "First Acquaintance," in *Freud, Master and Friend* (Cambridge, MA: Harvard University Press, 1945), p. 61.

[20] Wilhelm Stekel, "Introduction to Freud and Psychoanalysis," in *The Autobiography of Wilhelm Stekel: The Life Story of a Pioneer Psychoanalyst*, ed. Emil A. Gutheil (New York, NY: Liveright, 1950), p. 106.

[21] Max Graf, "Reminiscences of Professor Sigmund Freud," *Psychoanalytic Quarterly*, vol. 11 (1942), p. 471.

[22] C. G. Jung, "Letter to Sabina Spielrein—September 21/22, 1911," quoted in C. G. Jung, "The Letters of C. G. Jung to Sabina Spielrein," *Journal of Analytical Psychology*, vol. 46, no. 1 (January 2001), p. 181.

[23] A. A. Brill, "The Zurich School and Psychoanalysis," in *Freud's Contribution to Psychiatry* (New York, NY: W. W. Norton & Company, 1944), p. 95. "To Brill and others on the staff Freud was known as Allah and Jung as his prophet" (Harry K. Wells, "Psychoanalysis Comes to America," in *The Failure of Psychoanalysis: From Freud to Fromm* [New York, NY: International Publishers, 1963], p. 22).

[24] Isador Coriat "Letter to Ernest Jones—April 4, 1921," quoted in George Makari, *Revolution in Mind: The Creation of Psychoanalysis* (New York, NY: HarperCollins, 2008), p. 324.

[25] Paul Roazen, "Apostles," in *Freud and His Followers* (New York, NY: Meridian, 1974), p. 323.

[26] Hanns Sachs, "What and Why," in *Freud, Master and Friend* (Cambridge, MA: Harvard University Press, 1945), pp. 3–4.

[27] Frederick S. Perls, "Past and Present," in *Ego, Hunger and Aggression* (New York, NY: Vintage Books, 1969), p. 103.

[28] Max Graf, "Reminiscences of Professor Sigmund Freud," *Psychoanalytic Quarterly*, vol. 11 (1942), pp. 470–71.

[29] Hanns Sachs, quoted in Paul Roazen, "Apostles," in *Freud and His Followers* (New York, NY: Meridian, 1974), p. 323.

[30] Abram Kardiner, *My analysis with Freud: Reminiscences* (New York, NY: W. W. Norton & Company, 1977), p. 121.

[31] Adolf Meyer, quoted in Mikkel Borch-Jacobsen and Sonu Shamdasani, *The Freud Files: An Inquiry into the History of Psychoanalysis* (Cambridge, UK: Cambridge University Press, 2012), p. 121. "Those who imagine that all psychiatry and psychopathology and therapy have to resolve themselves into a smattering of claims and hypotheses of psychoanalysis and that they stand or fall with one's feelings about psychoanalysis, are equally misguided" (Adolf Meyer, "Thirty-Five Years of Psychiatry in the United States and Our Present Outlook," *American Journal of Psychiatry*, vol. 8, no. 1 [July 1928], p. 25).

[32] Karl Abraham, quoted in Peter Gay, "The Wednesday Psychological Society," in *Freud: A Life for Our Time* (New York, NY: Anchor Books, 1989), p. 178.

[33] Sigmund Freud, "Letter to Georg Groddeck—June 5, 1917," in Ernst L. Freud (ed.), *Letters of Sigmund Freud*, trans. Tania Stern and James Stern (New York, NY: Basic Books, 1975), p. 316.

[34] Karl Abraham, "Letter to Sigmund Freud—February 26, 1924," in *The Complete Correspondence of Sigmund Freud and Karl Abraham, 1907–1925*, trans. Caroline Schwarzacher, Christine Trollope and Klara Majthényi King, ed. Ernst Falzeder (London, UK: Karnac, 2002), p. 486.

[35] Erich Fromm, "Freud's Passion for Truth and His Courage," in *Sigmund Freud's Mission: An Analysis of His Personality and Influence* (New York, NY: Grove Press, 1963), p. 7.

[36] James Strachey, "Letter to Alix Strachey—November 10, 1924," in *Bloomsbury/Freud: The Letters of James and Alix Strachey, 1924–1925*, eds. Perry Meisel and Walter Kendrick (New York, NY: Basic Books, 1985), p. 113.

[37] Sigmund Freud, "Letter to Fritz Wittels—December 18, 1923," in Fritz Wittels, *Sigmund Freud: His Personality, His Teaching, and His School*, trans. Eden Paul and Cedar Paul (New York, NY: Routledge, 2014), p. 12. "People shouldn't interest themselves in my person they should interest themselves in analysis" (Sigmund Freud, quoted in Joseph Wortis, "Fragments of a Freudian Analysis," *American Journal of Orthopsychiatry*, vol. 10, no. 4 [October 1940], p. 849).

[38] Helen Walker Puner, "See How It Grows," in *Freud: His Life and His Mind* (New York, NY: Howell, Soskin, 1947), p. 153.

[39] Sigmund Freud, "Psycho-Analysis and Telepathy" (1941 [1921]), in *The Standard Edition of the Complete Psychological Works of Sigmund Freud, Vol. 18*, trans. and ed. James Strachey (London, UK: Hogarth Press and the Institute of Psycho-Analysis, 1975), p. 180.

[40] Erich Fromm, "The Fate of Both Theories," in *Beyond the Chains of Illusion: My Encounter with Marx and Freud* (New York, NY: Simon & Schuster, 1962), p. 138.

[41] Sigmund Freud, "The Dissection of the Psychical Personality" (1933 [1932]), in *New Introductory Lectures on Psycho-Analysis*, trans. and ed. James Strachey (New York, NY: W. W. Norton & Company, 1989), p. 87.

[42] John B. Watson, "The Psychology of Wish Fulfilment," *Scientific Monthly*, vol. 3, No 5 (November 1916), p. 480.

[43] Sigmund Freud, quoted in C. G. Jung, "Lecture Three—April 6, 1925," in *Analytical Psychology: Notes of the Seminar Given in 1925*, ed. William McGuire (London, UK: Routledge, 1992), p. 20.

[44] Alfred Hoche, quoted in Mikkel Borch-Jacobsen and Sonu Shamdasani, *The Freud Files: An Inquiry into the History of Psychoanalysis* (Cambridge, UK: Cambridge University Press, 2012), pp. 83–84.

[45] See Richard Noll, *The Jung Cult: Origins of a Charismatic Movement* (Princeton, NJ: Princeton University Press, 1994); Richard Noll, *The Aryan Christ: The Secret Life of Carl Jung* (New York, NY: Random House, 1997).

[46] C. G. Jung, "Introduction to Toni Wolff's *Studies in Jungian Psychology*" (1959), in *The Collected Works of C. G. Jung, Vol. 10: Civilization in Transition*, trans. R.F.C. Hull (Princeton, NJ: Princeton University Press, 1970), p. 469.

[47] Paul J. Stern, "The Psychological Club," in *C. G. Jung: The Haunted Prophet* (New York, NY: Dell, 1977), pp. 152–53.

[48] Fanny Bowditch Katz, quoted in Richard Noll, "Fanny Bowditch Katz—'Analysis Is Religion,'" in *The Aryan Christ: The Secret Life of Carl Jung* (New York, NY: Random House, 1997), p. 185.

[49] Liliane Frey-Rohn, quoted in Richard Noll, "'The Secret Church': The Transmission of Charismatic Authority," in *The Jung Cult: Origins of a Charismatic Movement* (Princeton, NJ: Princeton University Press, 1994), p. 285.

[50] Jolande Jacobi, quoted in Richard Noll, "'The Secret Church': The Transmission of Charismatic Authority," in *The Jung Cult: Origins of a Charismatic Movement* (Princeton, NJ: Princeton University Press, 1994), p. 286.

[51] Christiana Morgan, quoted in Richard Noll, "From Volkish Prophet to Wise Old Man," in *The Aryan Christ: The Secret Life of Carl Jung* (New York, NY: Random House, 1997), p. 266.

[52] Sigmund Freud, "On the History of the Psychoanalytic Movement" (1914), in *The History of the Psychoanalytic Movement*, ed. Philip Rieff (New York, NY: Collier Books, 1963), p. 95.

[53] Sigmund Freud, "On the History of the Psychoanalytic Movement" (1914), in *The History of the Psychoanalytic Movement*, ed. Philip Rieff (New York, NY: Collier Books, 1963), p. 93.

[54] Henri F. Ellenberger, quoted in Sonu Shamdasani, "Cult and Association," in *Cult Fictions: C. G. Jung and the Founding of Analytical Psychology* (London, UK: Routledge, 1998), pp. 4–5.

[55] Viktor von Weizsäecker, "Reminiscences of Freud and Jung," in *Freud and the 20th Century*, ed. Benjamin Nelson (New York, NY: Meridian, 1958), p. 72.

[56] C. G. Jung, "Letter to Sigmund Freud—August 11, 1910," in William McGuire (ed.), *The Freud/Jung Letters: The Correspondence Between Sigmund Freud and C. G. Jung*, trans. Ralph Manheim and R.F.C. Hull (Princeton, NJ: Princeton University Press, 1994), pp. 345–46. Jung emphasizes the need for a secret committee to awaken humanity and guide it according to the principles of this new secular religion: "Here I am alluding to a problem that is far more significant than these few simple words would seem to suggest: mankind is, in essentials, psychologically still in a state of childhood— a stage that cannot be skipped. The vast majority needs authority, guidance, law. This fact cannot be overlooked. The Pauline overcoming of the law falls only to the man who knows how to put his soul in the place of conscience. Very few are capable of this ('Many are called, but few are chosen'). And these few tread this path only from inner necessity, not to say suffering, for it is sharp as the edge of a razor" (C. G. Jung, "The Mana-Personality," in *Two Essays on Analytical Psychology*, trans. R.F.C. Hull [New York, NY: Meridian, 1956], p. 251).

[57] C. G. Jung, "Adaptation, Individuation, Collectivity" (1916), in *The Collected Works of C. G. Jung, Vol. 18: The Symbolic Life: Miscellaneous Writings*, trans. R.F.C. Hull (Princeton, NJ: Princeton University Press, 1980), p. 453.

[58] Ernest Jones, "Letter to Sigmund Freud—December 5, 1912," in *The Complete Correspondence of Sigmund Freud and Ernest Jones, 1908–1939*, ed. R. Andrew Paskauskas (Cambridge, MA: Belknap Press of Harvard University Press, 1993), p. 180.

[59] Sigmund Freud, "Letter to Ernest Jones—December 8, 1912," in *The Complete Correspondence of Sigmund Freud and Ernest Jones, 1908–1939*, ed. R. Andrew Paskauskas (Cambridge, MA: Belknap Press of Harvard University Press, 1993), p. 182.

[60] Sigmund Freud, "Letter to Sándor Ferenczi—June 8, 1913," in *The Correspondence of Sigmund Freud and Sándor Ferenczi, Vol. 1: 1908–1914*, trans. Peter T. Hoffer, eds. Ernst Falzeder, Eva Brabant and Patrizia Giampieri-Deutsch (Cambridge, MA: Belknap Press of Harvard University Press, 1993), p. 490.

[61] William M. Johnston, "Freud and His Followers," in *The Austrian Mind: An Intellectual and Social History, 1848–1938* (Berkeley, CA: University of California Press, 2000), p. 252.

[62] Erich Fromm, "Appendix: Freud's Theory of Aggressiveness and Destructiveness," in *The Anatomy of Human Destructiveness* (New York, NY: Holt, Rinehart and Winston, 1974), p. 478.

[63] Sigmund Freud, "Letter to C. G. Jung—January 1, 1907," in William McGuire (ed.), *The Freud/Jung Letters: The Correspondence Between Sigmund Freud and C. G. Jung*, trans. Ralph Manheim and R.F.C. Hull (Princeton, NJ: Princeton University Press, 1994), p. 18.

[64] Sigmund Freud, "(A) The Forgetting of Dreams," in *The Interpretation of Dreams*, trans. and ed. James Strachey (New York, NY: Science Editions, 1963), p. 517.

[65] Sándor Ferenczi, "Letter to Sigmund Freud—December 26, 1912," in *The Correspondence of Sigmund Freud and Sándor Ferenczi, Vol. 1: 1908–1914*, trans. Peter T. Hoffer, eds. Ernst Falzeder, Eva Brabant, and Patrizia Giampieri-Deutsch (Cambridge, MA: Belknap Press of Harvard University Press, 1993), p. 449.

[66] Erwin Stransky, quoted in Mikkel Borch-Jacobsen and Sonu Shamdasani, *The Freud Files: An Inquiry into the History of Psychoanalysis* (Cambridge, UK: Cambridge University Press, 2012), pp. 97–98.

[67] Thomas Szasz, "Freud as a Leader," *Antioch Review*, vol. 23, no. 2 (Summer 1963), pp. 140, 141.

[68] Peter J. Swales, "Freud, Filthy Lucre, and Undue Influence," *Review of Existential Psychology and Psychiatry*, vol. 23, nos. 1–3 (1997), p. 131.

[69] Max Graf, "Reminiscences of Professor Sigmund Freud," *Psychoanalytic Quarterly*, vol. 11 (1942), p. 471.

[70] Phyllis Grosskurth, "The Unruly Son," in *The Secret Ring: Freud's Inner Circle and the Politics of Psychoanalysis* (Reading, MA: Addison-Wesley Publishing, 1991), p. 48.

[71] Jeffrey Moussaieff Masson, "Anna Freud and I," in *Final Analysis: The Making and Unmaking of a Psychoanalyst* (Reading, MA: Addison-Wesley Publishing Company, 1990), p. 152.

[72] Ibid.

[73] Thomas Szasz, "Kraus's Place in Cultural History," in *Karl Kraus and the Soul-Doctors: A Pioneer Critic and His Criticism of Psychiatry and Psychoanalysis* (Baton Rouge, LA: Louisiana State University Press, 1976), p. 72.

[74] Sigmund Freud, "Letter to C. G. Jung—November 15, 1907," in William McGuire (ed.), *The Freud/Jung Letters: The Correspondence Between Sigmund Freud and C. G. Jung*, trans. Ralph Manheim and R.F.C. Hull (Princeton, NJ: Princeton University Press, 1994), p. 98.

[75] Sigmund Freud, quoted in Ernest Jones, "Dissensions," in *The Life and Work of Sigmund Freud, Vol. 2: Years of Maturity, 1901–1919* (New York, NY: Basic Books, 1955), p. 129.

[76] E. Michael Jones, "Part II, Chapter 3: Bremen, 1909," in *Libido Dominandi: Sexual Liberation and Political Control* (South Bend, IN: St. Augustine's Press, 2000), p. 124.

[77] Ernest Jones, "The Committee," in *The Life and Work of Sigmund Freud, Vol. 2: Years of Maturity, 1901–1919* (New York, NY: Basic Books, 1955), p. 164.

[78] Sigmund Freud, "Letter to Eugen Bleuler—September 28, 1910," quoted in Franz Alexander and Sheldon T. Selesnick, "Freud-Bleuler Correspondence," *Archives of General Psychiatry*, vol. 12 (January 1965), p. 2.

[79] Sigmund Freud, "Letter to Eugen Bleuler—October 16, 1910," quoted in Franz Alexander and Sheldon T. Selesnick, "Freud-Bleuler Correspondence," *Archives of General Psychiatry*, vol. 12 (January 1965), p. 4.

[80] Eric Hoffer, "Suspicion," in *The True Believer: Thoughts on the Nature of Mass Movements* (New York, NY: Harper & Row, 1966), p. 115.

[81] Erich Fromm, "Summary and Conclusion," to *Sigmund Freud's Mission: An Analysis of His Personality and Influence* (New York, NY: Grove Press, 1963), p. 111.

Chapter 4: The Censoring and Mythologizing of Psychoanalytic History

[1] Sigmund Freud, "Further Recommendations in the Technique of Psychoanalysis: Observations on Transference-Love" (1915), in *Therapy and Technique*, ed. Philip Rieff (New York, NY: Collier Books, 1963), p. 172.

[2] Russell Jacoby, "Revisionism: The Repression of a Theory," in *Social Amnesia: A Critique of Conformist Psychology from Adler to Laing* (Boston, MA: Beacon Press, 1975), p. 44.

[3] David E. Stannard, "The Failure of Psychohistory," in *Shrinking History: On Freud and the Failure of Psychohistory* (New York, NY: Oxford University Press, 1980), p. 151.

[4] Edgar A. Levenson, "'Things Fade: Alternatives Exclude'—Psychoanalytic Theory in Flux," in *The Fallacy of Understanding: An Inquiry into the Changing Structure of Psychoanalysis* (New York, NY: Basic Books, 1972), p. 19.

[5] Ernest Jones, "The Committee," in *The Life and Work of Sigmund Freud, Vol. 2: Years of Maturity, 1901–1919* (New York, NY: Basic Books, 1955), p. 157.

[6] Erich Fromm, "Introduction: Instincts and Human Passions," in *The Anatomy of Human Destructiveness* (New York, NY: Holt, Rinehart and Winston, 1974), p. 7.

[7] Hans J. Eysenck, "Psycho-Babble and Pseudo-History," in *Decline and Fall of the Freudian Empire* (New York, NY: Penguin Books, 1991), p. 181.

[8] Frank J. Sulloway, "The Myth of the Hero in the Psychoanalytic Movement," in *Freud, Biologist of the Mind: Beyond the Psychoanalytic Legend* (New York, NY: Basic Books, 1979), pp. 445–56.

[9] Sigmund Freud, "Anxiety and Instinctual Life" (1933 [1932]), in *New Introductory Lectures on Psycho-Analysis*, trans. and ed. James Strachey (New York, NY: W. W. Norton & Company, 1989), p. 118.

[10] Sigmund Freud, "Chapter Ten," in *The Future of an Illusion*, trans. and ed. James Strachey (New York, NY: W. W. Norton & Company, 1989), p. 71. See also Sigmund Freud, "Fixation to Traumas—The Unconscious," in *Introductory Lectures on Psycho-Analysis*, trans. and ed. James Strachey (New York, NY: W. W. Norton & Company, 1977), p. 285; Sigmund Freud, "Psycho-Analysis and Telepathy" (1941 [1921]), in *The Standard Edition of the Complete Psychological Works of Sigmund Freud, Vol. 18*, trans. and ed. James Strachey (London, UK: Hogarth Press and the Institute of Psycho-Analysis, 1975), p. 177; Sigmund Freud, "Psychical Qualities" (1940 [1938]), in *An Outline of Psycho-Analysis*, trans. and ed. James Strachey (New York, NY: W. W. Norton & Company, 1989), p. 31.

[11] Sigmund Freud, "The Psychical Apparatus" (1940 [1938]), in *An Outline of Psycho-Analysis*, trans. and ed. James Strachey (New York, NY: W. W. Norton & Company, 1989), p. 14.

[12] Thomas Szasz, "Freud as a Leader," *Antioch Review*, vol. 23, no. 2 (Summer 1963), pp. 136–37.

[13] Sigmund Freud, "Letter to Wilhelm Fliess—July 27, 1904," in *The Complete Letters of Sigmund Freud to Wilhelm Fliess, 1887–1904*, trans. and ed. Jeffrey Moussaieff Masson (Cambridge, MA: Belknap Press of Harvard University Press, 1985), p. 466.

[14] Sigmund Freud, "The Question of a *Weltanschauung*" (1933 [1932]), in *New Introductory Lectures on Psycho-Analysis*, trans. and ed. James Strachey (New York, NY: W. W. Norton & Company, 1989), p. 198.

[15] Sigmund Freud, "Why War?" (1933 [1932]), in *The Standard Edition of the Complete Psychological Works of Sigmund Freud, Vol. 22*, trans. and ed. James Strachey (London, UK: Hogarth Press and the Institute of Psycho-Analysis, 1953), p. 211.

[16] Sigmund Freud, "Anxiety and Instinctual Life" (1933 [1932]), in *New Introductory Lectures on Psycho-Analysis*, trans. and ed. James Strachey (New York, NY: W. W. Norton & Company, 1989), p. 118.

[17] Theodor W. Adorno, "Dwarf fruit," in *Minima Moralia: Reflections on a Damaged Life*, trans. E.F.N. Jephcott (London, UK: Verso, 2005), p. 49. See also Theodor W. Adorno, Else Frenkel-Brunswik, Daniel Levinson, and Nevitt Sanford, *The Authoritarian Personality* (New York, NY: Harper & Row, 1950).

[18] E. Michael Jones, "Part II, Chapter 3: Bremen, 1909," in *Libido Dominandi: Sexual Liberation and Political Control* (South Bend, IN: St. Augustine's Press, 2000), p. 124.

[19] Ernest Jones, "Contributions to Technique," in *The Life and Work of Sigmund Freud, Vol. 2: Years of Maturity, 1901–1919* (New York, NY: Basic Books, 1955), p. 230.

[20] Henri F. Ellenberger, quoted in Jacques Mousseau, "Freud in Perspective: A Conversation with Henri F. Ellenberger," *Psychology Today*, vol. 6, no. 10 (March 1973), p. 54.

[21] Philip Rieff, "Preface to the First Edition," in *Freud: The Mind of the Moralist* (Chicago, IL: University of Chicago Press, 1979), p. xiv.

[22] Erich Fromm, "Psychoanalysis—Science or Party Line?" in *The Dogma of Christ: And Other Essays on Religion, Psychology and Culture* (Greenwich, CT: Fawcett, 1973), p. 126.

[23] Richard Webster, "Freud, Fliess and the Theory of Infantile Sexuality," in *Why Freud Was Wrong: Sin, Science, and Psychoanalysis* (New York, NY: Basic Books, 1995), p. 226.

[24] Peter J. Swales, "Freud, Filthy Lucre, and Undue Influence," *Review of Existential Psychology and Psychiatry*, vol. 23, nos. 1–3 (1997), p. 127.

[25] Ernest Jones, "Medical Career," in *The Life and Work of Sigmund Freud, Vol. 1: The Formative Years and the Great Discoveries, 1856–1900* (New York, NY: Basic Books, 1959), p. 61.

[26] Sigmund Freud, "Letter to C. G. Jung—December 6, 1906," in William McGuire (ed.), *The Freud/Jung Letters: The Correspondence Between Sigmund Freud and C. G. Jung*, trans. Ralph Manheim and R.F.C. Hull (Princeton, NJ: Princeton University Press, 1994), p. 12

[27] Mikkel Borch-Jacobsen and Sonu Shamdasani, "Policing the Past," in *The Freud Files: An Inquiry into the History of Psychoanalysis* (Cambridge, UK: Cambridge University Press, 2012), p. 292.

[28] Ibid., pp. 236-237.

[29] Sigmund Freud, "Letter to Martha Bernays—April 28, 1885," in Ernst L. Freud (ed.), *Letters of Sigmund Freud*, trans. Tania Stern and James Stern (New York, NY: Basic Books, 1975), pp. 140–41.

[30] Sigmund Freud, "Letter to Edward L. Bernays—August 10, 1929," in Ernst L. Freud (ed.), *Letters of Sigmund Freud*, trans. Tania Stern and James Stern (New York, NY: Basic Books, 1975), p. 391.

[31] John B. Watson, "Feed Me on Facts," *Saturday Review of Literature*, vol. 4, no. 47 (June 1928), p. 967.

[32] John B. Watson, quoted in Kerry W. Buckley, *Mechanical Man: John Broadus Watson and the Beginnings of Behaviorism* (New York, NY: Guilford Press, 1989), p. 182.

[33] Sigmund Freud, "Chapter Six," in *Leonardo Da Vinci: A Study in Psychosexuality*, trans. A. A. Brill (New York, NY: Vintage Books, 1947), p. 109.

[34] Sigmund Freud, "Letter to Arnold Zweig—May 31, 1936," in Ernst L. Freud (ed.), *Letters of Sigmund Freud*, trans. Tania Stern and James Stern (New York, NY: Basic Books, 1975), p. 430.

[35] Richard Webster, "From Caul to Cocaine," in *Why Freud Was Wrong: Sin, Science, and Psychoanalysis* (New York, NY: Basic Books, 1995), p. 34.

[36] Hans J. Eysenck, "Psycho-Babble and Pseudo-History," in *Decline and Fall of the Freudian Empire* (New York, NY: Penguin Books, 1991), p. 190.

[37] Philip Rieff, "The Therapeutic as Theologian: Jung's Psychology as a Language of Faith," in *The Triumph of the Therapeutic: Uses of Faith After Freud* (Chicago, IL: University of Chicago Press, 1987), p. 110.

[38] René Guénon, "Tradition and Traditionalism," in *The Reign of Quantity and the Signs of the Times*, trans. Lord Northbourne (Ghent, NY: Sophia Perennis, 2001), p. 208.

[39] David E. Stannard, "The Problem of Theory," in *Shrinking History: On Freud and the Failure of Psychohistory* (New York, NY: Oxford University Press, 1980), p. 116.

Chapter 5: The Deification of Freud and the Birth of the Freudian Myth of the Hero

[1] Sigmund Freud, quoted in Ernest Jones, "Personal Life," in *The Life and Work of Sigmund Freud, Vol. 1: The Formative Years and the Great Discoveries, 1856–1900* (New York, NY: Basic Books, 1959), p. 348.

[2] David Bakan, "Freud's Messianic Identification," in *Sigmund Freud and the Jewish Mystical Tradition* (London, UK: Free Association Books, 1990), p. 170.

[3] Siegfried Bernfeld, "Freud's Scientific Beginnings," *American Imago*, vol. 6, no. 3 (September 1949), p. 185.

[4] Sigmund Freud, "On the History of the Psychoanalytic Movement" (1914), in *The History of the Psychoanalytic Movement*, ed. Philip Rieff (New York, NY: Collier Books, 1963), p. 55.

[5] Helen Walker Puner, "See How It Grows," in *Freud: His Life and His Mind* (New York, NY: Howell, Soskin, 1947), p. 158.

[6] Peter J. Swales, "Freud, Filthy Lucre, and Undue Influence," *Review of Existential Psychology and Psychiatry*, vol. 23, Nos. 1–3 (1997), p. 130.

[7] Ernest Jones, "Non-Medical Applications of Psychoanalysis," in *The Life and Work of Sigmund Freud, Vol. 2: Years of Maturity, 1901–1919* (New York, NY: Basic Books, 1955), p. 366. "Freud's self-identification with Moses...in later years became very evident" (Ernest Jones, "The Beginning of International Recognition," in *The Life and Work of Sigmund Freud, Vol. 2: Years of Maturity, 1901–1919* [New York, NY: Basic Books, 1955], p. 33).

[8] Philip Rieff, "The Religion of the Fathers" (1959), in *The Jew of Culture: Freud, Moses, and Modernity*, eds. Arnold M. Eisen and Gideon Lewis-Kraus (Charlottesville, VA: University of Virginia Press, 2008), p. 60.

[9] Reuben Fine, "The Unconscious: Creativity, Language, and Communication," in *History of Psychoanalysis* (New York, NY: Jason Aronson, 1990), p. 266.

[10] Erich Fromm, "The Quasi-Political Character of the Psychoanalytic Movement," in *Sigmund Freud's Mission: An Analysis of His Personality and Influence* (New York, NY: Grove Press, 1963), p. 100.

[11] Peter J. Swales, "Freud, Filthy Lucre, and Undue Influence," *Review of Existential Psychology and Psychiatry*, vol. 23, nos. 1–3 (1997), p. 130.

[12] Sigmund Freud, "Letter to Alexander Lipschütz—August 12, 1931," in Ernst L. Freud (ed.), *Letters of Sigmund Freud*, trans. Tania and James Stern (New York, NY: Basic Books, 1975), p. 407.

[13] Peter Gay, "Defiance as Identity," in *Freud: A Life for Our Time* (New York, NY: Anchor Books, 1989), p. 604.

[14] Richard Webster, "'Freud, who was my Christ!'," in *Why Freud Was Wrong: Sin, Science, and Psychoanalysis* (New York, NY: Basic Books, 1995), p. 300.

[15] Helen Walker Puner, "See How It Grows," in *Freud: His Life and His Mind* (New York, NY: Howell, Soskin, 1947), pp. 147–48.

[16] Richard Webster, "Anna Freud: Daughter and Disciple," in *Why Freud Was Wrong: Sin, Science, and Psychoanalysis* (New York, NY: Basic Books, 1995), p. 433.

[17] Kurt R. Eissler, "Talent and Genius," in *Talent and Genius: The Fictitious Case of Tausk contra Freud* (New York, NY: Quadrangle Books, 1971), pp. 279–80.

[18] Hanns Sachs, "A Considerable Protuberance," in *Freud, Master and Friend* (Cambridge, MA: Harvard University Press, 1945), p. 91.

[19] James Strachey, "Sigmund Freud: A Sketch of His Life and Ideas," in Sigmund Freud, *On the History of the Psycho-Analytic Movement*, trans. Joan Riviere, ed. James Strachey (New York, NY: W. W. Norton & Company, 1989), pp. xxxviii-xxxix.

[20] Raymond Recouly, "A Visit to Freud," *Outlook* (September 5, 1923), p. 27.

[21] Sigmund Freud, quoted in Ernest Jones, "Character and Personality," in *The Life and Work of Sigmund Freud, Vol. 2: Years of Maturity, 1901–1919* (New York, NY: Basic Books, 1955), p. 415.

[22] Sigmund Freud, "Letter to Wilhelm Fliess—October 6, 1893," in *The Complete Letters of Sigmund Freud to Wilhelm Fliess, 1887–1904*, trans. and ed. Jeffrey Moussaieff Masson (Cambridge, MA: Belknap Press of Harvard University Press, 1985), p. 57.

[23] Sigmund Freud, "Letter to Karl Abraham—March 25, 1917," quoted in Ernest Jones, "Expositions," in *The Life and Work of Sigmund Freud, Vol. 2: Years of Maturity, 1901–1919* (New York, NY: Basic Books, 1955), p. 226.

[24] Ernest Jones, "Case Histories," in *The Life and Work of Sigmund Freud, Vol. 2: Years of Maturity, 1901–1919* (New York, NY: Basic Books, 1955), p. 257.

[25] Sigmund Freud, "If Moses was an Egyptian...." in *Moses and Monotheism*, trans. Katherine Jones (New York, NY: Vintage Books, 1967), p. 22.

[26] Titus Burckhardt, "Traditional Cosmology and Modern Science: Cosmologia Perennis," in *Mirror of the Intellect: Essays on Traditional Science and Sacred Art*, trans. and ed. William Stoddart (Albany, NY: State University of New York Press, 1987), pp. 25–26.

[27] René Guénon, "The Misdeeds of Psychoanalysis," in *The Reign of Quantity and the Signs of the Times*, trans. Lord Northbourne (Ghent, NY: Sophia Perennis, 2001), pp. 233–34.

[28] Mikkel Borch-Jacobsen and Sonu Shamdasani, "The Politics of Self-Analysis," in *The Freud Files: An Inquiry into the History of Psychoanalysis* (Cambridge, UK: Cambridge University Press, 2012), p. 49.

[29] Sigmund Freud, "Recommendations to Physicians Practicing Psycho-Analysis" (1912), in *The Standard Edition of the Complete Psychological Works of Sigmund Freud, Vol. 12*, trans. and ed. James Strachey (London, UK: Hogarth Press and the Institute of Psycho-Analysis, 1958), p. 116.

[30] Philip Rieff, "The Tactics of Interpretation," in *Freud: The Mind of the Moralist* (Chicago, IL: University of Chicago Press, 1979), p. 104.

[31] C. G. Jung, "Psychological Commentary," in *The Tibetan Book of the Dead*, ed. W. Y. Evans-Wentz (London, UK: Oxford University Press, 1968), p. xlix.

[32] Jacques Lacan, quoted in Bice Benvenuto, *Concerning the Rites of Psychoanalysis: Or the Villa of the Mysteries* (New York, NY: Routledge, 1994), p. 150.

[33] Philip Rieff, "Community and Therapy," in *The Triumph of the Therapeutic: Uses of Faith After Freud* (Chicago, IL: University of Chicago Press, 1987), p. 77. Regarding the meaning of "counter-initiation" see René Guénon, *The Reign of Quantity and the Signs of the Times*, trans. Lord Northbourne (Ghent, NY: Sophia Perennis, 2001); Charles Upton, *Vectors of the Counter-Initiation: The Course and Destiny of Inverted Spirituality* (San Rafael, CA: Sophia Perennis, 2012).

[34] Frithjof Schuon, "The Psychological Imposture," in *Survey of Metaphysics and Esoterism*, trans. Gustavo Polit (Bloomington, IN: World Wisdom Books, 1986), p. 195.

[35] Sigmund Freud, "On the History of the Psychoanalytic Movement" (1914), in *The History of the Psychoanalytic Movement*, ed. Philip Rieff (New York, NY: Collier Books, 1963), p. 72.

[36] Ibid., p. 42.

[37] Ibid., p. 41.

[38] Ibid., pp. 42–43.

[39] Ernest Jones, "The Breuer Period," in *The Life and Work of Sigmund Freud, vol. 1: The Formative Years and the Great Discoveries, 1856–1900* (New York, NY: Basic Books, 1959), pp. 221–22.

[40] C. G. Jung, "A Review of the Early Hypothesis" (1912), in *Critique of Psychoanalysis*, trans. R.F.C. Hull (Princeton, NJ: Princeton University Press, 1975), p. 6.

[41] Sigmund Freud, "On the History of the Psychoanalytic Movement" (1914), in *The History of the Psychoanalytic Movement*, ed. Philip Rieff (New York, NY: Collier Books, 1963), p. 42.

[42] Ibid., pp. 41–42.

[43] Sigmund Freud, "The Future Prospects of Psycho-Analytic Therapy" (1910), in *The Standard Edition of the Complete Psychological Works of Sigmund Freud, Vol. 11*, trans. and ed. James Strachey (London, UK: Hogarth Press and the Institute of Psycho-Analysis, 1957), p. 146.

[44] Sigmund Freud, "An Autobiographical Study" (1925 [1924]), in *An Autobiographical Study*, trans. and ed. James Strachey (New York, NY: W. W. Norton & Company, 1989), p. 55.

[45] Frank J. Sulloway, "The Myth of the Hero in the Psychoanalytic Movement," in *Freud, Biologist of the Mind: Beyond the Psychoanalytic Legend* (New York, NY: Basic Books, 1979), p. 446.

[46] Henri F. Ellenberger, "Sigmund Freud and Psychoanalysis," in *The Discovery of the Unconscious: The History and Evolution of Dynamic Psychiatry* (New York, NY: Basic Books, 1970), pp. 547–48.

[47] Richard Noll, "The Problem of the Historical Jung," in *The Jung Cult: Origins of a Charismatic Movement* (Princeton, NJ: Princeton University Press, 1994), p. 18.

[48] Sigmund Freud, "Letter to Otto Rank—August 18, 1912," quoted in Peter Gay, "Psychoanalytic Politics," in *Freud: A Life for Our Time* (New York, NY: Anchor Books, 1989), p. 231.

[49] Ernest Jones, "Retrospect," in *The Life and Work of Sigmund Freud, Vol. 3: The Last Phase, 1919–1939* (New York, NY: Basic Books, 1957), p. 441.

Chapter 6: The Making of Psychological Man: From *Imago Dei* to *Homo Naturalis*

[1] Philip Rieff, "Preface to the Third Edition," in *Freud: The Mind of the Moralist* (Chicago, IL: University of Chicago Press, 1979), p. xxiii.

[2] Richard LaPiere, "Preface," to *The Freudian Ethic* (New York, NY: Duell, Sloan and Pearce, 1959), p. vii.

[3] Rollo May, quoted in Maurice Friedman, *Contemporary Psychology: Revealing and Obscuring the Human* (Pittsburgh, PA: Duquesne University Press, 1984), p. 4.

[4] Eric Fromm, "Freud's Model of Man and Its Social Determinants," in *The Crisis of Psychoanalysis* (Greenwich, CT: Fawcett, 1970), p. 44.

[5] Jeffrey B. Rubin, "A Well-Lived Life: Psychoanalytic and Buddhist Contributions," in *Psychoanalysis and Buddhism: An Unfolding Dialogue*, ed. Jeremy D. Safran (Somerville, MA: Wisdom Publications, 2003), p. 395.

[6] Eric Fromm, "Mental Health and Society," in *The Sane Society* (Greenwich, CT: Fawcett, 1955), p. 67.

[7] Gai Eaton, "Introduction," to *King of the Castle: Choice and Responsibility in the Modern World* (Cambridge, UK: Islamic Texts Society, 1990), p. 8.

[8] Irving Yalom, "Comparative Value of the Therapeutic Factors: The Client's View," in *The Theory and Practice of Group Psychotherapy* (New York, NY: Basic Books, 1975), p. 85.

[9] Jacob Needleman, "Freud and Human Possibility," in *Lost Christianity* (Garden City, NY: Doubleday, 1980), p. 60.

[10] Christopher Lasch, "The Awareness Movement and the Social Invasion of the Self," in *The Culture of Narcissism: American Life in an Age of Diminishing Expectations* (New York, NY: W. W. Norton & Company, 1978), p. 13.

[11] Meister Eckhart, "Selections from the Commentaries on Genesis," in *Meister Eckhart: The Essential Sermons, Commentaries, Treatises, and Defense*, trans. Edmund Colledge, O.S.A. and Bernard McGinn (Mahwah, NJ: Paulist Press, 1981), p. 106.

[12] Meister Eckhart, "Selected Sermons," in *Meister Eckhart: The Essential Sermons, Commentaries, Treatises, and Defense*, trans. Edmund Colledge, O.S.A. and Bernard McGinn (Mahwah, NJ: Paulist Press, 1981), p. 184.

[13] Karl Menninger, "The Motives," in *Man Against Himself* (New York, NY: Harcourt, Brace and World, 1938), p. 17.

[14] Victor Tausk, quoted in *Minutes of the Vienna Psychoanalytic Society, Vol. II: 1908–1910*, trans. Margarethe Nunberg, eds. Herman Nunberg and Ernst Federn (New York, NY: International Universities Press, 1967), p. 467.

[15] Charles Darwin, "Recapitulation and Conclusion," in *The Origin of Species* (London, UK: John Murray, 1866), p. 576; "The implications of evolutionary theory for [modern] psychology have been profound" (L. S. Hearnshaw, *The Shaping of Modern Psychology* [London, UK: Routledge, 1989], p. 115); see also James Rowland Angell, "The Influence of Darwin on Psychology," *Psychological Review*, vol. 16, no. 3 (May 1909), pp. 152–69.

[16] Sigmund Freud, "Letter to Georg Groddeck—June 5, 1917," in Ernst L. Freud (ed.), *Letters of Sigmund Freud*, trans. Tania Stern and James Stern (New York, NY: Basic Books, 1975), p. 317.

[17] C. G. Jung, "Student Years," in *Memories, Dreams, Reflections*, trans. Richard Winston and Clara Winston, ed. Aniela Jaffé (New York, NY: Vintage Books, 1965), p. 100.

[18] Frithjof Schuon, "Survey of Integral Anthropology," in *To Have a Center* (Bloomington, IN: World Wisdom Books, 1990), p. 39.

[19] Sigmund Freud, "Chapter Three," in *Civilization and Its Discontents*, trans. and ed. James Strachey (New York, NY: W. W. Norton & Company, 1989), pp. 43–45.

[20] In example, Rūmī is speaking here to the original Unity underlying all phenomena and not *evolutionism*: "I died as mineral and became a plant,/I died as plant and rose to animal,/I died as animal and I was a man./Why should I fear? When was I less by dying?/Yet once more I shall die as man, to soar\With angels blest; but even from angelhood/I must pass on: all except God doth perish./When I have sacrificed my angel soul,/I shall become what no mind e'er conceived./Oh, let me not exist! For Non-existence/Proclaims in organ tones, 'To Him we shall return'" (Rūmī, quoted in Reynold A. Nicholson, *Rūmī: Poet and Mystic* [London, UK: George Allen and Unwin, 1978], p. 103).

See also Wolfgang Smith, *Theistic Evolution: The Teilhardian Heresy* (Tacoma, WA: Angelico Press/Sophia Perennis, 2012).

[21] Śri Ramana Maharshi, quoted in B. Sanjiva Rao, "Bhagavan Sri Ramana and the Modern Age," in *Golden Jubilee Souvenir* (Tiruvannamalai: Sri Ramanasramam, 1995), p. 87.

[22] Ananda K. Coomaraswamy, "Letter to Anonymous Person—Date Unknown," in *Selected Letters of Ananda K. Coomaraswamy*, eds. Alvin Moore, Jr. and Rama P. Coomaraswamy (Oxford, UK: Oxford University Press, 1988), p. 211.

[23] E. F. Schumacher, "The Four Fields of Knowledge: 4," in *A Guide for the Perplexed* (New York, NY: Harper & Row, 1977), pp. 114–15. "We are told dogmatically that evolution is an established fact; but we are never told who has established it, and by what means. We are told, often enough, that the doctrine is founded upon evidence, and that indeed this evidence 'is hence-forward above all verification, as well as being immune from any subsequent contradiction by experience'; but we are left entirely in the dark on the crucial question wherein, precisely, this evidence consists" (Wolfgang Smith, "Evolution: A Closer Look," in *Teilhardism and the New Religion: A Thorough Analysis of the Teachings of Pierre Teilhard de Chardin* [Rockford, IL: Tan Books and Publishers, 1988], p. 2). "Darwinism is not in truth a scientific theory, but is simply an ideological postulate masquerding in scientific garb" (Wolfgang Smith, "Science and Myth," in *Science and Myth: What We Are Never Told* [San Rafael, CA: Sophia Perennis, 2010], p. 11).

[24] Frithjof Schuon, "The Message of the Human Body," in *From the Divine to the Human*, trans. Gustavo Polit and Deborah Lambert (Bloomington, IN: World Wisdom Books, 1982), p. 87.

[25] Jules H. Masserman, "Sexuality Re-Evaluated," *Canadian Journal of Psychiatry*, vol. 11, no. 5 (October 1966), p. 379.

[26] Ibid.

[27] Jacques Lacan, "The Word Brings Jouissance," in *The Triumph of Religion*, trans. Bruce Fink (Malden, MA: Polity, 2013), p. 74.

[28] Jean-Claude Larchet, "The Pathology of Fallen Man," in *Therapy of Spiritual Illnesses, Vol 1: An Introduction to the Ascetic Tradition of the Orthodox Church*, trans. Fr. Kilian Sprecher (Montréal: Alexander Press, 2012), p. 77.

[29] Saint Irenaeus, quoted in Frithjof Schuon, "The Path," in *Understanding Islam* (Bloomington, IN: World Wisdom, 1998), p. 139.

[30] Saint Mark the Ascetic, "Letter to Nicolas the Solitary," in *The Philokalia, Vol. 1: The Complete Text; Compiled by St. Nikodimos of the Holy Mountain and St. Makarios of Corinth*, trans. and ed. G.E.H. Palmer, Philip Sherrard, and Kallistos Ware (London, UK: Faber and Faber, 1983), p. 155.

[31] Frithjof Schuon, "Gnosis, Language of the Self," in *Gnosis: Divine Wisdom*, trans. G.E.H. Palmer (Bedfont, Middlesex, UK: Perennial Books, 1990), p. 71.

[32] Frithjof Schuon, "The Path," in *Understanding Islam* (Bloomington, IN: World Wisdom, 1998), p. 139.

[33] Frithjof Schuon, "Māyā," in *Light on the Ancient Worlds*, trans. Lord Northbourne (Bloomington, IN: World Wisdom Books, 1984), p. 96.

[34] Shankara, quoted in Reza Shah-Kazemi, *Paths to Transcendence: According to Shankara, Ibn Arabi, and Meister Eckhart* (Bloomington, IN: World Wisdom, 2006), p. 207.

[35] Sigmund Freud, "Letter to Richard S. Dyer-Bennet—December 9, 1928," in Ernst L. Freud (ed.), *Letters of Sigmund Freud*, trans. Tania and James Stern (New York, NY: Basic Books, 1975), p. 384.

[36] Leo Schaya, "Creation, the Image of God," in *The Universal Meaning of the Kabbalah*, trans. Nancy Pearson (Baltimore, MD: Penguin Books, 1974), p. 70.

[37] Sigmund Freud, "Thoughts for the Times on War and Death" (1915), in *The Standard Edition of the Complete Psychological Works of Sigmund Freud, Vol. 14*, trans. and ed. James Strachey (London, UK: Hogarth Press and the Institute of Psycho-Analysis, 1953), p. 281. "[I]t [the sexual instinct] is, in the first place, the deepest and most volcanic of human impulses..." (Havelock Ellis, "The Immense Part in Life Played by Transmuted Auto-Erotic Phenomena," in *Studies in the Psychology of Sex: The Evolution of Modesty, the Phenomena of Sexual Periodicity Auto-Erotism* [Philadelphia, PA: F. A. Davis Company, 1904], p. 203).

[38] Gregory of Nyssa, quoted in Jean-Claude Larchet, "Lust," in *Therapy of Spiritual Illnesses, Vol 1: An Introduction to the Ascetic Tradition of the Orthodox Church*, trans. Fr. Kilian Sprecher (Montréal: Alexander Press, 2012), p. 163.

[39] Sigmund Freud, "The Dissection of the Psychical Personality" (1933 [1932]), in *New Introductory Lectures on Psycho-Analysis*, trans. and ed. James Strachey (New York, NY: W. W. Norton & Company, 1989), pp. 91–92.

[40] Sigmund Freud, "The Clinical Picture" (1905 [1901]), in *Dora: An Analysis of a Case of Hysteria*, ed. Philip Rieff (New York, NY: Touchstone, 1997), p. 69

[41] Sigmund Freud, "Chapter Two," in *The Future of an Illusion*, trans. and ed. James Strachey (New York, NY: W. W. Norton & Company, 1989), p. 13.

[42] Joseph Jastrow, "Metapsychology," in *Freud: His Dream and Sex Theories* (Cleveland, OH: World Publishing Company, 1948), p. 89.

[43] Sigmund Freud, "Chapter Five," in *Civilization and Its Discontents*, trans. and ed. James Strachey (New York, NY: W. W. Norton & Company, 1989), pp. 67–69.

[44] Sigmund Freud, "Letter to Oskar Pfister—September 10, 1918," in *Psychoanalysis and Faith: The Letters of Sigmund Freud and Oskar Pfister*, trans. Eric Mosbacher, eds. Heinrich Meng and Ernst L. Freud (New York, NY: Basic Books, 1963), p. 61.

[45] Sigmund Freud, "Letter to Lou Andreas-Salomé—July 30, 1915," in Ernst L. Freud (ed.), *Letters of Sigmund Freud*, trans. Tania and James Stern (New York, NY: Basic Books, 1975), p. 311.

[46] Sigmund Freud, "Chapter Two," in *Civilization and Its Discontents*, trans. and ed. James Strachey (New York, NY: W. W. Norton & Company, 1989), p. 25.

[47] C. G. Jung, "Epilogue," in *Essays on Contemporary Events: The Psychology of Nazism*, trans. R.F.C. Hull (Princeton, NJ: Princeton University Press, 1989), p. 78.

[48] C. G. Jung, "Letter to Sabina Spielrein—August 12, 1908," quoted in C .G. Jung, "The Letters of C. G. Jung to Sabina Spielrein," *Journal of Analytical Psychology*, vol. 46, no. 1 (January 2001), p. 175.

[49] Sigmund Freud, "Chapter Seven," in *Civilization and Its Discontents*, trans. and ed. James Strachey (New York, NY: W. W. Norton & Company, 1989), p. 87.

[50] St. Isaac the Syrian, quoted in Jean-Claude Larchet, "Man's Original Health," in *Therapy of Spiritual Illnesses, Vol 1: An Introduction to the Ascetic Tradition of the Orthodox Church*, trans. Fr. Kilian Sprecher (Montréal: Alexander Press, 2012), p. 35.

[51] Titus Burckhardt, "The Branches of the Doctrine," in *Introduction to Sufi Doctrine*, trans. D. M. Matheson (Bloomington, IN: World Wisdom, 2008), pp. 28–29.

[52] Ibid., p. 29.

[53] Ibid.

[54] Sigmund Freud, "Beyond the Pleasure Principle" (1920), in *Beyond the Pleasure Principle*, trans. and ed. James Strachey (New York, NY: W. W. Norton & Company, 1989), p. 46.

[55] Sigmund Freud, "The Economic Problem in Masochism" (1924), in *General Psychological Theory: Papers on Metapsychology*, ed. Philip Rieff (New York, NY: Touchstone, 2008), pp. 192–93.

[56] Erich Fromm, "Freud's Instinct Theory and Its Critique," in *Greatness and Limitations of Freud's Thought* (New York, NY: Mentor Books, 1981), p. 114.

[57] Erich Fromm, "Appendix: Freud's Theory of Aggressiveness and Destructiveness," in *The Anatomy of Human Destructiveness* (New York, NY: Holt, Rinehart and Winston, 1974), p. 453.

[58] Sigmund Freud, "The Psychical Apparatus and the External World" (1940 [1938]), in *An Outline of Psycho-Analysis*, trans. and ed. James Strachey (New York, NY: W. W. Norton & Company, 1989), p. 85.

[59] Arthur Osborne, "The Death Wish," in *Be Still, It Is the Wind That Sings* (Tiruvannamalai, India: Sri Ramanasramam, 2003), p. 419.

[60] Rūmī, quoted in Seyyed Hossein Nasr, *The Garden of Truth: The Vision and Promise of Sufism, Islam's Mystical Tradition* (New York, NY: HarperCollins, 2008), p. 23.

[61] Meister Eckhart, "The Feast of Martyrs," in *Meister Eckhart, Vol. 1*, trans. C. de B. Evans, ed. Franz Pfeiffer (London, UK: John M. Watkins, 1924), p. 205.

[62] Quoted in Marco Pallis, "Is There Room for 'Grace' in Buddhism?" in *A Buddhist Spectrum: Contributions to Buddhist-Christian Dialogue* (Bloomington, IN: World Wisdom, 2003), pp. 68–69.

[63] Sigmund Freud, quoted in Bruno Goetz, "That is all I have to Say about Freud: Bruno Goetz's Reminiscences of Sigmund Freud," *International Review of Psycho-Analysis*, vol. 2 (1975), p 141.

[64] Sigmund Freud, "The Sexual Aberrations" (1905), in *The Basic Writings of Sigmund Freud*, trans. and ed. A. A. Brill (New York, NY: Modern Library, 1938), p. 2.

[65] Sigmund Freud, "Letter to Wilhelm Fliess—August 7, 1901," in Marie Bonaparte, Anna Freud and Ernst Kris (eds.), *The Origins of Psychoanalysis: Letters to Wilhelm Fliess, Drafts and Notes: 1887-1902*, trans. Eric Mosbacher and James Strachey (New York, NY: Basic Books, 1954), p. 334. "Human Bisexuality." (Sigmund Freud, "Letter to Wilhelm Fliess—August 7, 1901," in *The Complete Letters of Sigmund Freud to Wilhelm Fliess, 1887–1904*, trans. and ed. Jeffrey Moussaieff Masson [Cambridge, MA: Belknap Press of Harvard University Press, 1985], p. 448).

[66] Sigmund Freud, "The Sexual Aberrations" (1905), in *The Basic Writings of Sigmund Freud*, trans. and ed. A. A. Brill (New York, NY: Modern Library, 1938), p. 558.

[67] Sigmund Freud, "Femininity" (1933 [1932]), in *New Introductory Lectures on Psycho-Analysis*, trans. and ed. James Strachey (New York, NY: W. W. Norton & Company, 1989), p. 141.

[68] Sigmund Freud, "Letter to Wilhelm Fliess—December 6, 1896," in *The Complete Letters of Sigmund Freud to Wilhelm Fliess, 1887–1904*, trans. and ed. Jeffrey Moussaieff Masson (Cambridge, MA: Belknap Press of Harvard University Press, 1985), p. 212.

[69] Sigmund Freud, "Chapter Four," in *Civilization and Its Discontents*, trans. and ed. James Strachey (New York, NY: W. W. Norton & Company, 1989), p. 62.

[70] Philip Sherrard, "Towards a Theology of Sexual Love," in *Christianity and Eros: Essays on the Theme of Sexual Love* (Limni, Evia, Greece: Denise Harvey, 1995), p. 62.

[71] Kathleen Raine, *'What is Man?'* (Ipswich, UK: Golgonooza Press, 1980), p. 4.

[72] Frithjof Schuon, "The Message of the Human Body," in *From the Divine to the Human*, trans. Gustavo Polit and Deborah Lambert (Bloomington, IN: World Wisdom Books, 1982), p. 88.

[73] Kathleen Raine, *'What is Man?'* (Ipswich, UK: Golgonooza Press, 1980), p. 17.

[74] Abraham H. Maslow, quoted in Edward Hoffman, *The Right To Be Human: A Biography of Abraham Maslow* (Los Angeles, CA: Jeremy P. Tarcher, 1988), p. 236.

[75] Frithjof Schuon, "Concerning the Love of God," in *Logic and Transcendence*, trans. Peter N. Townsend (London, UK: Perennial Books, 1984), p. 195.

[76] Seyyed Hossein Nasr, "Man, Pontifical and Promethean," in *Knowledge and the Sacred* (Albany, NY: State University of New York Press, 1989), p. 183.

[77] Quoted in *Zohar: The Book of Enlightenment*, trans. Daniel Chanan Matt (Mahwah, NJ: Paulist Press, 1983), p. 56.

[78] Sigmund Freud, "Letter to Martha Bernays—August 29, 1883," in Ernst L. Freud (ed.), *Letters of Sigmund Freud*, trans. Tania Stern and James Stern (New York, NY: Basic Books, 1975), p. 50.

[79] Seyyed Hossein Nasr, "Modern Western Philosophy and Schools of Thought," in *A Young Muslim's Guide to the Modern World* (Chicago, IL: Kazi Publications, 1994), p. 174.

[80] Jean-Claude Larchet, "Man's Original Health," in *Therapy of Spiritual Illnesses, Vol 1: An Introduction to the Ascetic Tradition of the Orthodox Church*, trans. Fr. Kilian Sprecher (Montréal: Alexander Press, 2012), p. 21.

[81] Sigmund Freud, "Anxiety and Instinctual Life" (1933 [1932]), in *New Introductory Lectures on Psycho-Analysis*, trans. and ed. James Strachey (New York, NY: W. W. Norton & Company, 1989), p. 131.

[82] Clinias, "Laws—Book I," in *The Collected Dialogues of Plato: Including the Letters*, eds. Edith Hamilton and Huntington Cairns (Princeton, NJ: Princeton University Press, 1980), p. 1228.

[83] B. F. Skinner, "Chapter Fourteen," in *Walden Two* (New York, NY: Macmillan, 1962), p. 104.

[84] Frithjof Schuon, "Forward," to *The Transfiguration of Man* (Bloomington, IN: World Wisdom Books, 1995), p. vii.

[85] Karl Kraus, quoted in Thomas Szasz, "On Psychoanalysis and Psychology," in *Karl Kraus and the Soul-Doctors: A Pioneer Critic and His Criticism of Psychiatry and Psychoanalysis* (Baton Rouge, LA: Louisiana State University Press, 1976), p. 105.

[86] Philip Rieff, "Introductory: Toward a Theory of Culture," in *The Triumph of the Therapeutic: Uses of Faith After Freud* (Chicago, IL: University of Chicago Press, 1987), pp. 24–25.

[87] Richard LaPiere, "The Freudian Ethic," in *The Freudian Ethic* (New York, NY: Duell, Sloan and Pearce, 1959), p. 60.

[88] Nisargadatta Maharaj, "Awareness is Free," in *I Am That: Talks with Sri Nisargadatta Maharaj*, trans. Maurice Frydman, ed. Sudhakar S. Dikshit (Durham, NC: Acorn Press, 1999), p. 226.

[89] Philip Rieff, "The Analytic Attitude: Freud's Legacy and Its Inheritors," in *The Triumph of the Therapeutic: Uses of Faith After Freud* (Chicago, IL: University of Chicago Press, 1987), p. 39.

⁹⁰ St. Augustine of Hippo, "Book One," in *The Confessions of Saint Augustine*, trans. E. B. Pusey (Oxford, UK: John Henry Parker, 1853), p. 1.

Chapter 7: Psychologism: The Reduction of Reality to Psychological Criteria

[1] Ira Progoff, "Sigmund Freud and the Foundations of Depth Psychology," in *The Death and Rebirth of Psychology: An Integrative Evaluation of Freud, Adler, Jung and Rank and the Impact of Their Insights on Modern Man* (New York, NY: McGraw-Hill, 1969), p. 45.

[2] Sigmund Freud, "Chapter Six," in *The Future of an Illusion*, trans. and ed. James Strachey (New York, NY: W. W. Norton & Company, 1989), p. 38.

[3] Harry Oldmeadow, "The Not-So-Close Encounters of Western Psychology and Eastern Spirituality," in *Journeys East: 20th Century Western Encounters with Eastern Traditions* (Bloomington, IN: World Wisdom, 2004), p. 314.

[4] See René Guénon, "Fundamental Distinction Between the 'Self' and the 'Ego,'" in *Man and His Becoming According to the Vedanta*, trans. Richard C. Nicholson (New York, NY: Noonday Press, 1958), p. 28; see also Martin Lings, "Intellect and Reason," in *Ancient Beliefs and Modern Superstitions* (Cambridge, UK: Archetype, 2001), pp. 51–60.

[5] Seyyed Hossein Nasr, "The Western World and its Challenges to Islam," in *Islam and the Plight of Modern Man, Revised and Enlarged Edition* (Chicago, IL: ABC International Group, 2001), p. 215.

[6] C. G. Jung, "In Memory of Sigmund Freud" (1939), in *The Collected Works of C. G. Jung, Vol. 15: The Spirit in Man, Art and Literature*, trans. R.F.C. Hull (Princeton, NJ: Princeton University Press, 1971), p. 47. "Freud's psychological system suffers from the main error which was part of the mechanistic materialism" (Erich Fromm, "Survival and Trans-survival Needs," in *The Revolution of Hope: Toward a Humanized Technology* [New York, NY: Bantam Books, 1971], p. 71).

[7] Mark Perry, "Capital Punishment," in *The Mystery of Individuality: Grandeur and Delusion of the Human Condition* (Bloomington, IN: World Wisdom, 2012), p. 187.

[8] Jean Borella, "From Hegel to Freud: The Agony of the Sacred," in *The Crisis of Religious Symbolism and Symbolism & Reality*, trans. G. John Champoux (Kettering, OH: Angelico Press/Sophia Perennis, 2016), p. 165.

[9] Otto Rank, "Dream and Reality," in *Psychology and the Soul: A study of the Origin, Conceptual Evolution, and Nature of the Soul*, trans. Gregory C. Richter and E. James Lieberman (Baltimore, MD: Johns Hopkins University Press, 1998), p. 94.

[10] Ernest Jones, "Freud's Theory of the Mind," in The Life and Work of Sigmund Freud, vol. 1: The Formative Years and the Great Discoveries, 1856–1900 (New York, NY: Basic Books, 1959), p. 368.

[11] Otto Rank, "Introduction: Self-Knowledge and Human Nature," in *Psychology and the Soul: A study of the Origin, Conceptual Evolution, and Nature of the Soul*, trans. Gregory C. Richter and E. James Lieberman (Baltimore, MD: Johns Hopkins University Press, 1998), p. 3.

[12] Jean Borella, "Freud and the Inversion of the Sacred," in *The Crisis of Religious Symbolism and Symbolism & Reality*, trans. G. John Champoux (Kettering, OH: Angelico Press/Sophia Perennis, 2016), p. 194.

[13] Otto Rank, "Introduction: Self-Knowledge and Human Nature," in *Psychology and the Soul: A study of the Origin, Conceptual Evolution, and Nature of the Soul*, trans. Gregory C. Richter and E. James Lieberman (Baltimore, MD: Johns Hopkins University Press, 1998), p. 3.

[14] Ibid., p. 1.

[15] Philip Rieff, "In Defense of the Analytic Attitude," in *The Triumph of the Therapeutic: Uses of Faith After Freud* (Chicago, IL: University of Chicago Press, 1987), p. 81.

[16] Frithjof Schuon, "The Psychological Imposture," in *Survey of Metaphysics and Esoterism*, trans. Gustavo Polit (Bloomington, IN: World Wisdom Books, 1986), p. 195.

[17] Titus Burckhardt, "Traditional Cosmology and Modern Science: Modern Psychology," in *Mirror of the Intellect: Essays on Traditional Science and Sacred Art*, trans. and ed. William Stoddart (Albany, NY: State University of New York Press, 1987), p. 50.

[18] Titus Burckhardt, "Traditional Cosmology and Modern Science: Modern Psychology," in *Mirror of the Intellect: Essays on Traditional Science and Sacred Art*, trans. and ed. William Stoddart (Albany, NY: State University of New York Press, 1987), p. 47.

[19] C. G. Jung, "Some Crucial Points in Psychoanalysis: A Correspondence between Dr. Jung and Dr. Loÿ," (1914) in *Critique of Psychoanalysis*, trans. R.F.C. Hull (Princeton, NJ: Princeton University Press, 1975), p. 189.

[20] Sigmund Freud, "The Technique of Psycho-Analysis" (1940 [1938]), in *An Outline of Psycho-Analysis*, trans. and ed. James Strachey (New York, NY: W. W. Norton & Company, 1989), p. 52.

[21] Sigmund Freud, "The Future Prospects of Psycho-Analytic Therapy" (1910), in *The Standard Edition of the Complete Psychological Works of Sigmund Freud, Vol. 11*, trans. and ed. James Strachey (London, UK: Hogarth Press and the Institute of Psycho-Analysis, 1956), p. 286.

[22] Sigmund Freud, "The Technique of Psycho-Analysis" (1940 [1938]), in *An Outline of Psycho-Analysis*, trans. and ed. James Strachey (New York, NY: W. W. Norton & Company, 1989), p. 53.

[23] Sigmund Freud, "Analytic Therapy," in *Introductory Lectures on Psychoanalysis*, trans. and ed. James Strachey (New York, NY: W. W. Norton & Company, 1977), p. 448.

24 Sigmund Freud, "The Future Prospects of Psycho-Analytic Therapy" (1910), in *The Standard Edition of the Complete Psychological Works of Sigmund Freud, Vol. 11*, trans. and ed. James Strachey (London, UK: Hogarth Press and the Institute of Psycho-Analysis, 1956), pp. 141–42.

25 Wolfgang Smith, "The Ego and the Beast," in *Cosmos & Transcendence: Breaking Through the Barrier of Scientistic Belief* (Peru, IL: Sherwood Sugden & Company, 1990), p. 108.

26 Andrew Salter, "Analysis Terminable and Interminable," in *The Case Against Psychoanalysis* (New York, NY: Citadel Press, 1963), p. 124.

27 Gail Kennedy, "Psychoanalysis: Protoscience and Metapsychology," in *Psychoanalysis, Scientific Method, and Philosophy*, ed. Sidney Hook (New York, NY: New York University Press, 1964), p. 274.

28 Frithjof Schuon, "Understanding Esoterism," in *Esoterism as Principle and as Way*, trans. William Stoddart (Bedfont, Middlesex, UK: Perennial Books, 1981), p. 32.

29 Pope Pius XII, "On Psychotherapy and Religion: An Address of His Holiness Pope Pius XII to the Fifth International Congress on Psychotherapy and Clinical Psychology," April 13, 1953 (Washington, DC: National Catholic Welfare Conference, 1953), p. 4.

30 Hans Küng, "Critique of the Critique," in *Freud and the Problem of God*, trans. Edward Quinn (New Haven, CT: Yale University Press, 1979), p. 101.

31 Sigmund Freud, "Psychical Qualities" (1940 [1938]), in *An Outline of Psycho-Analysis*, trans. and ed. James Strachey (New York, NY: W. W. Norton & Company, 1989), p. 31.

32 C. G. Jung, "The Problem of the Attitude-Type," in *Two Essays on Analytical Psychology*, trans. R.F.C. Hull (New York, NY: Meridian, 1956), p. 56.

33 Erich Fromm, "Freud and Jung," in *Psychoanalysis and Religion* (New Haven, CT: Yale University Press, 1974), p. 20.

34 C. G. Jung, "Dream-Analysis in Its Practical Application," in *Modern Man in Search of a Soul*, trans. W. S. Dell and Cary F. Baynes (New York, NY: Harcourt, Brace & World, 1933), p. 17.

35 C. G. Jung, "Late Thoughts," in *Memories, Dreams, Reflections*, trans. Richard Winston and Clara Winston, ed. Aniela Jaffé (New York, NY: Vintage Books, 1965), pp. 350–52.

36 C. G. Jung, "Psychological Commentary," in *The Tibetan Book of the Dead*, ed. W. Y. Evans-Wentz (London, UK: Oxford University Press, 1968), p. xxxviii.

37 C. G. Jung, "Freud and Jung—Contrasts," in *Modern Man in Search of a Soul*, trans. W. S. Dell and Cary F. Baynes (New York, NY: Harcourt, Brace & World, 1933), p. 118.

38 Sri Anirvan, quoted in Lizelle Reymond, "Emotions," in *To Live Within*, trans. Nancy Pearson and Stanley Spiegelberg (New York, NY: Penguin Books, 1973), pp. 204–7.

[39] Frithjof Schuon, "The Psychological Imposture," in *Survey of Metaphysics and Esoterism*, trans. Gustavo Polit (Bloomington, IN: World Wisdom Books, 1986), pp. 196–97.

[40] Wolfgang Smith, "The Ego and the Beast," in *Cosmos & Transcendence: Breaking Through the Barrier of Scientistic Belief* (Peru, IL: Sherwood Sugden & Company, 1990), p. 109.

[41] Ken Wilber, "Freud and Buddha," in *A Brief History of Everything* (Boston, MA: Shambhala, 1996), p. 155.

[42] Frithjof Schuon, "No Activity Without Truth," in *The Betrayal of Tradition: Essays on the Spiritual Crisis of Modernity*, ed. Harry Oldmeadow (Bloomington, IN: World Wisdom, 2005), pp. 11–12.

[43] Charles Brenner, "Two Fundamental Hypotheses," in *An Elementary Textbook of Psychoanalysis* (New York, NY: Anchor Books, 1974), p. 2.

[44] Sigmund Freud, "Determinism, Belief in Chance and Superstition—Some Points of View" (1901), in *The Psychopathology of Everyday Life*, trans. and ed. James Strachey (New York, NY: W. W. Norton & Company, 1989), p. 324.

[45] Jacob Needleman, "Psychotherapy and the Sacred," in *A Sense of the Cosmos: The Encounter of Modern Science and Ancient Truth* (New York, NY: E. P. Dutton and Company, 1976), p. 116.

[46] Sigmund Freud, "Letter to Wilhelm Fliess—September 21, 1897," in *The Complete Letters of Sigmund Freud to Wilhelm Fliess, 1887–1904*, trans. and ed. Jeffrey Moussaieff Masson (Cambridge, MA: Belknap Press of Harvard University Press, 1985), p. 264.

[47] Karl Popper, "Science: Conjectures and Refutations," in *Conjectures and Refutations: The Growth of Scientific Knowledge* (New York, NY: Routledge, 2002), p. 49.

[48] Sigmund Freud, "Letter to Wilhelm Fliess—September 21, 1897," in *The Complete Letters of Sigmund Freud to Wilhelm Fliess, 1887–1904*, trans. and ed. Jeffrey Moussaieff Masson (Cambridge, MA: Belknap Press of Harvard University Press, 1985), p. 265.

[49] Sigmund Freud, "Explanations, Applications and Orientations" (1933 [1932]), in *New Introductory Lectures on Psycho-Analysis*, trans. and ed. James Strachey (New York, NY: W. W. Norton & Company, 1989), p. 175.

[50] Sigmund Freud, "The Future Prospects of Psycho-Analytic Therapy" (1910), in *The Standard Edition of the Complete Psychological Works of Sigmund Freud, Vol. 11*, trans. and ed. James Strachey (London, UK: Hogarth Press and the Institute of Psycho-Analysis, 1957), p. 145. Alternatively translated as: "we have noticed that every analyst's achievement is limited by what his own complexes and resistances permit" (Sigmund Freud, "The Future Prospects of Psychoanalytic Therapy" (1910), in *Therapy and Technique*, ed. Philip Rieff [New York, NY: Collier Books, 1963], p. 81).

[51] C. G. Jung, "Introduction to Kranefeldt's 'Secret Ways of the Mind'" (1930), in *Critique of Psychoanalysis*, trans. R.F.C. Hull (Princeton, NJ: Princeton University Press, 1975), p. 217.

[52] Sigmund Freud, "The Dissection of the Psychical Personality" (1933 [1932]), in *New Introductory Lectures on Psycho-Analysis*, trans. and ed. James Strachey (New York, NY: W. W. Norton & Company, 1989), p. 85.

[53] C. G. Jung, "The Stages of Life," in *Modern Man in Search of a Soul*, trans. W. S. Dell and Cary F. Baynes (New York, NY: Harcourt, Brace & World, 1933), p. 101.

[54] C. G. Jung, "The Mana-Personality," in *Two Essays on Analytical Psychology*, trans. R.F.C. Hull (New York, NY: Meridian, 1956), p. 244.

[55] Pope Pius XII, "On Psychotherapy and Religion: An Address of His Holiness Pope Pius XII to the Fifth International Congress on Psychotherapy and Clinical Psychology," April 13, 1953 (Washington, DC: National Catholic Welfare Conference, 1953), p. 8.

Chapter 8: Freudianism: The Counter-Religion to Replace Sacred Tradition

[1] Philip Rieff, "The Religion of the Fathers," in *Freud: The Mind of the Moralist* (Chicago, IL: University of Chicago Press, 1979), p. 257.

[2] Ernest Jones, "The Choice of Profession," in *The Life and Work of Sigmund Freud, Vol. 1: The Formative Years and the Great Discoveries, 1856–1900* (New York, NY: Basic Books, 1959), p. 34.

[3] Peter Homans, "Introduction," to *Jung in Context: Modernity and the Making of a Psychology* (Chicago, IL: University of Chicago Press, 1979), pp. 8–9.

[4] Whitall N. Perry, "The Revival of Interest in Tradition," in *The Unanimous Tradition: Essays on the Essential Unity of All Religions*, ed. Ranjit Fernando (Colombo: Sri Lanka Institute of Traditional Studies, 1999), p. 4. See also René Guénon, "Tradition and Traditionalism," in *The Reign of Quantity and the Signs of the Times*, trans. Lord Northbourne (Ghent, NY: Sophia Perennis, 2001), pp. 208–14; Marco Pallis, "Preface," to *The Way and the Mountain* (Bloomington, IN: World Wisdom, 2008), pp. xxvii–xxviii; Seyyed Hossein Nasr, "The Recovery of the Sacred: Tradition and Perennialism in the Contemporary World," *Sacred Web: A Journal of Tradition and Modernity*, vol. 19 (Summer 2007), pp. 15–37; Reza Shah-Kazemi, "Tradition as Spiritual Function: A 'Perennialist' Perspective," *Sacred Web: A Journal of Tradition and Modernity*, vol. 7 (Summer 2001), pp. 37–58.

[5] Ananda K. Coomaraswamy, "The Myth," "Notes to Hinduism," in *Hinduism and Buddhism* (New York, NY: Philosophical Library, 1943), pp. 6, 33.

[6] Ananda K. Coomaraswamy, "Primitive Mentality," in *Coomaraswamy, Vol. 1: Selected Papers, Traditional Art and Symbolism*, ed. Roger Lipsey (Princeton, NJ: Princeton University Press, 1977), p. 287.

[7] Rollo May, "The Therapist and the Journey into Hell," in *The Cry for Myth* (New York, NY: Delta Book, 1992), p. 151.

[8] Sigmund Freud, "Letter to Oskar Pfister—April 11, 1926," in *Psychoanalysis and Faith: The Letters of Sigmund Freud and Oskar Pfister*, trans. Eric Mosbacher, eds. Heinrich Meng and Ernst L. Freud (New York, NY: Basic Books, 1963), p. 103.

[9] Paul Ricoeur, "The Atheism of Freudian Psychoanalysis," in *On Psycho–analysis: Writings and Lectures, Vol. 1*, trans. David Pellauer (Cambridge, UK: Polity Press, 2012), p. 147.

[10] "Curious parallels have been pointed out between some of Freud's basic ideas and those of Marx. Marx and Freud each had rabbis among his ancestors; each belonged to a family within that circle of Jewry that had come under the influence of the Enlightenment; in the work of each theory is indissolubly linked to practice (in the form of revolutionary activity for Marx, of psychotherapy for Freud). Each man considered religion as an 'illusion'" (Henri F. Ellenberger, "The Background of Dynamic Psychiatry," in *The Discovery of the Unconscious: The History and Evolution of Dynamic Psychiatry* [New York, NY: Basic Books, 1970], p. 239). "The internal contradiction of Marxism is that it wants to build a perfect humanity while destroying man" (Frithjof Schuon, "No Initiative without Truth," in *The Play of Masks* [Bloomington, IN: World Wisdom Books, 1992], p. 78).

[11] Karl Marx, "A Contribution to the Critique of Hegel's 'Philosophy of Right': Introduction," in *Critique of Hegel's 'Philosophy of Right,'* trans. Annette Jolin and Joseph O'Malley (Cambridge, UK: Cambridge University Press, 1982), p. 131.

[12] Ibid.

[13] See Gustavo Polit, *Breaking the New Atheist Spell in the Light of Perennial Wisdom* (London, UK: Matheson Trust, 2017).

[14] See Richard Dawkins, *The God Delusion* (New York, NY: Houghton Mifflin, 2006).

[15] See Christopher Hitchens, *God Is Not Great: How Religion Poisons Everything* (New York: Twelve, Hachette Book Group, 2007).

[16] See Sam Harris, *The End of Faith: Religion, Terror, and the Future of Reason* (New York, NY: W. W. Norton & Company 2004).

[17] See Daniel C. Dennett, *Breaking the Spell: Religion as a Natural Phenomenon* (New York, NY: Viking, 2006).

[18] Eric Hoffer, "Fanaticism," in *The True Believer: Thoughts on the Nature of Mass Movements* (New York, NY: Harper & Row, 1966), p. 81.

[19] Wolfgang Smith, "The Ego and the Beast," in *Cosmos & Transcendence: Breaking Through the Barrier of Scientistic Belief* (Peru, IL: Sherwood Sugden & Company, 1990), p. 103.

[20] Sigmund Freud, "The Question of a *Weltanschauung*" (1933 [1932]), in *New Introductory Lectures on Psycho-Analysis*, trans. and ed. James Strachey (New York, NY: W. W. Norton & Company, 1989), p. 198.

[21] Sigmund Freud, "The Question of a *Weltanschauung*" (1933 [1932]), in *New Introductory Lectures on Psycho-Analysis*, trans. and ed. James Strachey (New York, NY: W. W. Norton & Company, 1989), p. 209.

[22] Sigmund Freud, "Letter to Charles Singer—October 31, 1938," in Ernst L. Freud (ed.), *Letters of Sigmund Freud*, trans. Tania Stern and James Stern (New York, NY: Basic Books, 1975), p. 453.

[23] Peter Gay, "Human Nature at Work," in *Freud: A Life for Our Time* (New York, NY: Anchor Books, 1989), p. 526.

[24] Peter Gay (ed.), *The Freud Reader* (New York, NY: W. W. Norton & Company, 1995), p. 429.

[25] Frank J. Sulloway, "Reassessing Freud's Case Histories: The Social Construction of Psychoanalysis," *Isis*, vol. 82, no. 2 (June 1991), p. 270.

[26] Sigmund Freud, "Postscript to a Discussion on Lay Analysis" (1927), in *The History of the Psychoanalytic Movement*, ed. Philip Rieff (New York, NY: Collier Books, 1963), p. 108.

[27] David Cohen, "Introduction," to *Psychologists on Psychology* (New York, NY: Taplinger Publishing Company, 1977), p. 1.

[28] Friedrich Nietzsche, "Book One," in *Daybreak: Thoughts on the Prejudices of Morality*, trans. R. J. Hollingdale, eds. Maudemarie Clark and Brian Leiter (New York, NY: Cambridge University Press, 2003), p. 33.

[29] Sigmund Freud, "Postscript" (1927), to *The Question of Lay Analysis*, trans. and ed. James Strachey (New York, NY: W. W. Norton & Company, 1989), p. 93.

[30] Sigmund Freud, "Postscript to a Discussion on Lay Analysis" (1927), in *The History of the Psychoanalytic Movement*, ed. Philip Rieff (New York, NY: Collier Books, 1963), p. 108.

[31] Erich Fromm, "The Psychoanalyst as 'Physician of the Soul,'" in *Psychoanalysis and Religion* (New Haven, CT: Yale University Press, 1974), p. 76.

[32] Sigmund Freud, "Letter to Oskar Pfister—February 9, 1909," in *Psychoanalysis and Faith: The Letters of Sigmund Freud and Oskar Pfister*, trans. Eric Mosbacher, eds. Heinrich Meng and Ernst L. Freud (New York, NY: Basic Books, 1963), p. 17.

[33] Thomas Szasz, "On Psychoanalysis and Psychology," in *Karl Kraus and the Soul-Doctors: A Pioneer Critic and His Criticism of Psychiatry and Psychoanalysis* (Baton Rouge, LA: Louisiana State University Press, 1976), p. 117. "[P]sychotherapy is secular ethics. It is the religion of the formally irreligious—with its language, which is not Latin but medical jargon; with its codes of conduct, which are not ethical but legalistic; and with its theology, which is not Christianity but positivism" (Thomas Szasz, "The Myth of Psychotherapy: Metaphorizing Medical Treatment," in *The Myth of Psychotherapy: Mental Healing as Religion, Rhetoric, and Repression* [Garden City, NY: Anchor Press, 1979], p. 8).

[34] Eric Hoffer, "Preface," to *The True Believer: Thoughts on the Nature of Mass Movements* (New York, NY: Harper & Row, 1966), p. x.

[35] Egon Friedell, "Epilogue: The Collapse of Reality," in *A Cultural History of the Modern Age, Vol. 3: The Crisis of the European Soul*, trans. C. F. Atkinson (New York, NY: Alfred A. Knopf, 1932), p. 480.

[36] Knight Dunlap, "Freud and the Psychoanalysts," in *Mysticism, Freudianism and Scientific Psychology* (St. Louis, MO: C. V. Mosby Company, 1920), p. 44.

[37] Seyyed Hossein Nasr, "Modern Western Philosophy and Schools of Thought," in *A Young Muslim's Guide to the Modern World* (Chicago, IL: Kazi Publications, 1994), p. 174.

[38] Paul Roazen, "The Future of Depth Psychology," in *Erik H. Erikson: The Power and Limits of a Vision* (Northvale, NJ: Jason Aronson, 1997), p. 183.

[39] Frederick S. Perls, *In and Out of the Garbage Pail* (Lafayette, CA: Real People Press, 1969), unpaginated.

[40] See Sigmund Freud, "A Religious Experience" (1928), in *The Standard Edition of the Complete Psychological Works of Sigmund Freud, Vol. 21*, trans. and ed. James Strachey (London, UK: Hogarth Press and the Institute of Psycho-Analysis, 1961), pp. 167–72; Sigmund Freud, "The Question of a *Weltanschauung*" (1933 [1932]), in *New Introductory Lectures on Psycho-Analysis*, trans. and ed. James Strachey (New York, NY: W. W. Norton & Company, 1989), pp. 195–225.

[41] Sigmund Freud, quoted in Peter Gay, "Human Nature at Work," in *Freud: A Life for Our Time* (New York, NY: Anchor Books, 1989), p. 526.

[42] Sigmund Freud, "Obsessive Actions and Religious Practices" (1907), in *The Standard Edition of the Complete Psychological Works of Sigmund Freud, Vol. 9*, trans. and ed. James Strachey (London, UK: Hogarth Press and the Institute of Psycho-Analysis, 1981), pp. 117, 119.

[43] Sigmund Freud, "Letter to Sándor Ferenczi—January 1, 1910," quoted in Ernest Jones, "Non-Medical Applications of Psychoanalysis," in *The Life and Work of Sigmund Freud, Vol. 2: Years of Maturity, 1901–1919* (New York, NY: Basic Books, 1955), p. 350.

[44] Sigmund Freud, "The Question of a *Weltanschauung*" (1933 [1932]), in *New Introductory Lectures on Psycho-Analysis*, trans. and ed. James Strachey (New York, NY: W. W. Norton & Company, 1989), p. 207.

[45] Sigmund Freud, "Chapter Five," in *Leonardo Da Vinci: A Study in Psychosexuality*, trans. A. A. Brill (New York, NY: Vintage Books, 1947), p. 98.

[46] Sigmund Freud, "The Return of Totemism in Childhood" (1913), in *Totem and Taboo*, trans. and ed. James Strachey (New York, NY: W. W. Norton & Company, 1989), pp. 190–91.

[47] Sigmund Freud, "An Example of Psycho-Analytic Work" (1940 [1938]), in *An Outline of Psycho-Analysis*, trans. and ed. James Strachey (New York, NY: W. W. Norton & Company, 1989), pp. 75–76.

[48] Erich Fromm, "Mechanisms of Escape," in *Escape from Freedom* (New York, NY: Henry Holt and Company, 1994), p. 176.

[49] Sigmund Freud, "Psychoanalysis and Religious Origins" (1919), in *Character and Culture*, ed. Philip Rieff (New York, NY: Collier Books, 1963), p. 226.

[50] Sigmund Freud, "Chapter Seven," in *Civilization and Its Discontents*, trans. and ed. James Strachey (New York, NY: W. W. Norton & Company, 1989), p. 93.

[51] Erich Fromm, "Ethics and Psychoanalysis," in *Man for Himself: An Inquiry into the Psychology of Ethics* (New York, NY: Rinehart and Company, 1947), p. 35.

[52] See C. G. Jung, *The Theory of Psychoanalysis* (New York, NY: Journal of Nervous and Mental Disease Publishing Company, 1915).

[53] Sigmund Freud, "Chapter Eight," in *The Future of an Illusion*, trans. and ed. James Strachey (New York, NY: W. W. Norton & Company, 1989), p. 55.

[54] Sigmund Freud, quoted in Ludwig Binswanger, "Reciprocal Visits between Binswanger and Freud" in *The Sigmund Freud—Ludwig Binswanger Correspondence, 1908–1938*, trans. Arnold J. Pomerans and Thomas Roberts, ed. Gerhard Fichtner (New York, NY: Other Press, 2003), p. 238. "[R]eligion is comparable to a childhood neurosis" (Sigmund Freud, "Chapter Ten," in *The Future of an Illusion*, trans. and ed. James Strachey [New York, NY: W. W. Norton & Company, 1989], p. 68).

[55] Sigmund Freud, "Chapter Eight," in *The Future of an Illusion*, trans. and ed. James Strachey (New York, NY: W. W. Norton & Company, 1989), pp. 55–56.

[56] Sigmund Freud, "Letter to Oskar Pfister—November 26, 1927," in *Psychoanalysis and Faith: The Letters of Sigmund Freud and Oskar Pfister*, trans. Eric Mosbacher, eds. Heinrich Meng and Ernst L. Freud (New York, NY: Basic Books, 1963), p. 117.

[57] Sigmund Freud, "Chapter Six," in *The Future of an Illusion*, trans. and ed. James Strachey (New York, NY: W. W. Norton & Company, 1989), p. 38.

[58] Sigmund Freud, "An Autobiographical Study" (1925 [1924]), in *The Standard Edition of the Complete Psychological Works of Sigmund Freud, Vol. 20*, trans. and ed. James Strachey (London, UK: Hogarth Press and the Institute of Psycho-Analysis, 1959), p. 68.

[59] Sigmund Freud, "An Autobiographical Study" (1925 [1924]), in *The Standard Edition of the Complete Psychological Works of Sigmund Freud, Vol. 20*, trans. and ed. James Strachey (London, UK: Hogarth Press and the Institute of Psycho-Analysis, 1959), p. 68.

[60] Christopher Lasch, "Culture and Personality," in *Haven in a Heartless World: The Family Besieged* (New York, NY: W. W. Norton & Company, 1995), p. 63.

[61] C. G. Jung, "Dream-Analysis in Its Practical Application," in *Modern Man in Search of a Soul*, trans. W. S. Dell and Cary F. Baynes (New York, NY: Harcourt, Brace & World, 1933), p. 16.

[62] Edward Sapir, "The Contribution of Psychiatry to an Understanding of Behavior in Society," *American Journal of Sociology*, vol. 42, no. 6 (May 1937), p. 865.

[63] Harry K. Wells, "Classical Psychoanalysis: Orthodox and Revised," in *The Failure of Psychoanalysis: From Freud to Fromm* (New York, NY: International Publishers, 1963), pp. 40–41.

[64] Claude Lévi-Strauss, "The Effectiveness of Symbols," in *Structural Anthropology*, trans. Claire Jacobson and Brooke Grundfest Schoepf (New York, NY: Basic Books, 1963), p. 199.

[65] Géza Róheim, "Summary," in *Psychoanalysis and Anthropology: Culture, Personality and the Unconscious* (New York, NY: International Universities Press, 1968), p. 488.

[66] Claude Lévi-Strauss, "The Effectiveness of Symbols," in *Structural Anthropology*, trans. Claire Jacobson and Brooke Grundfest Schoepf (New York, NY: Basic Books, 1963), pp. 197, 198.

[67] Franz Boas, "The Methods of Ethnology," *American Anthropologist*, vol. 22, no. 4 (October/December 1920), p. 321.

[68] Sigmund Freud, "The Question of a *Weltanschauung*" (1933 [1932]), in *New Introductory Lectures on Psycho-Analysis*, trans. and ed. James Strachey (New York, NY: W. W. Norton & Company, 1989), pp. 207–8.

[69] See Wilhelm Schmidt, *The Origin and Growth of Religion*, trans. H. J. Rose (New York, NY: Cooper Square Publishers, 1971).

[70] Joseph Epes Brown, "The Question of 'Mysticism'," in *The Spiritual Legacy of the American Indian: Commemorative Edition with Letters While Living with Black Elk*, eds. Marina Brown Weatherly, Elenita Brown and Michael Oren Fitzgerald (Bloomington, IN: World Wisdom, 2007), p. 82.

[71] Sigmund Freud, "Chapter Eight," in *The Future of an Illusion*, trans. and ed. James Strachey (New York, NY: W. W. Norton & Company, 1989), p. 56.

[72] Sigmund Freud, "Chapter Six," in *The Future of an Illusion*, trans. and ed. James Strachey (New York, NY: W. W. Norton & Company, 1989), p. 40.

[73] Sigmund Freud, "The Question of a *Weltanschauung*" (1933 [1932]), in *New Introductory Lectures on Psycho-Analysis*, trans. and ed. James Strachey (New York, NY: W. W. Norton & Company, 1989), p. 216.

[74] Sigmund Freud, "Chapter Two," in *Civilization and Its Discontents*, trans. and ed. James Strachey (New York, NY: W. W. Norton & Company, 1989), p. 22.

[75] Philip Rieff, "Preface to the Second Edition," in *Freud: The Mind of the Moralist* (Chicago, IL: University of Chicago Press, 1979), p. xix.

[76] Ibid.

[77] See Darrell Smith, "Trends in Counseling and Psychotherapy," *American Psychologist*, vol. 37, no. 7 (July 1982), p. 807.

[78] Albert Ellis, "The Case Against Religion: A Psychotherapist's View," in *The Case Against Religion: A Psychotherapist's View and The Case Against Religiosity* (Austin, TX: American Atheist Press, 1980), p. 15.

[79] Frederick S. Perls, "Neurosis," in *Ego, Hunger and Aggression* (New York, NY: Vintage Books, 1969), p. 67.

[80] Sigmund Freud, "Letter to Wilhelm Fliess—February 6, 1899," in Marie Bonaparte, Anna Freud and Ernst Kris (eds.), *The Origins of Psychoanalysis: Letters to Wilhelm Fliess, Drafts and Notes: 1887–1902*, trans. Eric Mosbacher and James Strachey (New York, NY: Basic Books, 1954), p. 276. Alternatively translated as: "the religion of science...is supposed to have taken the place of the old religion" (Sigmund Freud, "Letter to Wilhelm Fliess—February 6, 1899," in *The Complete Letters of Sigmund Freud to Wilhelm Fliess, 1887–1904*, trans. and ed. Jeffrey Moussaieff Masson [Cambridge, MA: Belknap Press of Harvard University Press, 1985], p. 343).

[81] Jean Borella, "Freud and the Inversion of the Sacred," in *The Crisis of Religious Symbolism and Symbolism & Reality*, trans. G. John Champoux (Kettering, OH: Angelico Press/Sophia Perennis, 2016), p. 193.

[82] C. G. Jung, "Letter to Sigmund Freud—February 11, 1910," in William McGuire (ed.), *The Freud/Jung Letters: The Correspondence Between Sigmund Freud and C. G. Jung*, trans. Ralph Manheim and R.F.C. Hull (Princeton, NJ: Princeton University Press, 1994), p. 294.

[83] Ibid.

[84] C. G. Jung, "Psychological Commentary," in *The Tibetan Book of the Great Liberation*, ed. W. Y. Evans-Wentz (London, UK: Oxford University Press, 2000), p. xxxvi.

[85] C. G. Jung, "Psychology and Religion" (1938/1940), in *The Collected Works of C. G. Jung, Vol. 11: Psychology and Religion: West and East*, trans. R.F.C. Hull, ed. Gerhard Adler (Princeton, NJ: Princeton University Press, 1975), p. 89.

[86] Sigmund Freud, "Letter to C. G. Jung—February 13, 1910," in William McGuire (ed.), *The Freud/Jung Letters: The Correspondence Between Sigmund Freud and C. G. Jung*, trans. Ralph Manheim and R.F.C. Hull (Princeton, NJ: Princeton University Press, 1994), p. 295. Jung wrote Freud on February 20, 1910, in an apologetic tone: "My last letter [on February 13, 1910] was naturally another of those rampages of fantasy I indulge in from time to time" (C. G. Jung, "Letter to Sigmund Freud—February 20, 1910," in William McGuire (ed.), *The Freud/Jung Letters: The Correspondence Between Sigmund Freud and C. G. Jung*, trans. Ralph Manheim and R.F.C. Hull [Princeton, NJ: Princeton University Press, 1994], p. 296).

[87] Sigmund Freud, "Letter to Eugen Bleuler—September 28, 1910," quoted in Franz Alexander and Sheldon T. Selesnick, "Freud-Bleuler Correspondence," *Archives of General Psychiatry*, vol. 12 (January 1965), p. 2.

[88] Sigmund Freud, "Revision of the Theory of Dreams" (1933 [1932]), in *New Introductory Lectures on Psycho-Analysis*, trans. and ed. James Strachey (New York, NY: W. W. Norton & Company, 1989), p. 8.

[89] C. G. Jung, quoted in Peter Gay, "Psychoanalytic Politics," in *Freud: A Life for Our Time* (New York, NY: Anchor Books, 1989), p. 239.

[90] Philip Sherrard, "Christianity and the Religious Thought of C. G. Jung," in *Christianity: Lineaments of a Sacred Tradition* (Brookline, MA: Holy Cross Orthodox Press, 1998), p. 154.

[91] C. G. Jung, "Psychotherapists or the Clergy," in *Modern Man in Search of a Soul*, trans. W. S. Dell and Cary F. Baynes (New York, NY: Harcourt, Brace & World, 1933), pp. 240–41.

[92] Erich Fromm, "Freud, the World Reformer" and "Summary and Conclusion," in *Sigmund Freud's Mission: An Analysis of His Personality and Influence* (New York, NY: Grove Press, 1963), pp. 87, 111.

[93] Robert S. Woodworth, "Followers of Freud and Jung," *The Nation*, vol. 103, no. 2678 (October 26, 1916), p. 396.

[94] John B. Watson, "The Myth of the Unconscious: A Behavioristic Explanation," *Harper's Magazine* (September 1927), p. 502.

[95] John B. Watson, "The Myth of the Unconscious," *The Ways of Behaviorism* (New York, NY: Harper & Brothers Publishers, 1928), p. 95. See also John B. Watson, "The Myth of the Unconscious: A Behavioristic Explanation," *Harper's Magazine* (September 1927), pp. 502–8.

[96] Richard Webster, "Critics and Dissidents," in *Why Freud Was Wrong: Sin, Science, and Psychoanalysis* (New York, NY: Basic Books, 1995), p. 362

[97] Sigmund Freud, "Prefatory Notes," in *Moses and Monotheism*, trans. Katherine Jones (New York, NY: Vintage Books, 1967), p. 68.

[98] Sigmund Freud, "Letter to Oskar Pfister—February 9, 1909," in *Psychoanalysis and Faith: The Letters of Sigmund Freud and Oskar Pfister*, trans. Eric Mosbacher, eds. Heinrich Meng and Ernst L. Freud (New York, NY: Basic Books, 1963), p. 16.

[99] Sigmund Freud, "Recommendations to Physicians Practicing Psycho-Analysis" (1912), in *The Standard Edition of the Complete Psychological Works of Sigmund Freud, Vol. 12*, trans. and ed. James Strachey (London, UK: Hogarth Press and the Institute of Psycho-Analysis, 1958), p. 115.

[100] Sigmund Freud, "Recommendations to Physicians Practicing Psycho-Analysis" (1912), in *The Standard Edition of the Complete Psychological Works of Sigmund Freud, Vol. 12*, trans. and ed. James Strachey (London, UK: Hogarth Press and the Institute of Psycho-Analysis, 1958), p. 115.

[101] Sigmund Freud, "Chapter Seven," in *The Future of an Illusion*, trans. and ed. James Strachey (New York, NY: W. W. Norton & Company, 1989), p. 47.

[102] Sigmund Freud, "Letter to Oskar Pfister—October 9, 1918," in *Psychoanalysis and Faith: The Letters of Sigmund Freud and Oskar Pfister*, trans. Eric Mosbacher, eds. Heinrich Meng and Ernst L. Freud (New York, NY: Basic Books, 1963), p. 63.

[103] Sigmund Freud, "Explanations, Applications and Orientations" (1933 [1932]), in *New Introductory Lectures on Psycho-Analysis*, trans. and ed. James Strachey (New York, NY: W. W. Norton & Company, 1989), p. 188.

[104] Sigmund Freud, "Chapter Seven," in *The Future of an Illusion*, trans. and ed. James Strachey (New York, NY: W. W. Norton & Company, 1989), p. 47.

[105] Ernest Jones, "The Psycho-Analytical 'Movement'," in *Free Associations: Memories of a Psychoanalyst* (New York, NY: Basic Books, 1959), p. 205.

[106] Sigmund Freud, "Letter to Oskar Pfister—February 16, 1929," in *Psychoanalysis and Faith: The Letters of Sigmund Freud and Oskar Pfister*, trans. Eric Mosbacher, eds. Heinrich Meng and Ernst L. Freud (New York, NY: Basic Books, 1963), p. 129.

[107] Sigmund Freud, "Chapter Eight," in *The Future of an Illusion*, trans. and ed. James Strachey (New York, NY: W. W. Norton & Company, 1989), p. 56.

[108] C. G. Jung, "Letter to Sigmund Freud—November 11, 1908," in William McGuire (ed.), *The Freud/Jung Letters: The Correspondence Between Sigmund Freud and C. G. Jung*, trans. Ralph Manheim and R.F.C. Hull (Princeton, NJ: Princeton University Press, 1994), p. 176.

[109] Bernard Hart, quoted in Peter Gay, *A Godless Jew: Freud, Atheism, and the Making of Psychoanalysis* (New Haven, CT: Yale University Press, 1987), p. 20.

[110] Gregory Zilboorg, "Psyche, Soul, and Religion," in *Mind, Medicine, & Man* (New York, NY: Harcourt, Brace & Company, 1943), p. 326.

[111] Sigmund Freud, "Psychoanalysis" (1922), in *Character and Culture*, ed. Philip Rieff (New York, NY: Collier Books, 1963), p. 247.

[112] Richard LaPiere, "The Freudian Doctrine of Man," in *The Freudian Ethic* (New York, NY: Duell, Sloan and Pearce, 1959), p. 53.

[113] Philip Rieff, "The Authority of the Past," in *Freud: The Mind of the Moralist* (Chicago, IL: University of Chicago Press, 1979), p. 214.

[114] Philip Rieff, "The Analytic Attitude: Freud's Legacy and Its Inheritors," in *The Triumph of the Therapeutic: Uses of Faith After Freud* (Chicago, IL: University of Chicago Press, 1987), p. 40.

Chapter 9: From Metaphysics to Metapsychology

[1] Pope Pius XII, "On Psychotherapy and Religion: An Address of His Holiness Pope Pius XII to the Fifth International Congress on Psychotherapy and Clinical Psychology, April 13, 1953" (Washington, D.C.: National Catholic Welfare Conference, 1953), pp. 5–6.

[2] Rama P. Coomaraswamy, "Modernism in the Church: The Road to Hell Is Paved with Good Intentions," in *The Destruction of the Christian Tradition: Updated and Revised* (Bloomington, IN: World Wisdom, 2006), p. 391.

[3] Sigmund Freud, "Determinism, Belief in Chance and Superstition—Some Points of View" (1901), in *The Psychopathology of Everyday Life*, trans. and ed. James Strachey (New York, NY: W. W. Norton & Company, 1989), p. 330.

[4] Ernest Jones, "Occultism," in *The Life and Work of Sigmund Freud, Vol. 3: The Last Phase, 1919–1939* (New York, NY: Basic Books, 1957), p. 398.

[5] Peter Gay, "Aggressions," in *Freud: A Life for Our Time* (New York, NY: Anchor Books, 1989), p. 363.

[6] See E. A. Burtt, *The Metaphysical Foundations of Modern Science* (Mineola, NY: Dover Publications, 2003).

[7] Philip Rieff, "Introduction," to Sigmund Freud, *General Psychological Theory: Papers on Metapsychology*, ed. Philip Rieff (New York, NY: Touchstone, 2008), p. ix.

[8] Sigmund Freud, "Determinism, Belief in Chance and Superstition—Some Points of View" (1901), in *The Psychopathology of Everyday Life*, trans. and ed. James Strachey (New York, NY: W. W. Norton & Company, 1989), p. 330.

[9] Sigmund Freud, "Determinism, Belief in Chance and Superstition—Some Points of View" (1901), in *The Psychopathology of Everyday Life*, trans. and ed. James Strachey (New York, NY: W. W. Norton & Company, 1989), p. 330.

[10] Ibid.

[11] René Guénon, "Sacred and Profane Science," in *The Crisis of the Modern World*, trans. Arthur Osborne, Marco Pallis and Richard C. Nicholson (Hillsdale, NY: Sophia Perennis, 2004), pp. 46–47.

[12] Philip Sherrard, "The Meaning and Necessity of Sacred Tradition," in *Christianity: Lineaments of a Sacred Tradition* (Brookline, MA: Holy Cross Orthodox Press, 1998), p. 16.

[13] Titus Burckhardt, "The Branches of the Doctrine," in *Introduction to Sufi Doctrine*, trans. D. M. Matheson (Bloomington, IN: World Wisdom, 2008), pp. 26–27.

[14] Frithjof Schuon, "Rationalism, Real and Apparent," in *Logic and Transcendence*, trans. Peter N. Townsend (London, UK: Perennial Books, 1984), p. 34.

[15] Paul Tournier, "The Rift between the Spiritual and the Temporal," in *The Whole Person in a Broken World*, trans. John and Helen Doberstein (New York, NY: Harper & Row, 1964), p. 93.

[16] Fulton J. Sheen, "The Philosophy of Anxiety," in *Peace of Soul* (Liguori, MO: Liguori/Triumph, 1996), p. 17.

[17] William C. Chittick, "Intellectual Knowledge," in *Science of the Cosmos, Science of the Soul: The Pertinence of Islamic Cosmology in the Modern World* (Oxford, UK: Oneworld, 2009), p. 26.

[18] Sigmund Freud, "Letter to Werner Achelis—January 30, 1927," in Ernst L. Freud (ed.), *Letters of Sigmund Freud*, trans. Tania Stern and James Stern (New York, NY: Basic Books, 1975), p. 375.

[19] Plato, *Apology* 38a

[20] Sigmund Freud, "Letter to Marie Bonaparte—August 13, 1937," in Ernst L. Freud (ed.), *Letters of Sigmund Freud*, trans. Tania and James Stern (New York, NY: Basic Books, 1975), p. 436.

[21] Ernest Jones, "Character and Personality," in *The Life and Work of Sigmund Freud, Vol. 2: Years of Maturity, 1901–1919* (New York, NY: Basic Books, 1955), p. 433.

[22] C. G. Jung, "The Philosophical Tree" (1945/1954), in *The Collected Works C. G. Jung, Vol. 13: Alchemical Studies*, trans. R.F.C. Hull, ed. Gerhard Adler (Princeton, NJ: Princeton University Press, 1983), pp. 265–66.

[23] Clement of Alexandria, "Book III—'On the True Beauty,'" in *The Writings of Clement of Alexandria*, trans. Rev. William Wilson (Edinburgh: T. & T. Clark, 1884), p. 273.

[24] Ibn al-'Arabī, quoted in William C. Chittick, *The Self-Disclosure of God: Principles of Ibn al-'Arabī's Cosmology* (Albany, NY: State University of New York Press, 1998), p. 134.

[25] Ibn al-'Arabī, quoted in William C. Chittick, *The Sufi Path of Knowledge: Ibn al-'Arabī's Metaphysics of Imagination* (Albany, NY: State University of New York Press, 1989), p. 322.

[26] Hakuin Ekaku, "The Difficulty of Repaying the Debt to the Buddhas and the Patriarchs," in *The Essential Teachings of Zen Master Hakuin*, trans. Norman Waddell (Boston, MA: Shambhala Publications, 1994), p. 62.

[27] William C. Chittick, "Veils of Light," in *The Self-Disclosure of God: Principles of Ibn al-'Arabī's Cosmology* (Albany, NY: State University of New York Press, 1998), p. 120.

[28] René Guénon, "The Realization of the Being through Knowledge," in *The Multiple States of the Being*, trans. Henry D. Fohr, ed. Samuel D. Fohr (Ghent, NY: Sophia Perennis, 2001), p. 77.

[29] René Guénon, "Knowledge and Action," in *The Crisis of the Modern World*, trans. Arthur Osborne, Marco Pallis, and Richard C. Nicholson (Hillsdale, NY: Sophia Perennis, 2004), p. 38.

[30] Śrī Ramana Maharshi, "Upadesa Saram (The Essence of Instruction)," in *The Collected Works of Ramana Maharshi*, ed. Arthur Osborne (Boston, MA: Weiser Books, 1997), p. 85.

[31] Śrī Śaṅkarācārya, quoted in *Vivekachudamani of Sri Sankaracharya: Text with English Translation, Notes and an Index*, trans. Swami Madhavananda (Almora: Advaita Ashrama, 1921), p. 170.

[32] Meister Eckhart, quoted in Ananda K. Coomaraswamy, "Theology and Autology," in *Hinduism and Buddhism* (New York, NY: Philosophical Library, 1943), p. 13. See also Samuel Bendeck Sotillos, "The Self and the Other in the Light of the One: The Metaphysics of Human Diversity," *Sacred Web: A Journal of Tradition and Modernity*, vol. 41 (Summer 2018), pp. 34–76.

[33] Sigmund Freud, "A Difficulty in the Path of Psycho-Analysis" (1917), in *The Standard Edition of the Complete Psychological Works of Sigmund Freud, Vol. 17*, trans. and ed. James Strachey (London, UK: Hogarth Press and the Institute of Psycho-Analysis, 1955), p. 143.

[34] Ernest Jones, "Character and Personality," in *The Life and Work of Sigmund Freud, Vol. 2: Years of Maturity, 1901–1919* (New York, NY: Basic Books, 1955), p. 423.

[35] Moses Maimonides, "Chapter Eleven," in *The Guide of the Perplexed, Vol. 2*, trans. Shlomo Pines (Chicago, IL: University of Chicago Press, 1963), pp. 440–41.

[36] Sigmund Freud, quoted in Siegfried Bernfeld, "Freud's Scientific Beginnings," *American Imago*, vol. 6, no. 3 (September 1949), p. 193.

[37] Sigmund Freud, "Freud's Psychoanalytic Method" (1904), in *Therapy and Technique*, ed. Philip Rieff (New York, NY: Collier Books, 1963), p. 59.

[38] Sigmund Freud, "Freud's Psycho-Analytic Procedure" (1904 [1903]), in *The Standard Edition of the Complete Psychological Works of Sigmund Freud, Vol. 7*, trans. and ed. James Strachey (London, UK: Hogarth Press and the Institute of Psycho-Analysis, 1953), pp. 252–53.

[39] C. G. Jung, "General Aspects of Psychoanalysis" (1913), in *Critique of Psychoanalysis*, trans. R.F.C. Hull (Princeton, NJ: Princeton University Press, 1975), p. 148.

[40] C. G. Jung, "Some Crucial Points in Psychoanalysis: A Correspondence between Dr. Jung and Dr. Loÿ" (1914), in *Critique of Psychoanalysis*, trans. R.F.C. Hull (Princeton, NJ: Princeton University Press, 1975), p. 189.

[41] Sigmund Freud, "Fixation to Traumas—The Unconscious" (1916–1917 [1915–1917]), in *Introductory Lectures on Psychoanalysis*, trans. and ed. James Strachey (New York, NY: W. W. Norton & Company, 1977), p. 282.

[42] Sigmund Freud, "The Method of Interpreting Dreams: An Analysis of a Specimen Dream," in *The Interpretation of Dreams*, trans. and ed. James Strachey (New York, NY: Science Editions, 1963), p. 100.

[43] Sigmund Freud, "Analytical Therapy" (1917), in *A General Introduction to Psychoanalysis* (New York, NY: Horace Liveright, 1920), p. 393.

[44] Sigmund Freud, "Taboo and Emotional Ambivalence" (1913), in *Totem and Taboo*, trans. and ed. James Strachey (London, UK: Routledge & Kegan Paul, 1961), p. 24.

[45] Henry Corbin, "The Question of Comparative Philosophy: Convergences in Iranian and European Thought," *Spring: An Annual of Archetypal Psychology and Jungian Thought* (1980), p. 3.

[46] Sigmund Freud, "Fixation to Traumas—The Unconscious" (1916–1917 [1915–1917]), in *Introductory Lectures on Psychoanalysis*, trans. and ed. James Strachey (New York, NY: W. W. Norton & Company, 1977), p. 282.

[47] Sigmund Freud, "The Psychogenesis of a Case of Female Homosexuality," *International Journal of Psycho-Analysis*, vol. 1, no. 2 (1920), p. 145.

[48] A. R. Natarajan, "M. A. Pigot," in *Timeless in Time: Sri Ramana Maharshi* (Bloomington, IN: World Wisdom, 2006), pp. 107–8.

[49] Sigmund Freud, "Letter to Wilhelm Fliess—February 13, 1896," in *The Complete Letters of Sigmund Freud to Wilhelm Fliess, 1887–1904*, trans. and ed. Jeffrey Moussaieff Masson (Cambridge, MA: Belknap Press of Harvard University Press, 1985), p. 172. Alternatively translated as, "I am continually occupied with psychology—it is really metapsychology...I hope something will come of it" (Sigmund Freud, "Letter to Wilhelm Fliess—February 13, 1896," in Marie Bonaparte, Anna Freud and Ernst Kris (eds.), *The Origins of Psychoanalysis: Letters to Wilhelm Fliess, Drafts and Notes: 1887–1902*, trans. Eric Mosbacher and James Strachey [New York, NY: Basic Books, 1954], p. 157).

[50] Sigmund Freud, "Letter to Wilhelm Fliess—December 17, 1896," in *The Complete Letters of Sigmund Freud to Wilhelm Fliess, 1887–1904*, trans. and ed. Jeffrey Moussaieff Masson [Cambridge, MA: Belknap Press of Harvard University Press, 1985], p. 216.

[51] Sigmund Freud, "Letter to Wilhelm Fliess—March 10, 1898," in Marie Bonaparte, Anna Freud and Ernst Kris (eds.), *The Origins of Psychoanalysis: Letters to Wilhelm Fliess, Drafts and Notes: 1887–1902*, trans. Eric Mosbacher and James Strachey (New York, NY: Basic Books, 1954), p. 246. Alternatively translated as: "I am going to ask you seriously...whether I may use the name metapsychology for my psychology that leads behind consciousness" (Sigmund Freud, "Letter to Wilhelm Fliess—March 10, 1898," in *The Complete Letters of Sigmund Freud to Wilhelm Fliess, 1887–1904*, trans. and ed. Jeffrey Moussaieff Masson [Cambridge, MA: Belknap Press of Harvard University Press, 1985], pp. 301–2).

[52] Sigmund Freud, quoted in Ernest Jones, "Letter to Wilhelm Fliess—March 10, 1898," in *The Life and Work of Sigmund Freud, Vol. 1: The Formative Years and the Great Discoveries, 1856–1900* (New York, NY: Basic Books, 1959), p. 357.

[53] Sigmund Freud, quoted in Ludwig Binswanger, "Reciprocal Visits between Binswanger and Freud" in *The Sigmund Freud—Ludwig Binswanger Correspondence, 1908–1938*, trans. Arnold J. Pomerans and Thomas Roberts, ed. Gerhard Fichtner (New York, NY: Other Press, 2003), p. 234.

[54] C. G. Jung, "The Aims of Psychotherapy," in *Modern Man in Search of a Soul*, trans. W. S. Dell and Cary F. Baynes (New York, NY: Harcourt, Brace & World, 1933), p. 64.

[55] C. G. Jung, "Psychological Commentary," in *The Tibetan Book of the Dead*, ed. W.Y. Evans-Wentz (London, UK: Oxford University Press, 1968), p. xxxvii.

[56] C. G. Jung, "Psychological Commentary," in *The Tibetan Book of the Great Liberation*, ed. W. Y. Evans-Wentz (London, UK: Oxford University Press, 2000), p. xxix.

[57] Sigmund Freud, "The Unconscious" (1915), in *General Psychological Theory: Papers on Metapsychology*, ed. Philip Rieff (New York, NY: Touchstone, 2008), p. 124.

[58] Sigmund Freud, "An Autobiographical Study" (1925 [1924]), in *An Autobiographical Study*, trans. and ed. James Strachey (New York, NY: W. W. Norton & Company, 1989), p. 66.

[59] Sigmund Freud, "Analysis Terminable and Interminable" (1937), in *The Standard Edition of the Complete Psychological Works of Sigmund Freud, Vol. 23*, trans. and ed. James Strachey (London, UK: Hogarth Press and the Institute of Psycho-Analysis, 1964), p. 225.

[60] René Guénon, "Essential Characteristics of Metaphysics," in *Introduction to the Study of the Hindu Doctrines*, trans. Marco Pallis (Ghent, NY: Sophia Perennis, 2001), p. 71.

[61] Ibid., p. 74.

[62] Richard LaPiere, "The Freudian Doctrine of Man," in *The Freudian Ethic* (New York, NY: Duell, Sloan and Pearce, 1959), p. 41.

[63] Frithjof Schuon, "The Contradiction of Relativism," in *Logic and Transcendence*, trans. Peter N. Townsend (London, UK: Perennial Books, 1984), p. 14.

Chapter 10: The Freudian Colonization of the Human Psyche: Id, Ego, and Super-Ego

[1] Sigmund Freud, "(F) The Unconscious and Consciousness—Reality," in *The Interpretation of Dreams*, trans. and ed. James Strachey (New York, NY: Science Editions, 1963), p. 613.

[2] Angelus Silesius, "Book Four," in *The Cherubinic Wanderer*, trans. Maria Shrady (Mahwah, NJ: Paulist Press, 1986), p. 97.

[3] Sigmund Freud, "(F) The Unconscious and Consciousness—Reality" (1899), in *The Interpretation of Dreams*, trans. and ed. James Strachey (New York, NY: Science Editions, 1963), p. 615.

[4] Ibid., p. 616.

[5] References made to the three-fold constitution of the human being can be found in St Paul's first epistle to the Thessalonians: "May the God of peace Himself sanctify you wholly; and may your *spirit and soul and body* be kept sound and blameless at the coming of our Lord Jesus Christ" (1 Thessalonians 5:23). See also René Guénon, "Spirit and Intellect," in *Miscellanea*, trans. Henry D. Fohr, Cecil Bethell, Patrick Moore, and Hubert Schiff (Hillsdale, NY: Sophia Perennis, 2001), pp. 20–24; René Guénon, "*Spiritus, Anima, Corpus*," in *The Great Triad*, trans. Henry D. Fohr, ed. Samuel D. Fohr (Hillsdale, NY: Sophia Perennis, 2004), pp. 68–73; William Stoddart, "What is the Intellect?" in *Remembering in a World of Forgetting: Thoughts on Tradition and Postmodernism*, eds. Mateus Soares de Azevedo and Alberto Vasconcellos Queiroz (Bloomington, IN: World Wisdom, 2008), pp. 45–50.

[6] Sigmund Freud, "Chapter Five," in *The Future of an Illusion*, trans. and ed. James Strachey (New York, NY: W. W. Norton & Company, 1989), p. 35.

7 See Sigmund Freud, *Totem and Taboo*, trans. and ed. James Strachey (New York, NY: W. W. Norton & Company, 1989).

8 Sigmund Freud, "The Ego and the Super-Ego (Ego Ideal)" (1923), in *The Ego and the Id*, trans. Joan Riviere, ed. James Strachey (New York, NY: W. W. Norton & Company, 1989), pp. 33–34.

9 Fulton J. Sheen, "Frustration," in *Peace of Soul* (Liguori, MO: Liguori/ Triumph, 1996), p. 3.

10 Richard LaPiere, "The Freudian Doctrine of Man," in *The Freudian Ethic* (New York, NY: Duell, Sloan and Pearce, 1959), p. 51.

11 Wolfgang Smith, "The Ego and the Beast," in *Cosmos & Transcendence: Breaking Through the Barrier of Scientific Belief* (Peru, IL: Sherwood Sugden & Company, 1990), p. 94.

12 Ibid., pp. 94–95.

13 Erich Fromm, "The Greatness and Limitations of Freud's Discoveries," in *Greatness and Limitations of Freud's Thought* (New York, NY: Mentor Books, 1981), p. 21.

14 Ernest Jones, "Freud's Theory of the Mind," in *The Life and Work of Sigmund Freud, vol. 1: The Formative Years and the Great Discoveries, 1856– 1900* (New York, NY: Basic Books, 1959), p. 397.

15 Sigmund Freud, quoted in Lionel Trilling, "Freud and Literature," in *The Liberal Imagination: Essays on Literature and Society* (New York, NY: New York Review of Books, 2008), p. 34.

16 Hans J. Eysenck, "The Experimental Study of Freudian Concepts," in *Decline and Fall of the Freudian Empire* (New York, NY: Penguin Books, 1991), p. 168.

17 Peter Gay, "Psychoanalysis," in *Freud: A Life for Our Time* (New York, NY: Anchor Books, 1989), p. 127.

18 Sigmund Freud, quoted in Lionel Trilling, "Freud and Literature," in *The Liberal Imagination: Essays on Literature and Society* (New York, NY: New York Review of Books, 2008), p. 34.

19 Wolfgang Smith, "The Ego and the Beast," in *Cosmos & Transcendence: Breaking Through the Barrier of Scientific Belief* (Peru, IL: Sherwood Sugden & Company, 1990), p. 95.

20 Sigmund Freud, "The Dissection of the Psychical Personality" (1933 [1932]), in *New Introductory Lectures on Psycho-Analysis*, trans. and ed. James Strachey (New York, NY: W. W. Norton & Company, 1989), p. 96.

21 Sigmund Freud, "Analysis Terminable and Interminable" (1937), in *The Standard Edition of the Complete Psychological Works of Sigmund Freud, Vol. 23*, trans. and ed. James Strachey (London, UK: Hogarth Press and the Institute of Psycho-Analysis, 1964), p. 235.

22 Erich Fromm, "The Sick Individual and the Sick Society," in *Beyond the Chains of Illusion: My Encounter with Marx and Freud* (New York, NY: Simon & Schuster, 1962), p. 59.

[23] Sigmund Freud, "The Dependent Relationships of the Ego" (1923), in *The Ego and the Id*, trans. Joan Riviere, ed. James Strachey (New York, NY: W. W. Norton & Company, 1989), p. 58.

[24] Sigmund Freud, "The Dissection of the Psychical Personality" (1933 [1932]), in *New Introductory Lectures on Psycho-Analysis*, trans. and ed. James Strachey (New York, NY: W. W. Norton & Company, 1989), pp. 96–97.

[25] "*No man can serve two masters*: for either he will hate the one, and love the other; or else he will hold to the one, and despise the other. Ye cannot serve God and mammon" (Matthew 6:24).

[26] Sigmund Freud, "The Psycho-Analytical Method," in *Collected Papers of Sigmund Freud, Vol. 1*, trans. Joan Riviere (London, UK: Hogarth Press and the Institute of Psycho-Analysis, 1950), p. 269.

[27] Sigmund Freud, "Symptom Formation" (1926), in *The Problem of Anxiety*, trans. H.A. Bunker (New York: W. W. Norton & Company, 1963), p. 19.

[28] Sigmund Freud, "The Dependent Relationships of the Ego" (1923), in *The Ego and the Id*, trans. Joan Riviere, ed. James Strachey (New York, NY: W. W. Norton & Company, 1989), p. 59. "[T]he ego is the sole seat of anxiety" (Sigmund Freud, "Anxiety and Instinctual Life" (1933 [1932]), in *New Introductory Lectures on Psycho-Analysis*, trans. and ed. James Strachey [New York, NY: W. W. Norton & Company, 1989], p. 106.

[29] Sigmund Freud, "Anxiety and Instinctual Life" (1933 [1932]), in *New Introductory Lectures on Psycho-Analysis*, trans. and ed. James Strachey (New York, NY: W. W. Norton & Company, 1989), p. 106.

[30] Sigmund Freud, "The Dissection of the Psychical Personality" (1933 [1932]), in *New Introductory Lectures on Psycho-Analysis*, trans. and ed. James Strachey (New York, NY: W. W. Norton & Company, 1989), p. 100.

[31] Sigmund Freud, "Analysis Terminable and Interminable" (1937), in *The Standard Edition of the Complete Psychological Works of Sigmund Freud, Vol. 23*, trans. and ed. James Strachey (London, UK: Hogarth Press and the Institute of Psycho-Analysis, 1964), p. 238.

[32] Sigmund Freud, "The Dissection of the Psychical Personality" (1933 [1932]), in *New Introductory Lectures on Psycho-Analysis*, trans. and ed. James Strachey (New York, NY: W. W. Norton & Company, 1989), pp. 99–100.

[33] Muriel Ivimey, "How Does Analysis Help?," in *Are You Considering Psychoanalysis?*, ed. Karen Horney (New York, NY: W. W. Norton & Company, 1962), p. 211.

[34] Meister Eckhart, "Sermon Ten," in *Meister Eckhart: Teacher and Preacher*, ed. Bernard McGinn (Mahwah, NJ: Paulist Press, 1986), p. 265.

[35] Frithjof Schuon, "Modes of Spiritual Realization," in *The Eye of the Heart* (Bloomington, IN: World Wisdom Books, 1997), p. 129. "[T]he Intellect [can know] everything that is knowable" (Frithjof Schuon, "The Alchemy of the Sentiments," in *Logic and Transcendence*, trans. Peter N. Townsend [London, UK: Perennial Books, 1984], p. 159).

[36] Moses Maimonides, "On the Terms: The Intellectus, the Intelligens and the Intelligible," in *The Guide for the Perplexed*, trans. Michael Friedländer (New York, NY: Dover, 1956), p. 100.

[37] Rūmī, quoted in A. J. Arberry, *Discourses of Rumi* (London, UK: RoutledgeCurzon, 2004), p. 152.

[38] Moses Maimonides, "On the Limit of Man's Intellect," in *The Guide for the Perplexed*, trans. Michael Friedländer (New York, NY: Dover, 1956), p. 41.

[39] Meister Eckhart, "Sermon Twelve," in *Meister Eckhart: Teacher and Preacher*, ed. Bernard McGinn (Mahwah, NJ: Paulist Press, 1986), p. 270.

[40] Meister Eckhart, quoted in *Ye Shall Know the Truth: Christianity and the Perennial Philosophy*, ed. Mateus Soares de Azevedo (Bloomington, IN: World Wisdom, 2005), p. 3.

[41] Black Elk, quoted in Frithjof Schuon, "The Sacred Pipe," in *The Feathered Sun: Plains Indians in Art and Philosophy* (Bloomington, IN: World Wisdom Books, 1990), p. 51.

[42] Sigmund Freud, "The Psychical Apparatus and the External World" (1940 [1938]), in *An Outline of Psycho-Analysis*, trans. and ed. James Strachey (New York, NY: W. W. Norton & Company, 1989), p. 84.

[43] Sigmund Freud, "Psychical Qualities" (1940 [1938]), in *An Outline of Psycho-Analysis*, trans. and ed. James Strachey (New York, NY: W. W. Norton & Company, 1969), p. 20.

[44] Sigmund Freud, "The Psychical Apparatus" (1940 [1938]), in *An Outline of Psycho-Analysis*, trans. and ed. James Strachey (New York, NY: W. W. Norton & Company, 1989), p. 14.

[45] Sigmund Freud, "The Ego and the Id" (1923), in *The Ego and the Id*, trans. Joan Riviere, ed. James Strachey (New York, NY: W. W. Norton & Company, 1989), pp. 18–19.

[46] Sigmund Freud, "The Dependent Relationships of the Ego" (1923), in *The Ego and the Id*, trans. Joan Riviere, ed. James Strachey (New York, NY: W. W. Norton & Company, 1989), p. 48.

[47] Sigmund Freud, "The Ego and the Id" (1923), in *The Ego and the Id*, trans. Joan Riviere, ed. James Strachey (New York, NY: W. W. Norton & Company, 1989), p. 19. "[T]he ego stands for reason and good sense while the id stands for untamed passions" (Sigmund Freud, "The Dissection of the Psychical Personality" (1933 [1932]), in *New Introductory Lectures on Psycho-Analysis*, trans. and ed. James Strachey [New York, NY: W. W. Norton & Company, 1989], p. 95).

[48] Huston Smith, "Science and Theology: The Unstable Détente," in *Beyond the Post-Modern Mind* (New York, NY: Crossroad, 1982), p. 115.

[49] René Guénon, "Materia Signata Quantitate," in *The Reign of Quantity and the Signs of the Times*, trans. Lord Northbourne (Ghent, NY: Sophia Perennis, 2001), p. 20.

[50] Erik H. Erikson, "Foundations in Observation," in *Identity: Youth and Crisis* (New York, NY: W. W. Norton & Company, 1968), p. 50.

[51] Georg Groddeck, "Letter XIV," in *The Book of the It* (New York, NY: Vintage Books, 1949), p. 114.

[52] Georg Groddeck, "Letter XXXII," in *The Book of the It* (New York, NY: Vintage Books, 1949), p. 240.

[53] Wolfgang Smith, "The Ego and the Beast," in *Cosmos & Transcendence: Breaking Through the Barrier of Scientistic Belief* (Peru, IL: Sherwood Sugden & Company, 1990), p. 109.

[54] Sigmund Freud, "The Ego and the Super-Ego (Ego Ideal)" (1923), in *The Ego and the Id*, trans. Joan Riviere, ed. James Strachey (New York, NY: W. W. Norton & Company, 1989), p. 33.

[55] Upon Jung's return from the September 1909 conference held at Clark University, he had a dream that has become well-known because it claims to have given him his initial ideas for the doctrine of the collective unconscious. Jung describes the dream: "On my way back from America, I had a dream that was the origin of my book on the *Psychology of the Unconscious* [1912]. In those times I had no idea of the collective unconscious; I thought of the conscious as of a room above, with the unconscious as a cellar underneath and then the earth wellspring, that is, the body, sending up the instincts. These instincts tend to disagree with our conscious ideas and so we keep them down. That is the figure I had always used for myself, and then came this dream which I hope I can tell without being too personal. I dreamed I was in a medieval house, a big, complicated house with many rooms, passages, and stairways. I came in from the street and went down into a vaulted Gothic room, and from there into a cellar. I thought to myself that now I was at the bottom, but then I found a square hole. With a lantern in my hand I peeped down this hole, and saw stairs leading further down, and down these I climbed. They were dusty stairs, very much worn, and the air was sticky, the whole atmosphere very uncanny. I came to another cellar, this one of very ancient structure, perhaps Roman, and again there was a hole through which I could look down into a tomb filled with prehistoric pottery, bones, and skulls; as the dust was undisturbed, I thought I had made a great discovery. There I woke up" (C. G. Jung, "Lecture Three—April 6, 1925," in *Analytical Psychology: Notes of the Seminar Given in 1925*, ed. William McGuire [London, UK: Routledge, 1992], pp. 22–23).

[56] C. G. Jung, "Sigmund Freud in His Historical Setting" (1934), in *The Collected Works of C. G. Jung, Vol. 15: The Spirit in Man, Art and Literature*, trans. R.F.C. Hull (Princeton, NJ: Princeton University Press, 1971), p. 40.

[57] C. G. Jung, "Letter to Sabina Spielrein—December 28, 1917," quoted in C. G. Jung, "The Letters of C. G. Jung to Sabina Spielrein," *Journal of Analytical Psychology*, vol. 46, no. 1 (January 2001), p. 191.

[58] Sigmund Freud, "The Historical Development," in *Moses and Monotheism*, trans. Katherine Jones (New York, NY: Vintage Books, 1967), p. 170.

[59] Arthur J. Deikman, "Spirituality Expands a Therapist's Horizons," *Yoga Journal*, Issue 88 (September/October 1989), p. 49.

[60] Sigmund Freud, quoted in Viktor E. Frankl, "Man's Search for Ultimate Meaning," in *On the Way to Self Knowledge*, eds. Jacob Needleman and Dennis Lewis (New York, NY: Alfred A. Knopf, 1976), p. 183.

[61] Frithjof Schuon, "Appendix," in *Light on the Ancient Worlds: A New Translation with Selected Letters*, trans. Deborah Casey, Mark Perry, Jean-Pierre Lafouge, and James S. Cutsinger. ed. Deborah Casey (Bloomington, IN: World Wisdom, 2005), p. 136.

[62] Jean Klein, "Chapter Five," in *Be Who You Are*, trans. Mary Mann (Salisbury, UK: Non-Duality Press, 2006), p. 46.

[63] Allen Esterson, "The Basic Concepts of Psychoanalysis," in *Seductive Mirage: An Exploration of the Work of Sigmund Freud* (Chicago, IL: Open Court, 1993), p. 230.

[64] E. M. Thornton, "Introduction," to *The Freudian Fallacy: An Alternative View of Freudian Theory* (Garden City, NY: Dial Press, 1984), p. ix.

Chapter 11: The "Oceanic Feeling": Mysticism versus Regression

[1] Alan W. Watts, "Psychotherapy and Liberation," in *Psychotherapy East and West* (New York, NY: Mentor Books, 1963), p. 23.

[2] Whitall N. Perry, "The Zodiac of the Soul: Observations on the Differences between Traditional and Empirical Psychology," in *Challenges to a Secular Society* (Oakton, VA: Foundation for Traditional Studies, 1996), p. 201.

[3] Sigmund Freud, "Chapter One," in *Civilization and Its Discontents*, trans. and ed. James Strachey (New York: W. W. Norton & Company, 1989), pp. 10–21; see also Mark Epstein, "Freud's Influence on Transpersonal Psychology" in *Textbook of Transpersonal Psychiatry and Psychology*, eds. Bruce W. Scotton, Allan B. Chinen, and John R. Battista (New York: Basic Books, 1996), pp. 29–38; Bruno Bettelheim, *Freud and Man's Soul* (New York, NY: Vintage Books, 1984).

[4] Sigmund Freud, "Chapter One," in *Civilization and Its Discontents*, trans. and ed. James Strachey (New York, NY: W. W. Norton & Company, 1989), p. 15.

[5] Ibid., pp. 12-13.

[6] Romain Rolland, "Letter to Sigmund Freud—December 5, 1927," quoted in William B. Parsons, "The Enigma of the Oceanic Feeling," in *The Enigma of the Oceanic Feeling: Revisioning the Psychoanalytic Theory of Mysticism* (New York, NY: Oxford University Press, 1999), p. 36.

[7] Sigmund Freud, "Letter to Romain Rolland—July 14, 1929," in Ernst L. Freud (ed.), *Letters of Sigmund Freud*, trans. Tania Stern and James Stern (New York, NY: Basic Books, 1975), p. 388.

[8] Sigmund Freud, "Chapter One," in *Civilization and Its Discontents*, trans. and ed. James Strachey (New York, NY: W. W. Norton & Company, 1989), p. 10.

[9] Sigmund Freud, "Letter to Romain Rolland—July 20, 1929," in Ernst L. Freud (ed.), *Letters of Sigmund Freud*, trans. Tania Stern and James Stern (New York, NY: Basic Books, 1975), p. 389.

[10] Sigmund Freud, "Letter to Romain Rolland—January 19, 1930," in Ernst L. Freud (ed.), *Letters of Sigmund Freud*, trans. Tania Stern and James Stern (New York, NY: Basic Books, 1975), p. 392.

[11] Ibid., p. 393.

[12] Ibid., p. 393.

[13] Ibid.

[14] Sigmund Freud, "Letter to Romain Rolland—March 4, 1923," in Ernst L. Freud (ed.), *Letters of Sigmund Freud*, trans. Tania Stern and James Stern (New York, NY: Basic Books, 1975), p. 341.

[15] Sigmund Freud, "Chapter One," in *Civilization and Its Discontents*, trans. and ed. James Strachey (New York, NY: W. W. Norton & Company, 1989), p. 11.

[16] See Jeffrey Moussaieff Masson, *The Oceanic Feeling: The Origins of Religious Sentiment in Ancient India* (Dordrecht, Netherlands: D. Reidel, 1980); Jeffrey J. Kripal, *Kali's Child: The Mystical and the Erotic in the Life and Teachings of Ramakrishna* (Chicago, IL: University of Chicago Press, 1998); Swami Tyagananda and Pravrajika Vrajaprana, *Interpreting Ramakrishna: Kali's Child Revisited* (India: Motilal Banarsidass Publishers, 2010).

[17] Stanislav Grof, "Spirituality and Religion," in *Psychology of the Future: Lessons from Modern Consciousness Research* (Albany, NY: State University of New York Press, 2000), p. 215. "Medical materialism finishes up Saint Paul by calling his vision on the road to Damascus a discharging lesion of the occipital cortex, he being an epileptic. It snuffs out Saint Teresa [of Avila] as an hysteric, Saint Francis of Assisi as an hereditary degenerate" (William James, "Religion and Neurology," in *The Varieties of Religious Experience* [New York, NY: Penguin Books, 1985], p. 13).

[18] Ernst Kris, "The Psychology of Caricature" (1934), in *Psychoanalytic Explorations in Art* (New York, NY: International Universities Press, 1952), p. 177. See also Raymond Prince and Charles Savage, "Mystical States and the Concept of Regression," *Psychedelic Review*, no. 8 (1966), pp. 59–75.

[19] Abraham H. Maslow, "Health as Transcendence of Environment," in *Toward a Psychology of Being* (Princeton, NJ: Van Nostrand, 1968), p. 182. "Regression in the psycho-analytical sense is a historical regression, a sliding back to infancy. Is there not a possibility of interpreting it differently? Regression might mean nothing more than a falling back to the true Self, a breakdown of pretenses and of all those character features which have not become part and parcel of the personality and which have not been assimilated into the neurotic's 'whole.'" (Frederick S. Perls, "Classical Psycho-Analysis," in *Ego, Hunger and Aggression* [New York, NY: Vintage Books, 1969], p. 82).

[20] Philip Rieff, "Sexuality and Domination," in *Freud: The Mind of the Moralist* (Chicago, IL: University of Chicago Press, 1979), p. 168.

[21] Saint Teresa, "Chapter Eighteen," in *The Complete Works of Saint Teresa of Jesus, Vol. 1: General Introduction, Life, Spiritual Relations*, trans. and ed. E. Allison Peers (New York, NY: Sheed & Ward, 1946), pp. 106, 108, 109, 110.

[22] Sigmund Freud, quoted in Ernest Jones, "Occultism," in *The Life and Work of Sigmund Freud, Vol. 3: The Last Phase, 1919–1939* (New York, NY: Basic Books, 1957), p. 392.

[23] Sigmund Freud, "Letter to Hereward Carrington—July 24, 1921," in Ernst L. Freud (ed.), *Letters of Sigmund Freud*, trans. Tania Stern and James Stern (New York, NY: Basic Books, 1975), p. 334.

[24] Sigmund Freud, "Psycho-Analysis and Telepathy" (1941 [1921]), in *The Standard Edition of the Complete Psychological Works of Sigmund Freud, Vol. 18*, trans. and ed. James Strachey (London, UK: Hogarth Press and the Institute of Psycho-Analysis, 1975), p. 178.

[25] Sigmund Freud, "Dreams and Occultism" (1933 [1932]), in *New Introductory Lectures on Psycho-Analysis*, trans. and ed. James Strachey (New York, NY: W. W. Norton & Company, 1989), p. 68.

[26] Ernest Jones, "Occultism," in *The Life and Work of Sigmund Freud, Vol. 3: The Last Phase, 1919–1939* (New York, NY: Basic Books, 1957), p. 381.

[27] Sigmund Freud, "Psycho-Analysis and Telepathy" (1941 [1921]), in *The Standard Edition of the Complete Psychological Works of Sigmund Freud, Vol. 18*, trans. and ed. James Strachey (London, UK: Hogarth Press and the Institute of Psycho-Analysis, 1975), p. 180.

[28] C. G. Jung, "On the Psychology and Pathology of So-called Occult Phenomena" (1902), in *The Collected Works of C. G. Jung, Vol. 1: Psychiatric Studies*, trans. R.F.C. Hull, ed. Gerhard Adler (Princeton, NJ: Princeton University Press, 1983), pp. 3–88. See also F. X. Charet, *Spiritualism and the Foundations of C. G. Jung's Psychology* (Albany, NY: State University of New York Press, 1993); James Webb, "The Hermetic Academy," in *The Occult Establishment* (La Salle, IL: Open Court, 1976), pp. 345–416.

[29] Frithjof Schuon, "Introduction," to *Logic and Transcendence*, trans. Peter N. Townsend (London, UK: Perennial Books, 1984), p. 1. See also René Guénon, *Theosophy: History of a Pseudo-Religion*, trans. Alvin Moore, Jr., Cecil Bethell, Hubert and Rohini Schiff (Hillsdale, NY: Sophia Perennis, 2004); René Guénon, *The Spiritist Fallacy*, trans. Alvin Moore, Jr. and Rama P. Coomaraswamy (Hillsdale, NY: Sophia Perennis, 2004).

[30] Frithjof Schuon, "The Psychological Imposture," in *Survey of Metaphysics and Esoterism*, trans. Gustavo Polit (Bloomington, IN: World Wisdom Books, 1986), pp. 197–98.

[31] Sigmund Freud, "Findings, Ideas, Problems" (1938), in *The Standard Edition of the Complete Psychological Works of Sigmund Freud, Vol. 23*, trans. and ed. James Strachey (London, UK: Hogarth Press and the Institute of Psycho-Analysis, 1981), p. 300.

[32] Sigmund Freud, "(F) The Unconscious and Consciousness—Reality" (1899), in *The Interpretation of Dreams*, trans. and ed. James Strachey (New York, NY: Science Editions, 1963), p. 615.

[33] René Guénon, "Tradition and the 'Unconscious,'" in *Symbols of Sacred Science*, trans. Henry D. Fohr, ed. Samuel D. Fohr (Hillsdale, NY: Sophia Perennis, 2004), pp. 39–40.

[34] Arthur Osborne, "Modern Idolatries," in *Be Still, It Is The Wind That Sings* (Tiruvannamalai, India: Sri Ramanasramam, 2003), p. 378.

[35] See Richard Maurice Bucke, *Cosmic Consciousness* (New York, NY: Arkana Books, 1991).

[36] René Guénon, "The Confusion of the Psychic and the Spiritual," in *The Reign of Quantity and the Signs of the Times*, trans. Lord Northbourne (Ghent, NY: Sophia Perennis, 2001), pp. 239–40.

[37] C. G. Jung, "The Psychology of the Transference" (1946), in *The Collected Works of C. G. Jung, Vol. 16: The Practice of Psychotherapy*, trans. R.F.C. Hull (Princeton, NJ: Princeton University Press, 1985), p. 192.

[38] René Guénon, "Individualism," in *The Crisis of the Modern World*, trans. Arthur Osborne, Marco Pallis and Richard C. Nicholson (Hillsdale, NY: Sophia Perennis, 2004), p. 58.

[39] René Guénon, "The Misdeeds of Psychoanalysis," in *The Reign of Quantity and the Signs of the Times*, trans. Lord Northbourne (Ghent, NY: Sophia Perennis, 2001), p. 228.

[40] Śrī Aurobindo, quoted in René Guénon, "Reviews of Books: Other Authors," in *Studies in Hinduism*, trans. Henry D. Fohr, ed. Samuel D. Fohr (Ghent, NY: Sophia Perennis, 2001), p. 168.

[41] Sigmund Freud, "The Primary and Secondary Processes—Repression" (1899), in *The Interpretation of Dreams*, trans. and ed. James Strachey (New York, NY: Science Editions, 1963), p. 608.

[42] Sigmund Freud, "(C) The Means of Representation in Dreams" (1899), in *The Interpretation of Dreams*, trans. and ed. James Strachey (New York, NY: Science Editions, 1963), p. 322.

[43] Black Elk, quoted in John G. Neihardt, "Early Boyhood," in *Black Elk Speaks: Being the Life Story of a Holy Man of the Oglala Sioux* (Lincoln, NE: University of Nebraska Press, 1988), p. 10.

[44] Sigmund Freud, "(F) The Unconscious and Consciousness—Reality" (1899), in *The Interpretation of Dreams*, trans. and ed. James Strachey (New York, NY: Science Editions, 1963), p. 621.

[45] Ibid.

[46] Sigmund Freud, "Third Lecture" (1910), in *Five Lectures on Psycho-Analysis*, trans. and ed. James Strachey (New York, NY: W. W. Norton & Company, 1989), pp. 34-35.

[47] Sigmund Freud, "The Technique of Psycho-Analysis" (1940 [1938]), in *An Outline of Psycho-Analysis*, trans. and ed. James Strachey (New York, NY: W. W. Norton & Company, 1969), p. 29.

[48] Mircea Eliade, "Patanjali's Yoga," in *Patanjali and Yoga*, trans. Charles Lam Markmann (New York, NY: Schocken Books, 1976), p. 58.

[49] Rūmī, quoted in A.J. Arberry, *Discourses of Rumi* (London, UK: RoutledgeCurzon, 2004), p. 200.

[50] Frithjof Schuon, "The Psychological Imposture," in *Survey of Metaphysics and Esoterism*, trans. Gustavo Polit (Bloomington, IN: World Wisdom Books, 1986), pp. 195–96.

[51] Michael Washburn, "Introduction," to *Transpersonal Psychology in Psychoanalytic Perspective* (Albany, NY: State University of New York Press, 1994), p. 16.

[52] Frederick S. Perls, "Philosophy of the Obvious," in *The Gestalt Approach and Eye Witness to Therapy* (Palo Alto, CA: Science and Behavior Books, 1973), p. 178.

[53] A. H. Almaas, "The Retrieval of Essence," in *Essence: The Diamond Approach to Inner Realization* (York Beach, ME: Samuel Weiser, 1986), p. 122.

[54] Sigmund Freud, "Letter to Ludwig Binswanger—October 8, 1936," in *The Sigmund Freud—Ludwig Binswanger Correspondence, 1908–1938*, trans. Arnold J. Pomerans and Thomas Roberts, ed. Gerhard Fichtner (New York, NY: Other Press, 2003), p. 211. Alternatively translated as, "I have always lived on the ground floor and in the basement of the building—you maintain that on changing one's viewpoint one can also see an upper floor housing such distinguished guests as religion, art, and others. You are not the only one; most cultivated specimens of *homo natura* think likewise. In this respect you are the conservative, I the revolutionary. If I had another life of work ahead of me, I would dare to offer even those high-born people a home in my lowly hut. I already found one for religion when I stumbled on the category 'neurosis of mankind.'" (Sigmund Freud, "Letter to Ludwig Binswanger—October 8, 1936," in Ernst L. Freud (ed.), *Letters of Sigmund Freud*, trans. Tania Stern and James Stern [New York, NY: Basic Books, 1975], p. 431).

[55] Sigmund Freud, quoted in Ludwig Binswanger, *Sigmund Freud: Reminiscences of a Friendship*, trans. Norbert Guterman (New York, NY: Grune & Stratton, 1957), p. 96.

[56] Harry Oldmeadow, "The Not-So-Close Encounters of Western Psychology and Eastern Spirituality," in *Journeys East: 20th Century Western Encounters with Eastern Traditions* (Bloomington, IN: World Wisdom, 2004), p. 317.

Chapter 12: The Eclipse of the Sacred and the Rise of Psychopathology

[1] Mark Perry, "Satan Is Not an Atheist," in *The Mystery of Individuality: Grandeur and Delusion of the Human Condition* (Bloomington, IN: World Wisdom, 2012), p. 173.

[2] Sigmund Freud, "Chapter Two," in *Civilization and Its Discontents*, trans. and ed. James Strachey (New York, NY: W. W. Norton & Company, 1989), p. 32.

[3] Sigmund Freud, "The Future Prospects of Psycho-Analytic Therapy" (1910), in *The Standard Edition of the Complete Psychological Works of Sigmund Freud, Vol. 11*, trans. and ed. James Strachey (London, UK: Hogarth Press and the Institute of Psycho-Analysis, 1957), p. 146.

[4] C. G. Jung, "Introduction to Kranefeldt's 'Secret Ways of the Mind'" (1930), in *Critique of Psychoanalysis*, trans. R.F.C. Hull (Princeton, NJ: Princeton University Press, 1975), p. 218.

[5] C. G. Jung, "Freud and Jung: Contrasts" (1929), in *Critique of Psychoanalysis*, trans. R.F.C. Hull (Princeton, NJ: Princeton University Press, 1975), p. 232. "[T]he ego is ill for the very reason that it is cut off from the whole, and has lost its connection with mankind as well as with the spirit." (C. G. Jung, "Freud and Jung—Contrasts," in *Modern Man in Search of a Soul*, trans. W. S. Dell and Cary F. Baynes [New York, NY: Harcourt, Brace & World, 1933], p. 123).

[6] St. John Chrysostom, quoted in Jean-Claude Larchet, "The First Origin of Illnesses; The Ancestral Sin," in *Therapy of Spiritual Illnesses, Vol 1: An Introduction to the Ascetic Tradition of the Orthodox Church*, trans. Fr. Kilian Sprecher (Montréal: Alexander Press, 2012), p. 46.

[7] Wolfgang Smith, quoted in Bernard Janzen, "Science, Scientism and Christological Cosmology," in *Unmasking the Faces of Antichrist: Interview with Dr. Wolfgang Smith* (Davidson, Saskatchewan, Canada: Triumph Communications, 2017), p. 21.

[8] Carl G. Jung, "The Soul of Man," in *Man and His Symbols*, ed. Carl G. Jung (New York, NY: Laurel, 1968), p. 85.

[9] Sigmund Freud, "Fifth Lecture" (1910), in *Five Lectures on Psycho-Analysis*, trans. and ed. James Strachey (New York, NY: W. W. Norton & Company, 1989), p. 56.

[10] Fulton J. Sheen, "Frustration," in *Peace of Soul* (Liguori, MO: Liguori/Triumph, 1996), p. 1.

[11] E. Fuller Torrey and Judy Miller, "Introduction," to *The Invisible Plague: The Rise of Mental Illness from 1750 to the Present* (New Brunswick, NJ: Rutgers University Press, 2007), p. 5. See also Michel Foucault, *Madness and Civilization: A History of Insanity in the Age of Reason*, trans. Richard Howard (New York, NY: Vintage Books, 1988); Erich Fromm, *The Pathology of Normalcy*, ed. Rainer Funk (Riverdale, NY: American Mental Health Foundation, 2010).

[12] Jean Borella, "Nature and Culture," in *The Crisis of Religious Symbolism and Symbolism & Reality*, trans. G. John Champoux (Kettering, OH: Angelico Press/Sophia Perennis, 2016), p. 159. "[M]ental pathology has always been considered, by all human civilizations, as naturally dependent on the sacred" (Jean Borella, "Freud and the Inversion of the Sacred," in *The Crisis of Religious Symbolism and Symbolism & Reality*, trans. G. John Champoux

[Kettering, OH: Angelico Press/Sophia Perennis, 2016], p. 194).

[13] Sigmund Freud, "Letter to Minna Bernays—December 3, 1885," in Ernst L. Freud (ed.), *Letters of Sigmund Freud*, trans. Tania Stern and James Stern (New York, NY: Basic Books, 1975), p. 188.

[14] Jean-Claude Larchet, "Conclusion," to *Therapy of Spiritual Illnesses, Vol 3: An Introduction to the Ascetic Tradition of the Orthodox Church*, trans. Fr. Kilian Sprecher (Montréal: Alexander Press, 2012), p. 258.

[15] Erich Fromm, "Foreword," to *Man for Himself: An Inquiry into the Psychology of Ethics* (New York, NY: Rinehart and Company, 1947), p. viii.

[16] Christopher Lasch, "The Survival Mentality," in *The Minimal Self: Psychic Survival in Troubled Times* (New York, NY: W. W. Norton & Company, 1984), p. 61.

[17] Mark Perry, "On Authority," in *The Mystery of Individuality: Grandeur and Delusion of the Human Condition* (Bloomington, IN: World Wisdom, 2012), p. 215.

[18] Sigmund Freud, "On the Mechanism of Paranoia" (1911), in *General Psychological Theory: Papers on Metapsychology*, ed. Philip Rieff (New York, NY: Touchstone, 2008), p. 23.

[19] Tage Lindbom, "The Veil of Maya," in *The Tares and the Good Grain or the Kingdom of Man at the Hour of Reckoning*, trans. Alvin Moore, Jr. (Macon, GA: Mercer University Press, 1983), pp. 82–83.

[20] Tage Lindbom, "Lucifer," in *Every Branch in Me: Essays on the Meaning of Man*, ed. Barry McDonald (Bloomington, IN: World Wisdom, 2002), p. 81.

[21] Sigmund Freud, "Chapter Two," in *Civilization and Its Discontents*, trans. and ed. James Strachey (New York, NY: W. W. Norton & Company, 1989), p. 33.

[22] Ibid.

[23] Paul Ricoeur, "Illusion," in *Freud and Philosophy: An Essay on Interpretation*, trans. Denis Savage (New Haven, CT: Yale University Press, 1970), p. 232.

[24] Philip Rieff, "The Religion of the Fathers," in *Freud: The Mind of the Moralist* (Chicago, IL: University of Chicago Press, 1979), p. 290.

[25] Paul C. Vitz, "Epilogue: A Biographical Critique of Freud's Atheism," in *Sigmund Freud's Christian Unconscious* (New York, NY: Guilford Press, 1988), p. 221.

[26] Paul C. Vitz, "Epilogue: A Biographical Critique of Freud's Atheism," in *Sigmund Freud's Christian Unconscious* (New York, NY: Guilford Press, 1988), p. 221.

[27] Philip Sherrard, "The Desanctification of Nature" in *The Rape of Man and Nature: An Inquiry into the Origins and Consequences of Modern Science* (Ipswich, UK: Golgonooza Press, 1991), p. 100.

[28] Carl G. Jung, "The Importance of Dreams," in *Man and His Symbols*, ed. Carl G. Jung (New York, NY: Laurel, 1968), p. 31.

[29] C. G. Jung, "Psychotherapists or the Clergy," in *Modern Man in Search of a Soul*, trans. W. S. Dell and Cary F. Baynes (New York, NY: Harcourt, Brace & World, 1933), pp. 230–31, 232.

[30] R. D. Laing, "Normal Alienation from Experience," in *The Politics of Experience* (New York, NY: Ballantine Books, 1972), pp. 25–26.

[31] Otto Rank, "Psychology and Social Change," in *Beyond Psychology* (New York, NY: Dover, 1958), p. 49.

[32] Arthur Janov, "The Problem," in *The Primal Scream: Primal Therapy, The Cure for Neurosis* (New York, NY: Dell Publishing, 1970), p. 16.

[33] Sigmund Freud, "Analysis Terminable and Interminable" (1937), in *The Standard Edition of the Complete Psychological Works of Sigmund Freud, Vol. 23*, trans. and ed. James Strachey (London, UK: Hogarth Press and the Institute of Psycho-Analysis, 1964), p. 235.

[34] Sigmund Freud, "(E) Representation by Symbols in Dreams—Some Further Typical Dreams" (1899), in *The Interpretation of Dreams*, trans. and ed. James Strachey (New York, NY: Science Editions, 1963), p. 373.

[35] Sigmund Freud, "The Relation of the Poet to Day-Dreaming" (1908), in *Character and Culture*, ed. Philip Rieff (New York, NY: Collier Books, 1963), p. 37.

[36] Sigmund Freud, "Analytic Therapy" (1916–1917 [1915–1917]), in *Introductory Lectures on Psychoanalysis*, trans. and ed. James Strachey (New York, NY: W. W. Norton & Company, 1977), p. 457.

[37] Sigmund Freud, "Representation by Symbols in Dreams—Some Further Typical Dreams" (1899), in *The Interpretation of Dreams*, trans. and ed. James Strachey (New York, NY: Science Editions, 1963), pp. 400–1.

[38] R. D. Laing, "The Existential-Phenomenological Foundations for a Science of Persons," in *The Divided Self: An Existential Study in Sanity and Madness* (New York, NY: Penguin Books, 1976), p. 25.

[39] C. G. Jung, "The Spiritual Problem of Modern Man," in *Modern Man in Search of a Soul*, trans. W. S. Dell and Cary F. Baynes (New York, NY: Harcourt, Brace & World, 1933), p. 206.

[40] Arthur J. Deikman, "Sufism and The Mental Health Sciences," in *Beyond Health and Normality: Explorations of Exceptional Psychological Well-Being*, eds. Roger Walsh and Deane H. Shapiro (New York, NY: Van Nostrand Reinhold, 1983), p. 273.

[41] Sigmund Freud, "The Dissection of the Psychical Personality" (1933 [1932]), in *New Introductory Lectures on Psycho-Analysis*, trans. and ed. James Strachey (New York, NY: W. W. Norton & Company, 1989), p. 73.

[42] Egon Friedell, "Epilogue: The Collapse of Reality," in *A Cultural History of the Modern Age, Vol. 3: The Crisis of the European Soul*, trans. C. F. Atkinson (New York, NY: Alfred A. Knopf, 1932), p. 482.

[43] Sigmund Freud, "Chapter Four," in *The Question of Lay Analysis*, trans. Nancy Procter-Gregg (New York, NY: W. W. Norton & Company, 1950), p. 54.

[44] Sigmund Freud, "Turning in the Ways of Psychoanalytic Therapy" (1919), in *Therapy and Technique*, ed. Philip Rieff (New York, NY: Collier Books, 1963), p. 189.

[45] Sigmund Freud, "Chapter Eight," in *Civilization and Its Discontents*, trans. and ed. James Strachey (New York, NY: W. W. Norton & Company, 1989), pp. 109–10.

[46] C. G. Jung, "New Paths in Psychology" (1912), in *Two Essays on Analytical Psychology*, trans. R.F.C. Hull (New York, NY: Meridian, 1956), p. 274.

[47] Sigmund Freud, "Letter to Wilhelm Fliess—May 16, 1897," in *The Complete Letters of Sigmund Freud to Wilhelm Fliess, 1887–1904*, trans. and ed. Jeffrey Moussaieff Masson (Cambridge, MA: Belknap Press of Harvard University Press, 1985), p. 243.

[48] Sigmund Freud, "Femininity" (1933 [1932]), in *New Introductory Lectures on Psycho-Analysis*, trans. and ed. James Strachey (New York, NY: W. W. Norton & Company, 1989), p. 150.

[49] Sigmund Freud, "Analytical Therapy" (1917), in *A General Introduction to Psychoanalysis* (New York, NY: Horace Liveright, 1920), pp. 395–96.

[50] Sigmund Freud, "Letter to Oskar Pfister—January 18, 1909," in Ernst L. Freud (ed.), *Letters of Sigmund Freud*, trans. Tania Stern and James Stern (New York, NY: Basic Books, 1975), p. 278.

[51] Sigmund Freud, quoted in Joseph Wortis, "Fragments of a Freudian Analysis," *American Journal of Orthopsychiatry*, vol. 10, no. 4 (October 1940), p. 845.

[52] Philip Rieff, "The Emergence of Psychological Man," in *Freud: The Mind of the Moralist* (Chicago, IL: University of Chicago Press, 1979), p. 330.

[53] C. G. Jung, "Psychotherapy and a Philosophy of Life" (1943), in *The Collected Works of C. G. Jung, Vol. 16: The Practice of Psychotherapy*, trans. R.F.C. Hull (Princeton, NJ: Princeton University Press, 1985), p. 78.

[54] C. G. Jung, "The State of Psychotherapy Today" (1934), in *The Collected Works of C. G. Jung, Vol. 10: Civilization in Transition*, trans. R.F.C. Hull (Princeton, NJ: Princeton University Press, 1970), p. 167.

Chapter 13: The Couch and the Confessional

[1] Pope Pius XII, "On Psychotherapy and Religion: An Address of His Holiness Pope Pius XII to the Fifth International Congress on Psychotherapy and Clinical Psychology," April 13, 1953 (Washington, D.C.: National Catholic Welfare Conference, 1953), p. 9.

[2] Sigmund Freud, quoted in Giovanni Papini, "A Visit to Freud," in *Freud as We Knew Him*, ed. Hendrik M. Ruitenbeek (Detroit, MI: Wayne State University Press, 1973), p. 100.

[3] Karl Kautsky, quoted in Peter Gay, *A Godless Jew: Freud, Atheism, and the Making of Psychoanalysis* (New Haven, CT: Yale University Press, 1987), pp. 39–40.

[4] Paul Tournier, "Everything Must be Paid For," in *Guilt and Grace: A Psychological Study*, trans. Arthur W. Heathcote, J. J. Henry and P. J. Allcock (New York, NY: Harper & Row, 1962), p. 177.

[5] Sigmund Freud, "Freud's Psycho-Analytic Procedure" (1904 [1903]), in *The Standard Edition of the Complete Psychological Works of Sigmund Freud, Vol. 7*, trans. and ed. James Strachey (London, UK: Hogarth Press and the Institute of Psycho-Analysis, 1953), p. 250.

[6] Sigmund Freud, "The Technique of Psycho-Analysis" (1940 [1938]), in *An Outline of Psycho-Analysis*, trans. and ed. James Strachey (New York, NY: W. W. Norton & Company, 1989), pp. 51-52.

[7] Richard Webster, "Priests, Penitents and Patients," in *Why Freud Was Wrong: Sin, Science, and Psychoanalysis* (New York, NY: Basic Books, 1995), p. 355.

[8] Max Rosenbaum, "Anna O. (Bertha Pappenheim): Her History," in *Anna O.: Fourteen Contemporary Reinterpretations*, eds. Max Rosenbaum and Melvin Muroff (New York, NY: Free Press, 1984), p. 20.

[9] Henri F. Ellenberger, "The Story of 'Anna O.': A Critical Review with New Data" (1972), in *Beyond the Unconscious: Essays of Henri F. Ellenberger in the History of Psychiatry*, trans. Françoise Dubor and Mark S. Micale, ed. Mark S. Micale (Princeton, NJ: Princeton University Press, 1993), p. 272.

[10] Titus Burckhardt, "Traditional Cosmology and Modern Science: Modern Psychology," in *Mirror of the Intellect: Essays on Traditional Science and Sacred Art*, trans. and ed. William Stoddart (Albany, NY: State University of New York Press, 1987), p. 49.

[11] Sigmund Freud, "Chapter One," in *The Question of Lay Analysis*, trans. Nancy Procter-Gregg (New York, NY: W. W. Norton & Company, 1950), p. 24.

[12] Alexander Reid Martin, "Why Psychoanalysis?" in *Are You Considering Psychoanalysis?*, ed. Karen Horney (New York, NY: W. W. Norton & Company, 1962), p. 26.

[13] Otto Rank, "Will and Force," in *Truth and Reality*, trans. Jessie Taft (New York, NY: W. W. Norton & Company, 1978), p. 16.

[14] Paul Tournier, "Psychoanalysis and Guilt," in *Guilt and Grace: A Psychological Study*, trans. Arthur W. Heathcote, J. J. Henry and P. J. Allcock (New York, NY: Harper & Row, 1962), p. 129.

[15] Ibid.

[16] C. G. Jung, "A Rejoinder to Dr. Bally" (1934), in *The Collected Works of C. G. Jung, Vol. 10: Civilization in Transition*, trans. R.F.C. Hull (Princeton, NJ: Princeton University Press, 1970), p. 540.

[17] C. G. Jung, "Problems of Modern Psychotherapy," in *Modern Man in Search of a Soul*, trans. W. S. Dell and Cary F. Baynes (New York, NY: Harcourt, Brace & World, 1933), p. 31.

[18] C. G. Jung, "Psychoanalysis and Association Experiments" (1906), in *The Collected Works of C. G. Jung, Vol. 2: Experimental Researches*, trans. Leopold Stein and Diana Riviere (Princeton, NJ: Princeton University Press, 1981), p. 316.

[19] Tage Lindbom, "The Veil of Maya," in *The Tares and the Good Grain or the Kingdom of Man at the Hour of Reckoning*, trans. Alvin Moore, Jr. (Macon, GA: Mercer University Press, 1983), pp. 81–82.

[20] Mark Perry, "The Iconic Figure," in *The Mystery of Individuality: Grandeur and Delusion of the Human Condition* (Bloomington, IN: World Wisdom, 2012), p. 78.

[21] Fulton J. Sheen, "Morbidity and the Denial of Guilt," in *Peace of Soul* (Liguori, MO: Liguori/Triumph, 1996), p. 79.

[22] Ibid.

[23] Fulton J. Sheen, "Psychoanalysis and Confession," in *Peace of Soul* (Liguori, MO: Liguori/Triumph, 1996), p. 121.

[24] Fulton J. Sheen, "The Philosophy of Anxiety," in *Peace of Soul* (Liguori, MO: Liguori/Triumph, 1996), p. 19.

[25] Mark Perry, "Introduction," to *The Mystery of Individuality: Grandeur and Delusion of the Human Condition* (Bloomington, IN: World Wisdom, 2012), p. 10.

[26] C. G. Jung, "Psychotherapists or the Clergy," in *Modern Man in Search of a Soul*, trans. W. S. Dell and Cary F. Baynes (New York, NY: Harcourt, Brace & World, 1933), p. 237.

[27] Ernest Jones, "The God Complex," in *Essays in Applied Psycho-Analysis* (London, UK: International Psycho-Analytical Press, 1923), pp. 209, 211–12, 213.

[28] Sigmund Freud, "On the History of the Psychoanalytic Movement" (1914), in *The History of the Psychoanalytic Movement*, ed. Philip Rieff (New York, NY: Collier Books, 1963), p. 42.

[29] Josef Breuer and Sigmund Freud, "On the Psychical Mechanism of Hysterical Phenomena: Preliminary Communication" (1893), in *Studies on Hysteria*, trans. and ed. James Strachey (New York, NY: Basic Books, 2000), p. 17.

[30] Sigmund Freud, "Letter to Wilhelm Fliess—June 28, 1892," in Marie Bonaparte, Anna Freud and Ernst Kris (eds.), *The Origins of Psychoanalysis: Letters to Wilhelm Fliess, Drafts and Notes: 1887–1902*, trans. Eric Mosbacher and James Strachey (New York, NY: Basic Books, 1954), p. 62.

[31] Sigmund Freud, "Sexuality in the Aetiology of the Neuroses" (1898), in *The Standard Edition of the Complete Psychological Works of Sigmund Freud, Vol. 3*, trans. and ed. James Strachey (London, UK: Hogarth Press and the Institute of Psycho-Analysis, 1981), p. 282.

[32] Sigmund Freud, "Freud's Psycho-Analytic Procedure" (1904 [1903]), in *The Standard Edition of the Complete Psychological Works of Sigmund Freud, Vol. 7*, trans. and ed. James Strachey (London, UK: Hogarth Press and the Institute of Psycho-Analysis, 1953), p. 249.

[33] Sigmund Freud, "On Psychotherapy" (1905 [1904]), in *The Standard Edition of the Complete Psychological Works of Sigmund Freud, Vol. 7*, trans. and ed. James Strachey (London, UK: Hogarth Press and the Institute of Psycho-Analysis, 1953), p. 259.

[34] Sigmund Freud, "A Short Account of Psycho-Analysis" (1924 [1923]), in *The Standard Edition of the Complete Psychological Works of Sigmund Freud, Vol. 19*, trans. and ed. James Strachey (London, UK: Vintage Books, 2001), p. 194.

[35] C. G. Jung, "Problems of Modern Psychotherapy," in *Modern Man in Search of a Soul*, trans. W. S. Dell and Cary F. Baynes (New York, NY: Harcourt, Brace & World, 1933), p. 35.

[36] Joseph Jastrow, "Hysterical Impairment," in *Freud: His Dream and Sex Theories* (Cleveland, OH: World Publishing Company, 1948), p. 19.

[37] Fulton J. Sheen, "Frustration," in *Peace of Soul* (Liguori, MO: Liguori/Triumph, 1996), p. 7.

[38] St. Symeon the New Theologian, quoted in Jean-Claude Larchet, "The Therapeutic Role of the Spiritual Father," in *Therapy of Spiritual Illnesses, Vol 2: An Introduction to the Ascetic Tradition of the Orthodox Church*, trans. Fr. Kilian Sprecher (Montréal: Alexander Press, 2012), p. 194.

[39] Abba Poemen, quoted in Jean-Claude Larchet, "The Manifestation of Thoughts," in *Therapy of Spiritual Illnesses, Vol 2: An Introduction to the Ascetic Tradition of the Orthodox Church*, trans. Fr. Kilian Sprecher (Montréal: Alexander Press, 2012), p. 222.

[40] Paul Tournier, "The Way of Confession," in *Guilt and Grace: A Psychological Study*, trans. Arthur W. Heathcote, J. J. Henry and P. J. Allcock (New York, NY: Harper & Row, 1962), p. 204.

Chapter 14: The Satanic Pact and the Psychologizing of Evil

[1] Fyodor Dostoyevsky, "Part One—Chapter Six," in *Crime and Punishment* (New York, NY: P. F. Collier & Son, 1917), p. 73.

[2] Rollo May, "Psychotherapy as Faustian," in *The Cry for Myth* (New York, NY: Delta Book, 1992), p. 268.

[3] Janet Malcolm, "Chapter Eight," in *In the Freud Archives* (New York, NY: Vintage Books, 1985), p. 81.

[4] Bernie Zilbergeld, "The Therapeutic Sensibility," in *The Shrinking of America: Myths of Psychological Change* (Boston, MA: Little, Brown and Company, 1983), p. 13.

[5] Bernie Zilbergeld, "The Therapeutic Sensibility," in *The Shrinking of America: Myths of Psychological Change* (Boston, MA: Little, Brown and Company, 1983), p. 13.

[6] C. G. Jung, "Psychotherapists or the Clergy," in *Modern Man in Search of a Soul*, trans. W. S. Dell and Cary F. Baynes (New York, NY: Harcourt, Brace & World, 1933), p. 232.

[7] René Guénon, "The Question of Satanism," in *The Spiritist Fallacy*, trans. Alvin Moore, Jr. and Rama P. Coomaraswamy (Hillsdale, NY: Sophia Perennis, 2004), p. 259.

[8] Ibid., p. 276.

[9] Frithjof Schuon, "Fifth Collection—XCVII," in *World Wheel, Volumes IV–VII* (Bloomington, IN: World Wisdom, 2006), p. 75.

[10] Ananda K. Coomaraswamy, "Who Is 'Satan' and Where Is 'Hell'?" in *Coomaraswamy, Vol. 2: Selected Papers: Metaphysics*, ed. Roger Lipsey (Princeton, NJ: Princeton University Press, 1978), p. 23.

[11] Seraphim Rose, "Epilogue," to *Orthodoxy and the Religion of the Future* (Platina, CA: Saint Herman of Alaska Brotherhood, 1990), p. 234. "The Christian world is now truly confronted by the principle of evil...This manifestation of naked evil has assumed apparently permanent form" (C. G. Jung, "Late Thoughts," in *Memories, Dreams, Reflections*, trans. Richard Winston and Clara Winston, ed. Aniela Jaffé [New York, NY: Vintage Books, 1965], p. 328).

[12] René Guénon, "The Fissures in the Great Wall," in *The Reign of Quantity and the Signs of the Times*, trans. Lord Northbourne (Ghent, NY: Sophia Perennis, 2001), p. 172.

[13] René Guénon, "The Confusion of the Psychic and the Spiritual," in *The Reign of Quantity and the Signs of the Times*, trans. Lord Northbourne (Ghent, NY: Sophia Perennis, 2001), p. 239. See also René Guénon, "The Question of Satanism," in *The Spiritist Fallacy*, trans. Alvin Moore, Jr. and Rama P. Coomaraswamy (Hillsdale, NY: Sophia Perennis, 2004), pp. 253–76.

[14] Ananda K. Coomaraswamy, "Who Is 'Satan' and Where Is 'Hell'?" in *Coomaraswamy, Vol. 2: Selected Papers: Metaphysics*, ed. Roger Lipsey (Princeton, NJ: Princeton University Press, 1978), p. 33. See also Charles Upton, *The System of the Antichrist: Truth and Falsehood in Postmodernism and the New Age* (Ghent, NY: Sophia Perennis, 2001).

[15] Sigmund Freud, "Letter to Wilhelm Fliess—January 24, 1897," in *The Complete Letters of Sigmund Freud to Wilhelm Fliess, 1887–1904*, trans. and ed. Jeffrey Moussaieff Masson (Cambridge, MA: Belknap Press of Harvard University Press, 1985), p. 227.

[16] Josef Breuer, "Theoretical," in Josef Breuer and Sigmund Freud, *Studies on Hysteria*, trans. and ed. James Strachey (New York, NY: Basic Books, 2000), p. 250.

[17] Sigmund Freud, "A Neurosis of Demonical Possession in the Seventeenth Century" (1923 [1922]), in *Studies in Parapsychology*, ed. Philip Rieff (New York, NY: Collier Books, 1966), p. 92.

[18] Immanuel Velikovsky, "The Dreams Freud Dreamed," *Psychoanalytic Review*, vol. 28 (October 1941), p. 490.

[19] Sigmund Freud, "Letter to Wilhelm Fliess—March 23, 1900," in Marie Bonaparte, Anna Freud and Ernst Kris (eds.), *The Origins of Psychoanalysis:*

Letters to Wilhelm Fliess, Drafts and Notes: 1887–1902, trans. Eric Mosbacher and James Strachey (New York, NY: Basic Books, 1954), p. 314. See also Sigmund Freud, "Letter to Wilhelm Fliess—March 23, 1900," in *The Complete Letters of Sigmund Freud to Wilhelm Fliess, 1887–1904*, trans. and ed. Jeffrey Moussaieff Masson (Cambridge, MA: Belknap Press of Harvard University Press, 1985), p. 405.

[20] Sigmund Freud, quoted in Ernest Jones, "Marriage," in *The Life and Work of Sigmund Freud, Vol. 1: The Formative Years and the Great Discoveries, 1856–1900* (New York, NY: Basic Books, 1959), p. 147.

[21] Sigmund Freud, "Letter to Wilhelm Fliess—August 14, 1897," in Marie Bonaparte, Anna Freud and Ernst Kris (eds.), *The Origins of Psychoanalysis: Letters to Wilhelm Fliess, Drafts and Notes: 1887–1902*, trans. Eric Mosbacher and James Strachey (New York, NY: Basic Books, 1954), p. 213. Alternatively translated as, "I am now enjoying a period of bad humor." (Sigmund Freud, "Letter to Wilhelm Fliess—August 14, 1897," in *The Complete Letters of Sigmund Freud to Wilhelm Fliess, 1887–1904*, trans. and ed. Jeffrey Moussaieff Masson [Cambridge, MA: Belknap Press of Harvard University Press, 1985], p. 261).

[22] Ernest Jones, "The Cocaine Episode," in *The Life and Work of Sigmund Freud, Vol. 1: The Formative Years and the Great Discoveries, 1856–1900* (New York, NY: Basic Books, 1959), p. 84.

[23] David Bakan, "Accretion of Meanings to the Devil Image," in *Sigmund Freud and the Jewish Mystical Tradition* (London, UK: Free Association Books, 1990), p. 236.

[24] Sigmund Freud, "Preface to the Second Edition" (1908), in *The Interpretation of Dreams*, trans. and ed. James Strachey (New York, NY: Science Editions, 1963), p. xxvi.

[25] See Peter J. Swales, "Freud, Filthy Lucre, and Undue Influence," *Review of Existential Psychology and Psychiatry*, vol. 23, Nos. 1–3 (1997), pp. 115–41.

[26] Sigmund Freud, "Letter to Martha Bernays—September 4, 1883," in Ernst L. Freud (ed.), *Letters of Sigmund Freud*, trans. Tania Stern and James Stern (New York, NY: Basic Books, 1975), p. 54.

[27] Sigmund Freud, "Letter to Martha Bernays—March 10, 1885," in Ernst L. Freud (ed.), *Letters of Sigmund Freud*, trans. Tania Stern and James Stern (New York, NY: Basic Books, 1975), p. 138.

[28] Sigmund Freud, "Letter to Martha Bernays—February 14, 1884," in Ernst L. Freud (ed.), *Letters of Sigmund Freud*, trans. Tania Stern and James Stern (New York, NY: Basic Books, 1975), p. 99.

[29] Sigmund Freud, "Letter to Wilhelm Fliess—September 21, 1899," in Marie Bonaparte, Anna Freud and Ernst Kris (eds.), *The Origins of Psychoanalysis: Letters to Wilhelm Fliess, Drafts and Notes: 1887–1902*, trans. Eric Mosbacher and James Strachey (New York, NY: Basic Books, 1954), p. 298.

Alternatively translated as, "My mood also depends very strongly on my earnings...I came to know the helplessness of poverty and continually fear it" (Sigmund Freud, "Letter to Wilhelm Fliess—September 21, 1899," in *The Complete Letters of Sigmund Freud to Wilhelm Fliess, 1887–1904*, trans. and ed. Jeffrey Moussaieff Masson [Cambridge, MA: Belknap Press of Harvard University Press, 1985], p. 374).

[30] Sigmund Freud, "Letter to Martha Bernays—February 2, 1886," in Ernst L. Freud (ed.), *Letters of Sigmund Freud*, trans. Tania Stern and James Stern (New York, NY: Basic Books, 1975), p. 201.

[31] Sigmund Freud, "Letter to C .G. Jung—March 14, 1911," in William McGuire (ed.), *The Freud/Jung Letters: The Correspondence Between Sigmund Freud and C. G. Jung*, trans. Ralph Manheim and R.F.C. Hull (Princeton, NJ: Princeton University Press, 1994), p. 402.

[32] Sigmund Freud, "Letter to C. G. Jung—March 9, 1909," in William McGuire (ed.), *The Freud/Jung Letters: The Correspondence Between Sigmund Freud and C. G. Jung*, trans. Ralph Manheim and R.F.C. Hull (Princeton, NJ: Princeton University Press, 1994), p. 210.

[33] Sigmund Freud, "Letter to Wilhelm Fliess—September 21, 1899," in *The Complete Letters of Sigmund Freud to Wilhelm Fliess, 1887–1904*, trans. and ed. Jeffrey Moussaieff Masson (Cambridge, MA: Belknap Press of Harvard University Press, 1985), p. 374.

[34] Sigmund Freud, "A Neurosis of Demonical Possession in the Seventeenth Century" (1923 [1922]), in *Studies in Parapsychology*, ed. Philip Rieff (New York, NY: Collier Books, 1966), p. 97.

[35] David Bakan, "Freud's Paper on Demoniacal Possession," in *Sigmund Freud and the Jewish Mystical Tradition* (London, UK: Free Association Books, 1990), p. 219.

[36] Sigmund Freud, "A Neurosis of Demonical Possession in the Seventeenth Century" (1923 [1922]), in *Studies in Parapsychology*, ed. Philip Rieff (New York, NY: Collier Books, 1966), p. 100.

[37] Paul C. Vitz, "Freud and the Devil: Literature and Cocaine," in *Sigmund Freud's Christian Unconscious* (New York, NY: Guilford Press, 1988), p. 113.

[38] René Guénon, "The Fissures in the Great Wall," in *The Reign of Quantity and the Signs of the Times*, trans. Lord Northbourne (Ghent, NY: Sophia Perennis, 2001), p. 172.

[39] Paul C. Vitz, "Freud and the Devil: Sexual Seduction and Splitting," in *Sigmund Freud's Christian Unconscious* (New York, NY: Guilford Press, 1988), p. 146.

[40] Leonard Shengold, "The Freud/Jung Letters," in *Freud and His Self-Analysis*, eds. Mark Kanzer and Jules Glenn (New York, NY: Jason Aronson, 1983), p. 200.

[41] C. G. Jung, "Psychological Interpretation of Children's Dreams" (Winter Term 1939/1940), in *Children's Dreams: Notes from the Seminar Given in 1936–1940*, trans. Ernst Falzeder and Tony Woolfson, eds. Lorenz Jung and

Maria Meyer-Grass (Princeton, NJ: Princeton University Press, 2008), p. 372.

[42] C. G. Jung, "The Archetypes of the Collective Unconscious," in *Two Essays on Analytical Psychology*, trans. R.F.C. Hull (New York, NY: Meridian, 1956), p. 106.

[43] Karen Horney, "Alienation from Self," in *Neurosis and Human Growth: The Struggle Toward Self-Realization* (New York, NY: W. W. Norton & Company, 1950), p. 155.

[44] Sigmund Freud, "A Neurosis of Demonical Possession in the Seventeenth Century" (1923 [1922]), in *Studies in Parapsychology*, ed. Philip Rieff (New York, NY: Collier Books, 1966), p. 102.

[45] Ibid., p. 91.

[46] Ibid.

[47] Ibid., p. 101.

[48] Ibid..

[49] Ibid., pp. 104–5.

[50] David Bakan, "Moses as an Egyptian," in *Sigmund Freud and the Jewish Mystical Tradition* (London, UK: Free Association Books, 1990), pp. 158–59.

[51] David Bakan, "Accretion of Meanings to the Devil Image," in *Sigmund Freud and the Jewish Mystical Tradition* (London, UK: Free Association Books, 1990), p. 233.

[52] Whitall N. Perry, "The Revolt Against Moses: A New Look at Psychoanalysis," in *Challenges to a Secular Society* (Oakton, VA: Foundation for Traditional Studies, 1996), p. 31.

[53] David Bakan, "The 'Flectere...' of the Interpretation of Dreams," in *Sigmund Freud and the Jewish Mystical Tradition* (London, UK: Free Association Books, 1990), p. 211.

[54] Ibid., p. 212.

[55] Sigmund Freud, "Beyond the Pleasure Principle" (1920), in *Beyond the Pleasure Principle*, trans. and ed. James Strachey (New York, NY: W. W. Norton & Company, 1989), p. 41.

[56] Ernest Jones, "The Medical Student," in *The Life and Work of Sigmund Freud, Vol. 1: The Formative Years and the Great Discoveries, 1856–1900* (New York, NY: Basic Books, 1959), p. 54.

[57] Ibid.

[58] René Guénon, "The Hatred of Secrecy," in *The Reign of Quantity and the Signs of the Times*, trans. Lord Northbourne (Ghent, NY: Sophia Perennis, 2001), p. 88.

[59] Sigmund Freud, quoted in Hanns Sachs, "'The Man Moses' and the Man Freud," *Psychoanalytic Review*, vol. 28 (1941), p. 159.

[60] Sigmund Freud, "Letter to C. G. Jung—November 12, 1908," in William McGuire (ed.), *The Freud/Jung Letters: The Correspondence Between Sigmund Freud and C. G. Jung*, trans. Ralph Manheim and R.F.C. Hull (Princeton, NJ: Princeton University Press, 1994), p. 178.

[61] Frederick Crews, "The Revenge of the Repressed," in *The Memory Wars: Freud's Legacy in Dispute* (New York, NY: New York Review of Books, 1995), p. 219.

[62] Sigmund Freud, "Letter to Wilhelm Fliess—January 17, 1887," in *The Complete Letters of Sigmund Freud to Wilhelm Fliess, 1887-1904*, trans. and ed. Jeffrey Moussaieff Masson (Cambridge, MA: Belknap Press of Harvard University Press, 1985), p. 224.

[63] C. G. Jung, "Letter to Hans Schmid—November 6, 1915," in *Selected Letters of C. G. Jung, 1909–1961*, ed. Gerhard Adler (Princeton, NJ: Princeton University Press, 1984), p. 5.

[64] Sigmund Freud, "Fragment of an Analysis of a Case of Hysteria" (1905 [1901]), in *The Standard Edition of the Complete Psychological Works of Sigmund Freud, Vol. 7*, trans. and ed. James Strachey (London, UK: Hogarth Press and the Institute of Psycho-Analysis, 1953), p. 109.

[65] Sigmund Freud, quoted in David Bakan, "Freud's Messianic Identification," in *Sigmund Freud and the Jewish Mystical Tradition* (London, UK: Free Association Books, 1990), p. 181.

[66] Philip Sherrard, "Christianity and the Religious Thought of C. G. Jung," in *Christianity: Lineaments of a Sacred Tradition* (Brookline, MA: Holy Cross Orthodox Press, 1998), p. 141.

[67] C. G. Jung, "The Stages of Life," in *Modern Man in Search of a Soul*, trans. W. S. Dell and Cary F. Baynes (New York, NY: Harcourt, Brace & World, 1933), p. 96.

[68] René Guénon, "Neo-Spiritualism," in *The Reign of Quantity and the Signs of the Times*, trans. Lord Northbourne (Ghent, NY: Sophia Perennis, 2001), p. 219.

[69] Jean-Louis Michon, "The Spiritual Practices of Sufism," in *Islamic Spirituality: Foundations*, ed. Seyyed Hossein Nasr (New York, NY: Crossroad, 1997), pp. 271–72.

[70] Titus Burckhardt, "Traditional Cosmology and Modern Science: Modern Psychology," in *Mirror of the Intellect: Essays on Traditional Science and Sacred Art*, trans. and ed. William Stoddart (Albany, NY: State University of New York Press, 1987), p. 61.

Chapter 15: The Ethical Void and the Crisis of the Super-Ego

[1] D.H. Lawrence, "Psychoanalysis vs. Morality," in *Psychoanalysis and the Unconscious* (New York, NY: Thomas Seltzer, 1921), p. 12.

[2] Sigmund Freud, "The Dependent Relationships of the Ego," in *The Ego and the Id*, trans. Joan Riviere, ed. James Strachey (New York, NY: W. W. Norton & Company, 1989), p. 56.

[3] Sigmund Freud, "Chapter Two," in *Civilization and Its Discontents*, trans. and ed. James Strachey (New York, NY: W. W. Norton & Company, 1989), p. 34.

[4] Christopher Lasch, "The Politics of the Psyche," in *The Minimal Self: Psychic Survival in Troubled Times* (New York, NY: W. W. Norton & Company, 1984), p. 198. See also Arnold A. Rogow, *The Dying of the Light: A Searching Look at America Today* (New York, NY: G.P. Putnam's Sons, 1975).

[5] Sigmund Freud, "The Internal World" (1940 [1938]), in *An Outline of Psycho-Analysis*, trans. and ed. James Strachey (New York, NY: W. W. Norton & Company, 1989), p. 95.

[6] Ibid.

[7] E. Michael Jones, "Part II, Chapter 1: Paris, 1885," in *Libido Dominandi: Sexual Liberation and Political Control* (South Bend, IN: St. Augustine's Press, 2000), p. 103.

[8] Philip Rieff, "In Defense of the Analytic Attitude," in *The Triumph of the Therapeutic: Uses of Faith After Freud* (Chicago, IL: University of Chicago Press, 1987), p. 89.

[9] Sigmund Freud, "Chapter Eight," in *Civilization and Its Discontents*, trans. and ed. James Strachey (New York, NY: W. W. Norton & Company, 1989), p. 97.

[10] "[Herbert] Marcuse is essentially an example of an alienated intellectual, who presents his personal despair as a theory of radicalism" (Erich Fromm, "The Paradox and Nature of Hope," in *The Revolution of Hope: Toward a Humanized Technology* [New York, NY: Bantam Books, 1971], p. 9).

[11] Herbert Marcuse, "The Hidden Trend in Psychoanalysis," in *Eros and Civilization: A Philosophical Inquiry into Freud* (New York, NY: Vintage Books, 1962), p. 11.

[12] Sigmund Freud, "The Ego and the Super-Ego (Ego Ideal)" (1923), in *The Ego and the Id*, trans. Joan Riviere, ed. James Strachey (New York, NY: W. W. Norton & Company, 1989), p. 32.

[13] Neil Postman, "When There Were No Children," in *The Disappearance of Childhood* (New York, NY: Vintage Books, 1994), p. 9.

[14] Christopher Lasch, "The Attack on the Nuclear Family and the Search for 'Alternate Life-styles,'" in *Haven in a Heartless World: The Family Besieged* (New York, NY: W. W. Norton & Company, 1995), p. 140.

[15] Sigmund Freud, "Letter to James J. Putnam—March 30, 1914," in James Jackson Putnam and Psychoanalysis: Letters between Putnam and Sigmund Freud, Ernest Jones, William James, Sándor Ferenczi, and Morton Prince, 1877–1917, trans. Judith Bernays Heller, ed. Nathan G. Hale, Jr. (Cambridge, MA: Harvard University Press, 1971), p. 171.

[16] Sigmund Freud, "Transference" (1916–1917 [1915–1917]), in *Introductory Lectures on Psychoanalysis*, trans. and ed. James Strachey (New York, NY: W. W. Norton & Company, 1977), p. 434.

[17] Philip Rieff, "The Ethic of Honesty," in *Freud: The Mind of the Moralist* (Chicago, IL: University of Chicago Press, 1979), p. 315.

[18] Karen Horney, "Auxiliary Approaches to Artificial Harmony," in *Our Inner Conflicts: A Constructive Theory of Neurosis* (New York, NY: W. W. Norton & Company, 1972), p. 134.

[19] Nathaniel S. Lehrman, "Moral Aspects of Mental Health," *The Humanist*, vol. 22, nos. 2–3 (1962), p. 60.

[20] Herbert Marcuse, "Epilogue: Critique of Neo-Freudian Revisionism," in *Eros and Civilization: A Philosophical Inquiry into Freud* (New York, NY: Vintage Books, 1962), p. 224.

[21] Anna Freud, *The Psychoanalytical Treatment of Children: Lectures and Essays* (New York, NY: Schocken Books, 1964), p. 61.

[22] Philip Rieff, "The Emergence of Psychological Man," in *Freud: The Mind of the Moralist* (Chicago, IL: University of Chicago Press, 1979), p. 355.

[23] Ibid.

[24] C. G. Jung, "From Esther Harding's Notebooks: 1922, 1925," in *C. G. Jung Speaking: Interviews and Encounters*, eds. William McGuire and R.F.C. Hull (Princeton, NJ: Princeton University Press, 1993), p. 29.

[25] Ernest Jones, "The Committee," in *The Life and Work of Sigmund Freud, Vol. 2: Years of Maturity, 1901–1919* (New York, NY: Basic Books, 1955), p. 166.

[26] C. G. Jung, "The State of Psychotherapy Today" (1934), in *The Collected Works of C. G. Jung, Vol. 10: Civilization in Transition*, trans. R.F.C. Hull (Princeton, NJ: Princeton University Press, 1970), p. 169.

[27] "Thou shalt love thy neighbor as thyself" (Mark 12:31). The Prophet Muhammad made a similar pronunciation: "None of you has faith until you love for your neighbor what you love for yourself" (Sahih Muslim).

[28] Sigmund Freud, "Chapter Eight," in *Civilization and Its Discontents*, trans. and ed. James Strachey (New York, NY: W. W. Norton & Company, 1989), p. 109.

[29] Ibn al-'Arabī, quoted in William C. Chittick, *The Sufi Path of Knowledge: Ibn al-'Arabī's Metaphysics of Imagination* (Albany, NY: State University of New York Press, 1989), p. 283.

[30] St. Makarios of Egypt, "Spiritual Perfection," in *The Philokalia, Vol. 3: The Complete Text; Compiled by St. Nikodimos of the Holy Mountain and St. Makarios of Corinth*, trans. and ed. G.E.H. Palmer, Philip Sherrard, and Kallistos Ware (London, UK: Faber and Faber, 1995), p. 291.

[31] Walpola Rahula, "The Words of Truth (*Dhammapada*)," in *What the Buddha Taught* (New York, NY: Grove Press, 1974), p. 128.

[32] See also Lorenzo Scupoli, *Unseen Warfare: The Spiritual Combat and Path to Paradise of Lorenzo Scupoli*, ed. Nicodemus of the Holy Mountain and revised by Theophan the Recluse, trans. E. Kadloubovsky and G.E.H. Palmer (Crestwood, NY: St. Vladimir's Seminary Press, 2000).

[33] Thomas Yellowtail, quoted in Michael Oren Fitzgerald, "Outdoor Ceremonies," in *Yellowtail, Crow Medicine Man and Sun Dance Chief: An Autobiography* (Norman, OK: University of Oklahoma Press, 1994), pp. 139–40.

[34] Rūmī, quoted in A.J. Arberry, *Discourses of Rumi* (London, UK: RoutledgeCurzon, 2004), pp. 68–69.

[35] Śrī Ramana Maharshi, "Who am I?" in *The Collected Works of Ramana Maharshi*, ed. Arthur Osborne (Boston, MA: Weiser Books, 1997), p. 46.

[36] C. S. Lewis, "Men without Chests," in *The Abolition of Man* (New York, NY: Collier Books, 1986), pp. 33–34.

[37] See Titus Burckhardt, *Introduction to Sufi Doctrine*, trans. D. M. Matheson (Bloomington, IN: World Wisdom, 2008).

[38] Javad Nurbakhsh, "The Passions of the Nafs," in *The Psychology of Sufism* [Del wa Nafs] (London, UK: Khaniqahi-Nimatullahi Publications, 1992), p. 39.

[39] Javad Nurbakhsh, "The Passions of the Nafs," in *The Psychology of Sufism* [Del wa Nafs] (London, UK: Khaniqahi-Nimatullahi Publications, 1992), p. 39.

[40] Frithjof Schuon, "A View of Yoga," in *Language of the Self* (Bloomington, IN: World Wisdom Books, 1999), p. 57.

[41] Richard Krafft-Ebing, "Fragments of a System of Psychology of Sexual Life," in *Psychopathia Sexualis* (New York, NY: Rebman Company, 1906), p. 5.

[42] Sigmund Freud, "Repression" (1915), in *The Standard Edition of the Complete Psychological Works of Sigmund Freud, Vol. 14*, trans. and ed. James Strachey (London, UK: Hogarth Press and the Institute of Psycho-Analysis, 1971), p. 151.

[43] Sigmund Freud, "On the History of the Psychoanalytic Movement" (1914), in *The History of the Psychoanalytic Movement*, ed. Philip Rieff (New York, NY: Collier Books, 1963), p. 50.

[44] Alain Daniélou, "Contents of the Book," in *The Complete Kāma Sūtra: The First Unabridged Modern Translation of the Classic Indian Text by Vātsyāyana*, trans. Alain Daniélou (Rochester, VT: Park Street Press, 1994), p. 23.

[45] Arthur Osborne, "Quest and Egoism," in *For Those with Little Dust: Selected Writings of Arthur Osborne* (Sarasota, FL: Ramana Publications, 1990), p. 125.

[46] Jean-Claude Larchet, "The Pathology of Fallen Man," in *Therapy of Spiritual Illnesses, Vol 1: An Introduction to the Ascetic Tradition of the Orthodox Church*, trans. Fr. Kilian Sprecher (Montréal: Alexander Press, 2012), p. 81.

[47] C. G. Jung, "Dream-Analysis in Its Practical Application," in *Modern Man in Search of a Soul*, trans. W. S. Dell and Cary F. Baynes (New York, NY: Harcourt, Brace & World, 1933), pp. 16–17.

[48] Sigmund Freud, "Chapter One," in *Leonardo Da Vinci: A Study in Psychosexuality*, trans. A. A. Brill (New York, NY: Vintage Books, 1947), p. 26.

[49] Sigmund Freud, "Letter to James J. Putnam—May 14, 1911," in *James Jackson Putnam and Psychoanalysis: Letters between Putnam and Sigmund Freud, Ernest Jones, William James, Sándor Ferenczi, and Morton Prince,*

1877–1917, trans. Judith Bernays Heller, ed. Nathan G. Hale, Jr. (Cambridge, MA: Harvard University Press, 1971), p. 121.

[50] Sigmund Freud, "The Dependent Relationships of the Ego" (1923), in *The Ego and the Id*, trans. Joan Riviere, ed. James Strachey (New York, NY: W. W. Norton & Company, 1989), p. 58.

[51] Sigmund Freud, "Infantile Sexuality" (1905), in *The Basic Writings of Sigmund Freud*, trans. and ed. A. A. Brill (New York, NY: Modern Library, 1938), p. 584.

[52] Sigmund Freud, "Introduction" (1917), to *A General Introduction to Psychoanalysis* (New York, NY: Horace Liveright, 1920), p. 8.

[53] Ibid..

[54] Sigmund Freud, "Recommendations to Physicians Practicing Psycho-Analysis" (1912), in *The Standard Edition of the Complete Psychological Works of Sigmund Freud, Vol. 12*, trans. and ed. James Strachey (London, UK: Hogarth Press and the Institute of Psycho-Analysis, 1958), p. 119

[55] Sigmund Freud, "The Theory of the Instincts" (1940 [1938]), in *An Outline of Psycho-Analysis*, trans. and ed. James Strachey (New York, NY: W. W. Norton & Company, 1969), p. 7.

[56] Erich Fromm, "Appendix: Freud's Theory of Aggressiveness and Destructiveness," in *The Anatomy of Human Destructiveness* (New York, NY: Holt, Rinehart and Winston, 1974), p. 465.

[57] Mark Perry, "Satan Is Not an Atheist," in *The Mystery of Individuality: Grandeur and Delusion of the Human Condition* (Bloomington, IN: World Wisdom, 2012), p. 173.

[58] Mark Perry, "Introduction," to *The Mystery of Individuality: Grandeur and Delusion of the Human Condition* (Bloomington, IN: World Wisdom, 2012), p. 2.

[59] Pope Pius XII, "On Psychotherapy and Religion: An Address of His Holiness Pope Pius XII to the Fifth International Congress on Psychotherapy and Clinical Psychology," April 13, 1953 (Washington, DC: National Catholic Welfare Conference, 1953), p. 5.

[60] Theodore Dalrymple, "Chapter One," in *Admirable Evasions: How Psychology Undermines Morality* (New York, NY: Encounter Books, 2015), p. 23.

Chapter 16: Freud and the Question of Jewish Identity

[1] Sigmund Freud, "Preface to the Hebrew Translation" (1930), in *Introductory Lectures on Psychoanalysis*, trans. and ed. James Strachey (New York, NY: W. W. Norton & Company, 1977), p. 11.

[2] Goethe, quoted in Sigmund Freud, "The Internal World" (1940 [1938]), in *An Outline of Psycho-Analysis*, trans. and ed. James Strachey (New York, NY: W. W. Norton & Company, 1989), p. 96.

3 Yosef Hayim Yerushalmi, "The Fourth Humiliation," in *Freud's Moses: Judaism Terminable and Interminable* (New Haven, CT: Yale University Press, 1991), pp. 9–10.

4 Andrew R. Heinze, "Benjamin Franklin in Hebrew: The *Musar* Sage of Philadelphia," in *Jews and the American Soul: Human Nature in the Twentieth Century* (Princeton, NJ: Princeton University Press, 2004), p. 49.

5 Kevin MacDonald, "Jewish Involvement in the Psychoanalytic Movement," in *The Culture of Critique* (Bloomington, IN: 1stBooks, 2002), p. 105.

6 Sigmund Freud, "An Autobiographical Study" (1925 [1924]), in *An Autobiographical Study*, trans. and ed. James Strachey (New York, NY: W. W. Norton & Company, 1989), p. 6.

7 Sigmund Freud, quoted in Ernest Jones, "Fame and Suffering," in *The Life and Work of Sigmund Freud, Vol. 3: The Last Phase, 1919–1939* (New York, NY: Basic Books, 1957), p. 124.

8 Sigmund Freud, "Letter to Lou Andreas-Salomé—January 6, 1935," in Sigmund Freud and Lou Andreas-Salomé, *Letters*, trans. William Robson-Scott and Elaine Robson-Scott, ed. Ernst Pfeiffer (New York, NY: W. W. Norton & Company, 1985), p. 205.

9 Ernest Jones, "Boyhood and Adolescence," in *The Life and Work of Sigmund Freud, vol. 1: The Formative Years and the Great Discoveries, 1856–1900* (New York, NY: Basic Books, 1959), p. 22.

10 Sigmund Freud, "Letter to Sabina Spielrein—August 20, 1912," quoted in Aldo Carotenuto, *A Secret Symmetry: Sabina Spielrein between Jung and Freud*, trans. Arno Pomerans, John Shepley and Krishna Winston (New York, NY: Pantheon Books, 1982), p. 117.

11 Kevin MacDonald, "Jewish Involvement in the Psychoanalytic Movement," in *The Culture of Critique* (Bloomington, IN: 1stBooks, 2002), p. 111.

12 Dennis B. Klein, "The Particular and the Universal," in *Jewish Origins of the Psychoanalytic Movement* (Chicago, IL: University of Chicago Press, 1985), p. 143.

13 Philip Rieff, "Preface to the Second Edition," in *Freud: The Mind of the Moralist* (Chicago, IL: University of Chicago Press, 1979), p. xx.

14 Peter Gay, "Sigmund Freud: A Brief Life," in Sigmund Freud, *Jokes and Their Relation to the Unconscious*, trans. and ed. James Strachey (New York, NY: W. W. Norton & Company, 1989), p. xi.

15 Ernest Jones, "Religion," in *The Life and Work of Sigmund Freud, Vol. 3: The Last Phase, 1919–1939* (New York, NY: Basic Books, 1957), p. 351.

16 Ernest Jones, "Boyhood and Adolescence," in *The Life and Work of Sigmund Freud, Vol. 1: The Formative Years and the Great Discoveries, 1856–1900* (New York, NY: Basic Books, 1959), p. 19.

[17] Sigmund Freud, "Letter to the Editor of the *Jewish Press Centre in Zürich*" (1925), in *The Standard Edition of the Complete Psychological Works of Sigmund Freud, Vol. 19*, trans. and ed. James Strachey (London, UK: Hogarth Press and the Institute of Psycho-Analysis, 1961), p. 291.

[18] George Sylvester Viereck, "Sigmund Freud Confronts the Sphinx," in *Glimpses of the Great* (New York, NY: Macaulay Company, 1930), p. 30.

[19] Ernest Jones, "Boyhood and Adolescence," in *The Life and Work of Sigmund Freud, Vol. 1: The Formative Years and the Great Discoveries, 1856–1900* (New York, NY: Basic Books, 1959), p. 19.

[20] Sigmund Freud, "An Autobiographical Study" (1925 [1924]), in *The Standard Edition of the Complete Psychological Works of Sigmund Freud, Vol. 20*, trans. and ed. James Strachey (London, UK: Hogarth Press and the Institute of Psycho-Analysis, 1959), p. 8.

[21] Jakob Freud, quoted in Ernest Jones, "Boyhood and Adolescence," in *The Life and Work of Sigmund Freud, Vol. 1: The Formative Years and the Great Discoveries, 1856–1900* (New York, NY: Basic Books, 1959), p. 19.

[22] Sigmund Freud, "Letter to Enrico Morselli—February 18, 1926," in Ernst L. Freud (ed.), *Letters of Sigmund Freud*, trans. Tania Stern and James Stern (New York, NY: Basic Books, 1975), p. 365.

[23] Sigmund Freud, "Letter to Marie Bonaparte—May 10, 1926," in Ernst L. Freud (ed.), *Letters of Sigmund Freud*, trans. Tania Stern and James Stern (New York, NY: Basic Books, 1975), p. 368.

[24] C. G. Jung, "Letter to Edith Schroder—April [Undated], 1957," in *Selected Letters of C.G. Jung, 1909–1961*, ed. Gerhard Adler (Princeton, NJ: Princeton University Press, 1984), p. 153.

[25] Sigmund Freud, "Letter to C. G. Jung—April 16, 1909," in William McGuire (ed.), *The Freud/Jung Letters: The Correspondence Between Sigmund Freud and C. G. Jung*, trans. Ralph Manheim and R.F.C. Hull (Princeton, NJ: Princeton University Press, 1994), p. 220. "Here is another instance where you will find confirmation of the specifically Jewish character of my [Freud's] mysticism" (Sigmund Freud, quoted in C. G. Jung, "Appendix I: Letters from Freud to Jung," in *Memories, Dreams, Reflections*, trans. Richard Winston and Clara Winston, ed. Aniela Jaffé [New York, NY: Vintage Books, 1965], p. 363).

[26] Sigmund Freud, "Letter to Karl Abraham—July 20, 1908," quoted in Ernest Jones, "The Beginning of International Recognition," in *The Life and Work of Sigmund Freud, Vol. 2: Years of Maturity, 1901–1919* (New York, NY: Basic Books, 1955), p. 49. "On the whole it is easier for us Jews, as we lack the mystical element." (Sigmund Freud, "Letter to Karl Abraham—July 20, 1908," in *The Complete Correspondence of Sigmund Freud and Karl Abraham, 1907–1925*, trans. Caroline Schwarzacher, Christine Trollope and Klara Majthényi King, ed. Ernst Falzeder [London, UK: Karnac, 2002], p. 52).

[27] David Bakan, "Freud's Positive Identification as a Jew," in *Sigmund Freud and the Jewish Mystical Tradition* (London, UK: Free Association Books, 1990), pp. 52–53.

[28] Sigmund Freud, "Letter to Oskar Pfister—October 9, 1918," in *Psychoanalysis and Faith: The Letters of Sigmund Freud and Oskar Pfister*, trans. Eric Mosbacher, eds. Heinrich Meng and Ernst L. Freud (New York, NY: Basic Books, 1963), p. 63.

[29] Sigmund Freud, "The Resistances to Psychoanalysis" (1925), in *Character and Culture*, ed. Philip Rieff (New York, NY: Collier Books, 1963), p. 262.

[30] Alphonse Maeder, "Letter to Sigmund Freud—October 24, 1912," quoted in John Kerr, *A Most Dangerous Method: The Story of Jung, Freud, and Sabina Spielrein* (New York, NY: Alfred A. Knopf, 1993), p. 424.

[31] A. A. Brill, "Introduction," to *The Basic Writings of Sigmund Freud*, trans. and ed. A. A. Brill (New York, NY: Modern Library, 1938), p. 4.

[32] See Editors of Executive Intelligence Review, *The Ugly Truth about the Anti-Defamation League* (Washington, DC: Executive Intelligence Review, 1992).

[33] See Hugo Knoepfmacher, "Sigmund Freud and the B'nai B'rith," *Journal of the American Psychoanalytic Association*, vol. 27, no. 2 (April 1979), pp. 441–49.

[34] Sigmund Freud, "Address to the Society of B'nai B'rith" (1926), in *The Standard Edition of the Complete Psychological Works of Sigmund Freud, Vol. 20*, trans. and ed. James Strachey (London, UK: Hogarth Press and the Institute of Psycho-Analysis, 1959), p. 274.

[35] Sigmund Freud, "Letter to Members of the B'nai B'rith Lodge—May 6, 1926," in Ernst L. Freud (ed.), *Letters of Sigmund Freud*, trans. Tania Stern and James Stern (New York, NY: Basic Books, 1975), p. 366.

[36] Wilhelm Reich, "Interview with Kurt R. Eissler—October 18, 1952," in *Reich Speaks of Freud: Wilhelm Reich Discusses his Work and his Relationship with Sigmund Freud*, trans. Therese Pol, eds. Mary Higgins and Chester M. Raphael (New York, NY: Farrar, Straus and Giroux, 1972), pp. 60, 62.

[37] Sigmund Freud, "Analysis of a Phobia in a Five-Year-Old Boy" (1909), in *The Standard Edition of the Complete Psychological Works of Sigmund Freud, Vol. 10*, trans. and ed. James Strachey (London, UK: Hogarth Press and the Institute of Psycho-Analysis, 1962), p. 36.

[38] Sigmund Freud, "Moses, His People, and Monotheistic Religion," in *Moses and Monotheism*, trans. Katherine Jones (New York, NY: Vintage Books, 1967), p. 66.

[39] Sigmund Freud, "Chapter Seven," in *The Future of an Illusion*, trans. and ed. James Strachey (New York, NY: W. W. Norton & Company, 1989), p. 46.

[40] Sigmund Freud, "Moses an Egyptian," in *Moses and Monotheism*, trans. Katherine Jones (New York, NY: Vintage Books, 1967), p. 3.

[41] Sigmund Freud, "If Moses was an Egyptian...," in *Moses and Monotheism*, trans. Katherine Jones (New York, NY: Vintage Books, 1967), pp. 49–50.

[42] Paul Ricoeur, "The Genetic Stage of Explanation: Totemism and Monotheism," in *Freud and Philosophy: An Essay on Interpretation*, trans. Denis Savage (New Haven, CT: Yale University Press, 1970), p. 244.

[43] Sigmund Freud, "Letter to Anonymous Individual—December 14, 1937," in Ernst L. Freud (ed.), *Letters of Sigmund Freud*, trans. Tania Stern and James Stern (New York, NY: Basic Books, 1975), p. 439.

[44] David Bakan, "The Moses of Michelangelo," in *Sigmund Freud and the Jewish Mystical Tradition* (London, UK: Free Association Books, 1990), p. 127.

[45] Sigmund Freud, "If Moses was an Egyptian...," in *Moses and Monotheism*, trans. Katherine Jones (New York, NY: Vintage Books, 1967), p. 52.

[46] Ibid..

[47] R. M. Jurjevich, "Freudian Corrosion of Civilized Values," in *The Hoax of Freudism: A Study of Brainwashing the American Professionals and Laymen* (Philadelphia, PA: Dorrance and Company, 1974), p. 128.

[48] Peter Gay, "A Greed for Knowledge," in *Freud: A Life for Our Time* (New York, NY: Anchor Books, 1989), p. 6.

[49] Sigmund Freud, "A Religious Experience" (1928), in *The Standard Edition of the Complete Psychological Works of Sigmund Freud, Vol. 21*, trans. and ed. James Strachey (London, UK: Hogarth Press and the Institute of Psycho-Analysis, 1961), p. 170.

[50] Sigmund Freud, "Letter to Members of the B'nai B'rith Lodge—May 6, 1926," in Ernst L. Freud (ed.), *Letters of Sigmund Freud*, trans. Tania and James Stern (New York, NY: Basic Books, 1975), p. 366.

[51] Sigmund Freud, "Letter to Charles Singer—October 31, 1938," in Ernst L. Freud (ed.), *Letters of Sigmund Freud*, trans. Tania Stern and James Stern (New York, NY: Basic Books, 1975), p. 453.

Chapter 17: Anti-Semitism and the Vengeance on Christianity

[1] Erich Fromm, "Malignant Aggression: Cruelty and Destructiveness," in *The Anatomy of Human Destructiveness* (New York, NY: Holt, Rinehart and Winston, 1974), p. 273.

[2] Sigmund Freud, quoted in René Laforgue, "Personal Memories of Freud" (1956), in *Freud as We Knew Him*, ed. Hendrik M. Ruitenbeek (Detroit, MI: Wayne State University Press, 1973), p. 344.

[3] Thomas Szasz, "Sigmund Freud: The Jewish Avenger," in *The Myth of Psychotherapy: Mental Healing as Religion, Rhetoric, and Repression* (Garden City, NY: Anchor Press, 1979), p. 151. "Freud was, throughout his life, *a proud, chauvinistic*, even *vengeful* Jew" (Thomas Szasz, "Sigmund Freud: The Jewish Avenger," in *The Myth of Psychotherapy: Mental Healing as Religion, Rhetoric, and Repression* [Garden City, NY: Anchor Press, 1979], p. 144).

[4] Sigmund Freud, "Prefatory Notes," in *Moses and Monotheism*, trans. Katherine Jones (New York, NY: Vintage Books, 1967), p. 67.

[5] Sigmund Freud, "Letter to Wilhelm Fliess—February 4, 1888," in *The Complete Letters of Sigmund Freud to Wilhelm Fliess, 1887–1904*, trans. and

ed. Jeffrey Moussaieff Masson (Cambridge, MA: Belknap Press of Harvard University Press, 1985), p. 19.

[6] Stanley Rothman and S. Robert Lichter, "Radical Jews: The Dilemmas of Marginality," in *Roots of Radicalism: Jews, Christians, and the Left* (New Brunswick, NJ: Transaction Publishers, 1996), p. 125.

[7] Kevin MacDonald, "Psychoanalysis as a Political Movement," in *The Culture of Critique* (Bloomington, IN: 1stBooks, 2002), p. 133.

[8] Andrew R. Heinze, "Jews and the Crisis of the Psyche," in *Jews and the American Soul: Human Nature in the Twentieth Century* (Princeton, NJ: Princeton University Press, 2004), p. 56.

[9] Andrew R. Heinze, "Introduction," to *Jews and the American Soul: Human Nature in the Twentieth Century* (Princeton, NJ: Princeton University Press, 2004), p. 3.

[10] Fritz Wittels, quoted in Dennis B. Klein, "The Particular and the Universal," in *Jewish Origins of the Psychoanalytic Movement* (Chicago, IL: University of Chicago Press, 1985), p. 142.

[11] "The Jewish Peril and The Catholic Church," *Catholic Gazette* (February 1936), p. 46.

[12] Max Horkheimer and Theodor W. Adorno, "Elements of Anti-Semitism: Limits of Enlightenment," in *Dialectic of Enlightenment: Philosophical Fragments*, trans. Edmund Jephcott, ed. Gunzelin Schmid Noerr (Stanford, CA: Stanford University Press, 2002), p. 145. See also Michael Minnicino, "The Frankfurt School and 'Political Correctness'," *Fidelio*, vol. 1, no. 1 (Winter 1992), pp. 4–27; Roger Scruton, *Fools, Frauds and Firebrands: Thinkers of the New Left* (London, UK: Bloomsbury, 2016); Kevin MacDonald, *The Culture of Critique* (Bloomington, IN: 1stBooks, 2002); Michael Walsh, *The Devil's Pleasure Palace: The Cult of Critical Theory and the Subversion of the West* (New York, NY: Encounter Books, 2015); Stuart Jeffries, *Grand Hotel Abyss: The Lives of the Frankfurt School* (London, UK: Verso, 2017); Michael Minnicino, "Freud and the Frankfurt School," *Executive Intelligence Review*, vol. 21, no. 16 (1994), pp. 36–38.

[13] Arnold Zweig, "Letter to Sigmund Freud—December 2, 1930," in *The Letters of Sigmund Freud and Arnold Zweig*, trans. William Robson-Scott and Elaine Robson-Scott, ed. Ernst L. Freud (London, UK: Hogarth Press and the Institute of Psycho-Analysis, 1970), p. 23.

[14] Sigmund Freud, "Letter to Martha Bernays—February 2, 1886," in Ernst L. Freud (ed.), *Letters of Sigmund Freud*, trans. Tania Stern and James Stern (New York, NY: Basic Books, 1975), p. 202.

[15] Sigmund Freud, "Letter to Oskar Pfister—October 16, 1910," in *Psychoanalysis and Faith: The Letters of Sigmund Freud and Oskar Pfister*, trans. Eric Mosbacher, eds. Heinrich Meng, and Ernst L. Freud (New York, NY: Basic Books, 1963), pp. 45–46.

[16] Sigmund Freud, "Letter to Members of the B'nai B'rith Lodge—May 6, 1926," in Ernst L. Freud (ed.), *Letters of Sigmund Freud*, trans. Tania Stern and James Stern (New York, NY: Basic Books, 1975), p. 367.

[17] Sigmund Freud, "The Resistances to Psychoanalysis" (1925), in *Character and Culture*, ed. Philip Rieff (New York, NY: Collier Books, 1963), p. 262.

[18] Sigmund Freud, "Application," in *Moses and Monotheism*, trans. Katherine Jones (New York, NY: Vintage Books, 1967), p. 117.

[19] Sigmund Freud, "Letter to Arnold Zweig—September 30, 1934," in Ernst L. Freud (ed.), *Letters of Sigmund Freud*, trans. Tania and James Stern (New York, NY: Basic Books, 1975), p. 421.

[20] Sigmund Freud, "Letter to Wilhelm Fliess—September 19, 1901," in Marie Bonaparte, Anna Freud and Ernst Kris (eds.), *The Origins of Psychoanalysis: Letters to Wilhelm Fliess, Drafts and Notes: 1887–1902*, trans. Eric Mosbacher and James Strachey (New York, NY: Basic Books, 1954), p. 336. Alternatively translated as, "the lie concerning man's redemption" (Sigmund Freud, "Letter to Wilhelm Fliess—September 19, 1901," in *The Complete Letters of Sigmund Freud to Wilhelm Fliess, 1887–1904*, trans. and ed. Jeffrey Moussaieff Masson [Cambridge, MA: Belknap Press of Harvard University Press, 1985], p. 449.

[21] Sigmund Freud, "Application," in *Moses and Monotheism*, trans. Katherine Jones (New York, NY: Vintage Books, 1967), p. 112.

[22] Sigmund Freud, "Infantile Material as a Source of Dreams" (1899), in *The Interpretation of Dreams*, trans. and ed. James Strachey (New York, NY: Science Editions, 1963), pp. 196–97.

[23] Peter Gay, "A Greed for Knowledge," in *Freud: A Life for Our Time* (New York, NY: Anchor Books, 1989), p. 12.

[24] Ernst Simmel, "Anti-Semitism and Mass Psychopathology," in *Anti-Semitism: A Social Disease*, ed. Ernst Simmel (New York, NY: International Universities Press, 1946), p. 50.

[25] Sigmund Freud, "Application," in *Moses and Monotheism*, trans. Katherine Jones (New York, NY: Vintage Books, 1967), p. 116.

[26] Sigmund Freud, quoted in Jacob Meitlis, "The Last Days of Sigmund Freud," *Jewish Frontier*, vol. 18, no. 9 (September 1951), p. 20.

[27] Sigmund Freud, "An Autobiographical Study" (1925 [1924]), in *An Autobiographical Study*, trans. and ed. James Strachey (New York, NY: W. W. Norton & Company, 1989), p. 7.

[28] David C. McClelland, "Religious Overtones in Psychoanalysis," *Princeton Seminary Bulletin*, vol. 52, no. 3 (January 1959), p. 32.

[29] René Guénon, "The Misdeeds of Psychoanalysis," in *The Reign of Quantity and the Signs of the Times*, trans. Lord Northbourne (Ghent, NY: Sophia Perennis, 2001), p. 227.

[30] Saint John Chrysostom, "Discourse Five," in *Discourses Against Judaizing Christians*, trans. Paul W. Harkins (Washington, D.C.: Catholic University of America Press, 1999), p. 136.

[31] Freud, quoted in Peter Gay, "The Question of a Jewish Science: 'A Title of Honor,'" in *A Godless Jew: Freud, Atheism, and the Making of Psychoanalysis* (New Haven, CT: Yale University Press, 1987), p. 121.

[32] Kevin MacDonald, "Jewish Involvement in the Psychoanalytic Movement," in *The Culture of Critique* (Bloomington, IN: 1stBooks, 2002), p. 110.

[33] Anna Freud, "Inaugural Lecture for the Sigmund Freud Chair at the Hebrew University, Jerusalem," *International Journal of Psycho-Analysis*, vol. 59 (1978), p. 148.

[34] Phyllis Grosskurth, "Open Warfare," in *The Secret Ring: Freud's Inner Circle and the Politics of Psychoanalysis* (Reading, MA: Addison-Wesley Publishing, 1991), p. 137.

[35] David Bakan, "The Moses of Michelangelo," in *Sigmund Freud and the Jewish Mystical Tradition* (London, UK: Free Association Books, 1990), p. 122.

[36] Sigmund Freud, "Letter to C. G. Jung—April 16, 1909," in William McGuire (ed.), *The Freud/Jung Letters: The Correspondence Between Sigmund Freud and C. G. Jung*, trans. Ralph Manheim and R.F.C. Hull (Princeton, NJ: Princeton University Press, 1994), p. 218.

[37] Helen Walker Puner, "See How It Splits," in *Freud: His Life and His Mind* (New York, NY: Howell, Soskin, 1947), p. 168.

[38] Fritz Wittels, "Freud's Personal Characteristics," in *Sigmund Freud: His Personality, His Teaching, and His School*, trans. Eden and Cedar Paul (New York, NY: Routledge, 2014), p. 138.

[39] Sigmund Freud, "Letter to Ludwig Binswanger—March 14, 1911," in *The Sigmund Freud—Ludwig Binswanger Correspondence, 1908–1938*, trans. Arnold J. Pomerans and Thomas Roberts, ed. Gerhard Fichtner (New York, NY: Other Press, 2003), p. 64.

[40] Sigmund Freud, quoted in Fritz Wittels, "Freud's Personal Characteristics," in *Sigmund Freud: His Personality, His Teaching, and His School*, trans. Eden Paul and Cedar Paul (New York, NY: Routledge, 2014), p. 140.

[41] Sigmund Freud, quoted in Ernest Jones, "The Beginning of International Recognition," in *The Life and Work of Sigmund Freud, Vol. 2: Years of Maturity, 1901–1919* (New York, NY: Basic Books, 1955), p. 51.

[42] Sigmund Freud, "Letter to C. G. Jung—February 25, 1908," in William McGuire (ed.), *The Freud/Jung Letters: The Correspondence Between Sigmund Freud and C. G. Jung*, trans. Ralph Manheim and R.F.C. Hull (Princeton, NJ: Princeton University Press, 1994), p. 62.

[43] Sigmund Freud, "Letter to C. G. Jung—January 17, 1909," in William McGuire (ed.), *The Freud/Jung Letters: The Correspondence Between Sigmund Freud and C. G. Jung*, trans. Ralph Manheim and R.F.C. Hull (Princeton, NJ: Princeton University Press, 1994), pp. 196–97.

[44] C. G. Jung, "Letter to Mr. President—April 20, 1914," in William McGuire (ed.), *The Freud/Jung Letters: The Correspondence Between Sigmund Freud and C. G. Jung*, trans. Ralph Manheim and R.F.C. Hull (Princeton, NJ: Princeton University Press, 1994), p. 358.

[45] C. G. Jung, "Letter to Sigmund Freud—March 3, 1912," in William McGuire (ed.), *The Freud/Jung Letters: The Correspondence Between Sigmund*

Freud and C. G. Jung, trans. Ralph Manheim and R.F.C. Hull (Princeton, NJ: Princeton University Press, 1994), p. 491.

[46] Ibid.

[47] Sigmund Freud, "On the History of the Psychoanalytic Movement" (1914), in *The History of the Psychoanalytic Movement*, ed. Philip Rieff (New York, NY: Collier Books, 1963), p. 76.

[48] C. G. Jung, "The State of Psychotherapy Today" (1934), in *The Collected Works of C. G. Jung, Vol. 10: Civilization in Transition*, trans. R.F.C. Hull (Princeton, NJ: Princeton University Press, 1970), p. 166.

[49] Ibid., pp. 165-166.

[50] H. R. Knickerbocker, "Diagnosing the Dictators: An Interview with Dr. Jung," *Hearst's International-Cosmopolitan*, vol. 106 (January 1939), pp. 108, 110. See also *C. G. Jung Speaking: Interviews and Encounters*, eds. William McGuire and R.F.C. Hull (Princeton, NJ: Princeton University Press, 1993).

[51] C. G. Jung, "Letter to James Kirsch—May 26, 1934," in *C. G. Jung Letters, Vol. 1: 1906–1950*, trans. R.F.C. Hull, eds. Gerhard Adler and Aniela Jaffé (New York, NY: Routledge, 1992), pp. 161–62. See also Ernest Harms, "Carl Gustav Jung—Defender of Freud and the Jews: A Chapter of European Psychiatric History under the Nazi Yoke," *Psychiatric Quarterly*, vol. 20, no. 2 (April 1946), pp. 199–230.

[52] C. G. Jung, quoted in Richard Noll, "'The Secret Church': The Transmission of Charismatic Authority," in *The Jung Cult: Origins of a Charismatic Movement* (Princeton, NJ: Princeton University Press, 1994), p. 286.

[53] Charles Upton, "Can Jung be Saved? A Sufic Re-Envisioning of the Jungian Archetypes," in *The Science of the Greater Jihad: Essays in Principial Psychology* (San Rafael, CA: Sophia Perennis, 2011), p. 95.

[54] Marie-Louise von Franz, "Introduction," to *The Collected Works of C. G. Jung, Supplementary Volume A: The Zofingia Lectures*, trans. Jan van Heurck, eds. Sir Herbert Read, Michael Fordham, and Gerhard Adler (New York, NY: Routledge, 2014), p. xxiv.

[55] Wolfgang Smith, "The Deification of the Unconscious," in *Cosmos & Transcendence: Breaking Through the Barrier of Scientistic Belief* (Peru, IL: Sherwood Sugden & Company, 1990), p. 129.

[56] C. G. Jung, "Confrontation with the Unconscious," in *Memories, Dreams, Reflections*, trans. Richard Winston and Clara Winston, ed. Aniela Jaffé (New York, NY: Vintage Books, 1965), p. 171.

[57] C. G. Jung, "Some Crucial Points in Psychoanalysis: A Correspondence between Dr. Jung and Dr. Loÿ" (1914), in *Critique of Psychoanalysis*, trans. R.F.C. Hull (Princeton, NJ: Princeton University Press, 1975), p. 207.

[58] C. G. Jung, "New Paths in Psychology" (1912), in *The Collected Works C. G. Jung, Vol. 7: Two Essays on Analytical Psychology*, trans. R.F.C. Hull, eds. Sir Herbert Read, Michael Fordham and Gerhard Adler (Princeton, NJ: Princeton University Press, 1972), p. 268.

[59] Sigmund Freud, "Letter to Wilhelm Fliess—October 3, 1897," in Marie Bonaparte, Anna Freud, and Ernst Kris (eds.), *The Origins of Psychoanalysis: Letters to Wilhelm Fliess, Drafts and Notes: 1887–1902*, trans. Eric Mosbacher and James Strachey (New York, NY: Basic Books, 1954), pp. 219–20. Alternatively translated as: "in my case the 'prime originator' was an ugly, elderly, but clever woman, who told me a great deal about God Almighty and hell and who instilled in me a high opinion of my own capacities...If...I succeed in resolving my own hysteria, then I shall be grateful to the memory of the old woman who provided me at such an early age with the means for living and going on living. As you see, the old liking is breaking through again today" (Sigmund Freud, "Letter to Wilhelm Fliess—October 3, 1897," in *The Complete Letters of Sigmund Freud to Wilhelm Fliess, 1887–1904*, trans. and ed. Jeffrey Moussaieff Masson [Cambridge, MA: Belknap Press of Harvard University Press, 1985], pp. 268–69).

[60] Sigmund Freud, "Letter to Wilhelm Fliess—October 15, 1897," in Marie Bonaparte, Anna Freud and Ernst Kris (eds.), *The Origins of Psychoanalysis: Letters to Wilhelm Fliess, Drafts and Notes: 1887–1902*, trans. Eric Mosbacher and James Strachey (New York, NY: Basic Books, 1954), p. 221.

[61] Paul C. Vitz, "The First Three Years," in *Sigmund Freud's Christian Unconscious* (New York, NY: Guilford Press, 1988), p. 18.

[62] The Talmud, quoted in Gershom Scholem, "After the Apostasy (1667–1668)," in *Sabbatai Ṣevi: The Mystical Messiah, 1626–1676*, trans. R. J. Zwi Werblowsky (Princeton, NJ: Princeton University Press, 2016), p. 805.

[63] Within every religion similar passages can be found as the founder of each faith tradition represents the *Logos*: In Christianity: "Jesus saith unto him, I am the way, the truth, and the life: no man cometh unto the Father, but by me" (John 14:6); in Islam, "No man shall meet God who has not first met the Prophet" (Ḥadīth); in Buddhism: "He who sees the *Dhamma* [Dharma] sees me, and he who sees me sees the *Dhamma* [Dharma]" (Samyutta Nikāya 3:120). "If 'no man cometh unto the Father, but by me,' it is because this 'me' as such possesses a saving and unitive virtuality; every subjectivity as such is in principle a door towards its own transpersonal Essence" (Frithjof Schuon, "The Enigma of Diversified Subjectivity," in *Roots of the Human Condition* [Bloomington, IN: World Wisdom Books, 1991], p. 50).

Chapter 18: Psychoanalysis and the Heretical Jewish Messianic Movements

[1] David Bakan, "Anti-Semitism in Vienna," in *Sigmund Freud and the Jewish Mystical Tradition* (London, UK: Free Association Books, 1990), p. 25.

[2] See also Whitall N. Perry, "The Revolt Against Moses: A New Look at Psychoanalysis," in *Challenges to a Secular Society* (Oakton, VA: Foundation for Traditional Studies, 1996), pp. 17–38; Mateus Soares de Azevedo, "Freudian Psychoanalysis as Secular Fundamentalism," in *Men of*

a Single Book: Fundamentalism in Islam, Christianity, and Modern Thought (Bloomington, IN: World Wisdom, 2010), pp. 67–79.

[3] Sigmund Freud, quoted in David Bakan, "Preface," to *Sigmund Freud and the Jewish Mystical Tradition* (London, UK: Free Association Books, 1990), p. xix. Jung was also influenced by Jewish mysticism, as he indicates in the following: "In a tract of the *Lurianic Kabbalah*, the remarkable idea is developed that man is destined to become God's helper in the attempt to restore the vessels which were broken when God thought to create a world. Only a few weeks ago, I came across this impressive doctrine which gives meaning to man's status exalted by the incarnation. I am glad that I can quote at least one voice in favour of my rather involuntary manifesto" (C. G. Jung, "Letter to Reverend Erastus Evans—February 17, 1954," in *C. G. Jung Letters, Vol. 2: 1951–1961*, trans. R.F.C. Hull, ed. Gerhard Adler [London, UK: Routledge, 2011], p. 157).

[4] David Bakan, "Anti-Semitism in Vienna," in *Sigmund Freud and the Jewish Mystical Tradition* (London, UK: Free Association Books, 1990), p. 26.

[5] Gershom Scholem, "Sabbetai Ẓevi and the Shabbatean Movement," in *Kabbalah* (New York, NY: Meridian, 1978), p. 244.

[6] Gershom Scholem, "The Background of the Sabbatain Movement," in *Sabbatai Ṣevi: The Mystical Messiah, 1626–1676*, trans. R. J. Zwi Werblowsky (Princeton, NJ: Princeton University Press, 2016), p. 2.

[7] Samuel H. Dresner, "Bashevis Singer," in *Can Families Survive in Pagan America?* (Lafayette, LA: Huntington House Publishers, 1995), p. 184.

[8] Gershom Scholem, "Notes," in *The Messianic Idea in Judaism: And Other Essays on Jewish Spirituality* (New York, NY: Schocken Books, 1995), pp. 355–56.

[9] Gershom Scholem, "Redemption through Sin," in *The Messianic Idea in Judaism: And Other Essays on Jewish Spirituality* (New York, NY: Schocken Books, 1995), p. 78.

[10] Gershom Scholem, "Redemption through Sin," in *The Messianic Idea in Judaism: And Other Essays on Jewish Spirituality* (New York, NY: Schocken Books, 1995), pp. 80–81. "Here, then, we have all the prerequisites for the sectarian disposition, for the sect serves the *illuminati* as both a rallying point for their own kind and a refuge from the incomprehension of the carnal and unenlightened masses. The sectarians regard themselves as the vanguard of a new world..." (Gershom Scholem, "Redemption through Sin," in *The Messianic Idea in Judaism: And Other Essays on Jewish Spirituality* [New York, NY: Schocken Books, 1995], p. 90). See Rabbi Marvin S. Antelman, *To Eliminate the Opiate, Vol. 1* (Jerusalem, Israel: Zionist Book Club, 1974); Rabbi Marvin S. Antelman, *To Eliminate the Opiate, Vol. 2* (Jerusalem, Israel: Zionist Book Club, 2002).

[11] Gershom Scholem, "The Beginnings of Sabbatai Ṣevi (1626–1664)," in *Sabbatai Ṣevi: The Mystical Messiah, 1626–1676*, trans. R. J. Zwi Werblowsky (Princeton, NJ: Princeton University Press, 2016), p. 198.

[12] Gershom Scholem, "The Beginnings of the Movement in Palestine (1665)," in *Sabbatai Ṣevi: The Mystical Messiah, 1626–1676*, trans. R. J. Zwi Werblowsky (Princeton, NJ: Princeton University Press, 2016), p. 215.

[13] Solomon Laniado, quoted in Gershom Scholem, "The Beginnings of the Movement in Palestine (1665)," in *Sabbatai Ṣevi: The Mystical Messiah, 1626–1676*, trans. R. J. Zwi Werblowsky (Princeton, NJ: Princeton University Press, 2016), p. 215.

[14] Gershom Scholem, "The Beginnings of the Movement in Palestine (1665)," in *Sabbatai Ṣevi: The Mystical Messiah, 1626–1676*, trans. R. J. Zwi Werblowsky (Princeton, NJ: Princeton University Press, 2016), p. 207.

[15] Samuel Primo, quoted in Heinrich Graetz, "Spinoza and Sabbatai Zevi," in *History of the Jews, Vol. V*, trans. Bella Löwy (London, UK: David Nutt, 1892), p. 152.

[16] Quoted in Gershom Scholem, "The Beginnings of the Movement in Palestine (1665)," in *Sabbatai Ṣevi: The Mystical Messiah, 1626–1676*, trans. R. J. Zwi Werblowsky (Princeton, NJ: Princeton University Press, 2016), p. 247.

[17] Gershom Scholem, "The Background of the Sabbatian Movement," in *Sabbatai Ṣevi: The Mystical Messiah, 1626–1676*, trans. R. J. Zwi Werblowsky (Princeton, NJ: Princeton University Press, 2016), p. 2.

[18] Gershom Scholem, "Redemption through Sin," in *The Messianic Idea in Judaism: And Other Essays on Jewish Spirituality* (New York, NY: Schocken Books, 1995), p. 96.

[19] Nathan of Gaza, quoted in Gershom Scholem, "The Beginnings of the Movement in Palestine (1665)," in *Sabbatai Ṣevi: The Mystical Messiah, 1626–1676*, trans. R. J. Zwi Werblowsky (Princeton, NJ: Princeton University Press, 2016), p. 204.

[20] Gershom Scholem, "The Beginnings of the Movement in Palestine (1665)," in *Sabbatai Ṣevi: The Mystical Messiah, 1626–1676*, trans. R. J. Zwi Werblowsky (Princeton, NJ: Princeton University Press, 2016), p. 211.

[21] Quoted in Gershom Scholem, "Sabbatianism and Mystical Heresy," in *Major Trends in Jewish Mysticism* (New York, NY: Schocken Books, 1974), p. 319. "Blessed art Thou, O Lord, who permittest that which is forbidden." (Quoted in Gershom Scholem, "The Beginnings of the Movement in Palestine (1665)," in *Sabbatai Ṣevi: The Mystical Messiah, 1626–1676*, trans. R. J. Zwi Werblowsky [Princeton, NJ: Princeton University Press, 2016], p. 242).

[22] Quoted in Gershom Scholem, "Shabbetai Ẓevi and the Shabbatean Movement," in *Kabbalah* (New York, NY: Meridian, 1978), p. 248.

[23] Gershom Scholem, "Sabbatianism and Mystical Heresy," in *Major Trends in Jewish Mysticism* (New York, NY: Schocken Books, 1974), p. 319.

[24] Gershom Scholem, "Shabbetai Ẓevi and the Shabbatean Movement," in *Kabbalah* (New York, NY: Meridian, 1978), p. 247.

[25] Quoted in Gershom Scholem, "The Beginnings of Sabbatai Ṣevi (1626–1664)," in *Sabbatai Ṣevi: The Mystical Messiah, 1626–1676*, trans. R. J. Zwi Werblowsky (Princeton, NJ: Princeton University Press, 2016), p. 113.

[26] Gershom Scholem, "The Beginnings of Sabbatai Ṣevi (1626–1664)," in *Sabbatai Ṣevi: The Mystical Messiah, 1626–1676*, trans. R. J. Zwi Werblowsky (Princeton, NJ: Princeton University Press, 2016), p. 125.

[27] Ibid., p. 126.

[28] Gershom Scholem, "Shabbetai Ẓevi and the Shabbatean Movement," in *Kabbalah* (New York, NY: Meridian, 1978), p. 246.

[29] Samuel Gandor, quoted in Gershom Scholem, "Sabbatianism and Mystical Heresy," in *Major Trends in Jewish Mysticism* (New York, NY: Schocken Books, 1974), pp. 290–91.

[30] Gershom Scholem, "The Beginnings of the Movement in Palestine (1665)," in *Sabbatai Ṣevi: The Mystical Messiah, 1626–1676*, trans. R. J. Zwi Werblowsky (Princeton, NJ: Princeton University Press, 2016), p. 311.

[31] Gershom Scholem, "After the Apostasy (1667–1668)," in *Sabbatai Ṣevi: The Mystical Messiah, 1626–1676*, trans. R. J. Zwi Werblowsky (Princeton, NJ: Princeton University Press, 2016), p. 793.

[32] We might add that Mustafa Kemal Atatürk (1881–1938), the founder of modern secular Turkey, was himself a Dönmeh crypto-Jew. See Marc David Baer, *The Dönme: Jewish Converts, Muslim Revolutionaries, and Secular Turks* (Stanford, CA: Stanford University Press, 2010); Cengiz Sisman, *The Burden of Silence: Sabbatai Sevi and the Evolution of the Ottoman-Turkish Dönmes* (New York, NY: Oxford University Press, 2015); Joachim Prinz, *The Secret Jews* (New York, NY: Random House, 1973); Andrew Mango, *Atatürk: The Biography of the Founder of Modern Turkey* (New York, NY: Overlook Press, 2002).

[33] Gershom Scholem, "The Last Years of Sabbatai Ṣevi (1668–1676)," in *Sabbatai Ṣevi: The Mystical Messiah, 1626–1676*, trans. R. J. Zwi Werblowsky (Princeton, NJ: Princeton University Press, 2016), p. 836.

[34] Gershom Scholem, "Redemption through Sin," in *The Messianic Idea in Judaism: And Other Essays on Jewish Spirituality* (New York, NY: Schocken Books, 1995), p. 84.

[35] Sabbatai Ẓevi, quoted in Gershom Scholem, "The Last Years of Sabbatai Ṣevi (1668–1676)," in *Sabbatai Ṣevi: The Mystical Messiah, 1626–1676*, trans. R. J. Zwi Werblowsky (Princeton, NJ: Princeton University Press, 2016), p. 837.

[36] Gershom Scholem, "Jacob Frank and the Frankists," in *Kabbalah* (New York, NY: Meridian, 1978), p. 287.

[37] Gershom Scholem, "Redemption through Sin," in *The Messianic Idea in Judaism: And Other Essays on Jewish Spirituality* (New York, NY: Schocken Books, 1995), p. 128.

[38] Gershom Scholem, "Redemption through Sin," in *The Messianic Idea in Judaism: And Other Essays on Jewish Spirituality* (New York, NY: Schocken Books, 1995), p. 126.

[39] Gershom Scholem, "Sabbatianism and Mystical Heresy," in *Major Trends in Jewish Mysticism* (New York, NY: Schocken Books, 1974), p. 308.

[40] Gershom Scholem, "Redemption through Sin," in *The Messianic Idea in Judaism: And Other Essays on Jewish Spirituality* (New York, NY: Schocken Books, 1995), p. 127.

[41] Gershom Scholem, "Shabbetai Ẓevi and the Shabbatean Movement," in *Kabbalah* (New York, NY: Meridian, 1978), p. 284.

[42] Jacob Frank, quoted in Gershom Scholem, "Redemption through Sin," in *The Messianic Idea in Judaism: And Other Essays on Jewish Spirituality* (New York, NY: Schocken Books, 1995), p. 130.

[43] Gershom Scholem, "Redemption through Sin," in *The Messianic Idea in Judaism: And Other Essays on Jewish Spirituality* (New York, NY: Schocken Books, 1995), pp. 130–31.

[44] Jacob Frank, quoted in Gershom Scholem, "Redemption through Sin," in *The Messianic Idea in Judaism: And Other Essays on Jewish Spirituality* (New York, NY: Schocken Books, 1995), p. 130.

[45] Jacob Frank, quoted in Gershom Scholem, "Religious Authority and Mysticism," in *On the Kabbalah and Its Symbolism*, trans. Ralph Manheim (New York, NY: Schocken Books, 1969), pp. 28–29.

[46] Gershom Scholem, "Redemption through Sin," in *The Messianic Idea in Judaism: And Other Essays on Jewish Spirituality* (New York, NY: Schocken Books, 1995), p. 85.

[47] C. G. Jung, "Prefaces to *Collected Papers on Analytical Psychology*" (1916), in *Critique of Psychoanalysis*, trans. R.F.C. Hull (Princeton, NJ: Princeton University Press, 1975), p. 209. "The programme of becoming happy, which the pleasure principle imposes on us, cannot be fulfilled; yet we must not—indeed, we cannot—give up our efforts to bring it nearer to fulfillment by some means or other" (Sigmund Freud, "Chapter Two," in *Civilization and Its Discontents*, trans. and ed. James Strachey [New York, NY: W. W. Norton & Company, 1989], p. 34).

[48] Gershom Scholem, "The Crypto-Jewish Sect of the Dönmeh (Sabbatians) in Turkey," in *The Messianic Idea in Judaism: And Other Essays on Jewish Spirituality* (New York, NY: Schocken Books, 1995), p. 160.

[49] René Guénon, "Conversions," in *Initiation and Spiritual Realization*, trans. Henry D. Fohr, ed. Samuel D. Fohr (Ghent, NY: Sophia Perennis, 2001), p. 63.

[50] Gershom Scholem, "Jacob Frank and the Frankists," in *Kabbalah* (New York, NY: Meridian, 1978), p. 304.

[51] Ibid., p. 305.

[52] See Gershom Scholem, "The Crypto-Jewish Sect of the Dönmeh (Sabbatians) in Turkey," in *The Messianic Idea in Judaism: And Other Essays on Jewish Spirituality* (New York, NY: Schocken Books, 1995), pp. 142–66.

[53] Junayd of Baghdad, quoted in Gershom Scholem, *Sabbatai Ṣevi: The Mystical Messiah, 1626–1676*, trans. R. J. Zwi Werblowsky (Princeton, NJ: Princeton University Press, 2016), p. 164.

[54] Ibn al-'Arabī, quoted in William C. Chittick, "The People of Blame," in *The Sufi Path of Knowledge: Ibn al-'Arabī's Metaphysics of Imagination* (Albany, NY: State University of New York Press, 1989), p. 372.

[55] Bāyazīd Bisṭāmī, quoted in Gerhard Böwering, "Ideas of Time in Persian Sufism," in *The Heritage of Sufism, Vol. 1: Classical Persian Sufism from its Origins to Rumi (700–1300)*, ed. Leonard Lewisohn (Oxford, UK: Oneworld, 1999), p. 218.

[56] William C. Chittick, "The Entities," in *Ibn 'Arabi: Heir to the Prophets* (Oxford, UK: Oneworld, 2007), p. 40.

[57] Mansūr al-Hallāj, quoted in Carl W. Ernst, "Introduction," to *Words of Ecstasy in Sufism* (Albany, NY: State University of New York Press, 1985), p. 3.

[58] Ibid.

[59] René Guénon, "The Necessity of Traditional Exoterism," in *Initiation and Spiritual Realization*, trans. Henry D. Fohr, ed. Samuel D. Fohr (Ghent, NY: Sophia Perennis, 2001), p. 42. See also Frithjof Schuon, "The Limitations of Exoterism," in *The Transcendent Unity of Religions* (Wheaton, IL: Quest Books, 1993), pp. 7–32.

[60] Moses Maimonides, quoted in Gershom Scholem, "Religious Authority and Mysticism," in *On the Kabbalah and Its Symbolism*, trans. Ralph Manheim (New York, NY: Schocken Books, 1969), p. 26.

[61] *Yigdal*, quoted in Gershom Scholem, "The Last Years of Sabbatai Ṣevi (1668–1676)," in *Sabbatai Ṣevi: The Mystical Messiah, 1626–1676*, trans. R. J. Zwi Werblowsky (Princeton, NJ: Princeton University Press, 2016), p. 841.

[62] See Charles Upton, *Vectors of the Counter-Initiation: The Course and Destiny of Inverted Spirituality* (San Rafael, CA: Sophia Perennis, 2012); Samuel Bendeck Sotillos, "New Age or the Kali-Yuga?" *AHP Perspective* (April/May 2013), pp. 15–21.

[63] René Guénon, "Christianity and Initiation," in *Insights into Christian Esoterism*, trans. Henry D. Fohr, ed. Samuel D. Fohr (Ghent, NY: Sophia Perennis, 2001), p. 12.

[64] 'Ali b. 'Uthman al-Jullabi al-Hujwiri, "On Blame (*Malamat*)," in *The Kashf al-Mahjub: The Oldest Persian Treatise on Sufism*, trans. R. A. Nicholson (London, UK: Luzac and Company, 1976), p. 65.

[65] "As they have realized (the 'Divine Truth') in the higher degrees (of the Microcosm), as they have been affirmed among 'the men of concentration,' of the *Al-Qurbah*, the *Al-Uns*, and the *Al-Wasl*, God is (so to speak) too jealous of them to let them reveal themselves to the world as they really are. So he gives them an appearance that corresponds to the state of 'separation from Heaven,' an appearance made of ordinary knowledge, of Shariite preoccupations—ritual or priestly—as well as the obligation to work, to follow a

profession, and to act among men. Nevertheless, their interiors remain in continual connection with the 'True-Divine,' as much in concentration (*al-jarq*) as in dispersion (*al jam'*), that is to say in all the states of existence. This mentality is one of the highest man can attain even though nothing of it appears on the outside. It resembles the state of the Prophet—may Allah pray for him and proclaim him!—who was raised to the highest degrees of the 'Divine Proximity' indicated by the Koranic formula, 'And he was distant by two lengths of a bow or even closer.' When they turn toward creatures they speak with them only of outward things. Of their intimate conversation with God, nothing appears on their person. This state is higher than that of Moses, whose face no one could look upon after he had spoken with God...The *Shaykh* of the group of Abu-Hafs en-Nisabūrī said: 'The Malamite disciples progress by exerting themselves. They care not for themselves. The world has no hold on them and cannot reach them, for their outer life is all uncovered while the subtleties of their inner life are rigorously hidden...' Abu-Hafs was one day asked 'why the name Malamatiyah?' He responded: 'The Malamatiyah are continually with God by the fact that they always dominate themselves and never cease to be conscious of *their lordly secret*. They blame themselves for all that they cannot prevent from showing with regard to their 'Divine Proximity,' in the office of prayer or otherwise. They conceal their merits and expose what is blameworthy in themselves. People then make their outward appearance a point of accusation; they blame themselves inwardly for they understand human nature. But God favors them by uncovering the mysteries, by the contemplation of the hypersensible world, by the art of knowing the intimate reality of things from outward signs (*al-ferāsah*), as well as by miracles. The world finally leaves them in peace with God, removed from them by their display of what is blamable or contrary to respectability. Such is the discipline of the *ṭarīqah* of the people of blame." (Abdul-Ḥādi's fragments of *Principles of the Malamatiyah* by Sayed Abu Abdur-Rahman, quoted in René Guénon, "Appendices," in *Initiation and Spiritual Realization*, trans. Henry D. Fohr, ed. Samuel D. Fohr [Ghent, NY: Sophia Perennis, 2001], pp. 183–84).

[66] Ibn al-'Arabī, quoted in William C. Chittick, "The People of Blame," in *The Sufi Path of Knowledge: Ibn al-'Arabī's Metaphysics of Imagination* (Albany, NY: State University of New York Press, 1989), pp. 373–74. "To revere the shaykh is to show reverence for none but God, so revere him out of courtesy toward God in God./The shaykhs are the courteous, and proximity aids them in guiding and strengthening in God./They are the inheritors of all the messengers, so their words come only from God./You see them like the prophets among their enemies, never asking from God anything but God./ But if a state should appear in them which distracts them from the Shari'a, leave them with God—/Follow not after them and walk not in their tracks, for they are God's freedmen in God./Be not guided by them from whom the Shari'a has gone, even if he brings news from God!" (Ibn al-'Arabī, quoted in William C. Chittick, "Spiritual Mastery," in *The Sufi Path of Knowledge:*

Ibn al-'Arabī's Metaphysics of Imagination [Albany, NY: State University of New York Press, 1989], p. 271).

[67] Aleister Crowley, "The Law of Thelema," in *The Book of the Law* (Boston, MA: Red Wheel/Weiser Books, 1976), p. 9. Regarding Freud's influence on Crowley, it has been written: "Crowley cured psychoses and neuroses in this wise. He saw that the mind or psyche was divided into consciousness and unconsciousness (the bottom level, so to speak); that was part of the occult tradition. But the conception of the unconscious (or as Crowley calls it, the 'subconscious') as a dynamic and disturbing force, he took from Freud, without any acknowledgment. (It would, incidentally, have been rather difficult for Crowley to have made this acknowledgement in the light of his belief in himself as the greatest living psychologist)" (John Symonds, *The Magic of Aleister Crowley* [London, UK: Frederick Muller, 1958], p. 78). There is also another important connection here between the founder of Scientology, L. Ron Hubbard (1911–86), and Aleister Crowley. According to Hubbard's son, Ronald DeWolf, formerly L. Ron Hubbard Jr. (1934–91), Hubbard saw himself not only as a devoted disciple of Crowley, but his successor: "According to Ron [Hubbard] Jr. his father considered himself to be the one 'who came after'; that he was Crowley's successor; that he had taken on the mantle of the 'Great Beast.' He told him that Scientology actually began on December the 1st, 1947. This was the day Aleister Crowley died" (Bent Corydon and L. Ron Hubbard, Jr., "L. Ron and the Beast," in *L. Ron Hubbard: Messiah or Madman* [Secaucus, NJ: Lyle Stuart, 1987], p. 50). "The one super-secret sentence that Scientology is built on is: 'Do as thou wilt.' That is the whole of the law. It also comes from the black magic, from Alistair [*sic*] Crowley...[L. Ron Hubbard] was sixteen [when] he got hold of the book...*The Book of the Law*...he thought of himself as the Beast 666 Incarnate...What a lot of people don't realize is that Scientology is black magic...Black magic is the inner core of Scientology...my father did not worship Satan. He thought he was Satan...I consider him a victim of his own involvement with black magic, drugs, and his own delusions. He became a victim of himself...he fell into his own insanity..." (L. Ron Hubbard, Jr., quoted in Allan Sonnenschein, "Inside the Church of Scientology: An Exclusive Interview with L. Ron Hubbard, Jr.," *Penthouse* [June 1983], pp. 173, 113, 175). Hubbard's Scientology and its mapping of the human psyche appear to have similarities with Freudian psychology. For example, what in Scientology is termed the *analytical mind* appears similar to the conscious mind and the *reactive mind* appears similar to the unconscious mind in psychoanalysis. Traumatic memories or *engrams* are stored in the unconscious mind and can be made conscious through *auditing*, which is similar to the psychoanalytic concept of abreaction. L. Ron Hubbard's creation of Scientology needs to be viewed similarly to Freud's creation of psychoanalysis as one man's attempt to remedy his own psychological unbalance. In October 1947, Hubbard was requesting psychiatric treatment and wrote a letter to the Veterans Administration: "After trying and failing for two years to regain

my equilibrium in civil life, I am utterly unable to approach anything like my own competence. My last physician informed me that it might be very helpful if I were to be examined and perhaps treated psychiatrically or even by a psychoanalyst. Toward the end of my service I avoided out of pride any mental examinations, hoping that time would balance a mind which I had every reason to suppose was seriously affected. I cannot account for nor rise above long periods of moroseness and suicidal inclinations, and have newly come to realize that I must first triumph above this before I can hope to rehabilitate myself at all...I cannot, myself, afford such treatment. Would you please help me?" (L. Ron Hubbard, quoted in Russell Miller, "The Mystery of the Missing Research," in *Bare-Faced Messiah: The True Story of L. Ron Hubbard* [New York, NY: Henry Holt and Company, 1987], pp.137–38). American psychologist Timothy Leary (1920–96), 1960's counter-culture hero and key proponent of the psychedelic revolution, in an interview on PBS's *Late Night America* confessed to continuing the work that began with Aleister Crowley: "Well, I've been an admirer of Aleister Crowley; I think that I'm carrying on much of the work that he started over 100 years ago. And I think the 60's themselves you know Crowley said he was in favor of finding your own self and 'Do what thou wilt shall be the whole of the law' under love. It was a very powerful statement. I'm sorry he isn't around now to appreciate the glories that he started." See Janet Reitman, *Inside Scientology: The Story of America's Most Secretive Religion* (New York, NY: Houghton Mifflin Harcourt, 2011); W. Vaughn McCall, "Psychiatry and Psychology in the Writings of L. Ron Hubbard," *Journal of Religion and Health*, vol. 46, no. 3 (September 2007), pp. 437–47.

[68] Voltaire, "Zaïre—Scene Four," in *The Works of Voltaire: The Dramatic Works of Voltaire, Vol. 5* (New York, NY: E. R. DuMont, 1901), p. 59.

[69] St. Augustine of Hippo, "Ten Homilies on the First Epistle of John," in *A Select Library of the Nicene and Post-Nicene Fathers of the Christian Church*, ed. Philip Schaff (New York, NY: Christian Literature Company, 1888), p. 504.

[70] Sigmund Freud, "Psychoanalysis" (1922), in *Character and Culture*, ed. Philip Rieff (New York, NY: Collier Books, 1963), p. 249.

[71] Peter J. Swales, "Freud, Filthy Lucre, and Undue Influence," *Review of Existential Psychology and Psychiatry*, vol. 23, nos. 1–3 (1997), p. 132.

[72] Walter Benjamin, "Critique of Violence," in *Reflections: Essays, Aphorisms, Autobiographical Writing*, ed. Peter Demetz (New York, NY: Schocken Books, 1986), p. 300.

[73] Gershom Scholem, "After the Apostasy (1667–1668)," in *Sabbatai Ṣevi: The Mystical Messiah, 1626–1676*, trans. R. J. Zwi Werblowsky (Princeton, NJ: Princeton University Press, 2016), p. 691.

[74] Ibid., p. 728.

[75] Gershom Scholem, "The Last Years of Sabbatai Ṣevi (1668–1676)," in *Sabbatai Ṣevi: The Mystical Messiah, 1626–1676*, trans. R.J. Zwi Werblowsky (Princeton, NJ: Princeton University Press, 2016), p. 915.

[76] David Bakan, "Moses as an Egyptian," in *Sigmund Freud and the Jewish Mystical Tradition* (London, UK: Free Association Books, 1990), p. 148.

[77] Ibid.

[78] Samuel H. Dresner, "The Return of Paganism," in *Can Families Survive in Pagan America?* (Lafayette, LA: Huntington House Publishers, 1995), p. 160.

[79] Moses Maimonides, quoted in Gershom Scholem, "The Background of the Sabbatian Movement," in *Sabbatai Ṣevi: The Mystical Messiah, 1626–1676*, trans. R. J. Zwi Werblowsky (Princeton, NJ: Princeton University Press, 2016), p. 13. "[O]ur Torah is for all eternity, nothing can be added to it and nothing taken away from it" (Moses Maimonides, quoted in Frithjof Schuon, "The Ternary Aspect of Monotheism," in *The Transcendent Unity of Religions* [Wheaton, IL: Quest Books, 1993], p. 100).

[80] Moses Maimonides, quoted in Gershom Scholem, "The Background of the Sabbatian Movement," in *Sabbatai Ṣevi: The Mystical Messiah, 1626–1676*, trans. R. J. Zwi Werblowsky (Princeton, NJ: Princeton University Press, 2016), p. 13.

[81] Eric Hoffer, "Imitation and Fanaticism," in *The Ordeal of Change* (New York, NY: Harper & Row, 1963), pp. 22–23.

[82] Tage Lindbom, "Lucifer," in *Every Branch in Me: Essays on the Meaning of Man*, ed. Barry McDonald (Bloomington, IN: World Wisdom, 2002), p. 80.

Chapter 19: Psychoanalysis as Pseudo-Science

[1] Frederick Crews, "Introduction," to *The Memory Wars: Freud's Legacy in Dispute* (New York, NY: New York Review of Books, 1995), p. 9.

[2] Richard Webster, "Psychoanalysis, Science and Human Nature," in *Why Freud Was Wrong: Sin, Science, and Psychoanalysis* (New York, NY: Basic Books, 1995), p. 438.

[3] Richard von Krafft-Ebing, quoted in Sigmund Freud, "Letter to Wilhelm Fliess—April 26, 1896," in *The Complete Letters of Sigmund Freud to Wilhelm Fliess, 1887–1904*, trans. and ed. Jeffrey Moussaieff Masson (Cambridge, MA: Belknap Press of Harvard University Press, 1985), p. 184. See also Max Schur, *Freud: Living and Dying* (New York, NY: International Universities Press, 1972).

[4] Thomas Szasz, "Preface," to *Anti-Freud: Karl Kraus's Criticism of Psychoanalysis and Psychiatry* (Syracuse, NY: Syracuse University Press, 1990), p. xiii.

[5] Ibid.

[6] Frank Cioffi, "Freud and the Idea of a Pseudoscience," in *Freud and the Question of Pseudoscience* (Chicago, IL: Open Court, 1998), p. 118.

[7] Sigmund Freud, "Explanations, Applications and Orientations" (1933 [1932]), in *New Introductory Lectures on Psycho-Analysis*, trans. and ed. James Strachey (New York, NY: W. W. Norton & Company, 1989), p. 188.

[8] Sigmund Freud, "Analytical Therapy" (1917), in *A General Introduction to Psychoanalysis* (New York, NY: Horace Liveright, 1920), p. 400. "[S]tatistics are worthless if the items assembled in them are too heterogeneous" (Sigmund Freud, "Analytic Therapy" (1916–1917 [1915–1917])), in *Introductory Lectures on Psychoanalysis*, trans. and ed. James Strachey [New York, NY: W. W. Norton & Company, 1977], p. 461).

[9] Sigmund Freud, "Explanations, Applications and Orientations" (1933 [1932]), in *New Introductory Lectures on Psycho-Analysis*, trans. and ed. James Strachey (New York, NY: W. W. Norton & Company, 1989), p. 188.

[10] Paul Ricoeur, "The Question of Proof in Freud's Psychoanalytic Writings," in *Hermeneutics and the Human Sciences: Essays on Language, Action and Interpretation*, trans. John B. Thompson (Cambridge, UK: Cambridge University Press, 1998), p. 248.

[11] Wolfgang Smith, "The Ego and the Beast," in *Cosmos & Transcendence: Breaking Through the Barrier of Scientistic Belief* (Peru, IL: Sherwood Sugden & Company, 1990), p. 100.

[12] William C. Chittick, "The Rehabilitation of Thought," in *Science of the Cosmos, Science of the Soul: The Pertinence of Islamic Cosmology in the Modern World* (Oxford, UK: Oneworld, 2009), p. 48. See also Rupert Sheldrake, *The Science Delusion* (London, UK: Coronet, 2013).

[13] Sigmund Freud, "Chapter Ten," in *The Future of an Illusion*, trans. and ed. James Strachey (New York, NY: W. W. Norton & Company, 1989), p. 71.

[14] Bertrand Russell, "Science of Ethics," in *Religion and Science* (Oxford, UK: Oxford University Press, 1997), p. 243.

[15] Sigmund Freud, "The Question of a *Weltanschauung*" (1933 [1932]), in *New Introductory Lectures on Psycho-Analysis*, trans. and ed. James Strachey (New York, NY: W. W. Norton & Company, 1989), p. 196.

[16] Huston Smith, "The Way Things Are," in *Forgotten Truth: The Common Vision of the World's Religions* (New York, NY: HarperCollins, 1992), p. 16.

[17] Jacob Needleman, "Psychotherapy and the Sacred," in *A Sense of the Cosmos: The Encounter of Modern Science and Ancient Truth* (New York, NY: E. P. Dutton and Company, 1976), p. 131.

[18] Wilhelm Reich, "The Development of the Orgasm Theory," in *The Function of the Orgasm*, trans. Theodore P. Wolfe (New York, NY: Noonday Press, 1970), p. 69.

[19] Sigmund Freud, "Psycho-Analysis and Psychiatry," in *Introductory Lectures on Psychoanalysis*, trans. and ed. James Strachey (New York, NY: W. W. Norton & Company, 1977), p. 244.

[20] Ira Progoff, "Sigmund Freud and the Foundations of Depth Psychology," in *The Death and Rebirth of Psychology: An Integrative Evaluation of Freud, Adler, Jung and Rank and the Impact of Their Insights on Modern Man* (New York, NY: McGraw-Hill, 1969), p. 26.

[21] Immanuel Velikovsky, "The Dreams Freud Dreamed," *Psychoanalytic Review*, vol. 28 (October 1941), p. 487.

[22] Sigmund Freud, "Letter to Wilhelm Fliess—February 1, 1900," in *The Complete Letters of Sigmund Freud to Wilhelm Fliess, 1887–1904*, trans. and ed. Jeffrey Moussaieff Masson (Cambridge, MA: Belknap Press of Harvard University Press, 1985), p. 398. "Charles Darwin was Freud's only real competitor as a modern cultural conquistador" (Peter Gay, "The Question of a Jewish Science: 'A Title of Honor,'" in *A Godless Jew: Freud, Atheism, and the Making of Psychoanalysis* [New Haven, CT: Yale University Press, 1987], p. 140).

[23] Sigmund Freud, "Letter to Wilhelm Fliess—April 2, 1896," in Ernst L. Freud (ed.), *Letters of Sigmund Freud*, trans. Tania Stern and James Stern (New York, NY: Basic Books, 1975), p. 232. See also Sigmund Freud, "Letter to Wilhelm Fliess—April 2, 1896," in Marie Bonaparte, Anna Freud, and Ernst Kris (eds.), *The Origins of Psychoanalysis: Letters to Wilhelm Fliess, Drafts and Notes: 1887–1902*, trans. Eric Mosbacher and James Strachey (New York, NY: Basic Books, 1954), p. 162; Sigmund Freud, "Letter to Wilhelm Fliess—April 2, 1896," in *The Complete Letters of Sigmund Freud to Wilhelm Fliess, 1887–1904*, trans. and ed. Jeffrey Moussaieff Masson (Cambridge, MA: Belknap Press of Harvard University Press, 1985), p. 180.

[24] Sigmund Freud, "Letter to Lou Andreas-Salomé—July 30, 1915," in Ernst L. Freud (ed.), *Letters of Sigmund Freud*, trans. Tania and James Stern (New York, NY: Basic Books, 1975), p. 310.

[25] Sigmund Freud, "Postscript" (1927), to *The Question of Lay Analysis*, trans. and ed. James Strachey (New York, NY: W. W. Norton & Company, 1989), p. 90.

[26] Sigmund Freud, quoted in Joseph Wortis, "The Analysis," in *Fragments of an Analysis with Freud* (New York, NY: Simon & Schuster, 1954), p. 84.

[27] Sigmund Freud, "Hypothesis and Technique of Interpretation" (1917), in *A General Introduction to Psychoanalysis* (New York, NY: Horace Liveright, 1920), p. 78.

[28] Sigmund Freud, "Traumatic Fixation—the Unconscious" (1917), in *A General Introduction to Psychoanalysis* (New York, NY: Horace Liveright, 1920), p. 240.

[29] Sigmund Freud, "Letter to Sándor Ferenczi—November 17, 1918," in *The Correspondence of Sigmund Freud and Sándor Ferenczi, Vol. 2: 1914–1919*, trans. Peter T. Hoffer, eds. Ernst Falzeder, Eva Brabant and Patrizia Giampieri-Deutsch (Cambridge, MA: Belknap Press of Harvard University Press, 1996), p. 311.

[30] Jules H. Masserman, "Sexuality Re-Evaluated," *Canadian Journal of Psychiatry*, vol. 11, no. 5 (October 1966), p. 386.

[31] Aldous Huxley, "Our Contemporary Hocus-Pocus," *Forum*, vol. 73 (March 1925), p. 315.

[32] Richard LaPiere, "The Freudian Ethic," in *The Freudian Ethic* (New York, NY: Duell, Sloan and Pearce, 1959), p. 56.

[33] Hans J. Eysenck, "Psycho-Babble and Pseudo-History," in *Decline and Fall of the Freudian Empire* (New York, NY: Penguin Books, 1991), p. 189.

[34] Lewis M. Terman, "Trails to Psychology," in *A History of Psychology in Autobiography, Vol. 2*, ed. Carl Murchison (Worcester, MA: Clark University Press, 1932), p. 330.

[35] Sigmund Freud, "Explanations, Applications and Orientations" (1933 [1932]), in *New Introductory Lectures on Psycho-Analysis*, trans. and ed. James Strachey (New York, NY: W. W. Norton & Company, 1989), p. 171.

[36] Karen Horney, "The Denial of the Vagina: A Contribution to the Problem of the Genital Anxieties Specific to Women," in *Feminine Psychology*, ed. Harold Kelman (New York, NY: W. W. Norton & Company, 1973), p. 150.

[37] Sigmund Freud, "Psycho-Analysis and Psychiatry" (1916–1917 [1915–1917]), in *Introductory Lectures on Psychoanalysis*, trans. and ed. James Strachey (New York, NY: W. W. Norton & Company, 1977), p. 255.

[38] C. G. Jung, "Sigmund Freud in His Historical Setting" (1934), in *The Collected Works of C. G. Jung, Vol. 15: The Spirit in Man, Art and Literature*, trans. R.F.C. Hull (Princeton, NJ: Princeton University Press, 1971), p. 38.

[39] Ibid., p. 39.

[40] Sigmund Freud, "The Future Prospects of Psychoanalytic Therapy" (1910), in *Therapy and Technique*, ed. Philip Rieff (New York, NY: Collier Books, 1963), p. 86.

[41] Maurice Natenberg, "Unconditional Surrender," in *Freudian Psycho-Antics: Fact and Fraud in Psychoanalysis* (Chicago, IL: Regent House, 1953), p. 51.

[42] Sigmund Freud, "Preface" (1940 [1938]), to *An Outline of Psycho-Analysis*, trans. and ed. James Strachey (New York, NY: W. W. Norton & Company, 1989), p. 9.

[43] Sigmund Freud, "Preface to the First Edition" (1899), in *The Interpretation of Dreams*, trans. and ed. James Strachey (New York, NY: Science Editions, 1963), p. 176.

[44] Sigmund Freud, "A Child Is Being Beaten" (1919), in *Sexuality and the Psychology of Love*, ed. Philip Rieff (New York, NY: Collier Books, 1978), p. 132.

[45] Knight Dunlap, "Preface," to *Mysticism, Freudianism and Scientific Psychology* (St. Louis, MO: C. V. Mosby Company, 1920), p. 8

[46] Emil Kraepelin, "Frequency and Causes," in *Dementia Praecox and Paraphrenia*, trans. R. Mary Barclay, ed. George M. Robertson (Edinburgh, UK: E & S Livingstone, 1919), p. 250.

[47] Heinz Kohut, "Preface," to *The Restoration of the Self* (Chicago, IL: University of Chicago Press, 2009), p. xviii.

[48] Aldous Huxley, "Our Contemporary Hocus-Pocus," *Forum*, vol. 73 (March 1925), pp. 318–19.

[49] Otto Fenichel, "Comments on the Literature of Psychoanalytic Technique," in *Problems of Psychoanalytic Technique* (New York, NY: Psychoanalytic Quarterly, 1941), p. 98.

[50] Sigmund Freud, "The Psychology of the Dream-Processes" (1899), in *The Interpretation of Dreams*, trans. and ed. James Strachey (New York, NY: Science Editions, 1963), p. 511.

[51] Karen Horney, "Psychogenic Factors in Functional Female Disorders," in *Feminine Psychology*, ed. Harold Kelman (New York, NY: W. W. Norton & Company, 1973), p. 163.

[52] Erich Fromm, "Freud's Instinct Theory and Its Critique," in *Greatness and Limitations of Freud's Thought* (New York, NY: Mentor Books, 1981), p. 132.

[53] Aldous Huxley, "Our Contemporary Hocus-Pocus," *Forum*, vol. 73 (March 1925), p. 319.

[54] Sigmund Freud, "The Psychotherapy of Hysteria," in Josef Breuer and Sigmund Freud, *Studies on Hysteria*, trans. and ed. James Strachey (New York, NY: Basic Books, 2000), p. 295.

[55] Sigmund Freud, "The Psychotherapy of Hysteria," in Josef Breuer and Sigmund Freud, *Studies on Hysteria*, trans. and ed. James Strachey (New York, NY: Basic Books, 2000), p. 281.

[56] Sigmund Freud, "Letter to Wilhelm Fliess—August 7, 1901," in *The Complete Letters of Sigmund Freud to Wilhelm Fliess, 1887–1904*, trans. and ed. Jeffrey Moussaieff Masson (Cambridge, MA: Belknap Press of Harvard University Press, 1985), p. 446. Alternatively translated as: "My clients are sick people, and therefore quite peculiarly irrational and unpredictable" (Sigmund Freud, "Letter to Wilhelm Fliess—August 7, 1901," in Marie Bonaparte, Anna Freud, and Ernst Kris (eds.), *The Origins of Psychoanalysis: Letters to Wilhelm Fliess, Drafts and Notes: 1887-1902*, trans. Eric Mosbacher and James Strachey [New York, NY: Basic Books, 1954], pp. 333–34).

[57] Sigmund Freud, "Analytical Therapy" (1917), in *A General Introduction to Psychoanalysis* (New York, NY: Horace Liveright, 1920), p. 388.

[58] Ibid., p. 391.

[59] Sigmund Freud, "Constructions in Analysis" (1937), in *The Standard Edition of the Complete Psychological Works of Sigmund Freud, Vol. 23*, trans. and ed. James Strachey (London, UK: Hogarth Press and the Institute of Psycho-Analysis, 1964), p. 262.

[60] Sigmund Freud, "Constructions in Analysis" (1937), in *The Standard Edition of the Complete Psychological Works of Sigmund Freud, Vol. 23*, trans. and ed. James Strachey (London, UK: Hogarth Press and the Institute of Psycho-Analysis, 1964), p. 259.

[61] Sigmund Freud, "Freud's Psycho-Analytic Procedure" (1904 [1903]), in *The Standard Edition of the Complete Psychological Works of Sigmund Freud, Vol. 7*, trans. and ed. James Strachey (London, UK: Hogarth Press and the Institute of Psycho-Analysis, 1953), p. 252.

[62] Sigmund Freud, "(A) The Work of Condensation," in *The Interpretation of Dreams*, trans. and ed. James Strachey (New York, NY: Science Editions, 1963), p. 280.

⁶³ Sigmund Freud, "(A) The Work of Condensation," in *The Interpretation of Dreams*, trans. and ed. James Strachey (New York, NY: Science Editions, 1963), pp. 280–81.

⁶⁴ Sigmund Freud, quoted in Joseph Wortis, "The Analysis," in *Fragments of an Analysis with Freud* (New York, NY: Simon & Schuster, 1954), p. 64.

⁶⁵ Sigmund Freud, "The Method of Interpreting Dreams: An Analysis of a Specimen Dream," in *The Interpretation of Dreams*, trans. and ed. James Strachey (New York, NY: Science Editions, 1963), p. 108.

⁶⁶ Sigmund Freud, "The Aetiology of Hysteria" (1896), in *The Standard Edition of the Complete Psychological Works of Sigmund Freud, Vol. 3*, trans. and ed. James Strachey (London, UK: Hogarth Press and the Institute of Psycho-Analysis, 1981), p. 205.

⁶⁷ Maurice Natenberg, "The Sorcery Behind the Couch," in *Freudian Psycho-Antics: Fact and Fraud in Psychoanalysis* (Chicago, IL: Regent House, 1953), p. 43.

⁶⁸ Andrew Salter, "Analysis Terminable and Interminable," in *The Case Against Psychoanalysis* (New York, NY: Citadel Press, 1963), p. 145.

⁶⁹ Richard LaPiere, "The Freudian Ethic," in *The Freudian Ethic* (New York, NY: Duell, Sloan and Pearce, 1959), p. 69.

⁷⁰ Robert Graves, "A Motley Hero," *Sewanee Review*, vol. 57, no. 4 (Autumn 1949), pp. 698–99.

⁷¹ Mikkel Borch-Jacobsen, "Neurotica: Freud and the Seduction Theory," in *Making Minds and Madness: From Hysteria to Depression* (New York, NY: Cambridge University Press, 2009), p. 55.

⁷² William Barrett, "Homeless in the World," in *The Illusion of Technique: A Search for Meaning in a Technological Civilization* (Garden City, NY: Anchor Books, 1979), p. 165.

⁷³ Karl Menninger, "Neutrality and Ethics of the Therapist," in *Theory of Psychoanalytic Technique* (New York, NY: Harper & Row, 1964), p. 93.

⁷⁴ Judd Marmor, "Psychoanalytic Therapy as an Educational Process," in *Psychiatry in Transition: Selected Papers* (New Brunswick, NJ: Transaction Publishers, 1994), p. 201.

⁷⁵ Aldous Huxley, "Our Contemporary Hocus-Pocus," *The Forum*, vol. 73 (March 1925), p. 319.

⁷⁶ Sigmund Freud, "An Autobiographical Study" (1925 [1924]), in *An Autobiographical Study*, trans. and ed. James Strachey (New York, NY: W. W. Norton & Company, 1989), p. 45.

⁷⁷ C. G. Jung, "Some Crucial Points in Psychoanalysis: A Correspondence between Dr. Jung and Dr. Loÿ" (1914), in *Critique of Psychoanalysis*, trans. R.F.C. Hull (Princeton, NJ: Princeton University Press, 1975), p. 199.

⁷⁸ Sigmund Freud, "Psychoanalysis" (1922), in *Character and Culture*, ed. Philip Rieff (New York, NY: Collier Books, 1963), p. 248.

⁷⁹ Sigmund Freud, "Letter to Wilhelm Fliess—September 22, 1898," in Ernest Jones, *The Life and Work of Sigmund Freud, Vol. 1: The Formative Years and the Great Discoveries, 1856–1900* (New York, NY: Basic Books, 1959),

p. 395. "I...have no desire at all to leave the psychology hanging in the air with no organic basis. But, beyond a feeling of conviction [that there must be such a basis], I have nothing, either theoretical or therapeutic, to work on, and so I must behave as if I were confronted by psychological factors only" (Sigmund Freud, "Letter to Wilhelm Fliess—September 22, 1898," in Marie Bonaparte, Anna Freud and Ernst Kris (eds.), *The Origins of Psychoanalysis: Letters to Wilhelm Fliess, Drafts and Notes: 1887-1902*, trans. Eric Mosbacher and James Strachey [New York, NY: Basic Books, 1954], p. 264).

[80] C. G. Jung, "General Aspects of Psychoanalysis" (1913), in *Critique of Psychoanalysis*, trans. R.F.C. Hull (Princeton, NJ: Princeton University Press, 1975), p. 148.

[81] Judd Marmor, "Psychoanalytic Therapy as an Educational Process," in *Psychiatry in Transition: Selected Papers* (New Brunswick, NJ: Transaction Publishers, 1994), pp. 198–99. "Patients under Freudian analysis dream Freudian dreams, discover their Oedipus complex, their castration anxieties, and establish strong transferences with their analysts. Patients under Jungian analysis dream Jungian dreams, discover their projections and their animas, and realize their individuations. And so on for every dynamic school and subschool. It is as if Descartes' famous 'evil genius' really existed and self-confirmed all the theories of dynamic psychiatry" (Henri F. Ellenberger, quoted in Jacques Mousseau, "Freud in Perspective: A Conversation with Henri F. Ellenberger," *Psychology Today*, vol. 6, no. 10 [March 1973], p. 56).

[82] Michael Franz Basch, "Genetic Investigation and Interpretation," in *Doing Psychotherapy* (New York, NY: Basic Books, 1980), pp. 70–71.

[83] Hans J. Eysenck, "The Interpretation of Dreams and the Psychopathology of Everyday Life," in *Decline and Fall of the Freudian Empire* (New York, NY: Penguin Books, 1991), p. 129.

[84] Bernard Hart, "Lecture Three," in *Psychopathology: Its Development and Its Place in Medicine* (Cambridge, UK: Cambridge University Press, 1950), p. 74.

[85] Malcolm Macmillan, "Psychoanalysis as Science," in *Freud Evaluated: The Complete Arc* (Cambridge, MA: Massachusetts Institute of Technology Press, 1997), pp. 625, 626.

[86] John Kerr, "Afterward," to *A Most Dangerous Method: The Story of Jung, Freud, and Sabina Spielrein* (New York, NY: Alfred A. Knopf, 1993), p. 509.

[87] Joseph Jastrow, "'Kobold im Keller'," in *Freud: His Dream and Sex Theories* (Cleveland, OH: World Publishing Company, 1948), pp. 37, 38.

[88] Jacques Lacan, "My Teaching, Its Nature and Its Ends," in *My Teaching*, trans. David Macey (London, UK: Verso, 2008), p. 71.

[89] Thomas Szasz, "Psychoanalysis as Base Rhetoric: Oedipus, from Rex to Complex," in *The Myth of Psychotherapy: Mental Healing as Religion, Rhetoric, and Repression* (Garden City, NY: Anchor Press, 1979), p. 127.

[90] Robert P. Knight, "Evaluation of the Results of Psychoanalytic Therapy," *American Journal of Psychiatry*, vol. 98, no. 3 (November 1941), p. 437.

[91] Richard Noll, "Religion Can Only Be Replaced by Religion," in *The Aryan Christ: The Secret Life of Carl Jung* (New York, NY: Random House, 1997), p. 59.

[92] Adolf Grünbaum, "Did Freud Vindicate His Method of Clinical Investigation?" in *The Foundations of Psychoanalysis: A Philosophical Critique* (Los Angeles, CA: University of California Press, 1985), p. 165.

Chapter 20: Psychoanalysis and Its Discontents: Corrosive Ideology and Debunked Case Histories

[1] Jacques Maritain, "Freudianism and Psychoanalysis," *CrossCurrents*, vol. 6, no. 4 (Fall 1956), p. 310.

[2] Karl Menninger, "Neurotic Invalidism," in *Man Against Himself* (New York, NY: Harcourt, Brace and World, 1938), p. 137.

[3] Sybil B. G. Eysenck, quoted in "Preface," to Hans J. Eysenck, *Decline and Fall of the Freudian Empire* (New Brunswick, NJ: Transaction Publishers, 2004), p. vii.

[4] Alfred Hoche, quoted in Mikkel Borch-Jacobsen and Sonu Shamdasani, *The Freud Files: An Inquiry into the History of Psychoanalysis* (Cambridge, UK: Cambridge University Press, 2012), p. 97.

[5] Louise Bates Ames, quoted in Martin L. Gross, "Our Psychologized Young," in *The Psychological Society: A Critical Analysis of Psychiatry, Psychotherapy, Psychoanalysis and the Psychological Revolution* (New York, NY: Random House, 1978), p. 247.

[6] Richard LaPiere, "The Freudian Doctrine of Man," in *The Freudian Ethic* (New York, NY: Duell, Sloan and Pearce, 1959), p. 54.

[7] C. G. Jung, "The Spiritual Problem of Modern Man," in *Modern Man in Search of a Soul*, trans. W. S. Dell and Cary F. Baynes (New York, NY: Harcourt, Brace & World, 1933), pp. 208–9. "No wonder that to unearth buried fragments of psychic life we have first to drain a miasmal swamp. Only a great idealist like Freud could devote a lifetime to the unclean work. This is the beginning of our psychology. For us acquaintance with the realities of psychic life could start only at this end, with all that repels us and that we do not wish to see" (C. G. Jung, "The Spiritual Problem of Modern Man," in *Modern Man in Search of a Soul*, trans. W. S. Dell and Cary F. Baynes [New York, NY: Harcourt, Brace & World, 1933], p. 214).

[8] Sigmund Freud, "Analytical Therapy" (1917), in *A General Introduction to Psychoanalysis* (New York, NY: Horace Liveright, 1920), p. 401.

[9] C. G. Jung, "Letter to Sigmund Freud—December 3, 1912," in William McGuire (ed.), *The Freud/Jung Letters: The Correspondence Between Sigmund Freud and C. G. Jung*, trans. Ralph Manheim and R.F.C. Hull (Princeton, NJ: Princeton University Press, 1994), p. 527.

[10] C. G. Jung, "Letter to Sigmund Freud—December 3, 1912," in William McGuire (ed.), *The Freud/Jung Letters: The Correspondence Between Sigmund Freud and C. G. Jung*, trans. Ralph Manheim and R.F.C. Hull (Princeton, NJ: Princeton University Press, 1994), p. 526.

[11] Robert R. Holt, "The Current Status of Psychoanalytic Theory," *Psychoanalytic Psychology*, vol. 2, no. 4 (1985), p. 297.

[12] William James, "Letter to Théodore Flournoy—September 28, 1909," in *The Letters of William James, Vol. II*, ed. Henry James (Boston, MA: Atlantic Monthly Press, 1920), p. 328.

[13] William James, "Letter to Théodore Flournoy—September 28, 1909," in *The Letters of William James, Vol. II*, ed. Henry James (Boston, MA: Atlantic Monthly Press, 1920), p. 328. "[H]e seems almost like a man obsessed" (Jacques Maritain, "Freudianism and Psychoanalysis," *CrossCurrents*, vol. 6, no. 4 [Fall 1956], p. 307).

[14] C. G. Jung, "Introduction to Kranefeldt's 'Secret Ways of the Mind'" (1930), in *Critique of Psychoanalysis*, trans. R.F.C. Hull (Princeton, NJ: Princeton University Press, 1975), p. 218.

[15] Phyllis Bottome, "Adler and the Freudian Circle," in *Alfred Adler: A Biography* (New York, NY: G. P. Putnam's Sons, 1939), p. 66. Not long before Adler's death in 1937, Adler had dinner with Abraham Maslow. When Maslow asked Adler about being a disciple of Freud, Adler "became very angry...He said that this was a lie and a swindle for which he blamed Freud entirely, whom he then called names like swindler, sly, schemer, as nearly as I can recall. He said that he had never been a student of Freud, or a disciple or a follower. He made it clear from the beginning that he didn't agree with Freud and that he had his own opinions" (Abraham H. Maslow, "Was Adler a Disciple of Freud? A Note," *Journal of Individual Psychology*, vol. 18, no. 2 [1962], p. 125).

[16] Frederick S. Perls, "A Life Chronology," *Gestalt Journal*, vol. 16, no. 2 (1993), p. 8.

[17] Havelock Ellis, "Letter to Joseph Wortis—September 14, 1934," quoted in Joseph Wortis, "First Meetings," in *Fragments of an Analysis with Freud* (New York, NY: Simon & Schuster, 1954), p. 11.

[18] Seymour Fisher and Roger P. Greenberg, "Freud's Psychoanalytic Therapy and the Realities of Current Analytic Practices," in *The Scientific Credibility of Freud's Theories and Therapy* (New York, NY: Columbia University Press, 1985), p. 285.

[19] Frank J. Sulloway, "Reassessing Freud's Case Histories: The Social Construction of Psychoanalysis," *Isis*, vol. 82, no. 2 (June 1991), p. 261.

[20] Mikkel Borch-Jacobsen and Sonu Shamdasani, "Case Histories," in *The Freud Files: An Inquiry into the History of Psychoanalysis* (Cambridge, UK: Cambridge University Press, 2012), p. 180.

[21] Kurt R. Eissler, "Appendix 1. The Desegregation of Psychoanalytic Institutes and Medical Schools," in *Medical Orthodoxy and the Future of Psychoanalysis* (New York, NY: International Universities Press, 1965), p. 395.

[22] Charles Brenner, "Psychoanalysis: Philosophy or Science?" in *Psychoanalysis and Philosophy*, eds. Charles Hanly and Morris Lazerowitz (New York, NY: International Universities Press, 1970), p. 42.

[23] Ernest Jones, "Case Histories," in *The Life and Work of Sigmund Freud, Vol. 2: Years of Maturity, 1901–1919* (New York, NY: Basic Books, 1955), p. 257.

[24] Erik H. Erikson, "Reality and Actuality," *Journal of the American Psychoanalytic Association*, vol. 10, no. 3 (July 1962), p. 455.

[25] Patrick J. Mahony, "Conclusions," to *Freud's Dora: A Psychoanalytic, Historical, and Textual Study* (New Haven, CT: Yale University Press, 1996), pp. 148–49.

[26] Sigmund Freud, "The Clinical Picture" (1905 [1901]), in *Dora: An Analysis of a Case of Hysteria*, ed. Philip Rieff (New York, NY: Touchstone, 1997), p. 38.

[27] Sigmund Freud, "An Autobiographical Study" (1925 [1924]), in *The Standard Edition of the Complete Psychological Works of Sigmund Freud, Vol. 20*, trans. and ed. James Strachey (London, UK: Hogarth Press and the Institute of Psycho-Analysis, 1959), p. 18.

[28] Mikkel Borch-Jacobsen, "Anna O.: The First Tall Tale," in *Unauthorized Freud: Doubters Confront a Legend*, ed. Frederick C. Crews (New York, NY: Viking, 1998), p. 14.

[29] Richard Webster, "Anna O. and the Birth of Psychoanalysis," in *Why Freud Was Wrong: Sin, Science, and Psychoanalysis* (New York, NY: Basic Books, 1995), p. 131.

[30] Sigmund Freud, "Traumatic Fixation—the Unconscious" (1917), in *A General Introduction to Psychoanalysis* (New York, NY: Horace Liveright, 1920), p. 242.

[31] Peter Gay, "The Theory in the Making," in *Freud: A Life for Our Time* (New York, NY: Anchor Books, 1989), p. 63.

[32] Ernest Jones, "The Breuer Period," in *The Life and Work of Sigmund Freud, Vol. 1: The Formative Years and the Great Discoveries, 1856–1900* (New York, NY: Basic Books, 1959), p. 225.

[33] Ibid.

[34] Albrecht Hirschmüller, quoted in *Why Freud Was Wrong: Sin, Science, and Psychoanalysis* (New York, NY: Basic Books, 1995), p. 134.

[35] Sigmund Freud, "Letter to C. G. Jung—April 19, 1908," in William McGuire (ed.), *The Freud/Jung Letters: The Correspondence Between Sigmund Freud and C. G. Jung*, trans. Ralph Manheim and R.F.C. Hull (Princeton, NJ: Princeton University Press, 1994), p. 141.

[36] Frank J. Sulloway, "Reassessing Freud's Case Histories: The Social Construction of Psychoanalysis," *Isis*, vol. 82, no. 2 (June 1991), p. 245.

[37] Barbara Von Eckardt, "Can Intuitive Proof Suffice?" in *Unauthorized Freud: Doubters Confront a Legend*, ed. Frederick C. Crews (New York, NY: Viking, 1998), p. 115.

[38] Sigmund Freud, "Letter to Wilhelm Fliess—February 4, 1888," in Marie Bonaparte, Anna Freud, and Ernst Kris (eds.), *The Origins of Psychoanalysis: Letters to Wilhelm Fliess, Drafts and Notes: 1887–1902*, trans. Eric Mosbacher and James Strachey (New York, NY: Basic Books, 1954), p. 55. Alternatively translated as, "talking people into or out of things...is what my occupation consists in" (Sigmund Freud, "Letter to Wilhelm Fliess—February 4, 1888," in *The Complete Letters of Sigmund Freud to Wilhelm Fliess, 1887-1904*, trans. and ed. Jeffrey Moussaieff Masson [Cambridge, MA: Belknap Press of Harvard University Press, 1985], p. 18).

[39] C. G. Jung, "Lecture Three—April 6, 1925," in *Analytical Psychology: Notes of the Seminar Given in 1925*, ed. William McGuire (London, UK: Routledge, 1992), p. 16.

[40] Janet Malcolm, "Chapter Six," in *Psychoanalysis: The Impossible Profession* (New York, NY: Alfred A. Knopf, 1981), p. 97.

[41] Robert S. Woodworth, "Some Criticisms of the Freudian Psychology," *Journal of Abnormal Psychology*, vol. 12, no. 3 (August 1917), p. 177.

[42] Egon Friedell, "Epilogue: The Collapse of Reality," in *A Cultural History of the Modern Age, Vol. 3: The Crisis of the European Soul*, trans. C. F. Atkinson (New York, NY: Alfred A. Knopf, 1932), p. 482.

[43] Ernest Jones, "Case Histories," in *The Life and Work of Sigmund Freud, Vol. 2: Years of Maturity, 1901–1919* (New York, NY: Basic Books, 1955), p. 258.

[44] Hans J. Eysenck, "Freud and the Development of the Child," in *Decline and Fall of the Freudian Empire* (New York, NY: Penguin Books, 1991), p. 105.

[45] Joseph Wolpe and Stanley Rachman, "Psychoanalytic 'Evidence': A Criticism Based on Freud's Case of Little Hans," *Journal of Nervous and Mental Disease*, vol. 131, no. 2 (August 1960), pp. 146–47.

[46] Sigmund Freud, "Analysis of a Phobia in a Five-Year-Old Boy" (1909), in *The Standard Edition of the Complete Psychological Works of Sigmund Freud, Vol. 10*, trans. and ed. James Strachey (London, UK: Hogarth Press and the Institute of Psycho-Analysis, 1962), p. 104.

[47] Ibid.

[48] Patrick J. Mahony, *Freud and the Rat Man* (New Haven, CT: Yale University Press, 1986), p. 213.

[49] Ernest Jones, "Case Histories," in *The Life and Work of Sigmund Freud, Vol. 2: Years of Maturity, 1901–1919* (New York, NY: Basic Books, 1955), p. 274.

[50] Erich Fromm, "The Relevance of Psychoanalysis for the Future," in *Beyond Freud: From Individual to Social Psychoanalysis*, ed. Rainer Funk (Riverdale, NY: American Mental Health Foundation, 2010), p. 131.

[51] Wolf Man, quoted in Karin Obholzer, "The Sister Complex," in *The Wolf-Man: Conversations with Freud's Controversial Patient—Sixty Years Later*, trans. Michael Shaw (New York, NY: Continuum, 1982), p. 113.

[52] Wolf Man, quoted in Karin Obholzer, "I, the Most Famous Case," in *The Wolf-Man: Conversations with Freud's Controversial Patient—Sixty Years Later*, trans. Michael Shaw (New York, NY: Continuum, 1982), pp. 171–72.

[53] Ibid., p. 112.

[54] Sigmund Freud, "From the History of an Infantile Neurosis" (1918 [1914]), in *The Standard Edition of the Complete Psychological Works of Sigmund Freud, Vol. 17*, trans. and ed. James Strachey (London, UK: Hogarth Press and the Institute of Psycho-Analysis, 1955), p. 112.

[55] Ernst Falzeder, "The Threads of Psychoanalytic Filiations or Psychoanalysis Taking Effect," in *100 Years of Psychoanalysis, Contributions to the History of Psychoanalysis*, eds. André Haynal and Ernst Falzeder (Geneva: Cahiers Psychiatriques Genevois, Special Issue, 1994), p. 182.

[56] Sigmund Freud, "Letter to C. G. Jung—April 2, 1911," in William McGuire (ed.), *The Freud/Jung Letters: The Correspondence Between Sigmund Freud and C. G. Jung*, trans. Ralph Manheim and R.F.C. Hull (Princeton, NJ: Princeton University Press, 1994), p. 413.

[57] Mikkel Borch-Jacobsen and Sonu Shamdasani, "Policing the Past," in *The Freud Files: An Inquiry into the History of Psychoanalysis* (Cambridge, UK: Cambridge University Press, 2012), pp. 283–84.

[58] Peter Gay, "Anna," in *Freud: A Life for Our Time* (New York, NY: Anchor Books, 1989), p. 439.

[59] Ibid., p. 440.

[60] Phyllis Grosskurth, "The Protégée," in *Melanie Klein: Her World and Her Work* (London, UK: Hodder and Stoughton, 1986), p. 99. See also Esther Menaker, "Anna Freud's Analysis by Her Father: The Assault on the Self," *Journal of Religion and Health*, vol. 40, no. 1 (Spring 2001), pp. 89–95.

[61] Peter Gay, "Anna," in *Freud: A Life for Our Time* (New York, NY: Anchor Books, 1989), p. 440.

[62] Sigmund Freud, quoted in Lavinia Edmunds, "His Master's Choice," *John Hopkins Magazine*, vol. 40, no. 2 (April 1988), p. 42.

[63] "Dear Freud: Recently I am informed by the participants, two patients presented themselves to you, a man and a woman, and made it clear that on your judgment depended whether they had a right to marry one another or not. The man is at present married to another woman, and the father of two children by her, and bound in honor by the ethics of his profession not to take advantage of his confidential position toward his patients and their immediate relatives. The woman he now wants to marry was his patient. He says you sanction his divorcing his wife and marrying his patient, but yet you have never seen the wife and learned to judge her feelings, interests and real wishes. The woman, this man's patient, is my wife...How can you know you are just to me; how can you give a judgment that ruins a man's home and happiness, without at least knowing the victim so as to see if he is worthy of the punishment, or if through him a better solution cannot be found?...Great Doctor, are you savant or charlatan? Doktor, please write me the truth. The woman is my wife whom I love..." (Abraham Bijur, quoted in Lavinia

Edmunds, "His Master's Choice," *John Hopkins Magazine*, vol. 40, no. 2 [April 1988], p. 44).

[64] Sigmund Freud, quoted in Lavinia Edmunds, "His Master's Choice," *John Hopkins Magazine*, vol. 40, no. 2 (April 1988), p. 45.

[65] Sigmund Freud, "The Technique of Psycho-Analysis" (1940 [1938]), in *An Outline of Psycho-Analysis*, trans. and ed. James Strachey (New York, NY: W. W. Norton & Company, 1969), p. 33.

[66] Horace Frink, quoted in Lavinia Edmunds, "The Marriage Counselor," in *Unauthorized Freud: Doubters Confront a Legend*, ed. Frederick C. Crews (New York, NY: Viking, 1998), p. 261.

[67] Anthony Storr, "The Concept of Cure," in *Psychoanalysis Observed*, ed. Charles Rycroft (Baltimore, MD: Penguin Books, 1968), p. 57.

[68] Abraham Myerson, "The Attitude of Neurologists, Psychiatrists, and Psychologists Towards Psychoanalysis," *American Journal of Psychiatry*, vol. 96, no. 3 (November 1939), p. 640.

[69] Fredric Wertham, "What to Do Till the Doctor Goes," *The Nation* (September 2, 1950), p. 206. See also Albert Ellis, "Is Psychoanalysis Harmful?" *Psychiatric Opinion*, vol. 5, no. 1 (January 1968), pp. 16–25.

[70] Sigmund Freud, "Analytical Therapy" (1917), in *A General Introduction to Psychoanalysis* (New York, NY: Horace Liveright, 1920), p. 390.

[71] Ibid., p. 397.

[72] Ibid., p. 398.

[73] Sigmund Freud, "On Beginning the Treatment (Further Recommendations on the Technique of Psycho-Analysis I)" (1913), in *The Standard Edition of the Complete Psychological Works of Sigmund Freud, Vol. 12*, trans. and ed. James Strachey (London, UK: Hogarth Press and the Institute of Psycho-Analysis, 1958), p. 128.

[74] Sigmund Freud, "A Short Account of Psycho-Analysis" (1924 [1923]), in *The Standard Edition of the Complete Psychological Works of Sigmund Freud, Vol. 19*, trans. and ed. James Strachey (London, UK: Vintage Books, 2001), p. 209.

[75] Frank J. Sulloway, "Reassessing Freud's Case Histories: The Social Construction of Psychoanalysis," *Isis*, vol. 82, no. 2 (June 1991), p. 252.

[76] Ernest Jones, "Case Histories," in *The Life and Work of Sigmund Freud, Vol. 2: Years of Maturity, 1901–1919* (New York, NY: Basic Books, 1955), p. 268.

[77] Karl Kraus, quoted in Thomas Szasz, "On Psychoanalysis and Psychology," in *Karl Kraus and the Soul-Doctors: A Pioneer Critic and His Criticism of Psychiatry and Psychoanalysis* (Baton Rouge, LA: Louisiana State University Press, 1976), p. 109.

[78] Karl Kraus, quoted in Thomas Szasz, "On Language, Life, and Love," in *Karl Kraus and the Soul-Doctors: A Pioneer Critic and His Criticism of Psychiatry and Psychoanalysis* (Baton Rouge, LA: Louisiana State University Press, 1976), p. 152.

[79] Sigmund Freud, "Fräulein Elisabeth von R.," in Josef Breuer and Sigmund Freud, *Studies on Hysteria*, trans. and ed. James Strachey (New York, NY: Basic Books, 2000), p. 160.

[80] Philip Rieff, "Introduction," to Sigmund Freud, *Dora: An Analysis of a Case of Hysteria* (New York, NY: Touchstone, 1997), p. xii.

[81] Karl Kraus, quoted in Thomas Szasz, "On Psychoanalysis and Psychology," in *Karl Kraus and the Soul-Doctors: A Pioneer Critic and His Criticism of Psychiatry and Psychoanalysis* (Baton Rouge, LA: Louisiana State University Press, 1976), p. 106.

Chapter 21: Freud on the Psychoanalytic Couch: A Case History of Unfinished Self-Analysis

[1] Friedrich Nietzsche, "Request," in *The Gay Science*, trans. Walter Kaufmann (New York, NY: Vintage Books, 1974), p. 49.

[2] Heinz Hartmann, quoted in Elisabeth Young-Bruehl, *Anna Freud: A Biography* (New Haven, CT: Yale University Press, 2008), p. 301.

[3] Harry K. Wells, *Pavlov and Freud, Vol. 2: Sigmund Freud: A Pavlovian Critique* (New York, NY: International Publishers, 1960), p. 189.

[4] Philip Rieff, "The Hidden Self," in *Freud: The Mind of the Moralist* (Chicago, IL: University of Chicago Press, 1979), p. 65.

[5] C. G. Jung, "Letter to Sigmund Freud—December 18, 1912," in William McGuire (ed.), *The Freud/Jung Letters: The Correspondence Between Sigmund Freud and C .G. Jung*, trans. Ralph Manheim and R.F.C. Hull (Princeton, NJ: Princeton University Press, 1994), p. 535.

[6] C. G. Jung, "Letter to Sigmund Freud—December 18, 1912," in William McGuire (ed.), *The Freud/Jung Letters: The Correspondence Between Sigmund Freud and C. G. Jung*, trans. Ralph Manheim and R.F.C. Hull (Princeton, NJ: Princeton University Press, 1994), p. 534.

[7] C. G. Jung, "Sigmund Freud," in *Memories, Dreams, Reflections*, trans. Richard Winston and Clara Winston, ed. Aniela Jaffé (New York, NY: Vintage Books, 1965), p. 158.

[8] Ibid.

[9] C. G. Jung, "Letter to Sigmund Freud—December 18, 1912," in William McGuire (ed.), *The Freud/Jung Letters: The Correspondence Between Sigmund Freud and C. G. Jung*, trans. Ralph Manheim and R.F.C. Hull (Princeton, NJ: Princeton University Press, 1994), p. 535.

[10] Jacques Lacan, "Excommunication," in *The Four Fundamental Concepts of Psychoanalysis*, trans. Alan Sheridan, ed. Jacques-Alain Miller (New York, NY: W. W. Norton & Company, 1998), p. 12.

[11] Philip Rieff, "The Hidden Self," in *Freud: The Mind of the Moralist* (Chicago, IL: University of Chicago Press, 1979), p. 65.

[12] Sigmund Freud, "Recommendations to Physicians Practicing Psycho-Analysis" (1912), in *The Standard Edition of the Complete Psychological Works of Sigmund Freud, Vol. 12*, trans. and ed. James Strachey (London,

UK: Hogarth Press and the Institute of Psycho-Analysis, 1958), p. 116.

[13] Sigmund Freud, "The Method of Interpreting Dreams: An Analysis of a Specimen Dream" (1899), in *The Interpretation of Dreams*, trans. and ed. James Strachey (New York, NY: Science Editions, 1963), p. 105.

[14] Sigmund Freud, "Letter to Wilhelm Fliess—October 15, 1897," in Sigmund Freud, *The Origins of Psychoanalysis: Letters to Wilhelm Fliess, Drafts and Notes (1887–1902)*, trans. Eric Mosbacher and James Strachey, eds. Marie Bonaparte, Anna Freud, and Ernst Kris (New York, NY: Basic Books, 1954), p. 221. Alternatively translated as: "My self-analysis is in fact the most essential thing I have at present and promises to become of the greatest value to me if it reaches its end" (Sigmund Freud, "Letter to Wilhelm Fliess—October 15, 1897," in *The Complete Letters of Sigmund Freud to Wilhelm Fliess, 1887–1904*, trans. and ed. Jeffrey Moussaieff Masson [Cambridge, MA: Belknap Press of Harvard University Press, 1985], p. 270).

[15] Sigmund Freud, "Letter to Wilhelm Fliess—November 14, 1897," in Sigmund Freud, *The Origins of Psychoanalysis: Letters to Wilhelm Fliess, Drafts and Notes (1887–1902)*, trans. Eric Mosbacher and James Strachey, eds. Marie Bonaparte, Anna Freud, and Ernst Kris (New York, NY: Basic Books, 1954), pp. 234–35. Alternatively translated as: "My self-analysis remains interrupted. I have realized why I can analyze myself only with the help of knowledge obtained objectively (like an outsider). True self-analysis is impossible; otherwise there would be no [neurotic] illness. Since I am still contending with some kind of puzzle in my patients, this is bound to hold me up in my self-analysis as well" (Sigmund Freud, "Letter to Wilhelm Fliess—November 14, 1897," in *The Complete Letters of Sigmund Freud to Wilhelm Fliess, 1887–1904*, trans. and ed. Jeffrey Moussaieff Masson [Cambridge, MA: Belknap Press of Harvard University Press, 1985], p. 281).

[16] Otto Rank, "Psychology Beyond the Self," in *Beyond Psychology* (New York, NY: Dover, 1958), p. 278.

[17] Sigmund Freud, "Letter to Wilhelm Fliess—November 14, 1897," in Sigmund Freud, *The Origins of Psychoanalysis: Letters to Wilhelm Fliess, Drafts and Notes (1887–1902)*, trans. Eric Mosbacher and James Strachey, eds. Marie Bonaparte, Anna Freud, and Ernst Kris (New York, NY: Basic Books, 1954), p. 235. "Since I am still contending with some kind of puzzle in my patients, this is bound to hold me up in my self-analysis as well" (Sigmund Freud, "Letter to Wilhelm Fliess—November 14, 1897," in *The Complete Letters of Sigmund Freud to Wilhelm Fliess, 1887–1904*, trans. and ed. Jeffrey Moussaieff Masson [Cambridge, MA: Belknap Press of Harvard University Press, 1985], p. 281).

[18] Sigmund Freud, "Lecture I: Introduction" (1916–1917 [1915–1917]), in *Introductory Lectures on Psychoanalysis*, trans. and ed. James Strachey (New York, NY: W. W. Norton & Company, 1977), p. 19.

[19] Sigmund Freud, "On the History of the Psychoanalytic Movement" (1914), in *The History of the Psychoanalytic Movement*, ed. Philip Rieff (New York, NY: Collier Books, 1963), p. 54.

[20] Sigmund Freud, "Letter to Wilhelm Fliess—July 7, 1897," quoted in Ernest Jones, "The Fliess Period," in *The Life and Work of Sigmund Freud, Vol. 1: The Formative Years and the Great Discoveries, 1856–1900* (New York, NY: Basic Books, 1959), p. 306. Alternatively translated as: "my own neurosis set itself against any advance in the understanding of the neuroses" (Sigmund Freud, "Letter to Wilhelm Fliess—July 7, 1897," in *The Complete Letters of Sigmund Freud to Wilhelm Fliess, 1887–1904*, trans. and ed. Jeffrey Moussaieff Masson [Cambridge, MA: Belknap Press of Harvard University Press, 1985], p. 255).

[21] Jacob Freud, quoted in Sigmund Freud, "(B) Infantile Material as a Source of Dreams" (1899), in *The Interpretation of Dreams*, trans. and ed. James Strachey (New York, NY: Science Editions, 1963), p. 216.

[22] Sigmund Freud, "Letter to Wilhelm Fliess—October 15, 1897," in *The Complete Letters of Sigmund Freud to Wilhelm Fliess, 1887–1904*, trans. and ed. Jeffrey Moussaieff Masson (Cambridge, MA: Belknap Press of Harvard University Press, 1985), p. 272.

[23] Sigmund Freud, "(D) Typical Dreams" (1899), in *The Interpretation of Dreams*, trans. and ed. James Strachey (New York, NY: Science Editions, 1963), p. 262.

[24] Ibid.

[25] Ernest Jones, "Character and Personality," in *The Life and Work of Sigmund Freud, Vol. 2: Years of Maturity, 1901–1919* (New York, NY: Basic Books, 1955), p. 409.

[26] Erich Fromm, "His Relationship to His Mother; Self-Confidence and Insecurity," in *Sigmund Freud's Mission: An Analysis of His Personality and Influence* (New York, NY: Grove Press, 1963), p. 22.

[27] Maryse Choisy, "The Fear of Death," in *Sigmund Freud: A New Appraisal* (New York, NY: Philosophical Library, 1963), p. 48.

[28] Whitall N. Perry, "The Revolt Against Moses: A New Look at Psychoanalysis," in *Challenges to a Secular Society* (Oakton, VA: Foundation for Traditional Studies, 1996), p. 30.

[29] Sigmund Freud, "Letter to Wilhelm Fliess—June 12 [correct date is June 22], 1897," in Marie Bonaparte, Anna Freud and Ernst Kris (eds.), *The Origins of Psychoanalysis: Letters to Wilhelm Fliess, Drafts and Notes: 1887–1902*, trans. Eric Mosbacher and James Strachey (New York, NY: Basic Books, 1954), pp. 210–11. Alternatively translated as: "I have been through some kind of neurotic experience, curious states incomprehensible to Cs., twilight thoughts, veiled doubts, with barely a ray of light here or there" (Sigmund Freud, "Letter to Wilhelm Fliess—June 22, 1897," in *The Complete Letters of Sigmund Freud to Wilhelm Fliess, 1887–1904*, trans. and ed. Jeffrey Moussaieff Masson [Cambridge, MA: Belknap Press of Harvard University Press, 1985], p. 254).

[30] Sigmund Freud, "Letter to Wilhelm Fliess—June 12 [correct date is June 22], 1897," in Marie Bonaparte, Anna Freud and Ernst Kris (eds.), *The Origins of Psychoanalysis: Letters to Wilhelm Fliess, Drafts and Notes: 1887–*

1902, trans. Eric Mosbacher and James Strachey (New York, NY: Basic Books, 1954), p. 211. Alternatively translated as: "I believe I am in a cocoon, and God knows what sort of beast will crawl out" (Sigmund Freud, "Letter to Wilhelm Fliess—June 22, 1897," in *The Complete Letters of Sigmund Freud to Wilhelm Fliess, 1887–1904*, trans. and ed. Jeffrey Moussaieff Masson [Cambridge, MA: Belknap Press of Harvard University Press, 1985], p. 254).

31 Sigmund Freud, "Letter to Wilhelm Fliess—March 23, 1900," in *The Complete Letters of Sigmund Freud to Wilhelm Fliess, 1887–1904*, trans. and ed. Jeffrey Moussaieff Masson (Cambridge, MA: Belknap Press of Harvard University Press, 1985), p. 406.

32 Sigmund Freud, "Letter to Wilhelm Fliess—August 14, 1897," in Sigmund Freud, *The Origins of Psychoanalysis: Letters to Wilhelm Fliess, Drafts and Notes (1887–1902)*, trans. Eric Mosbacher and James Strachey, eds. Marie Bonaparte, Anna Freud, and Ernst Kris (New York, NY: Basic Books, 1954), pp. 213–14. Alternatively translated as: "After having become very cheerful here, I am now enjoying a period of bad humor. The chief patient I am pre-occupied with is myself. My little hysteria, though greatly accentuated by my work, has resolved itself a bit further. The rest is still at a standstill. That is what my mood primarily depends on. The analysis is more difficult than any other. It is, in fact, what paralyzes my psychic strength for describing and communicating what I have won so far. Still, I believe it must be done and is a necessary intermediate stage in my work" (Sigmund Freud, "Letter to Wilhelm Fliess—August 14, 1897," in *The Complete Letters of Sigmund Freud to Wilhelm Fliess, 1887–1904*, trans. and ed. Jeffrey Moussaieff Masson [Cambridge, MA: Belknap Press of Harvard University Press, 1985], p. 261).

33 Ernest Jones, "The Fliess Period," in *The Life and Work of Sigmund Freud, Vol. 1: The Formative Years and the Great Discoveries, 1856–1900* (New York, NY: Basic Books, 1959), pp. 304–6.

34 Sigmund Freud, "Letter to Wilhelm Fliess—July 10, 1900," in Marie Bonaparte, Anna Freud, and Ernst Kris (eds.), *The Origins of Psychoanalysis: Letters to Wilhelm Fliess, Drafts and Notes: 1887–1902*, trans. Eric Mosbacher and James Strachey (New York, NY: Basic Books, 1954), p. 323. Alternatively translated as: "Everything is in flux and dawning, an intellectual hell, with layer upon layer; in the darkest core, glimpses of the contours of Lucifer-Amor." (Sigmund Freud, "Letter to Wilhelm Fliess—July 10, 1900," in *The Complete Letters of Sigmund Freud to Wilhelm Fliess, 1887–1904*, trans. and ed. Jeffrey Moussaieff Masson [Cambridge, MA: Belknap Press of Harvard University Press, 1985], p. 421).

35 William James, "Imagination," in *The Principles of Psychology, Vol. 2* (New York, NY: Dover, 1950), p. 64.

36 Sigmund Freud, "Recommendations to Physicians Practicing Psycho-Analysis" (1912), in *The Standard Edition of the Complete Psychological Works of Sigmund Freud, Vol. 12*, trans. and ed. James Strachey (London,

UK: Hogarth Press and the Institute of Psycho-Analysis, 1958), p. 111.

[37] Sigmund Freud, "Preface to the Second Edition" (1908), in *The Interpretation of Dreams*, trans. and ed. James Strachey (New York, NY: Science Editions, 1963), p. xxvi.

[38] Sigmund Freud, "(H) Affects in Dreams" (1899), in *The Interpretation of Dreams*, trans. and ed. James Strachey (New York, NY: Science Editions, 1963), p. 472.

[39] Ibid., p. 483.

[40] Ernest Jones, "The Fliess Period," in *The Life and Work of Sigmund Freud, Vol. 1: The Formative Years and the Great Discoveries, 1856–1900* (New York, NY: Basic Books, 1959), p. 308.

[41] Sigmund Freud, "Letter to C. G. Jung—November 12, 1908," in William McGuire (ed.), *The Freud/Jung Letters: The Correspondence Between Sigmund Freud and C. G. Jung*, trans. Ralph Manheim and R.F.C. Hull (Princeton, NJ: Princeton University Press, 1994), p. 178.

[42] Frank McLynn, "Stormclouds Gather," in *Carl Gustav Jung: A Biography* (New York, NY: St. Martin's Press, 1996), p. 157.

[43] Peter Homans, "Psychological Factors in the Formation of Jung's Thought: The First Three Phases, 1900–1913," in *Jung in Context: Modernity and the Making of a Psychology* (Chicago, IL: University of Chicago Press, 1979), p. 57.

[44] C. G. Jung, "Letter to Sabina Spielrein—October 7, 1919," quoted in C. G. Jung, "The Letters of C. G. Jung to Sabina Spielrein," *Journal of Analytical Psychology*, vol. 46, no. 1 (January 2001), p. 195.

[45] Sigmund Freud, "Letter to Georg Groddeck—June 5, 1917," in Ernst L. Freud (ed.), *Letters of Sigmund Freud*, trans. Tania Stern and James Stern (New York, NY: Basic Books, 1975), p. 317.

[46] Sigmund Freud, "Beyond the Pleasure Principle" (1920), in *Beyond the Pleasure Principle*, trans. and ed. James Strachey (New York, NY: W. W. Norton & Company, 1989), p. 23.

[47] Sigmund Freud, "The Subtleties of Faulty Action" (1935), in *The Standard Edition of the Complete Psychological Works of Sigmund Freud, Vol. 22*, trans. and ed. James Strachey (London, UK: Hogarth Press and the Institute of Psycho-Analysis, 1953), p. 234.

[48] C. G. Jung, "Therapeutic Principles of Psychoanalysis" (1912), in *Critique of Psychoanalysis*, trans. R.F.C. Hull (Princeton, NJ: Princeton University Press, 1975), p. 117.

[49] Ernest Jones, "Emergence from Isolation," in *The Life and Work of Sigmund Freud, Vol. 2: Years of Maturity, 1901–1919* (New York, NY: Basic Books, 1955), p. 4.

[50] Albert Ellis and Robert A. Harper, "How Far Can You Go with Self-Analysis?" in *A Guide to Rational Living* (Hollywood, CA: Wilshire Book Company, 1971), pp. 1, 6.

[51] Sigmund Freud, "Letter to Josef Breuer—May 3, 1889," in Ernst L. Freud (ed.), *Letters of Sigmund Freud*, trans. Tania Stern and James Stern (New

York, NY: Basic Books, 1975), p. 226.

[52] Josef Breuer, quoted in Paul F. Cranefield, "Josef Breuer's Evaluation of His Contribution to Psycho-Analysis," *International Journal of Psycho-Analysis*, vol. 39 (1958), p. 320.

[53] Mikkel Borch-Jacobsen and Sonu Shamdasani, "The Politics of Self-Analysis," in *The Freud Files: An Inquiry into the History of Psychoanalysis* (Cambridge, UK: Cambridge University Press, 2012), p. 49.

[54] Sigmund Freud, quoted in Peter Gay, "Death against Life," in *Freud: A Life for Our Time* (New York, NY: Anchor Books, 1989), p. 469.

[55] Sigmund Freud, "Letter to Wilhelm Fliess—October 15, 1897," in Sigmund Freud, *The Origins of Psychoanalysis: Letters to Wilhelm Fliess, Drafts and Notes (1887–1902)*, trans. Eric Mosbacher and James Strachey, eds. Marie Bonaparte, Anna Freud, and Ernst Kris (New York, NY: Basic Books, 1954), p. 223. Alternatively translated as: "Being totally honest with oneself is a good exercise" (Sigmund Freud, "Letter to Wilhelm Fliess—October 15, 1897," in *The Complete Letters of Sigmund Freud to Wilhelm Fliess, 1887–1904*, trans. and ed. Jeffrey Moussaieff Masson [Cambridge, MA: Belknap Press of Harvard University Press, 1985], p. 272).

[56] Helen Walker Puner, "The Stuff of Dreams," in *Freud: His Life and His Mind* (New York, NY: Howell, Soskin, 1947), pp. 122–23.

[57] John Farrell, "Paranoid Psychology," in *Freud's Paranoid Quest: Psychoanalysis and Modern Suspicion* (New York, NY: New York University Press, 1996), pp. 43–44.

[58] José Brunner, "Big Daddy," in *Freud and the Politics of Psychoanalysis* (New Brunswick, NJ: Transaction Publishers, 2001), p. 179.

[59] E. Michael Jones, "Part II, Chapter 3: Bremen, 1909," in *Libido Dominandi: Sexual Liberation and Political Control* (South Bend, IN: St. Augustine's Press, 2000), p. 129.

[60] Egon Friedell, "Epilogue: The Collapse of Reality," in *A Cultural History of the Modern Age, Vol. 3: The Crisis of the European Soul*, trans. C. F. Atkinson (New York, NY: Alfred A. Knopf, 1932), pp. 479–80.

[61] Cicero, quoted in John T. McNeill, "Philosophers as Physicians of the Soul," in *A History of the Cure of Souls* (New York, NY: Harper & Row, 1977), p. 27. "The wise man will seek out the wisdom of all the ancients, and will be occupied in the prophets..." (Ecclesiastes 39:1).

[62] Hans J. Eysenck, "Freud the Man," in *Decline and Fall of the Freudian Empire* (New York, NY: Penguin Books, 1991), p. 19.

[63] C. G. Jung, "Letter to Sigmund Freud—January 30, 1910," in William McGuire (ed.), *The Freud/Jung Letters: The Correspondence Between Sigmund Freud and C. G. Jung*, trans. Ralph Manheim and R.F.C. Hull (Princeton, NJ: Princeton University Press, 1994), p. 289.

Chapter 22: Freud's Cocaine Episode

[1] Siegfried Bernfeld, "Freud's Studies on Cocaine, 1884–1887," *Journal of the American Psychoanalytic Association*, vol. 1, no. 4 (October 1953), p. 582.

[2] See William Golden Mortimer, *Peru: The History of Coca, "The Divine Plant" of the Incas* (New York, NY: J. H. Vail & Company, 1901).

[3] Sigmund Freud, quoted in Siegfried Bernfeld, "Freud's Studies on Cocaine, 1884–1887," *Journal of the American Psychoanalytic Association*, vol. 1, no. 4 (October 1953), p. 597. Alternatively translated as: "I [Freud] realize that such self-observations have the shortcoming, for the person engaged in conducting them, of claiming two sorts of objectivity for the same thing. I had to proceed in this manner for reasons beyond my control and because none of the subjects at my disposal had such a regular reaction to cocaine. The results, though, were also confirmed by my testing of others, mainly colleagues" (Sigmund Freud, "Contribution to the Knowledge of the Effect of Cocaine" (1885), in *Cocaine Papers*, ed. Robert Byck [New York, NY: Stonehill, 1974], pp. 98–99).

[4] Sigmund Freud, "On the General Effect of Cocaine" (1885), in *Cocaine Papers*, ed. Robert Byck (New York, NY: Stonehill, 1974), p. 117.

[5] Sigmund Freud, "On Coca" (1884), in *Cocaine Papers*, ed. Robert Byck (New York, NY: Stonehill, 1974), p. 325; Sigmund Freud, quoted in Siegfried Bernfeld, "Freud's Studies on Cocaine, 1884–1887," *Journal of the American Psychoanalytic Association*, vol. 1, no. 4 (October 1953), p. 583.

[6] Sigmund Freud, "The Method of Interpreting Dreams: An Analysis of a Specimen Dream" (1899), in *The Interpretation of Dreams*, trans. and ed. James Strachey (New York, NY: Science Editions, 1963), p. 111.

[7] Hans J. Eysenck, "Freud the Man," in *Decline and Fall of the Freudian Empire* (New York, NY: Penguin Books, 1991), p. 40.

[8] Sigmund Freud, "Determinism, Belief in Chance and Superstition—Some Points of View" (1901), in *The Psychopathology of Everyday Life*, trans. and ed. James Strachey (New York, NY: W. W. Norton & Company, 1989), p. 333.

[9] Ernest Jones, "The Cocaine Episode," in *The Life and Work of Sigmund Freud, Vol. 1: The Formative Years and the Great Discoveries, 1856–1900* (New York, NY: Basic Books, 1959), p. 84.

[10] Ibid. p. 97.

[11] Sigmund Freud, "Letter to Wilhelm Fliess—June 12, 1895," in *The Complete Letters of Sigmund Freud to Wilhelm Fliess, 1887–1904*, trans. and ed. Jeffrey Moussaieff Masson (Cambridge, MA: Belknap Press of Harvard University Press, 1985), p. 132.

[12] Ernest Jones, "Letter to Siegfried Bernfeld—April 28, 1952," quoted in Harry Trosman and Ernest S. Wolf, "The Bernfeld Collaboration in the Jones Biography of Freud," *International of Journal of Psycho-Analysis*, vol. 54 (1973), p. 231.

[13] Sigmund Freud, "Letter to Martha Bernays—June 2, 1884," quoted in Ernest Jones, *The Life and Work of Sigmund Freud, Vol. 1: The Formative Years and the Great Discoveries, 1856–1900* (New York, NY: Basic Books, 1959), p. 84.

[14] Sigmund Freud, "Letter to Martha Bernays—February 2, 1886," in Ernst L. Freud (ed.), *Letters of Sigmund Freud*, trans. Tania Stern and James Stern (New York, NY: Basic Books, 1975), p. 201.

[15] E. M. Thornton, "The Unconscious Mind and the Oedipus Complex," in *The Freudian Fallacy: An Alternative View of Freudian Theory* (Garden City, NY: Dial Press, 1984), p. 199.

[16] Louis Lewin, quoted in Sigmund Freud, *Cocaine Papers*, ed. Robert Byck (New York, NY: Stonehill, 1974), p. 251.

Chapter 23: Childhood Sexual Abuse and the Betrayal of Truth

[1] Sigmund Freud, "Letter to Wilhelm Fliess—April 26, 1896," in *The Complete Letters of Sigmund Freud to Wilhelm Fliess, 1887–1904*, trans. and ed. Jeffrey Moussaieff Masson (Cambridge, MA: Belknap Press of Harvard University Press, 1985), p. 184.

[2] See Elizabeth F. Loftus and Jacqueline E. Pickrell, "The Formation of False Memories," *Psychiatric Annals*, vol. 25, no. 12 (December 1995), pp. 720–25; Elizabeth F. Loftus and Katherine Ketcham, *The Myth of Repressed Memory: False Memories and Allegations of Sexual Abuse* (New York, NY: St. Martin's Press, 1996).

[3] See Vincent J. Felitti, Robert F. Anda, Dale Nordenberg, David F. Williamson, Alison M. Spitz, Valerie Edwards, Mary P. Koss, and James S. Marks, "Relationship of Childhood Abuse and Household Dysfunction to Many of the Leading Causes of Death in Adults: The Adverse Childhood Experiences (ACE) Study," *American Journal of Preventive Medicine*, vol. 14, no. 4 (May 1998), pp. 245–58.

[4] Jeffrey Moussaieff Masson, "'The Aetiology of Hysteria'," in *The Assault on Truth: Freud's Suppression of the Seduction Theory* (New York, NY: Farrar, Straus and Giroux, 1984), p. 9.

[5] Sigmund Freud, "Letter to Wilhelm Fliess—October 15, 1895," in *The Complete Letters of Sigmund Freud to Wilhelm Fliess, 1887–1904*, trans. and ed. Jeffrey Moussaieff Masson (Cambridge, MA: Belknap Press of Harvard University Press, 1985), p. 144.

[6] Sigmund Freud, "The Aetiology of Hysteria" (1896), in *The Standard Edition of the Complete Psychological Works of Sigmund Freud, Vol. 3*, trans. and ed. James Strachey (London, UK: Hogarth Press and the Institute of Psycho-Analysis, 1981), p. 203.

[7] Ibid., p. 199.

[8] Ibid.

[9] Sigmund Freud, "Screen Memories" (1899), in *The Standard Edition of the Complete Psychological Works of Sigmund Freud, Vol. 3*, trans. and ed. James Strachey (London, UK: Hogarth Press and the Institute of Psycho-Analysis, 1981), p. 318.

[10] See Jeffrey Moussaieff Masson, *The Assault on Truth: Freud's Suppression of the Seduction Theory* (New York, NY: Farrar, Straus and Giroux, 1984); Sigmund Freud, *The Complete Letters of Sigmund Freud to Wilhelm Fliess, 1887–1904*, trans. and ed. Jeffrey Moussaieff Masson (Cambridge, MA: Belknap Press of Harvard University Press, 1985); Jeffrey Moussaieff Masson, *A Dark Science: Women, Sexuality, and Psychiatry in the Nineteenth Century* (New York, NY: Farrar, Straus and Giroux, 1986).

[11] A. H. Almaas, "The Retrieval of Essence," in *Essence: The Diamond Approach to Inner Realization* (York Beach, ME: Samuel Weiser, 1986), p. 108.

[12] Frederick Crews, "The Unknown Freud," in *Follies of the Wise: Dissenting Essays* (Emeryville, CA: Shoemaker and Hoard, 2006), p. 34.

[13] Sigmund Freud, "The Paths to the Formation of Symptoms" (1916–1917 [1915–1917]), in *Introductory Lectures on Psychoanalysis*, trans. and ed. James Strachey (New York, NY: W. W. Norton & Company, 1977), p. 367.

[14] Ernest Jones, "Emergence from Isolation," in *The Life and Work of Sigmund Freud, Vol. 2: Years of Maturity, 1901–1919* (New York, NY: Basic Books, 1955), p. 5.

[15] Sigmund Freud, "Letter to Wilhelm Fliess—September 21, 1897," in *The Complete Letters of Sigmund Freud to Wilhelm Fliess, 1887–1904*, trans. and ed. Jeffrey Moussaieff Masson (Cambridge, MA: Belknap Press of Harvard University Press, 1985), p. 264.

[16] Ibid.

[17] Sigmund Freud, "Letter to Wilhelm Fliess—March 7, 1897," in *The Complete Letters of Sigmund Freud to Wilhelm Fliess, 1887–1904*, trans. and ed. Jeffrey Moussaieff Masson (Cambridge, MA: Belknap Press of Harvard University Press, 1985), p. 232.

[18] Anna Freud, quoted in Jeffrey Moussaieff Masson, "Freud's Renunciation of the Theory of Seduction," in *The Assault on Truth: Freud's Suppression of the Seduction Theory* (New York, NY: Farrar, Straus and Giroux, 1984), p. 113.

[19] Sigmund Freud, "Femininity" (1933 [1932]), in *New Introductory Lectures on Psycho-Analysis*, trans. and ed. James Strachey (New York, NY: W. W. Norton & Company, 1989), p. 149.

[20] Sigmund Freud, "(I) Secondary Revision" (1899), in *The Interpretation of Dreams*, trans. and ed. James Strachey (New York, NY: Science Editions, 1963), p. 491.

[21] C. G. Jung, "Letter to Sigmund Freud—April 27, 1912," in William McGuire (ed.), *The Freud/Jung Letters: The Correspondence Between Sigmund Freud and C. G. Jung*, trans. Ralph Manheim and R.F.C. Hull (Princeton, NJ: Princeton University Press, 1994), p. 502.

[22] C. G. Jung, "Letter to Sigmund Freud—May 17, 1912," in William McGuire (ed.), *The Freud/Jung Letters: The Correspondence Between Sigmund Freud and C. G. Jung*, trans. Ralph Manheim and R.F.C. Hull (Princeton, NJ: Princeton University Press, 1994), p. 506.

[23] Sigmund Freud, "Letter to C. G. Jung—May 23, 1912," in William McGuire (ed.), *The Freud/Jung Letters: The Correspondence Between Sigmund Freud and C. G. Jung*, trans. Ralph Manheim and R.F.C. Hull (Princeton, NJ: Princeton University Press, 1994), p. 507.

[24] Janet Malcolm, "Chapter Four," in *In the Freud Archives* (New York, NY: Vintage Books, 1985), p. 51.

[25] Elizabeth F. Loftus, "The Power of Suggestion," in *Memory* (New York, NY: Ardsley House, 1988), p. 163.

[26] Frederick S. Perls, "Talk Three," in *Gestalt Therapy Verbatim* (Lafayette, CA: Real People Press, 1969), pp. 42–43.

[27] Sigmund Freud, "Constructions in Analysis" (1937), in *The Standard Edition of the Complete Psychological Works of Sigmund Freud, Vol. 23*, trans. and ed. James Strachey (London, UK: Hogarth Press and the Institute of Psycho-Analysis, 1964), pp. 265–66.

[28] Richard Webster, "The Seduction Theory," in *Why Freud Was Wrong: Sin, Science, and Psychoanalysis* (New York, NY: Basic Books, 1995), p. 202.

[29] Sigmund Freud, "The Aetiology of Hysteria" (1896), in *The Standard Edition of the Complete Psychological Works of Sigmund Freud, Vol. 3*, trans. and ed. James Strachey (London, UK: Hogarth Press and the Institute of Psycho-Analysis, 1981), p. 204.

[30] Sigmund Freud, "The Psychotherapy of Hysteria," in Josef Breuer and Sigmund Freud, *Studies on Hysteria*, trans. and ed. James Strachey (New York, NY: Basic Books, 2000), p. 300.

[31] Sigmund Freud, "The Aetiology of Hysteria" (1896), in *The Standard Edition of the Complete Psychological Works of Sigmund Freud, Vol. 3*, trans. and ed. James Strachey (London, UK: Hogarth Press and the Institute of Psycho-Analysis, 1981), pp. 195–96.

[32] Sigmund Freud, "An Autobiographical Study" (1925 [1924]), in *An Autobiographical Study*, trans. and ed. James Strachey (New York, NY: W. W. Norton & Company, 1989), p. 34.

[33] Sigmund Freud, "From the History of an Infantile Neurosis" (1918 [1914]), in *The Standard Edition of the Complete Psychological Works of Sigmund Freud, Vol. 17*, trans. and ed. James Strachey (London, UK: Hogarth Press and the Institute of Psycho-Analysis, 1955), pp. 50–51.

[34] Sigmund Freud, "An Autobiographical Study" (1925 [1924]), in *An Autobiographical Study*, trans. and ed. James Strachey (New York, NY: W. W. Norton & Company, 1989), p. 34.

[35] Sigmund Freud, "The Archaic Features and Infantilism of Dreams," in *Introductory Lectures on Psychoanalysis*, trans. and ed. James Strachey (New York, NY: W. W. Norton & Company, 1977), p. 201.

[36] Richard Webster, "The Seduction Theory," in *Why Freud Was Wrong: Sin, Science, and Psychoanalysis* (New York, NY: Basic Books, 1995), p. 210.

[37] Frank J. Sulloway, "Sexuality and the Etiology of Neurosis: The Estrangement of Breuer and Freud," in *Freud, Biologist of the Mind: Beyond the Psychoanalytic Legend* (New York, NY: Basic Books, 1979), p. 95.

Chapter 24: Freud, Eros, and the Sexual Revolution

[1] Osho [Bhagwan Shree Rajneesh], "The Understanding in Practice," in *Sex Matters: From Sex to Superconsciousness* (New York, NY: St. Martin's Press, 2002), p. 277.

[2] Sigmund Freud, "Letter to James J. Putnam—July 8, 1915," in Ernst L. Freud (ed.), *Letters of Sigmund Freud*, trans. Tania and James Stern (New York, NY: Basic Books, 1975), p. 308.

[3] Rollo May, quoted in Harry Stack Sullivan, *Conceptions of Modern Psychiatry* (New York, NY: W. W. Norton & Company, 1953), quote is taken from the back cover of book.

[4] Sigmund Freud, "The Sexual Enlightenment of Children (An Open Letter to Dr. M. Fürst)" (1907), in *The Standard Edition of the Complete Psychological Works of Sigmund Freud, Vol. 9*, trans. and ed. James Strachey (London, UK: Hogarth Press and the Institute of Psycho-Analysis, 1981), p. 138.

[5] C. G. Jung, "New Paths in Psychology" (1912), in *Two Essays on Analytical Psychology*, trans. R.F.C. Hull (New York, NY: Meridian, 1956), p. 269.

[6] Sigmund Freud, quoted in Ilse Ollendorff Reich, "Vienna: 1918–1930," in *Wilhelm Reich: A Personal Biography* (New York, NY: Avon Books, 1970), p. 36.

[7] "I [Wilhelm Reich] coined the term 'Sexual Revolution' in the 1930's" (Wilhelm Reich, "Interview with Kurt R. Eissler—October 18, 1952," in *Reich Speaks of Freud: Wilhelm Reich Discusses his Work and his Relationship with Sigmund Freud*, trans. Therese Pol, eds. Mary Higgins and Chester M. Raphael [New York, NY: Farrar, Straus and Giroux, 1972], p. 44). See also Wilhelm Reich, *The Sexual Revolution: Toward a Self-Regulating Character Structure*, trans. Therese Pol (New York, NY: Farrar, Straus and Giroux, 1986); Michael Minnicino, "The Frankfurt School and 'Political Correctness'," *Fidelio*, vol. 1, no. 1 (Winter 1992), pp. 4–27.

[8] Ilse Ollendorff Reich, "Author's Preface," to *Wilhelm Reich: A Personal Biography* (New York, NY: Avon Books, 1970), p. 19.

[9] Frederick S. Perls, "Classical Psycho-Analysis," in *Ego, Hunger and Aggression* (New York, NY: Vintage Books, 1969), p. 82.

[10] See Mary Eberstadt, "The Zealous Faith of Secularism," *First Things*, vol. 279 (January 2018), pp. 35–40.

[11] See Judith A. Reisman and Edward W. Eichel, *Kinsey, Sex and Fraud: The Indoctrination of a People*, eds. J. Gordon Muir and John H. Court (Lafayette, LA: Huntington House, 1990); Judith A. Reisman, *Kinsey: Crimes and*

Consequences (Crestwood, KY: Institute for Media Education, 2003); Judith A. Reisman, *Sexual Sabotage: How One Mad Scientist Unleashed a Plague of Corruption and Contagion on America* (Washington, DC: WND Books, 2010).

[12] In 1955, Kinsey traveled to Cefalù in Sicily (Italy), at the invitation of the filmmaker Kenneth Anger (b. 1927), who is a disciple of Crowley. He visited the ruins of Crowley's residence known as "The Abbey of Thelema," which was a central location for Crowley's sex magic. Kinsey admired Crowley and had great interest in obtaining his day-to-day sex diaries and is reported to have been successful in obtaining them likely for his sex research. See Bill Landis, *Anger: An Unauthorized Biography of Kenneth Anger* (New York, NY: HarperCollins, 1995); Jonathan Gathorne-Hardy, *Sex the Measure of All Things: A Life of Alfred C. Kinsey* (Bloomington, IN: Indiana University Press, 2000).

[13] Aleister Crowley, "At the Abbey of Thelema," in *The Confessions of Aleister Crowley: An Autobiography*, eds. John Symonds and Kenneth Grant (New York, NY: Arkana Books, 1989), p. 851.

[14] Alfred C. Kinsey, quoted in Judith Reisman, "The Homosexual in America," *Time*, vol. 87, no. 3 (January 21, 1966), p. 52.

[15] Paul Robinson, "Alfred Kinsey," in The Modernization of Sex: Havelock Ellis, Alfred Kinsey, William Masters, and Virginia Johnson (New York, NY: Harper & Row, 1976), p. 59.

[16] Alfred C. Kinsey, quoted in Wardell B. Pomeroy, "The Project Begins," in *Dr. Kinsey and the Institute for Sex Research* (New Haven, CT: Yale University Press, 1982), p. 77.

[17] James H. Jones, "Be Pure in Thought and Clean in Habit," in *Alfred C. Kinsey: A Life* (New York, NY: W. W. Norton & Norton, 2004), p. 82.

[18] Thomas Weyr, "The State of the Art," in *Reaching for Paradise: The Playboy Vision of America* (New York, NY: Times Books, 1978), p. 11.

[19] Bill Zehme, "Playboy Interview: Hugh M. Hefner," *Playboy*, vol. 47, no. 1 (January 2000), p. 244.

[20] Havelock Ellis, quoted in John Stewart Collis, *An Artist of Life: A Study of the Life and Work of Havelock Ellis* (London, UK: Cassell & Company, 1959), p. 8.

[21] John H. Gagnon, "Sex Research and Social Change," *Archives of Sexual Behavior*, vol. 4, no. 2 (March 1975), p. 111.

[22] Wardell Pomeroy and Leah C. Schaefer, "Impact of Published Surveys and Research on Public Concepts of Human Sexuality," in *Medical Sexology: The Third International Congress*, eds. Romano Forleo and Willy Pasini (Littleton, MA: PSG Publishing, 1980), p. 76.

[23] E. Michael Jones, "Introduction: Internet in Gaza: Sexual Liberation as Political Control," in *Libido Dominandi: Sexual Liberation and Political Control* (South Bend, IN: St. Augustine's Press, 2000), p. 2.

[24] E. Michael Jones, "Part I, Chapter 4: Paris, 1792," in *Libido Dominandi: Sexual Liberation and Political Control* (South Bend, IN: St. Augustine's Press, 2000), pp. 60–61.

[25] David F. Foxon, "Nicolas Chorier: Satyra Sotadica," in *Libertine Literature in England, 1660–1745* (New Hyde Park, NY: University Books, 1966), p. 48.

[26] Richard Webster, "Mysterious Mechanisms," in *Why Freud Was Wrong: Sin, Science, and Psychoanalysis* (New York, NY: Basic Books, 1995), p. 181.

[27] Joseph Jastrow, "Course of Libido," in *Freud: His Dream and Sex Theories* (Cleveland, OH: World Publishing Company, 1948), p. 48.

[28] Sigmund Freud, "Chapter Four," in *Civilization and Its Discontents*, trans. and ed. James Strachey (New York, NY: W. W. Norton & Company, 1989), p. 56.

[29] Sigmund Freud, "Letter to Wilhelm Fliess—[Undated] 1893," in Marie Bonaparte, Anna Freud, and Ernst Kris (eds.), *The Origins of Psychoanalysis: Letters to Wilhelm Fliess, Drafts and Notes: 1887–1902*, trans. Eric Mosbacher and James Strachey (New York, NY: Basic Books, 1954), p. 75. See also Sigmund Freud, "Letter to Wilhelm Fliess—[Undated] 1893," in *The Complete Letters of Sigmund Freud to Wilhelm Fliess, 1887–1904*, trans. and ed. Jeffrey Moussaieff Masson (Cambridge, MA: Belknap Press of Harvard University Press, 1985), pp. 45–46.

[30] Sigmund Freud, "My Views on the Part Played by Sexuality in the Aetiology of the Neuroses" (1905), in *Sexuality and the Psychology of Love*, ed. Philip Rieff (New York, NY: Collier Books, 1978), p. 14.

[31] Sigmund Freud, "'Civilized' Sexual Morality and Modern Nervousness" (1908), in *Sexuality and the Psychology of Love*, ed. Philip Rieff (New York, NY: Collier Books, 1978), p. 35.

[32] Sigmund Freud, "Some Character-Types Met with in Psychoanalytic Work" (1916), in *Character and Culture*, ed. Philip Rieff (New York, NY: Collier Books, 1963), p. 162.

[33] Sigmund Freud, "Fifth Lecture" (1910), in *Five Lectures on Psycho-Analysis*, trans. and ed. James Strachey (New York, NY: W. W. Norton & Company, 1989), p. 54.

[34] Sigmund Freud, "Sexuality in the Aetiology of the Neuroses" (1898), in *The Standard Edition of the Complete Psychological Works of Sigmund Freud, Vol. 3*, trans. and ed. James Strachey (London, UK: Hogarth Press and the Institute of Psycho-Analysis, 1981), p. 268.

[35] Ibid.

[36] Sigmund Freud, quoted in Joseph Wortis, "Fragments of a Freudian Analysis," *American Journal of Orthopsychiatry*, vol. 10, no. 4 (October 1940), p. 849.

[37] C. G. Jung, "Letter to Sabina Spielrein—November 24, 1911," quoted in C. G. Jung, "The Letters of C. G. Jung to Sabina Spielrein," *Journal of Analytical Psychology*, vol. 46, no. 1 (January 2001), p. 182.

[38] Sigmund Freud, "An Autobiographical Study" (1925 [1924]), in *An Auto-biographical Study*, trans. and ed. James Strachey (New York, NY: W. W. Norton & Company, 1989), p. 41.

[39] Sigmund Freud, "My Views on the Part Played by Sexuality in the Aetiology of the Neuroses" (1905), in *Sexuality and the Psychology of Love*, ed. Philip Rieff (New York, NY: Collier Books, 1978), p. 17.

[40] Sigmund Freud, "The Transformation of Puberty" (1905), in *Three Essays on the Theory of Sexuality*, trans. and ed. James Strachey (New York, NY: Basic Books, 2000), p. 92.

[41] Sigmund Freud, "Female Sexuality" (1931), in *Sexuality and the Psychology of Love*, ed. Philip Rieff (New York, NY: Collier Books, 1978), p. 194. "[T]he Oedipus complex may justly be regarded as the nucleus of the neuroses" (Sigmund Freud, "The Development of the Libido and the Sexual Organizations," in *Introductory Lectures on Psychoanalysis*, trans. and ed. James Strachey [New York, NY: W. W. Norton & Company, 1977], p. 337).

[42] Ernest Jones, "The Fliess Period," in *The Life and Work of Sigmund Freud, Vol. 1: The Formative Years and the Great Discoveries, 1856–1900* (New York, NY: Basic Books, 1959), p. 307.

[43] Sigmund Freud, "On the Universal Tendency to Debasement in the Sphere of Love (Contributions to the Psychology of Love II)" (1912), in *The Standard Edition of the Complete Psychological Works of Sigmund Freud, Vol. 11*, trans. and ed. James Strachey (London, UK: Hogarth Press and the Institute of Psycho-Analysis, 1956), p. 186.

[44] Sigmund Freud, "The Economic Problem in Masochism" (1924), in *General Psychological Theory: Papers on Metapsychology*, ed. Philip Rieff (New York, NY: Touchstone, 2008), p. 201.

[45] Ernest Jones, "Anthropology," in *The Life and Work of Sigmund Freud, Vol. 3: The Last Phase, 1919–1939* (New York, NY: Basic Books, 1957), p. 329.

[46] Sigmund Freud, "Letter to Wilhelm Fliess—May 31, 1897," in Marie Bonaparte, Anna Freud, and Ernst Kris (eds.), *The Origins of Psychoanalysis: Letters to Wilhelm Fliess, Drafts and Notes: 1887–1902*, trans. Eric Mosbacher and James Strachey (New York, NY: Basic Books, 1954), p. 206. Alternatively translated as: "I shall very soon uncover the source of morality" (Sigmund Freud, "Letter to Wilhelm Fliess—May 31, 1897," in *The Complete Letters of Sigmund Freud to Wilhelm Fliess, 1887–1904*, trans. and ed. Jeffrey Moussaieff Masson [Cambridge, MA: Belknap Press of Harvard University Press, 1985], p. 249).

[47] Sigmund Freud, "Letter to Wilhelm Fliess—May 31, 1897," in Marie Bonaparte, Anna Freud, and Ernst Kris (eds.), *The Origins of Psychoanalysis: Letters to Wilhelm Fliess, Drafts and Notes: 1887-1902*, trans. Eric Mosbacher and James Strachey (New York, NY: Basic Books, 1954), p. 206. Alternatively translated as: "The dream of course shows the fulfillment of my wish to catch a *Pater* [father] as the originator of neurosis and thus [the dream] puts an end to my ever-recurring doubts." (Sigmund Freud, "Letter

to Wilhelm Fliess—May 31, 1897," in *The Complete Letters of Sigmund Freud to Wilhelm Fliess, 1887–1904*, trans. and ed. Jeffrey Moussaieff Masson [Cambridge, MA: Belknap Press of Harvard University Press, 1985], p. 249).

[48] Jean Borella, "Freud and the Inversion of the Sacred," in *The Crisis of Religious Symbolism and Symbolism & Reality*, trans. G. John Champoux (Kettering, OH: Angelico Press/Sophia Perennis, 2016), p. 203.

[49] C. G. Jung, "Sigmund Freud," in *Memories, Dreams, Reflections*, trans. Richard Winston and Clara Winston, ed. Aniela Jaffé (New York, NY: Vintage Books, 1965), p. 149.

[50] Sigmund Freud, "An Example of Psycho-Analytic Work" (1940 [1938]), in *An Outline of Psycho-Analysis*, trans. and ed. James Strachey (New York, NY: W. W. Norton & Company, 1989), p. 71.

[51] Wilhelm Reich, "Interview with Kurt R. Eissler—October 18, 1952," in *Reich Speaks of Freud: Wilhelm Reich Discusses his Work and his Relationship with Sigmund Freud*, trans. Therese Pol, eds. Mary Higgins and Chester M. Raphael (New York, NY: Farrar, Straus and Giroux, 1972), p. 15.

[52] Sigmund Freud, "The Transformations of Puberty" (1905), in *The Basic Writings of Sigmund Freud*, trans. and ed. A. A. Brill (New York, NY: Modern Library, 1938), p. 611.

[53] Sigmund Freud, "The Theory of the Instincts" (1940 [1938]), in *An Outline of Psycho-Analysis*, trans. and ed. James Strachey (New York, NY: W. W. Norton & Company, 1989), p. 21.

[54] Douglas N. Morgan, "Freudian Love and Platonic Love," in *Love: Plato, the Bible and Freud* (Englewood Cliffs, NJ: Prentice-Hall, 1964), p. 165.

[55] Wilhelm Reich, "Interview with Kurt R. Eissler—October 18, 1952," in *Reich Speaks of Freud: Wilhelm Reich Discusses his Work and his Relationship with Sigmund Freud*, trans. Therese Pol, eds. Mary Higgins, and Chester M. Raphael (New York, NY: Farrar, Straus and Giroux, 1972), pp. 15–16.

[56] Ibid., pp. 22–23.

[57] Sigmund Freud, "The Transformations of Puberty" (1905), in *The Basic Writings of Sigmund Freud*, trans. and ed. A. A. Brill (New York, NY: Modern Library, 1938), p. 612.

[58] C. G. Jung, "Sigmund Freud," in *Memories, Dreams, Reflections*, trans. Richard Winston and Clara Winston, ed. Aniela Jaffé (New York, NY: Vintage Books, 1965), p. 150.

[59] Ibid. p. 151.

[60] C. G. Jung, "Psychoanalysis and Neurosis" (1916), in *Critique of Psychoanalysis*, trans. R.F.C. Hull (Princeton, NJ: Princeton University Press, 1975), p. 165.

[61] Ibid. "Jung had never really grasped Freud's concept of the libido and that he continued wittingly or unwittingly to equate it with the energy of adult

sexual instincts...Only in Jung's later writings does it become uncompromisingly clear that in his view libido is nothing more than a synonym for psychic energy" (Edward Glover, "Mental Energy," in *Freud or Jung?* [New York, NY: Meridian, 1956], pp. 57, 58).

[62] C. G. Jung, "General Remarks on the Therapeutic Approach to the Unconscious," in *Two Essays on Analytical Psychology*, trans. R.F.C. Hull (New York, NY: Meridian, 1956), p. 128.

[63] C. G. Jung, "Aspects of the Libido," in *Psychology of the Unconscious*, trans. Beatrice M. Hinkle (New York, NY: Moffat, Yard and Company, 1917), pp. 127–28.

[64] Karen Horney, "The Flight from Womanhood: The Masculinity Complex in Women as Viewed by Men and by Women," in *Feminine Psychology*, ed. Harold Kelman (New York, NY: W. W. Norton & Company, 1973), p. 54. See also Elisabeth Young-Bruehl (ed.), *Freud on Women: A Reader* (New York, NY: W. W. Norton & Company, 1990).

[65] Sigmund Freud, "The Dissolution of the Oedipus Complex" (1924), in *The Standard Edition of the Complete Psychological Works of Sigmund Freud, Vol. 19*, trans. and ed. James Strachey (London, UK: Vintage Books, 2001), p. 178.

[66] Sigmund Freud, "Chapter Four," in *The Question of Lay Analysis*, trans. Nancy Procter-Gregg (New York, NY: W. W. Norton & Company, 1950), pp. 61-62.

[67] C. G. Jung, "The Work," in *Memories, Dreams, Reflections*, trans. Richard Winston and Clara Winston, ed. Aniela Jaffé (New York, NY: Vintage Books, 1965), p. 201.

[68] Sigmund Freud, "Femininity" (1933 [1932]), in *New Introductory Lectures on Psycho-Analysis*, trans. and ed. James Strachey (New York, NY: W. W. Norton & Company, 1989), p. 156.

[69] Karen Horney, "On the Genesis of the Castration Complex in Women," in *Feminine Psychology*, ed. Harold Kelman (New York, NY: W. W. Norton & Company, 1973), p. 38.

[70] Sigmund Freud, "Chapter Four," in *The Question of Lay Analysis*, trans. Nancy Procter-Gregg (New York, NY: W. W. Norton & Company, 1950), p. 61.

[71] Sigmund Freud, quoted in Ernest Jones, "Character and Personality," in *The Life and Work of Sigmund Freud, Vol. 2: Years of Maturity, 1901–1919* (New York, NY: Basic Books, 1955), p. 421.

[72] Sigmund Freud, "Letter to Stefan Zweig—July 20, 1938," in Ernst L. Freud (ed.), *Letters of Sigmund Freud*, trans. Tania Stern and James Stern (New York, NY: Basic Books, 1975), p. 449.

[73] Sigmund Freud, "Sexuality in the Aetiology of the Neuroses" (1898), in *The Standard Edition of the Complete Psychological Works of Sigmund Freud, Vol. 3*, trans. and ed. James Strachey (London, UK: Hogarth Press and the Institute of Psycho-Analysis, 1981), p. 278.

[74] Josef Breuer, "Innate Disposition—Development of Hysteria," in Josef Breuer and Sigmund Freud, *Studies on Hysteria*, trans. and ed. James Strachey (New York, NY: Basic Books, 2000), p. 246.

[75] Ibid., p. 244.

[76] Sigmund Freud, "'Civilized' Sexual Morality and Modern Nervous Illness" (1908), in *The Standard Edition of the Complete Psychological Works of Sigmund Freud, Vol. 9*, trans. and ed. James Strachey (London, UK: Hogarth Press and the Institute of Psycho-Analysis, 1981), p. 195.

[77] See also Peter J. Swales, "Freud, Minna Bernays, and the Conquest of Rome: New Light on the Origins of Psychoanalysis," *New American Review*, vol. 1 (Spring/Summer 1982), pp. 1–23; Franz Maciejewski, "Freud, His Wife, and His 'Wife'," *American Imago*, vol. 63, no. 4 (Winter 2006), pp. 497–506.

[78] Ernest Jones, "Freud's Theory of the Mind," in *The Life and Work of Sigmund Freud, Vol. 1: The Formative Years and the Great Discoveries, 1856–1900* (New York, NY: Basic Books, 1959), p. 153.

[79] Peter Gay, "Sigmund and Minna? The Biographer as Voyeur," *New York Times Book Review*, January 29, 1989, p. 1.

[80] Ernest Jones, "Mode of Life and Work," in *The Life and Work of Sigmund Freud, Vol. 2: Years of Maturity, 1901–1919* (New York, NY: Basic Books, 1955), pp. 386–87.

[81] C. G. Jung, quoted in John M. Billinsky, "Jung and Freud (The End of a Romance)," *Andover Newton Quarterly*, vol. 10, no. 2 (1969), p. 42.

[82] Frederick Crews, "Sexual Healing," in *Freud: The Making of an Illusion* (New York, NY: Metropolitan Books, 2017), p. 564.

[83] C. G. Jung, "Letter to Sigmund Freud—January 30, 1910," in William McGuire (ed.), *The Freud/Jung Letters: The Correspondence Between Sigmund Freud and C. G. Jung*, trans. Ralph Manheim and R.F.C. Hull (Princeton, NJ: Princeton University Press, 1994), p. 289.

[84] Karen Horney, "The Problem of the Monogamous Ideal," in *Feminine Psychology*, ed. Harold Kelman (New York, NY: W. W. Norton & Company, 1973), pp. 95-96.

[85] Sigmund Freud, *Three Essays on the Theory of Sexuality*, trans. and ed. James Strachey (New York, NY: Basic Books, 2000), pp. 97, 26.

[86] Sigmund Freud, "The Clinical Picture" (1905 [1901]), in *Dora: An Analysis of a Case of Hysteria*, ed. Philip Rieff (New York, NY: Touchstone, 1997), p. 44.

[87] Sigmund Freud, "Infantile Sexuality" (1905), in *Three Essays on the Theory of Sexuality*, trans. and ed. James Strachey (New York, NY: Basic Books, 2000), p. 57.

[88] E. Michael Jones, "Part III, Chapter 15: Notre Dame, Indiana, 1970," in *Libido Dominandi: Sexual Liberation and Political Control* (South Bend, IN: St. Augustine's Press, 2000), p. 520.

[89] Ibid..

[90] Nathan Abrams, "Triple Ethnics," *Jewish Quarterly*, vol. 51, no. 4 (2004), p. 27.

[91] Al Goldstein, quoted in Nathan Abrams, "Triple Ethnics," *Jewish Quarterly*, vol. 51, no. 4 (2004), p. 27.

[92] Norman Doidge, "Acquiring Tastes and Loves," in *The Brain That Changes Itself: Stories of Personal Triumph from the Frontiers of Brain Science* (New York, NY: Penguin Books, 2007), p. 108.

[93] C. G. Jung, "The Archetypes of the Collective Unconscious," in *Two Essays on Analytical Psychology*, trans. R.F.C. Hull (New York, NY: Meridian, 1956), p. 116.

[94] Sigmund Freud, "Letter to Anonymous Individual—April 9, 1935," in Ernst L. Freud (ed.), *Letters of Sigmund Freud*, trans. Tania and James Stern (New York, NY: Basic Books, 1975), p. 277.

[95] Sigmund Freud, "The Sexual Aberrations" (1905), in *Three Essays on the Theory of Sexuality*, trans. and ed. James Strachey (New York, NY: Basic Books, 2000), p. 2.

[96] Sigmund Freud, "The Sexual Life of Man" (1917), in *A General Introduction to Psychoanalysis* (New York, NY: Horace Liveright, 1920), p. 266.

[97] Sigmund Freud, "Chapter Three," in *Leonardo Da Vinci: A Study in Psychosexuality*, trans. A. A. Brill (New York, NY: Vintage Books, 1947), p. 61.

[98] Sigmund Freud, "The Libido Theory and Narcissism" (1916–1917 [1915–1917]), in *Introductory Lectures on Psychoanalysis*, trans. and ed. James Strachey (New York, NY: W. W. Norton & Company, 1977), p. 426.

[99] Sigmund Freud, "Chapter Three," in *Leonardo da Vinci and a Memory of His Childhood*, trans. Alan Tyson, ed. James Strachey (New York, NY: W. W. Norton & Company, 1989), p. 55.

[100] Burness E. Moore and Bernard D. Fine, "Homosexuality," in *A Glossary of Psychoanalytic Terms and Concepts* (New York, NY: American Psychoanalytic Association, 1968), p. 48.

[101] Sigmund Freud, "The Psychogenesis of a Case of Female Homosexual," *International Journal of Psycho-Analysis*, vol. 1, no. 2 (1920), p. 148.

[102] See Charles W. Socarides, "Sexual Politics and Scientific Logic: The Issue of Homosexuality," *Journal of Psychohistory*, vol. 19, no. 3 (Winter 1992), pp. 307–29.

[103] Julius Evola, "Introduction," to *The Metaphysics of Sex* (New York, NY: Inner Traditions, 1983), p. 5.

[104] Julius Evola, "Man and Woman," in *Revolt Against the Modern World*, trans. Guido Stucco (Rochester, VT: Inner Traditions International, 1995), p. 166.

[105] Albert Ellis, "The Sex Tease of Courtship," in *The American Sexual Tragedy* (New York, NY: Lyle Stuart, 1962), p. 79.

[106] Ibid.

[107] Roshi Philip Kapleau, "Do I Have to Abandon My Family to Get Fully into Zen?" in *Zen: Dawn in the West* (Garden City, NY: Anchor Books, 1980), p. 225.

[108] Frithjof Schuon, "The Forbidden Fruit," in *Islam and the Perennial Philosophy*, trans. J. Peter Hobson (London, UK: World of Islam Festival Publishing Company, 1976), p. 191.

[109] Frithjof Schuon, "The Problem of Sexuality," in *Esoterism as Principle and as Way*, trans. William Stoddart (Bedfont, Middlesex, UK: Perennial Books, 1981), p. 129.

[110] Julius Evola, "Gods and Goddesses, Man and Women," in *The Metaphysics of Sex* (New York, NY: Inner Traditions, 1983), p. 115.

[111] Julius Evola, "Conclusion," to *The Metaphysics of Sex* (New York, NY: Inner Traditions, 1983), p. 276.

[112] Carl G. Jung, "The Importance of Dreams," in *Man and His Symbols*, ed. Carl G. Jung (New York, NY: Laurel, 1968), pp. 13–14.

[113] Knight Dunlap, "The Pragmatic Advantage of Freudo-Analysis: (A Criticism)," *Psychoanalytic Review*, vol. 1, no. 2 (1913–1914), p. 151.

[114] Sigmund Freud, "(E) Representation by Symbols in Dreams—Some Further Typical Dreams" (1899), in *The Interpretation of Dreams*, trans. and ed. James Strachey (New York, NY: Science Editions, 1963), p. 351.

[115] René Guénon, "Tradition and the 'Unconscious,'" in *Symbols of Sacred Science*, trans. Henry D. Fohr, ed. Samuel D. Fohr (Hillsdale, NY: Sophia Perennis, 2004), p. 38.

[116] René Guénon, "The Holy Grail," in *Symbols of Sacred Science*, trans. Henry D. Fohr, ed. Samuel D. Fohr (Hillsdale, NY: Sophia Perennis, 2004), p. 28. "First, symbolism seems to us to be particularly well adapted to the exigencies of human nature, which is not a purely intellectual nature but requires a sensory basis from which to raise itself to higher spheres...[S]ymbolism in the strict sense is essentially synthetic and thereby 'intuitive' as it were, which renders it more apt than language to serve as a support for intellectual intuition...[which] is higher than reason...Thus the highest truths, not communicable or transmissible in any other way, can be communicated up to a certain point when they are, so to speak, incorporated in symbols which will no doubt conceal them for many, but which will manifest them in all their brilliance to those with eyes to see" (René Guénon, "Word and Symbol," in *Symbols of Sacred Science*, trans. Henry D. Fohr, ed. Samuel D. Fohr [Hillsdale, NY: Sophia Perennis, 2004], pp. 7–8).

[117] Frithjof Schuon, quoted in Deborah Casey, "The Basis of Religion and Metaphysics: An Interview with Frithjof Schuon," *The Quest*, vol. 9, no. 2 (Summer 1996), p. 77. "Given the spiritual degeneration of mankind, the highest possible degree of beauty, that of the human body, plays no role in ordinary piety; but this theophany may be a support in esoteric spirituality, as is shown in Hindu and Buddhist sacred art. Nudity means inwardness, essentiality, primordiality and thus universality; clothing signifies social function, and in this framework the sacerdotal function as well. Nudity

means glory, radiation of spiritual substance or energy; the body is the form of the essence and thus the essence of the form" (Frithjof Schuon, "The Art of Dress and Ambience," in *Art from the Sacred to the Profane: East and West*, ed. Catherine Schuon [Bloomington, IN: World Wisdom, 2007], p. 133); "A remark is necessary here regarding the symbolism of nudity. It is common knowledge that in Hinduism, as in most other ancient religions—and notably also with American Indians—nudity has a sacred connotation. It manifests both the primordial and the universal, and it is not without reason that one speaks of the 'paradisal innocence' which was before the Fall. Again, there is in hieratic nudity a moral meaning as well as an intellectual one: under the first aspect, nudity—of the Hindu goddesses, in particular—expresses the generosity that welcomes and provides, likewise exemplified in the mystical *lactatio* of the Blessed Virgin; and under the second aspect, nudity indicates the esoteric 'unveilings,' and it is in this sense that one speaks of the 'naked truth.' And lastly, let us remember that, according to St. Paul: 'Unto the pure, all things are pure'" (Barbara Perry, quoted in Michael Oren Fitzgerald, "An Artistic Dimension," in *Frithjof Schuon: Messenger of the Perennial Philosophy* [Bloomington, IN: World Wisdom, 2010], p. 110).

[118] Martin Lings, *Mecca: From Before Genesis Until Now* (Cambridge, UK: Archetype, 2004), pp. 33–34; "In pre-Islamic times, the circumambulation of the Kaaba was probably performed naked, as sacred nudity is well known in ancient religious traditions" (Annemarie Schimmel, "Sacred Action," in *Deciphering the Signs of God: A Phenomenological Approach to Islam* [Albany, NY: State University of New York Press, 1994], p. 93).

[119] Titus Burckhardt, "Traditional Cosmology and Modern Science: Modern Psychology," in *Mirror of the Intellect: Essays on Traditional Science and Sacred Art*, trans. and ed. William Stoddart (Albany, NY: State University of New York Press, 1987), p. 63.

[120] Gershom Scholem, "The Zohar II. The Theosophic Doctrine of the Zohar," in *Major Trends in Jewish Mysticism* (New York, NY: Schocken Books, 1974), p. 228.

[121] Ibid.

[122] *Zohar: The Book of Splendor*, ed. Gershom Scholem (New York, NY: Schocken Books, 1977), pp. 89–90.

[123] Gershom Scholem, "The Zohar II. The Theosophic Doctrine of the Zohar," in *Major Trends in Jewish Mysticism* (New York, NY: Schocken Books, 1974), p. 227.

[124] Talmud, quoted in Gershom Scholem, "Tsaddik: The Righteous One," in *On the Mystical Shape of the Godhead: Basic Concepts in the Kabbalah* (New York, NY: Schocken Books, 1991), p. 111.

[125] August Forel, quote in Henri F. Ellenberger, *The Discovery of the Unconscious: The History and Evolution of Dynamic Psychiatry* (New York, NY: Basic Books, 1970), p. 814.

[126] *Caṇḍamahāroṣaṇa-tantra*, quoted in Miranda Shaw, *Passionate Enlightenment: Women in Tantric Buddhism* (Princeton, NJ: Princeton University

Press, 1994), p. 153.

[127] Saraha, quoted in Miranda Shaw, *Passionate Enlightenment: Women in Tantric Buddhism* (Princeton, NJ: Princeton University Press, 1994), p. 22.

[128] Alain Daniélou, "Virile Behavior in Women [*Purushāyita*]," in *The Complete Kāma Sūtra: The First Unabridged Modern Translation of the Classic Indian Text by Vātsyāyana*, trans. Alain Daniélou (Rochester, VT: Park Street Press, 1994), p. 179.

[129] Philip Sherrard, "Towards a Theology of Sexual Love," in *Christianity and Eros: Essays on the Theme of Sexual Love* (Limni, Evia, Greece: Denise Harvey, 1995), p. 61.

[130] Alain Daniélou, "Petting and Caresses [*Ālingana*]," in *The Complete Kāma Sūtra: The First Unabridged Modern Translation of the Classic Indian Text by Vātsyāyana*, trans. Alain Daniélou (Rochester, VT: Park Street Press, 1994), p. 122.

[131] Alain Daniélou, "The Three Aims of Life," in *The Complete Kāma Sūtra: The First Unabridged Modern Translation of the Classic Indian Text by Vātsyāyana*, trans. Alain Daniélou (Rochester, VT: Park Street Press, 1994), p. 36.

[132] *Caṇḍamahāroṣaṇa-tantra*, quoted in Miranda Shaw, *Passionate Enlightenment: Women in Tantric Buddhism* (Princeton, NJ: Princeton University Press, 1994), p. 41.

[133] Śrī Rāmakrishna, "The Master and Vijay Goswami," in *The Gospel of Ramakrishna: Originally recorded in Bengali by M., a disciple of the Master*, trans. Swami Nikhilananda (New York, NY: Ramakrishna-Vivekananda Center, 1977), p. 168. "I clearly perceived that the Divine Mother Herself had become everything" (Śrī Rāmakrishna, "With the Devotees at Dakshineswar (II)," in *The Gospel of Ramakrishna: Originally recorded in Bengali by M., a disciple of the Master*, trans. Swami Nikhilananda [New York, NY: Ramakrishna-Vivekananda Center, 1977], p. 346). "I worshipped all women as representatives of the Divine Mother. I realized the Mother of the universe in every woman's form" (Śrī Rāmakrishna, "Divinity Everywhere," in *The Original Gospel of Rāmakrishna: Based on M.'s English Text, Abridged*, eds. Swāmī Abhedānanda and Joseph A. Fitzgerald (Bloomington, IN: World Wisdom, 2011), p. 92).

[134] Ibn al-'Arabī, "From the Wisdom of the Singularity (*al-hikmat al-fardiyah*) in the Word of Muhammed," in *The Wisdom of the Prophets (Fusus al-Hikam)*, trans. Titus Burckhardt and Angela Culme-Seymour (Gloucestershire, UK: Beshara, 1975), p. 120.

[135] St. John Climacus, quoted in Philip Sherrard, "Towards a Theology of Sexual Love," in *Christianity and Eros: Essays on the Theme of Sexual Love* (Limni, Evia, Greece: Denise Harvey, 1995), p. 51.

[136] Black Elk, quoted in Joseph Epes Brown, "The Gift of the Sacred Pipe," in *The Sacred Pipe: Black Elk's Account of the Seven Rites of the Oglala Sioux* (Norman, OK: University of Oklahoma Press, 1989), p. 4.

137 Reinhold Niebuhr, "Sex Standards in America," *Christianity and Crisis*, vol. 8, no. 9 (May 1948), p. 66.

138 Jean-Claude Larchet, "The Pathology of Fallen Man," in *Therapy of Spiritual Illnesses, Vol 1: An Introduction to the Ascetic Tradition of the Orthodox Church*, trans. Fr. Kilian Sprecher (Montréal: Alexander Press, 2012), p. 76.

139 Saint Augustine, "Book IV: Divine Justice and the Growth of the Roman Empire," in *City of God* (New York, NY: Image Books, 1953), p. 56.

Chapter 25: The Neo- and Post-Freudian Revolution: Apologists, Heretics, and Revisionists

1 Harry K. Wells, "Classical Psychoanalysis: Orthodox and Revised," in *The Failure of Psychoanalysis: From Freud to Fromm* (New York, NY: International Publishers, 1963), p. 47.

2 Harry K. Wells, "Reformation of Psychoanalysis," in *The Failure of Psychoanalysis: From Freud to Fromm* (New York, NY: International Publishers, 1963), p. 138.

3 Erich Fromm, "The Psychoanalytic Approach to the Understanding of Aggression," in *The Anatomy of Human Destructiveness* (New York, NY: Holt, Rinehart and Winston, 1974), p. 84.

4 See J.A.C. Brown, *Freud and the Post-Freudians* (Baltimore, MD: Penguin Books, 1967).

5 Erich Fromm, "The Psychoanalytic Approach to the Understanding of Aggression," in *The Anatomy of Human Destructiveness* (New York, NY: Holt, Rinehart and Winston, 1974), p. 79.

6 Erich Fromm, "The Theory of Love," in *The Art of Loving* (New York, NY: Bantam Books, 1963), p. 8.

7 Wolfgang Smith, "The Ego and the Beast," in *Cosmos & Transcendence: Breaking Through the Barrier of Scientistic Belief* (Peru, IL: Sherwood Sugden & Company, 1990), p. 104.

8 Erich Fromm, "What Does It Mean to Be Human?" in *The Revolution of Hope: Toward a Humanized Technology* (New York, NY: Bantam Books, 1971), p. 58.

9 Valer Barbu, "What Schools of Psychoanalysis Are There?" in *Are You Considering Psychoanalysis?*, ed. Karen Horney (New York, NY: W. W. Norton & Company, 1962), p. 46.

10 Wilhelm Reich, "Interview with Kurt R. Eissler—October 18, 1952," in *Reich Speaks of Freud: Wilhelm Reich Discusses his Work and his Relationship with Sigmund Freud*, trans. Therese Pol, eds. Mary Higgins and Chester M. Raphael (New York, NY: Farrar, Straus and Giroux, 1972), p. 4.

11 Frederick S. Perls, "Classical Psycho-Analysis," in *Ego, Hunger and Aggression* (New York, NY: Vintage Books, 1969), p. 81.

[12] Wilhelm Reich, "Sexual Stasis: The Source of Energy of the Neurosis," in *The Function of the Orgasm*, trans. Theodore P. Wolfe (New York: The Noonday Press, 1970), p. 89.

[13] Morris Eagle, "The Dynamics of Theory Change in Psychoanalysis," in *Philosophical Problems of the Internal and External Worlds: Essays on the Philosophy of Adolf Grünbaum*, eds. John Earman, Allen I. Janis, Gerald J. Massey and Nicholas Rescher (Pittsburgh, PA: University of Pittsburgh Press, 1993), p. 404.

[14] A. H. Almaas, "Depth Psychology and the Mind," in *The Void: Inner Spaciousness and Ego Structure* (Boston, MA: Shambhala, 2003), pp. 4, 6.

[15] Sigmund Freud, "Lines of Advance in Psycho-Analytic Therapy" (1919), in *The Standard Edition of the Complete Psychological Works of Sigmund Freud, Vol. 17*, trans. and ed. James Strachey (London, UK: Hogarth Press and the Institute of Psycho-Analysis, 1955), p. 168.

[16] A. A. Brill, "Introduction," to *The Basic Writings of Sigmund Freud*, trans. and ed. A.A. Brill (New York, NY: Modern Library, 1938), p. 31.

[17] Ibid.

[18] Sigmund Freud, "Psycho-Analysis" (1926 [1925]), in *The Standard Edition of the Complete Psychological Works of Sigmund Freud, Vol. 20*, trans. and ed. James Strachey (London, UK: Hogarth Press and the Institute of Psycho-Analysis, 1959), p. 266.

[19] Ibid.

[20] Karen Horney, "Introduction," to *The Neurotic Personality of Our Time* (New York, NY: W. W. Norton & Company, 1964), p. ix.

[21] Sigmund Freud, "Psycho-Analysis and Psychiatry" (1916–1917 [1915–1917]), in *Introductory Lectures on Psychoanalysis*, trans. and ed. James Strachey (New York, NY: W. W. Norton & Company, 1977), p. 246.

[22] Karen Horney, "Introduction," to *The Neurotic Personality of Our Time* (New York, NY: W. W. Norton & Company, 1964), p. ix.

[23] Ibid., p. 8.

[24] Ibid.

[25] Paul Tournier, "The Inner Conflict of Modern Man," in *The Whole Person in a Broken World*, trans. John Doberstein and Helen Doberstein (New York, NY: Harper & Row, 1964), p. 34.

[26] Stanislav Grof, "Architecture of Emotional and Psychosomatic Disorders," in *Psychology of the Future: Lessons from Modern Consciousness Research* (Albany, NY: State University of New York Press, 2000), pp. 71–72.

[27] Otto Rank, "Individualism and Collectivism," in *Psychology and the Soul: A Study of the Origin, Conceptual Evolution, and Nature of the Soul*, trans. Gregory C. Richter and E. James Lieberman (Baltimore, MD: John Hopkins University Press, 1998), p. 61.

[28] Herbert Marcuse, "The Social Implications of Freudian 'Revisionism'," *Dissent: A Quarterly of Socialist Opinion*, vol. 2, no. 3 (Summer 1955), pp. 226–27.

[29] Christopher Lasch, "Culture and Personality," in *Haven in a Heartless World: The Family Besieged* (New York, NY: W. W. Norton & Company, 1995), pp. 80–81.

[30] Christopher Lasch, "Notes," in *Haven in a Heartless World: The Family Besieged* (New York, NY: W. W. Norton & Company, 1995), p. 202.

[31] Erich Fromm, "Values and Goals in Freud's Psychoanalytic Concepts," in *Zen Buddhism and Psychoanalysis*, eds. D. T. Suzuki, Erich Fromm, and Richard De Martino (New York, NY: Grove Press, 1963), p. 86.

[32] Sigmund Freud, quoted in Ernest Jones, "Freud's Theory of the Mind," in *The Life and Work of Sigmund Freud, Vol. 1: The Formative Years and the Great Discoveries, 1856–1900* (New York, NY: Basic Books, 1959), p. 395.

[33] Sigmund Freud, "Letter to Marie Bonaparte—January 15, 1930," in Ernest Jones, *The Life and Work of Sigmund Freud, Vol. 3: The Last Phase, 1919–1939* (New York, NY: Basic Books, 1957), p. 449.

[34] Sigmund Freud, "Letter to C. G. Jung—December 6, 1906," in William McGuire (ed.), *The Freud/Jung Letters: The Correspondence Between Sigmund Freud and C. G. Jung*, trans. Ralph Manheim and R.F.C. Hull (Princeton, NJ: Princeton University Press, 1994), pp. 12–13.

[35] Paul Heelas, "Developments," in *The New Age Movement* (Oxford, UK: Blackwell Publishers, 2003), p. 47. See also Samuel Bendeck Sotillos, "Prometheus and Narcissus in the Shadows of the Human Potential Movement," *AHP Perspective* (December 2012/January 2013), pp. 6–12.

[36] Rollo May, "Kierkegaard, Nietzsche, and Freud," in *The Discovery of Being: Writings in Existential Psychology* (New York, NY: W. W. Norton & Company, 1983), p. 87.

[37] James F. T. Bugental, "The Analytic Phase of the Therapeutic Work," in *The Search for Authenticity: An Existential-Analytic Approach to Psychotherapy* (New York, NY: Holt, Rinehart and Winston, 1965), p. 63.

[38] E. Fuller Torrey, "Freud Goes to Esalen," in *Freudian Fraud: The Malignant Effects of Freud's Theory on American Thought and Culture* (New York, NY: HarperCollins, 1992), p. 207.

[39] Paul Tournier, "The Task of the Church," in *The Whole Person in a Broken World*, trans. John Doberstein and Helen Doberstein (New York, NY: Harper & Row, 1964), p. 147.

[40] C. G. Jung, "Letter to Sabina Spielrein—April 3, 1919," quoted in C. G. Jung, "The Letters of C. G. Jung to Sabina Spielrein," *Journal of Analytical Psychology*, vol. 46, no. 1 (January 2001), p. 194.

[41] Marco Pallis, "Considerations on the Tantric Alchemy," in *A Buddhist Spectrum: Contributions to Buddhist-Christian Dialogue* (Bloomington, IN: World Wisdom, 2003), p. 90. There are commonalities between the Freudian and Jungian psychologies that are often minimized or altogether ignored as is outlined here: "The popular view according to which Jung's unconscious system is somehow broader or deeper than that of Freud is entirely fanciful. The concept of the dynamic unconscious originally advanced by Freud has been split up by Jung. One part has been assigned to a new container and

branded with Jung's trade mark—the 'Collective Unconscious.' Another has been dissociated, reduced in dynamic significance and allocated to the Personal Unconscious. This latter superficial and mainly pre-conscious Jungian system is however represented as being Freud's whole stock-in-trade and returned to him labelled in a way calculated to mislead the uninformed" (Edward Glover, "Mental Structure," in *Freud or Jung?* [New York, NY: Meridian, 1956], p. 28).

[42] C. G. Jung, "Therapeutic Principles of Psychoanalysis" (1912), in *Critique of Psychoanalysis*, trans. R.F.C. Hull (Princeton, NJ: Princeton University Press, 1975), p. 118.

[43] C. G. Jung, "Appendix: Answers to Questions on Freud" (1953), in *Critique of Psychoanalysis*, trans. R.F.C. Hull (Princeton, NJ: Princeton University Press, 1975), p. 237. "[T]he most consistent trend of Jungian psychology is its negation of every important part of Freudian theory" (Edward Glover, "Conclusion: The Eclectic's Dilemma," in *Freud or Jung?* [New York, NY: Meridian, 1956], p. 190).

[44] Frithjof Schuon, "The Contradiction of Relativism," in *Logic and Transcendence*, trans. Peter N. Townsend (London, UK: Perennial Books, 1984), p. 16.

[45] Philip Rieff, "The Analytic Attitude: Freud's Legacy and Its Inheritors," in *The Triumph of the Therapeutic: Uses of Faith After Freud* (Chicago, IL: University of Chicago Press, 1987), p. 30.

Conclusion: Founder of the Greatest Revolution in Psychology or "the Greatest Con Man in the History of Medicine"?

[1] Philip Rieff, "The Analytic Attitude: Freud's Legacy and Its Inheritors," in *The Triumph of the Therapeutic: Uses of Faith After Freud* (Chicago, IL: University of Chicago Press, 1987), p. 42. "[Freud's *oeuvre*] the most important body of thought committed to paper in the twentieth century" (Philip Rieff, "Preface to the First Edition," in *Freud: The Mind of the Moralist* [Chicago, IL: University of Chicago Press, 1979], p. x).

[2] Patricia Cohen, "Freud Is Widely Taught at Universities, Except in the Psychology Department," *New York Times* (November 25, 2007).

[3] Sam Keen, "Psychological Man," in *Fire in the Belly: On Being a Man* (New York, NY: Bantam Books, 1991), p. 108.

[4] Sigmund Freud, "Postscript" (1927), to *The Question of Lay Analysis*, trans. and ed. James Strachey (New York, NY: W. W. Norton & Company, 1989), p. 89.

[5] Poul Bjerre, "Points of View and Outlooks," in *The History and Practice of Psychoanalysis*, trans. Elizabeth N. Barrow (Boston, MA: Richard G. Badger, 1920), p. 321.

[6] C. G. Jung, "The Psychological Diagnosis of Evidence," in *The Collected Works of C. G. Jung, Vol. 2: Experimental Researches*, trans. Leopold Stein

and Diana Riviere (Princeton, NJ: Princeton University Press, 1981), pp. 332–33.

[7] C. G. Jung, "Letter to Sabina Spielrein—October 10, 1917," quoted in C. G. Jung, "The Letters of C. G. Jung to Sabina Spielrein," *Journal of Analytical Psychology*, vol. 46, no. 1 (January 2001), pp. 188–89.

[8] Peter B. Medawar, "Further Comments on Psychoanalysis," in *The Hope of Progress: A Scientist Looks at Problems in Philosophy, Literature and Science* (London, UK: Methuen, 1972), p. 68. "The opinion is gaining ground that doctrinaire psychoanalytic theory is the most stupendous intellectual confidence trick of the twentieth century" (Peter B. Medawar, "Victims of Psychiatry." Review of *The Victim Is Always the Same*, by I. S. Cooper. *The New York Review of Books* (January 23, 1975), p. 17.

[9] Nehemiah Jordan, "Whither Scientific Psychology?" in *Themes in Speculative Psychology* (New York, NY: Routledge, 2014), p. 230.

[10] Mortimer J. Adler, "Psychoanalysis as Psychology," in *What Man Has Made of Man: A Study of the Consequences of Platonism and Positivism in Psychology* (New York, NY: Frederick Ungar Publishing, 1938), p. 122.

[11] Seymour Fisher and Roger P. Greenberg, "Preface," to *The Scientific Credibility of Freud's Theories and Therapy* (New York, NY: Columbia University Press, 1985), p. viii.

[12] René Guénon, "The Hatred of Secrecy," in *The Reign of Quantity and the Signs of the Times*, trans. Lord Northbourne (Ghent, NY: Sophia Perennis, 2001), pp. 87–88.

[13] Robert S. Woodworth, "Followers of Freud and Jung," *The Nation*, vol. 103, no. 2678 (October 26, 1916), p. 396.

[14] Thomas Szasz, "Curing Souls: Religion of Remedy," in *The Myth of Psychotherapy: Mental Healing as Religion, Rhetoric, and Repression* (Garden City, NY: Anchor Press, 1979), p. 27.

[15] Christopher Lasch, "The Attack on the Nuclear Family and the Search for 'Alternate Life-styles,'" in *Haven in a Heartless World: The Family Besieged* (New York, NY: W. W. Norton & Company, 1995), p. 135.

[16] Frederick Crews, "The Verdict on Freud," *Psychological Science*, vol. 7, no. 2 (March 1996), p. 63.

[17] Erich Fromm, "Freud, the World Reformer," in *Sigmund Freud's Mission: An Analysis of His Personality and Influence* (New York, NY: Grove Press, 1963), p. 86.

[18] Frank Cioffi, "Why Are We Still Arguing about Freud?" in *Freud and the Question of Pseudoscience* (Chicago, IL: Open Court, 1998), pp. 1–2. "To read a prolonged case history by Freud is to wonder at the non sequiturs, the leaps of faith, the illogic, the arguments from authority in which they abound, but which were not, apparently, apparent to generations of readers. And although Freud was personally conservative in his manner and morality, except where his incestuous adultery with his sister-in-law was concerned, his effect, if not his intention, was to loosen Man's sense of responsibility for his

own actions, freedom from responsibility being the most highly valued freedom of all, albeit one that is metaphysically impossible to achieve. For Freud powerfully alienated men from their own consciousness by claiming that what went on in their conscious minds was but a shadow play, and that the real action lay deep beneath it, all undiscovered (and undiscoverable) without many hours of talking about oneself in the presence of an analyst who might from time to time offer an interpretation of the real meaning of non-acceptance, which would itself be interpreted as resistance in need of further analysis, and so on more or less *ad infinitum*" (Theodore Dalrymple, "Chapter One," in *Admirable Evasions: How Psychology Undermines Morality* [New York, NY: Encounter Books, 2015], p. 18).

[19] Eric Fromm, "Man in Capitalistic Society," in *The Sane Society* (Greenwich, CT: Fawcett, 1955), p. 151.

[20] Theodor W. Adorno, Else Frenkel-Brunswik, Daniel Levinson, and Nevitt Sanford, "Conclusions," to *The Authoritarian Personality* (New York, NY: Harper & Row, 1950), p. 976. See Herbert Marcuse, *Eros and Civilization: A Philosophical Inquiry into Freud* (New York, NY: Vintage Books, 1962).

[21] Bertrand Russell, "General Effects of Scientific Technique," in *The Impact of Science on Society* (New York, NY: Routledge, 1976), pp. 40, 41. "The social psychologists of the future will have a number of classes of school children on whom they will try different methods of producing an unshakable conviction that snow is black. Various results will soon be arrived at. First, that the influence of home is obstructive. Second, that not much can be done unless indoctrination begins before the age of ten. Third, that verses set to music and repeatedly intoned are very effective. Fourth, that the opinion that snow is white must be held to show a morbid taste for eccentricity. But I anticipate. It is for future scientists to make these maxims precise and discover exactly how much it costs per head to make children believe that snow is black, and how much less it would cost to make them believe it is dark gray...When the technique has been perfected, every government that has been in charge of education for a generation will be able to control its subjects securely without the need of armies or policemen" (Bertrand Russell, "General Effects of Scientific Technique," in *The Impact of Science on Society* [New York, NY: Routledge, 1976], p. 41). See also William Sargant, *Battle for the Mind: A Physiology of Conversion and Brain-Washing* (Cambridge, MA: Malor Book, 1997); Joost A. M. Meerloo, *The Rape of the Mind: The Psychology of Thought Control, Menticide, and Brainwashing* (New York, NY: Grosset & Dunlap, 1956); Neil Postman, *Amusing Ourselves to Death: Public Discourse in the Age of Show Business* (New York, NY: Penguin Books, 1988).

[22] C. S. Lewis, "The Abolition of Man," in *The Abolition of Man* (New York, NY: Collier Books, 1986), p. 72.

[23] Sigmund Freud, "The Dissection of the Psychical Personality" (1933 [1932]), in *New Introductory Lectures on Psycho-Analysis*, trans. and ed. James Strachey (New York, NY: W. W. Norton & Company, 1989), p. 72.

[24] Philip Rieff, "The Hidden Self," in *Freud: The Mind of the Moralist* (Chicago, IL: University of Chicago Press, 1979), p. 77.

[25] "[M]an in his integral nature, man who is not only a physical datum but, at one and the same time, body, soul, and spirit" (Titus Burckhardt, "The Traditional Sciences in Fez," in *Mirror of the Intellect: Essays on Traditional Science and Sacred Art*, trans. and ed. William Stoddart [Albany, NY: State University of New York Press, 1987], p. 173).

[26] Janet Malcolm, "Chapter Two," in *In the Freud Archives* (New York, NY: Vintage Books, 1985), p. 25.

[27] W. B. Yeats, "The Second Coming," in *The Collected Poems of W. B. Yeats* (London, UK: Wordsworth Editions, 2000), p. 158.

[28] Merton M. Gill, "Preface," to *Psychoanalysis in Transition: A Personal View* (Hillsdale, NJ: Analytic Press, 2000), p. xiii.

[29] Sigmund Freud, "Analysis Terminable and Interminable" (1937), in *The Standard Edition of the Complete Psychological Works of Sigmund Freud, Vol. 23*, trans. and ed. James Strachey (London, UK: Hogarth Press and the Institute of Psycho-Analysis, 1964), p. 228.

[30] C. G. Jung, "The Aims of Psychotherapy," in *Modern Man in Search of a Soul*, trans. W. S. Dell and Cary F. Baynes (New York, NY: Harcourt, Brace & World, 1933), pp. 72–73.

[31] David E. Stannard, "The Failure of Psychohistory," in *Shrinking History: On Freud and the Failure of Psychohistory* (New York, NY: Oxford University Press, 1980), p. 154.

[32] Joseph Jastrow, "Prospect," in *Freud: His Dream and Sex Theories* (Cleveland, OH: World Publishing Company, 1948), p. 285.

[33] John Kerr, "Afterword," to *A Most Dangerous Method: The Story of Jung, Freud, and Sabina Spielrein* (New York, NY: Alfred A. Knopf, 1993), p. 511.

[34] Hans J. Eysenck, "Psychoanalysis as a Method of Treatment," in *Decline and Fall of the Freudian Empire* (New York, NY: Penguin Books, 1991), p. 65.

[35] Sigmund Freud, "Le Bon's Description of the Group Mind" (1921), in *Group Psychology and the Analysis of the Ego*, trans. James Strachey (New York, NY: W. W. Norton & Company, 1989), pp. 16-17.

[36] C. G. Jung, "Introduction to Kranefeldt's 'Secret Ways of the Mind'" (1930), in *Critique of Psychoanalysis*, trans. R.F.C. Hull (Princeton, NJ: Princeton University Press, 1975), p. 217.

[37] David Bakan, "Freud's Messianic Identification," in *Sigmund Freud and the Jewish Mystical Tradition* (London, UK: Free Association Books, 1990), p. 170.

[38] Frederick S. Perls, "Intensive Workshop—June," in *Gestalt Therapy Verbatim*, ed. John O. Stevens (Lafayette, CA: Real People Press, 1969), p. 224.

[39] E. M. Thornton, "Epilogue" and "Introduction," to *The Freudian Fallacy:*

An Alternative View of Freudian Theory (Garden City, NY: Dial Press, 1984), pp. ix, 252.

[40] René Guénon, quoted in Ananda K. Coomaraswamy, "The Doctrine," in *Hinduism and Buddhism* (New York, NY: Philosophical Library, 1943), p. 61.

Index of Names

A

Abraham, Karl, 40
Adler, Alfred, 228
Adorno, Theodor W., 51, 186
Almaas, A. H., 286
Ames, Louise Bates, 227
Anna O., 151, 231
Aristotle, 155
Ashkenazi, Abraham Nathan
  b. Elisha Hayyim. *See*
  Nathan of Gaza
Augustine of Hippo, Saint,
  207, 283

B

Bakan, David, 2, 161, 163,
  164, 180, 183, 195, 208,
  301
Bakan, Siegfried, 57
Barbu, Valer, 28
Bauer, Ida, 230–31, 230–31,
  230–31
Bāyazīd Bisṭāmī, 204, 205
Benjamin, Walter, 207
Bernays, Edward, 4
Bernays, Jacob, 155
Bernays, Martha, 253
Bernays, Minna, 271
Bernfeld, Siegfried, 113, 251
Bijur, Abraham, 237
Bijur, Angelika, 236, 237
Bjerre, Poul, 293
Black Elk, 124, 137, 283
Bleuler, Eugen, 6, 12, 17
Boas, Franz, 101
Boethius, 23
Bonaparte, Marie, 271

Borch-Jacobsen, Mikkel, 231
Borella, Jean, 104, 142
Breger, Louis, 37
Brenner, Charles, 6, 88, 230
Breuer, Josef, 63, 64, 155,
  156, 160, 231, 232, 249,
  271
Brill, A. A., 39, 180, 287
Brown, Joseph Epes, 102
Brunner, José, 249
Buddha, 75, 170
Bugental, James F. T., 12,
  291
Burckhardt, Titus, 61, 73, 83,
  110, 151, 166, 279

C

Chittick, William C., 112, 204
Choisy, Maryse, 245
Chrysostom, Saint John, 141,
  189
Churchland, Paul M., 13
Cicero, Marcus Tullius, 250
Cleland, John, 265
Clement of Alexandria, 112
Climacus, Saint John, 282
Collingwood, R. G., 22
Coomaraswamy, Ananda K.,
  70, 109, 160
Coomaraswamy, Rama P., 27
Copernicus, Nicolaus, 19, 21,
  22, 23
Coriat, Isador, 39
Covington, Coline, 17
Crews, Frederick, 11, 257,
  296
Crowley, Aleister, 207, 264

Guénon, René, 5, 55, 61, 110, 112, 116, 135, 136, 159, 189, 203, 205, 206, 277, 301

H

Haitzmann, Christoph, 162
Ḥallāj, Manṣūr al-, 204, 205
Hart, Bernard, 108
Hartmann, Heinz, 241
Hefner, Hugh, 264
Heinze, Andrew R., 186
Hirschmüller, Albrecht, 231
Hitler, Adolf, 192
Hoche, Alfred, 42, 227
Hoffer, Eric, 47, 94, 209
Homans, Peter, 28, 91
Horkheimer, Max, 186
Horney, Karen, 215, 217, 270, 272, 288
Hug-Hellmuth, Hermine von, 236
Hujwīrī, 'Ali b. 'Uthman al-Jullabi al-, 206

I

Ibn 'Arabī, 112, 206, 282
Isaac the Syrian, St., 73
Ivimey, Muriel, 123

J

Jacobi, Jolande, 43
Jacoby, Russell, 49
James, Apostle, 149
James, William, 228, 246
Janet, Pierre, 9
Janov, Arthur, 145
Jastrow, Joseph, 72, 224, 300

Jones, E. Michael, 47, 250, 265, 272
Jones, Ernest, 2, 25, 38, 44, 46, 49, 51, 58, 63, 65, 82, 91, 107, 109, 115, 121, 155, 161, 164, 177, 178, 179, 181, 190, 230, 231, 233, 234, 236, 239, 246, 247, 248, 252, 258, 267, 271
Jones, James H., 264
Jones, Philip, 244
Junayd, al (of Baghdad), 204
Jung, Carl, 3, 6, 27, 32, 33, 39, 42, 43, 44, 62, 64, 69, 73, 81, 83, 86, 90, 97, 99, 104, 105, 108, 114, 115, 126, 134, 135, 141, 144, 145, 147, 152, 153, 156, 159, 162, 165, 169, 170, 173, 179, 190, 191, 192, 193, 215, 221, 227, 228, 232, 241, 242, 247, 248, 250, 259, 263, 266, 267, 269, 270, 273, 276, 291, 292, 294, 300
Jung, Ernest, 272
Jurjevich, R. M., 183

K

Kapleau, Roshi Philip, 275
Kardiner, Abram, 40
Katina, Rab, 280
Katz, Fanny Bowditch, 43
Kautsky, Karl, 149
Kennedy, Gail, 84
Kerr, John, 300
Kinsey, Alfred C., 263
Kinsey, Paul Robinson, 264
Klein, Dennis B., 177
Klein, Jean, 127

485

About the Author

SAMUEL BENDECK SOTILLOS is a practicing psychotherapist who has focused especially on the interface between spirituality and psychology. He is an Advisor to the Institute of Traditional Psychology, a former Board Affiliate of the Association for Humanistic Psychology, and on the Editorial Boards both of the journal *Spiritual Psychology and Counseling* and the *Armonia Journal*. His works include *Paths That Lead to the Same Summit: An Annotated Guide to World Spirituality* and *Behaviorism: The Quandary of a Psychology without a Soul*, and his articles have appeared in numerous journals, including *Sacred Web*, *Sophia*, *Parabola*, *Resurgence*, and the *Temenos Academy Review*. He lives on the Central Coast of California.

www.ingramcontent.com/pod-product-compliance
Lightning Source LLC
Chambersburg PA
CBHW020813270326
41928CB00006B/363